FFEL TOWER ▲ 296 | THE CHAMPS-ÉLYSÉES ▲ 3

LA VILLETTE ✪

CANAL DE L'OURCQ

PARC DE LA VILLETTE

XVIII

MONTMARTRE ✪

XIX

Stalingrad

GARE DU NORD

GARE DE L'EST

CANAL ST-MARTIN

PARC DES BUTTES-CHAUMONT

IX

X

PARC DE BELLEVILLE

II

République

XX

III

BEAUBOURG ✪

PÈRE-LACHAISE CEMETERY ✪

THE LOUVRE

THE MARAIS ✪

XI

NOTRE-DAME ✪

IV

Bastille

ÎLE ST-LOUIS

TIN QUARTER ✪

Nation

DIN DU MBOURG

SEINE

GARE DE LYON

XII

V

JARDIN DES PLANTES

GARE D'AUSTERLITZ

0   0.6   1.2 miles

PÈRE-LACHAISE ▲ 412 | MONTMARTRE ▲ 414 | LA VILLETTE ▲ 428

NOTRE-DAME
A Gothic masterpiece, the cathedral dominates the Île de la Cité. Tours start in the cathedral square.
BEAUBOURG
A colorful temple to modern art and architecture. Tours start on the piazza beside the museum.
THE MARAIS
A unique microcosm of old Paris, the Marais is a network of ancient narrow streets. Tours start on Place des Vosges.

PÈRE-LACHAISE
A cemetery with a multitude of architectural styles and the largest green space in Paris.
MONTMARTRE
One of the city's best-known villages, set on a hill. Tours start from the Place des Abbesses, winding up the narrow streets to take in the view from Sacré-Cœur.
LA VILLETTE
Center of learning and culture with a modern outlook, set in an 85-acre park.

PARIS

● Encyclopedia section

HISTORY The impact of international historical events on local history, from the arrival of the first inhabitants, with key dates appearing in a timeline above the text.

PARISIAN SCENES Parisian customs and traditions and their expression in the modern world.

ARCHITECTURE The architectural heritage, focusing on style and topology, a look at rural and urban buildings, major civil, religious and military monuments.

AS SEEN BY PAINTERS A selection of paintings of the city by different artists and schools, arranged thematically.

AS SEEN BY WRITERS An anthology of texts focusing on the city, taken from works of all periods and countries, arranged thematically.

▲ Itineraries

FIVE SIDES OF PARIS Five major aspects of the Parisian identity.

■ NATURE The natural heritage: species and habitats characteristic to the area covered by the guide, annotated and illustrated by naturalist authors and artists.

Each itinerary begins with a map of the area to be explored.

✪ SPECIAL INTEREST These sites are not to be missed. They are highlighted in gray boxes in the margins.

★ EDITOR'S CHOICE Sites singled out by the editor for special attention.

INSETS On richly illustrated double pages, these insets turn the spotlight on subjects deserving more in-depth treatment.

◆ Practical information

All the travel information you will need before you go and when you get there.

USEFUL ADDRESSES A selection of hotels and restaurants compiled by an expert.

PLACES TO VISIT A handy table of addresses and opening hours.

APPENDICES Bibliography, list of illustrations and general index.

MAP SECTION Maps of areas covered by the guide, followed by an index; these maps are marked out with letters and figures making it easy for the reader to pinpoint a town, region or site.

◆ LOUVRE, MARAIS, ÎLE DE LA CITÉ, QUARTIER LATIN

◆ LOUVRE, MARA

Each map in the map section is designated by a letter. In the itineraries, all the sites of interest are given a map reference (for example: ◆ **2** D8).

The mini-map pinpoints the itinerary within the wider area covered by the guide.

The itinerary map shows the main sites, the editor's choices and the places of special interest.

★ The star symbol signifies sites singled out by the editor for special attention.

▲ ÎLE DE LA CITÉ

1. SQUARE DU VERT-GALANT 2. PLACE DAUPHINE 3. SAINTE-CHAPELLE 4. CONCIERGERIE 5. PALAIS DE JUSTICE 6. PRÉFECTURE DE POLICE 7. CHAMBRE DE COMMERCE 8. MARCHÉ AUX FLEURS 9. HÔTEL-DIEU 10. NOTRE-DAME 11. SQUARE JEAN XXIII 12. SQUARE DE L'ÎLE 13. SAINT-LAMBERT 14. HÔTEL LAUZUN

☐ One day

The Île de la Cité is the historical heart of Paris: from the time of the Late Empire (3rd to 5th centuries AD), this strip of land was the focus of royal, judiciary and religious power. The Gallo-Roman palace which stood on the western part of the island was later taken over by the Merovingians and then rebuilt by Philippe le Bel in the 14th century. Today's Palais de Justice stands on the same site. The Parlement and other institutions were based here, including the Chambre des Comptes (Chamber of Revenue), the Chambre du Trésor (Treasury) and so on. The eastern part of the island was devoted to religion in the Gallo-Roman era onward. A cathedral already stood on the site of today's Notre-Dame in 362. Gradually an entire ecclesiastical center grew up around this building: a baptistry, bishop's palace, the Hôtel-Dieu (general hospital), and

Vedettes du Pont Neuf island's population was regarded as the most destitute in Paris: it fell from 15,000 inhabitants in 1858 to 5,000 in 1868.

PLACE DAUPHINE AND THE PONT-NEUF ★ (2 C7)

In 1584, Henri III decided to sell off the end of the Île de la Cité in order to raise funds to build the Pont-Neuf: an area of sand and water made up of three small islands which had to be filled in and joined together, significantly increasing the island's surface area. In 1601, Henri IV decided to build a three-sided square here (the base of the triangle, on the Rue de Harlay, was demolished in 1874). The land was sold in 12 lots, on which 32 identical houses were built in red brick with stone facing. The houses had an arcade on the first floor, and three stories above this; the façades on the Seine side were identical. Only the two symmetrical buildings at the end of the square are still in their original form. The square itself is charming – the poet Malherbe, in the 17th century, described it as "the most beautiful and the most practical in Paris".

NOTRE-DAME DE PARIS ★ (2 D8)

A CLASSICAL CATHEDRAL
Today it is thought that the Île de la Cité had a

A HIVE OF ACTIVITY
Up until the 19th century, the Pont-Neuf (above, during construction) buzzed with activity. Below, opposite: the bridge in the 17th century.

PONT-NEUF
This was the first bridge across the Seine ● 27 without houses on it. The humpback bridge with semicircular arches was designed by the architects Pierre Des Illes and Androuet du Cerceau and opened in 1607. The statue of Henri IV which dates from 1818, replaced a statue by Franqueville which was erected in 1635 and destroyed in 1792.

NOTRE-DAME
This masterpiece set between the arms of the Seine justly deserves the moniker "ship of stone". Building began when Paris was chosen as the capital of France. In the crypt is the Musée de l'Histoire de Paris. Do not miss the view from the top of the towers and the official center of Paris, marked in the square in front of the west end.

46 houses occupied by canons. As these institutions were built it became necessary to raise the level of the island, which has grown in size from 20 to 40 acres over ten centuries. The island was completely transformed under Haussmann, who razed the medieval city to create an administrative center. This center is now the base of two institutions devoted to maintaining public order – the Judiciary and the police. In the 19th century, the

cathedral as far back as the 4th century, at a time when Christianity was spreading, thanks to the policies of Emperor Constantine. A group of episcopal buildings was established, consisting of the bishop's house, the baptistry (destroyed in 1748) and an exceptionally long basilica (230 to 260 feet long). The beginnings of what was to become the Hôtel-Dieu (general hospital) probably go back to this period. This episcopal

355

❂ This symbol indicates places of special interest.

☐ The clock symbol beneath the mini-map, at the start of the intinerary, indicates the time taken to cover the featured area.

The bracketed map references alongside a title or within the text refer to the maps at the back of the guide (e.g.: 2 D8).

● ▲ ◆
The above symbols within the text provide cross-references to a place or a theme discussed elsewhere in

03

◆ Practical information

ST-GERMAIN-DES-PRÉS ▲ 234
My first is a legendary quarter frequented by the Parisian intelligentsia, and is full of students and publishers. My second is a shopping zone that attracts a well-heeled, cosmopolitan clientele. My whole appears on café terraces at the first hint of summer.

LATIN QUARTER ▲ 246
Between catching a movie at an art movie-theater and drinking mint tea at the city's mosque, take time to admire the view of the Île de la Cité from the terrace of the Institut du Monde Arabe. Then meld with the crowds of students who flock to the universities.

FAUBOURG ST-GERMAIN ▲ 262
At the west end, elegant 18th-century town houses can sometimes be glimpsed behind richly carved gateways. Toward the east end, antique dealers keep alive the tradition of the Faubourg St-Germain as a rich source of collector's pieces and works of art.

MONTPARNASSE ▲ 272
Paris in all its dimensions, from the heights of the Eiffel Tower to the depths the Catacombs of the Place Denfert-Rochereau. There is also the cemetery, the area's unique concentration of artists and writers, and the Atlantic Garden, underneath the station.

INVALIDES AND CHAMP-DE-MARS ▲ 290
A quiet, middle-class quarter with wide avenues giving equally fine views of the Eiffel Tower and the Invalides, the two principal landmarks in this part of Paris.

THE 16TH ARRONDISSEMENT: PASSY – CHAILLOT ▲ 300
Smart and modern. Small local stores and exclusive retail outlets line the Rue de Passy and Rue des Belles-Feuilles, the Avenue Victor-Hugo and Avenue Mozart. At the Trocadéro, café terraces are still a favorite meeting place for the local inhabitants.

THE 16TH ARRONDISSEMENT: AUTEUIL ▲ 304
The out-of-town exclusivity that pervades this area emanates from the peaceful village of Auteuil. Here also are the restrained and unique architectural styles of Guimard and Mallet-Stevens, and comfortable detached houses set in wide expanses of greenery.

THE CHAMPS-ÉLYSÉES ▲ 308
Beneath the serene golden apex of the obelisk of the Concorde Square, the Champs-Élysées are fashionable once again. Ladurée and Louis Vuitton have shops there; Fouquet's, the famous restaurant, has been refurbished; and major open-air exhibitions take place in the gardens.

LA DÉFENSE ▲ 318
Running the gamut of modern and contemporary architectural styles, La Défense is now firmly part of the Parisian skyline. From the top of the Grande Arche, the view stretches uninterrupted as far as the Louvre, almost 5 miles away.

THE LOUVRE AND THE TUILERIES ▲ 322
The Louvre and its gardens set the tone of this area, where there are many princely buildings and vistas, the result of tasteful development over the centuries. Old stores and modern boutiques nestle under arcades, along alleys and around small squares.

FAUBOURG ST-HONORÉ TO THE OPÉRA ▲ 342
With exclusive boutiques on the Rue du Faubourg-St-Honoré and department stores on the boulevards, this is the place to shop till you drop. Further west the district becomes more residential, and the well-to-do can be seen strolling in the Parc Monceau.

ÎLES DE LA CITÉ AND ST-LOUIS ▲ 354
Notre-Dame is the main attraction, but the Île de la Cité also has such gems as the Place Dauphine, the flower market and the Square du Vert-Galant. The Île St-Louis, the smaller island, has a secluded village atmosphere, with a host of 17th-century mansions.

BEAUBOURG – LES HALLES ▲ 372
Superlatives abound: here is Europe's largest pedestrianized street (rue Montorgueuil), the world's greatest number of travelers (to Châtelet-Les Halles station), the vast museum of modern art at Beaubourg, and the largest discrict in Europe for clothing industry (Sentier).

THE MARAIS ▲ 384
The north of the Marais, with clothes and accessories wholesalers, has an industrious atmosphere. The south, with the Rue des Rosiers, throbs with life and is one of the most prominent gay areas in the capital. The Place des Vosges, to the east, invites leisurely Sunday strolls.

BASTILLE – FAUBOURG ST-ANTOINE ▲ 402
Contrasting itineraries: the Bastille and its nightlife, right next to the traditional furniture-making area, the Opéra with its flowery promenade, and Bercy, an area in which the old wine warehouses have found a new lease of life.

BELLEVILLE – MÉNILMONTANT ▲ 408
The popular face of multicultural Paris, with Arab, African, Asian and Jewish communities, as well as more recently established groups, around the Rue Oberkampf.

MONTMARTRE ▲ 414
Beneath the hill, the Place Pigalle has enticing street stalls luring young late-night passers-by. There is also the Place des Abbesses, the heart of the area, the Place du Tertre, with a village feel, and the great vantage point of the Sacré-Cœur.

FROM ST-LAZARE TO ST-MARTIN ▲ 424
Step back into 19th-century Paris. The pride of the post-Napoleonic era, this was to be a latter-day Athens in the neoclassical style: *grand boulevards* laid out by Haussmann, centers where traditional crafts flourished, and, bringing a bucolic touch, the St-Martin canal.

LA VILLETTE ▲ 428
The only multidisciplinary complex of its kind in the world, La Villette subsumes the city and its suburbs. Town and country come together in the 85-acre landscaped park, with the Canal de l'Ourcq, the Cité des Sciences et de l'Industrie and the Cité de la Musique.

EVERYMAN GUIDES
Published by Alfred A Knopf

Completely revised and updated in 2003

Originally published in France by
Nouveaux-Loisirs, a subsidiary of Editions
Gallimard, Paris, 1995 © 1995 Editions
Nouveaux-Loisirs.

Translated by
Wendy Allatson, Michael Cunningham,
Susan Mackervoy and Sue Rose

Edited and typeset by
Book Creation Services, London

Printed in Italy by
Editoriale Lloyd

EVERYMAN GUIDES
Gloucester Mansions
140a Shaftesbury Avenue
London WC2H 8HD
guides@everyman.uk.com

PARIS

EDITORS Clotilde Lefebvre; Anne-Josyane Magniant and
Veronika Vollmer (updates)
ADVISORS Danièle Chadych, M. A. Corcuff, Jean-Pierre Le
Dantec, Alfred Fierro, Marc Gaillard, Jean-Claude Garreta,
Brigitte Gournay, Bertrand Lemoine, Jean-Marc Léri, Guilhem
Lesaffre, Michel Le Moël, Marguerite Pennec
GALLIMARD AUTHORS Marie-Hélène Albertini-Viennot,
Laurence de Bélizal, Liesel Couvreur Schiffer, Gilles Février,
Corinne Hewlett, Catherine Ianco, Béatrice Jaulin, Anne-
Josyane Magniant, Sybille d'Oiron, Nina Paronian, Édouard de
Pazzis, Christine Puget, Nicolas Ragonneau, Michel Spagnol
AUTHORS G. Adam, J.-P. Adam, M.-C. Adès, M. Amandry,
I. Bachelard, S. Baratte, C. Barbillon, M.-N. Baudoin Matuszeck,
G. Bauer, A. Bavelier, B. Blache, F. Bellec, V. Berecz, L. Bergeron,
M. Bernus-Taylor, D. Blaizot, Mme Bordaz, N BottaKouznetzoff,
M. Bouchard, G. Boulinier, M. Bruson, T. Burogard, T. Burollet,
D. Cailleaux, M. F. Callas, M. Carlier, T. Carneiro, A. Caubet,
A.-M. Châtelet, G. Cheyssial, M. Courant-Vidal, Mme Causse
Fouqueray, M.-V. Clin, N. Daliès, M. Deming, M. Dunoyer de
Segonzac, D. Ferriot, Alfred Fierro, M. de Fleury, D. Freignac,
J. Fritsch, N. Gasc, C. Genet-Bondeville, G. Genty, L. Gervereau,
P. Georgel, S. Gohel, P-M. Grineval, S. Grossiord, L. Guyard,
R. Herbaut, C. Horel, A. Jacob, M. Jaoul, M. Kuraszewski, G.
Lacambre, S. Lecombre, J.-M. Leniaud, J.-M. Léri, C. Levisse-
Touzé, S. de Lisle, A. Lefébure, M.-C. Le Floch, C. Madoni,
H. Marraud, M. Maucuer, J. Mayer, J.-H. Martin, C. Merle-
Portalès, K. Michel-Haciski, B. Mons, J.-P. Midant, J. Mouliérac,
I. Neto, A. Nardin, C. Nossoc, A. Okada, I. Ottaviani, A.Panchont,
F. Pascaud, A. Pasquier, J.-D. Pariset, P-P. Perraud, A Perrot,
J.-M. Peyronnet, P. Pinon, D. Petermüller, M. Polonovski, V.
Pomarède, B. Quette, C. de Quiqueran Beaujeu, T. du Regard,
B. Rondot, V. Roudot, C. Savary, N. Sainte-Fare-Garnot, D. Soutat,
H. Seckel, M Werner Szanbien, J. Treuttel, G. Viatte,
F. Viatte, V. Vignon, P. de Vogüe, V. Wiesinger
PRACTICAL INFORMATION UPDATE
Jean-François Chougnet, GaultMillau for the hotels and
Fiona Beeston for the restaurants
LAYOUT Michèle Bisgambiglia, Olivier Brunot, François
Chentrier, Béatrice Desrousseaux, Carole Gaborit, Alain
Gouessant, Roberta Maranzano, Philippe Marchand, Riccardo
Tremori, Isabelle Roller
PICTURE RESEARCH Nathalie Beaud, Marie-Amélie Beri,
Carine Lepied, Nils Warolin, assisted by Annie-Claire Auliard
and Mélanie Tissandier
ILLUSTRATIONS Architecture: François Brosse, P. Biard,
P. Candé, D. Grant, J.-M. Guillou, J.-B. Héron, O. Hubert, P. de
Hugo, J.-F. Lecomte, P. Lhez, J.-F. Peneau, J.-P. Pocabare,
C. Quiec, C. Rivière, J.-S. Roveri, A. Soro **Itineraries**: F. Moireau
A. Pladière **Nature**: F. Bony, J. Chevallier, F. Desbordes, C. Felloni,
B. Duhem, J.-M. Kacédan, J. Wilkinson, C. Lachaud, P. Robin
MAPS: Atelier de Bayonne (F. Callède, D. Duplantier, F. Liéval;
R. Etcheberry, coloring: M. Gros, L. Dousset, G. Mersch)
COMPUTER MAPS: Edigraphie **PHOTOGRAPHY**: X. Richer,
P. Delance, L. de Selva, F. Buxin, E. Valentin

SPECIAL THANKS TO: the RATP, the Musées de la Ville
de Paris and the Direction des affaires culturelles de la Ville
de Paris, whose support has made this guide reality; in
particular, thanks to Jean-Jacques Aillagon, directeur des
affaires culturelles de la Ville de Paris, Bernard Schotter,
sous-directeur du Patrimoine de la Ville de Paris and
Sophie Durrleman, chef du Bureau des Musées, direction
des affaires culturelles de la Ville de Paris.

Encyclopedia section

In the late 19th century, huge building projects ripped holes in the capital. When photographs were commissioned to chart this technological progress, a close partnership sprang up between engineer and photographer. This transformed the photographer from artist to skilled technician, methodically recording the metamorphosis of the site. These candid photographs (c. 1890) convey a celebration of modernity and an absolute confidence in a new world.

Photographers at the end of the 19th century took a special interest in the capital's heritage. Their patrons, principally institutions, preferred the pictures not to include people. As a result, the photographs were long shots, accentuating the documentary quality of these topographical views. At the same time, the tradition of photographing people, usually in humble occupations, grouped Parisians into socioprofessional categories. Atget, Paul Géniaux, Louis Vert and Lansiaux, among others, patiently recorded an unusual Paris in the throes of change.
(Below, *Tourists in St-Germain, Floods* by Lansiaux, 1920.)

After the austere, horror-filled years of World War Two, France began to rebuild. Humanitarian values and a desire to work together were the keynotes of this new society. Illustrated magazines played their part in the country's rebirth by publishing photographs of simple, evocative moments which showed a love of life. In the leading journals of the day, photographers like Boubat (*Quai du Louvre et l'Institut*, 1952, below), Doisneau, Ronis and Izis published sensitive, highly subjective pictures which were, quite naturally, dubbed humanist photography. On their solitary walks, they re-created a personal record of a bygone Parisian society.

History

● HISTORY

| Bronze Age | The Parisii settle in the Cité. | Lutetia spreads along the Left Bank. | **280** Walls are erected around the Cité. |

-5000   -3000   -500   0   200   400

| Hunter-fishermen inhabit the banks of the Seine near Bercy. | Bronze weapons and implements from the second millennium. | **52** Battle of Lutetia. | **14–37** Parisii boatmen's pillar is raised to the glory of Jupiter. | **250** Saint Denis is martyred. | **451** Invasion by the Huns. |

PREHISTORY

THE PALEOLITHIC PERIOD TO ROMANIZATION

Prehistoric man, whose chief occupation was hunting and gathering food, occupied the Paris Basin from around 700,000 BC: in fact, evidence of Paleolithic settlement has been excavated in Paris itself. In the Neolithic period, around 5000 BC, Danubian tribes who farmed and lived in villages of wooden or cob houses had settled in what is now the Île de France region. The population boom of the middle Neolithic period caused territorial disputes, forcing the population to take refuge behind palisades, embankments and

ditches. Traces of this so-called ribbon pottery culture have been found on the sites of the Jardin du Carrousel, the Place du Châtelet and the Porte de Vitry. In September 1991 building work at Bercy uncovered an arch dating from the Cerny period (4500–4200 BC), three oak dugout canoes from the mid-Neolithic period (4200–3400 BC) and an array of

implements and pottery proving that a permanent settlement existed there. Megaliths dating from the final Neolithic period (3400–1800 BC) have been discovered near Châtelet, behind the Hôtel de Ville, near St-Merri and in the Rue St-Dominique. In the Bronze Age (1800–750 BC) the Seine became a key trade route for English tin bound for the Mediterranean

and Central Europe. The Celts settled on the banks of the river during the late Iron Age (475–52 BC), and around 250–225 BC the Gallic tribe of the Parisii settled along the Seine between its confluences with the Marne and the Oise. At that time Lutetia was confined to the Île de la Cité and served as a refuge in times of war and as a ford for crossing the river. Gold coins dating from around 100 BC bear witness to the Parisii's thriving economic activity.

ANTIQUITY AND THE EARLY MIDDLE AGES

In 58 BC Julius Caesar began his conquest of Gaul. The battle of Lutetia in 52 BC and the surrender of

Vercingetorix and the Gallic chief Camulogenes assured Rome's victory. Lutetia was rebuilt in stone with a grid of paved streets ● 56 after the model of Italian cities. The Roman governor settled in the Île de la Cité, and the town spread along the Left

Bank, down the slopes of Mount Ste-Geneviève, on top of which stood the forum. The neglected Right Bank had only a temple to Mercury, erected on the hill at Montmartre.

The city covered some 124 acres at this point and had about five thousand inhabitants.

THE GRAND INVASIONS

Three centuries of Roman peace ended in AD 275 with the first of a series of raids by tribes of the outer Rhine. Lutetia was pillaged and the inhabitants fled back to the Cité, which was hastily fortified. This fortification was given the name of Paris toward the end

of the 3rd century. Christianity, which according to tradition appeared around 250 with Saint Denis the first bishop, triumphed in the 5th century with Saint Geneviève, the city's patroness. Her faith helped her to turn back Attila's hordes in 451, who were

defeated by the Roman general Actius in what is now known as the Champagne area. In 486 the Franks, a Germanic tribe who were native to the Rhine estuary and commanded by Clovis, seized the city, which served sporadically as their

capital. Their Carolingian successors abandoned it for the valley of the Meuse and Aix-la-Chapelle. The Normans looted the area around the Cité but were unable to seize the island despite a lengthy siege in 885–6.

511–558	987	1190–1210
Notre-Dame is constructed.	Huguès Capet is crowned king.	The Philippe-Auguste wall is built.
600	800	1000	1100	1200	1300

| 508 | 756 | 885 | 1163 | 1215 | 1257–74 |
| Clovis makes Paris his capital. | Pippin the Short is crowned in the Abbey of St-Denis. | Normans lay siege to the Cité. The Parisians resist. | Notre-Dame is reconstructed. | Foundation of the University of Paris. | The Sorbonne is founded by Robert de Sorbon. |

THE MIDDLE AGES

PARIS, CAPITAL OF FRANCE

With the coronation of Huguès Capet in 987, Paris became the kingdom's capital. Having considered Orléans, the kings settled for good in the Palais de la Cité under the reign of Louis VI the Fat (1108–37). In 1141 an undeveloped area on the site of what is now the Hôtel de Ville was granted in perpetuity by Louis VII to the bourgeoisie for their trading operations. Between 1310 and 1830 executions were carried out on this square. Philippe-Auguste (1180–1223) founded Les Halles, had the streets paved, and surrounded the city with a fortified wall. In 1215 the Pope founded the University of Paris

● 22. Colleges sprang up in the late 12th century and thrived in the 13th century.

Louis IX's chaplain, Robert de Sorbon, founded one of the most famous of these colleges, the Sorbonne, in 1257: this was to be the home of the Faculty of Theology in the 15th century. Under the reigns of Louis IX (1226–70) and Philippe the Fair ● 23 (1285–1314) Paris became the most densely populated city in Europe, with over 200,000 inhabitants in 1328.

ÉTIENNE MARCEL (1315–58). Provost of the merchants of Paris, Étienne Marcel came from a family of wealthy drapers and was the leader of the Third Estate in the States-General of 1355 and 1356. Protesting poor royal administration, he encouraged the estates to call for the foundation of a regency council and for institutional reform. For a year he commanded the capital. On February 22, 1358, the conflict culminated in the murder of two of the Dauphin's key counselors. Supporters of the Dauphin assassinated Étienne Marcel on July 31.

MUNICIPAL GOVERNMENT IS BORN

The boatmen's guild held the monopoly on river trade upstream and downstream of Paris. Based in the Place de Grève, the municipal government of the Parloir aux Bourgeois was formed to regulate this traffic administratively and legally. In the records kept, the first provosts of the merchants and aldermen appear in 1263.

ROYAL AUTHORITY CHALLENGED

Despite the ever-increasing burden of taxes, relations between the monarchy and the bourgeoisie remained excellent until the outbreak of war between France and England, which ended in disaster at Crécy (1346). The Great Plague of 1348 decimated the population, and the defeat of John the Good by the English created a terrible crisis. When the dauphin, Charles, brought together the estates in a bid to raise more money to continue the war, he crossed swords with the provost of the merchants, Étienne Marcel.

PARISIAN CRISES

Devastated by war, the Île de France was rocked by a peasant uprising in May 1358. The assassination of Étienne Marcel on July 31 restored civil peace and royal authority in Paris. Once on the throne, Charles V built the Bastille, as well as a city wall on the Right Bank around the newly built quarters. In March 1382 taxation triggered the Maillotin revolt. In retaliation, municipal autonomy was revoked. The King's madness and his uncles' struggle for power enabled Parisians to regain control of their institutions. The butchers' faction, led first by Simon Caboche, then by the executioner Capeluche, unleashed a reign of terror on the city in 1413 and 1418. After the Duke of Burgundy was murdered, his supporters allied themselves with the English, who entered Paris. Henry VI of England assumed the crown of France on the death of Charles VI. His son, Charles VII, took refuge in Bourges until 1436. After eighty years of stormy dealings with the capital, the monarchy withdrew to the Loire. Paris became a city peopled by citizens of independent means and civil servants.

1300		1350		1400		1500		1550		1600

1364–80
City wall built by
Charles V.

1528
The new Louvre is
constructed.

1606
Place des Vosges
is built.

1348
Widespread
epidemic of the
Great Plague.

1358
Étienne Marcel
stirs up Paris
against Charles V.

1418
Plague
epidemic.

1420
The English
occupy Paris.

1528
François I takes
up residence in
Paris.

1572
St Bartholomew's
Day massacre.

1610
Assassination
of Henri IV.

FROM THE RENAISSANCE TO THE ENLIGHTENMENT

RELIGION AND HUMANISM

The religious crisis which set Catholics against Protestants was started in 1517 by Luther's protests against the decadence of the Church and culminated in the St Bartholomew's Day massacre in 1572 ● 24. The crisis had forced the monarchy in 1528 to take up residence once again in its capital, which in turn boosted town-planning activity in Paris. François I entrusted the Italian architect Pietro da Cortona with the task of transforming the fortress of the Louvre ▲ 324 into a Renaissance palace. He also reformed the education system. At the request of the Hellenist Guillaume Budé, he founded the Collège de France to counteract the inflexibility of the University ● 22, which was hostile to Italian humanism. The city joined forces with the Holy League against the King and was besieged twice, in 1589 and 1590, and yielded to Henri IV only after he had abjured Protestantism in 1594.

Guillaume Budé.

THE GLOOMY 17TH CENTURY

During the 17th century French sovereigns worked hard to improve the appearance of Paris. The Place des Vosges was constructed in the reign of Henri IV,

the Île St-Louis started to take shape in 1614, and the Marais spread under Louis XIII. Louis XIV had the old rampart walls of Paris knocked down and replaced with wide boulevards, started the fashion for public gardens, and oversaw the widespread installation of street lighting. In the reign of Louis XV, Gabriel designed the Place Royale, which was to become the Place de la Concorde. But the capital was rocked by political disturbances. In 1635 France's entry into the Thirty Years' War caused epidemics and shortages in Paris and eventually landed the Parisians in a civil war, the Fronde, which lasted from 1648 to 1652. In 1666, traumatized by the events of his childhood, Louis XIV abandoned Paris for Versailles, where he had a palace built. He undertook increasingly dangerous campaigns, which sparked dreadful revolts in the capital in 1692 and 1709. The monarchy's desertion of the city caused discontent among Parisians. Undermined by the disputes between Jesuits and Jansenists, religious faith came under open attack in the 18th century salons, where the ideas of the philosophers were discussed. Even the commoners were opposed to the power of an absolute and remote monarch. The construction of tollhouses around the city increased hostilities.

*THE FRONDE.
The parliament of Paris, opposed to the government's financial measures, attempted to restrict royal power. The arrest of the leaders triggered protest among the populace, who barricaded the streets. Various princes joined the "frondeurs", including Condé. While marching on Paris, he clashed with Turenne's troops. Deserted by the bourgeoisie, he was forced to flee. From that time onward the heads of state steered clear of the capital.*

The Prince of Condé.
(Below) The Holy League
marching to the
Place de Grève.

1633 Creation of the Jardin des Plantes.		1763 Inauguration of the Place Louis XV.		1786 Construction of the toll-houses.	

1700   **1750**   **1770**   **1780**   **1790**

| 1648 The Fronde. | 1715 Death of Louis XIV. | 1751–72 Publication of the *Encyclopédie*. | 1774 Louis XVI restores the former parliament of Paris. | 1789 Convocation of the States General at Versailles. | July 14 Taking of the Bastille. | January 21, 1793 Execution of Louis XVI. |

THE REVOLUTION

Even on the eve of the Revolution, Paris continued to grow. The thoroughfare connecting the Louvre with the Tuileries was finally completed, and an ordinance of 1783 prescribed a minimum width of 30 feet for new streets ● 52. From the Chaussée d'Antin to the Faubourg St-Martin there was an unbroken vista of new buildings under construction. However, in 1789 this expansion was brought to an abrupt halt. The bankruptcy of state finances led to the collapse of the monarchy. Haunted by the specter of food shortages, unrest swept through the Faubourg St-Antoine and Faubourg St-Marcel. The nobility and the clergy refused to attend the States General with the Third Estate, who set themselves up as a National Assembly. The announcement of the dismissal of Finance Minister Necker was the last straw. On July 14 the

Bastille was stormed. Louis XVI returned to the capital. For five years revolutionary Paris, with the Jacobin *sans-culottes* at the helm and dominated by the imposing figure of Robespierre, forced the rest of the nation to toe the line. The populace invaded the Tuileries on August 10, 1792, and overthrew the monarchy. The moderate Girondins were ousted on June 2, 1793, and from September 1793 to July 1794, the *sans-culottes* instituted the official Reign of Terror. In March and April 1794, the Hébertists and the Dantonists were eliminated. Then came the about-turn. With the Thermidorian reaction, the

Robespierrists were marched to the scaffold in July 1794, to the delight of a population pushed too far by the Terror. Famine riots in the French revolutionary months of Germinal and Prairial (March and May 1795) and the abortive Royalist insurrection in Vendémiaire (October 1795) marked the death throes of the capital.

THE CONSULATE AND THE EMPIRE

Victorious in battle, Napoleon had himself elected First Consul, then crowned himself Emperor in 1804 and stripped Paris of all municipal power, for fear of a repeat of the excesses of the Revolution. Foreign visitors saw imperial Paris as a thriving city. The Vendôme column, a symbol of Napoleonic glory decorated with a bas-relief retracing the feats of the Grande Armée, was inaugurated on August 15, 1810. At the instigation of the prefect Frochot, an ambitious town-planning program was launched. Bridges, fountains, sewers, markets and slaughterhouses were opened, and work started on the Rue de Rivoli. Nevertheless, the financial crises of 1805 and 1810 and the instability caused by a sharp rise in the population due to rural depopulation, caused unrest in the capital. The Napoleonic saga ended in disaster: in March 1814, Paris was besieged by foreign armies, who restored the Bourbons, exiled since 1791, to the throne. Napoleon's return to the Tuileries a year later during the Hundred Days was merely incidental; Waterloo forced the Emperor to abdicate once again.

| **1853**
Haussmann starts
work. | **1860**
Division into twenty
arrondissements. | **1875**
Paris Opera House
is completed. | **1889**
Completion of
the Eiffel Tower. |

1800   **1820**   **1840**   **1860**   **1880**   **1900**

| **1804**
Bonaparte is
crowned Emperor in
Notre-Dame. | **July 27–9, 1830**,
Les Trois Glorieuses, the
three-day revolution. | **December 2, 1851**
Coup d'état by
Napoleon
Bonaparte. | **1870–1**
Paris besieged by
the Germans. | **1871**
Paris Commune. | **1894–9**
Dreyfus affair. |

THE 19TH CENTURY

REVOLUTIONS IN PARIS

Paris was modernized during the Restoration: markets and canals improved the city's access to supplies. Bridges, sidewalks, gas lighting and buses made it easier for its inhabitants to get around. The capital acquired a stock exchange, the Palais de la Bourse ▲ 353, which opened for business in 1825. Parisians wasted no time in opposing an outmoded moral code and political regime. The July Revolution, *Les Trois Glorieuses*, forced Charles X to abdicate. The younger branch of the Orléans family succeeded the Bourbons to the French throne with Louis-Philippe. The July Monarchy represented a golden age for the bourgeoisie. Arcades and showy monuments like the obelisk in the Place de la Concorde and the Arc de Triomphe ▲ 316 were all the rage: many artists and writers reaped the benefits of this growing affluence. In 1832 a cholera epidemic swept Paris, hitting the poverty-stricken quarters in the center and southeast particularly hard. Fearing another foreign invasion, prime minister Thiers surrounded Paris with a wall on the site of what is now the ring road circling Paris. In 1847 an economic crisis broke out: Louis-Philippe showed little patience with the rules of parliamentary monarchy, and as a result of his behavior a new revolution overthrew the regime and set up the Second Republic in February 1848. This abortive working-class and socialist revolution, which was suppressed in June 1848, threw the bourgeoisie into the arms of Napoleon's nephew. The future Napoleon III had himself elected Emperor one year after his coup d'état of December 2, 1851.

HAUSSMANN'S PARIS

In 1853 Napoleon III appointed Haussmann ● 72 prefect of the Seine. He demolished entire districts, built avenues and boulevards, and created parks and gardens. Europeans who had come for the various universal exhibitions ● 30 were dazzled by the street lighting. The improvement of the sewer system and the supply of running water to all buildings went hand in hand with the growth of a city which attracted thousands of immigrants every year. Paris, which had topped a million inhabitants in 1846, now had 700,000 more. On January 1, 1860, the inner suburbs were annexed to the capital in order to rationalize town planning, which increased the number of arrondissements from twelve to twenty. But the Franco-German war was to topple the regime on September 4, 1870. While the Emperor was a prisoner of the Prussians, an interim government was set up in Paris, several days before the enemy surrounded the city. The siege,

capitulation and loss of Alsace-Lorraine infuriated the populace, sparking off the bloody revolt of the Commune ● 28.

THE BELLE ÉPOQUE

Under the Third Republic the city continued to expand, but it was not until the end of the century, during the Belle Époque, that the capital regained the dynamism it had known under Haussmann. The Exhibition of 1889 ● 30 ushered in this new era. The regime withstood the unrest caused by the Boulanger affair (1889) and the Dreyfus affair (1894). Paris, along with Vienna, was a cultural center of Europe. As Haussmann's work was being completed, Art Nouveau was demolishing the prefect's concepts. The construction of the Metro ● 40 was finally started in 1900.

THE JULY REVOLUTION
Charles X wanted nothing to do with a parliamentary monarchy, and his authoritarianism provoked violent opposition. Between July 27 and 29, 1830, the Days of the Barricades, there were some bloody clashes. The royal troops under the command of Marshal Marmont were defeated by the rebels.

1921	1925	1969	1977	1998 Opening of
Fortifications of	Exhibition of	Creation of	Inauguration of	Météor driverless
Paris demolished.	Decorative Arts.	the RER.	Beaubourg.	metro, line 14.

| 1920 | 1940 | 1960 | 1980 | 1990 | 2000 | 2010 |

1914	June 14, 1940	August 1944	March 25, 1977	1986–8	1989
Assassination of	Germans occupy	Liberation of	Paris elects its	First	Bicentenary of
Jaurès. Outbreak of	Paris.	Paris.	first mayor.	coalition.	the Revolution.
World War One.					

MODERN TIMES

In the early years of the 20th century, the population of Paris increased by 25 percent, but war arrested this trend. Paris peaked at just under three million inhabitants in 1921. Construction ground almost completely to a halt between 1919 and 1939. After this, the inner suburbs absorbed the new arrivals, and Paris suffered urban sprawl. Parisian industry relocated there, taking advantage of lower costs and an abundant supply of labor. The formation of a *ceinture rouge*, a ring of left-wing suburbs around Paris, gradually highlighted the divide between the capital and its suburbs. The capital still fascinated the world, with the bohemian lifestyle of painters of the School of Paris, mainly led by foreigners who had settled in Montparnasse ▲ *272*. Despite the Roaring Twenties, the international prestige enjoyed by the City of Light during the Belle Époque had become tarnished: the Universal Exhibitions of 1925 and 1931 were pale reflections of those in 1889 and 1900.

THE MEGALOPOLIS

After the Nazi occupation ● *32*, which deeply affected the city, Paris and its suburbs resumed their growth. The housing shortage was worsened by the demolitions. The bistros reaped the benefits of widespread overcrowding, which favored the growing popularity of literary cafés like the Flore and the Deux-Magots. Nightclubs and Boris Vian's St-Germain-des-Prés sprang up partly as a result of the recession and the general need to forget. The terrible winter of 1954 saw the appearance of Abbot Pierre and led to the launch of an extensive building program. This activity was speeded up when a new political group came to power in 1958. The outer suburbs outstripped the inner suburbs in 1962, while the city's population dropped to some two million inhabitants. Paris began to revamp its older quarters – especially the Marais, helped by the 1962 Malraux Law – in an attempt to justify its image as the showcase of France. Large-scale public works carried out under the Fifth Republic created a modern transport system for a city and suburbs of around ten million people. In 1969, the first RER line was opened.

The suburbs were now just a stone's throw from the capital, and five new towns were built around Paris. The city, now largely populated by the middle and upper classes, became more gentrified. Although the regime was rocked by the student revolts of 1968 ● *34*, the fear of a new Commune had vanished. The Pompidou years were marked by the realization of large-scale public works projects planned by De Gaulle: les Halles, Beaubourg, Rungis, la Défense and the Montparnasse Tower. Treating any controversy with contempt, the new leaders drastically altered the face of the capital. The period of economic expansion in France (1945–75) came to an end with the oil crisis. France under Valéry Giscard d'Estaing became more conservative. Paris rehabilitated, protected and developed its open spaces and private facilities. In 1976 the city was granted municipal status similar to that of other cities in France, and the following year it elected its first mayor in modern times. One of Pompidou's most eccentric projects, running the A10 freeway through Paris, was abandoned. Elected president in

1981 and again in 1988, François Mitterrand gave Paris a dazzling array of public buildings, including the Opéra Bastille, the Grande Arche de la Défense, the Grand Louvre and the library that bears his name. At the same time the boom in the construction of offices that began in 1988 was hit by the economic slump, so that empty office space is now being converted into housing. The city's population has ceased its decline. The Stade de France stadium in St-Denis was opened in 1998 for the soccer World Cup. Districts in the east of Paris (Bercy ● *80* and Tolbiac) were redeveloped. Finally the opening of Meteor, the driverless metro (line 14), in 1998 and of RER's Line E in 1999 greatly improved public transport in and between Paris and the suburbs.

Descended from the chapter school of Notre-Dame cathedral, the University of Paris took shape during the 17th century. The restrictions imposed by the chancellor of Notre-Dame, who supervised the teaching and awarded the diplomas, very soon prompted some teachers to put themselves beyond the reach of his authority, taking up residence on the Left Bank, where the Abbey of Ste-Geneviève allowed them to teach. One of the first to cross the Seine was Abelard, who was persecuted in the Cité.

THE BIRTH

A studious but unruly throng of students and teachers took over the hitherto deserted slopes of Ste-Geneviève. Before the colleges were built, classes were held in stables or barns. Fond of brawling and carousing, the students provoked hostility and fear. Following a brawl in a tavern which claimed the lives of five people in 1200, Philippe-Auguste decided that the students would come under the exclusive jurisdiction of the Church and not that of the state. In 1215 the University was given its statutes by Robert de Courson, the papal legate. A compromise drawn up in 1238 by Pope Gregory IX outlined a division of powers: teachers in the faculties of Theology and Canonic Law would receive their degrees from the chancellor of Notre-Dame, while the chancellor of Ste-Geneviève would award arts degrees. The vice-chancellor, who represented the University after 1211, was merely the head of the Faculty of Arts, elected by the bursars from the four nations.

THE NATIONS

These were clubs, guilds and brotherhoods at one and the same time. The nation of France was divided into five clans, corresponding to Paris and the archdioceses of Sens, Reims, Tours and Bourges. The other nations were those of Picardy, Normandy and England along with Belgium, Germany and Scandinavia.

GREAT DISPUTES

The University interfered in all the major political and religious disputes of the Middle Ages. Not satisfied with fighting heretical ideas and trying to find a way of resolving the Great Schism, it also tried to impose its will on royal authority during John the Good's captivity and Étienne Marcel's rebellion.

STUDIES

These began around the age of fourteen at the Faculty of Arts and included the *trivium* (grammar, rhetoric and dialectics) and the *quadrivium* (mathematics, geometry, music and astronomy). After six years students sat for their baccalauréat, then a master's degree, which enabled them to teach. Bachelors of arts could then study canonic law or medicine and obtain a doctorate. A doctorate from the Faculty of Theology, the crowning glory of the university required some further fifteen years of study.

THE SORBONNE

Colleges, which sprang up around 1250, were originally hotels or boarding houses lodging people from the provinces or abroad who had come to study in Paris. In the 14th century tutors living on site gave the boarders extra tuition. There were, in the following century, some sixty colleges housing nearly seven hundred students. The most famous was founded in 1257 by Robert de Sorbon and became the seat of the Sorbonne's Faculty of Theology in the 15th century. The major religious orders, especially the Dominicans, Franciscans and Cistercians, had their own colleges for monks who came to study theology.

Seal of the University of Paris.

THE MARTINETS

Martinets catered for their own needs, studied under form-masters, and threw in their lot with a professor only for examinations. Having no means of support, they lived by their wits, often engaging in criminal activities. Their scandalous lifestyles painted a shady picture of the student world, evoked by the life of poet François Villon.

● St Bartholomew's Day

Catherine de' Medici.

The French Reformed Church, founded in Paris in 1559, remained a minority in the face of widespread Catholicism: its only power base was south of the Loire. The massacre of Protestants at Wassy in March 1562, perpetrated by the Duc de Guise's men, triggered the first of the eight Wars of Religion which were to ravage the country until 1598. The atrocities reached their climax with the St Bartholomew's Day massacre on August 24, 1572, in Paris. Peace was restored when Henri IV abjured Calvinism in 1593 and granted freedom of worship to the Protestants with the Edict of Nantes in 1598.

THE PROTESTANTS IN PARIS

The bulk of the Reformation's urban contingent was supplied by petty magistrates, well-educated craftsmen, furriers, drapers, silversmiths and booksellers. In high society the noblest lineages – Bourbon, Condé, Bouillon, Turenne and La Rochefoucauld – rallied to Calvinism. The illiterate and superstitious lower classes, surrounded by their priests and mendicant sermonizing monks, developed a hatred of the Huguenots, whose wealth they coveted.

THE BACKGROUND TO THE TRAGEDY

Henri II's widow, Catherine de' Medici, wielded power in the name of her son, Charles IX. Despised as much by the Protestants as by the Catholics, she vacillated between the two camps. Unable to overcome the Calvinists by force of arms, she negotiated with them out of fear of King Philippe II of Spain, whose lands surrounded France. The marriage of her daughter Marguerite to Henri de Bourbon, King of Navarre, was meant to seal the reconciliation between French citizens of both denominations.

THE MAIN PLAYERS

On July 9 or 10, the King of Navarre, his cousin Condé, Admiral de Coligny and La Rochefoucauld entered Paris with a thousand Gascon gentlemen. The infuriated Catholic Parisians welcomed the De Guise family, who had arrived from Lorraine. The latter took up residence in their mansion and their retinue in the inns around the Louvre.

Coligny persuaded the weak Charles IX to come to the aid of the Protestants in the Netherlands, who had revolted against the King of Spain. The Queen Mother threatened to leave for Florence if her son complied and at the same time decided to get rid of Coligny, who had become too influential.

THE BLOODY WEDDING

On August 18 the King of Navarre married Marguerite de Valois. On the morning of August 22, Coligny was shot twice but was saved by Ambroise Paré. On the following evening Catherine de' Medici confessed to her son that she had bribed the would-be assassin Maurevert and resumed her blackmail: she would go back to Florence if the King refused to annihilate the Huguenots. Charles IX resigned himself to the task. The provost of the merchants was ordered to close the city gates and put the militia on alert.

THE MASSACRE

The signal for the slaughter was given at around three or four in the morning by the bell of St-Germain-l'Auxerrois. The Duc de Guise and his men killed Admiral de Coligny first. The King of Navarre's most loyal companions had their throats slit while in bed at the Louvre. The massacre lasted until August 29 and claimed between fifteen hundred and two thousand lives, wiping out the cream of the Protestant nobility. Only Henri de Bourbon was spared and kept prisoner. The capital's Calvinist bourgeoisie was also severely hit, and Protestantism was practically eradicated in Paris. The St Bartholomew's Day massacre was to be the root cause of a further twenty years of civil war in France.

● PARIS AND THE FRENCH REVOLUTION

The French Revolution began at the Bastille, the symbol of absolute monarchy: the constitutional monarchy was overthrown in the Palais des Tuileries and wiped out in the Place de la Concorde, where Louis XVI was beheaded. A few paces from where the Terror had begun, it ended with the massacre of the final victims in the Place de la Nation. After a bitter four-year struggle along this east–west axis, Paris gained local power for itself in place of the absolutism of Versailles.

THE TOLLHOUSES BURNT

From the point of view of the city, if not the nation, a highly symbolic event took place in the summer of 1789: the barely completed tollhouses, which embellished Paris' new customs barrier, were burnt down.

As a result, some of Claude Nicolas Ledoux's work was lost to the country's architectural heritage.

A POLITICAL MAP
Paris inherited a political geography from the Revolution. The Faubourg St-Antoine became the stronghold of a democratic artisan community. The old working-class quarters on the Right Bank acquired a new importance in Parisian political life: the mouthpieces of power – the Assembly and the Jacobin and Feuillant clubs – were set up around the château between what are now Rue St-Honoré and Rue de Rivoli. The Champs-de-Mars, a symbol of national unity at the Festival of Federation in 1790, was the scene of some of the clashes which heralded civil war in July 1791.

> "Over Paris, which has no bread, rises the hard wheat of pikes. With its cornflowers of steel, its poppies of blood, here is the harvest of protracted anger."

Max-Pol Fouchet

THE TERROR

The whole population was affected by the Terror: 115 priests were killed including 2 bishops and 1 archbishop; more than 2,800 people were guillotined in the Place de la Concorde. Picpus cemetery is full of graves belonging to the nobility as well as to working-class people.

THE CHANGING FACE OF PARIS

During the Terror, a great deal of property changed hands due to the institutional and social upheaval. Goods belonging to the Church, the city and the aristocracy were sold. The finest mansions and convents fell into the hands of architects, lawyers, notaries, bankers, tradesmen and manufacturers or became the property of the state. Part of the prestigious Faubourg St-Germain was transformed into a ministerial quarter, while the Elysée Palace started its glorious career in the Faubourg St-Honoré. Speculators were busy demolishing many great structures including the convent buildings belonging to the Abbey of St-Germain-des-Prés. The result was a great loss to the Roman-Gothic architectural heritage of Paris.

● THE COMMUNE

The Commune marked one of the most serious crises in the history of Paris: even during the June days of 1848 and the St Bartholomew's Day massacre, blood had never flowed so freely. The Franco-Prussian war was at the root of this bloodbath. After the defeat of Sedan and the fall of the Empire, the enemy arrived at the walls of Paris and besieged the recently fortified capital. This widened the rift between the patriotic Parisians and the government, which, forced to surrender in early 1871, fell back to Bordeaux. When the government returned to Versailles, it convoked the National Assembly and forced Paris to capitulate, triggering the hostilities.

WAR ABROAD

The events of the spring of 1871 were preceded by the siege of Paris by the Prussians, the final military and political episode in the war waged during the summer of 1870. The enemy bombarded the city with twelve thousand shells between January 5 and 27, 1871. These shells fell mainly on the Left Bank, hitting

1,400 houses, the Museum, the greenhouse in the Jardin des Plantes, the Necker Hospital, the Institut des Jeunes Aveugles and many other buildings. Outside Paris the Prussians destroyed Château de St-Cloud (October 23, 1870) and the Château de Meudon (January 31, 1871) just after the armistice had been signed.

THE COMMUNE

The Parisian working-class movement was infuriated by the siege and the government's capitulation, as well as the political hijacking of patriotic fervor. This resulted in a confrontation between Paris and Versailles which was the seat of the legal government under the leadership of Thiers on March 18, 1871. Two armies clashed: the regular troops and the Federalists of the National Guard. The latter imbued Montmartre with its revolutionary spirit by preventing the men of Versailles from taking away the guns belonging by right to Parisians, which had been stored on a piece of wasteland on top of the hill. Ironically, ten years later the monumental staircase leading to the basilica of the Sacré-Coeur was built on the same site.

It was no mean task to regain Paris; despite Haussmann's thoroughfares, the dense and virtually impenetrable city hindered the deployment of an army. This problem was compounded by the fact that the streets were bristling with barricades.

THE BLOODY WEEK (MAY 21–7, 1871)

The Federalists' Wall in the Père Lachaise cemetery ▲ *412* witnessed the death of only a small number of the Commune's 20,000 victims (according to some estimates, the figure was as high as 35,000 deaths), but the massacre took its toll on the surrounding quarter. The street battles here were bitter, earning residents of Belleville the epithet of "barbarians". The Bloody Week badly scarred the city. Falling back gradually toward the east of Paris, the Communards resorted to arson and whole streets were destroyed. The Tuileries Palace was torched, later razed in 1882 and replaced by gardens. The Cour des Comptes on the banks of the Seine remained in ruins until 1898. The Louvre itself only barely escaped damage.

● THE UNIVERSAL EXHIBITIONS

Five universal exhibitions were held in Paris during the 19th century but only one in the 20th century, in 1937. The difficulties of recovering from the devastation of World War One partly account for the decline in the number of exhibitions. These temporary exhibitions were first and foremost a showcase for the industrial skills of the participating nations and the great strides made in the domain of technical progress, which they helped to popularize. France was particularly fond of these events, which provided ample opportunity to show off its artistic and scientific creativity, as well as its high-quality production, geared to luxury items. Paris had inherited a rich architectural heritage, making it an ideal setting for international exhibitions.

1855 AND 1867
The innovative nature of the exhibitions during the Second Empire rivaled that of Crystal Palace in London in 1851. They ushered in the era of great halls with metal frames, and vast glass roofs, like that of the breathtaking Palais de l'Industrie. The exhibitions also encouraged huge influxes of tourists (eleven million visitors atttended in 1867) and helped to give the hotel industry a boost. The first Parisian luxury hotels date from this period.

THE EXHIBITIONS OF 1878 AND 1889

These two exhibitions were organized in praise of the Third Republic. The exhibition in 1878 helped blot out the bad memories of 1871, while that of 1889 coincided with the centenary of the Revolution. They formed a strong link between the Left and Right banks near the 7th and 8th arrondissements and these areas became the most elegant parts of Paris.

The Trocadero, the palace built on a hill at Chaillot, and the Eiffel Tower were also the fruits of these exhibitions. The plan for the Eiffel Tower was the object of much public derision but once erected it became the most popular monument in Paris. The École Militaire, which until then had been tucked away on the outer edges of the working-class district of Grenelle, now became part of the capital.

THE EXHIBITION OF 1937

This strange event provided a forum for the shaky prestige of the democratic states of the world, while the two showiest pavilions confronting each other on the banks of the Seine were those of the Soviet Union and the Third Reich. All that remains of this exhibition is the memory of social unrest which nearly jeopardized the completion of construction work and the new neoclassical Palais de Chaillot.

THE UNIVERSAL EXHIBITION OF 1900

The Grand Palais replaced the Palais de l'Industrie, facing the Petit Palais on a new triumphal avenue linking the Élysée Palace to the Hôtel des Invalides via the Alexandre III bridge, which had been built for the occasion. For the first time the monuments of a universal exhibition were built to last. The two palaces and the bridge were the showpieces of a new architectural style which combined conventional stonework and decorative motifs with the innovative use of metalwork. This triumphant industrial architecture blended in perfectly with the state buildings of the Left Bank, which were built by Louis XIV and Louis XV.

● OCCUPIED PARIS, LIBERATED PARIS

From June 14, 1940, to August 25, 1944, the German army had military command over the occupied zone. When the French government departed on June 10, 1940, Paris was proclaimed an open city and was spared Allied bombing raids. Its liberation, however, gave rise to violent street fighting.

OCCUPIED PARIS

Imagine a city without buses or taxis and with few gas-fueled vehicles; instead there were some diesel vehicles, bicycles, tandem bicycles with passenger trailers for hire, and horse-driven vehicles. The Metro, closed from 11am to 3pm and at weekends, ran until 11pm; this famous

Der Militärbefehlshaber in Frankreich.

O.Qu.West
Rue d'Astorg 25-27

General der Luftwaffe Paris

GL/Paris

Bekleidungslager
Kdt. von Gross-Paris

"last Metro" enabled people to get home before curfew.

The army's presence could not be ignored; all signs were in German, and red flags flew from the tops of public buildings guarded by armed sentries. The commander-in-chief of the Luftwaffe was based at the Palais du Luxembourg, the governor of Paris at the Hôtel Meurice, and the government of occupied France at the Majestic. The occupiers could also be found in black-market restaurants and luxury nightclubs such as the Shéhérazade and the Suzy Solidor.

SHADOWY AREAS

Grim memories abound at 74, avenue Foch and 9, rue des Saussaies, where the Gestapo officiated; the prisons of the Cherche-Midi (54, boulevard Raspail) and Mont-Valérien (4,500 were shot between 1941 and 1944); the Vélodrome d'Hiver, where Jews were rounded up in July 1942; not to mention the prisons in the suburbs: Drancy, Fresnes and Romainville. Occupied Paris also worked for Germany: the tunnel of St-Cloud housed a submarine torpedo factory employing as many as five thousand prisoners.

RESISTANCE PARIS

Colonel Fabien dared to commit the first public act of resistance on August 21, 1941, by killing a German officer at the Metro station that now bears his name. A convent on the Rue de la Glacière housed the representative of the Intelligence Service. Thirty-seven young Resistance fighters were executed in front of the waterfall in the Bois de Boulogne.

PARIS UNDER THREAT

The forty-five bridges crossing the Seine between Le Pecq and Choisy were not destroyed, unlike those farther down river. Consequently, Paris became a strategic thoroughfare, playing a key role in the German defense of northern and eastern France. Hitler gave Governor von Choltitz strict orders to defend every inch of Paris and to reduce the city to ashes in case of a withdrawal following defeat. So the bridges, state buildings, supply routes, railways and stations were all mined. The systematic destruction of any quarter which attempted rebellion was also ordered.

LIBERATED PARIS

The Liberation left its mark along the entire length of the Left Bank. On August 24 and 25, 1944, American forces entered Paris via the Porte d'Orléans, the Porte de Vanves and the Porte de Sèvres. The bells of Notre-Dame pealed out a welcome for the vanguard, while General de Gaulle's epic march down the Champs-Élysées blotted out the memory of the Wehrmacht march in 1940. There was fighting all over Paris. There are plaques on many of the capital's buildings reminding people of the dark hours that the city lived through.

Leclerc's Second Armored Division and assorted

PARIS IN REVOLT

The uprising of Paris began on the 1,518th day of the occupation, on August 19, 1944. The various branches of the Resistance seized the police headquarters and, from the Catacombs, called for barricades to be erected. More than two hundred were raised in three days. The fighting was particularly fierce along the south–north thoroughfares, especially boulevards St-Michel and St-Germain, the junction of which was called the "crossroads of death", as well as the Place de la République and the Rue La Fayette. The Grand Palais was partially destroyed. A representative of the Gaullist Resistance took up his post without difficulty in the Hôtel Matignon, which Pierre Laval had just deserted.

● MAY 1968

Although it is the city of revolutions, Paris was not in the vanguard of student unrest at the end of the 1960's. As early as 1964 in California and 1966 in Berlin, thousands of students joined forces to stage major sit-ins. But the Parisian movement, with its revolution of May 1968, was the only one to result in a major political crisis on a national scale, almost succeeding in overthrowing the government.

NANTERRE: BIRTH OF A MOVEMENT

The university academic year of 1967–8 was extremely turbulent, disrupted by general protest meetings, demonstrations and clashes with the police. A class strike ended the year at Nanterre, a new campus in the suburbs built cheek-by-jowl with the poor quarters, and whose name, like that of Berkeley, was to become famous. The protest movement got underway on March 22, 1968, when forty-two students invaded the university's administrative offices.

le grand chambardement

THE LATIN QUARTER

When Nanterre closed on May 2, the Sorbonne took over. On May 3 demonstrators in the courtyard were expelled by the military. From then on there were daily violent clashes on the Left Bank between university and high school students and the French riot police, the CRS. On May 7 the French student union, the UNEF, organized a huge march from the Latin Quarter to the Arc de Triomphe.

THE DAY OF MAY 10

The unrest took on another dimension during the night of May 10–11, when barricades were erected in the Latin Quarter, sparking a violent counter attack by the police with hundreds of casualties – but no deaths – on both sides. The students then changed their tactics and occupied a number of buildings. The universities of the Sorbonne and Censier and the Odéon Theater became hotbeds of student unrest. Today the only reminders of this turbulent period are the old posters and graffiti scrawled across the walls of the Sorbonne.

RENAULT

Amid total confusion, links were forged between the student movement and the trade-union movement; Billancourt, Flins and Cléon became the centers of a social unrest which threatened to spread to every sector of French society. And indeed by May 22 ten million French people were on strike. The old stadium of Charléty, near the recently rebuilt residence halls, was the site of a major political demonstration on May 27, which called for the formation of a transitional government.

TRAVAILLEURS
FRANÇAIS IMMIGRÉS
UNIS

RESTORING ORDER

In response to this chaos, there was a major demonstration down the Champs-Élysées on May 30 in support of General de Gaulle. The value of such a symbolic gesture, reminiscent of his march in 1944, was not lost on the country, and he was seen as the figure most able to restore order. However, the situation remained unstable for several weeks.

Parisian scenes

● PARISIAN STREET LIFE

Despite the three million cars that drive through Paris every day, the city remains the domain of pedestrians, whose lot was greatly improved at the end of the last century when sidewalks were laid across the city and public health became a concern. Nowadays, police officers and street cleaners have replaced the many peddlers who used to work the city's streets before the war. But the Parisian street retains much of its picturesque charm, and the open-air markets still echo with the cries of days gone by.

THE PEDESTRIANS OF PARIS

Under the Ancien Régime, only the more important citizens were allowed to walk on the sides of the street. Others were left to share the central part of the road with the waste water. In 1780 the first sidewalks were laid, but they did not become common until the Second Empire.

THE CLEAN PREFECT

In 1884 Eugène Poubelle (above), prefect of the Seine, made it obligatory for Parisians to use trash cans (to which he gave his name). Two years later, he introduced a sewer system. Despite the hostility of those who saw it as an infringement on their liberty, health became a public matter toward the end of that century. From then on, the streets which formed the nervous system of Haussmann's city were to be used by all and sundry.

POLICE OFFICERS

Emergency help, community policing and traffic control are the main responsibilities of the police, who ensure the safety of the Republic's most important institutions, based in the capital. It is administered by a central organization at police headquarters – *la préfecture de police*.

Photographed in 1904, one of the largest markets in Paris is still still held two mornings a week on the Boulevard de Belleville.

Every year traffic officers or members of the Paris security forces issue eight million parking tickets to motorists.

The glowing colors of the market in the Rue Mouffetard at the heart of the Latin Quarter.

Parisian garbage collectors now preach the virtues of recycling and "keeping Paris clean", a slogan found on every street corner.

THE CRIES OF PARIS

"Buy my tender artichokes!" If you want to hear the "cries of Paris", simply go to one of the city's fifty or so food markets, which spread out along the sidewalks and central islands in the streets. But only a few of the many peddlers who used to walk the streets of Paris before the war have survived. From time to time, you will still hear the ringing cries of the glazier and the knife grinder, as well as the refrain of the street musician who sings for coins thrown down from your window.

A woman selling roasted chestnuts (below).

THE CONCIERGE

he concierge is a colorful character in Parisian e, inherited from the 19th century, when every ented property had its own caretaker's room. ese caretakers have gradually been replaced by the electronic keypad.

La place de la Concorde vue de l'hôtel de la Marine

PARISIAN STREET LIFE

Carnivals disappeared from the streets of Paris in 1914, but the popular success of the Technoparade has given the genre a new lease of life.

Women from the suburbs marching on Versailles to clamor for bread, the Communards erecting barricades against the king's men from Versailles, the endless Front Populaire marches, the paving stones of May 1968 – at regular intervals throughout its history, Paris has been engulfed in strife, and angry crowds have rampaged through its streets. Although the capital does not spawn a revolution every day, it nevertheless continues to live up to its reputation: 1,500 protest demonstrations are held every year, an average of four a day.

POLITICAL ROUTES
After half a century, marches and demonstrations have split the city into two distinct political worlds. From 1934 on, the main Bastille–Nation and Bastille–République roads became left-wing demonstration routes; the political parties and unions which brought the Front Populaire to power once again commandeered the symbolic power of the revolutionary suburbs. On the other side of the political spectrum, Liberation transformed the Champs-Élysées into a Gaullist route. On May 30, 1968, one million people gathered there to demand an end to the *chienlit* (student protests).

ROUGH CUT
Weighing between 2 and 4 pounds, the Parisian *pavé*, a roughly cut granite paving stone, can be thrown as far as 65 feet. A favorite weapons of rioters, it was also their creed: "Sous les pavés la plage" (meaning "Beneath harsh reality lies a brighter tomorrow") declared the student protesters of May 1968.

BARRICADES
"Dreadful masterpieces of civil war" in Victor Hugo's words, the barricades were a characteristic feature of the revolutions of 1830 and 1848 and the Commune (left, Place de la Concorde, 1871). One of the sayings of the Liberation was: "Everyone to the barricades!" Dozens were erected in the Latin Quarter in May 1968.

DEMO INSTRUCTIONS
Any demonstration on a public road comes under the jurisdiction of the police, which prescribes a minimum of 3½ square yards per person if a crowd is to be able to move in complete safety.

38

STREET CELEBRATIONS

Concerts in the streets and dancing until the small hours of the morning: this is how Parisians have celebrated Midsummer's Eve since the summer music festival was created in 1981. On the evening of July 14 dances are held everywhere. Among the most popular are those held in fire stations and the one in the Place de la Bastille (left).

FIELD OF HONOR

In 1804, Napoleon I organized a spectacular party along the Champs-Élysées ▲ *312* to celebrate his marriage to Marie-Louise. The Champs-Élysées acquired its patriotic and official status with the victory parade on July 14, 1919. This was reinforced when the ashes of the Unknown Soldier were moved to the Arc de Triomphe in 1921.

● THE METRO

Packed like sardines in the Metro during the rush hour, Parisians dream of a different way of life. "Métro, boulot, dodo" ("metro, work, sleep") – a saying inherited from the 1970's – mocks the commuter's life style. But this underground kingdom created in 1900 by the engineer Fulgence Bienvenüe (left), after forty years of procrastination and conflict between the city and the state, has its finer moments: when a talented musician livens up your journey, when a station becomes a museum, or when a train crosses the Seine at sunset on the elevated section of the Metro.

PARIS VERSUS THE SUBURBS
Paris did not want a Metro system which served the suburbs and insisted that it run exclusively within the city boundaries, taking care that it traveled on the right, in the opposite direction of the trains, to prevent a future link-up.

HERITAGE
Guimard designed eighty-four Art Nouveau entrance signs (top, facing page) as well as advertisement panels composed of white earthenware tiles with carved borders.

PARALLEL LINES
Rather than negotiating with private landowners, the city excavated state-owned land. Hence, most lines followed the path of existing roads instead of plotting new routes ▲ 281.

SUBTERRANEAN CULTURE
Launched in 1967 by André Malraux, who transformed the Louvre Metro station into a museum, the policy for themed stations has endured. The Assemblée Nationale station (left).

PROFESSIONAL, AUTOMATON OR IDLER?
Passengers on the Metro fall into three categories: the first makes his daily journey as quickly and efficiently as possible, the second travels like an automaton, and the third wanders along, stopping to look at the slightest distraction.

REFUGE
The Metro has always been a refuge for some of the 25,000 homeless in Paris. They tell their life stories or sell magazines devoted to the issues of homelessness (below) in the Metro cars. They are all at one time or another pulled in by the "Blues" from the welfare service for homeless people or by SAMU, the ambulance and emergency service of the city of Paris, for medical treatment and checkups.

THE SONG OF THE METRO
Accordions, violins, tom-toms and guitars – the Metro echoes with all the rhythms of the world. After banishing amateur musicians from its subways for many years, RATP is now granting them licences and sites.

● THE CAFÉS

A handful of prestigious cafés have assured the fame of this most Parisian of institutions. The first of these, the Procope, buzzed with the rivalry between its illustrious customers, the philosophers of the Enlightenment. But just as legendary are the local bistros with their canvas canopies and their tables which spill out over the sidewalks at the break of dawn. Cafés are ideal for meeting people and doing business, and there are no fewer than one for every two hundred citizens.

FROM THE PROCOPE . . .
(13, rue de l'Ancienne Comédie, 75006) In 1686 a Sicilian, Francesco Procopio, opened a coffee shop in Paris. He decorated it lavishly – mirrors, chandeliers, gilt fittings – and attracted members of polite society who until then had hardly ever visited taverns. They regarded this new drink from the East, *Kahve*, as a tonic for the brain.

. . . TO THE LOCAL BISTRO
In the 19th century the luxurious cafés on the grand boulevards and the small bars in the working-class quarters, as pilloried by Zola in *L'Assommoir*, existed cheek-by-jowl. At the turn of the century the two types of establishments merged to give birth to the modern café.

CAFÉ GLOSSARY

Petit noir (espresso): 2 ounces of strong coffee, made by forcing steam through the ground beans.

Noisette: espresso with a dash of milk.
Petit crème, *grand crème*: coffee with milk, either *bien blanc* (very light) or *bien noir* (dark).
Ballon: 6 ounces of red or white wine served in a round wine glass.
Demi: 9 ounces of draft beer originally served in pint glasses.

DE CARBOU! N'IA ...

"Coal for sale!" was the call in patois of people from the Auvergne, who came to Paris in the 19th century to sell wine and coal. Gradually the coal merchants (*bougnats*) turned to barkeeping and they dominate the profession to this day. *Mastroquet* was the name formerly given to wine merchants. The word, from which *troquet* (meaning bar) is derived, comes from *demi-stroc*, which was a measure of wine.

"ZINC"

The *zinc*, or bar-counter, whose elongated shape often dictates that of the room, is the focal point of any café. It first appeared in the 19th-century *assommoirs* (cheap bars), as it enabled a greater number of customers to be served. At that time it was made of an alloy of tin and zinc, from which it derived its name: some fine examples still exist.

SALON ON THE STREET

With its glass façade tempting you to take some time out, the Parisian café functions as a salon on the street. Right from the start, this nonpartisan, democratic meeting place provided intellectuals with a perfect forum for debate and inspiration. Diderot and D'Alembert probably

launched the *Encyclopédie* at the Procope. Molière and Voltaire, who lived nearby, were regular customers. Camille Desmoulins incited the people to revolt from the Café de Foy in the Palais-Royal. The surrealists, followed by Sartre and De Beauvoir, transformed certain cafés in St-Germain-des-Prés into literary meccas.

THE WAITER

The traditional costume worn by a café waiter, or *rondin*, is black trousers, white shirt, bow tie and a waistcoat with many pockets for dividing up the loose change. A white apron encircles his waist, calling to mind a log of wood, or *rondin*. Every year a waiters' contest is organized in Paris.

Every twenty years or so, Paris invents new locations for entertainment, places where you can eat and drink while watching a show. The Revolution had its *cafés-chantants* (cafés with performing artists), the July Monarchy its musical societies and glee clubs, the Belle Époque its *café-concerts* (cafés with live music) and their working-class equivalent in music halls, the 20th century its music-hall revues and its cabarets. In the 1970's *café-théâtre* (cafés with live theater) took over, encouraging a new generation of actors and authors. Today, there is a revival of *cafés-chantants*, small bistros with performances by musicians and raconteurs in a friendly, informal location.

CAFÉS-CONCERTS
Derived from the simple cafés which welcomed appearances by artistes, the *cafés-concerts* became an institution under the Second Empire. From 1870, establishments, designed to stage shows (Folies-Bergère, Ba Ta Clan, Moulin-Rouge), developed similarities with music-hall.

THE RETURN OF CAFÉS-CHANTANTS
Music and song are making a decisive come-back in Parisian cafés. Often tiny, these cafés have strange and evocative names – Le Baron Rouge (the Red Baron), L'Ogre de Barbarie (the Barbaric Ogre), L'Oreille Cassée (the Split Ear), La Patate Bleue (the Blue Potato), La Liberté. Eclectic in style, they are also responsible for reviving the tradition of accordion music and French ballad.

PARISIAN REVUE
The revue consisted of various performances by scantily-clad women on a raised stage. The revue was at its height during the inter-war period with its stars Mistinguett and Josephine Baker.

ARTISTIC CABARETS

Heir to the glee clubs of the July Monarchy – working-class choirs singing songs by anti-establishment poets in the backrooms of small bars – the artistic cabaret was born in Montmartre at the end of the last century. Aristide Bruant and Yvette Guilbert invented the political and satirical song at the Mirliton and at the Divan Japonais. The impertinent and provocative spirit of cabaret was kept alive in the 1920's at the Boeuf sur le Toit, then after the war in St-Germain-des-Prés.

CAFÉ-THÉÂTRE

In the 1960's a generation of young authors and actors in search of unconventional places to perform directed their attention to cafés. A new genre and a new term was born – *café-théâtre*. Le Royal in Montparnasse, La Vieille Grille in the Latin Quarter and Le Fanal in Les Halles were among the trail-blazers. *Café-théâtre*, a melting pot of new talent which was responsible for the discovery of artists such as Coluche and Gérard Depardieu, is still going strong and favors witty and satirical material.

SCHOOL FOR ARTISTES

Cafés-chantants, cabarets and *café-théâtres*, where artistes perform to demanding audiences at close proximity, have always played a role in fostering new talent. Georges Brassens and Léo Ferré (left) made their debuts in cabarets during the 1950's.

MIDDLE-CLASS PARIS, WORKING-CLASS PARIS

Between Avenue Foch and Faubourg-St-Antoine, between the Étoile and the Bastille, two very different worlds are juxtaposed. The spotless rows of houses in the west provide a contrast with the motley collections of buildings in the east. However, the boundary between bourgeois Paris and working-class Paris, the residential west and the industrial east, is not quite so clear-cut. The phenomenon of fashionable quarters, which had become the exclusive property of the élite in the 19th century, is now on the wane. Paris, emptied of a working class which has moved out to the suburbs, and populated mainly by white-collar workers and professionals, is now only a small part of Greater Paris.

The victorious bourgeoisie of the 19th century, symbolized by the portrait of François Bertin (Ingres, 1832). Around 1900, gangs of hooligans ▲ *410* (below), who held sway in Belleville, embodied the insolent humor of working-class Paris.

THE FASHIONABLE QUARTERS
Paris was split in two during the 19th century with Haussmann's remodeling of the capital and the proliferation of buildings entirely devoted to the bourgeoisie. In the west were the stylish quarters, which annexed the suburb of Neuilly, making it part of the exclusive bourgeois domain. In the east were the working-class quarters, with their narrow streets and workshops.

> "The peaceful west, dotted with trees, with beautifully painted, bright buildings whose iron shutters . . . let out joy and warmth, security."
>
> Louis Aragon

THE PIANO NOBILE
Until the beginning of the 19th century, the different social classes lived in the same areas, and often under the same roof. But fortunes dwindled the higher you climbed (above). The *piano nobile*, with its high ceilings and lavishly decorated windows, was on the second or third floor.

NAP VERSUS RAP
Two types of Parisian youth. *Nap* refers to the epicenter of the stylish west, the quarters of Neuilly, Auteuil and Passy.

HOW THE EAST WAS WON
In the early 1980's many artists and professionals moved to the old workshops in eastern Paris. Restoration and large-scale public works – Bercy, Bastille, Tolbiac – have created some prestigious buildings in this area. The former divide between east and west is eroding.

● LEFT BANK, RIGHT BANK

"The wind of intellect does not blow across the Pont du Carrousel", stated the writer Roger Martin du Gard before World War Two.

6ᵉ Arrᵗ

PLACE
SAINT-GERMAIN
DES-PRÉS

**RIVE DROITE
ITINERAIRE
CONSEILLE** ▷

The Seine crisscrosses Paris and symbolically divides the city into two worlds. The Right Bank is the world of business, luxury and commerce, while the Left Bank represents the world of culture, education and the professions. This dichotomy, which dates back to the 12th century, reached its peak in the 1930's and 1940's, when St-Germain-des-Prés aspired to the title of cultural center of the world.

THE LATIN-SPEAKING BANK

The cultural calling of the 5th, 6th and 7th arrondissements, on the Left Bank, began to take shape in the 12th century with the foundation of the University. The Latin Quarter ▲ 246 was so called because the majority of its inhabitants spoke Latin. Although most of the universities and

important schools have moved out of the area, it has not lost its reputation, albeit purely symbolic today, of being the quarter of the intellectual élite. There are still some prestigious institutions here, such as the Louis-le-Grand and the Henri IV *lycées* and the École Normale Supérieure or "Normale Sup", a teacher-training college.

"LE VENTRE DE PARIS"

Among the first business activities to gain a foothold on the Right Bank were the markets on the site of what was to be the central covered market, or *ventre* (belly) *de Paris*. Haussmann's town-planning program was mainly on the Right Bank.

THE BUSINESS QUARTER

Dedicated to business, the Right Bank is the site of banks, insurance companies, head offices, prestigious hotels and department stores.

THE LITERARY REPUBLIC

Because of its schools and universities, the Left Bank acted as a magnet for publishing-related trades. As early as the Middle Ages illuminators took up residence in the Latin Quarter. This area still has the highest concentration of publishing houses and bookstores in Paris, and it is considered *de rigueur* for a writer to live on the Left Bank. Place St-Germain-des-Prés is the epicenter of this

literary republic, where even the cafés (Lipp, Flore and Deux Magots) award literary prizes.

Architecture

Because it was founded on a limestone basin, Paris has largely been built out of stone. Until the 18th century, the materials for its monuments came from quarries in the city's basements, and excavations accounted for nearly 10 percent of the capital's surface. Later on these materials were quarried from neighboring regions, particularly the Oise. Besides freestone, many of these quarries supplied rough-hewn limestone and gypsum, or plaster, which were the basic components used in everyday architecture. Brick, which was given pride of place in the town-planning programs of Henri IV and Louis XIII, made a comeback at the end of the 19th century. Zinc (used for roofs), glass and iron (often combined), and concrete were the three great innovations of the last century.

Roofs
Traditionally used for roofing details, zinc became a full roofing material at the beginning of the 1800's and was widely used by Haussmann instead of slate and tile. A soft material, it was suitable for the varied roof work in an increasingly built-up city.

BRICK
Regarded for many years as a filling material, brick was used in addition to stone at the end of the 19th century, playing its part in the revival of modern ornamental style. During the interwar period Parisian brick reached its apogee; it was used for many public buildings, such as the Institute of Art and Archeology, almost to the exclusion of all other materials.

STONE. Freestone was widely used in buildings designed by Haussmann. From the 1930's onward, stone was used in the form of a facing attached by clamps or cement. The modern Parisian building was created by the architect Roux-Spitz, who pioneered this technique. Today there is an ongoing debate between supporters of stone and champions of glass.

PLASTER

Until the 19th century stone was reserved for public buildings and mansions for the wealthy, while creators of more ordinary housing opted for a plaster façade over a wooden structure filled with brick, rough-hewn limestone and rubble. Plaster façades were often decorated with moldings, cornices or fluting, which were meant to imitate the appearance of stone. These composite buildings were said to be built of "Paris stone".

IRON AND GLASS

From the Eiffel Tower to Beaubourg, there has always been a whiff of revolt in the use of iron. Appearing in the late 1800's, it was soon used in conjunction with glass. The use of glass has recently been revived in the form of cemented glass walls.

555,000 GOLD LEAVES
This is the number of gold leaves which were used to regild the dome of Les Invalides. Often statues and railings were also gilded.

51

TOWN-PLANNING REGULATIONS

The first town-planning regulations were implemented in Paris as early as the Middle Ages. These have been modified and supplemented over the centuries in response to the vagaries of land apportionment, changing trends in housing, and large-scale town-planning projects. They governed land use, the height of buildings in relation to the road width, and the design of façades. Occasionally they determined the way buildings were decorated and the materials used in their construction. The uniformity of the urban landscape of Paris is due to their strict application.

The narrow plots of land and the cantilevered buildings of the Middle Ages.

Plot of land: 98 ft.
Road: 10 ft.
Façade

Plot of land: 98 ft.
Road: 20 ft.
Façade: 23 ft.

Alignment and widening of the streets in the 17th century.

57½ ft.
Façade: 98 ft.
Plot of land: 98 ft.
Road: 32 ft.

First thoroughfares by Rambuteau.

165 ft.
66 ft.
Road: 66 ft.
Façade: 66 ft.

1859: Haussmann's standards.

THE FIRST SIDEWALKS
Sidewalks first appeared at the end of the 18th century. They transformed the Parisian landscape, since their arrival led to the disappearance of the central gutter, which ran down the center of the road like an open sewer, in favor of cambered roads. Rambuteau, prefect of the Seine between 1833 and 1848, built the first wide avenues with side gutters, prefiguring Haussmann's system for the city.

HAUSSMANNIZATION
The 1859 regulations set extremely stringent building standards. The design and materials of façades were often prescribed, as was the size of buildings: they had to be between 49 to 82 feet long and measure 66 feet to the cornice, on top of which a further 16½ feet was allowed for the attic. This gave the new boulevards a square profile, their width being equal to the height of the buildings at the cornice.

1902: Buildings were higher and their decoration more lavish.

20 ft.

72 ft.

Façade: 115 ft.

STREETS IN THE MIDDLE AGES

Plots of land were long and narrow (16½ by 98 feet), a legacy from the agricultural system. Cantilevered wooden structures jutted out over the streets, which had no sidewalks and at best had been provided with a central gutter for drainage (opposite page, top).

1967: Irregularly spaced, high-rise buildings and sidewalks.

SPLENDORS OF THE BELLE ÉPOQUE

The 1902 regulations softened the severity of Haussmann's designs: bow windows were allowed to hang out over the street, buildings could be 115 feet wide and 72 feet high up to the cornice, and a further 20 feet was allowed for the story set back from the street. Attics and façades boasted a wealth of ornamentation, which was to disappear in the 1930's.

HEALTH AND EMBELLISHMENT

As early as the Middle Ages the city made recommendations regarding fire prevention, sewage disposal and street lighting, without a great deal of success. In 1607 the monarchy required that buildings be aligned along the street. At the end of the 17th century cantilevered structures projecting out over the road were prohibited, and the use of fire-resistant plaster as a revetment for façades, as well as the use of brick and stone for the first rented houses, became requirements.

Height of building = width of road.

1967: A BREAK WITH THE PAST

The 1967 regulations genuinely altered the Parisian landscape. Buildings could now soar as high as 121 feet, but they had to be set back from the road so as not to block the light. This change, which favored the erection of high-rise buildings, broke up the continuity of the streets.

CONTEMPORARY SYNTHESIS

In 1977 new regulations insisted that buildings must once again be aligned along the street and be a height in proportion with the width of the road. These regulations also preserved rulings made in the previous decade concerning light; consequently, inner courtyards had to be generously proportioned. On the other hand, façades were still of a considerable length. These regulations produced a series of Haussmann pastiches which soon gave way to a great architectural eclecticism, providing a showcase for every trend imaginable.

72 ft.

1977: The well-spaced, eclectic city.

Paris remained within its 14th-century city walls for many years despite its steady growth in population (2). The demolition of this wall by Louis XIV, and the later inclusion of extensive tracts of open land within the customs barrier of the Farmers General Wall (4), did nothing to encourage expansion, as the inhabitants preferred to congregate near the center of the city, with its thriving business activities. In the early decades of the 19th

THE PHILIPPE-AUGUSTE WALL (1213) (1). Over 3 miles long, this wall encompassed an equal area on either side of the Seine: the river was blocked by chains near the Pont des Arts in the west, and Pont Marie and Pont de la Tournelle in the east. The wall was never demolished, and some parts of it still survive, mainly in the Marais.

THE CHARLES V RAMPART WALL (1383) (2). This wall enlarged the area on the Right Bank encompassed by the Philippe-Auguste wall. It followed the present route of the Pont Royal, Porte St-Denis, Porte St-Martin and Bassin de l'Arsenal. Around 1635, Louis XIII enlarged it toward the northwest (3). It marked the boundaries of the area of the Right Bank that was not marshland; beyond that stretched an old channel of the Seine.

THE NEW COURSE (1705) (3). Since France's borders were now defended, Louis XIV demolished the fortifications built by Charles V and Louis XIII on the Right Bank, replacing them with a wide promenade. The main gates, like those of St-Denis and St-Martin, were adorned with triumphal arches. This wide boulevard became the center of Parisian life in the mid-19th century.

century, a rapid growth in population, the first affordable public transport systems, and the commitment of the authorities to ease traffic around the center reversed this trend. By the time the Thiers fortifications (5) were demolished, around 1920, the city wall had not been used for defensive purposes for many years. The famous *fortifs* had become popular places to take a stroll, and a huge shanty town stretched over the area, which was unsuitable for development.

THE FARMERS GENERAL WALL (1787) (4). Built in order to collect taxes on goods bound for the capital, the wall had no defensive function. Forming a ring over 328 feet wide, it followed a north–south route corresponding to the present Nation–Étoile Metro line. Sixty tollhouses, designed by the architect Ledoux of which four have survived were posted along the wall.

THE THIERS FORTIFICATIONS (1844) (5). Stretching 24 miles these fortifications form the longest city wall in the world. Replaced in the interwar period, they formed a 984-foot-wide barrier unsuitable for development. Sixteen isolated forts, such as Mount Valérien, stood several miles outside the fortifications.

THE PÉRIPHÉRIQUE (1973) (6). This ring road is 22 miles long, of which 4 miles are underground. Acting as a modern city wall, it can be crossed only in certain places. Unlike the uniform façades constructed along the boulevards, the landscape bordering the *périf* is as disordered as it is disparate. The *périphérique* marks the administrative limits of the capital.

Lutetia in the Gallo-Roman period.

In 52 BC, Caesar's general Labenius seized Lutetia, the city of the Parisii. Like other cities in Gaul, its architecture and layout were to be completely remodeled along Roman lines. The rustic Gallic houses were replaced by houses lining a grid of streets. A new town, supplied with water from an aqueduct, sprang up on Mount Ste-Geneviève, on the Left Bank of the river, where the main public monuments stood. Around the end of the 3rd century, the threat of barbarian invasion forced the inhabitants to fortify the island and convert the Forum into a fortress. The city had been renamed Paris and became the capital of the Frank kingdom under Clovis; it was to stagnate until the Capetians came to power in the 10th century.

PLAN OF LUTETIA
Shortly after the conquest, town planners imposed a typically Roman plan encompassing the Île de la Cité and Mount Ste-Geneviève; this was where the forum, three thermal baths, a theater and an amphitheater were built. The *cardo*, or north–south road, was laid and supplemented by a grid of secondary roads. The *cardo* continued toward Senlis and Orléans. The cemeteries were situated outside the town along the main roads.

BOATMEN'S PILLAR
Erected on the Île de la Cité in the early part of the 1st century, this public monument was dedicated to the emperor Tiberius and to Jupiter by the boatmen's guild. The combined images of Gallic and Roman gods bear witness to the early assimilation of indigenous divinities into the Roman pantheon.

THERMAL HEATING
Furnaces in the basement sent hot air into a cavity called the *hypocaust* beneath the *caldarium* and the *tepidarium*. Ceramic pipes, or *tabuli*, carried the warm air inside the partitions, heating floors, pools and walls.

FORUM
This building was a religious, political and commercial complex, the nerve center of any Roman city. Lutetia's Forum stretched over 590 feet on what is now the Rue Soufflot, from the Boulevard St-Michel to the Rue St-Jacques. Here, as everywhere, it formed a self-contained area closed to urban traffic.

CONSOLES
The vaulting of the *frigidarium* rests on the prows of merchant ships, the seal of the boatmen's guild.

MASONRY
The mortar masonry, alternating rubble and brick, was concealed by painted plaster.

THE HEART OF THE CITY
Within the Forum stood a great temple and a civic and judicial basilica running eastward along the *cardo*. The central area was surrounded by porticos housing shops, which doubled as a shelter and a meeting place. These shops opened onto the streets surrounding the Forum.

A VAST COMPLEX
Apart from the main buildings, the thermal-baths complex included a vast open space used as an outdoor gymnasium. This complex, along with Lutetia's two other thermal baths, reveals the great emphasis placed on physical fitness in Lutetia, like everywhere else in the Roman empire. The thermal baths played a key part in the Romanization of the city.

CLUNY
THERMAL BATHS
These thermal baths in the north are Lutetia's finest monument. The immense vaulted *frigidarium* (cold room) can still be seen, as can the remains of the *caldarium* and the *tepidarium*, as well as one of two gymnasiums (bottom left), formerly covered. Its water came from the Wissous aqueduct.

MEDIEVAL PARIS:
THE URBAN INFRASTRUCTURE

The city which Clovis made the center of his kingdom in 508 still b
the marks of its Gallo-Roman heritage, with its ramparts, network
public roads, thermal baths and arenas. The Île de la Cité was the
site of the kings' palace, while the episcopal complex which was to
give birth to Notre-Dame cathedral sprawled along the eastern
tip. Geographic and economic factors as much as
religious and intellectual considerations contributed
to the growth of Paris from the 6th century
through the Middle Ages, first on the Left
Bank, then the Right Bank. A series of
city walls marked the spread of Paris
and its suburbs.

PARIS AT THE DEATH OF CHARLES V
With 1,082 acres inside the city walls and a population of 100,000, Paris was the largest city in France.

Paris in 1380.

GEOGRAPHIC FACTORS

The waters of the Marne, the Oise, the Yonne, the Loing and the Seine converge in the Paris Basin, which was originally easily accessible. The Bièvre and the Sèvre also flowed into the Seine in Paris. The river, whose course was more convoluted at that time, and the *marais* (marsh), which gave its name to the oldest quarter on the Right Bank, used to form a double defense. This role was assumed by the city walls when the marsh was drained and the city spread along the banks. The Seine became the main artery of transport for foodstuffs and merchandise.

58

ECONOMIC FACTORS

From the Île de la Cité, businesses and shops sprawled along the existing roads around the bridges and gates, although growth was more dynamic on the Right Bank than the Left. Trading activity increased along the riverbank between St-Gervais and St-Merry, where it was easy to land. The butchers' guild, followed by many others, took up residence near the Châtelet, and the first markets were built in 1183.

RELIGIOUS FACTORS

Between the palace and the episcopal complex, a dense web of homes and businesses sprang up in the Île de la Cité, encircling the churches, hospices and monasteries. On the banks of the Seine around the fortified monasteries founded in the 6th century, various rural market towns appeared: St-Germain-des-Prés and Ste-Geneviève on the Left Bank, and St-Martin-des-Champs on the Right Bank.

INTELLECTUAL FACTORS

The first important intellectual development in Paris took place on the Île de la Cité and the Left Bank, where eminent lecturers such as Pierre Abelard attracted up to 10,000 students. The colleges founded to accommodate them were to become reputable schools.

THE NETWORK OF PUBLIC ROADS

The Île de la Cité was linked to the riverbanks by four bridges. The quays formed the city's first promenades.

MEDIEVAL PARIS: GOTHIC ARCHITECTURE

Gothic architecture, whose main innovations were the systematic use of ribbed vaults and pointed arches, was first used for royal residences in and around the Île-de-France in the early 12th century, taking the place of Romanesque architecture. There are several periods of Gothic architecture: early Gothic, from 1125 to 1290; classical Gothic, up to 1250; Rayonnant Gothic, up to 1380; and Flamboyant Gothic up to the beginning of the 16th century.

ST-MARTIN-DES-CHAMPS
Both the multifoil plan and the carving of this church, built around 1130,

ST-GERMAIN-DES-PRÉS
This church, with its radiating chapels and flying buttresses dating from the middle of the 12th century, reveals an architectural innovation in its treatment of the choir. This formula was to be widely adopted and developed by Gothic architecture.

are still Romanesque in inspiration. However, Gothic innovations can be seen in the spatial layout (double ambulatory, open radiating chapels and large central chapel), as well as in the vaults of the choir supported by buttresses and in the ribbed vaults.

NOTRE-DAME
When the upper windows of the choir were enlarged, flying buttresses rising 49 feet were added and chapels were built between them. The combination of stone and metal in Rayonnant-style Gothic architecture meant that windows could be larger, as can be seen in the south rose window of Notre-Dame (1258–70).

CAPITALS
The slender capitals of Ste-Chapelle, with their floral decoration and colors set off by gold, share the monument's mystic symbolism.

BASTILLE
Used first for defense, then as a state prison, the Bastille is an example of military art from the Gothic period: the firepower was concentrated in the base and on the flat roof.

REFECTORY OF ST-MARTIN-DES-CHAMPS
This building, whose dimensions (39 by 138 feet) make it unique, is a testimony to the consummate technical mastery of the classical Gothic architects, in this case Pierre de Montreuil. The two naves with their ribbed vaults, the slender columns which separate them, and the quality of the decoration are its crowning glories.

LOUVRE
The pillar in the *salle basse* of the royal château is an example of the intense stylistic development which took place during the classical period of Gothic architecture.

TOUR DE JEAN-SANS-PEUR
A rare example of Parisian feudal architecture, this early-15th-century tower still has its spiral staircase, which is crowned with a vault boasting some remarkable floral decoration.

STE-CHAPELLE
The spire of Ste-Chapelle dates from 1853. Its restoration, like that of the rest of the building, ranks among the most successful projects of the 19th century. Resting on a delicate cast-iron frame, the present spire is modeled on the one by the carpenter Robert Fouchier, who at the end of the 14th century erected a flawless gem of Rayonnant-style Gothic architecture.

TOUR ST-JACQUES
The archivolts (moldings around the arches), pinnacles and gables make this a masterpiece of Flamboyant-style Gothic architecture.

Royal squares – spaces created as settings for statues of sovereigns – are among the Ancien Régime's most enduring urban initiatives. The five in Paris bear witness to the dynastic continuity of the Bourbons from Henri IV to Louis XV, in spite of the fact that they do not adhere to a fixed model. Open-plan to a greater or lesser degree, their architecture as well as the symbolism of the décor and statuary evolved in line with the monarchy's changing political requirements.

THE WARRIOR KING
At night, four lamps in the Place des Victoires are used to illuminate this statue of Louis XIV surrounded by captives.

PLACE DAUPHINE
Henri IV set about changing the face of Paris by creating a coherent urban ensemble on the tip

of the Île de la Cité linked to the Pont-Neuf. This bridge, which was devoid of houses, at last made it possible for the city to open out onto the river. The ensemble of buildings did not assume its true significance until the addition of the statue of the king.

PLACE DE LA CONCORDE
The former Place-Louis-XV completed the Right Bank's triumphal perspective: buildings were constructed on one side only, thereby respecting continuity. The two palaces by Gabriel (right), which form the monumental decoration of the square, were inspired by the colonnade at the Louvre. The positioning of the equestrian statue of Louis XV at the intersection of the two main axes is in accordance with the traditional 17th-century scheme.

TO THE WEST
Initially on the outskirts of the city, Place de la Concorde paved the way for Paris to be extended westward.

PLACE DES VOSGES

Except for the two large pavilions which indicate the entrances, the brick and stone houses boast a uniformity accentuated by the closed nature of this urban cloister (above).

The individual houses can be distinguished only by looking at the division of the roofs.

PLACE DES VICTOIRES. This perfect circle (above), designed as a setting for the statue of Louis XIV, was one of the major sites dedicated to royalty.

LOUIS XV
Bouchardon revived the tradition of the equestrian statue by glorifying the virtues of the peacemaking king.

The concept of the town as a well-ordered organism took hold under Louis XIV. The fact that the kingdom was now defended at its borders made Paris an open city surrounded by wide boulevards, while triumphal gates, like those of St-Denis and St-Martin, replaced the old city gates. The Academy of Architecture, founded in 1671, created an appreciation for an increasingly austere style of architecture, which could be seen in the simplicity of the decoration, the moderate proportions and the constant preoccupation with symmetry. French-style classicism had arrived.

INVALIDES
The epitome of classical architecture, the Invalides' uncompromising symmetry drew its inspiration from the Escorial near Madrid.

OBSERVATORY
The first national observatory dates from 1667. Its façades are oriented toward the cardinal points of the compass and boast a precision which reflects that of the exact sciences, emphasized by the horizontal balustrade. The structure was built of top-quality stone laid with meticulous care. This building, which is reminiscent of a civil-engineering structure or a fortification, prefigures the rationalist architecture of the 18th century.

HÔTEL DES INVALIDES
In 1670, Louis XIV decided to erect a hospital for his soldiers. The building displays a long, austere façade, simply adorned by dormer windows shaped like trophies; at either end groups of statues serve as pediments. This severity acts as a foil for the central frontispiece, a genuine triumphal arch erected to the glory of the king. Long, sober buildings, gallery-covered arcades and enclosed square courts are evocative of a barracks or a convent.

FAÇADE OF ST-ROCH

This faithfully reflects the classical design of Jesuit style: a high bay with a pediment between two low bays, all punctuated by columns.

ST-LOUIS-DES-INVALIDES

Like St Peter's in Rome, the church of the Invalides incorporates both an elongated plan and a cruciform plan. The austere Soldiers' Church, with three naves and based on an elongated plan, opens into the sumptuous Royal Chapel, which is designed on a cruciform plan and is crowned by two superposed domes, a system which allowed the fresco of the lower dome to be illuminated indirectly.

CHURCH OF ST-ROCH

Begun in 1653 by Lemercier, the church (above) is, at 410 feet long, one of the largest in Paris. Its dimensions and the quality of its decoration also make it one of the finest examples of classical architecture.

Although its façade combines baroque and classical elements, its interior is medieval: a barrel-vaulted nave with lunettes, aisles with chapels, a deep choir and a transept with almost nonexistent arms. The two chapels beyond the choir, extended later by the Calvary chapel, create a sequence of theatrical effects which are highly baroque in flavor.

This unusual plan was never repeated.

BERNINI COLONNADE

In 1664 Bernini submitted a highly baroque plan for the colonnade of the Louvre. His plan was rejected after work was started, but the combination of a rusticated first floor and two stories joined by an order of colossal proportion was to be a source of inspiration for many architects.

COLONNADE OF THE LOUVRE

In 1667 Louis XIV accepted the plan by Charles Perrault for the Louvre's east façade, oriented toward the city. Although its high base reflects Italian tradition, the scale of its colonnade is baroque and the severity of its straight lines is classical.

65

At the end of the Middle Ages, the city's mansions, or *hôtels*, were built around an inner courtyard used by one family alone. In the 16th century this plan was codified: a main building in which every room overlooked both the courtyard and the garden, two wings forming a U-shape housing the outbuildings and a gallery, and an enclosed courtyard on the street side. Having made its first appearance in the Marais, the mansion spread to the faubourgs St-Germain and St-Honoré in the 17th century. It remained U-shaped in plan, but the layout of the rooms became more complicated. By the end of the 18th century, the wings had disappeared completely.

HÔTEL CARNAVALET

The only surviving 16th-century mansion in Paris, this has been greatly modified. With it, the plan of the mansion became truly urban: the modest building overlooking the street housed the kitchens and stables, while the main residence was sheltered at the back of the courtyard.

HÔTEL DE CLUNY

The mansion owned by the abbots of Cluny (above), whose construction was started in 1480, is a very early example of a typical Parisian mansion. Its main building is sandwiched between courtyard and garden, its left wing has a superposed portico and gallery, and its boundary wall overlooks the street. It is entered by an external turret staircase, a distinguishing feature of wealthy residences.

HÔTEL MATIGNON

The interior layout of the rooms in the double main buildings was improved in the 18th century, as seen in this mansion from 1720. The symmetry of two suites of rooms divided by a longitudinal wall was replaced by a more irregular layout. The two façades overlooking the courtyard and the garden are not aligned, a feature handed down from the early 17th century.

The recessed gateway allows carriages to maneuver more easily.

FRONT ELEVATION

Two large pavilions framing a small, flat-roofed entrance indicate the grandeur of this stone-built mansion.

HÔTEL DE SULLY

Impeccably restored, the Hôtel de Sully (below) is the epitome of the grand Parisian early-17th-century mansion. It faithfully reproduces the U-shaped plan of the previous century: it has a single main building, each room overlooks both garden and courtyard; and the central stairwell is crossed to get from one to the other. The lavish ornamentation of its façades is in keeping with Renaissance style. The mansion still has an orangery at the back of its gardens.

GALLERY OF THE HÔTEL LA VRILLIÈRE

The gallery (above), a room designed as a showcase for a mansion's splendor, was used for receptions. The heavy Rococo décor of this room dates from 1718.

ROOFS

Until the 17th century, mansions had steeply pitched Gothic roofs with high stone dormer windows. They then adopted curb or mansard roofs, with discrete wooden dormer windows, occasionally concealed by a balustrade. These roofs were much better suited to the double main buildings.

Tall, steeply pitched, medieval-style roofs.

Classical mansard roofs.

WINGS

Wings of the same height as the main building were characteristic of the early 17th century.

HÔTEL BIRON

Constructed in 1727, this mansion (right) typifies the move toward a greater sophistication in design with its isolated main building and borrowings from contemporary châteaux.

The architects of the Enlightenment did their utmost to contribute to social progress. Every type of building was remodeled so that its layout and character reflected its function. This craving for modernity was most clearly seen in public architecture, which enabled architects to reinterpret classical models using simplified forms and new techniques. By appealing both to the senses and to reason, this architecture applied a certain logic to the urban landscape.

ODÉON
The vogue for theatergoing in the second half of the 18th century transformed the urban auditorium (left). It was promoted to the rank of a public monument, reviving classical traditions. The Nouvelle-Comédie (1782) was a recognizable, autonomous block whose façade was graced with a portico but no pediment. The interior layout reflected an emphasis on audience comfort.

THE NATION'S FIRST TEMPLE
The basilica of Ste-Geneviève by Soufflot (1755–90), a meditation on the foundations of architecture, ushered in the neoclassical era.

AN ELOQUENT URBAN ART
The plan for a monumental theater presupposed an expressive urban setting. The Nouvelle-Comédie fitted into a new residential district, creating an unexpected rapport between a public building and its surroundings. It governed the way this quarter was divided up, with five radiating streets (above) leading to an amphitheatrical square which functioned as a curtain-raiser to the theater; these streets were lined with elegant uniform buildings. This was the first district in Paris to have English-style sidewalks.

BETWEEN CHÂTEAU AND MANSION
The desire for privacy, along with a courtly life style of conversation, music and amateur theatricals, accounted for the construction of small houses, or follies, around Paris and in its new quarters. In 1770, Ledoux erected a pavilion for a kept dancer, Mademoiselle Guimard. He made it a temple to Terpsichore, giving free reign to his fondness for visual contrasts.

THE VILLETTE BARRIER
Around the customs barrier erected on the eve of the Revolution, Claude Nicolas Ledoux built some fifty tollhouses, which were treated as monuments. Each one is different, although they were characterized by simple geometrical forms and by their free interpretation of ancient orders.

THE PERFECT CHURCH
Soufflot set out to reform church architecture by drawing up an extremely controversial plan based on a cruciform, which was both rational and poetic. The structure was to be kept very simple by bracing it with a metal framework within the masonry and supporting it with flying buttresses. In this way, the lightness of Gothic building was united with classical harmony, the complexity of the vaulting echoing the beauty of the weight-bearing columns. The dome was made up of three cup-shaped structures.

ÉCOLE DE CHIRURGIE
This building, constructed in 1775, proved that classical art could give a new lease on life to public architecture. An open colonnade includes a doorway in the guise of a triumphal arch opening onto a temple façade; the classical theater and a demi-cupola inspired by the Panthéon merge in the lecture hall.

The population of Paris doubled during this time, and the disparity between the wealthy western part of the city and the poverty-stricken central and eastern districts became even more pronounced. The authorities planned some new thoroughfares to clean up the city and improve access to certain areas in the capital.

The Arc de Triomphe.

The Restoration was marked by the dividing up of quarters in the west of the city and the building of churches.

ARC DE TRIOMPHE
This was based on a classical model like many public buildings of the time.

ST-VINCENT-DE-PAUL
Located in the heart of a new quarter, this church was built on the basilical plan, which was common at that time.

ASSEMBLÉE NATIONALE
The façade which decorates the front of the Assemblée Nationale (below) dates from 1806, while the building itself was the product of modifications made to the Palais Bourbon in 1795. Its Corinthian colonnade echoes that of the Madeleine, on the other side of the Place de la Concorde. It disguises the fact that the building is not in line with the bridge.

RUE DE RIVOLI
Initially designed to stretch as far as the Palais Royal, this urban promenade (below) overlooking the terrace of the Tuileries, was extended eastward after 1848. The homogenous façade gives the street its monumental nature, prefiguring Haussmann's grand thoroughfares.

DECORATION
This evolved from sober neoclassicism to elaborate eclecticism.

FONTAINE MOLIÈRE
Public spaces were rapidly modernized with gas street lighting, sidewalks and sewers. Hundreds of public drinking fountains and dozens of fountains improved the Parisian water supply. Between 1828 and 1848 the architect Visconti built several monumental fountains, including the Fontaine Molière (below).

ARCADES. The marriage of iron and glass became more widespread, particularly in new arcades (above).

ANGLOPHILIA
The rue de Rivoli adopted the repetitive English-style façades.

PARISIAN BUILDINGS
The typical Parisian building took shape in this period. For reasons of health and ventilation, the regulations of 1783 prescribed that the height of a building be in direct proportion to the width of the street. This led to the four-story buildings topped by a recessed story with a continuous balcony.

HAUSSMANN'S GRAND PUBLIC WORKS

The grand public works of Paris were the work of Georges-Eugène Haussmann, prefect of the Seine from 1853 to 1870. Besides providing buildings with a fresh water supply, extending the sewer system, creating gardens, squares and public buildings (churches, town halls, theaters, hospitals and barracks), he was also responsible for laying new roads. He envisioned a network of thoroughfares crossing Paris from one side to the other, which would move the congested center farther to the northwest. These wide roads cut across the city in an attempt to ease traffic and thereby make the city a healthier place to live, as well as to improve the appearance of the urban landscape. Some roads were even designed to combat possible civil unrest.

HAUSSMANN'S GREAT THOROUGHFARES

The Second Empire's program of road building presupposed specific financing, compulsory purchases and demolitions. However, the scheme swallowed up huge amounts of money and caused Haussmann's downfall before that of the regime. Although demolitions were carefully thought out in line with skillfully devised plans and confined to what was strictly necessary, they drove out many landlords and tenants. Only the landlords were ever compensated. The plan did not spare monuments from the Middle Ages, particularly in the Île de la Cité, whose dense infrastructure was largely destroyed.

PLACE DE L'OPÉRA

Before the competition of 1860 for the construction of the Opéra, Haussmann's architects designed the square and the surrounding streets and determined the size of the buildings and the disposition of the façades. The Avenue de l'Opéra remains one of the best examples of Haussmann's straight, uniform roads, in spite of the fact that Garnier, the architect, stopped the avenue from being planted with trees.

RÉSERVOIR MÉNILMONTANT

PARC MONCEAU
GARE ST-LAZARE
GARE DU NORD
GARE DE L'EST
BUTTES CHAUMONT
RÉSERVOIR MÉNILMONTANT
LOUVRE
TURBIGO
ÉCOLE
MONGE
GARE DE LYON
GARE MONTPARNASSE
GARE D'AUSTERLITZ
RÉSERVOIR DE MONTSOURIS
PARC MONTSOURIS

RAILWAY LINES
MAJOR INTERSECTIONS
EXISTING SECTIONS
OTHER ROUTES (PRINCIPAL)
RING ROADS
EXISTING SECTIONS
PRE 1860
POST 1860

THOROUGHFARE ESTHETICS

Thoroughfares in the Second Empire were characterized by straight lines. The lie of the land nitting, their axes had to coincide with impressive vistas. This concept was applied to roads from the mid-1800's onward. The Boulevard Henri-IV provides a visual link between the July Column in the Place de la Bastille and the dome of the Panthéon.

Haussmann did not devise a program for architecture in the way that he did for the layout of the city. Although the growing problem of working-class housing concerned Napoleon III, who financed the construction of several housing projects, it left Haussmann cold. However, construction became necessary as a result of the thoroughfares: houses had to be reconstructed, and the new quarters of Paris did not have any public buildings. Haussmann preferred to use humble practitioners like Gabriel Davioud because they were easier to manipulate.

THE URBAN LANDSCAPE

Davioud designed some meticulously ordered buildings for the Place St-Michel and a fountain to match the scale of these buildings. The square sets off the corner of the Rue Danton and the Boulevard St-Michel, drawing attention away from the lack of alignment between the boulevard and the bridge, which ran counter to Second Empire tastes.

CIVIC BUILDINGS

Like monuments, civic buildings can mark the focal points of the city's structure. This is the case with the town hall in the 11th arrondissement at the corner of the Boulevard Voltaire and Avenue Parmentier (above). The building was inspired by 18th-century French style.

Eclecticism was the order of the day, and the choice of style depended on the nature of the building: neo-Byzantine, Romanesque or Gothic for churches, neo-Renaissance or classical for civic buildings. The building program for the town halls became vitally important in 1860, when the districts around Paris were annexed.

A DISCRETE MONUMENTALITY

Although Haussmann accepted that buildings should display a certain monumentality, he also believed that monuments should blend in with their urban surroundings. The two theaters by Davioud flanking the Place du Châtelet are still the most striking example of this discretion. Despite the classically monumental façades, their architecture reflects the scale of the neighboring buildings, and only the volume essential for the auditorium makes it stand out. The façades overlooking the Seine observe the rhythm and alignment of the buildings on the quayside.

Attic

Façade overlooking the street

Recessed story with continuous balcony

Maids' rooms

Back staircase

Main staircase

Reception rooms

Bedrooms

Inner courtyard

Entrance

Shops

Cellars

Sewers

BALCONIES
Continuous balconies run the entire width of a Haussmann building on the third and sixth stories.

HAUSSMANN'S BUILDINGS
The typical features of a Haussmann building are its base, its carriage entrance and mezzanine, a *piano nobile* with balcony, another balcony on the top story, and a mansard roof with dormer windows. The internal plan is inspired by aristocratic 18th-century apartments: at the front is a suite made up of the salon, dining room and master bedroom; the servants' quarters overlook the courtyard.

DECORATION
The decoration is remarkable for its sobriety: the proportions and outline of the cornices and the balconies (above) were all that were needed. Haussmannian architecture was to survive the Second Empire by some thirty years.

IRON ARCHITECTURE

Iron architecture, of which Paris has an abundance, proved to be one of the successes of the 19th century. Linked to the growth of industrial society, it bears witness to a symbiosis peculiar to this period between technical progress and a liking for decoration. The extent of its triumph is revealed by the debates about its esthetic appeal and modernity.

IRON AND CAST IRON
Until 1880 iron structures were supported by columns made of cast iron, a material which lent itself to ornamentation, as can be seen by the capital above.

PONT ALEXANDRE-III
Built in 1900, this was the first bridge to cross the Seine in a single span which had an almost horizontal road.

GARE DU NORD
The great station halls, like the Gare du Nord, built in 1863 (above), are among the first examples of the marriage of iron and glass, which was to be repeated in a variety of ways for countless glass roofs.

STRUCTURE AND DÉCOR
The Alexandre III bridge was inspired by the technique used for stone bridges. This made it possible to build the road lower than usual, in order not to mar the perspective between the Invalides and the Grand Palais. The vault of fifteen arches is composed of cast-steel components called *voussoirs*, which are assembled with bolts. The elaborate decoration, typical of the end of the century, is the work of several sculptors.

It has been added to the arch without distorting its purity of line, reflecting the 19th-century spirit of synthesis between ornamentation and structure.

RIVETS
The rivets used in assembly were hot-welded.

GREENHOUSES: GLASS SETTINGS

The first entirely glazed roofs were designed for greenhouses. The roof at Auteuil for the overhead section of the Metro, designed by the architect Formigé, shows how "transparent" metal can become when combined with glass.

LES HALLES
A much-imitated model, the central market, by Baltard and Callet, succeeded for the first time in combining metal, brick and glass. Les Halles was completed in 1874 and demolished in 1971.

GLASS ROOFS
The strength of iron made it possible to reduce the thickness of the uprights and let in more light. The double dome in the Galeries Lafayette exploits this.

EIFFEL TOWER
The star attraction of the Universal Exhibition of 1889, the tower ▲ 296 is a skillful framework composed of a lattice of girders which reaches a height of 984 feet.

A RATIONALIST STYLE OF ARCHITECTURE
Iron architecture is the work of both engineers and architects who sought to find a language suitable for a new material: often concealed behind more worthy stone, iron eventually made its esthetic appeal felt.

ORNAMENTATION
Decoration had no structural role and kept to the building's lines of force.

ASSEMBLY
Small posts bonded by braces support the pavement.

77

At the beginning of the 20th century, architectural design was characterized by the construction of lavishly decorated buildings. This new style, so dear to Guimard, was altered under the influence of theories of hygienics, and low-cost housing was developed. Sauvage with his stepped buildings and Le Corbusier with his Cité du Refuge (Salvation Army Hostel) built versions of their own social ideal. Mallet-Stevens designed a new street as if it were an avant-garde stage set, while monumental architecture reigned victorious on the Chaillot hill up until the eve of World War Two.

CAST-IRON ORNAMENTS
Anchors shaped like seahorses and railings with cheerful masks adorned the Castel Béranger. Designed and cast to the specifications of the architect, they revealed his desire to control every detail of a building, which was regarded as a work of art.

CERAMICS
Ceramic decorations were much in demand by builders at the turn of the century. The

CASTEL BÉRANGER
The Castel Béranger reveals a chaotic interplay of volumes, a mix of materials and the desire by Guimard to pay attention to each detail within this luxury apartment building, in which every apartment was different. These features, characteristic of Parisian Art Nouveau as inspired by Viollet-le-Duc, were realized around 1900.

Perret brothers used this type of decoration in 1904 on a building in the 16th arrondissement when they dropped stoneware lozenges in concrete to form plantlike motifs.

TOKYO PALACE

With its colonnade on either side of a central axis and its terraces populated by hieratic sculptures, the Museum of Modern Art, built in 1937, reflects the international academic trend of the times.

STEPPED BUILDINGS

The receding steps of the buildings by Henri Sauvage made the streets lighter while allowing light into all the apartments. With the low-cost housing of the Rue des Amiraux, built ten years after the block on the Rue Vavin, modern architecture had arrived on the low-cost housing market.

LAYOUT

A rational internal layout and terraces were designed to create a new way of living.

PUBLIC AMENITIES

Hollowing out the center of this enormous block, Sauvage installed a swimming pool for relaxation, sport and hygiene, reflecting the social aspirations of the time.

AVANT-GARDE COLORS

Polychromy was the only form of decoration tolerated by the modernists, who despised bourgeois taste and excessive ornamentation: the architect became a self-styled colorist. The entrance to the Cité de Refuge, at 12, rue Cantagrel, a monumental portico built in 1933 by Le Corbusier, is treated like an exhibition pavilion. The façade of the main building was remodeled after World War Two.

RUE MALLET-STEVENS

In this uniform street by Mallet-Stevens, who ignored the burning issue of housing for the masses, there are five mansions and a caretaker's house. Inaugurated in 1927, this was to represent a manifesto for the modern city. However, despite the interplay of recessed stories, the overlapping of cubic and cylindrical volumes, and the flat roofs so admired today, these prototypes were used only by the architect, his friends and his patrons, and did not make it into general use.

Since the Renaissance, the banks of the Seine have had various urban monuments and groups of buildings erected on them. Today they are the site of projects and new districts which have extended the city center. The quarters of Bercy and Seine Rive Gauche – home of the Ministry of Finance, the Bibliothèque de France, the MK2 movie center and the planned Maison du Cinéma by Frank O. Gehry – bear witness to the attention now being paid to this part of the city center. The desire to provide the capital with public buildings which reflect its international standing, as well as the wish to revitalize architectural design in France, can be clearly seen in the remodeling of existing sites such as the Louvre.

ORSAY: A MUSEUM IN A TRAIN STATION ▲ *160* (left)
The conversion of the Gare d'Orsay into a museum, with a central nave measuring 459 feet long and 115 feet high, was designed in conflict rather than in stylistic accord with the 19th-century building: beneath the chasing of the arches of the vault is a massive monumental aisle, as well as galleries with solid walls and a balcony.

The new quarter of Bercy (below).

THE LOUVRE ▲ *324* (below)
In 1979 underground development was first used for Les Halles; it is now being applied to the heart of the city, where the infrastructure is extremely dense. The 15 acres created under the Louvre eased traffic problems and provided vital modern machinery.

BERCY ▲ *407*
The quarter of Bercy is an example of new-style Parisian town planning, with its perfectly straight continuation of existing streets. The park, the housing which borders it on one side, the Palais Omnisports, the hotel and business complex and the much talked-about Maison du Cinéma have created a new center, an initiative typical of the late 1980's. The eclectic architectural styles echo the diversity of the buildings.

BERCY PARK HOUSING
Each U-shaped block overlooking the park surrounds a smaller building. The entire development is the product of an original approach: the uniformity of the buildings, designed by several architects, is guaranteed by the balconies which link them together, along with a set of common building regulations.

INSTITUT DU MONDE ARABE ▲ *144* (below)
The IMA building combines the exterior and strict alignment of Haussmann's city with contemporary glass and a metal façade. The inner courtyard opening onto a narrow passage, the south façade with its Arabic shapes, the spiral library in the prow and the highly contemporary interplay of transparent effects provide endless references while successfully integrating the building into the historic heart of the city.

ARAB WINDOWS
Joining tradition and modernity, the windows of the IMA incorporate the technology of photoelectric cells within the motif of Arabic *moucharabieh*.

BIBLIOTHÈQUE FRANÇOIS MITTERRAND ▲ *232* (below right)
The Bibliothèque's towers frame a wooden podium; they delineate the Seine Rive Gauche quarter, created out of nothing over railway lines.

MK2 BIBLIOTHEQUE
▲ *232*
This movie complex, erected between the Très Grande Bibliothèque and the railtracks of Gare d'Austerlitz and financed by producer Marin M Karmitz, consists of 14 movie screens, two music stores and four restaurants.

PALAIS OMNISPORTS ▲ *407*
The Palais Omnisports is an unusual sight, blending in with the park owing to the turf which covers its sloping façades. This flattened pyramid, which provides a forum for sporting events and large concerts, is a showcase for numerous architectural feats.

MINISTRY OF FINANCE
▲ *231*
A truncated portico with monumental ambitions, this building is heir to the megastructures of the 1970's, which often never made it off the drawing board. It enjoys a unique position in the Parisian landscape.

81

Grande Arche

La Défense demonstrates how the ideas of the modern movement have been applied to the city: isolated high-rise buildings on either side of an esplanade, and traffic relegated to the outskirts or below the immense pedestrian podium. Although La Défense has been criticized for its scale, it is a fine realization of modernity. It has broken away from the traditional cityscape yet respects the vista from the west of Paris, which governs the central open space and the position of the buildings and of the Grande Arche.

1 ☐   5 ▨
2 ▨   6 ☐
3 ■   7 ▨
4 ☐

1. Residential buildings
2. Office buildings
3. Network of public roads
4. RER-Metro
5. Parking
6. Podium
7. Soil

LA TOUR SANS FIN
With a proposed height of 1,312 feet and a diameter of only 131 feet, giving a ratio of 1 : 10 instead of the customary 1 : 5, the "Tower of Infinity" project, the final progeny of the planners of La Défense, will now never be realized.

A TWO-TIERED CITY
La Défense resembles a ship whose water line would be marked by its podium: above, pedestrians and towers; below, layer upon layer of galleries. Trains, RER and Métro are found in the bed-rock: above these are the network of roads, then the station entrance halls, parking and various facilities.

AN ARCH OUT OF LINE

From the Carrousel, the perspective of the great axis passes under the Arc de Triomphe, then over a slope to terminate at the Grande Arche. The arch is slightly out of line with the axis, and this reveals its depth and volume. The construction suspended between its walls scales down the building's proportions for pedestrians at its threshold seeing it up close.

A GIANT CUBE

This almost perfect colossal cube, which measures about 361 feet high, wide and deep, could easily accommodate Notre-Dame cathedral, which rises to 305 feet.

THE GRANDE ARCHE

The Arche is supported by twelve piers, each 98 feet tall (right), integrated into a transport network where it was impossible to dig foundations. These piers carry the cube, whose upper and lower platforms and walls are held together by enormous frames. Prestressed concrete, which is commonly used in large civil engineering projects was used for the first time in this building.

CNIT

The Centre National des Industries et Techniques (CNIT), built in 1958, was La Défense's first building. It is a remarkable design owing to its concrete vault, at 781 feet one of the largest in the world. The three sections of this vault are composed of a double shell of thin concrete and rest on three abutment piers linked to each other by steel rods buried underground.

83

Davioud made a lasting impact on the Parisian landscape by furnishing Haussmann's boulevards and avenues with many utilitarian and decorative structures. These pieces of street furniture, supplemented from the early 1970's onward by small public conveniences in line with new requirements, still punctuate and emphasize the capital's boulevards.

FAITHFUL REPRODUCTIONS
These circular iron gratings were designed to surround the trees that were planted in rows during the Second Empire. The ones manufactured today are exact replicas.

LAMPS
These 19th-century lamps are still in use.

MORRIS COLUMNS
These columns, an early version of the hoardings which used to advertise forthcoming attractions, are topped by onion domes in the exotic style favored by the Second Empire. The current version can accommodate public toilets or telephones.

LIGHTING
With the advent of gas lighting, iron street lamps, often ornamented with plantlike motifs, made their appearance on the Parisian scene.

Double bench.

NEW FURNITURE
Bus shelters, portable toilets, public telephones and bulletin boards (below) satisfy new needs while respecting the rows of trees.

FONTAINE WALLACE
This iron drinking fountain is an archetypal example of street furniture of the 19th century. It reflected the hygienic concerns of the period.

Paris
as seen by painters

Paris provided the setting for many festivities connected with the presence of its kings, as well as for the celebrations of its populace. One of the most lavish royal celebrations was organized in 1615 on the occasion of the marriage of Louis XIII to Anne of Austria. A *carrousel* (parade) lasting three whole days took place against the backdrop of celebrations for the newly inaugurated Place Royale (now Place des Vosges). This ANONYMOUS ARTIST condensed the three days into one composition **(1)**, which serves to highlight the contrast between the attractive confusion of the entrances and the regularity of the façades. The most popular working-class festival under the Ancien Régime was the carnival. By the beginning of this century it had become a much quieter affair, amounting to a procession of floats on the third Thursday of Lent. LUIGI LOIR (1845–1916), whose prolific output was devoted almost exclusively to Paris, took the carnival as a subject for several canvases. In his *Mi-Carême à Paris* **(2)**, Loir widened the rue de Rivoli out of all proportion, making its severity, rendered in muted shades, a perfect foil for the dazzling colors of the floats. Another festival, the Universal Exhibition of 1878 ● *30*, provided France with the opportunity to show off its new-found prosperity. The streets of Paris were

decked with thousands of flags on the day of its opening, the result of a unanimous surge of patriotism. CLAUDE MONET (1840–1926) was moved by this spectacular sight. His *Rue Montorgeuil* (1878) **(4)** conveys

the shimmering effect of the moving colors and also recreates the lively confusion of movement in the street. Since July 14 was created a public holiday in 1880, this spectacle can be staged every year. RAOUL DUFY's (1877–1953) *Rue*

pavoisée **(3)** is still impressionistic in mood, but the broad strokes and the innovative use of color mark a distinct shift toward Fauvism.

| 1 |
| 2 | 3 | 4 |

Raoul Dufy

> "Nothing is more beautiful than the way the great hill looks when the sun shines on its soil of red ocher, veined with gypsum and clay...wound about by ravines and footpaths."
>
> Gérard de Nerval

As Canaletto did with Venice, JEAN-BAPTISTE RAGUENET (1715–93) specialized in painting the sights of Paris. With painstaking objectivity and charm, he preserved images of the city in the 18th century for future generations. One of his most meticulous paintings, *Joute des Mariniers* (4), brings to mind the water festivals which regularly took place on the Seine under the Ancien Régime and depicts the houses which crowded along the top of the Pont Notre-Dame at that time. In fact, all the bridges of Paris except the Pont-Neuf were covered with buildings which were eventually demolished by royal edict in 1786. The widespread demolitions in the reign of Napoleon III elicited a great deal of nostalgia. Many painters who loved the old medieval city strove to preserve a picture of the condemned sites for generations to come, in the same way that the photographer Atget did later on. PAUL SCHAAN, L. MEYER and ALBERT PIERSON were among these artists. Their output, although neglected, is full of charm. Schaan, with his *Bièvre au bief de la rue de Valence* (1) preserved the memory of the river which flowed through the 13th and 5th arrondissements to pour into the Seine at what is now the Gare Austerlitz. Meyer has handed down an extremely evocative view of the *Maquis de Montmartre* (2). This legendary spot, which inspired so many artists, covered the north slope of the hill. The vast area of open land was gradually covered with precarious shacks, forming an extensive shantytown which disappeared when the Avenue Junot was built. Pierson, with his *Passage des singes* (3), depicting the view of the thoroughfare between the Rue Vieille-du-Temple and the Rue des Guillemites, conjures up the intricate and complex network of courtyards and passageways which used to weave through the heart of Paris.

1	2	3

4

The metamorphosis of Paris under the Second Empire gave fresh impetus to the genre of the urban landscape: the pursuit of the picturesque was abandoned for a celebration of modernity. The most representative painter of this new type of urban landscape was CAMILLE PISSARRO (1830–1903). *L'Avenue de l'Opéra* (1897) **(2)** is typical of a whole series of bird's-eye views of the city's main thoroughfares. JEAN BÉRAUD (1849–1936), in his many *Vues du boulevard* **(3)**, shared a similar goal, but he was also fond of painting crowd scenes with a meticulous attention to detail, which gave his work a documentary quality. The Gare St-Lazare inspired MONET (1840–1926) on many occasions. In the painting *La Gare St-Lazare* (1877) **(1)**, which now hangs in the Musée d'Orsay, the immense iron-and-glass nave forms a rigid framework encompassing the thick scrolls of bluish steam belching out of the locomotive against a background of golden light. In *Toits sous la neige* **(4)**, GUSTAVE CAILLEBOTTE (1848–94) takes his search for the surprising to the extreme: his view of the capital's rooftops assumes an almost abstract quality, which gives it a singular charm.

1		
2	3	4

THE EIFFEL TOWER

The Eiffel Tower, that quintessential symbol of both modern Paris and the most daring of innovations in what was basically industrial architecture, found an admirer in ROBERT DELAUNAY (1885–1941) **(1)**. Seeing it as the steel muse of a new world which he observed, contemplated and adored from every angle, he adopted it as a favorite subject from 1909 until the end of his career. At first treated in a disjointed manner in the spirit of Cubism, the tower later became an excuse for juxtaposing rich colors which composed the painting unaided. This is the case with the canvas in the Musée d'Art Moderne **(2)**, dated 1923, in which Delaunay manages to highlight the tower's dizzy slenderness from below through a simple combination of vibrant colors. Although the Eiffel Tower had not been such a constant source of inspiration for anyone before Delaunay, many earlier painters had nevertheless taken it as a model. The most important of these is probably PAUL-LOUIS DELANCE, a little-known artist who painted an extremely attractive canvas dated January 1889 **(3)**.

> "Shepherdess O Eiffel Tower
> Your flock of bridges
> are bleating this morning."
>
> Guillaume Apollinaire

This painting depicts the progress of the work several months before the World Exhibition opened in 1889. Shrouding the metal structure in smoke from the building site, he successfully transforms the tower into a kind of allegory for industrial activity. Several years later LOUIS-WELDEN HAWKINS (1849–1910), an Englishman who became a naturalized French citizen, gave the tower a supporting role in a strange composition **(4)**: with its height and width chopped out of the picture, the tower is used as a foil for one of the former Trocadero's ornamental statues. After Delaunay's compositions, one of the most intense visions of the Eiffel Tower is probably that of NICOLAS DE STAËL (1914–55). After years of pure abstraction, the artist returned to a type of representation with this picture **(5)** in 1954. Despite the extremely simplified outlines, the monument remains perfectly recognizable.

THE SEINE

From the 17th century onward, the banks of the Seine have been a frequently depicted Parisian motif. Certain painters, such as JOHAN BARTHOLD JONGKIND (1819–91), were more receptive to its charms than others. Born and trained in Holland, he took pains to depict the many different faces of the Seine during his long stays in Paris. His *View of Notre-Dame* (3), dating from 1864, bears the stamp of his meeting with Monet, as can be seen by the innovative treatment of the play of light on moving water. ALBERT MARQUET (1875–1947) restricted his views of the Seine to a small number of vantage points, repeated endlessly, corresponding to what he could see from the windows of his successive studios. His *Vue de Notre-Dame sous la neige* (1) and *Vue du Pont-Neuf, effet de brouillard* (2) date from after the Fauvist period, which ended in 1907. The dazzling hues of his early views of Paris were replaced by a subtle chromatic quality, which he subsequently favored. Between 1899 and 1909, HENRI MATISSE (1869–1954) occupied a studio near Marquet's and also painted many views of the Seine during this period. His *Notre-Dame, en fin d'après-midi* (1902) (4) is vivid proof of this.

1	
2	4
3	

The Pont des Arts as painted by Paul Signac in 1928.

THE SEINE

PAUL SIGNAC (1863–1935), the theorist of Divisionism, applied his method to a great variety of subjects, including the sights of Paris. In *La Seine à Grenelle*, Signac strayed from the rules which he himself devised and broadened his stroke to such an extent that the canvas looks like a mosaic.

Paris
as seen by writers

Parisians

Impressions of Paris

The most celebrated English biography is a group portrait in which one extraordinary man paints the picture of a dozen more. At the center of a brilliant circle, James Boswell (1740-95) captures the powerful, troubled and witty figure of Samuel Johnson (1709-84), who, in the year 1775 went to travel through France, and spent some time in Paris.

66Oct. 10. Tuesday. We saw the *Ecole Militaire*, in which one hundred and fifty young boys are educated for the army. They have arms of different sizes, according to the age; – flints of wood. The building is very large, but nothing fine except the council-room. The French have large squares in the windows; – they make good iron palisades. Their meals are gross. **99**

66We passed through *Place de Vendôme*, a fine square, about as big as Hanover-square. – Inhabited by the high families. – Lewis XIV. on horse-back in the middle.**99**

66Oct. 12. Thursday. We went to the Gobelins. – Tapestry makes a good picture: imitates flesh exactly. – One piece with a gold ground; – the birds not exactly coloured. – Thence we went to the King's Cabinet; – very neat, not, perhaps, perfect. – Gold ore. – Candles of the candle-tree. – Seeds. – Woods. Thence to Gagnier's house, where I saw rooms nine, furnished with a profusion of wealth and elegance which I never had seen before. – Vases. – Pictures. – The dragon china. – The lustre said to be of crystal, and to have cost 3,500l. – The whole furniture said to have cost 125,000l. – Damask hangings covered with pictures. – Porphyry. – This house struck me.**99**

66Oct. 17. Tuesday. The sight of palaces, and other great buildings, leaves no very distinct images, unless to those who talk of them. As I entered, my wife was in my mind: she would have been pleased. Having now nobody to please, I am little pleased.**99**

66Oct. 19. Thursday. At Court, we saw the apartments; – the King's bed-chamber and council-chamber extremely splendid. – Persons of all ranks in the external rooms through which the family passes; – servants and masters. – Brunet with us the second time.
The introductor came to us; – civil to me. – Presenting. – I had scruples. – Not necessary. – We went and saw the King and Queen at dinner. – We saw the other ladies at dinner. – Madame Elizabeth, with the Princess of Guimené. – At night we went to a comedy. I neither saw nor heard. Drunken women. – Mrs Th. preferred one to the other.**99**

66Oct. 20. Friday. We saw the Queen mount in the forest. – Brown habit; rode aside: one lady rode aside. – The Queen's horse light grey; – martingale. – She galloped. – We then went to the apartment, and admired them. – Then wandered through the palace. In the passages, stalls and shops. – Painting in Fresco by a great master, worn out. – We saw the King's horses and dogs. – The dogs almost all English. – Degenerate. The horses not much commended. – The stables cool; the kennel filthy... The king fed himself with his left hand as we.**99**

❝OCT 28. Saturday. Hotel – a guinea a day. – Coach, three guineas a week. – Valet de place, three l. a day. – *Avantcoureur*, a guinea a week. – Ordinary dinner, six l. a head. – Our ordinary seems to be about five guineas a day. – Our extraordinary expences, as diversions, gratuities, clothes, I cannot reckon. – Our travelling is ten guineas a day.❞

JAMES BOSWELL, *THE LIFE OF SAMUEL JOHNSON*,
EVERYMAN'S LIBRARY, LONDON,
ALFRED A. KNOPF, INC. NEW YORK, 1992

THE BELLS

François Rabelais (c. 1494–c. 1553) was well known for his satirical tales of the two giants Gargantua and Pantagruel.

*How Gargantua payed his welcome to the Parisians, and how
he took away the great Bells of our Ladies Church.*

❝Some few dayes after that they had refresh't themselves, he went to see the city, and was beheld of every body there with great admiration; for the People of *Paris* are so sottish, so badot, so foolish and fond by nature, that a juglr, a carrier of indulgences, a sumpter-horse, or mule with cymbals, or tinkling bells, a blinde fidler in the middle of a crosse lane, shall draw a greater confluence of people together, then an Evangelical Preacher: and they prest so hard upon him, that he was constrained to rest himself upon the towers of our Ladies Church; at which place, seeing so many about him, he said with a loud voice, I beleeve th⸱t these buzzards wil have me to pay them here my welcom hither, and my *Proficiat⸱* ⸱t is but good reason, I will now give them their wine, but it shall be only in sport; Then smiling, he untied his faire *Braguette*, and drawing out his *mentul* into the open aire, he so bitterly all-to-bepist them, that he drowned two hundred and sixty thousand, foure hundred and eighteen, besides the women and little children: some neverthelesse of the company escaped this piss-flood by meer speed of foot, who when they were at the higher end of the University, sweating, coughing, spitting, and out of breath, they began to swear and curse, some in good hot earnest, and others in jest, *Carimari, Carimara: Golynoly, Golynolo*: by me sweet Sanctesse, we are wash't in sport, a sport truly to laugh at, in *French Par ris*, for which that city hath been ever since called Paris, whose name formerly was *Leucotia*, (as *Strabo* testifieth, *lib. quarto*) from the Greek word λευκστηζ, whitenesse, because of the white thighs of the Ladies of that place. And forasamuch as at this imposition of a new name, all the people that were there, swore every one by the Sancts of his parish, the *Parisians*, which are patch'd up of all nations, and all pieces of

99

countreyes, are by nature both good *Jurers*, and good *Jurists*, and somewhat overweening; whereupon *Joanninus de Barrauco libro de copiositate reverentiarum*, thinks that they are called *Parisians*, from the *Greek* word παρρησια, which signifies boldnesse and liberty in speech. This done, he considered the great bells, which were in the said tours, and made them sound very harmoniously, which whilest he was doing, it came into his minde, that they would serve very well for *tingling Tantans*, and *ringing Campanels*, to hang about his mares neck, when she should be sent back to his father, (as he intended to do) loaded with *Brie* cheese, and fresh herring; and indeed he forthwith carried them to his lodging. In the mean while there came a master begar of the Fryers of S. *Anthonie*, to demand in his canting way the usual benevolence of some hoggish stuffe, who, that he might be heard afar off, and to make the bacon, he was in quest of, shake in the very chimneys, made account to filch them away privily. Neverthelesse, he left them behinde very honestly, not for that they were too hot, but that they were somewhat too heavy for his carriage. This was not he of *Bourg*, for he was too good a friend of mine. All the city was risen up in sedition, they being (as you know) upon any slight occasion, so ready to uproars and insurrections, that forreign nations wonder at the patience of the Kings of *France*, who do not by good justice restrain them from such tumultuous courses, seeing the manifold incoveniences which thence arise from day to day. Would to God I knew the shop, wherein are forged these divisions, and factious combinations, that I might bring them to light in the confraternities of my parish. Beleeve for a truth, that the place wherein the people gathered together, were thus sulfured, hopurymated, moiled and bepist, was called *Nesle*, where then was, (but now is no more) the Oracle of *Leucotia*: There was the case proposed, and the inconvenience shewed of the transporting of the bells: After they had well *ergoted pro* and *con*, they concluded in *Baralipton*, that they should send the oldest and most sufficient of the facultie unto *Gargantua*, to signifie unto him the great and horrible prejudice they sustain by the want of those bells; and notwithstanding the good reasons given in by some of the University, why this charge was fitter for an Oratour then a Sophister, there was chosen for this purpose our Master *Janotus de Bragmardo*. **99**

FRANÇOIS RABELAIS, *GARGANTUA AND PANTAGRUEL*,
TRANS. SIR THOMAS URQUHART AND PIERRE LE MOTTEUX,
PUB. EVERYMAN'S LIBRARY, LONDON, 1994

NOTRE-DAME

Victor Hugo (1802–85) was a novelist, poet and dramatist, as well as a politician with changing affiliations. One of his best-known works "Notre-Dame de Paris" (translated into English as "The Hunchback of Notre Dame") tells the story of a wild romance against the medieval setting of the old cathedral.

❝That façade, as we now see it, has lost three important accessories: in the first place, the flight of eleven steps, which raised it above the level of the ground; in the next, the lower range of statues which filled the niches of the three porches, and the upper range of twenty-eight more ancient sovereigns of France which adorned the gallery of the first story, commencing with Childebert and ending with Philip Augustus, holding in his hand 'the imperial globe.'

Time, raising by a slow and irresistible progress the level of the city, occasioned the removal of the steps; but if this rising tide of the pavement of Paris has swallowed up, one after another, those eleven steps which added to the majestic height of the edifice, Time has given to the church more perhaps than it has taken away; for it is Time that has imparted to the façade that sombre hue of antiquity which makes the old age of buildings the period of their greatest beauty.

But who has thrown down the two ranges of statues? – who has left the niches empty? – who has inserted that new and bastard pointed arch in the middle of the beautiful central porch? – who has dared to set up that tasteless and heavy door of wood, carved in the style of Louis XV, beside the arabesques of Biscornette? – The men, the architects, the artists, of our days.❞

VICTOR HUGO, *THE HUNCHBACK OF NOTRE-DAME*,
PUB. RICHARD BENTLEY, EDINBURGH, 1838

HISTORY

COURT OF THE SUN KING

Louis, Duc de Saint-Simon (1675–1755), has depicted better than anyone else the reign of Louis XIV. The definitive text of his "Mémoires" was written between 1739 and 1750. He came from a grand family and from his birth was destined to the highest responsibilities in the kingdom. Louis XIV and Marie-Thérèse held him at his baptism, an early friend was the Duc de Chartres, the king's nephew and later Regent. His father was a favorite of Louis XIII, and a cousin of the Montmorency and the Condé families. On his mother's side, he was a cousin of Mme de Montespan. A politician and a diplomat, he was obsessed with history. For him the character of great men was what determined history, hence his care to note every detail of the court and the life of his contemporaries.

❝The Chevalier de Bouillon, who since the death of the Comte d'Auvergne's son had begun to call himself the Prince d'Auvergne, asked the Regent to allow public balls at the Opéra three times a week, with payment on entry, masked or unmasked, the boxes making a convenient refuge for those who wished to watch without joining the dance. It was thought that public balls, supervised as the Opéra always is during performances, would be safe from scandal, and might discourage people from attending shady little dance-halls scattered over Paris, where scandals so often originate. The Opéra balls were duly inaugurated, with huge crowds and all the desired effect. The proposer was at once given a pension of six thousand livres, and a wonderful new machine was invented that swiftly and easily covered the orchestra pit, bringing the stage and the auditorium to the same level, and perfectly flat. What was most unfortunate was that M. le Duc d'Orléans had only to walk a step to go there after his suppers, and very frequently showed himself in a most unseemly condition. The Duc de Noailles, ever anxious to pay his court, appeared at the first one of all, so drunk that there was no filthiness he did not commit.**

Tessé waited an entire day at Beaumont lest the Czar should arrive early. He at length appeared on Friday, 7 May, at noon precisely. Tessé made his bow at the coach door, had the honour of dining with him afterwards, and that same afternoon escorted him to Paris. When they arrived, however, the Czar chose to enter the city in one of the Marshal's coaches, but not in his company, preferring to drive with three members of his own staff. Thus Tessé followed in a second coach. They alighted at the Louvre at nine in the evening. The Czar inspected every room of the Queen-mother's suite, but thought them too luxurious and too brightly lit. He at once stepped back into his coach and went to the Hôtel de Lesdiguières, where he decided to lodge. There also he thought the rooms much too grand; and he had his camp-bed set up in one of the closets. The Maréchal de Tessé, whose duty it was to do the honours of his house and table and accompany him everywhere, also had rooms in the Hôtel de Lesdiguières. He had his work cut out in trying to stay with the Czar, and was sometimes reduced to chasing after him. Verton, one of the King's stewards, had charge of the service, and of the tables for the retinue, numbering altogether forty persons, twelve or fifteen of whom were of sufficient importance either by birth or function to eat at the Czar's table. Verton had his wits about him, and figured large in certain circles. He was a great one for good eating and gambling high. He ordered the household so efficiently and showed so much tact and goodwill that the Czar became remarkably friendly with him, and so did the suite.

HISTORICAL MEMOIRS OF THE DUC DE SAINT-SIMON,
VOL. III: 1715–23, ED. AND TRANS. LUCY NORTON,
PUB. HAMISH HAMILTON, LONDON, 1972

AFTER THE WAR

Alice B. Toklas (1877–1967) was the friend, secretary and companion of Gertrude Stein (1874–1946), and moved with her to Paris where Stein lived in the Rue de Fleurus, and developed a literary salon. The autobiography quoted below is Stein's own memoir, which she published using Toklas' name.

**It was a changed Paris. Everything was changed, and everybody was cheerful.

During our absence Eve had died and Picasso was now living in a little home in Montrouge. We went out to see him. He had a marvellous rose pink silk counterpane on his bed. Where did that come from Pablo, asked Gertrude Stein. Ah ça, said Picasso with much satisfaction, that is a lady. It was a well-known chilean society woman who had given it to him. It was a marvel. He was very cheerful. He was constantly coming to the house, bringing Paquerette a girl who was very nice or Irène a very lovely woman who came from the mountains and wanted to be free. He brought Erik Satie and the Princesse de Polignac and Blaise Cendrars.

It was a great pleasure to know Erik Satie. He was from Normandy and very fond of it. Marie Laurencin comes from Normandy, so also does Braque. Once when after the war Satie and Marie Laurencin were at the house for lunch they were delightully enthusiastic about each other as being normans. Erik Satie liked food and wine and knew a lot about both. We had at that time some very good eau de vie that the husband of Mildred Aldrich's servant had given us and Erik Satie, drinking his glass slowly and with appreciation, told stories of the country in his youth.

Only once in the half dozen times that Erik Satie was at the house did he talk about music. He said that it had always been his opinion and he was glad that it was being recognised that modern french music owed nothing to modern Germany. That after Debussy had led the way french musicians had either followed him or found their own french way. . . .

It was a changed Paris. Guillaume Apollinaire was dead. We saw a tremendous number of people but none of them as far as I can remember that we had ever known before. Paris was crowded. As Clive Bell remarked, they say that an awful lot of people were killed in the war but it seems to me that an extraordinary large number of grown men and women have suddenly been born.

As I say we were restless and we were economical and all day and all evening we were seeing people and at last there was the defile, the procession under the Arc de Triomphe, of the allies.

The members of the American Fund for French Wounded were to have seats on the benches that were put up the length of the Champs Elysées but quite rightly the people of Paris objected as these seats would make it impossible for them to see the parade and so Clémenceau promptly had them taken down. Luckily for us Jessie Whitehead's room in her hotel looked right over the Arc de Triomphe and she asked us to come to it to see the parade. We accepted gladly. It was a wonderful day.

We got up at sunrise, as later it would have been impossible for them to cross Paris in a car. This was one of the last trips Auntie made. By this time the red cross was painted off it but it was still a truck. . . .

Auntie then was making practically her last trip. We left her near the river and walked up to the hotel. Everybody was on the streets, men, women, children, soldiers, priests, nuns, we saw two nuns being helped into a tree from which they would be able to see. And we were admirably placed and we saw perfectly.

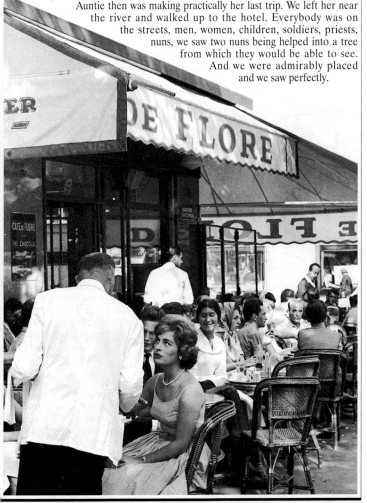

We saw it all, we saw first the few wounded from the Invalides in their wheeling chairs wheeling themselves. It is an old french custom that a military procession should always be preceded by the veterans from the Invalides. They all marched past through the Arc de Triomphe. Gertrude Stein remembered that when as a child she used to swing on the chains that were around the Arc de Triomphe her governess had told her that no one must walk underneath since the german armies had marched under it after 1870. And now everybody except the germans were passing through.

All the nations marched differently, some slowly, some quickly, the french carry their flags the best of all, Pershing and his officer carrying the flag behind him were perhaps the most perfectly spaced. It was this scene that Gertrude Stein described in the movie she wrote about this time that I have published in Operas and Plays in the Plain Edition.

However it all finally came to an end. We wandered up and we wandered down the Champs Elysées and the war was over and the piles of captured canon that had made two pyramids were being taken away and peace was upon us.**

THE AUTOBIOGRAPHY OF ALICE B. TOKLAS,
PUB. JOHN LANE, THE BODLEY HEAD,
LONDON, 1935

DAILY LIFE

LOCAL CUSTOMS

"Birds of America" by Mary McCarthy (1912–89) is a novel in which the protagonist is a young American boy living in Paris and Rome, and complaining about the tourist industry in both cities.

The French, like the Italians, only buy what they need for one day. I had a shock, though, yesterday, when I went to do my marketing at the Marché Buci – that big outdoor market, near the Odéon. At one stall, I asked for a carrot, and the *type* refused to sell me one. He said I had to buy a kilo. Like you, dearest Ma, I started to argue. I wanted to know why. How it would damage him to sell me one carrot or one apple or one pear. I explained that I didn't have an icebox and that I was just one person. '*Ça ne me regarde pas,*' he growled. Finally we compromised on a pound. That's quite a lot of carrots for a single man. While he was weighing them, I got into conversation with an Italian, who had been watching me and smiling – very nice, about the *babbo*'s age, an intellectual. He said that in Italy not only would they sell you one carrot but divide it in four. According to him, this only proved that Italy is a poor country, while France is a rich country. I said the Italians had more heart than the French even if they gyp you sometimes. The French *grudge* gypping you, Mother. Maybe, I said, people in poor countries had more heart than people in rich countries. After all, Poverty used to be represented as a virtue. I hadn't noticed any statues of Poverty on French churches.

That reminds me. Did you know that you're supposed to tip the usher in a French movie house? I didn't know and got hissed at by the woman the other day when I went to see an Antonioni flick. All the students in the vicinity stopped necking and turned to ogle me as I stumbled into my seat. I gather I was being called a '*sale américain*', but if she knew I was an American, she might have enlightened me about the local customs. It must happen all the time with foreigners. But I suppose that's what makes her mad. Usually when I'm in some place like a stand-up coffee bar, I watch what the other customers do and follow their example, but in a movie house you're literally in the dark. This little incident wrecked the film for me. I hardly saw Monica Vitti because of the rage I was in.

The picture was half over before I finally grasped what I'd done that was so horrible. Then it was too late to rectify it – at least without getting stared at some more. Besides, I couldn't see how much the other customers were giving. In case you want to know, it's a franc on the Champs-Elysées and fifty centimes in the little places. The clerk at my hotel told me. **99**

MARY MCCARTHY, *BIRDS OF AMERICA*,
PUB. WEIDENFELD AND NICOLSON,
LONDON, 1971

VISITING GERTRUDE STEIN

In "A Moveable Feast", Hemingway (1899–1961) writes with hindsight in the late 1950's about the ex-patriate literary set who lived in Paris in the 1920's. These included Ezra Pound, Ford Maddox Ford and Gertrude Stein.

66If I walked down by different streets to the Jardin du Luxembourg in the afternoon I could walk through the gardens and then go to the Musée du Luxembourg where the great paintings were that have now mostly been transferred to the Louvre and the Jeu de Paume. I went there nearly every day for the Cézannes and to see the Manets and the Monets and the other Impressionists that I had first come to know about in the Art Institute at Chicago. I was learning something from the painting of Cézanne that made writing simple true sentences far from enough to make the stories have the dimensions that I was trying to put in them. I was learning very much from him but I was not articulate enough to explain it to anyone. Besides, it was a secret. But if the light was gone in the Luxembourg I would walk up through the gardens and stop in at the studio apartment where Gertrude Stein lived at 27 rue de Fleurus.

My wife and I had called on Miss Stein, and she and the friend who lived with her had been very cordial and friendly and we had loved the big studio with the great paintings. It was like one of the best rooms in the finest museum except there was a big fireplace and it was warm and comfortable and they gave you good things to eat and tea and natural distilled liqueurs made from purple plums, yellow plums or wild raspberries. These were fragrant, colourless alcohols served from cut-glass carafes in small glasses and whether they were *quetsche, mirabelle* or framboise they all tasted like the fruits they came from, converted into a controlled fire on your tongue that warmed you and loosened it.

Miss Stein was very big but not tall and was heavily built like a peasant woman. She had beautiful eyes and a strong German-Jewish face that also could have been *friulano* and she reminded me of a northern Italian peasant woman with her clothes, her mobile face and her lovely thick, alive, immigrant hair which she wore put up in the same way she had probably worn it in college. She talked all the time and at first it was about people and places. **99**

ERNEST HEMINGWAY, *A MOVEABLE FEAST*,
PUB. JONATHAN CAPE, LONDON, 1964

RETURNING TO THE CITY

In the letter below, Gustave Flaubert (1821–80) writes to his friend from adolescence, Alfred Le Poittevin, on April 2, 1845. Flaubert studied law in Paris, from 1841–5.

66I enjoyed seeing Paris again; I looked at the boulevards, the rue de Rivoli, the sidewalks, as though I were back among them after being away a hundred years; and I don't know why, but I felt happy in the midst of all that noise and all that human flood. (But I have no one with me, alas! The moment you and I part, we set foot in some strange land where people do not speak our language nor we theirs.) No sooner was I off the train than I put on my city shoes, boarded a bus, and began my visits. The stairs of the Mint left me breathless, because there are a hundred of them and also because I remembered the evenings, gone never to return, when I used to climb them on my way to dinner. I greeted Mme and Mlle Darcet, who were in mourning; I sat down, talked for half an hour, and then decamped.

Everywhere I went I walked in my own past, pushing through it as though striding knee-deep against the current of a flowing, murmuring river. I went to the Champs-Elysées, to see the two women with whom I used to spend entire afternoons (which I probably wouldn't do now, I've become such a lout). The invalid was still half-lying in an armchair. She greeted me with the same smile and the same voice. The furniture was still the same, and the rug no more worn. In exquisite affinity, one of those rare harmonies that can be perceived only by the artist, a street-organ began to play under the windows, just as it used to when I would be reading them *Hernani* or *René*.❞

GUSTAVE FLAUBERT, *THE LETTERS OF GUSTAVE FLAUBERT 1830–1857*,
ED. AND TRANS. FRANCIS STEEGMULLER, PUB. FABER AND FABER, LONDON, 1981
AND HARVARD UNIVERSITY PRESS, HARVARD, 1979

JAMES JOYCE AT DINNER

Sylvia Beach published the first edition of Joyce's Ulysses in 1922 at her bookshop Librairie Shakespeare. She was a friend and patron of many of the ex-patriate literary set and wrote about them in the memoir "Shakespeare and Company".

❝In Paris, Joyce and his family dined out every evening. His particular restaurant – this was in the early 'twenties – was the one opposite the Gare Montparnasse, Les Trianons. The proprietor and the entire personnel were devoted to Joyce. They were at the door of his taxi before he alighted and they escorted him to a table reserved for him at the back, where he could be more or less unmolested by people who came to stare at him as he dined, or brought copies of his works to be autographed.

The head-waiter would read to him the items on the bill of fare so that he would be spared the trouble of getting out several pairs of glasses and perhaps a magnifying glass. Joyce pretended to take an interest in fine dishes, but food meant nothing to him, unless it was something to do with his work. He urged his family and the friends who might be dining with him to choose the best food on the menu. He liked to have them eat a hearty meal and persuaded them to try such and such a wine. He himself ate scarcely anything, and was satisfied with the most ordinary white wine just as long as there was plenty of it. As he never drank a drop all day long, he was pretty thirsty by dinnertime. The waiter kept his glass filled. Joyce would have sat there with his family and friends and his white wine till all hours if at a certain moment Nora hadn't decided it was time to go. He ended by obeying her – it was according to an understanding between them, one of the many understandings between this couple who understood each other so well.

Wherever Joyce went, he was received like royalty, such was his personal charm, his consideration for others. When he started on his way downstairs to the men's room, several waiters came hurrying to escort him. His blindness drew people to him a great deal.

Joyce's tips were famous; the waiters, the boy who fetched him a taxi, all those who served him, must have retired with a fortune. I never grudged tips, but, knowing the circumstances, it seemed to me that Joyce overtipped.❞

SYLVIA BEACH, *SHAKESPEARE AND COMPANY*,
PUB. FABER AND FABER, LONDON, 1960

PARIS 1787–90

Arthur Young (1741–1820) was an agricultural theorist who displayed acute powers of political and social observation in his writings.

1787
❝OCT 25TH. This great city appears to be in many respects the most ineligible and inconvenient for the residence of a person of small fortune of any that I have seen; and vastly inferior to London. The streets are very narrow, and many of them crowded, nine-tenths dirty, and all without foot pavements. Walking, which in London is so pleasant and so clean, that ladies do it every day, is here a toil and a fatigue to a man, and an impossibility to a well-dressed woman. The coaches are numerous, and, what are much worse, there are an

infinity of horse cabriolets, which are driven by young men of fashion and their imitators, alike fools, with such rapidity as to be real nuisances, and render the streets exceedingly dangerous, without an incessant caution. **99**

66 . . . in other respects I take it to be a most eligible residence for such as prefer a great city. The society for a man of letters, or [for one] who has any scientific pursuit, cannot be exceeded. The intercourse between such men and the great, which, if it is not upon an equal footing, ought never to exist at all, is respectable. Persons of the highest rank pay an attention to science and literature, and emulate the character they confer. I should pity the man who expected, without other advantages of a very different nature, to be well received in a brilliant circle at London, because he was a fellow of the Royal Society. But this would not be the case with a member of the Academy of Sciences at Paris; he is sure of a good reception everywhere. Perhaps this contrasts depends in a great measure on the difference of the governments of the two countries. Politics are too much attended to in England to allow a due respect to be paid to anything else; and should the French establish a freer government, academicians will not be held in such estimation, when rivalled in the public esteem by the orators who hold forth liberty and property in a free parliament. **99**

1789

66 JUNE 9TH. The business going forward at present in the pamphlet shops in Paris is incredible. I went to the Palais-Royal to see what new things were published, and to procure a catalogue of all. Every hour produces something new. Thirteen came out to-day, sixteen yesterday, and ninety-two last week. We think sometimes that Debrett's or Stockdale's shops at London are crowded, but they are mere deserts compared to Desein's [Desennes], and some others here, in which one can scarcely squeeze from the door to the counter. The price of printing two years ago was from 27 *livres* to 30 *livres* per sheet, but now it is from 60 *livres* to 80 *livres*. This spirit of reading political tracts, they say, spreads into the provinces, so that all the presses of France are equally employed. Nineteen-twentieths of these productions are in favour of liberty, and commonly violent against the clergy and nobility. **99**

❝It is easy to conceive the spirit that must thus be raised among the people. But the coffee-houses in the Palais-Royal present yet more singular and astonishing spectacles; they are not only crowded within, but other expectant crowds are at the doors and windows, listening *à gorge déployée* to certain orators, who from chairs or tables harangue each his little audience. The eagerness with which they are heard, and the thunder of applause they receive for every sentiment of more than common hardiness or violence against the present government, cannot easily be imagined.❞

❝JUNE 26TH. Every hour that passes seems to give the people fresh spirit: the meetings at the Palais-Royal are more numerous, more violent, and more assured; and in the assembly of electors, at Paris, for sending a deputation to the National Assembly, the language that was talked, by all ranks of people, was nothing less than a revolution in the government, and the establishment of a free constitution. What they mean by a free constitution is easily understood – *a republic*; for the doctrine of the times runs everyday more and more to that point; yet they profess, that the kingdom ought to be a monarchy too; or, at least, that there ought to be a king. In the streets one is stunned by the hawkers of seditious pamphlets, and descriptions of pretended events, that all tend to keep the people equally ignorant and alarmed. The supineness and even stupidity of the Court is without example; the moment demands the greatest decision, and yesterday, while it was actually a question whether he should be a doge of Venice, or a king of France, the King went a hunting!❞

1790

JAN. 4TH. After breakfast, walk in the gardens of the Tuileries, where there is the most extraordinary sight that either French or English eyes could ever behold at Paris. The King, walking with six grenadiers of the *milice bourgeoise*, with an officer or two of his household, and a page. The doors of the gardens are kept shut in respect to him, in order to exclude everybody but deputies, or those who have admission-tickets. When he entered the palace, the doors of the gardens were thrown open for all without distinction, though the Queen was still walking with a lady of her court. She also was attended so closely by the *gardes bourgeoises*, that she could not speak, but in a low voice, without being heard by them. A mob followed her, talking very loud, and paying no other apparent respect than that of taking off their hats wherever she passed, which was indeed more than I expected. Her Majesty does not appear to be in health; she seems to be much affected, and shows it in her face; but the King is as plump as ease can render him. By his orders, there is a little garden railed off for the Dauphin to amuse himself in, and a small room is built in it to retire to in case of rain; here he was at work with his little hoe and rake, but not without a guard of two grenadiers. He is a very pretty good-natured-looking boy, of five or six years old, with an agreeable countenance; wherever he goes, all hats are taken off to him, which I was glad to observe. All the family being kept thus close prisoners (for such they are in effect) affords, at first view, a shocking spectacle; and is really so, if the act were not absolutely necessary to effect the revolution; this I conceive to be impossible; but if it were necessary, no one can blame the people for taking every measure possible to secure that liberty they had seized in the violence of a revolution.❞

ARTHUR YOUNG, *TRAVELS IN FRANCE DURING THE YEARS 1787, 1788, 1789*, ED. CONSTANTIA MAXWELL, PUB. CAMBRIDGE UNIVERSITY PRESS, 1950

WALKING AT NIGHT

In "Nightwood", Djuna Barnes describes a nightmare world (chiefly based on Paris and New York), in which the characters are troubled and desperate.

❝Close to the church of *St. Sulpice*, around the corner in the *rue Servandoni*, lived a doctor. His small slouching figure was a feature of the *Place*. To the proprietor of the *Café de la Mairie du VIe* he was almost a son. This relatively small square, through which tram lines ran in several directions, bounded on the one side by the church and on the other by the court, was the doctor's 'city'. What he would not find here to answer to his needs, could be found in the narrow streets that ran into it. Here he had been seen ordering details for funerals in the parlour with its black broadcloth curtains and mounted pictures of hearses; buying holy pictures and *petits Jésus* in the boutique displaying vestments and flowering candles. . . .

He walked, pathetic and alone, among the pasteboard booths of the *Foire St. Germain* when for a time its imitation castles squatted in the square. He was seen coming at a smart pace down the left side of the church to go into Mass; bathing in the holy water stoup as if he were its single and beholden bird, pushing aside weary French maids and local tradespeople with the impatience of a soul in physical stress.

Sometimes, late at night, before turning into the *Café de la Mairie du VIe*, he would be observed staring up at the huge towers of the church which rose into the sky, unlovely but reassuring, running a thick warm finger around his throat, where, in spite of its customs, his hair surprised him, lifting along his back and creeping up over his collar. Standing small and insubordinate, he would watch the basins of the fountain loosing their skirts of water in a ragged and flowing hem, sometimes crying to a man's departing shadow: 'Aren't you the beauty!'❞

DJUNA BARNES, *NIGHTWOOD*,
PUB. FABER AND FABER,
LONDON, 1936

WALKING BY DAY

Henry James (1843–1916) describes his early years in "A Small Boy and Others". Here he describes walking in Paris with his elder brother, William James, later a philosopher and psychologist.

❝That autumn renewed, I make out, our long and beguiled walks, my own with W. J. in especial; at the same time that I have somehow the sense of the whole more broken appeal on the part of Paris, the scanter confidence and ease it inspired in us, the perhaps more numerous and composite, but obscurer and more baffled imitations. Not indeed – for all my brother's later vision of an accepted flatness in it – that there was not some joy and some grasp; why else were we forever (as I seem to conceive we were) measuring the great space that separated us from the gallery of the Luxembourg, every step of which, either way we took it, fed us with some interesting, some admirable image, kept us in relation to something nobly intended? That particular walk was not prescribed us, yet we appear to have hugged it, across the Champs-Elysées to the river, and so over the nearest bridge and the quays of the left bank to the Rue de Seine, as if it somehow held the secret of our future; to the extent even of my more or less sneaking off on occasion to take it by myself, to taste of it with a due undiverted intensity and the throb as of the finest, which *could* only mean the most Parisian, adventure. The further quays, with their innumerable old bookshops and print-shops, the long cases of each of these commodities, exposed on the parapets in especial, must have come to know us almost as well as we knew them; with plot thickening and emotion deepening steadily, however, as we mounted the long, black Rue de Seine – *such* a stretch of perspective, *such* an intensity of tone as it offered in those days; where every low-browed vitrine waylaid us and we moved in a world of which the dark message, expressed in we couldn't have said what sinister way too, might have been 'Art, art, art, don't you see? Learn, little gaping pilgrims, what *that* is!' Oh we learned, that is we tried to, as hard as ever we could, and were fairly well at it, I always felt, even by the time we had passed up into that comparatively short but wider and finer vista of the Rue de Tournon, which in those days more abruptly crowned the more compressed approach and served in a manner as a great outer vestibule to the Palace. Style, dimly described, looked down there, as with conscious encouragement, from the high grey-headed, clear-faced, straight-standing old houses – very much as if wishing to say 'Yes, small staring jeune homme, we are dignity and memory and measure, we are conscience and proportion and taste, not to mention strong sense too: for all of which good things take us – you won't find one of them when you find (as you're going soon to begin to at such a rate) vulgarity.' This, I admit, was an abundance of remark to such young ears; but it did all, I maintain, tremble in the air, with the sense that the Rue de Tournon, cobbled and a little grass-grown, might more or less have figured some fine old street *de province*: I cherished in short its very name and think I really hadn't to wait to prefer the then, the unmenaced, the inviolate Café Foyot of the left hand corner, the much-loved and so haunted Café Foyot of the old Paris, to its – well, to its roaring successor.❞

HENRY JAMES, *AUTOBIOGRAPHY VOL. I, A SMALL BOY AND OTHERS*,
PUB. CHARLES SCRIBNER, NEW YORK, 1913

ATMOSPHERE

TASTE

Evelyn Waugh (1903-66) had some typically caustic criticisms of the French reputation for good taste.

❝ There is nothing essentially modish in the atmosphere of Paris, any more than there is anything specifically medical in the atmosphere of Harley Street. In almost all matters except the business of dress-making, Parisian taste is notably lower and less progressive than Berlin or Vienna or even London. The French, through the defects rather than the qualities of their taste, are saved from the peculiarly English horrors of folk dancing, arts and crafts, and the collection of cottage antiquities, only to fall victim, one false thing driving out another, to the worst sort of sham modernity. If the choice is inevitable beween pewter-*cum*-warming-pan-*cum*-timbered-gables and the glass of M. Lalique, it is surely better to be imposed upon by a past which one has not seen than by a present of which one is one oneself a part ? **99**

EVELYN WAUGH, *LABELS: A MEDITERRANEAN JOURNAL*, PUB. DUCKWORTH, LONDON, 1930

LE BISTRO

George Orwell (1903-50) worked in a series of low-paid jobs in Paris and enjoyed the social life.

66 We had some jolly evenings, on Saturdays, in the little *bistro* at the foot of the Hôtel des Trois Moineaux.

The brick-floored room, fifteen feet square, was packed with twenty people, and the air dim with smoke. The noise was deafening, for everyone was either talking at the top of his voice or singing. Sometimes it was just a confused din of voices; sometimes everyone would burst out together in the same song – the 'Marseillaise', or the 'Internationale', or 'Madelon', or 'Les Fraises et les Framboises'. Azaya, a great clumping peasant girl who worked fourteen hours a day in a glass factory sang a song about, '*Il a perdu ses pantalons, tout en dans*ant *le Charleston*'. Her friend Marinette, a thin, dark Corsican girl of obstinate virtue, tied her knees together and danced the *danse du ventre*. The old Rougiers wandered in and out, cadging drinks and trying to tell a long, involved story about someone who had once cheated them over a bedstead. T., cadaverous and silent, sat in his corner quietly boozing. Charlie, drunk, half danced, half staggered to and fro with a glass of sham absinthe balanced in one fat hand, pinching the women's breasts and declaiming poetry. People played darts and diced for drinks. Manuel, a Spaniard, dragged the girls to the bar and shook the dice-box against their bellies, for luck. Madame F. stood at the bar rapidly pouring *chopines* of wine through the pewter funnel, with a wet dishcloth always handy, because every man in the room tried to make love to her. Two children, bastards of big Louis the bricklayer, sat in a corner sharing a glass of syrop. Every one was very happy, overwhelmingly certain that the world was a good place and we a notable set of people. **99**

GEORGE ORWELL, *DOWN AND OUT IN PARIS AND LONDON*, PUB. PENGUIN BOOKS, LONDON, 1940

Five sides of Paris

HERE ARE A FEW PARISIAN THEMES
TO GIVE YOU A TASTE OF VARIOUS DIFFERENT ASPECTS OF LIFE IN PARIS.

Paris chic: explore the world of fashion and couture ▲ *115–32.*

Museums: discover the great museums and the artists' studios ▲ *133–72.*

A city for gourmets: from famous restaurants to family-run eateries ▲ *173–90.*

Nature: discover the parks of Paris and their unexpected wildlife ▲ *191–212.*

Along the Seine: the bridges, quays and the most beautiful avenue in Paris ▲ *215–31.*

Paris chic

The proclamation of the Second Empire signaled the demise of the small, exclusive dressmaker. The rise of haute couture was dominated by two Paris-based English tailors, Redfern and Worth, and a Frenchman called Doucet. They imposed their own ideas and used fashionable embroiderers, feather dressers and pleaters. They also worked hard to ensure that their creations' renown established Paris's reputation for impeccable taste. Their illustrious successors have included Jean Patou, Robert Piguet, Elsa Schiaparelli and Cristóbal Balenciaga.

THE ELEGANCE OF DOUCET

Jacques Doucet inherited a lingerie shop at 21, rue de la Paix, and in 1875 turned it into a fashion house. He had an unmatched reputation for expensive gowns, designing clothes for the actresses Sarah Bernhardt and Réjane.

EUGÉNIE'S CONTRIBUTION

The Empress Eugénie was able to support luxury industries thanks to the pomp of the court. She was also responsible for launching an unusually ostentatious fashion that demanded large amounts of fabric.

A CITY OF COUTURIERS

Since the 19th century Paris has boasted of an abundance of talented couturiers and milliners: some are commemorated in pavement inscriptions. There are dedications at the corner of the Avenue

Montaigne and the Rue-François I to the following: Jeanne Paquin, a dressmaker from the Rue de la Paix who designed the high-waisted "Directoire" look; Madeleine Vionnet, a designer famous for her bias-cut crepes who opened her own house in 1912; and the Callot sisters. A creation by Lucien Lelong (left).

1950'S STYLE
Essential fashion
accessories of the
1950's included fans,
gloves, parasols and
highly acclaimed
Parisian hats.

anne Lanvin
ure, Mode, Fourrures, Lingerie
Faubourg Saint Honoré, Paris.

**JEANNE LANVIN, OR
MOTHERLY LOVE**
aul Iribe's design for the
ompany's future logo in
927 symbolized Lanvin's
ve for her daughter, her
ain source of inspiration.

**PAUL POIRET, SULTAN
AND REVOLUTIONARY**
Pupil of Worth and Doucet,
Paul Poiret, here caricatured
by Rip, influenced the world
of fashion from 1909 until
the interwar years. He
shocked society with his
extraordinary Eastern-
influenced shimmering
gowns with matching
turbans, which were
designed to be worn
without corsets.

WORTH, THE INVENTOR OF HAUTE COUTURE
Charles Frederick
Worth moved from
London to Paris in
1845, at the age of
twenty, and worked in
a draper's shop
until he was able to
open his own shop at
7, rue de la Paix, in
1858. Specializing in
well-cut clothes, he
lightened the female
silhouette and
instituted the seasonal
rhythms of fashion
by preparing his
collections in advance.
One of his
innovations
was to use live
models for
fashion shows.

Parisian women are acknowledged paragons of elegance and charm the world over: indeed, it is said that couturiers always have Parisian women in their mind's eye when dreaming up new creations. They are also admired for their natural chic, wit and smart appearance. Her image has changed, however, from the turn of-the-century *cocotte*, a woman of easy virtue kept by rich lovers, who launched fashion and spent a fortune shopping, to the assiduous, businesslike *Parisienne* of today.

Liane de Pougy, a celebrated Parisian courtesan.

IN BLACK AND WHITE

Parisian women have long been objects of admiration and jealousy, and have inspired many writers. Henri Becque (1837–99) entitled one of his plays *La Parisienne*; Colette described her impressions of a provincial woman who comes to Paris in *Claudine à Paris*; and in 1950, Jacques Laurent launched a literary review called *La Parisienne*.

LA PARISIENNE

HENRI BECQUE

LA PARISIENNE
COMÉDIE

WILLY ET COLETTE

Claudine à Paris

WORLDLY WOMEN

The reign of the *cocottes* began under the Second Empire: at that time they had little difficulty in eclipsing society ladies. Women in French high society were not only cultured but curious and loquacious; they took their revenge in the early years of the 20th century by opening literary *salons*. The most celebrated *salons* included those of the Countess Anna de Noailles (above), a noted storyteller and poet; the Duchess of La Rochefoucauld, who received the writer Paul Valéry in the Place des États-Unis; and the Comtesse de Fels, who wrote on her invitations: "A little tea, a little conversation."

A SILHOUETTE IN TOWN

This was how the couturier Olivier Lapidus described modern Parisian women, as represented by the actress Sabine Azéma, photographed here by Robert Doisneau.

THE INIMITABLE PARISIENNE

A character in Léon Gozlan's *Parisian Mistresses* says of the typical *Parisienne*: "She is a composite of grace and sensitivity; an inexhaustible source of seduction . . . the kind of woman you dream about when you're sixteen, and the only one you remember when you're sixty." Not all Parisian women are members of high society, but the one sketched here by Gruau is celebrated for her innate confidence in her appearance.

FREEDOM AND ELEGANCE
The *tailleur Bar*, created by Christian Dior after the end of World War Two, symbolized a return to opulent, affluent living standards after the privations of the German Occupation. However, the great sophistication of the New Look, which was quickly adopted by the majority of Parisian women, deterred others, who were afraid of losing their physical and social freedom.

AN AMBASSADRESS OF PARIS
These days, the catwalks are largely dominated by foreigners, such as the beautiful Somalian model Ebyan. However, even though Parisian women are sometimes born outside the capital, they can always be identified by their impeccable knowledge of the city, their open-minded, curious manner and their way of choosing what they like.

According to the sociologist Jean Baudrillard, "Couturiers are the modern world's last adventurers: they cultivate the gratuitous act." A virtual laboratory for French fashion and taste, haute couture brings together people with astonishing creative talent. The designers themselves are endowed with exceptional ability and work for a clientele of no more than two thousand women all over the world. A fashion house can describe itself as haute couture only if it meets certain criteria relating to fittings and presentations of collections in January and July; since 1994, these have taken place at the Carrousel du Louvre.

MODERN ELEGANCE FROM CHANEL
29–31, rue Cambon 75008
"Fashion passes; style remains." This was the byword of Gabrielle (Coco) Chanel, who is remembered for her comfortable yet chic women's clothes between the two wars. Her fashion house in the Rue Cambon was best known for its cardigans, black dresses decorated with costume jewelry, camellias and straw hats as well as the famous "little suit". Since taking over the firm in 1983, Karl Lagerfeld has continued to steer the same course, occasionally adding touches of irreverent humor.

YVES SAINT LAURENT'S IMPECCABLE CHIC
5, avenue Marceau 75008
After working as an assistant to Dior, Saint Laurent presented his first collection in 1962. At his retirement in 2002 he had conceived 77,751 designs. Through haute couture, and the ready-to-wear label Rive Gauche, he created the image of a woman who was sophisticated and elegant in any setting. The Texan Tom Ford became chief designer and creative director at YSL in 2000.

MYTHS AND RITES
The presentation of collections takes up a great deal of media space these days. The public revels in the life styles of famous models and loves to see the couturier emerging at the end of a fashion show.

SCHERRER: CLASSICISM AND REFINEMENT

Jean-Louis Scherrer's first show was held in a cellar in 1962. Since moving to the Avenue Montaigne, his house has acquired a reputation for a timeless style and lavish evening dresses.

CHRISTIAN DIOR:
ETERNAL FEMININITY

30, avenue Montaigne
75008

Once established in the Avenue Montaigne, Dior turned fashion upside down with the New Look. This marked a return to opulence and included flowing gowns made of luxurious materials and hemlines a good eight inches longer. Today a more minimalist, unstructured style is brought to Dior by John Galliano, who came to Dior in 1997 after two years at Givenchy.

GIVENCHY:
UNPARALLELED DISTINCTION

5, rue du Cherche-Midi 75006

Hubert de Givenchy, who was known as the gentleman of haute couture, discovered his vocation on a visit to the Pavilion of Elegance at the 1937 Universal Exhibition. He opened his own house in 1952. In March 2001 Julien MacDonald became the new artistic director for Givenchy womenswear.

OLIVIER LAPIDUS:
MODERN CRAFTSMANSHIP

12, rue François-Ier
75008

When Olivier inherited the house of Lapidus from his father, Ted, in 1982, he was very much the newcomer to the high-fashion scene. His creations, aimed at refined, modern women, employ the finest talents in the fashion business, including Lyons silk merchants, embroiderers and lacemakers.

CHRISTIAN LACROIX: LUXURY AND IMAGINATION

26, avenue Montaigne 75008

Lacroix, a native of Arles, devoted his first collection, in 1987, to Provence. He drew on Provençal folklore for his summery colors and rich, embroidered fabrics. He gives the female form an outline that is often extravagant but always seductive. In 2002 he became artistic director of the Florentine fashion house Pucci.

The 1960's focus on youth encouraged a new wave of creative designers. Of these, Daniel Hechter, Cacherel, Emmanuelle Khanh and Dorothée Bis defended the idea that fashion was no longer the preserve of the couturiers. Courrèges designed geometrically styled clothes made of synthetic materials, Paco Rabanne produced gowns made of aluminum, and Pierre Cardin developed his ready-to-wear line. These currents gave rise to an avant-garde which flourished during the 1980's in the Place des Victoires.

AGNÈS B. – THE SPIRIT OF "ANTI-FASHION"

Rue du Jour 75001
The work of Agnès B. evokes a relaxed, urban lifestyle. In 1979 she invented the cotton cardigan with metal poppers, available in a wide range of colors. This summed up perfectly the philosophy of a designer who loved to create simple clothes that you mix and match as you like, suitable for wearing day or night, in any combination and in any social situation.

ALAÏA, A DESIGNER WHO GLORIFIES WOMEN

7, rue de Moussy 75004
The gowns designed by Azzedine Alaïa, a proud Parisian originally from Tunisia, are meant for elegant women who are confident of their seductive powers. Alaïa ostentatiously underlines the female form and reveals parts of the body by the skillful use of soft fabrics.

He designed these low-cut shoes for the woman who is sensual and also has a sense of humor.

MUGLER: STRUCTURED ELEGANCE

49, av. Montaigne 75008
These designs were inspired by the ballerinas with whom Thierry Mugler worked when he trained as a dancer. He produces a sublime version of the female form and is well known for his spectacular shows.

CASTELBAJAC: WIT AND COLOR

6, pl. St-Sulpice 75006
Jean-Charles de Castelbajac is instantly recognizable for his motifs in primary colors and his use of unusual materials. An example was the "fur" coat he made out of Teddy Bear material.

SONIA RYKIEL AND "DÉMODE"

175, bd. St-Germain 75006
Rykiel's creations are intended to be worn exactly as the wearer wishes. Their sober hues and simple forms adorned with accessories are a rich combination of humor and sophistication.

JEAN-PAUL GAULTIER: ICONOCLAST

44, av. Georges V 75008
"Everything is beautiful if you think it is beautiful" says the man whose designs have revolutionized fashion. Gaultier has no taboos and easily moves from punk to frock coats.

MONTANA: SPIRIT OF THE 1980's

131, rue St-Denis 75001
Claude Montana has said he wants to design clothes that people will enjoy rediscovering. He achieves a rigorous, futuristic style with his use of leather and shoulder pads.

Dictionaries define accessory as something that is "extra", "additional" or "an adjunct"; the word comes from the Latin *accedere* which means to add. Objects of adornment, fashion accessories may be divided into two categories: those that are worn, like hats, and those that are carried, like handbags. The ways in which these objects are now used reflects how customs have changed: at one time a fan was a must for every society woman, and no lady would be seen without a hat.

ELVIS POMPILIO AND HIS FUNNY HATS
62, rue des Sts-Pères
75006
Elvis Pompilio was born in Belgium in 1961 from Italian parents. After graphic art studies he started designing hats, and in 1990 opened his first shop in Brussels. Soon clothes designers were commissioning hats from him. He now has shops in Paris, Antwerp and London. His creations, made of felt, velvet, cloth, straw or even objects he picked up in flea markets, are kitsch and colorful but chic, and advertise a strong sense of humor.

CHRISTIAN LOUBOUTIN'S SHOES
19, rue J.-J. Rousseau
75001
The extremely expensive and elegant shoes of this Parisian designer have been popular with fashionable women ever since he opened his boutique in the Galerie Vérot-Dodat. Louboutin selects from a wide variety of materials, including calfskin and eel skin, and is keen on fish-scale designs and a wide range of colors. His shoes with wooden heels decorated in gold leaf are minor masterpieces.

GEORGES GASPAR: UMBRELLAS, CANES AND PARASOLS
Georges Gaspar is the undisputed leader in the field of umbrellas: he supplies the most famous shops, boutiques, theater costume departments and department stores the world over. Gaspar came to Paris from Hungary in 1931 and started up his small company six years later. His daughter continues the tradition, making elegant and beautifully detailed objects sold in department stores such as the Bon Marché, Galeries Lafayette and Printemps.

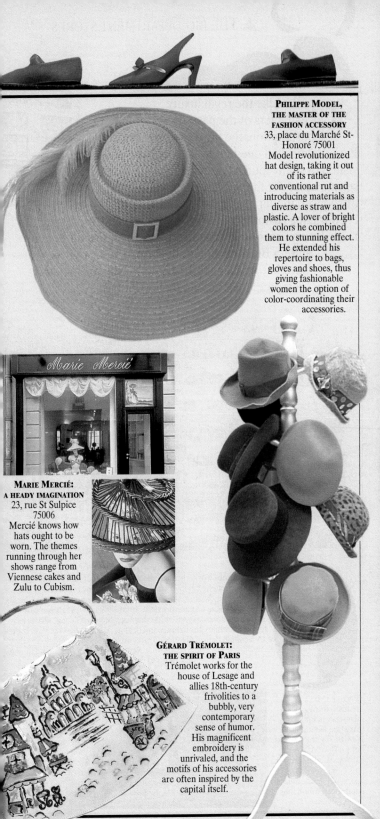

PHILIPPE MODEL, THE MASTER OF THE FASHION ACCESSORY

33, place du Marché St-Honoré 75001

Model revolutionized hat design, taking it out of its rather conventional rut and introducing materials as diverse as straw and plastic. A lover of bright colors he combined them to stunning effect. He extended his repertoire to bags, gloves and shoes, thus giving fashionable women the option of color-coordinating their accessories.

MARIE MERCIÉ: A HEADY IMAGINATION

23, rue St Sulpice 75006

Mercié knows how hats ought to be worn. The themes running through her shows range from Viennese cakes and Zulu to Cubism.

GÉRARD TRÉMOLET: THE SPIRIT OF PARIS

Trémolet works for the house of Lesage and allies 18th-century frivolities to a bubbly, very contemporary sense of humor. His magnificent embroidery is unrivaled, and the motifs of his accessories are often inspired by the capital itself.

▲ THE BIG DEPARTMENT STORES

Like the regal luxury ocean liners of the past or vast temples of consumption, the big department stores of Paris – almost all one hundred years old – are visited by many tourists each year. These stores sprang up under the Second Empire. They introduced modern sales techniques and, by encouraging customers to browse without obligation, they made luxury living accessible to all. Les Magasins du Louvre and La Belle Jardinière have gone, but surviving stores have hardly changed and now include prestigious designer labels among their offerings.

A CITY WITHIN A CITY

The luxurious world through which the customer moves gives no hint of the frenetic beehive atmosphere that reigns in the rest of the building. This cross-section (above) of Le Printemps, between Rue du Havre and Rue Caumartin, dates from 1889 and reveals some of the store's mysteries as well as its complex structure. Storage space, next to the machinery for lighting and heating, is in the basement, in order to facilitate daily deliveries. Offices are now on alternate floors; they used to be just underneath what were once the bedrooms and dining rooms used by resident staff.

PROFIT AND PHILANTHROPY
Entrepreneurs like Aristide Boucicault (1810–77), the founder of Le Bon Marché, also took an interest in his employees' personal development and social well-being.

CHRISTMAS WINDOWS
The windows of the *grands magasins* are famous the world over. The imaginatively thought-out scenes are designed to promote the sale of toys – and to cause crowds to gather on the sidewalks.

> "Apart from the murmur of the breeze, all that remained was the sense of an enormous Paris – one so enormous that it would always have enough to provide for shoppers."
>
> Émile Zola

LE BON MARCHÉ

22, rue de Sèvres 75007

This store opened on the Left Bank in 1852 and was the first of its type. It inspired Émile Zola's novel *Au bonheur des dames*.

The cupola of Le Printemps, which was built in 1923, is a fine example of Art Nouveau. It is 64 feet wide and 52½ feet high. The cupola was torn down during World War Two.

THE BEST USE OF ADVERTISING

Big department stores in Paris devote much of their advertising budgets to publicity, including brochures, shopping bags and calendars.

SYMBOLIC AND FUNCTIONAL ARCHITECTURE

These colossal cathedrals of commerce were built to inspire respect and to tempt customers to spend money. They were the work of such architects as Gustave Eiffel, who designed Le Bon Marché, and Paul Sédille, who was responsible for Le Printemps. The interiors have been redone many times and the current directors are commissioning well-known artists to give their establishments a younger look. This stairway in Le Bon Marché is the work of Andrée Putman.

127

The quick fortunes that were made during the Second Empire did muc for the prosperity of jewelers who I forsaken the Palais-Royal for the Rue de la Pa and the Place Vendôme: Mellerio (one of who creations is shown below, right) was the oldest these firms. The excesses of the Belle Époque gave the jewelers' skills a new boost, and fresh impetus was provided by the development of diamond mining in South Africa. The Place Vendôme has been the center of the jewelers' trade ever since.

TRADITION AND INNOVATION
The house of Cartier dates from 1847. This family firm was involved in the early days of baguette-cut stones and jewels set in platinum.

A BESTIARY BY CARTIER
23, place Vendôme 75001
These parrots made of diamonds are an example of the animal themes which Cartier loved. Other examples include a marvelous panther (1914) set on a bracelet watch and a pink flamingo brooch, both commissioned by the Duchess of Windsor.

MAUBOUSSIN:
A MASTER OF COLOR
20, place Vendôme 7500
The house of Maubouss was established in 1827. It is best known for its combinations of colored stones and carved moth of-pearl. This pearl colla includes a 130-carat eme

Chaumet's modern designs have the same peerless quality as these jewels designed specially for the Empress Marie-Louise.

CHAUMET, THE IMPERIAL JEWELER
12, place Vendôme 75001
A collection of diadems belonging to Nitot, founder of the house of Chaumet, is kept in the Hôtel Saint-James, which has also housed the shop since 1907. Nitot achieved prominence when Napoleon I made him responsible for the decorations for his coronation.

Frédéric Boucheron (1830–1902), the founder of a dynasty of jewelers.

BOUCHERON: A PASSION FOR PRECIOUS STONES
20, place Vendôme 75001
A gold medal at the Universal Exhibition of 1867 turned Boucheron into the favorite jewelry house of Paris' cosmopolitan high society. It has occupied premises in the Place Vendôme since 1893 and is credited with bringing rock crystal back into fashion.

THE CREATIVE GENIUS OF VAN CLEEF & ARPELS
22, place Vendôme 75001
This jeweler, which has been no. 22 since 1906, is well known for its worldwide search for precious stones and for innovations such as the *serti mystérieux*, a technique of mounting stones on a gold lattice but with no claws holding the stones in place. This method was used on the Galliéra necklace shown here.

Producers of luxury goods have promoted an image of sumptuous living that has given France, and Paris in particular, a worldwide reputation. They are the guardians of old traditions based on unique skills. These artists' talents combine creativity with exceptional technical skills requiring years of study. Their interests are served by the Colbert Committee, which was set up by the perfumer Jean-Jacques Guerlain in 1954 to promote these artists and protect them from fraudulent imitations.

LALIQUE FANTASIES
11, rue Royale 75008
The founder of the company René Lalique was a jeweler until 1911, when he turned to the design of perfume bottles, which are now collectors' items. Lalique's inimitable style – he often took his inspiration from nature – is based on a combination of transparent and glazed glass which gives his work a mysterious, almost unreal appearance. This modern statue (below) is a good example. The purity of crystal is sometimes enhanced by the use of bright colors.

CHRISTOFLE: TABLE SETTINGS
9, rue Royale, 75008
This coffee pot, which won a prize at the 1880 Concours Général des Arts en Métal, is the work of the designer Carrier-Belleuse. It shows Christofle's abiding interest in the decorative arts since the firm's foundation in 1833. He was also a notable designer of deluxe table decoration. At one time he supplied steamships: clients today include major restaurants.

HERMÈS AND THE EQUESTRIAN STYLE
24, rue du Faubourg St-Honoré 75008
This square of silk, one of Hermès' most notable products, is a reminder of the former saddlery which opened in the Faubourg St-Honoré in 1879. The Hermès style, which is both sporty and elegant, is celebrated for its high-quality leather and ingenious designs.

BACCARAT: A MASTER OF CRYSTAL WORK
30, rue de Paradis 75010
The Baccarat museum in the Rue de Paradis contains items that date from 1823: Baccarat's most important works, they are exhibited against a background of mirrors and wood. The collection also includes superb candelabra commissioned by Czar Nicholas II, paperweights, and vases (above) from the early 1900's.

LOUIS VUITTON: A PASSION FOR TRAVEL
54, avenue Montaigne 75008
This trunkmaker settled in Paris in 1854. One of his many innovations was a single key that would open every piece of a customer's luggage. Baggage marked with his initials is recognized the world over. The company today is also a patron of the arts: it funded the restoration of the Opéra's museum-library in 1989. It also publishes works written by great authors containing references to travel and slim, elegant travel guides on European cities, sold together in stylish slipcases.

THE POSSI LAMP
The style is inspired by plant motifs and by Daum's love of naturalism.

DAUM: AN ARTISTIC GLASSMAKER
32, rue de Paradis 75010
His small workshop specializing in hand-made glass was first opened in Nancy in 1874: Daum soon acquired a reputation for his exceptional skill at such techniques as *verre martelé* (its surface like hammered pewter) and the making of *pâte de verre*. The refractive index in these crystal pieces is comparable to that found in diamonds.

131

As the poet Charles Baudelaire (1821–67) wrote in *Correspondences*, "fragrances, colors and sounds correspond". Perfume bottles from the turn of the century have become collectors' items since François Coty commissioned designs from Lalique and Baccarat. Many fine artists have been employed on promotional work as perfumes have become flagships for the fashion houses which have made them so well known (an illustration by Gruau for Dior, above).

THE GUERLAIN TRADITION

The house of Guerlain has occupied these premises at 2, place Vendôme since 1828. The firm's most celebrated products are *Jicky*, *L'Heure Bleue*, *Shalimar* and *Mitsouko*.

THE LEGENDARY CHANEL No. 5

When Mlle Chanel said "luxury has its smells", she was undoubtedly thinking of this jasmine perfume which she created in 1921. *Chanel No. 5* has a timeless quality: it is the most widely sold perfume in the world.

THE FRAGRANCE OF DREAMS

Perfumes became fashionable during the 19th century, when it was customary to sprinkle them lightly on handkerchiefs and fans. During the Second Empire women wore Guerlain's *Bouquet de l'Impératrice*.

DIOR: THE CUTTING EDGE OF CHIC

Miss Dior, launched in 1947: the hound's-tooth bottle was also part of the New Look.

HERMÈS: LEATHER AND SCENTS

Bottles of *Calèche* and *Amazone* are sheathed in leather, a reminder of the horseriding that made Hermès famous.

Museums

MUSÉE D'ART MODERNE DE LA VILLE DE PARIS
11, av. du Président Wilson 75016 (1 B4)

Collections that predate the museum
The outbreak of World War Two prevented the installation of the museum's modern art collections in the Palais de Tokyo ▲ 303 – they remained in the Petit Palais. The Museum of Modern Art of the City of Paris did not open until 1961, but even before then its lasting prosperity had already been guaranteed by donors, collectors, artists and dealers (such as Ambroise Vollard). In 1937 the city of Paris acquired a number of major works, including Fernand Léger's *The Discs*.
Décor
The superb panels by Delaunay, Gleizes and Villon were made in 1938 for the Sculpture Room in the Tuileries, but presented to the Museum of Modern Art instead. They illustrate the revival that French abstract art enjoyed in the 1930's. The Matisse Room houses two huge triptychs: *The Unfinished Dance* and *The Dance in Paris*. They are two of the three versions of *The Dance*, which Dr Barnes commissioned from Matisse in 1930 for his foundation in Merion, near Philadelphia. The Dufy Room

contains *The Spirit of Electricity*, which Dufy produced for the Pavilion of Electricity at the 1937 Universal Exhibition.
Main currents of the 20th century
Fauvism was dominated by Matisse, Derain, Vlaminck, Braque and Dufy, while Cubism was mainly represented by Picasso and Braque. During the interwar period, Dadaism made an impact through the work of Picabia, as did Surrealism through Ernst and De Chirico. The Paris School brought together foreign painters and sculptors already living in Paris, including Soutine, Modigliani and Zadkine. A room in the museum is devoted to color and the works of Bonnard, Vuillard, Dufy and Matisse. In 1931 the Abstraction-Creation Group brought together the European avant-garde of nonfigurative art. The main trends in postwar art include the lyric abstraction of the 1950's, France's new realists of the 1960's and *arte povera* in Italy. The 1970's were shared by Support-Surface, BMPT groups and "daily mythologies". The objective of the museum's contemporary art department (ARC) is to bring young talent and innovative research to the public's attention.

WOMAN WITH FAN
(1919, Modigliani) This portrait of Lunia Czechowska is notable for its references to hieratic traditions and simplicity of design.

THE CARDIFF TEAM
(1912–13, Robert Delaunay) In this work the artist puts into practice his research into the action of light on moving color. Solidly constructed planes give the painting a very architectural structure.

THE DISCS
*(1918, Fernand Léger) This seminal work from the artist's
mechanical period illustrates Léger's fascination with modern life
and with the world of "implacable and beautiful machines".*

MUSÉE DES ARTS DÉCORATIFS

107, rue de Rivoli
75001 (1 J5)

Art and business working in tandem

The Union Centrale des Beaux-Arts Appliqués à l'Industrie was set up in 1864 after the Universal Exposition and later became the Union Centrale des Arts Décoratifs (UCAD). Founded to promote a revival in the creation of fine arts, it achieved this by bringing together artists and business people and enabling them to create "beauty in functional things". It opened a library and a museum with collections illustrating French domestic decoration. In 1905 the museum and the library (now housed in the pavilion in the Marsan Wing of the Louvre) benefited from new bequests, gifts and purchases of antique pieces (works by Jules Maciet, Raymond Koechlin, Émile Peyre and David David-Weill) and also began to buy contemporary works of importance.

Understanding techniques

The museum's collections, which span the Middle Ages to the present day, are exhibited by period and by theme. Some of the galleries contain objects that date from a particular period; this enables the visitor to draw comparisons between various techniques, such as carpentry, cabinetmaking, faïence decorated with high-temperature colors and low-temperature enamels, soft and hard porcelain, glassware, enamel work, bronzes, gold work, jewelry and tapestry. Certain techniques are also presented by category, including drawing, glassware, wallpaper and toys.

A style evolves

The period rooms have been restored with decoration and objects in the same style. The late-18th-century Barriol Room and Jeanne Lanvin's apartment were both created by Armand Rateau.

Other museums

In addition to the Musée des Arts Décoratifs, the UCAD manages two other museums within the Palais du Louvre: the Musée de la Mode et du Textile, established in 1982 by culture minister Jack Lang, and the Musée de la Publicité, a poster museum, which was restructured by Jean Nouvel in 1999.

A phased reopening

The Musée des Arts Décoratifs is undergoing a reorganization, and at present only the Middle Ages and Renaissance rooms are open to the public.

SLOPING DESK
(Mme de Pompadour, at Bellevue). This 18th-century piece illustrates the influence of contemporary enthusiasm for the Far East.

*Astrolabe (1567) by
G. Arsenius.*

MUSEÉ DES ARTS
ET MÉTIERS
292, rue St-Martin
75003 (2 F3)

Steeped in history
The Conservatory of
Arts and Crafts,
which was created by
the Convention in
1794, has been
described as a
collection of
machines, models,
tools, drawings,
descriptions and
books connected
with arts and crafts
of all kinds. It is
housed in the former
abbey of St-Martin-
des-Champs ▲ 382.
A unique museum
The museum has
been refurbished by
architect André
Bruno. It has a new
main entrance, and
the theme of its
collections is taken
up in the decoration,
by the artist Francois
Schuiten, of the
nearby
metro station. Over
70,000 objects are on
display, some in
fascinating
reconstructions,
such the laboratory
of the chemist
Lavoisier (1734–94)
and of the physicists
Charles and the
Abbé Nollet. All
important inventions
made since the
16th century are
exhibited here, from
Cugnot's artillery
transporter (1770) to
Clément Ader's
airplane (1897).
Whole sections are
devoted to the
history of
innovations and
technical advances.
Some of the 200
objects on display in
this part of the
museum are
brought to life
in working
demonstrations.

MUSÉE DES ARTS
ET TRADITIONS
POPULAIRES
6, avenue du
Mahatma-Gandhi
75016 (8 E2)

French ethnography
Since 1968 this
museum has been
divided into three
parts. The Gallery of
Culture contains
scenes from
traditional rural life
(reconstructions of
craft workshops,
domestic interiors,
ceramics, carved
wood, copper and
tin) as well as
exhibitions (colored
prints and costumes).
In the Scientific
Gallery objects are
carefully categorized
into various
groupings including
agricultural
implements, tools
and everyday objects,
while the Gallery of
Temporary
Exhibitions shows
new acquisitions.

MUSÉE DE
L'ASSISTANCE
PUBLIQUE
47, quai de la
Tournelle 75005
(2 E9)

A unique story
The Hôtel de
Miramion became
the Central
Pharmacy for
Hospitals in 1812,
and has housed this
museum of public
welfare since it

BLACKSMITH'S SIGN
*This wrought-iron
sign is decorated with
bouquets made of
iron showing scenes
from the artist's
apprenticeship and
his work at the forge.
At the top is the
figure of Saint Eligius,
the patron saint of
metalworkers.*

BOURDELLE IN HIS WORKSHOP WITH
"HERACLES THE ARCHER" (C. 1910)
*Once free of the influence of Rodin, Bourdelle
showed a rare talent for composition, a brilliant
use of space and a powerful
demonstration of tension.*

opened in 1934. The collections provide an account of the history of charity, public assistance and Parisian hospitals from the 12th century onward.

ABANDONED CHILDREN
Receptacles such as these (left) were installed in front of hospitals and foundlings' hospices, as places to deposit unwanted children.

Origins of the modern hospital

The museum's collections were first put together at the end of the 19th century, and additions have been made subsequently. Seven hundred years of charitable activity are recounted in illuminated manuscripts, religious paintings, portraits of great believers and men of action (such as Saint Vincent de Paul), and engravings and plans of Paris' oldest hospitals and hospices (Hôtel-Dieu, St-Louis Hospital and the Hospice des Enfants Trouvés – foundling hospital). The role played by medicine in 19th-century hospitals highlights stages in the development of the modern hospital.

MUSÉE BOURDELLE 18, rue Antoine-Bourdelle 75015 (6 G1)

An artist's studio...

The sculptor Antoine Bourdelle moved here in 1885, when the street was called Impasse du Maine. He lived here until his death in 1929. His widow and daughter later gave the land and part of his collection to the City of Paris.

... becomes a museum

The museum opened on July 4, 1949, and contains over five hundred carved works, pastels, paintings, and fresco cartoons, as well as the artist's private collection.

MUSÉE CARNAVALET
23 and 29, rue de
Sévigné, 75003 (2 G6)

**Museum of the
history of Paris**
Work was started on
the Hôtel Carnavalet
in 1548: it was
completed by the
City of Paris in 1866
to accommodate its
historical collections.
In 1989 the
revolutionary
collections of the
19th and 20th
centuries were put
on display at 29, rue
de Sévigné; the
Hôtel Le Peletier de
St-Fargeau, a
townhouse
completed around
1690.
Hôtel Carnavalet
▲ *390* This house

contains
archeological
remains and models
dating from
prehistory, the
Bronze and Iron
ages, the Gallo-
Roman town of
Lutetia, and Paris in
the Merovingian and
Carolingian eras.
The Middle Ages are
represented by
sculptures and by
stained glass from
buildings no longer
standing. Four
rooms on the first
floor recount the
history of Paris
during the
Renaissance and the
Wars of Religion.
Rooms on the
second floor trace
the life of Mme de
Sévigné, who lived in

the Hôtel
Carnavalet. The
remaining rooms
describe Paris
during the Ancien
Régime. The
decoration recalls
bourgeois and
aristocratic life in
the 17th and

18th centuries. The
museum also
contains a few
objects belonging to
Voltaire and
Rousseau.
**Hôtel Le Peletier de
St-Fargeau** ▲ *390*
The third floor
houses portraits,
objets d'art and

furniture which
recall the events that
shook Paris between
1789 and 1794. The
city in the 19th and
20th centuries is
illustrated by
portraits (*Madame*

Récamier by
Baron Gérard) and a
superb collection of
views that trace its
transformation in
the second half of
the 19th century. No
less remarkable is
the collection of

Opposite, top: Porcelain from Sèvres.
Opposite, bottom: Country picnic set in vermeil, belonging to Napoleon I. Below: "Plantation of the Tree of Freedom" by Jean-Jacques Champin, 1848.

The Musée Cernuschi will be closed for refurbishment until 2004.

terracotta caricatures by Jean-Pierre Dantan. The museum also boasts some marvelous rooms, including the shop of the jeweler Fouquet (1900) by Alphonse Mucha and the ballroom of the Hôtel de Wendel, decorated by José María Sert in 1924.

brought back from his trip to Asia. He bequeathed to the City of Paris his home and his collections of Chinese and Japanese bronzes and Chinese ceramics. The museum was opened in 1898. Since then, the building has been refurbished on several occasions. The Chinese collections from the end of the Sung

MUSÉE CERNUSCHI
7, avenue Vélasquez 75008 (9 E8)

Ancient Chinese art ...
The financier Henri Cernuschi (1826–96) commissioned the architect Bouwens to build this townhouse in 1873 on the edge of Monceau Park. It was here that Cernuschi displayed the objects he had

STONE STELE
This stele is, surmounted by entwined dragons. I t was carved during the Northern Ch'i Dynasty 550–570 and bears an inscription from the year 560.

Dynasty (13th century) have expanded significantly: they include Neolithic ceramics, ancient bronze and jade objects, and a remarkable group of funerary statuettes.
... and contemporary Chinese paintings
Thanks to a gift from Dr Kuo Yu-Shou in 1953, the museum now boasts a number of paintings, including works by Zhang Daqian (1899–1983), Fu Baoshi (1905–65) and Qi Baishi (1863–1957).

MUSÉE DE LA CHASSE ET DE LA NATURE
Hôtel Guénégaud 60, rue des Archives 75003 (2 F5) ▲ 387

A house built by Mansart
The City of Paris bought this townhouse and later handed it over to the Hunting and Nature Foundation, set up by François Sommer and his wife. They established a museum here and opened a private club for "defenders of nature".
Hunting weapons
The Museum of Hunting and Nature traces the history of

African Room, Musée de la Chasse.

firearms from matchlock harquebuses to more sophisticated weapons. The collection also includes hunting knives, swords, spears and crossbows.
Zoomorphic art
This art form reached its apogée in the 18th century with the work of Chardin, Oudry (*The Hound Bitch and Her Young*) and Desportes (portraits of Louis XIV's dogs). Important 19th-century artists in this field included Carle Vernet, Camille Corot and Alfred de Dreux.
African, Asian and American rooms
The stuffed animals are interspersed with trophies, weapons and objets d'art.

MUSÉE DE CLUNY
6, place Paul-Painlevé
75005 (2 C9)

From Gallo-Roman Antiquity to the Middle Ages
The Cluny Museum was formed in 1843 with the bringing together of Alexandre du Sommerard's collection of medieval and Renaissance objets d'art and the celebrated Gallo-Roman baths, containing a number of sculptures from Antiquity and the Middle Ages. There is now a museum specially devoted to Renaissance works at the Château d'Écouen and the Cluny Museum has established itself as the National Museum of Medieval Art and Culture.

Beautiful works of gold and enamel
Objects made of gold include 7th-century crowns from Gurrazar, Spain, and an early-11th-century altar from Basel. There are also objects of silver and copper. Some of them are enameled

LADY WITH UNICORN
To illustrate the theme of the vanity of the world (the pleasures of the five senses must yield to the asceticism of the spirit), the artist has combined the decorative and abstract spirit of a traditional mille-fleurs background with a newfound attachment to all the details of the real world.

(from workshops in Limousin) or adorned with precious stones. During the Middle Ages they constituted the treasuries of rich abbeys and princes.

Religious and profane tapestry
A 15th-century profane tapestry in six parts entitled *Lady with Unicorn* is housed in a specially built rotunda. The five senses are represented in five of the brightly colored, well-balanced pieces. The sixth, titled *My Sole Desire* (above), shows jewels placed in a chest: this symbolizes the renunciation of worldly goods.

A medieval garden, recreated by the landscape gardeners Éric Ossart and Arnaud Maurières, due to open in fall 2000, will complete the museum. The approach to the museum will be via a succession of parterres, including one with some of the flora that figure in the tapestries.

MUSÉE COGNACQ-JAY
Hôtel Donon
8, rue Elzévir
75003 (2 G6)

Businessman, philanthropist and collector
Like the English art collector and philanthropist Sir Richard Wallace, the founder of the Samaritaine

NYMPHS RESTING ON THEIR RETURN FROM THE HUNT *(1745, attributed to François Boucher). Boucher was Louis XV's favorite painter, a master of courtly and rococo works. Boucher's world was sensual and gracious, and consisted of undulating forms, light, bright colors and flesh tones that recall mother-of-pearl.*

RECLINING LEOPARD *(Kändler, 18th century). Johann Joachim Kändler was the director of the factory at Meissen, which jealously guarded the secret of making kaolin-based hard porcelain.*

MUSÉE DE LA CURIOSITÉ ET DE LA MAGIE
11, rue Saint-Paul 75004 (2 G8)

Magic has a museum all to itself in the Marais quarter. It is located

A historical scene from the Musée Grévin: Mozart at the harpsichord, aged 7.

in a maze of subterranean vaults that once served as a lodging house for travelers who arrived at night, in the era when the Marais was on the outskirts of Paris. In later years, the place was the scene of the Marquis de Sade's salacious activities. Since 1993, various curiosities have been brought together here – magic amusement

machines, colorful posters from the 19th century, automatons, fake objects – and classic tricks with evocative names – such as the Indian Trunk, the Hindu Basket, and the Devil's Mirror –

all tracing the long history of illusionism.

MUSÉE GRÉVIN
10, bd. Montmartre 75009 (2 B2)

Waxworks
In 1881 the Parisian journalist Arthur Meyer opened a waxworks with representations of prominent people of his day. He entrusted the task of designing the figures to Alfred Grévin. The museum now exhibits the most important figures in the arts, politics and sports. Various events are held in a second-floor theater (1900): the Palais des Mirages is well known for its magnificent sound-and-light shows.

CONJURING TRICKS
Evidence, in wood and metal, of the sheer ingenuity of conjurers. In the background is a reproduction of The Conjurer *by Hieronymus Bosch.*

department store, Ernest Cognacq, was a great admirer of the Age of Enlightenment. Together with his wife, Marie-Louise Jay, he collected over a thousand paintings, drawings, sculptures, pieces of furniture, tapestries and objets d'art, and bequeathed them to the City of Paris in 1928. The collection is now on display in the Hôtel Donon.
The 18th century: apex of French art
Court life is splendidly captured by Oeben's "mechanical" table and Jean-Marc Nattier's *Portrait of Marie Leczinska*. The museum paints an intimate vision of a century that had a passion for refined interiors. All four

floors contain work by various guilds: these highlight the roles played by women and children, and the developing taste for the exotic. There is also a fine collection of snuffboxes.

MUSÉE GUIMET
6, place d'Iéna
75016 (1 A4)

Asian art and religions

The National Museum of Asian Art, otherwise known as the Guimet Museum, was based on a collection which Émile Guimet

BUDDHA SHIELDED BY THE NAGA MUCILINDA *(12th century) Khmer art in the style of the Bayon Temple.*

(1836–1918) brought back from a trip to the Far East for a study of world religions. On his return to France, Guimet founded the Museum of the History of Religions in Lyons; then, in 1885, he gave his collections to the French state so that a similar museum could be established in Paris. The Guimet Museum was opened in 1889. It received sculptures from the Trocadéro Indo-Chinese museum, and in 1945 Asian works hitherto stored in the Louvre were also transferred here. The collection continued to expand with gifts, bequests and purchases, and

with objects given to the museum by French archeologists who worked in India, Afghanistan, central Asia, Indochina and the Far East. After a four-year program of renovation, the exhibits are now laid out in a logical succession of periods and geographical area. The first floor, devoted to statuary, focuses on India and areas with Indian influence (Khmer art, Javan bronzes). The second floor has two chronological displays; to the right, Chinese art of the 6th to the 8th centuries, and to the left Tibetan and Nepalese artifacts – the richest collection today – and arts of central Asia: objects from Afghanistan, Pakistan and northern India trace the Silk Road and link up with the Chinese displays. On the third floor, the Chinese theme continues in the new gallery of Chinese painting, and the arts of Japan and Korea

are newly laid out in a larger space. Crowning it all, the rotunda on the fifth floor features a display of Chinese screen paintings.

MUSÉE GUSTAVE-MOREAU
14, rue La Rochefoucauld
75009 (10 A9)

Symbolic mythology

As a young man Gustave Moreau (1826–98) was trained in the studio of the Academician François Picot.

However, he was more drawn to the Romantics and soon came under the influence of Théodore Chassériau. Later, on his trips to Italy, he discovered the genius of the ancient masters. Moreau's art was refined and sensual, and he eventually fell under the spell of medieval miniatures and enamel work. Through his allegorical and mythological subjects, he sought a spiritual vision of the world articulated by new means of expression.

THE APPARITION *After 1871, Gustave Moreau executed a series of variations on the theme of Salome and the beheading of John the Baptist.*

SHIVA NATARAJA
(Southern India, 11th-century bronze)
The god Shiva performs a cosmic dance within a circle of flames. The dance simultaneously destroys worlds and recreates and maintains them in existence.

Educational aims

The Gustave Moreau Museum is a rare example of a museum created by the artist for his work and preserved in its original state. After Moreau died in 1898, his sole heir, Henri Rupp, respected the artist's wishes regarding the displaying of his pictures. A series of pivoting panels enables visitors to see the thousands of drawings, water-colors and paintings; these cover the walls up as far as the ceiling and have served as models for subsequent generations.

MUSÉUM D'HISTOIRE NATURELLE

Jardin des Plantes
57, rue Cuvier
75005 (2 F10)

The Royal Medicinal Herb Garden opened in 1635 and was renamed the National Museum of Natural History in 1793. Its objectives – the preservation and expansion of collections, basic and applied research, and the teaching and diffusion of knowledge – have not changed since that time.

Gallery of Comparative Anatomy and Paleontology

This gallery provides a magnificent survey of the world of vertebrates. The Gallery of Paleontology, on the second floor, has a fine collection of fossils of invertebrates and extinct vertebrates, which trace the development of animal life on this planet. One room is devoted entirely to paleontology in the Paris Basin.

Grand Gallery

This glass-roofed building covers 10,700 square feet and was built at the end of the 1800's by Jules André. It contains a wide range of species and tells the story of man's role in the evolution of life. Animals selected from the collections – they were restored before being spectacularly exhibited – contribute to this graphic presentation. Another feature of the museum is the Gallery of Birds, which traces the history of ornithology.

Gallery of Paleobotany and Mineralogy

This gallery tells the story of plants since their first appearance on

Grand Gallery

Earth, using plant fossils, illustrations of the major groups in the plant world and dioramas.

The Gallery of Mineralogy contains over 600,000 items, ranging from giant crystals to meteorites.

DE L'HOMME – INSTITUT DU MONDE ARABE – DES INVALIDES

Skull of Tautavel Man (c. 450,000 BC) and Krishna (India, painted micro-syenite) below left.

MUSÉE DE L'HOMME
Palais de Chaillot
Place du Trocadéro
75016 (8 J8)

Prehistory, ethnology and anthropology
The Trocadéro Museum of Ethnography changed its name to the Museum of Mankind in 1937; for the Universal Exhibition of Arts and Technology it occupied premises in the Passy wing of the Palais de Chaillot. The aim of the Musée de

l'Homme is to bring together everything about mankind – the origins, evolution and diversity of human culture. When it opened, some of the exhibits came from the cabinets of curiosities that French kings had owned since the 16th century. It received a wide range of ethnological collections, the fruits of

archeological digs and human skeletons from the old ethnography museum. These were supplemented with items that were lent or donated by travelers and collectors, or provided by scientific missions throughout the world. The history of man and related issues are addressed using almost 35,000 skulls and several hundred full skeletons in the Laboratory of Biological Anthropology, and by more than 500,000 items in the Laboratory of Prehistory.

New additions
The displays are arranged on a geographical and thematic basis. The Gallery of the Night of Time traces the long evolution from the first primates to modern humans and describes the slow development of knowledge about our origins. The "All Parents, All Different" display underlines the enormous physical and biological diversity that marks the six billion people in the world who nonetheless all have a common and recent origin. The American Galleries take the visitor on a trip through the Americas from Alaska to Tierra del Fuego, and highlight the history of Native Americans from prehistoric times to the present day.

The Institut du Monde Arabe takes its key elements from Arab architecture.

MUSÉE DE L'INSTITUT DU MONDE ARABE
1, rue des Fossés-St-Bernard
75005 (2 F9)

Art and civilization
The Museum of the Institute of the Arab World opened in 1987. It recounts the history of Arab and Islamic art and civilization from the origins of Islam to modern times. The collections are still growing and they are flexible and adapt easily to the building. The satin-like finish of the anodized aluminum provides a sober setting for the illuminations, ceramics, textiles and inlaid metals that have come from this refined urban civilization.
Comprehensive collections
A visit to the museum starts with a presentation of the

pre-Islamic era. This is followed by a few ancient pages on the critical role of the source of all Islamic law for Muslims: the Koran. Outstanding successes in scientific and technical skills, a field in which Spain played an active role, encouraged a heightened awareness of the arts. This was especially true of ceramics, which are well represented here. From the 10th century onward, the Muslim world has been characterized by unity and variety; and a dual approach, both chronological and geographical, invites one to discover the links between forms, motifs and techniques in both time and space. The collections have been enlarged by long-term loans from Arab countries: following the first made by Syria and Tunisia, the museum was described as "the museum of all Arab museums". The Museum of the Institute of the Arab World also boasts a marvelous collection of contemporary Arab art, including paintings, sculptures, graphic art, tapestry and ceramics.

MUSÉES DES INVALIDES
Hôtel des Invalides
75007 (1 F7)

Musée de l'Armée
This museum, founded in 1905, grew out of two others: the Artillery Museum, which opened in 1797, and the Army Historical Museum, which opened in 1897. Today's museum is the largest in France devoted to the army. It traces the history of armies from medieval times to today, and the 300,000 items on display include fine examples of arms and armor, small artillery models, and historical memorabilia and uniforms from the Ancien Régime to World War Two.

Musée d'Histoire Contemporaine
This museum was founded in 1914 and transferred to the Invalides in 1973. The exhibits are of considerable political, social and cultural significance. The 1.5 million items (dating from 1870 to the present day), include paintings, posters, political cartoons and photographs, and focus on the major events in the history of France and other countries.

Musée de l'Ordre de la Libération
This museum was able to open thanks to gifts made by the Companions of the order of the Liberation, an Order created by General de Gaulle in Brazzaville in 1940. The North Gallery deals with Free France, the South Gallery covers the Resistance, and the second floor is devoted to deportation.

Musée des Plans-Reliefs
These models of fortresses were made between 1668 and 1875 and were used for

CHARLES IX'S ARMOR
(France, 1564–74, carved gilt iron)

strategic purposes. The collection was originally on display in the Grande Galerie of the Louvre.

145

HEAD OF DROPSICAL MAN
(Attributed to Hans Holbein the Elder; pen and brown-wash drawing, green tempera, highlights in white and green gouache)

MUSÉE DU LOUVRE – GRAPHIC ARTS
Palais du Louvre 75001 (1 A5)

Royal origins
The initial collection consisted of the King's Cabinet, which has been in the Louvre since it opened and was expanded through the addition of Louis XIV's purchases and by items produced by the king's favorite painters. By 1730 there were 8,593 items, and this number was increased through the acquisition of a thousand drawings sold by Pierre-Jean Mariette in 1775. The collection continued to expand with the incorporation of items seized during the Revolution,

INTERIOR
(Edgar Degas, oil on paper) This tantalizing, thought-provoking sketch recalls the backgrounds to be found in some of Degas' portraits of the 1860's.

purchases, bequests, gifts and donations. In 1989, the Louvre acquired two studies of Leonardo's *Draperies* from the collection of the Countess of Béhague.

Everything on paper
The Graphic Arts department has about 126,000 items on paper, covering a period from the 14th to the early 20th century, and exclusively representing Western art. The formats and techniques are varied, and the works are often kept in albums or notebooks. There are pastels, gouaches and large sketches in addition to more traditional drawings and watercolors. The 19th-century pastels were transferred to the Musée d'Orsay in 1986. There is also a collection of miniatures in ivory and enamel, which the museum acquired thanks to the Doisteau (1919) and David-Weill (1947) bequests. The opening of the Richelieu Wing in 1993 enabled the museum to devote a small section to the graphic art of northern Europe. The Graphic Arts department also has a collection of 16,000 copperplates originally used for royal commissions.

HEAD OF MAN WEARING A TURBAN
(Salvator Rosa, black stone, pastel, highlights in white and red chalk on beige paper) This idealized and detailed study of a head probably dates from Rosa's second stay in Rome, from 1649 to 1660.

MUSÉE DU LOUVRE – PAINTING

From royal collections to a museum

The private collections that once belonged to the kings of France now constitute the basis of the paintings hanging in the Louvre. These have been joined by works seized during the Revolution, commissions given to artists during the Restoration and the Second Empire, generous donations made by collectors at the end of the 19th and start of the 20th centuries, and purchases.

Paintings presented by school

French painting is exhibited in rooms on the third floor of the Richelieu Wing. This section also includes primitives, the Fontainebleau School, and 16th-century works, as well as paintings of the 17th, 18th and 19th century, which are on display in rooms encircling the Cour Carrée. The Salles Rouges of the Denon Wing (Daru, Denon and Mollien) house the large paintings of the neoclassical and Romantic periods. Another tour starting in the Richelieu Wing is devoted to Flemish and Dutch painting. The Louvre has a number of primitives and works by contemporaries of Van Eyck, and important works by Rembrandt,

VIRGIN AND CHILD WITH SAINT ANNE
(c. 1500, Leonardo da Vinci).
This work, which influenced many artists including the young Raphael, was brought to France by Leonardo when he was summoned there by François I. It became part of the royal collections on Leonardo's death.

Vermeer and Rubens. These include a magnificent cycle commissioned by Marie de' Medici for the glorification of royalty, which brings the tour to a close. A third sequence of rooms, 21 in all, designed by Lorenzo Piqueras and opened in 1999 in the Denon Wing, is devoted to Italian painting of the 17th and 18th centuries; the collection includes Titian's *Entombment of Christ* and Raphael's *Portrait of Balthazar Castiglione*. Paintings of the Spanish school of the 15th to 18th centuries is displayed in the rooms beyond those devoted to the Italian school. Paintings of other foreign schools and of the English school await a permanent display within the museum.

SPHINX HEAD OF KING DJEDEDFRE (c. 2570 BC, quartzite) This was found in a ditch alongside the king's pyramid near Giza. It is the head of a sphinx with the features of the king.

MUSÉE DU LOUVRE – EGYPT

The Department of Egyptian Antiquities reopened in 1997 after three years of restoration and building works. The department now exhibits more than 5,000 pieces.

The days of the archeologists

Egyptologist Jean-François Champollion was appointed director of the Charles X Museum in 1826. He acquired for the Louvre the 4,000 objects that Henry Salt, the British consul in Alexandria, had brought back from Egypt. Between 1850 and 1854, Auguste Mariette took part in archeological excavations of the sacred bulls at the Serapeum in Saqqara and sent 6,000 objects back to the Louvre. The French Institute of Oriental Archeology in Cairo, which was founded in 1880, provided many pieces from sites where it was taking part in digs.

A 4,000-year-old civilization

The first-floor rooms provide a picture of daily life through numerous objects connected with fishing, animal rearing, agriculture, hunting, writing, craft work, dwellings, dress, music and games. The Avenue of Sphinxes leads to the temple: here, the crypt opens out onto an area devoted to the dead and to funerary rites. The worship of animals is illustrated by objects from the Serapeum. The rooms on the second floor take the visitor on a historic tour which starts with the wealth that characterized the final centuries of prehistory; included are decorated vases and votive objects, such as the *Palette de la Chasse*. The first two dynasties witnessed the early days of writing and the foundation of royalty (*Stele of the Serpent-King*). The Old Empire is represented by statuary and reliefs that came from the pyramids and tombs (*Crouching Scribe*), while the Middle Empire reunited Egypt after 200 years of turbulence; this is illustrated by the statues of Senroswet III. The successes that crowned the New Empire fill five rooms (18th Dynasty, Amarna and Ramesside). The last thousand years were those of dynasties less famous and highly productive: an example is the *Triad of Osorkon*.

After Cleopatra died, Egypt fell under Roman control and, as the rooms surrounding the Visconti Courtyard show, converted to Christianity.

THE DIVINE CONSORT KAROMAMA (870–825 BC; bronze inlaid with gold, silver and electrum) Jean-François Champollion fell in love with this statuette of the Princess of Thebes, the "mystical spouse" of the god Amun.

PYX OF AL-MUGHIRA
(Cordoba, 968, ivory)
The detailed decoration has been sculpted, then carved again.

MUSÉE DU LOUVRE – THE ORIENT

Nonstop excavations
The Department of Oriental Antiquities has about 90,000 pieces which came from French digs in the Middle East carried out under Paul-Émile Botta ▲ *150*, Ernest Renan (Phoenicia, 1862) and Ernest de Sarzec (Tello, 1877), the man who rescued the Sumerians from oblivion. Marcel Dieulafoy's discovery of traces of the Persian Empire in Susa in 1884 was followed up by Jacques de Morgan (1897) and Roland de Mecquenem. In the 20th century, the Abbé de Genouillac was succeeded by André Parrot (Tello, Larsa and Mari, 1923) and Claude Schaeffer (Ugarit, 1929). Other major collections acquired by the Louvre include the finds made by Louis De Clercq in Syria at the beginning of the 20th century and given to the museum by Henri de Boisgelin in 1967.
The ancient Orient: Mesopotamia, Iran and the Levant
In the Richelieu Wing the rooms are divided according to geographical area (Mesopotamia, Iran and the Levant) and are then arranged chronologically. Treasures from Mesopotamia, Sumer, Babylon and Assur are grouped around the Khorsabad Court ▲ *150*. The Iran tour commences in the Richelieu Wing and continues in the north wing of the Cour Carrée with decorations from the palace of Darius in Susa. The Levant, from its origins to the second millennium BC, is located in rooms adjoining the west wing of the Cour Carré; near the north wing are large-scale exhibits from Palmyra, Cyprus and Phoenicia (1st millennium BC), and a collection of anthropoid sarcophagi.
The Islamic world
The royal collections contained luxurious objects for many years, but an Islamic section was set up only in 1890. The metal and ivory objects, ceramics, wainscoting, carpets, textiles, miniatures and drawings are exhibited in thirteen rooms on the mezzanine floor of Richelieu Wing. The first nine rooms are vaulted and have been specially adapted to house objects from the ancient and medieval periods. The remaining rooms are more modern in design and are situated under the Khorsabad Court. There are more than a thousand objects, from an area extending from Spain to India, omitting North Africa ▲ *158*.

MUSÉE DU LOUVRE – TRIBAL ART
The future museum of tribal art
Among 116 artifacts from Africa, Asia, Oceania, and the Americas, displayed by Jean-Michel Wilmotte, are some key pieces from the former Barbier-Muller collection.

BAPTISMAL FONT OF SAINT LOUIS
(13th–14th century, Syria or Egypt)
This large receptacle is an outstanding example of Mameluke art and bears the signature of Muhammad ibn Zayn. It forms part of the French royal collections and in the 18th century became known (incorrectly) as the Baptismal font of Saint Louis, a misnomer which has survived. The decoration consists of large inlaid pieces of silver gilt.

IBEX GOBLET
(Iran, 4th millennium, terracotta)
Painted vases from the tombs at Susa are notable for their highly skilled use of very stylized but figurative forms.

HEAD OF GUDEA
(Tello, c. 2130 BC, diorite)
The prince is wearing royal headgear consisting of a hat made of woolly curls. His face is unusually broad.

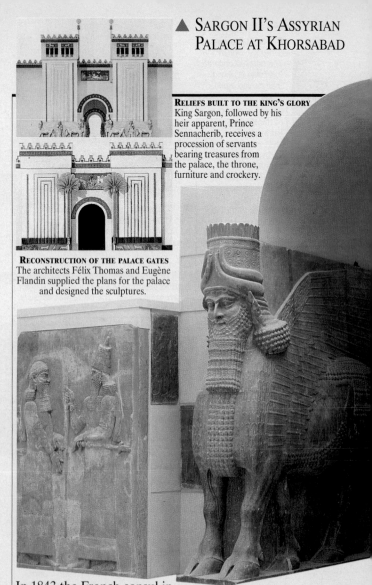

RELIEFS BUILT TO THE KING'S GLORY
King Sargon, followed by his heir apparent, Prince Sennacherib, receives a procession of servants bearing treasures from the palace, the throne, furniture and crockery.

RECONSTRUCTION OF THE PALACE GATES
The architects Félix Thomas and Eugène Flandin supplied the plans for the palace and designed the sculptures.

In 1843 the French consul in Mosul, Paul-Émile Botta, made important Assyrian finds in the course of his research on the Khorsabad site. His copies of cuneiform writings led to the deciphering of ancient Mesopotamian writing, and the large reliefs which he sent back to the Louvre were put on display in the world's first Assyrian museum (1847). This museum, which became the Napoleon III Museum in 1857, existed until 1991. The opening of the Richelieu Wing in 1993 made it possible to reorganize the Assyrian collections and to refurbish the Khorsabad Court, which strongly evokes the monumental entrance to Sargon II's palace.

Androcephalous bulls standing between the Cour Carrée and the Richelieu Wing.

MONUMENTAL STONE DECORATION
The carved frieze which protected the base of brickwork walls is interrupted by doors bored into the wall. They are framed by mythological figures 14½ to 16 feet high, including winged bulls with men's heads.

THE EXCAVATIONS
The photographer Gabriel Tranchand was a friend of the Assyriologist Victor Place and successor to Botta. In 1853–4 he took photographs at the Khorsabad site showing the stages of the excavations.

ENTRANCE TO THE THRONE ROOM
Its monumental decoration, on the east wall of the courtyard, is evoked by a bull turning its head (the original is in Chicago); it is next to the hero, who is strangling a lion (pseudo-Gilgamesh), whose strength is a measurement of the king's power.

MUSÉE DU LOUVRE – GREEK, ETRUSCAN AND ROMAN ANTIQUITIES

A museum of antiquities

This museum was founded in 1792 and officially opened in 1800. At the time, it mainly housed sculptures from royal collections, but it was rapidly enlarged through the addition of goods seized from émigrés and numerous important works brought back by victorious French armies. More conventional acquisitions included the

sculptures was increased by the addition of the Parthenon Metope (1818) and part of the Albani collection. The *Venus de Milo*, a gift from the Marquis of Rivière to Louis XVIII, came to the Louvre in 1821; shortly afterward, the Greek state presented the marbles from Zeus' temple in Olympia.

Three civilizations

With the acquisition of the Tochon collection in 1818 and the arrival of the Durand collection in 1825, the Louvre at last had a strong display of Greek and Etruscan

vases, and almost 2,000 bronzes. The *Winged Victory at Samothrace* was acquired under the Second Empire, together with the huge collection of the Marquès de Campana. This, at that time the most important collection in the world, consisted of around 12,000 objects, including hundreds of marbles, over 1,500 terracotta pieces, and 3,500 vases. The late 19th century saw the arrival of smaller

objects, such as statuettes from Tanagra and Myrina, larger statues from Ancient Greece, and a superb treasury of Roman silverware discovered in a villa at Boscoreale, near Pompeii. More recently, the Louvre acquired new collections, including finds from Elaious in Thrace, a marvelous series of mosaics excavated at Antioch, and bronzes and jewelry from the De Clercq-Boisgelin donation.

TOMB OF PHILIPPE POT
(15th century) This monumental tomb, an outstanding piece of medieval funerary art was found at Cîteaux.

KORE OF SAMOS
(Sámos, 570 BC, marble)
This representation of Persephone is typical of early Greek sculpture and is dedicated by Chéramýes to the goddess Hera.

prestigious Borghese collection in 1808. After 1815, the number of

MUSÉE DU LOUVRE – SCULPTURE

French sculpture
Since 1993, French sculpture has been displayed on the first floor of the Richelieu Wing, occupying some 30 rooms encircling the two main courtyards: one is devoted to statues, groups and vases from Marly (Cour Marly); the other contains outdoor sculptures from the 17th, 18th and 19th centuries (Cour Puget). The chronological tour takes the visitor from the oldest pre-Roman and Roman sculptures to neoclassicism and Romanticism, and

includes major works, ranging from Jean Goujon's *Nymphs* to Pierre Puget's *Milo of Croton* to Pigalle's *Mercury*.

Foreign sculpture
Italian sculpture from the late Middle Ages and early Renaissance is particularly well represented. Northern Europe, particularly Germany, boasts a treasury of late-medieval wooden sculptures with polychrome decoration. Spanish sculpture, which is often felt by the French to be characterized by excessive realism, is poorly represented.

The rooms in the Denon Wing which were given over to sculpture in 1994 are very different. A respect for spaces and interior decoration, and the need for disparate works to be displayed together, meant that Napoleon III's former stables have been used for the presentation of pre-16th-century Italian and northern European pieces. The stables' brick and stone vaults have been refurbished, and the windows give onto the Cour Lefuel. The Mollien Gallery (Michelangelo Gallery) on the floor above contains an outstanding collection of Italian sculptures from Michelangelo to Canova, including the *Gate of Cremona*. One of the aims of this new layout is to highlight the department's three most famous sculptures: Michelangelo's two *Slaves* and Canova's *Psyche Revived by the Kiss of Eros*.

COUR MARLY
The huge glass roof ▲ 327 allows large quantities of natural light to enter this courtyard. The architect Michel Macary has made use of the symmetry of the two groups carved by Coustou and Coysevox.

LOUISE BRONGNIART
(1777, Jean-Antoine Houdon, terracotta) This artist executed a large number of children's portraits notable for their supple contours and lively expressions. Houdon earned a great deal of money producing busts of famous people, including Diderot, Benjamin Franklin, George Washington, the Comte de Buffon and Jean-Jacques Rousseau.

The Grand Salon in Napoleon III's apartments ▲ 325.

tables adorned with gold and porcelain from the royal factory at Sèvres.

MUSÉE DU LOUVRE – OBJETS D'ART

Royal objets d'art
The department has inherited a number of royal collections, including bronzes and precious stones belonging to Louis XIV and the Crown Jewels, as well as part of the treasure from the

CHARLES IX'S SHIELD
(embossed gold-plated iron and enamel)
This ceremonial shield was made by Pierre Redon in Paris in 1572. It is symbolic of the luxurious life style and refinement enjoyed by the court of the Valois in its declining years.

SUGER'S EAGLE
(Rome, Imperial era, porphyry, St-Denis before 1147, mounting in nielloed silver gilt). Suger, the Abbot of St-Denis Abbey and a counselor to Louis VI and Louis VII, turned this into a liturgical vase by placing it on a mounting in the form of an eagle's head.

St-Denis Abbey: this included the regalia used in the coronations of French kings and vases collected by the French monk Suger in the 12th century. The decoration of paintings and gilt stucco in the Apollo Gallery was undertaken by Charles Lebrun in 1661; it was completed by Eugène Delacroix around 1850 with his *Triumph of Apollo*, which is in the center of the ceiling. There are also precious stones and some valuable snuffboxes.

Medieval and Renaissance collections
Chronological and geographical considerations have led to

these collections being located on the second floor of the Richelieu Wing. The most remarkable works are pieces made by goldsmiths (final years of the Valois), glassmakers, enamelers (workshops in Limousin), artists working in ivory and bronze, and tapestry makers.

17th and 18th centuries
This period is represented to the north of the Cour Carrée by a large collection of furniture, tapestries and objects whose diversity and quality reflect the huge advances made by French civilization at that time. An example of this refinement can be seen in

The first half of the 19th century
These collections have now been divided up: to the north of the Cour Marly are the most beautiful Empire pieces, particularly the furnishings of Mme Récamier's drawing room and bedchamber (1798). To the east of the Cour Carrée are decorative arts of the Restoration and the July Monarchy, together with innovations shown at the Expositions of Industrial Products. The chronological tour ends in the rooms that were decorated during the reign of Napoleon III and which served as reception rooms for the minister of finances from 1871 until 1989.

Portuguese sea compass, 1744.

LA DAUPHINE *(29-oar galley, 1736–92). Contemporary model (scale 1:24).*

ships of the royal fleets is told in the Navy Museum's Grand Gallery. The story starts with the *Couronne* (1637), the first large vessel built in France, and includes the magnificent series of *Ports of France* painted by Joseph Vernet (1754–65). It concludes with models of the most up-to-date commercial craft and submarines to be launched in France's shipyards.

MUSÉE DE LA MARINE
Palais de Chaillot
Place du Trocadéro
75016 (8 J8)

A long tradition
In 1748 the inspector general of the navy, Louis-Henri Duhamel du Monceau, brought together a remarkable collection of model ships and naval machines. The objective was to give instruction to apprentice shipbuilders for whom a school had just been started in Paris. When Charles X opened a public museum in 1827, the Dauphin Museum's collections were enlarged by the addition of paintings from Versailles and the Louvre, ornaments from ships in the navy's various dockyards and artillery pieces.
A reminder of France's great maritime past
The entire history of the construction and strategic use of the

MUSÉE MARMOTTAN
2, rue Louis-Boilly
75016 (8 E9)

Where Impressionism is worshipped
The Marmottan Museum was originally a hunting lodge and then a private townhouse. It was converted by Paul Marmottan into a Napoleonic museum with an unusual collection of furniture, bronzes, sculptures and paintings. It now houses most of the Impressionists including Sisley, Pissarro, Renoir, Caillebotte, Guillaumin and Jongkind. It has over a hundred paintings by Monet.
The Wildenstein donation
Daniel Wildenstein presented the museum with his father's marvelous collection of illuminations in 1980. This comprised 300 miniatures from antiphonaries, missals and books of hours from various European countries.

DÉSIRÉE CLARY *(Baron Gérard, 1770–1837) Désirée Clary, Joseph Bonaparte's sister-in-law, married Marshal Bernadotte, who became King of Sweden in 1818.*

A gold franc minted during the reign of Jean le Bon (1360)

MUSÉE DE LA MONNAIE

11, quai de Conti
75006 (2 B7)

The Museum of the Paris Mint is situated in the old room once used for striking coins. Its collections of 2,000 coins, 450 medals, tokens, sculptures, machines and tools, official documents, paintings, engravings and stained-glass windows are now housed in a more modern setting. The museum is unable to put its entire collection on display and has therefore opted to concentrate on key moments in French history from antiquity to the present day. This is achieved through coins and medals which commemorate acts of daily life as well as great historical events. The architecture of the former coin-press room suggests a basilica. It also underlines the educational nature of the museum's presentation: this includes glass casings which enable visitors to see both sides of the coins and medals.

MUSÉE NATIONAL D'ART MODERNE

Centre Pompidou
6, rue Beaubourg
75004 (2 E5)

A new look
The new MNAM, redesigned by the architect Jean-François Bodin, now contains 1,400 works of art laid out in displays arranged by Werner Spies. The approach is multidisciplinary and chronological. Design, photography and architecture complement the great scope of modern and contemporary art that make this museum the most important of its kind in the world. The purpose of the new displays, reinforcing the constantly innovative character of this museum "that never sleeps", was to put on public view a significant number of the 44,000 works in the collection that together represent the artists and major movements of the modern era. The spacious, airy layout also offers striking views over the rooftops of Paris and enhances the visitor's experience. Access (to level 4) is by escalators on the outside of the building.

Contemporary art (from 1960)
The displays are changed every year (or every six months in the case of the most modern exhibits). They illustrate the major movements in art since the 1960s (Pop Art, New Realism, Conceptual Art, Fluxus, Arte Povera, and others), with displays devoted exclusively to single artists, among them Joseph Beuys, Dan Graham and Yaacov Agam (room 10), an exponent of kinetic art. A major part of the museum is devoted to art from the 1990s to the present day. Three large areas concentrate on design and architecture: the 1960s (room 11), the 1970s and 1980s (room 16), dominated by Italian design, and the 1990s (rooms 32 and 33), where all is lightness and transparency.

Modern art (1905 to 1960)
The dispays are changed every eighteen months. Access (to level 5) is through the museum. There are some unusual juxtapositions; paintings by Georges Braque and Picasso can be seen alongside African

LOUIS XIV AS A CHILD WITH JEAN VARIN
(1654, attributed to François Lemaire)
The engraver Jean Varin initiated the young Louis XIV in the art of old coins.

THE SHEPHERD OF THE CLOUDS
(1953, Jean Arp)
Arp followed his early figurative, Cubist work with abstract creations in which he explored the element of chance.

NUDE WITH ORANGES
(1953, Matisse, India ink, gouache, cut and pasted paper) The museum has almost 150 works of Henri Matisse. It has been seeking to establish the artist's linear development by acquiring a series of key paintings, including "Greta Prozor" (1916), "French Window at Collioure" (1914) and the original sketches for "Jazz" (1943–6). This policy has now been implemented following a donation which the artist's son Pierre made to the museum on his death.

> "The first characteristic of modern art is not to tell a story."
> André Malraux

sculpture, throwing light on the ambiguous nature of Cubism, which draws on scientific progress while also looking to the beauty of nature. Surrealism (rooms 19 to 26) is given prominence; here are works by Luis Buñuel, Alberto Giacometti, René Magritte, Salvador Dali, Max Ernst and Picasso. Abstract art, De Stijl and the Bauhaus complete this survey of modern art; architecture and decorative arts (with echoes of Paul Klee and Kandinsky) can be seen in rooms 14 Finally, three terraces on which large-scale scupture is displayed add a further dimension to the collections.

NEW YORK CITY I
(1942, Mondrian; oil on canvas)
"New York City I" was painted during Mondrian's stay in that city. It makes a clean break with the black structure of his Parisian period and substitutes a range of primary colors which alone organize the rhythm and space of his paintings. This is one of the major pieces in a collection which also includes abstract works by Theo van Doesburg, Arp, Pevsner, Malevitch and Moholy-Nagy.

MUSÉE NATIONAL DES ARTS D'AFRIQUE ET D'OCÉANIE

293, avenue
Daumesnil 75012
(4 H4)

A 1930's setting

This building was
constructed from
plans by Jaussely
and Laprade for the
Colonial Exhibition
of 1931. It has
retained some of the
1930's decoration,
including a bas-
relief by Janniot on
the façade, frescos
by Ducos de La
Haille and interior
furnishings by
Ruhlmann and
Printz. The
museum was the
only building of
any size to survive
the Colonial
Exhibition,
and from
1935

onward, it housed
the Musée des
Colonies (Colonial
Museum). The
building was taken
over by the Ministry
of Cultural Affairs
in 1960, and André
Malraux turned it
into the National
Museum of African
and Oceanic Arts.

The Musée
National des Arts
d'Afrique et
d'Océanie is
closed. It will
reopen in 2005.

Museum move

The collections will
be transferred to the
new museum on the
Quai Branly which
will also include
the ethnographic
collections of the
Musée de l'Homme
▲ 144. The
collections of the
two museums will
be combined,
preserved and
enriched. The new
museum, measuring
419,800 square feet
and designed by
the architect Jean
Nouvel, will open in
2005 on a site near
the Eiffel Tower.

Aquarium

Located in the
building's basement,
the aquarium
remains open to
the public. The fish
are exhibited by
theme: evolution,
region (Africa,
Americas, Asia),
taxonomy and
physiological
characteristics (such
as reproduction and
locomotion). There
are in total some
79,260 gallons of
water including
13,210 gallons of
sea water, in
surroundings which
have retained the
Art Deco feel.
The ground-floor
furnished salons of
Paul Reynaud and
Field Marshal
Lyautey are also still
open to the public,
as is the great hall.

STATUE OF THE GOD RAO
*This wood statue
from Mangareva
Island, in the Gambier
Archipelago survived
the missionaries of
the 19th century. It is
remarkable for its thin
body and smooth
face, and the position
of the arms. It was
brought to Europe in
1836 by Fathers of
the Picputian Society.*

BIRD MASK
*This mask of wood and brass was made by
the Yaouré of the Ivory Coast. Carvings from
the borderlands of Liberia, Upper Guinea and
the Ivory Coast are usually masks of human
faces. They comprise a variety of images, in
a range of materials and decorations and are
remarkable for their fine, simple lines.*

"Rabâb" lute, created by an unknown lutemaker in Afghanistan

MUSÉE DE LA MUSIQUE

Cité de la Musique, 221, avenue Jean-Jaurès 75019 (11 D5)

Origins

The original Music Museum was founded in 1864 under the control of the Paris Music Conservatory, after their purchase of 300 instruments from the composer Louis Clapisson. Other prestigious acquisitions followed: in 1887, a Java gamelan thought to be one of the oldest in existence; in 1934, the rare instrument collection of Paul Cesbron; and in 1980, the Chambure collection, from the museum's director between 1961 and 1973.

A new museum

The idea of a new museum was born in the 1960's, and in 1979 the decision was taken to site it at La Villette, where plans already existed for the creation of a Cité de la Musique. Designed by Christian de Portzamparc, the Cité today houses two concert halls, information centres and a bookstore, as well as the new Musée de la Musique, which opened in 1997.

A unique collection

The museum displays in the region of 900 instruments from a total national collection of more than 4,500, grouped into nine major points in the history of music and the manufacture of instruments between the end of the 17th century and the present day. Each of the nine spaces is centred around one musical work, played by an ensemble and illustrated by a model of the setting in which it was composed. Thus the visitor moves from a room in the Mantoue Palace, where Monteverdi's *Orfeo* was created, to the Champs-Élysées theatre where the premiere of Igor Stravinsky's *The Rite of Spring* created a furore.

Early 17th-century Venetian arched lute.

MUSÉE NISSIM DE CAMONDO

63, rue de Monceau 75008 (9 F8)

The Hôtel de Camondo

Between 1911 and 1914, Moïse de Camondo, a wealthy banking heir with a strong enthusiasm for the decorative arts of the 18th century, chose a site at the edge of Monceau Park to build a mansion to house his large collection of objets d'art, consisting of furniture, paintings, carpets, tapestries, porcelain and gold plate. Following the death of his only son, Nissim de Camondo, in World War One, the count bequeathed the house and its collection to the Union Centrale des Arts Décoratifs (UCAD). The museum opened to the public in 1936.

Exceptional objets d'art

The collection created by Moïse de Camondo is devoted almost exclusively to the decorative arts of the second half of the 18th century. A few works represent the earlier Louis XIV period. One such is the carpet in the Grand Salon, which was commissioned from the house of Savonnerie for the Grande Galerie in the Louvre. From the neoclassical period, the collection shows the assembled works of the cabinet-makers to the king and court. These include curtained, balustrated pieces

The Blue Room at the Musée Nissim de Camondo

of furniture and a hollowed chiffonier table, both created by Jean-Henri Riesener, and a folding desk by Jean-François Leleu. A pair of vases covered in petrified wood, from the collection of Marie Antoinette, illustrates the refined nature of her Versailles apartments, of which Moïse de Camondo was so fond. Tableware holds a special place in this collection. Among the most spectacular of all the pieces are the large Sèvres porcelain dinner service decorated with a bird motif and known as the "Buffon", and the Orloff silverware commissioned by Catherine the Great.

M'O

M for Musée, <u>O</u> for Orsay: an attractive logo for one of the most successful gambles that the worlds of architecture and museums have ever known. The Gare d'Orsay was scheduled to be torn down in 1970 but survived by the skin of its teeth and became a landmarked building in 1978. The vast dimensions of this early 20th-century building have helped the new project and are ideally suited for a museum. The main hall is now bordered by a series of terraces and stepped landings, where the exhibits are housed. The whole building benefits from an abundance of natural light.

FROM PALACE TO RAILWAY STATION

In the middle of the 19th century, two buildings occupied the site of what is now the Musée d'Orsay: the barracks of a cavalry regiment and the offices of the Revenue Court and the Council of State. The fires of the Paris Commune (1870–1) left them in ruins. The Orléans Railway Company bought the land in 1897 with a view to constructing the Gare d'Orsay for trains serving Nantes, Bordeaux and Toulouse. The building was scheduled to be ready for the Universal Exhibition of 1900, and construction was completed in only two years.

QUAI D'ORSAY

The quai d'Orsay was built by Charles Boucher d'Orsay, Provost of the Merchants of Paris in 1708. It was used for storing wood until 1810.

STEEL ARCHES AND PLASTER CAISSONS
The ceiling illustrates the close working relationship between the construction workers and the architects. It is characterized by a highly skilled system of roof timbers with no tie beams and monumental ornamentation consisting of large caissons of molded plaster bound with vegetable fibers.

Vue de face

Bouche de soufflage

Orifice résonateur

Laine minérale

Résonateur (4 par caisson)

ONE OF MANY PLANS
When it was decided to put the station to a new use in 1935, Raymond Lopez proposed transforming the building into an enormous sports complex containing a sailing basin that could be covered over by a removable floor and used for other activities. The outside walls were to be completely reworked in a strikingly modern style.

THE BIRTH OF MODERN PAINTING
(*Le Déjeuner sur l'herbe*, Manet, 1863)
This painting's theme suggested new ways of treating space and volumes, heralding the birth of 20th-century art.

SCULPTURE AND REALISM
(*The Dance*, Carpeaux, 1869)
This contrasts with the carved groups decorating the Paris Opéra.

The collections in the Musée d'Orsay specialize in art of the late 19th and early 20th centuries. The museum seeks to capture the full diversity of this unusually dense and prolific period by focusing not only on painting, sculpture, and decorative and graphic arts but also on other visual arts such as architecture, town planning, movies, posters, the press and illustrated books. The abundant exhibits are displayed on three main floors, and a tour of the museum is chronological.

SCULPTURE AND CARICATURE (*Ratapoil*, Honoré Daumier, c. 1850, bronze) Daumier was a sculptor and painter, but above all he was a caricaturist who took delight in poking fun at the politics and customs of his time.

PHOTOGRAPHY AT THE MUSÉE D'ORSAY: 1839–1918 *Portrait of Charles Baudelaire* by Nadar.

THE PRE-EMINENCE OF COLOR (*Arearea*, Gauguin, 1892) Simplified forms, spaces lacking depth of field and flat colors were later taken up by the Pont-Aven School and then by the Nabis.

THE ARCHITECTS
The wide-ranging renovation was carried out by two architectural teams: ACT (Renaud Bardon, Pierre Colboc and Jean-Paul Philippon) and a team led by Gae Aulenti.

IMAGINATION: A MORE POTENT FORCE THAN CAUTION
It was highly appropriate that a place where journeys had once started should be turned into a haven of preservation and contemplation. In order to respect the structure of the original building, Laloux's cast-iron pillars and beams, together with his stucco decoration, were preserved, restored and then removed. The stone elements and steel geometry of the new structures exude colossal strength, and provide a contrast with the ornate style of the original interior.

THE ENTRANCE
The façade that overlooks Rue de Bellechasse is more peaceful than the windy quay that faces north and was therefore chosen for the main entrance.

A WARM WELCOME
The canopy, the old entrance hall and the café provide visitors with a warm welcome.

The quality materials used in the refurbishment work include an ocher-colored hard limestone from Buxy for the floors and certain moldings.

EARLY CUBISM
(*The Bridge at Maincy*, Cézanne, c. 1879) Cézanne broke with Impressionism at an early stage, opting for vigorous representation and classical composition; he also brought naturalism to simple geometric forms. His brush strokes, which were almost rectangular and very regular, became increasingly independent of what he was painting and varied only according to the direction in which it was inclined.

POINTILLISM
(*Woman with Umbrella*, Signac, 1893)
The two theoretical principles of pointillism were the division of tone and the simultaneous contrast of colors.

Vase with festooned neck (Gallé, 1880–84)

BETWEEN EXPRESSIONISM AND SYMBOLISM
(*Mature Age*, Claudel, 1894–1903, bronze)

NABIS

SCULPTURE (PRE-1870)

THEATER

THE NABIS: PROPHETS OF A NEW ART FORM
(*The Box*, Bonnard, 1908) Pierre Bonnard's fellow students at the Académie Julian and the École des Beaux-Arts included Vuillard and Maurice Denis; they all drew inspiration from Gauguin. They were no less influenced by Japanese prints, and here Bonnard combines the flat colors, the simplification, and the almost nonexistent depth of field of Japanese prints with a freedom of composition and a most unusual composition.

MUSÉE DE L'ORANGERIE
Place de la Concorde, Terrasse des Tuileries 75001 (1 H4)

> The Orangerie Museum will be closed for refurbishment until 2004.

permanent exhibition, much of the interior of the building was refurbished. Since then, the museum has been dedicated to the presentation of just two collections, the *Waterlilies* and the Walter–Guillaume Collection: they are and, through him, of Impressionism itself. It also represents several important threads in 20th-century art, extending from Kandinsky to Pollock, to which Monet contributed both chronologically and stylistically. The eight large personalities and tastes of its two creators. One of these was the man who bought the paintings, Paul Guillaume, a champion of modern art in Paris between 1914 and 1934. The other was the second wife of the architect Jean

"WATERLILIES" *(Claude Monet, room 2)*
This floating, seemingly limitless space is engulfed by an effusion of color and the artist's fluid, animated style. In this painting, in which the Impressionist revolution reaches its apogee, the viewer is invited to plunge headlong into a contemplative reverie, far removed from any neat description, nourished by an intense feeling for nature.

From gallery to museum
The Orangerie Museum in the Tuileries was built in a former Second Empire orangery on the south terrace of the Tuileries. It has housed Monet's *Waterlilies* since 1927, and between 1929 and 1978 it also contained a prestigious contemporary gallery. When the Jean Walter–Paul Guillaume Collection was presented to the state on condition that it remain on

very different but nonetheless share subtle affinities. It is hoped that restoration work (particularly on the presentation of the *Waterlilies*) will further enhance these collections, and that an extension will encourage a renewed interest in temporary exhibitions.

The "Waterlilies"
This remarkable work, which takes up the two *Waterlilies* Rooms, was the culmination of Monet's own work

compositions were inspired by the pond in the famous garden which he created on his land at Giverny. They cover the walls of two elliptical rooms: the layout projects a single, continuous sweep of painting incorporating the constant renewal of plant life and an unending flow of light, water and time.

The Jean Walter–Paul Guillaume Collection
This collection reflects the

"OX AND CALF'S HEAD" *(Chaim Soutine, 1925). Soutine examined his subjects in series of variations: they illustrate at once his weakness for perfection and his profoundly unhappy life.*

Walter, Juliette (also known as Domenica), who made small alterations to the collection and bought the major works of Cézanne. Altogether there are

"COURBET WITH BLACK DOG" *(Gustave Courbet, 1842). The contrast between the dark silhouettes of the painter and black dog and the whites and ochers of the rock provides a fine illustration of Courbet's sense of composition and command of color.*

144 paintings, dating from the 1870's to the 1930's, grouped by artist with various rooms devoted to artists the couple was particularly fond of: Cézanne, Renoir, Rousseau, Soutine, Modigliani, Matisse, Derain and Picasso. A "return to the classical

order", a movement that gained support after World War One, resulted in three major works: Matisse's *Three Sisters*, Picasso's *Grande Baigneuse* and Derain's *Harlequin and Pierrot*.

MUSÉE DU PETIT PALAIS
Avenue Winston-Churchill 75008 (1 F4)

> The Musée du Petit Palais will be closed for refurbishment until Jan. 2005.

A treasury of ancient art
The building was constructed by Charles Girault

▲ *312* for the Universal Exhibition of 1900: it houses a collection of ancient art based on two major donations. The first was a unique collection bequeathed by the brothers Eugène and Auguste Dutuit in 1902. This consisted of works of art of classical antiquity and medieval objects (not currently on show), priceless pieces from the French and Italian Renaissance (in particular terracotta objects from St-Porchaire), majolica figures, enamels from Limousin, glass objects, timepieces and the celebrated room of Flemish and Dutch paintings. In 1930 the Tuck Collection was added, largely made up of paintings, sculptures, tapestries and 18th-century objets d'art, and also including porcelain from China, Sèvres and

Meissen, English snuffboxes and some fine Louis XV and Louis XVI furniture.

An overview of 19th-century art
This feature of the collections is the result of judicious commissions and purchases made by the City of Paris in the 20th century. One of the highlights was the acquisition of Jules Dalou's workshop; other major donations have included works by Courbet, Carpeaux, Carriès and Cézanne. This section boasts neoclassical paintings and sculpture, examples of

troubadour art, and paintings from the Romantic, Realist, Impressionist, post-Impressionist, Symbolist and Nabis schools. It also contains a large number of naturalist and allegorical sculptures and a collection of splendid objets d'art dating from the 1900's including ceramic stoneware pieces by Jean Carriès, glassware by Gallé and jewelry by Fouquet. In 1998 4,500 drawings by Charles Jacqueau, Louis Cartier's most important assistant, were presented to the museum.

MODEL OF A MONUMENT FOR THE PLACE DE LA RÉPUBLIQUE
(Jules Dalou, 1879). This monument, eventually made in bronze, was commissioned by the City of Paris for the Place de la Nation; it was unveiled in 1899.

"PORTRAIT OF JACQUELINE WITH CROSSED HANDS"
(Vallauris, 1954) Jacqueline Roque was Picasso's haunting, ever-present model for almost twenty years: he married her in 1961. Here, he represents her as hieratic and compact, a true modern sphinx.

MUSÉE PICASSO
Hôtel Salé, 5, rue de Thorigny 75003 (2 G6)

The Picasso collection
Picasso liked to describe himself as "the world's leading collector of Picassos"; indeed, in his workshops and homes he kept a considerable proportion of his 80 years of artistic output. When he died in 1973 his heavy death duties were paid through the donation of some of his works. The selection, made in 1979, eventually formed the basis of a museum unique in the world for the number and range of his works. They included 203 paintings, 158 sculptures, 29 paintings in relief, 88 ceramic pieces, 15 *papiers collés*, almost 1,500 drawings, some 30 sketchbooks and over 1,600 prints.

They cover all periods of Picasso's working life. The collection of sculptures includes virtually all of his small Cubist constructions, the unique series of sand-coated reliefs from the summer of 1930, and the large carvings of heads that he did at Le Boisgeloup in the early 1930's. The sketchbooks, which include preparatory drawings for the *Demoiselles*

d'Avignon, throw light both on the creative direction that Picasso was taking and on the genesis of some of his works. A second donation was added after his wife Jacqueline died in 1986. This complemented the collection which was lacking certain items (for example, *Portrait of Jacqueline with Crossed Hands*) and contributed another 24 magnificent sketchbooks, 2 sculptures, about 40 drawings and a number of prints and ceramics. In addition to these works by Picasso himself were items from his private collection, including

works by Cézanne, Matisse, Rousseau, Derain, Braque and Miró and some pieces of primitive art.

The paintings find a home
An hôtel in the

"WOMAN'S HEAD"
(Le Boisgeloup, plaster original, 1931).

"STILL LIFE WITH CANE CHAIR"
(1912). This was the first time that Picasso used a real object (the oilcloth imitating the cane seating of a chair) in one of his paintings.

Marais, which had been empty, was chosen in 1976 to house the works that made up the first donation. Built

> **"In my view, modern sculpture needs to exaggerate forms from a moral point of view."**
>
> Rodis

between 1656 and 1659 for Pierre Aubert de Fontenoy, who had made a fortune collecting salt taxes, the house had been unusually expensive to build and came to be known as the Hôtel Salé ▲ 389 (salé, or "salty", means exorbitant prices). The most elaborate part of the original interior décor was a monumental

THE CATHEDRAL (stone, 1931). The two representations of the same hand face one another in such a way as to suggest a ribbed vault symbolizing the work's original title, the "Arche d'Alliance".

1729 and 1730, and was acquired by the state in 1911. Rodin handed his works over to the Hôtel de Biron in 1916; the drawings and sculptures, his private collection, the archives and the old photographs and works from the Villa des Brillants at Meudon formed the basis of the museum's collection when it opened in 1919.

movements: Romanticism, with its accent on pathos; Art Nouveau, with its fluidity and meandering curves; and Naturalism, with its concern for anatomical accuracy. Rodin's freedom of style can be seen in all the materials he used: the museum contains sculptures in marble, bronze and terracotta. There are works from his youth; representations of couples, groups, torsos and portraits; works by Camille Claudel, and studies of important monuments. There is also a selection of seven thousand drawings, and paintings by Carrières, Monet, Van Gogh (*Père Tanguy*) and Zuolaga from Rodin's private collection. The 8-acre garden, whose south-facing parterre has recently

staircase adorned with an abundance of carved wood made by the Marsy brothers and Martin Desjardins. The landmarked parts of the building were restored when the architect Roland Simounet carried out his refurbishments, and these have revealed its initial grandeur. The lamp and candelabra over the main stairway, the chandeliers in the hallway and second-floor drawing rooms, and the furniture in the other rooms were specially created for the museum by Diego Giacometti. The intermingled

paintings, sculptures, drawings and engravings provide eloquent illustration of the varied technical approaches adopted by Picasso during his lifetime.

MUSÉE RODIN
Hôtel de Biron, 77, rue de Varenne 75007 (1 G7)

A rococo house
Auguste Rodin (1840–1917) moved into the Hôtel de Biron ▲ 268 in 1908 on the advice of his secretary, Rainer Maria Rilke. At the time, the building was divided into a number of artists' workshops. This splendid example of rococo architecture was built by Jean Aubert between

Rodin, a sculptor of genius
Rodin was an independent spirit when it came to inspiration and its figurative application, but he nonetheless stood at the crossroads of a number of artistic

been renovated, contains monumental bronzes, including the *Gates of Hell*, the *Burghers of Calais* and *Balzac* as well as some antique pieces.

ZADKINE – CABINET DES MÉDAILLES

Gold medallion (1665).

THE ASSAS FOLLY
In 1928, Ossip Zadkine went to live in the Rue d'Assas, a curious rural oasis where he worked until his death in 1967.

MUSÉE ZADKINE
100 *bis*, rue d'Assas
75006 (5 A1)

From Primitivism to Abstraction
The sculptures in the garden and the five rooms illustrate each stage of Zadkine's work. Until the mid-1920's, Zadkine worked mainly in wood and stone in a style reminiscent of Brancusi and Modigliani; he did not produce his first Cubist works, such as *Woman with a Fan*, until 1923. During the 1930's, Zadkine pursued themes from Greco-Latin antiquity as revised and corrected by Cubism (*The Maenads*). His four projects for monuments to poets (1938) were forerunners of his postwar Baroque output. An outstanding example is the model for his most famous sculpture, *Destroyed City* (1951). Only when Zadkine was approaching the end of his career did the human form finally disappear from his work. This period was filled with projects for sculptures designed to contrast sharply with the austere styles of the 1960's: see *Floral Forms* (1967), below.

CABINET DES MÉDAILLES
Bibliothèque Nationale, 58, rue de Richelieu 75002 (2 B3)

Coins, medals and antiques
This department of the Bibliothèque Nationale (National Library), known as the Cabinet des Médailles, was initially based on the manuscripts, gold plate, carved stones and old coins which the kings of France collected from the Middle Ages

Statue designed to go with the monument to Vincent Van Gogh at Auvers-sur-Oise, 1956.

AMASIS VASE
This Attic amphora (550–530 BC) decorated with black figures is signed by the potter Amasis. On one side it shows Athena and Poseidon; on the other, Dionysus entertains two maenads. On the handles is a representation of hoplites fighting.

onward. Until the 19th century, old coins were known as *médailles* (medals). The museum itself, which has occupied these premises since 1917, contains over 500,000 coins and medals and 30,000 nonmonetary objects. It was renovated in 1981: four of the rooms house the most prestigious objects (including the throne of Dagobert and a treasury of Gallo-Roman silverplate found at Berthouville, northern France) and a choice selection of coins and medals. Two more rooms on the mezzanine are given over to minting techniques and a history of coins.

A city for gourmets

The first Paris restaurant was opened in 1785 by Boulanger in the Rue des Poulis. The sign read *"Venite ad me omnes qui stomacho laboratis et ego vos restaurato"* (Come all who are hungry and I will restore you). Over the years cooking has gradually acquired the status of an art form, both perfectible and transmissable. In the early years of the 20th century, Auguste Escoffier defined the precepts of modern cuisine to which all the great chefs of today still adhere: that the chefs' cooking should attract gourmets from all over the world, and that the décor and history of the restaurants should make the meal into an experience of unique pleasure.

ALAIN SENDERENS
Senderens is one of the great artists of modern French cuisine. The wood paneling at the Lucas-Carton (9, pl. de la Madeleine 75008) provides a superb setting for his talents. Senderens is famous for several creations including "La Cuisine Retrouvée de Marcel Proust", a dish which combines literature and gastronomy.

LA TOUR D'ARGENT
15–17, quai de la Tournelle 75005
This establishment, which has been an inn since the 16th century, is named for its stone tower which sparkles in the sunlight. Henri IV was often lured here by the heron pâté. The restaurant, on a promontory in the Seine, with endless bay windows in the upstairs dining room to take in the views of Notre-Dame and the Île de la Cité, is presided over by Claude Terrail.

RESTAURANT STAFF
The movements of staff, from the humblest waiter to the maître d'hôtel are strictly choreographed. Even their uniforms are designed for esthetic appeal.

> "The gourmet is above all a diner who knows what to eat, and who does not choose the wrong combinations of tastes, aromas, wines or spices."

Léon-Paul Fargue

NOUVELLE CUISINE

The emergence of nouvelle cuisine in 1968 had a profound impact on cooking. The prime mover was the chef Michel Guérard: although nouvelle cuisine initially eschewed rich sauces, many of them now contain dairy products. The success of nouvelle cuisine – based on its remarkable ability to bring out the flavors of the very best ingredients – was assured when it was given a formal definition by the food writers Christian Millau and Henri Gault.

MICHELIN GUIDE

Founded in 1900 and originally aimed at motorists, this is one of the most highly regarded restaurant guides. It is feared by chefs, who attach great importance to the guide's system of awarding stars.

A KEY FIGURE

Antonin Carême (1783–1833) came from a modest background but became a legend in the history of modern gastronomy. He was a great lover of the arts, particularly architecture, and after training with the pastry chef Bailly, set about producing dishes of extraordinary complexity. In 1815 he was in charge of the kitchens of the Prince Regent and later entered the service of the Czar Alexander of Russia. He spent the last few years of his life writing books on gastronomy.

THE SOMMELIER

Philippe Faure-Brac, the top wine waiter of 1992, will certainly go along with the view that there is no such thing as a restaurant that serves good food with poor quality wine. The sommelier is the person who advises on, and oversees the serving of wines in serious restaurants. Down in the wine cellar his word is law.

CLIMBING THE GASTRONOMIC HEIGHTS

A meal of the highest class – 410 feet above the streets of Paris – awaits patrons of the Jules Verne (Eiffel Tower, second floor 75007), a restaurant completed in 1983. Slavik's metal decoration is even more imaginative than the writings of Jules Verne himself and presents diners with a unique view of Paris.

France is bordered by three seas and an ocean, so it is hardly surprising that fish and seafood occupy an important place in French cuisine. Paris excels when it comes to fish because it is so conveniently close to the coasts of Brittany and Normandy. Fresh produce is essential to a restaurant's reputation: the quality of the meal absolutely depends on it. Fish-farming techniques have also made it possible for fresh fish and seafood to be supplied all year round. The days when oysters were available only in winter are long gone.

BOUILLABAISSE

This Provençal specialty was originally a fish ragout that fishermen made from what was left over from their catches. Bouillabaisse is ideally made with small pieces of fish such as scorpion fish, whiting and John Dory; these are allowed to simmer in a stock containing tomatoes, onions, garlic, fennel and bay leaves. In fact, it is made with whatever fish is available on that day, which is why there is no definitive recipe.

LE DÔME
108, bd. du Montparnasse 75014
The bustle of the Boulevard Montparnasse owes much to its restaurants especially, since 1923, Le Dôme. The menu boasts some of the best bouillabaisse in Paris, and the décor includes photos of artists looking down over the diners.

JACQUES LE DIVELLEC
107, rue de l'Université 75007
The most chic fish restaurant in Paris is named after this self-styled "ambassador of the sea", who left La Rochelle in 1983 and started a business near Les Invalides. He made a magnificent lobster press in collaboration with the silversmith Christofle.

QUENELLES OF PIKE

This is one of the great dishes of Lyon. The quenelles are made with a purée of fillets of pike and fresh cream, and the velvety texture is provided by the white sauce which is mixed in with crayfish paste. The dish is ideally accompanied by a mild white wine.

SOLE MEUNIÈRE

This dish is as magnificent as it is simple. The fillets of sole are seasoned and rolled in flour before being sautéed in butter. Lemon juice, parsley, salt and pepper bring a spicy tang to the golden flesh, and finally a knob of butter is added.

LA MÉDITERRANÉE

, pl. de l'Odéon 75006 his restaurant, which as built in the Place de Odéon in 1930, became amous for its murals. It as painted blue and eceived artists and riters of the Latin Quarter, like Picasso, althus and Cocteau, one f whose drawings, dated 960, decorates the enu. Patrons of this stablishment have ncluded Charlie haplin and Orson Velles.

FISH AND WINE

White wine is usually drunk with fish and other seafood. Vineyards close to the sea, such as Bordeaux, Loire and Côtes-de-Provence, produce wines which go extremely well with seafood recipes, while Chablis and Riesling are ideal with oysters and shrimp. More inland wines like Burgundy,

Jura and Côtes-du-Rhône are perfect partners for freshwater fish like trout, perch and pike.

Brasseries occupy dominant positions on the city's main thoroughfares and at innumerable crossroads, and are therefore of great importance to Paris' culinary landscape. The origins of the brasserie go back to the German annexation of Alsace-Lorraine in 1870, when the inhabitants of Alsace fled the oppressive régime and introduced this sort of eating establishment to Paris. The brasserie's unchanging décor – mirrors, glass, benches covered in moleskin and immaculate tablecloths – was ideally suited to a diet of sauerkraut and beer. The volume of conversation rises perceptibly at mealtimes and when Parisians drop by in the evening before or after a show, and then stay on long into the night.

BEER DRINKING IN BRASSERIES
Since the 16th century, the word brasserie has denoted a place that sells beer (*brasser* means to brew). In the 19th century it was a kind of bar that served not only drinks (mainly beer) but also food. Frédéric Bofinger, the owner of a brasserie in the Rue de la Bastille, was the first person to sell

BOFINGER
5–7, rue de la Bastille 75004
Bofinger opened in 1864 and was designated a protected landmark in 1982. It is one of the oldest brasseries in Paris. Its present décor is the work of the architect Legay and the decorator Mitgen: the magnificent cupola is by Neret and Royer.

SAUERKRAUT
Sauerkraut from Alsace is made by leaving shredded cabbage to ferment in salt for three weeks; it is served with sausages, potatoes, and other meats as *choucroute garnie*. In some restaurants, sauerkraut is accompanied by seafood.

bière à la pompe, or draft beer: this new, light-colored beverage was a huge success. Beer is drunk less these days with food, but it is still part of the atmosphere of the brasserie.

LIPP

151, bd. St-Germain 75006
A celebrated habitué of Lipp was the poet Léon-Paul Fargue (1876–1947), a customer well known for always being the last to arrive for dinner. His father and uncle had created the faience panels. He suffered a stroke here while dining with Picasso and remained paralyzed for the rest of his life.

FLO

7, cour des Petites-Écuries 75010
In 1914 this brasserie, then called "Hans", was damaged by anti-German demonstrators. It later took the name Flo, a diminutive form of the name of its new owner, Robert Floderer.

ALSATIAN WINES

Alsace is best known for white wines, either dry or fruity. It has three AOC (Appellation d'Origine Contrôlée) wines: Vin d'Alsace, Alsace Grand Cru and Crémant d'Alsace. Wines made with Sylvaner, Riesling and Gewürztraminer grapes are an ideal accompaniment for sauerkraut.

CONFIT

Brasseries often have various rustic dishes on their menus: these include confit, a dish that uses up the leftover fat of ducks or geese, which are very popular birds in southwest France. The meat is first salted and left in an earthenware pot for 24 hours. Then it is gently cooked in fat until it is very tender.

Restaurants specializing in regional cuisine and home-style cooking give the most accurate impression of French cooking generally and of what French people themselves today. These establishments are often family-run businesses with recipes and knowhow brought from the provinces. Regional restaurant specialties are like holiday postcards sent from Proven Burgundy or the southwest. Restaurants that go in for home-style cooking are more intimate and less fancy, but their simple and classical recipes are no less mouth-watering. Parisians particularl enjoy this type of food at lunch, typically opting for snails or chic and french fries before going back to work.

POT-AU-FEU
Alexandre Dumas claimed to have discovered this rustic dish; it comes from Lyons but is now eaten all over France. It takes 48 hours to prepare a good *pot au feu* and to bring out all the flavors. Place the vegetables (celery, carrots, turnips, leeks and cabbage) and meat (beef and marrow bones) in a pot of hot water in order to produce a good stock, then add a *bouquet garni*. The broth is eaten with croutons, and the meat and vegetables with various condiments.

CHARTIER
7, rue du Faubourg-Montmartre 75009

Chartier is still a cheap eatery (*bouillon*) and has the same sign that it had when it was opened by its founders, Camille and Édouard Chartier, in 1895. A revolving door leads into the enormous dining room. The staff are dressed in long white aprons, vests and bowties, and the décor is pre-1940's. All of these curious and unexpected details give customers the impression they are in a time warp.

THE BLACKBOARD
In the dining room is a blackboard that has the menu and the *plat du jour* written in chalk. This typically Parisian device is now widespread.

Boeuf Bourguignon

The meat is marinated in red Burgundy, and this wine is also the dish's ideal accompaniment. This rich, rustic meal is made with the rump cut into small pieces. Brown the meat in bacon fat with onions, add more wine and the marinade, and bring to a boil. Simmer for three hours with baby onions, garlic and a *bouquet garni*.

Lescure

7, rue de Mondovi
75001
Lescure is situated near the Place de la Concorde and is one of the most pleasant – and least expensive – restaurants in this business quarter. It is a family concern and both rustic and classical dishes have been served in this warm, welcoming setting since 1919.

Snails

Francis Ponge, a poet noted for his championing of *escargots* (snails), makes no references to how they should be cooked. Only two kinds of snail are of any interest to the gourmet, he says: the Burgundy snail, which is well known in eastern France, and the *petit-gris*, from

Restaurant PHARAMOND

24, Rue de la Grande-Truanderie... Les Halles

Unusual for Les Halles district, the elaborate décor has remained intact. *Tripes à la mode de Caen* is allowed to simmer for 15 hours. It is always served here on individual plate-warmers, as it has been since the establishment moved to its present location in 1879.

Pharamond

24, rue de la Grande Truanderie 75001
Normandy cuisine is represented in Paris by Pharamond.

Gascony and Provence. Snails are traditionally prepared with garlic butter and *fines herbes*, but different regions have many other ways of cooking them. In Burgundy, snails may be cooked in Chablis before they are placed back in their shells, which have been filled with butter; in this recipe, the mantle (the liver and other organs, and the most nutritious part) is not removed.

Cassoulet

Cassoulet (a stew made with lamb, pork, goose and white beans) is the great specialty of southwest France and, according to the chef Prosper Montagné, "the god of Provençal cooking". The name comes from *cassole*, the terracotta dish in which the recipe is cooked.

A tour of Paris' restaurants is something like a trip around the world. The innumerable foreign communities in Paris are well represented by their respective cuisines, and their restaurants make great efforts to serve food in appropriate settings. The many North African, Chinese, Japanese and Italian restaurants present excellent food at very good prices and are very popular. More off the beaten track are Russian, Caribbean, Portuguese and South American restaurants, providing lots of surprises for the more adventurous palate.

NORTH AFRICA
One of the great traditional specialties of North Africa is *tagine*, which takes its name from the round earthenware dish with a cone-shaped lid of the same name. This stew of spiced lamb, veal or chicken with vegetables, dried fruits and nuts varies from region to region.

JAPAN
The greatest triumph of Japanese cooking is sushi: a small packet of rice is sprinkled with rice vinegar, and a thin slice of raw fish is laid on top, then the whole thing is wrapped in a seaweed leaf.

SOUTHEAST ASIA
The most popular Vietnamese specialty in Paris is *cha gio*, a kind of spring roll filled with noodles, wrapped in mint and lettuce leaves, and sprinkled with *nuoc nam* (fish sauce).

SOUTH AMERICA
Of all the South American cuisines in Paris, the best known is Brazilian. The national Brazilian specialty is *feijoada*, a dish once cooked by slaves. The basic ingredients are black beans and pork, but like all such national dishes, *feijoada* can be cooked in many different ways.

PORTUGAL

Portuguese cuisine is difficult to find in Paris, although there are some excellent Portuguese restaurants. Fresh and salt cod figure among the specialties: salt cod is often cooked *en brandade* (pounded with garlic, oil and cream).

SPAIN

Paella is not the archetypal Spanish dish it is sometimes made out to be: it is a typical dish from Valencia and is based on rice with meat or fish. The name comes from the two-handled pan in which it is cooked.

ITALY

Italy has been the world's leading producer of wine for many years. Heady, powerful Chianti classico from Tuscany is the best known but Orvieto classico goes very well with fish and seafood.

RUSSIA

Russian restaurants always serve *borscht*. This soup of green cabbage, beets and various other vegetables was a great favorite of Simone de Beauvoir.

NEAR EAST

Lebanese restaurants offer genuine tabbouleh. Semolina is widely used in France but a different kind is found in this dish. It is prepared with chopped parsley, mint, tomatoes, onions and cracked wheat, then served on a bed of lettuce or cabbage.

CENTRAL EUROPE

This area is well represented by Ashkenazic Jewish restaurants, famous for *zakuski*, assorted hors d'oeuvres from Russia, and for stuffed carp. These restaurants use kosher products.

183

MOUTON-ROTHSCHILD 1926

French wine is celebrated throughout the world. The cultivation of grapevines in the South of France, and viticulture in other regions dates from the beginning of recorded history. The capital no longer keeps the majority of vines for itself, but the marketing of wine is closely linked to developments that have taken place in Paris. Events like the excitement surrounding the arrival each year of Beaujolais nouveau bring bistros and wine bars to life and give the whole city a holiday air. *Cavistes* will take every opportunity to remind one and all that wine drinking symbolizes the French art of living.

CAVISTES

Cavistes specialize in the selling of wine by the bottle. There are quite a number of independent *cavistes* in Paris, but most of them belong to chains like Nicolas and the Repaire de Bacchus.

Some *cavistes* organize general tastings for their customers; other tastings are based on a particular vineyard in order to stimulate interest in unknown grapes.

BLANC-CASSIS

The most popular aperitif in France is kir, a mixture of cassis and dry white wine, originally Bourgogne Aligoté. It was popularized by Canon Kir (1876–1968), a noted Resistance fighter and mayor of Dijon from 1945 to 1968.

CITY VINES

The last grapevines still growing in the capital owe their survival to the endeavors of a few hard-working Parisians. The Clos Montmartre, a vineyard dating back to the earliest years of our era, became operational again in 1935. The harvest takes place on the first weekend in October. The grapes produce a modest rosé. The Clos des Morillons, in the Georges-Brassens Park (15th arrondissement), has been producing grapes for red wine since 1982.

BERCY

Wines and brandies have been sold in Bercy since the 17th century, but the area's special interest in wine dates from 1790, when the autonomous commune escaped the city toll. Even 20 years ago, 20 percent of all wine drunk in France passed through Bercy. Despite development and its being turned over to entertainment and leisure, the area still retains traces of its oenophilic past.

RHÔNE VALLEY
Rhône Valley vineyards are situated on both sides of the Rhone. The wines have the powerful, individual characteristics of either the northern (Côte-Rôtie) or southern (Châteauneuf-du-Pape and Gigondas) slopes.

JUST A GLASS
Wine lovers flock to bars like the Ange Vin, where different wines can be sampled by the glass. The relaxed, intimate atmosphere of these establishments enables the real wine buff to indulge his or her passion – and talk nonstop about the color of a Chablis or the bouquet of a St-Émilion. These bars sometimes serve rustic dishes that go well with the wines.

BORDEAUX
This, the biggest wine-producing area in France, is governed by three kinds of *appellation: générale*, *régionale* and *communale*. The smaller the locality specified, the better the wine. Tannin-rich Bordeaux wines offer an extremely wide range of full-bodied reds (Médoc and St-Émilion), dry and sweet whites (Graves and Sauternes), as well as a few rosés.

BURGUNDY
This area extends from the northwest (Chablis) to the south (Beaujolais). In the middle are the great Côte-d'Or wines, such as Vosne-Romanée and Puligny-Montrachet, for which Burgundy is best known.

JURA
This small wine-making area – the main town is Arbois – produces a variety of wines, ranging from reds and rosés to sparkling whites. However, it is best known for its nutty-tasting white wines like the exceptional Château-Chalon, a yellow wine made from Savagnin grape: it is left to age for six years in sealed wooden barrels and can last for decades.

LOIRE
Between Nevers and Nantes, the Loire is surrounded by numerous vineyards that produce delightfully fresh wines such as Muscadet and Vouvray (dry and sparkling whites) and Saumur-Champigny and Anjou (reds).

CHAMPAGNE
Champagne, the most famous wine in the world, is perfect for celebrations. It is made from two red grapes, Pinot Noir and Pinot Meunier. Blanc de blanc is made with white Chardonnay grapes. Different amounts of sugar are needed to produce brut, sec and demi-sec Champagne.

France has a proud rural tradition and boasts over four hundred varieties of cheese made from cows', goats' and sheep's milk. Accordingly, an enormous selection of cheeses is available in Paris. As the writer Colette succinctly put it "Paris has every sweet, sharp, aperitif and extra-mature cheese from home and abroad – and consumes every bit." There is just as much variety in the different types of French breads, the best known of all being the *baguette*.

BREAD VARIETIES
1. Walnut bread
2. Organic whole-wheat bread
3. Rye bread with raisins
4. Decorated loaf
5. Boule de campagne
6. Flûte Gana
7. Baguette

STAPLE DIET AND SACRED RITUAL

There is documentary evidence of bread being eaten in Egypt as long ago as 2500 BC. Indeed, it has been the staple of most civilizations because of its nutritious value and the fact that it keeps for long periods. It also plays a part in the Christian (the body of Christ in the Eucharist) and Jewish (bread is blessed before being eaten at table) liturgies.

BAGUETTE

French bread arouses so much anxiety that the state has tried to protect master bakers from the predations of big businesses which produce frozen baguettes. Under a decree passed in 1993 only bread kneaded and baked at the point of sale may now be referred to as *pain maison* (homemade bread).

TO GO WITH EVERY DISH

Bread is a foodstuff in its own right and needs to be chosen carefully to accompany certain dishes. It contributes to the overall balance of a meal: rye bread, for instance, is ideal with oysters and sour dough bread is best with foie gras while lemon bread goes best with fish.

ROQUEFORT (D)

Blue cheeses made from sheep's or cow's milk are marked by blue veins. These are caused by a type of fungus known as *penicillium* which forms during the maturing process, and gives Roquefort from Aveyron its veined appearance.

ÉPOISSES (C)

This cheese is strong-smelling and fully flavored. The maturing process takes two to four months: at the end of this the cheese is soaked in water and Marc de Bourgogne. Other cheeses with washed rinds are flavored with cider or beer according to the region.

CHEESE EXPERT

Expert cheese makers supervise the entire maturing process and check on how the cheeses are developing. In 1909 a Breton cheese maker by the name of Henri Androuët opened a shop selling cheese he had matured on the premises. In 1934 he launched a cheese cuisine restaurant – the first of its type – which was very popular with Sacha Guitry and Maria Callas.

CAMEMBERT (A)

This Normandy cheese is made with milk either straight from the cow or pasteurized and is soft and sweet. A good Camembert is left in the maturing room for an average of three to six weeks.

CANTAL (E)

This Auvergne cheese was first referred to by Pliny the Elder. It is so-called pressed cheese and is the oldest of all the French varieties. It is eaten fresh or after maturing for three months.

BRIE (B)

Originally from Île-de-France, Brie was once voted "king of cheeses" by a jury of European ambassadors being entertained by Talleyrand. This creamy cheese matures quickly: it tastes mildly of hazelnuts.

GOAT'S CHEESE

There are numerous types of small goat's cheese: they may be fresh, dry, hard or smoked, according to the length of the maturing process. The flavor matures as the cheese ages and farmhouse cheeses develop a blue mold. The best-known is Crottin de Chavignol.

BEST OF FRIENDS

The respective tastes of wine and cheese complement each other and result in the most delicate of harmonies. However, there are no hard-and-fast rules about which wine goes with which

cheese, as the qualities of each vary from year to year. On the whole it is advisable to pair wines and cheeses from the same region.

The delights of restaurants are frequently concealed behind grand façades, but pastries, confectionery, ice creams and other wicked temptations flaunt themselves shamelessly in the windows of Parisian shops. Confectioners combine practical and esthetic skills to produce imaginative and mouth-watering delicacies. This tradition dates back to the end of the 19th century, when afternoon tea (or a short break from shopping) was the perfect excuse for a minor indulgence in a smart tea shop.

A BEVERAGE OF THE GODS

Chocolate is made from the beans of the cacao tree. The origin of chocolate as a cold drink dates back to pre-Colombian times, when it formed part of Aztec and Maya mythology: the god Quetzalcoatl is said to have gone mad after drinking it. His people viewed cocoa beans as valuable products and even used them as currency.

A DRAMATIC SUCCESS

The *opéra*, an almond pastry consisting of layers of coffee and chocolate, is a recent creation. Because its rectangular shape suggests a stage, Andrée Gavillon, the director of the Maison Dalloyau (99–101 rue du Faubourg St-Honoré 75001), chose the name as a tribute to the corps de ballet of the Paris Opera.

EATING CHOCOLATE

Chocolate was consumed only as a drink until 19th-century confectioners succeeded in making cacao paste into chocolate sweets. Cocoa beans are roasted and crushed, then mixed with sugar and lecithin: after the mixture hardens it is compressed.
Try La Maison du Chocolat 225, rue du Faubourg St-Honoré 75008.

Americain auec Sa Choco latiere et Son Gobelet

Jean Béraud, 1889

PARIS-BREST

At the end of the 19th century, a pastrychef in the Paris suburbs conceived the idea of a pastry in the shape of a bicycle wheel while watching competitors in the famous Paris-Brest cycle race. That is how this most Parisian of cakes – choux-pastry filled with almond cream – came to be made.

"MILLEFEUILLE"

Antonin Carême layered *crème pâtissière* with puff pastry to produce *millefeuille*. In medieval times similar pastries had been well known in the East, and the recipe was brought back by Crusaders.

BERTHILLON

31, rue St-Louis-en-l'Île 75004

Raymond Berthillon's tiny ice cream parlor on the Île St-Louis has been hugely popular ever since it opened in 1954. It offers a range of 72 flavors, including 8 kinds of chocolate ice cream, as well as blueberry and fig sorbets.

OLD-FASHIONED ICE CREAM

Ice cream was in existence long before the invention of the refrigerator. The development of a cooling mixture – combination of crushed ice and salt – allowed ice cream to be kept at around 42 °F.

LENÔTRE

Gaston Lenôtre, from Normandy, is one of today's great pastry chefs. His success with pastries, confectionery and ice cream has enabled him to build a gastronomic empire, including many shops and his own cooking school. In 1999 he opened his first gourmet boutique and café on American soil, in Las Vegas.

BÊTISES DE CAMBRAI

Legend has it that these candies of boiled sugar owe their name to an error (*bêtise* means blunder) made by the son of a confectioner called Afchain in Cambrai (northern France) while measuring ingredients. The *Bêtises de Cambrai* are a mixture of boiled sugar, mint and caramelized sugar.

FLOWER CANDIES

Violettes de Toulouse are among the most unusual and elegant sweets to be found anywhere in France. The petals, and sometimes entire flowers, of violets are coated in crystallized sugar to preserve their subtle perfume.

AUX VRAIES

Bêtises de Cambrai

AFCHAIN

TRADITION MENTHE

Spices were used in the Middle Ages to help preserve fruit and meat. Pepper, nutmeg and saffron were most commonly used, and their commercial importance prompted some of the great explorations of the Renaissance. Today spices are minor ingredients whose flavors are nonetheless considered essential. The modern "spice route" through Paris takes in large and small shops (*épicerie* is now the general term used to mean grocery store) where bottles and jars sit waiting for an opportunity to send forth their exotic perfumes.

CHUTNEY
This sweet and sour Indian condiment is made by cooking fresh fruit and vegetables in vinegar with sugar and spices.

HÉDIARD
21, pl. de la Madeleine 75008

In 1854 Ferdinand Hédiard opened an *épicerie* in Place de la Madeleine which specialized in imported produce. He realized that he could make money out of rare, exotic products and had papaya, guava, mango and loquat shipped to France. He is remembered for selling the writer Alexandre Dumas one of the first pineapples.

BALSAMIC VINEGAR
This originated in Modena in Italy. Its unique flavor comes from the must (unfermented juice) of white Trebbiano grapes. Aging in casks of various woods and sizes gives the vinegar its distinctive color and flavor.

FAUCHON
26–30, pl. de la Madeleine 75008

From a modest family in Calvados, August Fauchon (1856–1938) moved to Paris to sell fruits and vegetables in the vicinity of the Madeleine. He was soon the owner of a number of shops, one of which, in the Place de la Madeleine, he turned into an *épicerie de luxe*: since the 1930's it has sold rare and unusual products.

GINGER
Different forms of this root are used in seasoning a large number of Eastern dishes. Candied ginger is also delicious as a confectionery.

CURRY
This mixture of spices (including pepper and turmeric) is used in the meat, fish and vegetable dishes that form part of traditional Indian cuisine.

JAMS
The last course in medieval banquets consisted of fruit preserves: these jams were made from fruit and numerous spices caramelized in sugar.

Paris nature

THE ROOFTOPS OF PARIS

Summer

Winter

STARLING
The starling is well adapted to cities.
In the spring, it exchanges its
plumage scattered with white spots
for a dark, iridescent version.

Parisians and visitors alike are
generally unaware of the wealth of bird life in the city. Birds
live, eat and reproduce at roof level, far from the bustling
streets; they share television antennas, chimney stacks and the
skies while the pedestrians below completely ignore them.
There are many species to look for apart from sparrows and
pigeons: some of these, such as swifts and swallows, are
migratory birds that travel thousands of miles between Paris and
Africa every year.

House martin

Swift

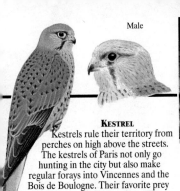

KESTREL

Kestrels rule their territory from perches on high above the streets. The kestrels of Paris not only go hunting in the city but also make regular forays into Vincennes and the Bois de Boulogne. Their favorite prey are sparrows and small rodents. There are about thirty pairs of kestrels in the city. When they are here, these small falcons normally take up their positions on ancient monuments or office blocks: such buildings presumably remind them of the cliffs where they spend most of their time.

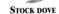

BLACK REDSTART

The black redstart occupies the rooftops from March to October or November. It likes to adopt a commanding position when singing or lying in wait for insects.

STOCK DOVE

This, one of the scarcest of the species to be found in Paris, makes its home in holes in walls or on disused chimney stacks. It can be recognized by its dark eye and blue-gray plumage.

ROCK PIGEON

The semi-domestic rock pigeon has its ferocious detractors as well as its faithful supporters. Measures have been taken to limit its numbers.

AERIAL HUNTERS

Swifts and house martins are perpetually on the lookout for flying insects, which they eat to the exclusion of anything else. They come to the capital only for a few months in the summer.

193

Magpie

■ PETITE CEINTURE RAILWAY

Even in the largest city in France there are still special areas
where nature has been left to its own devices and has partly
taken control of its own destiny. These forgotten corners –
abandoned gardens and other tranquil spots not generally
accessible to the public – are a secret paradise for the city's
nature-lovers. Over the years parts of the Petite Ceinture
railway have been overrun by flora and fauna: only a stone's
throw from the noise and bustle of the city, insects buzz, lizards
bask in the sun, and sparrows peacefully chirrup the afternoon
away.

CELANDINE
Its orange-yellow
juice is said to cure
warts.

TRAVELER'S JOY
This plant's feathery
fruit grows throughout
the winter.

COMMON ELDER
The elder's juicy berries
are eaten by a wide
variety of birds.

WHITE BRYONY
This climber bears
fruit until the autumn

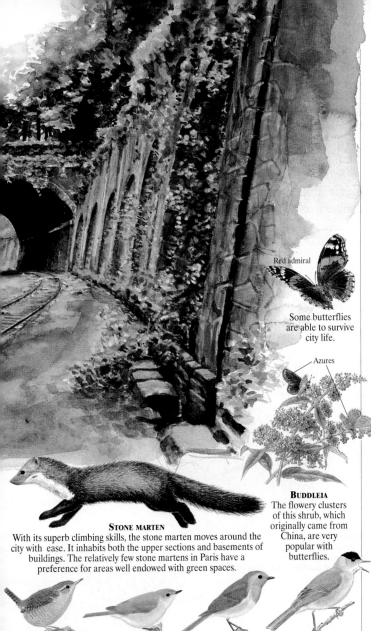

Red admiral

Some butterflies are able to survive city life.

Azures

BUDDLEIA
The flowery clusters of this shrub, which originally came from China, are very popular with butterflies.

STONE MARTEN
With its superb climbing skills, the stone marten moves around the city with ease. It inhabits both the upper sections and basements of buildings. The relatively few stone martens in Paris have a preference for areas well endowed with green spaces.

WINTER WREN
Despite its size, this wren sings with impressive volume.

CHIFFCHAFF
This warbler returns to wooded parts of the city each spring.

ROBIN
The robin builds its nest on the ground in well-hidden areas among thick vegetation.

BLACKCAP
The fluted song of the male blackcap is particularly melodious.

HOUSE MOUSE
This mouse lives only in buildings – or underground – where it can find food, shelter and warmth.

HEDGEHOG
Hedgehogs live in some parks (Buttes-Chaumont and Montsouris) and in abandoned sections of the Petite Ceinture railway.

WALL LIZARD
This lizard is seen less and less in Paris these days. The drop in numbers is largely attributable to cats.

UNUSUAL MICRO-HABITATS

A gillyflower on its balcony.

The visitor who takes enough time – and knows where to look – will soon realize that Paris is teeming with nooks and crannies where flowers, insects and spiders lead a quiet but tenacious existence. An urban world in miniature awaits the assiduous enthusiast in the cracks in concrete and asphalt and the spaces between paving stones.

These "secret" plants need only a little moisture and mineral nutrients.

Young ailanthus

The tiny flowers of the ivy-leaved toadflax are best seen close up.

WOOD LOUSE
This small crustacean loves moisture but loathes light.

Greater plaintain

Meadow grass

Chickwe

BEHIND BARS
Cavities sealed by iron grills sometimes provide shelter for plants and small invertebrates.

WILD CAMOMILE
This plant grows from April to October.

DANDELION
Dandelions are smaller in cities.

BETWEEN PAVING STONES
Where paving stones still exist, the gaps between them sometimes provide the settings for embryonic botanical gardens – as long as they are not disturbed by passing pedestrians.

JUMPING SPIDER
This small, energetic spider catches its insect prey by jumping on it suddenly.

FIRE BUG
This pretty little bug likes lying out in the sun.

Ivy

Spider waiting for its prey

Fossils

Wall rue

Moss

LOVERS OF OLD STONE
Old walls provide insects with plenty of hiding places. Here spiders spin their silky webs to catch flies and gnats.

Bumblebee

Small tortoiseshell

Cabbage white

Peacock

BUTTERFLIES OF PARIS
During the summer months butterflies can be found in flowerbeds and on balconies.

Nettles

A WILD BOUQUET OF PLANTS
A simple planter full of wild flowers and plants is all that is needed to attract butterflies of every color and other city-based booty hunters.

Ground ivy

Cabbage white

Shaggy soldier

leaved adflax

197

■ PARKS AND GARDENS

YEW
Both pruned and unpruned yew
trees are found everywhere in the
parks of Paris. Their red berries
are very popular with birds.

The parks and gardens of Paris are
welcome havens of green for numerous species of birds. The
selection presented here consists of resident species that can be
seen all year round. Some of them are very common and can be
seen anywhere, while others are either rarer or else lead more
discreet lives, demanding keen powers of observation from those
who want to see them. Each spring the capital's parks resound to
their cooing, warbling and trilling.

Male

Male

**LESSER SPOTTED
WOODPECKER**
This woodpecker,
hardly bigger than a
sparrow, is seen
mostly in the winter.

**SHORT-TOED
TREECREEPER**
These often avoid
detection because of
their bark-colored
plumage.

GREENFINCH
In spring, the male
indulges in elaborate
nuptial display
flights.

**HEDGE ACCENTOR
(DUNNOCK)**
This unassuming little
bird spends much of its
time shuffling jerkily
along on the ground.

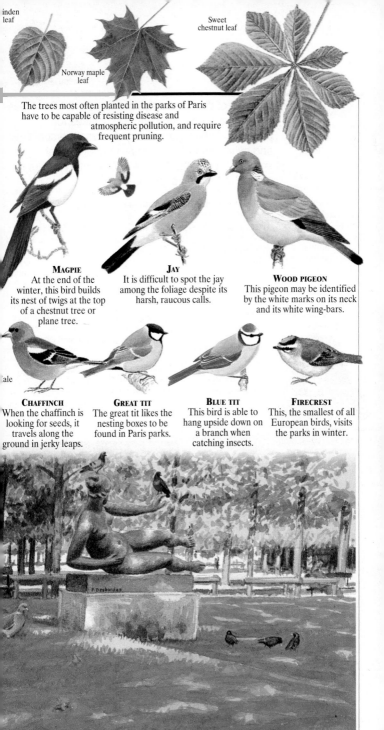

Linden leaf

Norway maple leaf

Sweet chestnut leaf

The trees most often planted in the parks of Paris have to be capable of resisting disease and atmospheric pollution, and require frequent pruning.

MAGPIE
At the end of the winter, this bird builds its nest of twigs at the top of a chestnut tree or plane tree.

JAY
It is difficult to spot the jay among the foliage despite its harsh, raucous calls.

WOOD PIGEON
This pigeon may be identified by the white marks on its neck and its white wing-bars.

CHAFFINCH
When the chaffinch is looking for seeds, it travels along the ground in jerky leaps.

GREAT TIT
The great tit likes the nesting boxes to be found in Paris parks.

BLUE TIT
This bird is able to hang upside down on a branch when catching insects.

FIRECREST
This, the smallest of all European birds, visits the parks in winter.

ale

The aim of the great classical gardens of Paris was to glorify the royal and princely palaces for posterity. These gardens created vast perspectives and by incorporating plants into geometrical shapes, they embodied the 17th-century desire for reason to triumph over nature.

TUILERIES AND JARDINS DU CARROUSEL (1 HI–J45)

Le Nôtre's garden
In the 16th century ▲ 332 Catherine de' Medici built a palace on the site of a former tile factory; attached to the site was an enclosed garden. André Le Nôtre turned it into a French-style

André Le Nôtre (1613–1700) studied architecture and painting before succeeding his grandfather, and then his father, as head gardener at the Tuileries.

garden in 1666. To establish the palace's domination over its natural environment – there was countryside to

the west and the river to the south – Le Nôtre erected two large terraces, forming a broad alley that extended the line of the palace some way beyond the garden boundaries. This followed the route of the future Champs-Élysées and traced the first section of the Grand Axis ▲ 308, the perspective that would one day run from the Louvre all the way to the Grande Arche of La Défense. The garden is divided into two parts. Next to the palace there is a wide-open expanse adorned by parterres with box-edged beds, including those in the shape of arabesques. There is also a wooded area, which becomes increasingly dense

Wall rue is a rare fern that grows in cracks in the old walls of the Tuileries.

and mysterious as it extends westward.
A prototype for a public park
The Tuileries were one of the first

gardens in Europe to open to the public. Long a favorite with visitors and Parisians alike, in the 18th century they became the model for public gardens throughout France and Europe. At the time it boasted cafés, kiosks, seats for rent and stone benches: it was also a place where all classes of society could come for relaxation. Until the end of the 19th century, successive

The Tuileries and Carrousel gardens contain about a hundred 17th-to-20th-century sculptures, including some by Aristide Maillol.

"The Tuileries" (1876, Claude Monet).

governments organized festivals here, illuminating the park with fireworks.

The new Tuileries

Work on the Tuileries and Carrousel gardens, which had lain in poor condition for some years, was recently completed. The aim was to reincorporate the gardens into the extended Louvre Palace and the Grand Axis vista, while reviving the site's historical associations.

The Carrousel Garden

This 19th-century garden was created after the

The parterres and private gardens of the Grand Carré (above) are to be restored to their original 19th-century layout. During the Restoration they were laid out beside the palace and reserved for the royal family. Napoleon III had the gardens enlarged.

Tuileries Palace was destroyed by fire; the triumphal arch, the focal point of a sunburst pattern of hedges, is the gateway to the Tuileries. It can be described as the "green room" of the Louvre, adorned with its Maillol sculptures and topiarised trees and hedges. It opens out onto a terrace-belvedere: this was constructed over the underground path, on the exact site of the palace's former terrace. Adorned with a central stairway, the terrace descends to the Tuileries,

where Le Nôtre's designs – the more manicured parterres of the Grand Carré as well as the wild thickets of the Grand Couvert – are unchanged: the latter have been restored to their former wildness. Some five hundred trees have been planted around the garden.

LE JARDIN DU PALAIS-ROYAL (2 AB4)

Virtually nothing remains of the original design for the garden which was built close to the Palais-Royal in the early 1600's. The garden was bigger than it is today: it consisted of parterres with box hedging and was decorated with pools and statues, while to the north it opened onto a small wood where Louis XIV went fox hunting as a child. The construction of nearby galleries and streets in the 18th century reduced the size of the grounds and shortened the perspective. Then it was turned into an English-style garden, before acquiring the layout we know today. The garden of the Palais-Royal covers an area of eight acres; it is shaded by four double rows of lime trees trimmed *en marquise*. The central pool with its fountain is flanked by two expanses of grass bordered by single-color flowerbeds decorated with 19th-century statues. In the years leading up to the Revolution and during the Directoire, this charming yet peaceful garden was one of the liveliest spots in all of Paris ▲ 338: today, the peace of the Palais-Royal Garden is disturbed only by the screeching of swifts as they arrive from Africa in April.

"The Shepherd and the Goat" (1830), a marble statue by Paul Lemoyne in the Palais-Royal Garden.

LE JARDIN DU LUXEMBOURG (2 A9)

The garden which Marie de' Medici had built for her palace is laid out around a central parterre dominated by terraces. Two thousand elm trees arranged in a square once framed a view that ended abruptly at the Carthusian monastery. The monks refused to give up any of their land, and as a result the southern extension was not completed until the end of the 18th century – after the monastery had been torn down during the Revolution. The garden was restored during the First Empire by Chalgrin, who widened and lengthened the central vista and built an English-style garden to the

from the upper floors of the palace. In the late 19th century, they were replaced by lawns bordered with flower beds.

southwest. The balustrades overhanging the central parterre and pool date from the same period. The construction of nearby streets and avenues during the Second Empire reduced the area covered by the garden, but its general appearance was not changed.

The Latin Quarter Garden
This princely park, where the painter Watteau paid clandestine visits to seek inspiration, was opened to the public in 1778. Since then, it has been a haunt for students and local residents, but,

The apiary in the Luxembourg Garden is home to some twenty colonies of bees (about twenty million individuals). Practical and theoretical courses are organized by the Société Centrale d'Apiculture.

Medici fountain (above), whose pediment bears the queen's coat of arms; the second is the Regard fountain (1869), and a fountain commemorating Eugène Delacroix, decorated with a bronze statue by Jules Dalou (1890).

Flora

The flower beds, which are replanted three times a year, are a riot of gillyflowers, salvias and dahlias; in summer they are joined by orange, date and pomegranate trees, and oleanders. The palace is surrounded on all sides by extensive wooded areas planted with white chestnut trees. The English Garden is cut off by a line of laurel, aucuba and privet hedges and boasts a huge variety of plants. There is

also an orchard – the remains of the Carthusian nursery – which contains two thousand varieties of apple and pear trees trained as espaliers.

The Observatory Gardens

These were laid out in 1867 but were recently renamed the Robert Cavelier

Between May and October plants are taken from the Luxembourg Orangerie and replanted in the central flowerbeds.

unlike other parks, it has rarely been used for grand festivities. The 19th century saw the introduction of a bandstand, a merry-go-round by Garnier and numerous shelters: a number of small areas designed for relaxation and entertainment have been added more recently.

Statues

About eighty statues, among them the renowned *Queens and Famous Women of France* series, are

distributed around the garden: they are the work of several 19th-century artists, including Cain, Frémiet, Bourdelle and Marqueste. There are three fountains: the

de La Salle and Marco Polo gardens: they form the final section of the perspective conceived by Chalgrin. The Observatory Gardens contain the superb Four-Corners-of-the-World fountain, a collective work completed in 1874 after plans by Davioud. The statues of four women supporting the globe, symbolizing the four corners of the world ▲ 272, are by Jean-Baptiste Carpeaux (1827–75).

Botanical gardens date from the Renaissance and were first used for educational purposes during the reign of Louis XIV. They have also been used for experiments on, and the conservation of, exotic specimens brought back from foreign expeditions.

Each century has made a contribution to the Jardin des Plantes. The numerous species of flora are meticulously labeled.

LE JARDIN DES PLANTES (5 FG1)

Louis XIII built the Royal Medicinal Herb Garden in 1633 for the use of medical students. In 1640, it became the first garden in Paris to open to the public. Under the supervision of Buffon (1739–88) the Botanical Gardens were enlarged and became a center of scientific learning. Scholars of the day included the three Jussieu brothers, who were botanists, and the naturalist Daubenton. In 1793 the National Convention awarded the garden the title of National Museum of Natural History; the museum's galleries were built during the 19th and 20th centuries ▲ *142*.

Botanical and horticultural collections

The collections of dahlias, cannas and geraniums are found in the French parterres, which extend from the Grande Galerie de l'Évolution to the railings by the entrance. There is also a rose garden and a section containing four hundred varieties of iris. The Ecological Park is set out in the English manner and boasts a fine collection of trees and shrubs growing wild; the Botany School identifies grasses and edible and medicinal plants. The rockery in the Alpine Garden is covered with two thousand species of alpine plants classified by region; it also has a curious microclimate which enables the temperature to vary by up to 46°F in different areas.

This 66-foot cedar of Lebanon, planted by

The two hothouses in the Jardin des Plantes, the Mexican and the Australian, were built by Charles Rohaut de Fleury in 1834. This was the first time that iron was used for this type of construction.

The maze

This was built around 1640 on an artificial mound, at the top of which is a bronze summer house, the oldest metal building in Paris. The column at the bottom stands over the tomb of Daubenton.

The menagerie

Added to the Jardin des Plantes during the Revolution, after the Royal Menagerie had been confiscated, the menagerie stands in an area laid out in the English style and incudes a vivarium containing snakes and crocodiles.

Bernard de Jussieu in 1734, is one of the oldest trees in Paris.

LE JARDIN DES SERRES D'AUTEUIL

This was laid out in 1898 by Jean-Camille Formigé on the site of Louis XV's former nurseries and included greenhouses. It is Paris' official orchard and is the supplier of indoor plants to the Hôtel de Ville and some of the mayors' offices. The Serres d'Auteuil Garden is also a botanical garden with well-labeled plants and trees. The most remarkable feature of the garden is the series of greenhouses which form the great hothouse: this is 325 feet long and has a central dome 53 feet high. It contains a palmarium and an abundance of tropical flora.

LE PARC FLORAL DE VINCENNES (4 GH7)

The floral park was opened in 1969 as a site for horticultural exhibitions. It covers 76 acres landscaped by Daniel Collin and abounds in valleys, artificial lakes and rivers. Groves of beech and cedar trees have been planted, which complement small clumps of Corsican pine and oaks. The style of the pavilions and patios, the design of the ponds and the fine statuary (works by Calder, Stahly and others) anchor the park in the esthetic traditions of the 1970's. Particularly striking is the Dahlia Garden, which winds its way through the pine forest like a long, multicolored river.

With a nod in the direction of pictorial art, the Valley of Flowers contains the flora that appear in Impressionist landscapes, including sunflowers, corn, sweet peas, hollyhocks and bindweed. The Pavillon des Papillons (Butterfly pavilion) of l'Île-de-France has

collections of wood lice, cockroaches, slugs and silkworms as well as butterflies.

The Chartres Folly, later Monceau Park, embodied the frivolous and refined behavior of high society at the end of the 18th century.

The picturesque garden (or *jardin anglo-chinois*) was very fashionable during the second half of the 18th century; it was the opposite of the French classical garden in every way. Here we are in a land of illusion dotted with curious and exotic ruins and buildings.

LE PARC MONCEAU (9 E8)

The Chartres Folly
Louis XVI's brother, the Duke of Chartres, had a folly built near the hamlet of Monceau in 1787: it was one of the first gardens in the *anglo-chinois*

The Naumachia in Monceau Park is in the form of a pond surrounded by a colonnade.

style. The architect Carmontelle – a dramatist, organizer of festivities and avant-garde landscape gardener – designed the park as an open-air Pandora's box of curiosities and as a location for festivities. The rivers, small woods, rockery and grottos which he built were set off by a number of extravagant constructions, of which only the Egyptian Tomb and the Naumachia have

Monceau Park contains one of the tallest trees in Paris: this Oriental plane is 200 years old and has a circumference of 23 feet.

survived. The park was enlarged in 1793 to include a rotunda by Claude Nicolas Ledoux ● 69,

the designer of the tollhouses of the Farmers-General Wall.

Haussmann's "renovations"
The park suffered as a result of Haussmann's apportionment of the Monceau Plain. Half of the land (20 acres) was sold to the Pereire brothers, who built streets and private houses; then the park was encircled

The tomb of the King of Hearts is on an island in Bagatelle Park.

by railings with monumental gates. It was later renovated by Alphand ▲ 208, who introduced rare species of plants and complemented the old buildings with an Italianate bridge and a grotto with stalactites.

Flora and fauna The park contains several specimens of trees planted in the 19th century and a number of rare species, including a fruit-bearing fig tree and the extraordinary *Davidia* (handkerchief tree). The bird life is exceptionally abundant and varied: there have even been sightings of the spotted fly-catcher, a rare visitor to Paris.

BAGATELLE (8 D3)

The Artois Folly In 1775, Louis XV's brother, the Count of Artois, had Bagatelle's castle and park built in only two months, in response to a challenge by Marie-Antoinette. Thomas Blaikie designed the park in the *anglo-chinois* style, introducing waterfalls, grottos, a pagoda and a lovers' pavilion. The grounds were further extended in the 19th century with an orangery and stables. A subsequent owner, Sir Richard Wallace, added two hunting lodges and the Trianon.

The property was bought by the City of Paris in 1904 and has since been used for horticultural shows. The park provides a remarkable cross-section of garden design spanning three centuries.

The English Garden, with its much-admired undergrowth, ponds and shaded grassy areas, also contains theme gardens, including an iris garden, a French-style parterre and an extraordinary rose garden built in 1904 by J.C.N. Forestier, the warden of parks and gardens and friend of Monet.

Of the many "lovers' pavilions" built in the Bois de Boulogne during the 19th century, Château Bagatelle (above) is the only one to have survived.

Bagatelle Park boasts a profusion of plants that grow all year round, but June is the best time to visit.

Landscape gardens, inspired by English parks, came into being during the Second Empire. Their irregular shapes gave the impression of a natural, varied landscape. Created as a pocket of greenery in the heart of a busy city, these hidden gardens offered private, winding paths for quiet walks.

LE PARC DES BUTTES-CHAUMONT
(11 B8)
As part of his drive to make Paris a healthier place in which to live, Napoleon III conceived an ambitious plan for green open spaces, and in seventeen years, no fewer than 4,950 acres of woods, parks, gardens and squares were laid out and 600,000 trees planted. Jean-Charles Alphand (1817–91) was in charge of

Two bridges lead across the ravines to the Temple of Sybil, on a cliff 292 feet high.

implementing the policy, assisted by the gardener Barillet-Deschamps, the architect Davioud and the engineer Belgrand. Behind the decision to build the Buttes-Chaumont Park in 1863 lay a desire to rehabilitate the surrounding slum area by creating one final park in the northeast.
An example of a landscape park Alphand used dynamite charges to give new forms to the Buttes-Chaumont; the results included a lake, a number of waterfalls and rivers, embankments and large plantations.

The lake in Montsouris Park is the only place in Paris where the moorhen regularly nests.

When the park was opened in 1867 it was a typical Haussmann design: paths plunging deep into the undergrowth, clambering up rocks, and then opening out onto higher land and winding their way through the countryside. All of this formed part of an idealized picture of nature adorned by features of much picturesque charm, including a temple and a grotto with stalactites.

Flora

The park contains several remarkable trees including an example of *Gymnocladus canadensis* and two *Gingko biloba*.

Haussmann's parks are noted for their artifice: they abound in false rocks, false grottos and false woods.

LE PARC MONTSOURIS (5 AB8)

Montsouris Park was designed to be a copy of Buttes-Chaumont to the south. It was laid out by Alphand between 1867 and 1878 over the site of old quarries that had been turned

Montsouris Park contains about ten sculptures realized between 1880 and 1960.

into catacombs in the late 18th century. As with the Buttes-Chaumont Park, Alphand was obliged to conceal the railway lines, and he produced a landscape dotted with valleys. He also dug an artificial lake, built waterfalls and grottos, and laid out grassy areas and thickets to produce alternating blocked and unrestricted views. The highest point was once occupied by the Palais du Bardo: this building, which burned down in 1991, was a

reproduction of the Bey of Tunis' summer residence, a typically Moorish design built for the Universal Exhibition of 1867. The park also contains a meteorological station, constructed in 1947 next to the south bearing of the old Paris Meridian; this once stood in an observatory designed by Vaudoyer in 1806.

Birds

The southern extremity of the old Petite Ceinture railway track is carpeted with pines and abundant herbaceous vegetation. The area attracts numerous species of rare birds.

These include the crested and coal tit, the wren, the serin and the spotted fly-catcher.

Modern landscape artists like their parks to be fully integrated into local life and history. Forms are generally classical, but more modern ideas, including expanses of grass, are common. These areas of greenery are surrounded by theme gardens designed for public use.

PARC DE LA VILLETTE (11 D4)

This park was built in 1987 on the site of the old Halles: it is crossed by L'Ourcq canal and its 86 acres make it the largest green space in Paris. It was designed by Bernard Tschumi as a prototype of a 21st-century "garden

city" and links two important cultural centers, the Cité des Sciences to the north and the Cité de la Musique and the Grande Halle to the south. La Villette Park is open day and night and is noted for its walks, entertainments, shows and displays of modern art: it is extremely popular. The most striking visual elements are twenty-one red follies arranged in a

The crested lark is particularly fond of the wide open spaces of La Villette.

geometric pattern around the park. There is also an architectural promenade that gives visitors a cinematic experience of space; this leads to the theme gardens. With the exception of the Bamboo Garden (left), these are somewhat disappointing: the themes include plant life and water, imagination, play, fog, islands, children's fears and dragons.

PARC DE BELLEVILLE (3 B2)

Belleville Park was built on the side of a hill on a site covering 11 acres. Several aspects of the park are linked to local history ▲ 408. Examples include: a vine and numerous open-air cafés which call to mind the wine-growing that was once a feature of these slopes; artificial grottos which recall the old gypsum quarries; and waterfalls and pools which are reminders of the water that still flows underground. The wide-ranging selection of plants and trees are laid out in both traditional and modern styles.

Belleville Park is situated on some of the highest ground in Paris: there is a magnificent view from a belvedere at the summit.

PARC DE BERCY (4 B4)

This park, built on a site where bonded warehouses once stood, was designed as a garden of remembrance. Landmarks recall the area's history, including a paved track, warehouses, the ruins of Château

Bercy and about a hundred trees. Bercy Park was built on a classical model with broad expanses of grass, parterres and a terrace which, as in the Tuileries, runs down to the Seine. In a style evoking picturesque gardens, the parterres have four buildings dedicated to the seasons. The recent creation of a romantic garden around a canal, ending in a little island, completes the picture.

White garden

Glasshouse

Small glasshouse

Moving ga

LE PARC ANDRÉ-CITROËN (7 G6)

Since 1993 this park has marked the center of a new district constructed over the site of the old motor car factory. The White Garden to the east underlines the closeness of the city, whereas the denser, more shaded Black Garden has the reverse effect. The main area, which runs down to the quays lining the Seine, is extremely classical and encircles a broad expanse of grass. There is an

The two large greenhouses in the Parc André-Citroën, designed by Patrick Berger: one is an orangery, while the other houses southern Mediterranean flora.

esplanade at the end of the perspective, which is also marked by two enormous greenhouses framing a peristyle adorned with 120 water jets. The ubiquitous theme of water is also taken up in the grassy section with its waterfalls and large canal. To the north is a line of six gardens each dedicated to one of the senses and, by virtue of its color, associated with a type of metal. Along the riverbank, vegetation grows freely in this untended garden, a huge, unspoilt area

dotted with wild flowers and *Graminaceae.* The fallow land is also rich in flora.

Black garden

André-Citroën Park on the Left Bank was built by a team of architects and landscape artists. Its view of the Seine complements those from Champ-de-Mars and the Esplanade des Invalides.

...amorphosis garden

Rock garden

The profusion of flowers and the wild nature of this garden attract numerous insects.

The Bois de Boulogne and the Bois de Vincennes are all that remain of an enormous forest that encircled Lutetia in the 1st century. The configuration of these two "green lungs" situated at the gates to Paris dates from the Second Empire.

LE BOIS DE BOULOGNE (Map 8)

A few pairs of green woodpeckers can still be found in the Bois de Boulogne: they spend a lot of time on the ground searching for anthills.

Thousands of Parisians flock to the Bois de Boulogne every weekend. Its 2,100 acres extend from Boulogne to Neuilly and contain wooded areas, lakes, footpaths, bridle paths, cycle tracks, sports facilities and restaurants. Contained within it are numerous gardens, including the Bagatelle ▲ 207, Pré-Catelan, Shakespeare and Serres d'Auteuil ▲ 205 gardens.

A royal park and lovers' rendezvous The Bois de Boulogne is now separated from the

Rouvray Forest, which stood to the northwest of Paris in medieval times. It became a royal park in the 13th century and acquired the name "Boulogne" after Philip the Fair had a small church built there in 1301 to commemorate a pilgrimage to Boulogne-sur-Mer. The forest was opened to the public by Louis XVI in the 18th century and gained a reputation as a place for loose living: following the example of the kings of France – Francis I had turned the Château de Madrid into a lovers' rendezvous – the nobility built the châteaux of La Muette, Neuilly, La Folie St-James and Bagatelle.

A fashionable promenade in the Belle Époque
Napoleon III renovated the area as soon as he came to power: it had been badly damaged during the Revolution and Allied occupation of 1814–15. The Bois de Boulogne was linked to Paris by the Allée de l'Impératrice (now Avenue Foch), and

it was then fundamentally redesigned by Alphand ▲ *208*, who between 1852 and 1858 built 60 miles of paths, constructed lakes and rivers, and planted 400,000 trees. The addition of a children's amusement area, the Jardin de l'Acclimatation (1860), and the Pré-Catelan Garden (1855), followed by the Longchamp and Auteuil racecourses (1857 and 1873, respectively), made the Bois de

The Moulin de Longchamp (above) stands among the ruins of Longchamp Abbey in the Bois de Boulogne. The abbey, founded in 1256, was destroyed during the Revolution.

Boulogne one of the most fashionable promenades of the Belle Époque.

Flora and fauna
Three kinds of oak account for over half the trees in the Bois de Boulogne: the *chêne rouvre* (which gave its name to Rouvray Forest), the pedunculate oak and the durmast oak. The area provides natural habitats for squirrels, bats and hedgehogs, as well as dozens of species of birds, including jays, tawny owls and

carrion crows. The Bois de Boulogne also contains a bird sanctuary.

Lac Supérieur and Lac Inférieur are at different levels and are linked by a waterfall: the lower lake contains two islands. Below: the Chalet des Îles.

Bank voles are normally reddish in color, but many in the Bois de Boulogne are black. This phenomenon often occurs among animals living close to or in the middle of big cities.

Le Bois de Vincennes (Map 4)

This forest was a royal hunting ground from the 12th century until it was turned into a public park during the reign of Louis XV. There was an unhappy period in the early years of the 19th century, when part of the land was cleared for military purposes.

The rock in Vincennes Zoo is entirely artificial and was recently restored.

In fact, it narrowly avoided being used for army maneuvers, but was dubbed "Canonville" just the same. Encouraged by the success of the Bois de Boulogne, Napoleon III and the planner Haussmann decided to lay out a park of comparable dimensions to the east in 1857. Alphand and his assistants built the relief topography (Gravelle Knoll) and three lakes (Minimes, St-Mandé and Gravelle); Lake Daumesnil was added later. The forest's 2,460 acres were then reforested and crisscrossed with new pathways, and the whole area was filled with expanses of greenery, hillocks, grottos, and restaurants and other buildings. The

forest acquired a hippodrome in 1863, the Imperial Farm in 1859, and in 1867 the School of Horticulture was established with its arboretum of 850 labeled species. Other attractions were added later: they included a zoo (1934), the Floral Park (1969) ▲ *205*, and the Georges-Ville Farm (1989), designed with the specific purpose of introducing children to aspects of agriculture.

Vincennes Zoo
This replaced the Zoological Garden, which had been temporarily laid out for the Colonial Exhibition of 1931.

The common heron is sometimes seen near the lakes in the Bois de Vincennes.

130,000 trees: mainly oaks and some fifteen other species, principally beech and maple. The most common animal is the *Crocidura russula*, a species of shrew that preys on grasshoppers. Tench, roach, carp, pike, and a range of insects and frogs

It contains 550 mammals, including endangered species such as the giant panda, rare species of seal and tapir, and 700 birds.

Flora and fauna
The Bois de Vincennes has

and toads can be found in the lakes, which also attract numerous aquatic birds, including the common heron and the black-headed gull.

Along the Seine

BLACK-HEADED GULL
Flocks of black-headed gulls live around the Seine, animating the scene with their buoyant flight and shrill cries.

Thanks to progress in techniques of water treatment, the Seine is now less polluted than it has been for many years. The present cloudy appearance of the water is due simply to suspended mineral particles. As a result of this significant improvement in water quality, aquatic plants have been reintroduced, and over twenty species of fish have returned, even in the stretch of the river which runs through the city center. There is also the winter parade of gulls with their circling flight, giving the city an unexpected seaside atmosphere.

Male

Female   Herring gull   Yellow-legged gull

GRAY WAGTAIL
The wagtail scurries along the quays, pecking away as it runs.

HERRING AND YELLOW-LEGGED GULLS
The herring gull can be seen throughout the year but is more common in winter. The yellow-legged gull is a seasonal visitor and can be spotted mainly in summer and autumn. Both species adapt well to city life.

Male

KINGFISHER
This is a migratory bird that is generally seen in Paris in autumn and spring.

MALLARD
These ducks are quite tame but cautious, especially during the nesting season. Variations in plumage are common.

COOT
Only in winter can a few coots be seen on the river, driven there from frozen ponds near the capital.

Two centuries ago the Seine was used as a trading route, a washing and watering place for animals; it also had high levels of organic pollution.

DACE
This fish can tolerate poor-quality water better than many other species.

GUDGEON
Gudgeons are very gregarious fish, swimming along the riverbed in shoals.

ON THE RIVERBANKS
The riverside supports plants well suited to the conditions, both above and below water-level. Plants which thrive in damp conditions grow in the tiniest crevices.

The pretty spikes of purple loosestrife can be seen from May to August.

Mosses and algae flourish close to outflows.

Young, hardy wall rocket manages to survive in cracks.

PIKE
This powerful, well-armed predator feeds on other fish, crayfish and ducklings.

BREAM
With their flat, curved bodies adult bream stay in deep water during the day.

ROACH
Shoals of roach thread through the underwater vegetation.

Curled pondweed

The introduced aquatic vegetation attracts the fish.

Water milfoil

The calm, meandering River Seine has never been used as a defensive barrier. Long ago the islands and the Left and Right banks joined forces to form the city of Paris, largely ignoring the water running between them. However, following the construction of the Pont-Neuf and Place Dauphine under Henri IV, the city began to come to terms with this river that flowed through its heart and to integrate it into city life. The resulting quays have now been named a World Heritage Site by UNESCO.

LIBERTY MADE TO MEASURE
This statue is a miniature of the American Statue of Liberty, presented to the United States by France in 1886 to commemorate the centenary of the Declaration of Independence. *Liberty Enlightening the World* and her tiny replica are the works of Auguste Bartholdi.

1 STATUE OF LIBERTY
2 MAISON DE LA RADIO
3 ALLÉE DES CYGNES
4 SEINE WATERFRONT
5 AUTONOMOUS PORT OF PARIS

— FOOTPATH

THE SEINE, CRADLE OF PARIS ✪
Paris is intimately linked to the Seine, as its motto – *Fluctuat nec mergitur* (It pitches but does not founder) – readily proclaims. The sunny quays of the Right Bank are perfect for a stroll at the end of the day, when the setting sun bathes the Pont-Neuf and the Île de la Cité in golden light. Every Sunday in summer the bankside walks team with cyclists, rollerstakers and pedestrians. Take a pleasure boat and watch the history of Paris unfold.

AV. DU PDT KENNEDY

AV. DU PDT KENNEDY

PONT DE GRENELLE

QUAI DE GRENELLE

QUAI DE GRENELLE,

(hor

returned from the front, he secretly acquired materials: the lights, which were completed in 1941, are telescopic.

ST-NICOLAS PORT
A large port grew up during the 17th and 18th centuries close to the Louvre (**27**): it supplied the court with corn, hay, wood, vegetables and meat. The Seine brought a large amount of merchandise into Paris, most of it from

QUAI DES TUILERIES

ES TUILERIES

QUAI DU LOUVRE

27

PONT ROYAL

PONT DU CARROUSEL

QUAI VOLTAIRE

QUAI MALAQUAIS

FRANCE **25**

26

28

D'HONNEUR

DELIGNY SWIMMING POOL
Floating pools were fashionable from the 18th century onward: there was one close to the Tuileries and others beneath Pont-Neuf and near the Tournelle Bridge. The Deligny swimming pool, built near the National Assembly, sank in 1993.

THE INSTITUT DE FRANCE AND THE LOUVRE IN THE 18TH CENTURY

BIR-HAKEIM BRIDGE

by the New York architect Richard Meier, this buildingIt is notable for its aluminum façade and glass walls.

THE TOWPATH

Before the invention of steam- and gas-driven engines, boats traveling along the River Seine upstream were towed by men or horses. The towpath upstream of Paris was on the Right Bank, and trees, ports and building works were not allowed to obstruct it.

AV. DE NEW YORK

PONT DE BIR-HAKEIM

QUAI BRANLY

PONT D'IÉNA

BUILDINGS OVERLOOKING THE SEINE (4)

These twenty towers range from 164 to 295 feet tall and between 1970 and 1990 they slowly replaced the working-class district of Grenelle. While it was under construction the media criticized this "little New York" for its arrogance, the inhumanity of its architecture and its proximity to the Eiffel Tower.

6 CHAMP-DE-MARS
7 EIFFEL TOWER
8 EMBARKATION POINT

ALEXANDRE III BRIDGE

By establishing an alliance with Russia in 1893, France broke free from the diplomatic isolation that Germany had orchestrated for the previous twenty years.

This newly built bridge was named after Czar Alexander III to mark the alliance.

The candelabra are copies of lamps on Trinity Bridge in St Petersburg, and the decoration includes lions made of stone, statues glistening with gold and keystones adorned with nymphs of the Seine and the Neva.

STATUE OF ALBERT I (17)

Albert I of Belgium remained in his invaded country throughout World War One and, with help from France, he never surrendered. This statue, built in 1938, commemorates Franco-Belgian friendship.

COURS LA REINE

PONT DES INVALIDES

COURS LA REINE

PONT ALEXANDRE III

QUAI D'ORSAY

QUAI D'ORSAY

ART NOUVEAU

THE ZOUAVE ON
PONT DE L'ALMA (11)
When the bridge was rebuilt in 1974, this was the only zouave to survive. Parisians use it to measure how level of the River Seine.

HÔTEL LALIQUE (13)
This house is notable for its pinnacled windows, glass doorway and railings decorated with fir cones. It was built in 1902 in keeping with the preferences of its codesigner and first owner René Lalique.

PONT ALEXANDRE-III

COURS ALBERT IER

QUAI D'ORSAY

PONT DES INVALIDES

QUAI D'ORSAY

11 THE ZOUAVE ON PONT DE L'ALMA

12 START OF SEWER TOURS AND EMBARKATION POINT FOR THE BATEAUX-MOUCHES

14 SEITA MUSEUM AND GALLERY

15 ESPLANADE DES INVALIDES

FOR BATEAUX-
PARISIENS AND THE
VEDETTES FOR
ÎLE-ST-LOUIS

⑨ TROCADÉRO PALACE

UNIVERSAL EXHIBITIONS

Of the nine exhibitions mounted worldwide between 1855 and 1900, five took place in Paris. The Exhibition of 1900, which featured the Seine, was celebrated with boat trips and a focus on the bridges. A reconstruction of medieval Paris on Cours la Reine provided a marked contrast with the Italian, Turkish, British, Belgian and Serbian pavilions erected on the Quai d'Orsay. The new Grand Palais housed an exhibition of foreign painters.

PERSPECTIVE

When the Military Academy was built, a perspective spanning the Seine was intended. Today the line joining the Eiffel Tower, Iéna Bridge and the Trocadéro Fountains now extends as far as the Palais de Chaillot.

⑩ MUSÉE D'ART MODERNE AT THE PALAIS DE TOKYO (▲ *134*)

AV. DE NEW YORK

AV. DE NEW YORK

PASSERELLE DEBILLY

QUAI BRANLY

THE TUILERIES BY THE RIVERSIDE

The Tuileries Garden was commissioned by Catherine de' Medici in 1564 and was the first large park to be built on the banks of the Seine. Marie de' Medici later introduced the Florentine fashion for horse-driven carriage rides. The river was not lined with trees until the time of Napoleon III.

SECRET LIGHTING
Raymond Subes started work on the lamps for the Pont du Carrousel just as war

16. GRAND PALAIS
17. STATUE OF ALBERT I
18. PETIT PALAIS (▲ 169)
20. PLACE DE LA CONCORDE (▲ 316)
21. MUSÉE DE L'ORANGERIE (▲ 168)
23. JARDIN DES TUILERIES (▲ 200)

QUAI DES TUILERIES

QUAI

PONT DE LA CONCORDE

PASSERELLE SOLFÉRINO

QUAI ANATOLE FRANCE

QUAI ANATOL

France date from 1905 and are typical of the period.

FROM THE MADELEINE TO THE NATIONAL ASSEMBLY

From the Pont de la Concorde, the façade of the National Assembly is clearly a copy of the Madeleine. Pont de la Concorde is the only bridge in Paris with freestone arches.

19. NATIONAL ASSEMBLY
22. ART NOUVEAU BUILDINGS OF THE QUAI ANATOLE-FRANCE
24. MUSÉE DE LA LÉGION

25. MUSÉE D'ORSAY (▲ 160)
26. CAISSE DE DÉPOTS ET CONSIGNATIONS
28. ÉCOLE DES BEAUX-ARTS

PONT DES ARTS
(rebuilt in 1982)
In 1804 a toll
payment restricted
its use to pedestrians.

BARGES
These craft were used from the 17th century
onward to provide cheap passenger transport
and were enormously popular until they were
replaced by the railway.

THE PONT-NEUF
WRAPPED BY
CHRISTO
(1985).

**THE KING'S
ORANGES**
Mandarins,

QUAI DE LA MÉGISSERIE

E LA MÉGISSERIE

Q DE L'HORLOGE

PONT NEUF

QUAI DE CONTI

QUAI DES ORFEVRES

QUAI DES GRANDS-AUGUSTINS

PONT ST-MICHEL

PONT AU

29. COUR CARRÉE
30. INSTITUT DE
FRANCE
31. MUSÉE DE LA
MONNAIE (▲ 156)
32. ÎLE DE LA CITÉ
33. EMBARKATION
POINT FOR THE
VEDETTES DU
PONT-NEUF
36. CONCIERGERIE
37. STE-CHAPELLE AND
PALAIS DE JUSTICE
42. PRÉFECTURE OF
POLICE
43. MAGISTRATES
COURT
44. STATUE OF
CHARLEMAGNE
45. NOTRE-DAME

46. HÔTEL DES URSINS
48. DEPORTATION
MEMORIAL
49. DEVICE FOR
MEASURING THE
SEINE'S LEVEL

JARDIN DES PLANTES

In the 1500's the Jardin des Plantes was a simple garden of medicinal herbs. Louis XIII and Louis XV converted it into an enormous park specializing in botanical research.

56. INSTITUT DU MONDE ARABE
57. UNIVERSITÉ DE JUSSIEU
62. JARDIN DES PLANTES
63. GARE D'AUSTERLITZ

THE LONG-FORGOTTEN BIÈVRE

This waterway became an open-air sewer. It is now covered and part of...

During the reign of François I the foul-smelling business of...

CHARLES DE GAULLE BRIDGE (64)

Shaped like an aircraft wing and laid out with broad sidewalks and dedicated cycle lanes, the new Charles de Gaulle Bridge, opened in 1997, is the thirty-seventh bridge in Paris. It spans the Seine between the Gare de Lyon and the Gare d'Austerlitz.

50. ÎLE ST-LOUIS
51. HÔTEL DE JASSAUD
52. CHURCH OF ST-LOUIS-EN-L'ÎLE
53. PORTICO OF THE FORMER HÔTEL DE

59. ARSENAL
60. PRÉFECTURE OF PARIS
61. BOULEVARD MORLAND
64. PONT CHARLES-DE-

WATER TOURNAMENTS
The *nautes* (Parisian boatmen) organized tournaments on public holidays: the events included races, the uprooting of targets and throwing competitors into the water. Tournaments are still organized in May on the Bassin de la Villette.

CÉLESTINS

QUAI HENRI-IV

ORGES-POMPIDOU

VOIE GEORGES-POMPIDOU

PONT MARIE

OURBON

QUAI D4ANJOU

BOURBON

QUAI DE BÉTHUNE

PONT DE LA TOURNELLE

PONT DE SULLY

PONT DE SULLY

QUAI ST-BERNARD

TOURNELLE

49

with holes in the hull. These occupations were probably carried out in tandem.

NOTRE-DAME FROM THE TOURNELLE BRIDGE

BOTTLENECKS ON THE SEINE

The worst bottlenecks on the Seine occurred during the 18th century when arches, quays, the pillars of houses and the foundations of mills began to encroach into the river. Near Châtelet the Seine has narrowed by 131 feet as a result of centuries of building. It was only in 1762 that the authorities decided to remove the corbeled houses from the riverside and bridges: with that Paris began to have a much less cluttered appearance, but lost some of its Venetian charm.

THE "BRIDGE SWALLOWERS" AND THE WATERMEN

During the Middle Ages the narrow arches of the upstream bridges made navigation hazardous and boatmen had

INSTITUTE OF THE ARAB WORLD (56)

The architects Jean

QUAI DE L'HOTEL DE VILLE

QUAI D

PONT LOUIS-PHILIPPE

PONT MARIE

PONT ST-LOUIS

50

51

52

PONT DE L'ARCHEVÊCHÉ

PONT DE LA TOURNELLE

QUAI MONTEBELLO

QUAI DE LA TOURNELLE

"bridge swallowers" were authorized to do this work. Boats could be hauled against the tide with the help of rings that can still be seen under the bridges.

WATER AND GAS SUPPLY
The Louis-Philippe and Bercy bridges are decorated with bull's-eye windows that mark the water and gas lines on them.

LOUVIERS ISLAND
A branch of the Seine once flowed over what is now Boulevard Morland. The island was used for storing wood: firewood was stacked out in the open to dry, while timber unloaded onto the Quai de la Rapée was for the use of woodworkers in nearby Faubourg St-Antoine.

isolation techniques in the construction of this building, including photo-electric cells in windows to filter light.

LOUIS XIV'S favorite fruit, were sold on this bridge during the 17th century.

BIRDCATCHERS
From 1600 onward canaries, warblers, quails, goldfinches, linnets, chaffinches, larks, starlings and blackbirds were sold between the Pont-Neuf and the Pont au Change. Bird catching has been forbidden between May and August.

CONCIERGERIE ▲ 366
SAINTE GENEVIÈVE
This woman's once dissuaded the Huns from attacking Lutetia: she became the patron saint of Paris. This statue made in 1928 by Paul Landowski has her facing east.

Q. DE GESVRES
QUAI DE L'HOTEL-DE-VILLE
PONT NOTRÉ-DAME
PONT D'ARCOLE
QUAI DE
LA CORSE
BD DU PALAIS
CHANGE
RUE DE LA CITÉ
RUE D'ARCOLE
PONT LOUIS-PHILIPPE
PONT ST-LOUIS
QUAI DE
DU-MARCHÉ-NEUF
PETIT PONT
PONT AU DOUBLE
PORT DE MONTEBELLO
PONT DE L'ARCHEVÊCHÉ
QUAI ST-MICHEL
QUAI DE MONTEBELLO
QUAI DE LA

No!
This poster was part of a campaign mounted by Paris-lovers in 1973 against a project to build a freeway on the Left Bank. The plan was withdrawn on the death of President Pompidou in 1974.

FLOATING WASH HOUSES AND FISHING BOATS
Washerwomen used to wash clothes in the Seine and dry them in the open air on their boats on the quayside. The current that ran past the Île de la Cité was slow and, to avoid epidemics, the washerwomen were sometimes banned from

MINISTRY OF FINANCE (66)
Paul Chemetov and Huidobro Borja designed this building as a combination of gate to the city and bridge half immersed in the Seine. The Ministry of Finance moved here from the Louvre in 1989.

THE APPLE PORT
Until World War One the fruit market was based at the port of Grève and mainly sold apples. The boats were turned into shops by having tarpaulins drawn over them: in winter the fruit was left out in the open.

PEE

QUAI DE BERCY

PONT DE BERCY

THE HALLES AT BERCY
Napoleon III's enormous Halles at Bercy supplied Paris with produce between 1860 and 1970. A few of the original buildings are preserved in Bercy Park.

C. BLANC

PARLOIR DE BERCY

▲ Bibliothèque François Mitterrand

The project to build the monumental Bibliothèque de France, known as the "Très Grande Bibliothèque", was first announced by President Mitterrand in 1988, but the design evolved greatly over the intervening years. Renamed for the late president, it opened to the public in 1996. Its four towers stand upriver from Gare d'Austerlitz and overlook the Left Bank of the Seine.

A TURBULENT HISTORY

President Mitterrand announced the decision to build a "very large library" (Très Grande Bibliothèque) of an entirely new type on July 14, 1988 – a construction project of great ambition. The library was to cover all fields of knowledge, be accessible to all, use the most modern data transmission technology, be available for consultation over long distances, and establish links with the other great libraries of Europe. One effect has been to highlight the plight of the present Bibliothèque Nationale ▲ 341; it is sent over fifty thousand books and other items of printed material every year, and its 75 miles of shelves are reaching saturation point. The new library holds between ten and twelve million books, including the books formerly held in Rue de Richelieu.

FOUR OPEN BOOKS

The design by architect Dominique Perrault consists of four open-book-shaped towers framing a ground-level garden, visible from the terraces or lecture rooms. The height of the towers has been reduced from 328 ft to 262 ft. The towers contain offices and book storage areas: the first floor and garden level are surrounded by storage areas and divided into open-access reading rooms and facilities for researchers. The two floors are divided into four sections: philosophy, history and human sciences; political, legal and economic science; science and technology; and literature and art.

COLLECTIVE CATALOGUE
This combines the computer networks of the eighty-four main libraries in France.

PRESERVING THE BOOKS
The glass towers have air conditioning, storage spaces made of reinforced concrete and covered with brass and copper, and wooden isolation shutters, in order to protect the books kept there.

Itineraries in Paris

1. Jardins du Luxembourg
2. Senate
3. Théâtre de l'Odéon
4. Réfectoire des Cordeliers

🕐 **Half a day**

WHERE CREATIVITY KNOWS NO BOUNDS
The spirit of St-Germain-des-Prés is embodied in detective stories such as the *Série noire* and magazines like *Les Temps Modernes*. Other examples include *Exercices de*

Style by Raymond Queneau, which Yves Robert made into a film entitled *La Rose rouge*, starring a team of athletic songsters, the Jacques Brothers (above); and Alfred Jarry's *Ubu Roi* and Jean-Paul Sartre's *No Exit* at the Théâtre du Vieux-Colombier.

The legendary rectangle of St-Germain-des-Prés is a round-the-clock melting pot of elderly residents, innumerable tourists, businesses that are constantly opening and closing down, street entertainers and the traditional hubbub of students and people visiting publishing houses. The most popular meeting places are the famous cafés and brasseries which date from the district's glory days (Lipp, Le Flore, Les Deux-Magots and La Rhumerie) and newer ones at the Odéon crossroads and Place St-André-des-Arts.

THE GRANDE ÉPOQUE

As early as the 1920's, St-Germain-des-Prés was a focal point for students, writers and artists living on the Left Bank. The war put a stop to this for a while, but writers and artists were soon lured back by the warmth of local cafés which had not been requisitioned: Jean-Paul Sartre and Simone de Beauvoir were only two of the many intellectuals who patronized Le Flore. The Liberation resulted in an explosion of intellectual fervor, and it was here that Existentialism found its natural breeding ground. This period not only had its high priests, like Sartre and Albert Camus, but also boasted temples in the form of wine bars such as Le Tabou and Le Lorientais. These echoed to new jazz rhythms – the clarinets of Sidney Bechet and Claude Luter and the trumpet of Boris Vian (left), an engineer, talented writer and organizer of local St-Germain activities. The period found its faithful in young people who were promptly carried away by their newfound freedom. The district also became immensely fashionable, and the American press was largely responsible for making St-Germain-des-Prés the "world meeting place for the intellectual and artistic élite".

TODAY. St-Germain is no longer the little village it was back in the 1950's, and reality has surpassed the legends: with its maze of winding, crisscrossing streets, its art galleries, its antique and book shops and its luxury boutiques, St-Germain is still a pleasure to live in and to visit. There are also wonderful strolls along the quays and in the Luxembourg Gardens.

ORIGINALLY AN ABBEY

HALF LEGEND, HALF HISTORY. When the son of Clovis, Childebert I, returned from the Iberian peninsula in 542, he brought back the tunic of Saint Vincent and rich booty, including a golden Toledan cross, probably the work of Salomon. Saint Germanus, then Bishop of Paris, advised the Merovingian king to construct a holy place to house these precious relics, and the Basilica of Ste-Croix and St-Vincent was built in 557; a monastery was added shortly afterward. The name St-Germain became established around the 9th century. Saint Germanus himself granted the abbey independence from episcopal jurisdiction. When he died in 576, large numbers of pilgrims gathered around his tomb, expecting a miracle. He was initially buried in the small St-Symphorien Chapel, close to the clock-tower porch; however, in 756 his remains were transferred to the basilica itself in the course of a religious ceremony that took place in the presence of Pippin the Short (715–68) and his son Charlemagne (747–814), then aged twelve. The basilica was used as a burial place for the Frankish kings until Dagobert.

LIBERTY! LIBERTY!
"Beneath a pack of lies and speculation there lay a sliver of reality. The anxiety of those searching for themselves with a crazy desire for meeting up, for friendship, for sharing and exchanging; the cruel laugh of youth and the learning about our newfound liberty. We derive pleasure from every iota of meaning we can squeeze out of the word liberty."
Juliette Gréco
Jujube

235

The abbey underwent further decoration and was given immense tracts of land. It attracted much envy, and the building was frequently pillaged by Barbarian invaders ● *16*.

THE ABBEY'S RENAISSANCE. A new basilica was built over the original Merovingian foundations in 990. A small town emerged and grew steadily. The abbey was situated beyond the confines of the royal walls (*enceintes*) ● *54* and was therefore obliged to develop its own system of defense.

After roads were built during the 14th century, the appearance of the town did not alter for another three hundred years.

SPIRITUAL RENEWAL AND INTELLECTUAL ASCENDANCY. After the Wars of Religion, a reform movement took hold of the Catholic Church, and in 1631 the abbey adopted the Rule of the Benedictines of Saint Maurus. By 1647, the Monastery of St-Germain-des-Prés had become the order's mother house, and it was soon one of Europe's leading intellectual centers, under such scholars as Dom Mabillon (1632–1717), the monastery's historian Dom Bouillart (1632–1707) and Dom Montfaucon (1655–1741).

THE REVOLUTION. After religious orders were abolished, on February 13, 1790, the monks were dispersed or, in many cases, executed. Their library, which was confiscated, contained about fifty thousand volumes and seven thousand manuscripts, including Pascal's *Pensées*; the Bibliothèque Nationale has around a thousand manuscripts which were saved from the fire of 1794. This splendid building was destroyed during the Revolution, and much of what remained was pulled down during construction work on the Rue de l'Abbaye in 1800. All that remains are the church and Abbot's Palace, and they survive only thanks to an energetic campaign that was led by Victor Hugo.

THE ABBOT'S CHURCH   ● *60* (1 J8)

The Church of St-Germain-des-Prés, which was reconsecrated in 1803, is notable for the abundant restoration work carried out between 1819 and the present day.

> "Place St-Germain-des-Prés . . . one of the few spots in the capital where you feel most up to date, and closest both to true reality and to the men who know what is really going on in the country, the world and in art."
>
> Léon-Paul Fargue

EXTERIOR ★. The Romanesque DOORWAY was badly damaged during the Revolution and is now covered over by a 17th-century porch. Only the side façades of the CLOCK-TOWER PORCH (990–1014), with bays adorned with Moorish arches, have preserved their original appearance. The flying buttresses of the chevet were among the first to be designed in a new architectural style.

INTERIOR. (Brochure available inside the entrance.) THE NAVE dates from the 11th century, and the original framework, still visible, was vaulted in the 17th century. The CHOIR was rebuilt around 1145 on the model of the St-Denis Basilica ▲ *432* and Sens Cathedral; it was consecrated in 1163 by Pope Alexander III. Of great interest are a 15th-century *Virgin and Child*, which comes from Notre-Dame; a splendid CRUCIFIX next to the left-hand pillar in the nave; and some 13th-century stained-glass windows in the Ste-Geneviève Chapel (the work of Pierre de Montreuil ▲ *362*), originally in the Virgin Chapel.

ST-SYMPHORIEN CHAPEL ★ (On the right, before the railing at the entrance to the church). This was built on the site of Saint Germanus' first burial place. Archeological excavations in the 1970's revealed both the Merovingian foundations and, on the intrados of the arch on the south wall, a FRAGMENT OF A MURAL PAINTING dating from the 13th century.

PALAIS ABBATIAL ★ (3 *bis*, rue de l'Abbaye). The bosses and pediments give the architecture of the Abbot's Palace (1586–1699) a strong classical sense of restraint. The palace prefigures much of the Place Royale ▲ *396*.

PLACE DE FÜRSTENBERG ★
This square is in the former courtyard of the Abbot's Palace. A pillar surmounted by a flame ornament on the corner of the Rue de Fürstenberg is a remnant of the monastery's northern entrance. The Delacroix Museum at no. 6 occupies what remains of the outhouses belonging to the Abbot's Palace.

PLACE
SAINT
SULPICE

"There is a lot to see in Place St-Sulpice, like the Mayor's Office, a financial institution, a police station, three cafés (one of which sells

tobacco), a cinema, a church with work by Le Vau, Gittard, Oppenord, Servandoni and Chalgrin (and dedicated to Clotaire II's chaplain who was Bishop of Bourges from 624 to 644 and whose feast day is January 17), a publishing house, an undertaker's, a travel agency, a bus stop, a tailor, a hotel, a fountain decorated by statues of the four great Christian orators (Bossuet, Fénelon, Fléchier and Massillon), a newspaper stall, a man selling devotional articles, a car park, a beauty clinic and many more things besides."

Georges Pérec
Attempt to Coax Everything out of Some Place in Paris

CHURCH OF ST-SULPICE (1 J9

Reconstruction work on this 13th-century building commenced during the 1600's but it took 135 years, and each stage was marked by developments in architectural style.

EXTERIOR. In 1733 this Jesuit-style church was given an extraordinarily austere monumental façade: first Doric and then Ionic pillars were added later. The façade, which was never completed, was designed by Jean-Nicolas Servandoni (1695–1766), a painter, architect, decorator and noted rococo artist. The unfinished south tower was built by Maclaurin in 1749 and the north tower by Chalgrin in 1777–8.

INTERIOR ★. The proportions of this church are stunning. The ground plan is similar to that found in Gothic churches. The plinths under the two fonts for holy water in the form of giant shellfish were carved by Jean-Baptiste Pigalle. The choir is adorned with statues by Edme Bouchardon (1698–1762) ▲ 268. Other fine rococo pieces include the tomb of the *curé* Languet de Gergy by Michel-Ange Slodtz and the wainscoting in the sacristy. The VIRGIN CHAPEL was built by Servandoni and restored by Charles de Wailly ▲ 240, who also designed the pulpit in 1788 (above, left). François Lemoyne ▲ 264 painted the frescos on the cupola, Pigalle carved the *Virgin and Child*, and Van Loo did the paintings on either side of the altar. The HOLY ANGELS' CHAPEL, decorated with three frescos by Delacroix between 1853 and 1863, is also of interest. The ORGAN by F.A. Cliquot (1781) was restored by Aristide Cavaillé-Coll in the 19th century: it has a beautiful Louis XVI organ case designed by Chalgrin. Among the virtuoso organists who have played here are Charles-Marie Widor and Marcel Dupré. Many people still come to listen to this fine instrument every Sunday.

THE SENATE ★ (2 A9)

On the Left Bank of the Seine is the Luxembourg Palace (the seat of the Senate) and its garden which harmoniously combines architecture and modernity, history and the art of garden design.

MARIE DE' MEDICI'S PALACE. Widow of Henry IV, this Florentine queen chose faubourg St-Germain-des-Prés in her search for a garden to add to her residence. Her architect, Salomon de Brosse, an artist greatly influenced by Androuet du Cerceau and the Renaissance, synthesized French tradition and Florentine ideas taken from the Pitti Palace. The palace, built 1612 to 1622, follows the classical ground plan of a French château.

INTERIOR DECORATION. During her regency for her son, Louis XIII, Marie added sumptuous decorations to her second-floor apartments in the southwest of the palace. The painted ceiling panels and the wainscoting are elaborately decorated in gold and azure, and are adorned with arabesques that provided settings for series of paintings. A cycle of twenty-four canvases representing the life of Marie de' Medici (above: *Marie de' Medici as Bellona*) was painted for the west gallery by Rubens. It now hangs in the Louvre. After her final break with her son the king and exile in 1630, the palace passed to her second son, Gaston d'Orléans, after whom it was named. In 1778, Louis XVI gave it to his brother, the future Louis XVIII.

A NATIONAL PALACE. When the palace was taken over by the state in 1792, all of its art collections were removed. The Constitution of the year III declared the palace to be the seat of the Directoire and thereby gave it a new lease on life. Chalgrin refurbished it by building a neoclassical peristyle in the main hall and adding a main staircase, conference room and museum. In 1814 the Restoration turned it into the Chamber of Peers, but

following alterations by Henri de Gisors in 1834, the palace took on the appearance of a national assembly. Gisors enlarged it on the side facing the garden by building a new, identical façade and doubled the number of pavilions. He also designed the conference chamber (above), the Throne Gallery, the library and several salons.

THE SENATE
The Senate is the direct successor to the Chamber of Peers and the Republican Senate, its functions having varied according to the political regime that happens to be in power. Under the Constitution of the Fifth Republic, the Senate and the National Assembly make up the French Parliament and vote on laws and control government activities; Senators themselves may propose and amend laws. In 1750 it became the first public museum in France and still has rooms managed by a museum built in 1886 and used for temporary exhibitions.

A house sign outside 18, rue des Canettes: it gave its name to one of the streets leading into Place St-Sulpice.

THÉÂTRE DE L'ODÉON

(2 B9) ● *68*

Peyre and Wailly's plan to build a theater on the grounds of
the Hôtel de Condé was one of the last examples of large-
scale building carried out during the Ancien Régime
(1778–81). It resolved the constraints imposed by traffic
(roads converging and thereby facilitating the comings and
goings of carriages) and responded to the new esthetic
imperatives of adorning the city with
styles inspired by ancient designs. The
Théâtre de l'Odéon opened on April 9,
1782 with a performance given by the
Comédiens du Roi (king's actors).
Decorations to the square added shortly
afterward respected the theater's
overall architectural design. The
theater was twice destroyed by
fire, and an identical model
was built in 1819, although
on this occasion the two
side arches flanked by
pavilions (above) were
omitted. The Odéon was
further damaged when it was
occupied by student protesters
in May 1968 ● *34*, but it is now
making a new name for itself
as the Odéon-Théâtre de
l'Europe.

INTERIOR. The ceiling was decorated by André Masson in
1965. The small Salle Roger-Blin was added in 1967, allowing
the introduction of experimental theater.

RUE DE L'ÉCOLE-DE-MÉDECINE

(2 B8 and 9)

Rue des Cordeliers follows the route of an old Gallo-Roman
road. It was renamed Rue de l'École-de-Médecine during the
Revolution, when the schools of Surgery (at no. 5) and
Medicine (in Rue de la Bûcherie) were brought together in a
single neoclassical building (1775) at no. 12.
REFECTORY OF THE CORDELIER MONASTERY ★ (no. 15). This
was started in the 14th century and completed in the 16th.
It consists of fourteen bays supported by fine buttresses which
may be seen on the side walls. The refectory was on the first
floor and the novices' sleeping quarters were on the second.
The west façade has preserved its original two doors. The

largely wooden interior has been badly damaged, although the original beams and posts are on view during special occasions.

SCHOOL OF MEDICINE AND SURGERY (no. 12). The school was constructed over the cloister of the Cordelier Monastery and was opened in 1775. It was built by Jacques Gondoin, an architect adept at the architecture of antiquity ● 68.

THE DEATH OF MARAT Charlotte Corday (1768–93) held Marat responsible for the fall of her Girondin friends and for the Reign of Terror. She asked to see him, and on July 13, 1793, Marat received her in his bath and she stabbed him to death. She was executed shortly afterward.

Danton (1759–94) founded the Club des Cordeliers in 1790 in what was left of the monastery: this club played a key role during the Revolution, particularly in the fall of the monarchy. Marat (1743–93), famous for his vehement attacks on those in power, was murdered by Charlotte Corday in his house in the nearby Rue Antoine-Dubois; he was buried in the monastery garden.

The School of Medicine was enlarged (toward Boulevard St-Germain and on either side) in the late 19th century by Paul Ginain and is now part of the Université René-Descartes-Paris-V. It has preserved its old library and today houses the Museum of the History of Medicine.

ST-ANDRÉ-DES-ARTS QUARTER ★   (2 BC8)

A stroll along these narrow streets lined with houses mostly dating from the 17th and 18th centuries is recommended. Much of their charm – balconies decorated with wrought iron, keystones and medallions – is above eye level.

PLACE AND RUE ST-ANDRÉ-DES-ARTS. The square (below) was built when Rue Danton was laid out over the site of both the Collège d'Autun and the former Church of St-André-des-Arts (1211–15), which was destroyed in the early 19th century. Rue St-André-des-Arts once led up to the St-Germain Abbey; it is now a bustling modern street.

Cour du Commerce-St-André is a small courtyard which leads into Cour de Rohan, a stunningly beautiful spot.

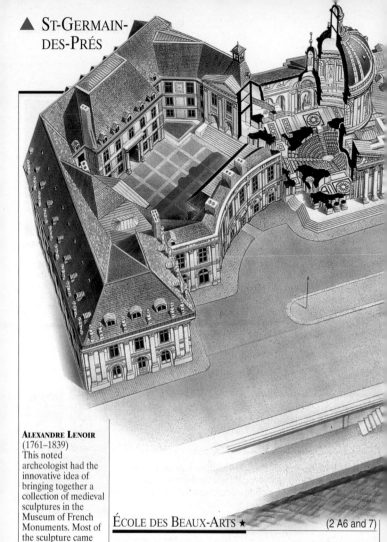

ALEXANDRE LENOIR
(1761–1839)
This noted
archeologist had the
innovative idea of
bringing together a
collection of medieval
sculptures in the
Museum of French
Monuments. Most of
the sculpture came
from churches taken
over by the state
during the
Revolution. The
museum was one of
Paris' main tourist
attractions until it was
closed down in 1816.

ÉCOLE DES BEAUX-ARTS ★   (2 A6 and 7)

This School of Fine Art is housed in three buildings: the
remains of the Petit-Augustin Monastery (since 1806), built by
Marguerite de Valois in the early 17th century; the 17th-to-
18th-century Hôtel de Chimay; and a striking building added
by François Debret and Félix Duban in the 19th century.
MONASTERY OF THE PETITS-AUGUSTINS (14, rue Bonaparte).
Against the gable over the entrance to the church (1617) is
the central avant-corps from the façade of the Château
d'Anet (Eure-et-Loir), a fine work executed by
Philibert Delorme between 1547 and 1555.
The church contains a museum of Renaissance
moldings, and under the oldest dome in Paris
(1608) the Louanges Chapel houses a
collection of Michelangelo replicas. Here in1795
the archeologist Alexandre Lenoir founded the
Museum of French Monuments (left) ▲ *158*.

INSTITUT DE FRANCE ★   (2 B7)

The Institut de France, which was founded by
the Directory in 1795 to replace the learned
societies suppressed in 1793 by the Convention,

Hôtel de la Monnaie (2 B8) ▲ 156

The reasoning behind this design for the Mint by Jacques-Denis Antoine (1733–1801) was the impossibility of building a factory to manufacture coins and medals in a palace that truly matched the nation's opulence. Industrial and monumental architecture were closely related and were in keeping with

the new neoclassical style of the period. The Administration of Coins and Medals comes under the Ministry of Finance. It issues French currency and is responsible for manufacturing all legal tender. The Mint is one of the few metal works in the center of Paris, and its coin press rooms also turn out collection coins, official decorations and jewels.

THE FIVE ACADEMIES
The most famous is the French Academy, founded by Richelieu in 1635. The others are the Academy of Inscriptions and Letters (1663), the Academy of Sciences (1666) and the Academy of Fine Arts – which combined the academies of Painting and Sculpture (1648) and Architecture (1671) in 1816 – were founded by Colbert. The Academy of Moral and Political Sciences was established in 1795.

brings together five academies that have elected 325 members. Since 1805 it has housed the Collège des Quatre-Nations, itself founded thanks to a bequest by Cardinal Mazarin (1612–61). The institute was constructed on a general plan by Le Vau, who located it on the banks of the Seine, in view of the royal apartments in the Louvre. The institute's magnificent architecture extends from the chapel, the celebrated cupola of academic assemblies to the two quarter-circle wings ending in two square pavilions. The East Pavilion houses the MAZARIN LIBRARY, the first public library in France; its superb wainscoting is all that survives from the religious and civic libraries that existed before the Revolution.

ROLE OF THE INSTITUTE. The institute now devotes itself to the patronage and encouragement of letters, arts and science. Thanks to a very substantial cultural heritage, mainly consisting of the Jacquemart-André Museum, and the châteaux of Chantilly and Langeais, the institute embodies a unique French tradition through the prizes it awards annually, the initiatives that it sponsors and through its learned publications and meetings.

The Seine flows through the middle of the longest library in the world. The secondhand-book stalls extend for 2½ miles, from the Musée d'Orsay to Pont de Sully, selling everything from masterpieces to minor works of little value. Rain or shine, these booksellers, known as the "peasants of Paris", cling to their sections of the parapet as if their lives depended on it. They are very much a part of the spirit of Paris.

Booksellers have given inspiration to many painters: (above) *Booksellers on Quai de la Mégisserie* (1900), by Galien-Laloue. They also have their eulogists: one was the writer Anatole France, an indefatigable friend of those men "so battered by the air, the rain, the frost, the fog and the sunshine that they end up looking like old statues in cathedrals".

The first booksellers worked along Quai Voltaire on the Left Bank and on Quai de la Mégisserie on the Right Bank. The more recent arrivals have their stalls on the Quai des Célestins.

The City of Paris has granted 245 bookseller concessions: they are renewable each year and give the bookseller use of 27 feet of parapet. Moreover, so as not to disturb the view of passersby, the stall may not be more than 3½ ft high with the canopy open. Stalls sell a wide range of goods, from tourist postcards to first editions of Baudelaire's *Les Fleurs du Mal*.

The booksellers are always getting into trouble with the authorities. When André Malraux was Minister of Culture (1959–69), he banned them from ever using the quays alongside the Louvre.

"Bouquinville"

The road to fortune – from the purgatory of Quai Voltaire, Quai St-Bernard and Quai des Célestins to the paradise of "Bouquinville" (literally "book city", a number of shops around Place St-Michel) – can take generations.

A LONG-ESTABLISHED TRADE

The history of Paris' secondhand-book sellers goes back some four hundred years: it takes in hawkers peddling "subversive" books and playing hide-and-seek with the police on the Pont-Neuf to their modern successors working their parapets along the quays. The word used to describe secondhand-book sellers (*bouquinistes*) dates from the 18th century and is derived from *bouc* (foul odor); it refers to the musty smell of leather and paper that emanated from their stalls or from the Dutch word *boekin* (small book). Their work was not legalized until 1859.

▲ LATIN QUARTER

1. CHURCH OF ST-SÉVERIN
2. CHURCH OF ST-JULIEN-LE-PAUVRE
3. MUSÉE CLUNY
4. THE SORBONNE
5. COLLÈGE DE FRANCE
6. CHURCH OF ST-ÉTIENNE-DU-MONT
7. THE PANTHÉON
8. VAL-DE-GRÂCE
9. PORT-ROYAL
10. CHURCH OF ST-MÉDARD
11. THE ARENA
12. THE MOSQUE
13. JARDIN DES PLANTES
14. INSTITUT DU MONDE ARABE

The Latin Quarter is somehow immutable yet still changing. Although it has not lost any of its soul or high spirits, it is also no longer what it once was. The fountain in Place St-Michel (2 C8) has become the meeting place for young people from all over the world – and also for individuals on the margins of society for whom Latin is not exactly the *lingua franca*. Today the Boul'Mich (Boulevard St-Michel) has been taken over by secondhand-clothes dealers and hamburger stalls, the RER drops off legions of suburban dwellers every morning, la Mouffe (Rue Mouffetard) and Rue St-Séverin have been colonized by Oriental restaurants and pizza parlors, the former École Polytechnique (2 D10) in Rue Descartes has emigrated to the suburbs, and the Sorbonne (2 C9) now occupies only part of what has become a fragmented university.

ST-VICTOR ABBEY
(2 EF10)
The famous scholar Guillaume de Champeaux (c. 1070–1121) taught here from 1108. It was on his advice that King Louis VI (1080–1137) built an abbey here in 1113. The abbey acquired an enviable reputation but was torn down in 1811.

COLLÈGE DE LOUIS LE GRAND

PRAYER AND STUDY

As the name suggests, the Latin Quarter has been marked by two traditions: religious and university life.

RELIGIOUS FOUNDATIONS. The foundation on the hilltop of a sanctuary, which later became Ste-Geneviève Abbey, is attributed to King Clovis (c. 456–511). In 1113 Louis IV founded St-Victor Abbey in the vicinity of Place Jussieu (2 EF10). Many religious communities subsequently settled around these two abbeys, which attracted large numbers of people, for whom parish churches were also built. The piety that marked the time of Louis XIV's reign accentuated the religious atmosphere of the place. Anne of Austria sought to revive the tradition of the early royal foundations and had the magnificent Val-de-Grâce monastery ▲ 258 constructed, older buildings extravagantly redecorated or partly rebuilt (including the nave and choir of the Church of St-Nicolas-du-Chardonnet) and new churches erected; these included the Church of St-Jacques-du-Haut-Pas, whose Jansenist austerity recalls the nearby Port-Royal Convent ▲ 257.

UNIVERSITY AND COLLEGES. The hilltop gained its intellectual standing with the arrival of dissident masters like Abelard during the 12th century, who brought with them their own retinues of scholars. This movement culminated in the establishment of the university statutes ● 22 and in the opening of colleges. Teaching at the University of Paris was of a higher standard than at Bologna and Oxford, but it was also rooted in scholasticism and soon yielded to the renewed assaults of humanism. In the 16th century François I founded the Collège de France ▲ 253 and the Jesuits opened the prestigious Clermont College; during the 17th century, science was served by the establishment of the Jardin des Plantes ▲ 204 and the Observatory ▲ 259. This concentration of learning continued with the foundation of the École Normale Supérieure and the École Polytechnique during the Revolution, the establishment of the two largest *lycées* in Paris (Louis-le-Grand, formerly Clermont College, and Henri IV, on the site of the Ste-Geneviève Abbey) under the Empire, and the revival of the Sorbonne ▲ 251 during the Third Republic.

THE FASHIONABLE LATIN QUARTER ✪
From October to May, on weekdays, why not join the crowds of students flocking to the Sorbonne? Few of the lecture theaters are open to visitors but it is pleasant to stroll in the courtyard or under the arcades. During exhibitions, the chapel of Ste-Ursule, where Richelieu is buried, is open to visitors. Nearby are the quiet streets of the hill of Ste-Geneviève, and Saint-Germain-des-Prés, is as lively and fashionable as ever.

ST-MICHEL FOUNTAIN
Haussmann ● 74 had the St-Michel Fountain built so as to create a focal point at the end of the Boulevard du Palais. Gabriel Davioud (1823–81), who was given the commission, drew his inspiration from the Trevi Fountain in Rome and the Marie de' Medici Fountain in the Luxembourg Gardens. Beneath a triumphal arch, the fountain's main decorative element, stands a bronze statue of Saint Michael slaying the dragon by François-Joseph Duret (1804–65). The result is a Second Empire pastiche.

St-Séverin (2 CD8)

The old cobbled streets of the St-Séverin Quarter are very popular with tourists. The first jazz club, Le Caveau de la Huchette, in Rue de la Huchette, has remained faithful to this kind of music, and the plays of Ionesco continue to be performed at the Petit Théâtre de la Huchette, as they have since 1957. Rue St-Séverin is another bustling street: on the other side of Rue St-Jacques, it turns into picturesque Rue Galande and leads into the Maubert district, also known as la Maube. The area between the Musée de la Police and the Musée de l'Assistance Publique ▲ *136* is a delightful place for a stroll. Above left, a charming little square on the corner of Rue de la Bûcherie and Rue des Grands-Degrés.

CHURCH OF ST-SÉVERIN ★ (1, rue des Prêtres-St-Séverin). The main attraction of this parish church, rebuilt in 1495, is the ingenious construction of its processional corridor: it contains an extraordinary PALM GROVE, which makes St-Séverin one of Paris' best examples of Flamboyant Gothic style. There is some confusion over the dedication to Saint Séverin the Solitary (he had an oratory on this site around a Merovingian necropolis) and another dedication to one Saint Severinus, the Abbot of St-Maurice-d'Agaune of Switzerland, who was a friend of King Clovis.

EXTERIOR. This church boasts many excellent examples of Flamboyant style; the clock tower (1250) contains the oldest bell in Paris (1412).

INTERIOR. The choir was restored in the Italianesque style of the 17th century; it contains what is probably the oldest triforium in Paris. The twenty rib vaults of the apse spring from the middle of the processional path around an EXTRAORDINARY

SHAKESPEARE AND CO.
(2 D8, 37, rue de la Bûcherie)
This unusual English-language
bookstore sells books both old and
new: it is run by the grandson of
Walt Whitman.

WREATHED PILLAR (right) and then separate before falling
back on the supporting pillars with a grace only the greatest
artists can execute. Also of interest are two paintings: *Saint
Luke Writing the Gospel* (against the wall of the clock tower),
from the French School of the 17th century, and a *Crucifixion*
(opposite) painted on wood by Jan Bruegel (1568–1625). The
stained-glass windows in the first three bays have been restored,
but they are the only surviving work of 14th-century glass
painting. The decoration in the upper part of the nave and apse
are excellent examples of 15th- and 16th-century art. The
Church of St-Séverin is also well known for its concerts: its
18th-century organ is considered to be one
of the finest in Paris.

ST-JULIEN-LE-PAUVRE. The tiny Church of
St-Julien-le-Pauvre stands in the Square
Viviani. Dante is said to have prayed here,
and the square boasts the oldest tree in
Paris, a false acacia planted in 1620
(below). The Cluniac monks from
Longpont Abbey, northwest of Paris, had
the 6th-century basilica rebuilt in 1165 over
the foundations and on the plan of the original church: they
enclosed it within a priory. The University ● *22* frequently
used the premises, but following the contested election of a
rector in 1564 students sacked the church, and the priory's
decline was further accelerated. It was finally razed in the
17th century: the nave and the south aisle were separated
from two bays and the Gothic façade was replaced. The
church was used for storing salt during the Revolution; since
1889, it has been run by the Catholic sect of Melchites.

Jazz ambience at the
Caveau de la
Huchette.

**THE FALSE ACACIA
IN THE SQUARE
VIVIANI** (2 D8)
This false acacia
(*robinier*) takes its
name from J. Robin,
who brought back
some acacia seeds
from America in 1661
and sowed them in his
garden. Many acacias
were later
transplanted, but this
one is probably the
doyen of all the
acacias in
Paris.

EXTERIOR. The buttresses supporting the apsidioles and the
apse are typical of 12th-century architecture. The absence of
flying buttresses is justified by the church's small dimensions.
INTERIOR. The capitals of the columns to the south are
decorated with four harpies, "heads of
women hatched in the nests of eagles",
according to Huysmans. The
iconostasis (a screen
separating the nave from
the sanctuary in
Byzantine churches)
conceals the full
glory of the Gothic
design: since 1900 it has
been decorated with a
supplication by
a Damascan
artist.

5ᵉ Arr¹
RUE DANTE
1265 · 1321 · POÈTE ITALIEN

THE WELL-CONSTRUCTED ROMAN BATHS
The walls of the Roman Baths consist of regular layers of rubble alternating with rows of bricks, which were probably covered with plaster in ancient times. The baths are in remarkably good condition – the vaults and mortar of the *frigidarium* have survived despite the weight of the hanging garden built in the Middle Ages.

THE HÔTEL DE CLUNY AND A NEW DECORATIVE STYLE
The Flamboyant, exuberant décor of curves and countercurves was challenged by a play of rectilinear forms that anticipated classicism. The top of

the accoladed arches in the West Gallery is an example of this challenge: note the vertical impact of the mullioned windows and the horizontal presentation of the lintels, which contrast with the parallel lines of the balustrade of the covered way.

ROMAN BATHS AND THE HÔTEL DE CLUNY ★

(2 C9) 6, place Paul-Painlevé. This Paris house of the monks of Cluny-en-Bourgogne is a rare example of late-medieval civil architecture and a magnificent illustration of Flamboyant Gothic style. It was built between 1485 and 1498 over the former Gallo-Roman baths ● 56. The medieval house and the Roman remains are now a museum ▲ 140.

THE TOWNHOUSE. The ground plan of this house, set between the courtyard and the garden and consisting of a main building with two wings at right angles, prefigured the design of Parisian townhouses (*hôtels*) ● 66. It was a kind of château within a town, and despite the military associations of the crenelated wall, central tower and covered way, it was notable for furnishings appropriate to a lavishly decorated country house devoted to leisure and comfortable living.

HYGIENE AND RELAXATION AT THE HÔTEL DE CLUNY. The 2nd-century baths to the north were constructed on the northern foothills of Mount Ste-Geneviève and on the edge of the marshes. The northern baths, the eastern baths (near the Collège de France) and the southern baths (beneath the Rue Gay-Lussac) constitute the three Gallo-Roman baths that have been discovered on the Left Bank. To the north, toward the Boulevard St-Germain, there are two symmetrical rooms (*palestrae*) linked by a corridor: these were used for exercising before bathing. The large *frigidarium*, which is encircled by oblong courtyards, is the best preserved room of the baths. It is over 46 feet high, and the roof with its three barrel vaults is supported by consoles in the form of ship's bows – a reference to the Paris boatmen. The *tepidarium* to the east was a warm room divided into individual bathing chambers: it was used after the *frigidarium* and before the *caldarium*, a hot room offering saunas, steam baths and massage.

THE SORBONNE   (2 C9)

(47, rue des Écoles). The Sorbonne today represents three great historical periods, which mirror the history of the nation.

THE MIDDLE AGES. This first period coincided with the expansion of the university during the 13th and 14th centuries ● *22*. The Collège de Sorbon (founded by Robert de Sorbon in 1257) became the Faculty of Theology, acquired an outstanding reputation, and had as many as ten thousand students. The first printing press in Paris was installed there, in 1470. The Sorbonne then shut itself off from the new ideas of the Renaissance and allowed Spain to organize the Counter Reformation. As a result the Faculty of Theology declined and was overtaken by the humanist teaching of the Jesuits and the future Collège de France.

THE MONARCHY. This period was associated with Cardinal Richelieu, who was in charge of the Collège de Sorbon from 1622 and decided that it should be rebuilt. The only surviving building, designed by Jacques Lemercier (1585–1654), is the chapel, with its opposed façades: one is a side of the main courtyard, while the other faces onto the Place de la Sorbonne.

THE SORBONNE: THESIS AND CEREMONY
The solemnity of the Turgot Amphitheater and the Louis-Liard Room is very popular with students doing the oral section of their doctorate examinations. This exam comes at a critical stage in a student's career, marking both the end of many years of study and the presentation

of the thesis; it is also supposed to catapult the student into higher education. The whole ritual is littered with fine compliments and harsh criticisms. It is like an academic joust, punctuated by calls of "honorable" or "very honorable", and the "congratulations of the jury" are – or are not – added. The oral presentation of a thesis makes a marked impression on those present, but it is invariably a very special moment in the life of any Sorbonne student. The miniature (above) shows a classroom in the Sorbonne during the 16th century.

The courtyard of the Old Sorbonne, by Lansyer.

THE NEW SORBONNE – 1883

The architect Henri-Paul Nénot achieved a splendid architectural compromise between the various constraints imposed by a long, narrow, sloping piece of land and the need to preserve the old 17th-century chapel. The New Sorbonne eschews pastiche and an excess of modernism; instead, it is characterized by great solemnity.

The university was closed down during the Revolution. The Emperor reopened it in 1806 as a lay institution based outside the Latin Quarter. At the behest of the Duke of Richelieu, the newly restored Ancienne Maison de Sorbonne was incorporated into the Académie de Paris in 1821. It became highly thought of in intellectual circles under such renowned thinkers as Guizot and Michelet, but during the Second Empire its reputation once again fell due to its concentration on academic teaching.

REPUBLICANISM. The Third Republic gave the Sorbonne a new look and a new reputation. One of the consequences of the Siege of Paris by the Germans in 1870 ● *20* was that the founders of a lay, scientific republic had to reorganize the higher-education system. The New Sorbonne (1883–1901) was constructed after a plan by Henri-Paul Nénot (1853–1934): the college became a complex machine responding to late-19th-century ideas with science laboratories, an observatory with a telescope (the Tower of Astronomy in the Rue St-Jacques), a library, classrooms and amphitheaters designed by official artists. All of these facilities gradually fell into disrepair. Immediately after the events of May 1968, the reforms of Edgar Faure finally brought the prestigious institutions together, forming the Académie de France and the Universities of Paris–III (New Sorbonne) and Paris–IV (Paris-Sorbonne).

SEATS OF LEARNING. The statues of Louis Pasteur (1822–95) and Victor Hugo (1802–85) symbolize the two buildings that line either side of the main courtyard. To the south, toward Rue Cujas, is the former Faculty of Sciences, dominated by the towers of Physics and Astronomy. The Faculty of Letters is to the north; inside the entrance on Rue des Écoles there is a double monumental staircase that leads up to a Pompeian peristyle and onto a large amphitheater (above: a door) and reception rooms.

CHAPEL OF STE-URSULE-DE-LA-SORBONNE (1635–42). The site of this early church built by Robert de Sorbon is marked by a double stipple in white on the floor of the courtyard.

ROBERT de SORBON

The entrances, one to the north (in the ancient style and preceded by a peristyle) and one to the south (in the Jesuit style), and the church's two axes (which are approximately the same length) represent the building's double function: part college chapel, part funerary chapel to house Richelieu's tomb. The mausoleum was designed by François Girardon in 1694 after plans by Le Brun: in accordance with custom, a cardinal's hat is suspended above the tomb. The cupola (opposite) over the crossing was decorated by Philippe de Champaigne (1602–74).

RICHELIEU'S TOMB
Richelieu's mausoleum, by François Girardon (1628–1715), is the finest example of French funerary sculpture from the 17th century. Girardon conceived

THE COLLÈGE DE FRANCE (2 D9)

(11, place Marcelin-Berthelot). The college was founded by François I in 1530 at the suggestion of the great humanist Guillaume Budé. In the 17th century it was renamed the Collège Royal de France, and it acquired its present name during the Revolution. At the time of the Renaissance the College was intended to provide the kind of modern education that the university had rejected. **"DOCET OMNIA" – IT TEACHES EVERYTHING.** Although continuing to increase the number of its professorships, the Collège de France has always been an unorthodox part of the French university system, since it does not award degrees and is under no obligation to recruit academics as teachers. This enabled the poet Paul Valéry to be elected there and allows Pierre Boulez to teach there today in the capacity of honorary professor. During the 19th century, when Napoleon III abolished the chairs held by Jules Michelet, Edgar Quinet, Adam Mickiewicz and Ernest Renan, the college had its moments of glory as part of the intellectual opposition. Later, Marcelin Berthelot, Claude Bernard and then Frédéric Joliot-Curie built up the science department, and Henri Bergson's classes were exceptionally popular. Courses run by François Jacob, Claude Lévi-Strauss, Raymond Aron and Michel Foucault have further diversified the college's teaching. **THE BUILDINGS.** The Collège de France did not have its own premises until the 17th century. The sober, solemn buildings, reconstructed between 1774 and 1780 by Chalgrin, encircle the main courtyard. Those buildings designed by Letarouilly (1831–42) extend to the west in the direction of the Rue St-Jacques; they are similar in style to Chalgrin's but are more heavily decorated, and are organized around two courtyards (Guillaume-Budé and Letarouilly) separated by a portico with arcades and Pompeian decorations (above). The recent interior decoration was designed by the architect Wilmotte.

this kind of tomb in the form of an altar. He was strongly influenced by Hellenistic statuary, and for his groups of people he also found inspiration in the pictorial representations of Poussin: the drape of the cloths, too, is in the style of the great painter. Richelieu's tomb escaped being destroyed during the Revolution thanks to Alexandre Lenoir, who removed it to the Museum of French Monuments.

THE PATRON SAINT OF PARIS
Genovefa (c. 422–502) performed many miracles during her life, saving Paris from invasion more than once. King Clovis, his wife Clotilde and the entre population held Genovefa in the very highest esteem. Well into the 18th century, whenever calamities befell the city, her assistance continued to be sought .

STE-GENEVIÈVE ABBEY

The summit of what the Gallic historian Camille Jullian has called the "sacred hill of pagan Lutetia" is crowned by the CLOVIS TOWER (Lycée Henri-IV, 2 D10, 23, rue de Clovis), the CHURCH OF ST-ÉTIENNE-DU-MONT and the PANTHÉON. They are reminders of Ste-Geneviève Abbey, which together with the Abbey of St-Germain-des-Prés ▲ 234 has long played a critical part in the spiritual, intellectual and economic life of the Left Bank.

ST-ÉTIENNE-DU-MONT ★　　(2 D10)

(1, place Ste-Geneviève). This church not only synthesizes Gothic style and new trends in Renaissance decorative art, it also contains elements of architectural confusion which give it great charm. It is a remarkably interesting church for several reasons: the shrine devoted to Saint Geneviève, the patron saint of Paris; the magnificently carved ROOD SCREEN – the only one in the city (opposite); and a fine series of 16th- and 17th-century stained-glass windows.

EXTERIOR. The unusual appearance of the façade is partly due to the imbalance brought about by the destruction of the former abbey church that once adjoined it (below): the two façades were architecturally symmetrical. The earliest parish church was dedicated to Saint Étienne in the 13th century and abutted the northern side of the Ste-Geneviève Abbey: it was rebuilt between 1492 and 1586. Part of the church's unique appeal lies in the exceptionally beautiful doorway in the main façade, completed around 1626. There are three pediments superimposed one behind the other, and each is marked by a distinct geometrical form: one is triangular, one is arched, and one, like the pediment of the early church, is gabled.

INTERIOR. The ground plan is Gothic, and the transept does not disturb the continuity of the chapels. The dominant style is Flamboyant, despite the addition of Renaissance decorative elements such as a semicircular arch instead of a Gothic arch in the nave. The vault with intersecting ribs in the choir is decorated with a range of different PENDANT KEYSTONES; the most extraordinary keystone, at the crossing, is 18 feet long and falls back on a network of star-shaped ribs.

STAINED-GLASS WINDOWS. The fourth chapel of the right-hand aisle contains a *Parable of the Wedding Guests* (1568) in painted glass, in the style of an enamel. It is the work of Nicolas Pinaigrier who was responsible for the stained glass in the nave's upper windows (1587–8) and who also worked on the windows in the Charnier Cloister .

> "Nothing in my early childhood made such an impression on me as seeing the Panthéon between me and the sun . . . That moment is still with me and continues to illuminate my inner self."
>
> Jules Michelet

PAINTINGS. The ex-votos to Saint Geneviève are the work of two famous portrait artists. The first, by Nicolas de Largillère (1696), commemorates August 10, 1696, when the shrine was carried in a procession praying for deliverance from the drought then gripping the country; it was a gift of the Provost of Merchants. The second, by François de Troy (1726), begs Saint Geneviève to halt the heavy rains that were ruining the crops; this was a gift from the aldermen of Paris.

PLACE DU PANTHÉON   (2 CD10)

This square was designed by Germain Soufflot (1709–80) as a natural exit from the church into the street and opened up the view after it was extended as far as the Luxembourg Gardens. Place du Panthéon has two classical buildings with curvilinear façades: on the north side there is the mayor's office of the 5th arrondissement (1844) by Hittorff, and on the south, at the corner of the Rue Cujas, is the Faculty of Law; partly built by Soufflot, this was completed in 1822 and has frequently been restored.

BIBLIOTHÈQUE STE-GENEVIÈVE. This building was erected in 1844 by Henri Labrouste (1801–75). The only major library in Paris to survive the Revolution, it contains about three million volumes originating from the library of the former abbey. It is both a public and a university library. The interior décor is in sharp contrast to the severity of the façade: the colors and pictorial representations show the influence of the paintings and ancient monuments which Labrouste studied during his stay in Rome.

BIBLIOTHÈQUE STE-GENEVIÈVE
In constructing this neoclassical building, Labrouste used new 19th-century materials such as iron and cast iron. They were resistant, non-combustible and inexpensive, and they enabled the artist to marry architectural lightness (making use of natural light) with new forms of plasticity (applying rich decoration). This was the first time that a steel framework ● 77 was used on a public building, and the library served as a model for many subsequent designs.

A SCIENTIFIC EXPERIMENT FROM THE CUPOLA OF THE PANTHÉON
It is possible to see the gallery of the first cupola, below which the physicist Léon Foucault (1819–68) carried out his celebrated public experiment with a pendulum: its oscillating movement was intended to demonstrate the rotation of the Earth. People flocked to the

THE PANTHÉON (2 CD10)

The Panthéon owes its existence to Louis XV's vow to rebuild the old Church of Ste-Geneviève: the king wished to give thanks for being cured of a serious illness during the Siege of Metz, in 1744.

THE NEW CHURCH. The design was entrusted to Jacques-Germain Soufflot, who sought to combine "the lightness of Gothic architecture and the magnificence of Greek architecture". The need to strengthen the basement impeded early progress, but work moved ahead thereafter until Soufflot's death in 1780. The project was taken over by Jean-Baptiste Rondelet (1743–1829), who embarked on a plan influenced by the Pantheon in Rome, building a church in the form of a Greek cross surmounted by an ovoid dome and preceded by a monumental portico.

Panthéon to watch the experiment (above) in 1851. The huge pendulum is now kept in the Conservatoire National des Arts et Métiers ▲ 136.

"A GRATEFUL FATHERLAND THANKS ITS GREAT MEN." In 1791, the Assembly decided to turn the church into a burial place for great men. The first to be chosen were Mirabeau, Voltaire, Rousseau and Marat, although Mirabeau and Marat were soon removed. After all the religious trappings had been taken out, Quatremère de Quincy (1782–1857) was given the task of making the building into a "visible Elyseum", so he walled up the forty-two windows to accentuate the sepulchral effect. Throughout the 19th century the Panthéon swung between civic and religious functions: it was reconsecrated by Napoleon in 1806 but became the Panthéon in 1831 under Louis-Philippe. The pediment was decorated by David d'Angers (1788–1856). It was converted once more into a church under Napoleon III in 1852, but when Victor Hugo's body was brought here at the end of his grand state funeral (above) in 1885, the Panthéon was once and for all established as the site for Republican rituals.

INTERIOR. The Panthéon is 360 feet wide and 272 feet high. Each of the naves is lined with aisles delimited by a hundred Corinthian columns, and the walling-up of the windows – traces of which can be seen from the outside – has provided space for the production of a vast mural. There is also a *Life of Saint Geneviève* by Puvis de Chavannes, the greatest fresco artist of the 19th century, and the center of the cupola is decorated with a fresco by Antoine-Jean Gros (1771–1835) entitled *The Apotheosis of Saint Geneviève*.

THE CRYPT. This contains the tombs of Voltaire and, facing it, Rousseau (both died in 1778). The Galerie des Couronnes houses the tombs of, among others, Victor Hugo, Émile Zola, the chemist Marcelin Berthelot (with his wife), Victor Schoelcher (the anti-slavery campaigner), the socialist Jean Jaurès, the lawyer René Cassin (1987) and the politician Jean Monnet (1988).

FINAL RESTING-PLACE. Numerous cermonies take place at the Panthéon. In 1964, during the transferring of Resistance hero Jean Moulin's ashes, the writer and then Minister for Cultural Affairs André Malraux delivered a speech in the presence of General de Gaulle. On May 21, 1980, François Mitterrand marked his first term as president by laying a rose on the tombs of Jean Jaurès, Victor Schoelcher and Jean Moulin. In 1989, the bicentenary of the Revolution, the Revolutionary figures Henry Grégoire, Gaspard Monge and Marquis de Condorcet were celebrated. Among others to have been given their final resting-place here are the scientists Pierre and Marie Curie (in 1995), André Malraux himself (in 1996), and, in 2002, the writer Alexandre Dumas, author of the much-loved novel *The Three Musqueteers*.

JACQUES-GERMAIN SOUFFLOT (1713–80) Soufflot was Controller of the King's Buildings in the final years of the Ancien Régime; he was also a representative figure in the artistic avant-garde of the Enlightenment. He achieved a unique synthesis of French classicism (which he

inherited), Greek design (which he had studied in the temples of southern Italy) and Gothic art. Several great national institutions were designed by him like the Gobelins and the Louvre, but the Panthéon is his greatest achievement.

257

THE VAL-DE-GRÂCE (5 B23)

The Val-de-Grâce Monastery, founded in 1621 by Louis XIII's wife, Anne of Austria, is in the center of the Faubourg St-Jacques, a district noted for its many religious buildings. The Val-de-Grâce is an imposing example of 17th-century ecclesiastical architecture. It is also well preserved, thanks to the military hospital which has occupied the premises since the Revolution. Henrietta of France, wife of Charles I and daughter of Henri IV, is buried here, as are the hearts of twenty-six members of the French royal family including the son, grandson and great grandson of Louis XIV.

A CHURCH DEDICATED TO THE NATIVITY (1, place Alphonse-Laveran). Anne of Austria vowed to build a magnificent temple in God's name if he sent her a son. The wish was granted twenty-three years later, when she gave birth to the future Louis XIV, but she was not able to discharge her obligation until she became regent in 1643. François Mansart (1598–1666) ▲ *291* was given the task of drawing up the plans, and the foundation stone was laid by the seven-year-old Louis XIV on April 1, 1645. The work, supervised first by Jacques Lemercier ▲ *249* and then by Pierre Le Muet, was completed by Gabriel Le Duc around 1669: all of the architectural interventions kept faith with Mansart's original plans.

A BAROQUE DOME. Gabriel Le Duc's dome is 62 feet in diameter and 135 feet high, with similarities between his design and the dome of St Peter's in Rome. There are also echoes of the Sorbonne ▲ *250* in the first floor (articulated with bays surmounted

BETWEEN BAROQUE AND CLASSICISM
The design of the canopy in Val-de-Grâce was influenced by the Bernini baldacchino in St Peter's in Rome, and the decoration of the cupola owes much to Lanfranco's fresco in the Church of Sant'Andrea della Valle in the same city. It earned the artist the sobriquet of "Mignard the Roman". However, the Italian atmosphere is tempered by the importance given to sculpture over

painting, particularly in the decoration of the vault and arcades of the nave. The carving is the work of Michel Anguier, and Philippe de Buyster was responsible for most of the decoration on the canopy, the capitals, the columns of the façade and the genies on the dome.

The well-preserved Port-Royal cloister has a serenity entirely suited to religious retreats.

by semicircular and triangular pediments), the four lanterns, the cupola with two lines of dormer windows, and also in the campanile adorned with openwork design, encircled by a railing and ending in a globe supporting a cross.

INTERIOR. Val-de-Grâce has been variously adapted to its triple functions of parish church (nave), royal chapel (Chapel of St Anne) and abbey chapel (Chapel of St-Louis). However, the overall architecture has continued to be influenced by the Gesù Church in Rome, demonstrated by its central nave, wide side chapels, uniform transept, a crossing dominated by a cupola resting on pendentives, and a façade of superimposed orders. The interior contains some fine examples of the Italianate influence found in French religious art of the 17th century. The overall décor was given over to sculpture dominated by a form of classicism that challenged the lyricism of the Italian Baroque. On either side of the entrance are two paintings (an *Ascension* and a *Pentecost*), from the school of Philippe de Champaigne, who had decorated the apartments of the Queen's Pavilion.

FORMER ABBEY OF PORT-ROYAL   (5 B3)

(123–5, boulevard de Port-Royal). The former Abbey of Port-Royal de Paris was transferred from the Jansenist Port-Royal-des-Champs by Mother Angélique Arnauld in 1626; what little remains is now part of the Baudelocque Maternity Home, where Chaptal founded a school for midwives in 1802. The cloister and the church are reminders that this abbey was once occupied by the Port-Royal hermits, who devoted their lives to caring for the sick. When Jansenism was banned by Louis XIV in 1664, the nuns refused to sign the censure of Jansenism and were expelled: their "maison des champs" was torn down in 1709.

A FORMER ABBEY CHURCH. (Open on Sundays). This church, which was built by Antoine Lepautre in 1646, consists of a single nave and a bay with side chapels. The crossing of the uniform transept is covered by a cupola resting on pendentives, and the overall decoration, including the wainscoting, is marked by characteristic Jansenist rigor.

THE AMPHITHEATER
The sloping ground
made it possible to
place the two tiers
of thirty-five steps
on the natural
inclination of the
land. Only the front
six steps have been
restored. The seating
higher up and close to
the exterior walls lies
on a construction
similar to that used in
the amphitheater at
Nîmes: these walls
contain semicircular
bays separated by
engaged columns and
supporting a cornice.

RUE MOUFFETARD

Despite the road building that convulsed life on the hill
during the 19th century, part of the township of St-Médard,
a district formed around the tomb of the saint (who died in
545), was somehow preserved. The medieval route, which is
popularly known as "La Mouffe" (Rue Mouffetard), tumbles
down the hill from Place de la Contrescarpe to the Church
of St-Médard, where a small market is encircled by a line of
stores and restaurants.

PLACE DE LA CONTRESCARPE (5 D1). This square (which is
actually a circle) was built in 1852 and is one of the most
colorful in all of Paris. At this point in the
counterscarp (the outer wall of a ditch built
for fortification purposes) stood the Bordelles
Gate, later known as St-Marcel Gate, which
was demolished in 1683. It formed part of the
Philippe-Auguste Wall ● *54*, and a fragment
of the rampart may still be seen at 3, rue Clovis. This entrance
to the city was famous for its inns.

5ᵉ Arrᵗ
**RUE
DU POT DE FER**

CHURCH OF ST-MÉDARD (5 D2) 141, rue Mouffetard. The
façade, nave and clock tower were rebuilt in the 15th century,
while the choir and the chapels date from the 16th and 17th
centuries. Louis-François Petit-Radel built the Virgin Chapel
in 1784 and recarved the columns in the choir in the Doric
manner to blend with the ancient styles then in fashion: the
porch was redone at the same time. The first chapel in the
choir on the left contains a painting of *Saint Joseph Walking
with the Child Jesus* (1636), attributed to
Francisco de Zurbarán (1598–1664).

LUTETIAN ARENA (5 E1)

(49, rue Monge). These remains dating
from the Gallo-Roman period (1st–2nd
centuries) were discovered when the
Rue Monge was under construction in
1869 and were later restored by Louis-
Joseph Capitant. The arena held fifteen

PLACE DE
LA CONTRESCARPE
A plaque on a 19th-century house at no. 1 recalls that a tavern, the Pomme de Pin (fir cone), once stood in the square, probably opposite. A fir cone was widely used by wine merchants as a sign: it alluded to the resin that was used to seal the casks. The most famous of these taverns was one on the Île de la Cité praised by Rabelais and patronized by many literary figures, including Villon, Ronsard, Boileau, Racine, La Fontaine and Molière.

thousand people; its richly decorated stage was used mainly for dramatic representations and games, including fights between men and animals. The oval arena measures 170½ feet by 151 feet, and it is serviced by two broad side entrances.

THE MOSQUE OF PARIS   (5 E1)

(1, place du Puits-de-l'Ermite). This was the first Muslim place of worship in Paris; it was built between 1922 and 1926 in recognition of the suffering that North African Muslims had undergone during World War One. Constructed by Charles Heubès, Robert Fournez and Maurice Mantout after plans by Maurice Tranchant de Lunel, the mosque is in the Moorish style and is influenced by the mosque at Fez. Local craftsmen, many of them Moroccan, were involved in applying the extremely elaborate decoration to the ornate doors, carved ceilings, mosaics and ceramics. The mosque is organized around courtyards and gardens, and consists of three groups of buildings encircled by a wall. Each is devoted to a particular activity: religious in the mosque surmounted by its square minaret; cultural at the Institute of Muslim Studies and in the main courtyard; and social around the Turkish baths, near the stores and café next to the exterior wall.

The 85-feet tall minaret and one of the interior courtyards of the Paris Mosque (above).

▲ FAUBOURG ST-GERMAIN

🕑 One day

Faubourg St-Germain now plays host to numerous ministries and embassies. Most of the district was built in the

THE PRÉ-AUX-CLERCS
This large field bordered by the Seine was once a favorite haunt of students (*clercs*) in the Latin Quarter.

It extended from the Monastery of St-Germain-des-Prés to the Champ-de-Mars. A ditch divided it, separating on one side the Petit-Pré-aux-Clercs (below), which ran from the Abbey to Rue Bonaparte, from the remainder of the park which was known as the Grand-Pré-aux-Clercs.

18th century and was, above all, a creation of the aristocracy; situated on the road that led to Versailles and two steps from the Louvre and Tuileries following the construction of the Pont Royal in 1685 – St-Germain became a fashionable district, overtaking the Marais ▲ *384*, which had become crowded and unfashionable. St-Germain had also been attracting prominent families and princes of the royal line since the end of Louis XV's reign. The decades between the death of the old king and the Revolution were notable for the emergence of a new life style and refined tastes which spread through all the European courts, leaving an indelible mark on architecture, interior design, furniture and objets d'art. Examples in architecture included the three hundred or so private townhouses (*hôtels*) built mostly during the 18th century, at the time of Voltaire and Rousseau, about a hundred of which survive today.

AROUND THE CARRÉ RIVE-GAUCHE ★

The rectangle known as the Carré Rive-Gauche is bounded by the Quai Voltaire, Rue du Bac, Rue des Sts-Pères and Rue de l'Université: it is remarkable for its unique mile-long stretch of 120 antique shops and art galleries which, since the 18th century, have perpetuated the Faubourg's passion for rare objects and works of art.

QUAI VOLTAIRE (1 I6). This quay was always very popular with artists: photographs below show the quay as it was at the beginning of this century and now it is today. The house at no. 9 was the home of Vivant Denon (1747–1825), an art lover, talented writer, engraver and diplomat who was also administrator of the Louvre during the Empire. The painters Ingres, Delacroix and Corot all

had studios here. Charles Baudelaire wrote *Les Fleurs du Mal* and Richard Wagner completed *Die Meistersinger* in the old house at no. 19. The quay was originally called Quai Malaquais, then Quai des Théatins after the Italian *teatini* who founded a convent there: one of the entrances can still be seen at 26, rue de Lille. It was renamed the Quai Voltaire in 1791, the year that the great philosopher died in the HÔTEL DE VILLETTE on the corner of the Rue de Beaune.
RUE DE L'UNIVERSITÉ (1 I1 to 6). The 18th-century building at no. 13, once known as the Hôtel Feydeau de Brou, was altered and enlarged in 1975 to accommodate the École Nationale d'Administration (ENA), a university institution for senior civil servants; most of the classes are now taught in Strasbourg. The long-established *Revue des Deux-Mondes*, which was founded in 1829 and made its reputation publishing the great names of 19th-century literature, now has premises at no. 15 in the 17th-century HÔTEL D'ALIGRE. The parliamentarian Tallemant des Réaux (1619–92) lived at no. 17 in the HÔTEL BOCHART DE SARON, a house built in 1639 and redecorated in 1770 by Jean-Baptiste Bochart de Saron. The Sieur des Réaux took a keen interest in the sciences and astronomy. He carried out some of the first experiments in the smelting of platinum and published historical works on his private printing press. The house now belongs to Éditions Gallimard.

29, QUAI VOLTAIRE (1 I6) During 1830 the beautiful Marie d'Agoult (1805–76), a writer and the companion of Franz Liszt, received guests here at the former Hôtel de Mailly-Nesle (1632). The ceiling (detail, above) was painted by Jean Bérain the Elder (1639–1711).

FAMILY RESIDENCES
A private townhouse – with the owner's coat of arms on the pediment – had reception rooms as well as private apartments with smaller rooms in which the furniture, often miniaturized, had been designed with new kinds of uses in mind. This was the era of boudoirs, "cabinets de curiosités" and secret rooms. It was also an age characterized by a hunger for novelty and intimacy. This weakness for beauty spelled ruin for many. When a house had to be sold, it usually acquired the name of its new owner.

ÉCOLE NATIONALE D'ADMINISTRATION (1 I7) 13, rue de l'Université.
The ENA was set up at the time of the Liberation to provide prospective senior civil servants with an appropriately democratic system of education and training. Graduates go on to work for the Quai d'Orsay (Foreign Office), the Tax Inspectorate, the Finance Office and the Council of State.

THE MUSÉE D'ORSAY: ART ON THE RAILS ✪
An extension of the National Museum of Modern Art, the Musée d'Orsay takes the same multidisciplinary approach to the display of its collections. It is quite easy to spend a whole morning in this fascinating place. The afternoon can be spent nosing out a treasure among the antique dealers of the Carré Rive Gauche or relaxing in the Tuileries gardens. It is best to arrive early or at the end of the day, avoiding term time and weekends.

RUE DES STS-PÈRES (1 I6). The chocolate shop DEBEAUVE ET GALLAIS, established in 1811 at no. 30, is notable for its beautiful façade by the First Empire architects Percier and Fontaine.

RUE DU BAC (1 I6). This old road was extended by a ferry (*bac*) which crossed over to the Right Bank of the Seine. The ferry was used in the 16th century to transport the stones required to construct the Tuileries Palace ▲ *200*. It was here that shops first sold articles at fixed prices and for cash in the 19th century. The former HÔTEL JACQUES-SAMUEL BERNARD (1740) at no. 46 has preserved its door with brackets surmounted by masks. The vast collection of animals and insects on sale at Deyrolle, the amazing taxidermist next door (opposite, bottom right), are a reminder of the popularity of such curiosities in the 18th century.

> 7ᵉ Arⁱ
> BOULEVARD
> SAINT
> GERMAIN

CHURCH OF ST-THOMAS AQUINAS (1 I7) Place St-Thomas d'Aquin. This church was originally the chapel of Dominican novitiates; the rest of the convent buildings are now occupied by the French Army. It was constructed in 1683 after plans by Pierre Bullet, and the Jesuit-style façade was built in 1770 by his brother Claude. The building extends behind the high altar by what was originally the choir; the ceiling was decorated in 1724 with a *Transfiguration* by François Lemoyne (1688–1737).

AROUND THE MUSÉE D'ORSAY ★ (1 HI6) ▲ *16c*

The outrage aroused by the tearing down of Les Halles in 1971, and the sudden interest in French 19th-century architecture, saved the Gare d'Orsay, which had been under threat of demolition since 1961, from this fate and turned it into a museum. The railway station was built in 1898–1900 on the site of the old Cours des Comptes, which set on fire in 1871 during the Commune like the former nearby Hôtel de Belle-Isle (56, rue de Lille) on whose site is now the Caisse des Dépôts et Consignations whose entrance is graced by a Dubuffet sculpture.

HÔTEL DE SALM (1 H5) 64, rue de Lille. This house, which was built between 1782 and 1788 by Pierre Rousseau for

Prince Frederic III of Salm Kyrbourg, boasts two contrasting faces: the monumental façade on the Rue de Lille has a double open colonnade with an Ionic order; the other façade, which overlooks the Seine, is more reminiscent of a country house (above: cross-section). Napoleon presented this house to the Chancellery of the Legion of Honor. It was later enlarged in order to provide premises for their museum. The interior was destroyed by fire during the Commune, but it was later rebuilt in the spirit of official 19th-century art (above, left).

HÔTEL DE BEAUHARNAIS AND HÔTEL DE SEIGNELAY (1 H5) 78 & 80, rue de Lille; German Embassy and Ministère du Commerce et de L'Artisanat. Germain Boffrand began work on these two adjoining houses in 1715. The Hôtel de Beauharnais was sold to J.B. Colbert de Torcy, nephew of the minister, and passed into the hands of Prince Eugène de Beauharnais, the stepson of Napoléon, who added Pompeian decoration fitting with imperial style (above: the bathroom and the Four Seasons drawing room). The prince sold the house to the Prussian Legation in 1817. The smaller Hôtel de Seignelay has a fine rococo drawing room on the garden side.

MAISON DES DAMES DE LA POSTE (1 I6) 41, rue de Lille. This house was built in 1907 for employees training to work for the Post Office. It provided accommodation for staff from the provinces, widows and spinsters. The Art Deco interior is unaltered, and the building is now used as a restaurant (Le Télégraphe).

HÔTEL POZZO DI BORGO, OR MAISONS, OR SOYÉCOURT (1 H6). 51, rue de l'Université. This house, built by Lassurance in 1707, contains a rococo drawing room by the celebrated Antwerp designer Jacob Verberckt (1704–71). The HÔTEL DE POULPRY, now a residence for École Polytechnique students, was built nearby in the same year at 12, rue de Poitiers. The decoration on one of the ceilings is attributed to Watteau.

THE ASSEMBLÉE NATIONALE (1 G5)

(126, rue de l'Université). The Palais-Bourbon has been the seat of the French government since 1798. Like the Hôtel de Lassay (no. 128), owned by the National Assembly since 1843, and the President's official residence, the palace's origins are aristocratic. It was built in 1726 by Lassurance, Aubert and Gabriel for Louise-Françoise, the legitimized daughter of Louis XIV and Mme de

nrf

ÉDITIONS GALLIMARD (1 I7) 5, rue Sébastien-Bottin. The publishing house of Gallimard was founded in 1911, two years after the appearance of the journal *Nouvelle Revue Française*, founded by André Gide and his friends. The firm has since been sustained by a family dynasty:

Gaston (1882–1975) published a number of writers of importance, and his son Claude (1914–91) consolidated the family empire by publishing the Folio Collection and founding his own distribution company, Sodis. Today the company is run by Antoine Gallimard, the founder's grandson.

265

ALTERATIONS TO THE PALAIS-BOURBON
The semicircular Council Chamber and the loggia were constructed by J.P. Gisors and E.C. Leconte under the Directoire. In 1806 Bernard Poyet erected the ancient-style façade overlooking the river, facing the Madeleine Church. This wall conceals the absence of any axial connection between

the palace and the Pont de la Concorde. The sculptures of Sully, L'Hospital, Colbert and d'Aguesseau have survived, but the pediment erected to the glory of the Emperor was replaced during the July Monarchy by one in honor of Jean-Pierre Cortot. After 1828, Jean-Baptiste de Joly enlarged the chamber and built a new portico, with a pediment on the side of the courtyard.

Montespan, widow of the Duke of Bourbon. The house next door was intended for the Marquis de Lassay, the lover of the Duchess of Bourbon. Nothing remains of the former building except the courtyard and the main façade, which has a colonnade and monumental porch facing the Rue de l'Université. Although a story was added in the 1840's, the Hôtel de Lassay has substantially preserved its original appearance. The Place du Palais-Bourbon and its Louis XVI houses form a jewel-box-like setting.

ALLEGORY ON THE PICTURE RAIL. Changes in government meant that certain styles of interior decoration went out of favor. Delacroix, whom Thiers imposed against the supporters of neoclassicism in 1833, added allegories to the decoration of the king's drawing room and the library: these were preserved by the Empire and the Republic.

MINISTÈRE DES AFFAIRES ÉTRANGÈRES
(1 F5) 130, rue de l'Université and 37, quai d'Orsay). The Ministry of Foreign Affairs was constructed in 1845 by J. Lacornée and was the first building in the district to be designed as a ministry.

> "But I don't dare speak of Paris, where I
> have lived for more than twenty years.
> To know it is the work of a lifetime."

Stendhal

RUE ST-DOMINIQUE (1 C TO H 6)

This former cattle trail takes its name from the Dominicans
who settled here in 1632. Rue St-Dominique (below, right)
was inhabited by many prominent families, and in the 18th
century it boasted a large number of townhouses. Many of
these disappeared when a third of the road was lost to the
newly constructed Boulevard St-Germain.

HÔTELS DE BRIENNE (1 G6) 14–16, Ministry of Defense.
These two houses were built in 1724 and 1728 by
F. Debias-Aubry and by President Duret, a gentleman who
had a hand in most property deals in the Faubourg
St-Germain. They had many owners, including Louis XVI's
treasury minister, M.-A. Loménie de Brienne, Lucien
Bonaparte and Napoleon's mother. After the buildings were
acquired by the state in 1817, they were extended on many
occasions along the Boulevard St-Germain. General de
Gaulle established his headquarters here on August 25, 1944.
The nearby Square Samuel-Rousseau contains the
Ste-Clothilde Basilica, which was constructed between 1846
and 1856 in the neo-Gothic style of the time by Gau and
Ballu.

HÔTEL DE ROQUELAURE ★
(1 H6) 246, boulevard
St-Germain, formerly 62, rue
St-Dominique. This house
was built by Lassurance in
1724 and later refurbished by
Leroux. Grotesque masks
ornament a superb Regency
façade, and the interior
contains some fine 18th-
century decoration, including
a magnificent rococo drawing
room.

RUE DE GRENELLE

There are many townhouses with large gardens between here
and the Boulevard des Invalides.

HÔTEL DE ROTHELIN-CHAROLAIS (1 G7) 101, Ministry of
Enterprises and Economic Development. This house was
built in 1704 by Lassurance, a supremely gifted architect who
had been influenced by Mansart. It was enlarged on the
orders of the Princess of Charolais in 1736, and the interior
was refurbished during the 19th century.

HÔTEL DE VILLARS (1 G7) 116, Mayor's Office of the 7th
arrondissement. This house, built in 1644, has been frequently
redecorated. There is a
beautiful Restoration drawing
room that was decorated by A.
Vauchelet in 1834.

HÔTEL DE ROCHECHOUART ★
(1 G7) 110, Ministry of
Education. M. Cherpitel built
this house in 1776 in Louis XVI
style. The Corinthian drawing
room has preserved its original
décor.

ROCOCO

Rococo style
represented a radical
departure from the
rigid principles of
classicism, with its
passion for frenzied
lines and
asymmetrical forms.
It takes its name
(*rocaille*) from the
rock-like materials
used in grottos and
fountains. One of its
many characteristics
is an enthusiasm for
shell ornament. The
style began to emerge
in France around
1725 and found its
most extreme
expression
in Germany.

In architecture, the
style's originality was
revealed through the
soundness of the
proportions allied to
ornamental sculpture;
the use of white Ile-
de-France stone did
much to emphasize
the harmony.
However, the true
innovation of rococo
in interior decoration
is seen in furniture,
ornaments, vases,
mirrors, bronzes and
gold pieces, tapestries
and carpets – in a
word, everything that
enlivens a house.

FOUNTAIN OF THE FOUR SEASONS (1 H7)
57–59, rue de Grenelle. Constrained by space, Edme Bouchardon produced a semicircular construction with the main body at the front flanked by two wing sections. The design anticipated by several years a return to ancient styles.

HÔTEL DE NOIRMOUTIER ★ (1 F6)
138, residence of the Prefect of the Île-de-France region. Built by Jean Courtonne, this is one of the most elegant and beautifully balanced houses in the district. The dining room has attractive boiserie representing La Fontaine's *Fables*.

HÔTEL DU CHÂTELET ★ (1 F6)
127, Ministry of Labor. This house was built between 1772 and 1774 by Cherpitel for the Duc du Châtelet, whose mother, the Marquise du Châtelet, was a friend of Voltaire. It is a magnificent example of the neoclassical style that dominated the final years of the century; features include the severe Doric order surrounding the main courtyard and the monumental façade, with its four massive columns.

The horizontal lines of the entablature and the attic story make a powerful contrast with these columns, and are further accentuated by balustrades that run along buildings that stand on either side of the courtyard, which have not been raised. The dining room and the drawing room give onto the garden; the original wood paneling has been preserved.

RUE DE VARENNE

Of the many spacious gardens in this area, only the garden of the Hôtel Matignon has preserved its original dimensions.
HÔTEL DE BOISGELIN (1 H7 and 8) 47, Italian Embassy. This townhouse (below), built around 1787 by Cartaud, was enlarged and restored during the 19th and 20th centuries. French and Italian 18th-century décor has been introduced and adapted to the new setting.
HÔTEL DE GALLIFFET (1 H7) Italian Cultural Institute. This house was built by F.E. Legrand, with the sculptor J.B. Boiston, for Simon de Galliffet in 1784, a time of renewed emphasis on ancient forms of art. The monumental façade overlooking the courtyard, which had originally faced the Rue du Bac, has Ionic columns on two stories; the first-floor reception rooms are articulated by Ionic columns with trompe l'oeil fluting and have only recently been decorated.

HÔTEL DE BIRON, MUSÉE RODIN ★ ▲ *171* (1 F7) no. 77. This residence was built for the financier Peyrenc de Moras in 1728 by Aubert and Gabriel, the architects of the Palais-Bourbon. Typically, the layout consists of a house standing between a courtyard and a garden. The house takes its name

SCIENCES-PO
(1 I8) 27, rue St-Guillaume. In 1945 the Institut d'Études Politiques, better known as "Sciences-Po", replaced the École Libre des Sciences Politiques, a private institution set up two years after the Siege of Paris (1870) by a group of liberals under Émile Goutmy (1835–1906) to educate senior officials. The school, which subtly adapted to the spirit of republicanism, uses teaching methods which draw on the German seminar system and the British tutorial system. It is also a major research institution and is now the country's leading training ground for high flyers in both the private and the public sectors.

from the Maréchal de Biron, who owned the house from 1753 to 1788. It was later occupied by the religious order of the Dames du Sacré-Coeur, who removed the interior decoration; some of it was restored when the Rodin Museum was opened on the first floor. (Below: *L'Ombre*, c. 1880, bronze statue by Rodin.)

HÔTEL MATIGNON ★ (1 G8) no. 57, residence of the Prime Minister. This townhouse is one of the most beautiful in the whole district. Like the Élysée Palace and the Place Beauvau, it has come to symbolize the pinnacle of state power. It was built by Jean Courtonne in 1722; Jean Mazin continued to work on it for the Prince de Tingry, who sold it to Jacques de Goyon, Sire de Matignon. As was customary in those days, the façade follows the semicircular line of the courtyard – this configuration made it easier for carriages to come and go. Jean Courtonne was responsible for the construction of the façades, with their elaborate and abundant ornamentation, the layout, and the interior decoration of both the large oval vestibule (by the courtyard) and the octagonal drawing room, (by the garden). The first-floor Golden drawing room, with decorations by Mazin, has preserved much of its original décor. In 1725 the Duc de Matignon had a small Louis XV pavilion built at the far end of the park, near the Rue de Babylone: this was the Petit Trianon (above right). Opposite the Hôtel Matignon (above), at no. 56, is the HÔTEL GOUFFIER DE THOIX, endowed with a remarkably beautiful rococo door.

notable for their severe and monumental design, with a return to order and straight lines: examples include the hôtels de Salm, du Châtelet, de Rochechouart and de Galliffet. Similar trends were to be found in interior decoration and furniture, with straight lines replacing curves and arcs.

BABYLON GARDEN ★ (1 G9)
33, rue de Babylone.
This garden was once the orchard of the Convent of the Daughters of Charity.

FOREIGN MISSIONS HOUSES (1 G8)
118–20, rue du Bac.
These houses, built around 1713 to be rented, look out over the Square des Missions-Étrangères and a bust of Chateaubriand: the writer spent his last years in this area. The two main doors

are decorated with medallions carved by L. Dupin, and the stone sculptures on the tympana are the work of J.B. Turreau, known as "Toro".

Right: the Hôtel de Galliffet, where in 1797 Mme de Staël met Bonaparte for the first time.

SÈVRES-BABYLONE ★

LE SÉMINAIRE DES MISSIONS-ÉTRANGÈRES (1 H8) 128, rue du Bac.
This institution has been operating in the district almost without a break for more than three hundred years. The seminary used to train priests as missionaries: in 1658, French vicars apostolic were appointed to Cochin China and Tonkin (now North and South Vietnam), more than two hundred years before France began to colonize these areas. The chapel (1689) at nos. 124–8 has a façade with two rectangular levels superimposed, as did other churches in the early years of the following century. Behind this is the seminary's main building, which dates from 1732.

CHAPEL OF THE MIRACULOUS MEDAL (1 H8) 136, rue du Bac.
"Strike a medal in the image of this one, and everyone who carries it will receive grace." These were the words of the Virgin Mary on an occasion in 1830 when she is said to have appeared to a young novice at the Convent of the Filles-de-la-Charité-de-St-Vincent-de-Paul. The nun in question, Catherine Labouré, died in 1876 and was canonized in 1947. The chapel is noted for its devotion to the Virgin and is the destination of pilgrims who come between November 27 and December 8, the anniversary of the Virgin's appearances.

BON MARCHÉ
Gustave Eiffel's use of steel architecture ● 77 created an abundance of space, and the big windows let in large amounts of natural light.

PAGODE ★
(1 FG8) 57 *bis*, rue de Babylone. The Pagode was built in 1895 by a director of the Bon Marché, who gave it to his wife. It was opened to the public in 1931. It is now a movie theater.

BON MARCHÉ ▲ *126* (1 H8 and 9) 140, rue du Bac. Originally a small shop selling novelties, the Bon Marché rapidly expanded, and by 1868 it employed four hundred people. The demolition of the Hospice des Petits-Ménages allowed the shop to expand even further between 1869 and 1882. One of Boucicaut's objectives was to complement his commercial success with a paternalistic social attitude: this was described by Émile Zola in his *Au Bonheur des dames*. Today it is Paris' chicest department store.

LAENNEC HOSPITAL (1 H9) 42, rue de Sèvres. The construction of this former Hospice for Incurables signaled the expansion of Faubourg St-Germain; it was founded in 1634 and was turned into a hospital in 1878. The chapel, built by Gamard at the same time, still has its original façade and spire. Large parts of the hospital were soon put to other uses, and it became a residential building. Only those parts with a preservation order on them were to remain.

CHAPEL OF PRIESTS OF THE CONGREGATION OF THE MISSION (1 H9) 95, rue de Sèvres. This chapel was built in 1826 by an order founded by Saint Vincent de Paul (1576–1660). The interior décor (right) has not been changed, and the embalmed body of the saint is kept above the high altar.

🕐 **One day**

FOUR-CORNERS-OF-THE-WORLD FOUNTAIN
Av. de l'Observatoire. This Davioud fountain is decorated by Carpeaux and Frémiet ▲ 203.

The atmosphere and myths surrounding the Bohemian district of Montparnasse have gone forever – supplanted by the urban growth that the area has embraced. However, for all the changes, the aura of old Montparnasse lingers on.

HISTORY. Montparnasse formed part of the fortifications built by Henri II (1519–59), but it was given its name – Mount Parnassus – by students in 1687. It is not known whether the hill was natural or simply a mound of rubbish and builder's rubble that was dumped when the Boulevard du Montparnasse was built. This fine thoroughfare designed during the reign of Louis XIV (1638–1715), was not completed until 1761. By the end of the 18th century it had become an elegant promenade with four rows of trees and lined with magnificent houses and gardens, overlooked by convents in the Rue Notre-Dame-des-Champs, which ran parallel to the boulevard.

THE BEGINNINGS OF MONTPARNASSE

This "admirable and deserted" spot, as Montparnasse was described in the early days, inspired a number of entrepreneurs to open dance halls and open-air cafés (*Bal Bullier*, below, opposite).

EARLY EVENTS. During this early period the GRANDE CHAUMIÈRE opened which proved an exceptionally popular café until 1853, when it was supplanted by La Closerie des Lilas. The latter name was adopted some thirty years later by the establishment that bears it to this day, while that of La Grande Chaumière was transferred to a street and to an art school. From 1814 onward there was a popular spot for dancing on the corner of the Boulevard du Montparnasse and the Boulevard d'Enfer (Raspail): it later became the CARREFOUR VAVIN, a focal point of international art. It is still dominated by RODIN'S *BALZAC*, a powerful figure which many feel speaks for all art and literature.

EARLY CELEBRITIES. Prominent figures of the day were attracted by the hushed, almost rural charm of the streets of Montparnasse. In November 1826, Victor Hugo (1802–85) rented a house in the Rue Notre-Dame-des-Champs. Meanwhile, living in exile in the marvelous 18th-century Hôtel du Silène, the beautiful Milanese Princess Belgioioso (1808–71) received young writers and members of Italian Risorgimento high society who had taken refuge in Paris; she later sold her mansion to the celebrated Collège Stanislas. Another local resident was the critic Sainte-Beuve (1804–69), who settled at no. 16 in 1850 – it was, he said, "my final nest for my declining years". In the late 19th century, nothing could be more peaceful than this district of establishment painters and artists. The Rue Notre-Dame-des-Champs could boast the workshop of Gérome (1824–1904) and the house of Bouguereau (1825–1905); Bartholdi (1834–1904) had already moved into a house-cum-workshop on the corner of the Rue d'Assas and the Rue Vavin. James Whistler (1834–1903) was resident in the Rue d'Assas and the Dutchman Johan Jongkind (1819–91) ● *94* lived in a building in the Boulevard du Montparnasse that would later house Le Jockey, a famous jazz club.

URBAN DEVELOPMENT. Houses and other residential property began to spring up along the boulevard and adjoining streets. The Midi Cemetery ▲ *287*, later renamed the Montparnasse, had been built in 1824: now enlarged, it extended the length of the Boulevard Edgar-Quinet. The charming STATE RAILWAY STATION in the Place de Rennes was opened at about the same time as the new Church of Notre-Dame-des-Champs.

"BALZAC" BY RODIN
The plaster roughcast of this sculpture was commissioned by the Société des Gens de Lettres and was shown at their 1898 *salon*. It caused such a scandal (for representing the great writer in his dressing gown) that it was not exhibited publicly until 1939.

PLACE DENFERT-ROCHEREAU
As the two symmetrical pavilions by Claude Nicolas Ledoux ● *68* demonstrate, the old Place d'Enfer was cut into the Farmers General Wall in 1784. The square was named after Colonel Denfert-Rochereau, who had so heroically defended the town of Belfort in 1878. A replica of a lion carved by Bartholdi in the wall of the Belfort citadel stands in the center of the square. It looks down over a busy crossroads. There is also an entrance to the Catacombs nearby.

Paris owes much to what lies beneath its streets – the stone used to make its famous buildings and the water that travels through miles of pipes before gushing up through the fountains.

Montsouris district

Winding stairway leading to the quarries

Subsidence dome

Support column

Rounded columns

Subsidence

Inspection galle

Ground water

THE PARIS QUARRIES

Paris was built with gypsum and limestone extracted from below ground level. The Left Bank alone has 186 miles of underground tunnels that are not accessible to the public.

Gypsum
Coarse limestone

The Right Bank was quarried mainly for gypsum; these deposits have now been exhausted. Some quarries in the suburbs (below) are still open to visitors.

Undercutting

Cutting with a blade

Driving wedges into the stone

Removing block on rollers

INSPECTING THE QUARRIES
Intensive mining caused subsidence, and the quarries also encouraged the trading of a wide range of goods. To put a stop to this, a team of inspectors was set up in 1777 under the Sieur Guillaumot. He and his successor,

Héricart de Thury, were responsible for some public works of great beauty, including this inspection gallery with a semicircular arch entrance with raised keystones

POMP
CLOIT
CHAR

The first inspectors plac
engraved signs on the ri
hand side of passagewa
and structures; these
enabled their successor
and catacomb enthusia
to find their way around
In the last ten years or s
the tunnels have been
infested with
another kind of
sign – graffiti.

The fountain in Square Louvois by Visconti.

The hill of Montmartre Sacré-Coeur

Inspection port

Access stairway

Water main

Reservoir

Aqueduct

Longitudinal section of a sewer

PARIS WATER

he earliest waterworks system was built by
e Romans. By the Middle Ages, however,
e city had no clean-water system at all: the
ound water had become seriously
ontaminated and was polluting the wells.
Philippe-Auguste inaugurated the city's first
public fountain using spring water in 1184.
Henri IV and Marie de' Medici constructed
a water system that was based largely on the
Roman network, but it was Haussmann who
introduced the modern system.

DRINKING WATER

In 1852, Belgrand commenced work on
diverting the springs which now supply half
the city with its drinking water. The

remaining inhabitants
rely on water pumped
from the Seine and
Marne, which is filtered
before distribution.

WATER CARRIERS

Until the end of the
19th century, many
Parisians used the
services of a water
carrier to bring water
to their homes.

MONTSOURIS RESERVOIR

This was built by
Belgrand to take
water from the River
Dhuis. Constructed
on two levels, it has a
capacity of 3.25
million cubic feet and
supplies some of
eastern Paris with
water.

View of the
lower level of
the Montsouris
reservoir.

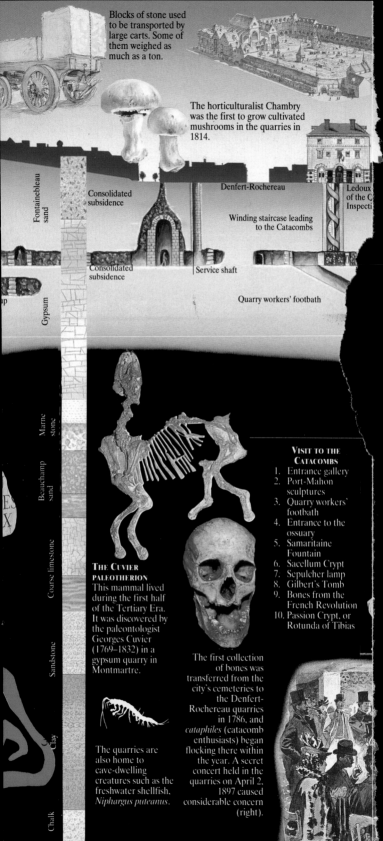

Blocks of stone used to be transported by large carts. Some of them weighed as much as a ton.

The horticulturalist Chambry was the first to grow cultivated mushrooms in the quarries in 1814.

Fontainebleau sand

Consolidated subsidence

Denfert-Rochereau

Ledoux of the Q Inspecti

Winding staircase leading to the Catacombs

Consolidated subsidence

Service shaft

up

Gypsum

Quarry workers' footbath

Marne stone

Beauchamp sand

Coarse limestone

Sandstone

Clay

Chalk

THE CUVIER PALEOTHERION

This mammal lived during the first half of the Tertiary Era. It was discovered by the paleontologist Georges Cuvier (1769–1832) in a gypsum quarry in Montmartre.

The quarries are also home to cave-dwelling creatures such as the freshwater shellfish, *Niphargus puteanus*.

The first collection of bones was transferred from the city's cemeteries to the Denfert-Rochereau quarries in 1786, and *cataphiles* (catacomb enthusiasts) began flocking there within the year. A secret concert held in the quarries on April 2, 1897 caused considerable concern (right).

VISIT TO THE CATACOMBS

1. Entrance gallery
2. Port-Mahon sculptures
3. Quarry workers' footbath
4. Entrance to the ossuary
5. Samaritaine Fountain
6. Sacellum Crypt
7. Sepulcher lamp
8. Gilbert's Tomb
9. Bones from the French Revolution
10. Passion Crypt, or Rotunda of Tibias

UNDERGROUND PARIS

EAU & GAZ
A TOUS LES ÉTAGES

Institut de France

Siphon underneath the Pont de l'Alma

THE CITY'S NERVOUS SYSTEM

The sewers also accommodate other elements of the city's nervous system. Facilities such as running water (drinking and nondrinking), telephone cables, the pneumatic-express letter system (there are still two such lines in Paris) and the cables that operate traffic lights all run through the sewer pipes.

SAGEP

A new addition to the sewer system is the Climespace distribution network; this is currently under construction.

Main sewer

Branch sewer

Runoff sewer

THE NETWORK

This consists of over 1,300 miles of sewer mains which collect water from 18,000 drains from the city's gutters, and liquid waste through 63,000 connections installed under buildings.

THE SEWERS OF PARIS

The architect Bruneseau built the first modern sewers in Paris in the early 19th century. After the cholera epidemic of 1832, the authorities decided to go further, and within ten years the capital possessed 62 miles of pipes. In 1853 Haussmann and his right-hand man, the engineer Eugène Belgrand, started work on a more wide-ranging scheme. The broad-based nature of today's sewer system owes much to the genius of these two great men.

The main pipes take much of the sewage that Paris produces to the purification plant at Achères, 12 miles northwest of the capital.

UNDERGROUND PARIS

Merovingian sarcophagus

THE BASTILLE CRYPT
A circular gallery beneath the July Column was used to shelter victims of the revolutions between 1830 and 1848.

The Louvre

Crypt

Archeological excavation of the Louvre

River Seine

CRYPTS AND CAVES

BERNARDINE CELLAR
Underneath the refectory of the former Bernardine Monastery in the Rue de Poissy, now used as an official building, there is a 14th-century Gothic cellar. This enormous room is banked up as high as the capitals of the 32 columns supporting the ceiling.

ST-SULPICE CRYPT
The Church of St-Sulpice ▲ 238 was built on the site of an older church in the domain of the Abbey of St-Germain-des-Prés. Organized tours use a staircase behind the sacristy to descend into the largest crypt in all of Paris. It contains a former cemetery, the foundations of the primitive church and the well that once stood in the square.

CRYPT OF ST DENIS
This chapel in Rue Pierre-Nicole is said to have been where Saint Denis made his first retreat.

ROMANESQUE REMAINS
The Church of Notre-Dame-des-Champs was constructed on this site in 1033 and enclosed all the existing buildings. It was taken over by the Carmelites in 1604 but was destroyed during the Revolution; only the primitive crypt remains. The nuns built a smaller convent in 1802 and restored the chapel but finally departed for good in 1902.

THE CEMETERY OF THE INNOCENTS

When the city authorities decided to close the parish churchyards for reasons of hygiene in 1786, this was the cemetery to be transferred to the Catacombs in the qua

Panthéon

Sorbonne

Pavilion (offices
quarries
on Service)

Vault

Nuclear fallout shelter

Ossuary

Gilbert's false tomb

nda of the Tibias

Gallery containing bones
(not open to the public).

French Resistance headquarters

THE PARIS CATACOMBS

THE WAR UNDERGROUND

This network of quarries was used during World War Two by both the Resistance and the occupying forces: they served as shelters, resting places and operations centers for active

ROTUNDA OF TIBIAS

Like the remaining catacombs that are open to the public, the Passion Crypt, or Rotunda of Tibias, was constructed in the 19th century as a way of stimulating visitors' imagination. A load-bearing pillar supports a barrel-shaped structure made of bones.

combatants.
(Above: door to a German bunker.)
The headquarters of the Rol-Tanguy network leader was extraordinarily close to a German bunker. During the cold war, a number of public buildings in Paris were provided with nuclear fallout shelters.

e hundred
s who
in the
round
k can inspect
oot of
they can
cess through
26,000
ion holes
ted all over
ital.

The fountain in Place de la Concorde ▲ 310 built by Hittorff.

Run-off sewer

Branch sewer

Main sewer

St-Martin Canal

Well

NTRUDERS
The sewer system is
nfested with brown
ats, and workers
have to be
accinated against
eptospirosis. The
nspection points
are also swarming
with cockroaches.

CLEARING OUT
Top: a sluice boat clearing out a sewer main.
Bottom: clearing out a siphon sewer with a cleaning ball.

THE PUMP AT LA SAMARITAINE
This hydraulic machine was built on piles abutting the Pont-Neuf during the reign of Henri IV. It supplied the Louvre and the Tuileries with water from the Seine.

Victor Hugo set part of *Les Misérables* in the Paris sewers.

ICI, AU CROISEME
DU BOULEVARD SÉBASTO
ET DE LA RUE DE RIVOL
LE CHEMIN DE FER MÉTROPOLI
PASSE AU DESSOUS DU

**THE MÉTRO
CRICKET**
This insect thrives in
the warm environment
of the tunnels.

TRANSPORT AND COMMUNICATIONS

A large number of pipes, mains and cables run along the shallow substratum under Paris: they are part of the telephone, gas, electricity, steam, water and sewer systems. Road tunnels and the Métro are built below them, and the RER and express rail links use the deepest tunnels.

1. Underground route for cars
2. RER elevator
3. Upper level of RER station
4. RER station
5. Météor (Métro 14)
6. Eole (RER E)
7. Métro station
8. Urban heating system
9. Water main
10. Cable
11. Gas main
12. Telephone cables
13. Vault
14. Parking lot

THE CURTAIN RISES

At the beginning of the 20th century, the scene was set for Montparnasse to become the CAPITAL OF CUBISM: the area was full of young artists from abroad who were later to constitute the Paris School. This Montparnasse, in Léon-Paul Fargue's description, "had neither walls nor doors. . . . The first lamp which shed light on the district – a district which has since become famous the world over – was the old 'bearded lamp' Henri Rousseau, also known as 'Le Douanier', who lived in the Avenue du Maine around 1895." (Above: *The Snake Charmer*, 1907.)

MODIGLIANI, KING OF MONTPARNASSE. An extraordinary set of newcomers moved into the area from central Europe and even from across the Atlantic. AMEDEO MODIGLIANI, a handsome Italian born in 1884 into an impoverished Jewish merchant family, came to Paris in 1906 and set up house in Montmartre. His health was not good and he

LA CLOSERIE DES LILAS (5 A2) Every Tuesday evening from 1890 onward, the poet Paul Fort presided over a gathering of young writers in this establishment, formerly an open-air dance hall. In 1925 the survivors of this learned assembly organized a banquet in honor of the symbolist poet Saint-Pol-Roux (1861–1940). This event celebrating the author of *La Dame à la Faulx* ended in an indescribable fracas instigated by the Surrealists, who considered Saint-Pol-Roux to be one of their own.

returned to Italy to spend a few months with his family. He returned to Paris in 1910, this time settling in Montparnasse. Here he created the works which made him famous – so famous that his name was to be forever linked with the history of this quarter.

LA ROTONDE (6 I2). This little bistro became a meeting place for several artists who had settled in Montparnasse. As a young man, the Swiss writer Blaise Cendrars (1887–1961) spent hours at the slot machines by the bar (at this stage he still had both his arms). In its back room, where the mirrors were completely covered with "one hundred thousand declarations of love", Modigliani and his inseparable companion, Soutine (1894–1943), accompanied by a young Japanese painter called Fujita (1886–1968) (opposite), used to rub shoulders with Russian exiles. Trotsky had a regular table here and Lenin is said to have visited La Rotonde.

LE DÔME (6 I1). On the other side of the street is the huge, sunny terrace of Le Dôme. This café became a meeting place for German artists, especially members of the Munich School, who had come to Paris from the banks of the Spree.

LA CLOSERIE DES LILAS (5 A2). Paul Fort (1872–1960), elected the "prince of poets" in 1912, used to hold court here every Tuesday evening from 1890 onward. Francis Carno dedicated a long chapter to the famous Tuesdays at La Closerie in his *Memoirs of Another Life*. The café with its charming Art Deco interior is still a meeting place for today's literary set.

A NEW STYLE. Buildings in the MODERN STYLE were put up all along the boulevards Montparnasse and Raspail (completed in 1906), as well as in the neighboring streets. The house built by the architect Henri Sauvage (6 I1) is one of the most interesting of these creations (right). Building sites sprang up everywhere, and the country-style houses of the 19th century made way for blocks of studios – some can still be seen today – which artists could rent at very low rates. Yet it is to a sculptor, Alfred Boucher, that we owe the existence of La Ruche ▲ 288, a curious and unusual building put up in 1902: it took in young artists arriving in Paris, whatever their origins, nationality or artistic tendencies. Between 1902 and 1939, La Ruche housed many artists – from Léger to Soutine, from Chagall to Lipchitz, from Zadkine ▲ 172 to Kisling – who were to become the stars of the Paris School and make fortunes thanks to the astuteness of their dealers.

"A SPORTY, TIERED HOUSE"
This is how architect Henri Sauvage (1873–1932) ● 79 described the building at 26, rue Vavin, which he built in 1912. Sauvage's house is covered with ceramic

tiles; its tiers, with their terrace gardens, allow more air and light into the interior. It was the forerunner of a new type of architectural design, heralding the post-war international style.

RUE SCHOELCHER
(6 J3) This door belongs to the building (no. 5) created by Bigot in 1911. Picasso lived at no. 5 *bis*, where he kept a studio (below) until 1917.

1914: THE END OF AN ERA

While La Ruche was a refuge for impoverished artists in the first decade of the 20th century, the center of Montparnasse was home to wealthier artists, like Van Dongen, who held a lavish party in his studio in the Rue Denfert-Rochereau on May 24, 1914. Picasso had also moved into the neighborhood, renting a luxurious apartment in the Rue Schoelcher which dazzled all his friends. On July 14, 1914, a grand ball with Chinese lanterns was held at the Carrefour Vavin, bringing together artists and locals from all over Montparnasse. These riotous celebrations were to be the swan song of an era which was to end two weeks later when war was declared, on August 2, 1914. This was the end of the golden age of Montparnasse.

ACT TWO: THE CRAZY YEARS

After World War One, Montparnasse became both a mecca for artists from all over the world and a fashionable place attracting anyone who desired to see and be seen. Thus the quarter gained in celebrity but lost much of its former charm.

TRANSFORMATION OF THE OLD CAFÉS. The Carrefour Vavin became one of the focal points of post-World War One Parisian life. LA ROTONDE was enlarged, renovated and given a grill room and a restaurant on the second story, where a jazz orchestra played for diners. Père Libron's old zinc-covered bar had changed from a modest bistro into a luxury establishment where the bourgeoisie came to dine in the vain hope of spotting famous local artists. LE DÔME also underwent a transformation: it took over the neighboring establishment, where it opened a café-bar decorated in red leather with nickel-plated Art Deco chairs and its terrace grew to vast dimensions. Customers could see Fujita with his beautiful new wife Yuki surrounded by the old celebrities of the area, like

KIKI OF MONTPARNASSE
After World War One, nightclubs sprang up all over Montparnasse. One of these was Le Jockey, founded by an American and initially located on the corner of the Rue Campagne-Première. Le Jockey had a main room and a bar with very distinctive décor: it was here that Kiki, the undisputed queen of Montparnasse, held court, regaling customers with her bawdy songs. Kisling, Man Ray and many other artists painted portraits of her.

Kisling, who lived nearby in the Rue Joseph-Bara. Americans of the "lost generation" used to meet at LE SELECT, the first bar in Paris to stay open all night. On December 20, 1927, a bitterly cold night, a new and luxurious establishment with a domed roof called LA COUPOLE opened on the same street.

FESTIVE EXTRAVAGANCE. Parisians had decided to put the tribulations of war behind them. The terraces of the large cafés were overrun with extravagantly dressed crowds of all ages. Well-known artists were treated like royalty. Parties and dances were held for any and every occasion, or even for no occasion at all – like the famous BAL NÈGRE in the newly fashionable Rue Blomet, where the entire population of Montparnasse gathered to celebrate Ubu, the eponymous character in Alfred Jarry's play *Ubu Roi*. Jarry's famous satirical vision of life premiered in 1896 and was the first literary work of the "Absurd" movement.

THE SEVENTH ART. Two movie theaters vied for the avant-garde audiences of the 1930's. One of these was LE VAVIN, in the Rue Jules-Chaplain, which specialized in Soviet and Judeo-Polish movies –Waszynsky's extraordinary *Dybbuk* (1937) was screened here. The other was RASPAIL 216 where Parisians were able to see Bette Davis in her first important role in *Of Human Bondage* (1934) directed by John Cromwell, adapted from a novel by Somerset Maugham.

RUE DE LA GAÎTÉ (6 H23). This aptly named street offered the liveliest spectacle at this time – a variety of delights with a mixture of restaurants, accordionists and bistros. The old THÉÂTRE MONTPARNASSE of Seveste and La Rochelle had been renovated, cleaned and modernized, and once again became a center of dramatic activity, delighting a whole generation with the skills of the gifted magician Gaston Baty. BOBINO, the home of the popular song, witnessed performances by the leading performers of this genre. Celebrities who have performed here include Maurice Chevalier, Edith Piaf and Juliette Gréco.

1940: THE CURTAIN FALL

The German occupation dealt a fatal blow to Montparnasse. The artists, many of them of Jewish origin, gradually left for safer places. The Germans took hold of Montparnasse in the first months of the occupation, requisitioning the large cafés for their personal use. For four years the terraces were "a sea of green", as a contemporary put it.

RUE DE LA GAÎTÉ
The Rue de la Gaîté no longer lived up to its name once it had lost Bobino, the famous home of the popular song, and many of its old bistros.

276, BOULEVARD RASPAIL (6 J4)
This turn-of-the-century building (above) is decorated on the theme of the couple: young love is portrayed on the left; in the middle is the arrival of the child; and old age is shown on the right.

TOUR MONTPARNASSE
Montparnasse Tower stands on the huge square in front of the new railway station, which serves Brittany with the high-speed TGV Atlantique. The tower has 58 stories of steel and smoked glass. It was widely criticized when it was first built in the mid-1940's, but has since become a familiar feature of the Paris landscape. From the top is a spectacular view of the city.

LIBERATION. On August 19, 1944, General Leclerc's 2nd Armored Division made a triumphal entry into Paris through the Avenue d'Orléans and the Boulevard du Montparnasse. The general set up his staff headquarters in the station on Place de Rennes, and it was here, on August 25, 1944, that General von Choltitz signed the treaty of surrender on behalf of the German occupying forces. Montparnasse did come alive again, but things were never the same: the area had been superseded by St-Germain-des-Prés ▲ *234*, where new trends had been set in the cafés which had escaped German control.

DECLINE. Vavin, La Rotonde, Le Dôme and La Coupole held onto their traditions, but times had changed, and Montparnasse was a shadow of its former self. The only streets to retain their character were the old ones between the Boulevard du Montparnasse and the Luxembourg Gardens, with their charming buildings from the 1890's:

rues Joseph-Bara, d'Assas and le Verrier are good examples. Léon-Paul Fargue, one of the last witnesses of the old Montparnasse, who spoke so eloquently of that "golden, ethereal, nervy Montparnasse which could banish the demons of solitude", went on a walk through the quarter in November 1947 – his last walk as a "pedestrian of Paris" through streets he knew so well, heading for Montparnasse Cemetery down the avenue which Louis XIV had dreamed of.

THE MODERN AGE

The old bohemian haunts have gradually been replaced or surrounded by contemporary buildings. The process started with the new station (6 G2) and the MAINE-MONTPARNASSE CENTER in which it is set, with its American-style Montparnasse Tower. Although the project had been proposed by Raoul Dautry as long ago as 1934, it began only in 1969 and continued on into the 1980's, with the redevelopment of the Guilleminot-Vercingétorix area on the other side of the Place de Catalogne (6 G3). The Place de Catalogne itself has a fountain designed by Shamaï Haber; it is bordered by two apartment blocks designed by Maurice Novarina in 1988, which follow the curve of the square, matching Ricardo Bofill's Échelles du Baroque building from 1983. Novarina's buildings are located on either side of a central alley: LES COLONNES is elliptical, while L'AMPHITHÉÂTRE is in the shape of a classical theater. The design of the façades is in keeping with the urban landscape and the inner green area, which surrounds a church.

NOTRE-DAME-DU-TRAVAIL. (6 G4) 35, rue Guilleminot. This church, Our Lady of Labor, was built especially for workers in 1899, following a popular subscription. Its striking metallic framework gives it the look of a factory, which is very apt. It is decorated with superb Art Deco friezes and contemporary works of art.

FONDATION CARTIER (6 J4) 261, boulevard Raspail. In 1994 the jeweler Cartier set up this institute devoted to contemporary art on the Left Bank, picking up on Montparnasse's long artistic tradition. The architect Jean Nouvel was commissioned to design the building. As Nouvel explained, "The style is one of lightness, using glass and finely woven steel to blur the tangible limits of the building and to dispel the impression of a solid volume in hazy evanescence. A style which allows the quarter to enjoy a beautiful garden which has long been hidden from view". The institute is located on the site of the former American Cultural Center, which was itself built on a place where the writer Chateaubriand lived between 1826 and 1838. In his *Memoirs from Beyond the Grave*, the writer records having "planted twenty-three Solomon cedars" in the garden; appropriately, one of these cedars now stands by the entrance to the institute.

MONTPARNASSE CEMETERY (6 IJ3)
This is the second largest cemetery in Paris. It was founded in 1824 and has become the traditional burial place of artists and literary figures. The Rue Émile-Richard, built in 1890, divided the cemetery's 48 acres into a small and a large cemetery. The poet Charles Baudelaire, buried in the sixth division, is without a doubt the star of the cemetery. The sculptor José de Charmoy created an unusual memorial for him (below) and for Sainte-Beuve's tomb in the seventh division. Zadkine, Tristan Tzara, Zao Wou-ki, and Brancusi are all buried here.

RIES LA

287

▲ La Ruche: a city of artists

La Ruche (The Beehive), the home of Expressionism, stands as a symbol of Montparnasse bohemianism. It was built thanks to the great generosity of "Père Boucher", sculptor and philanthropist, and housed some of the great names of the Paris School. Its studios were saved from decay and destruction by the Seydoux Foundation in the 1970's. Hidden away among the greenery of a peaceful garden, it still receives artists from all over the world.

ALFRED BOUCHER
He reached the height of his fame at the end of the 19th century. Having made a fortune from his flattering busts of society figures and sculptures of fleshy nymphs, he put part of it in the service of young, impecunious artists. Boucher bought a piece of land near the horsemeat slaughterhouses of Vaugirard for next to nothing and had La Ruche built there.

THE BEEHIVE IN DECLINE
La Ruche went into decline between the two world wars: by the beginning of the 1960's it had deteriorated into a decaying, unattractive ruin. It was saved due to the efforts of artists like Simone Dat and the financial assistance of René Seydoux. The studios have been designated a historical monument.

Lipchitz and his wife (below) by
Modigliani (right). *Sailor with Guitar*,
sculpture by Lipchitz. Sketch of
La Ruche by Fernand Léger (opposite).

LEGENDS OF LA RUCHE

Some of Père Boucher's "bees", like Chagall
and Léger, were good workers while others,
like Soutine, were incurable troublemakers.
In the midst of this artistic melting pot,
Modigliani and his mistress, Jeanne
Hébuterne, played out the drama of their
brief, tragic lives.

A MEDICI VILLA
FOR THE POOR

The artists of La Ruche
lived in poverty. Many
came from Eastern
Europe – Lipchitz,
Zadkine, Chagall,
Brancusi and Soutine –
drawn toward this
artistic crucible by
Montparnasse's
bohemian ambiance
and cheap rents. Some
French artists also
stayed here, including
Fernand Léger, drawing
in their wake the poets
and writers
    Apollinaire,
    Max Jacob,
    André Salmon
    and Blaise
    Cendrars.

THE ROTONDE DES VINS

Boucher took many ideas
from the Universal
Exhibition of 1900 – in
particular, the
Rotonde des Vins.
This polygonal
building in the shape
of a beehive was
divided into twenty-
four tiny studios. They
were nicknamed
"slices of brie"
because of their
wedge shape.

TODAY'S BEEHIVE

The studios at
91, quai de la Gare,
in former refrigerated
warehouses, are
today's successors
to the bohemian
artists' city. Since
1981 they have
housed a colorful
set of sculptors
and musicians.

▲ INVALIDES AND CHAMP-DE-MARS

1. HÔTEL DES INVALIDES
2. ESPLANADE DES INVALIDES
3. UNESCO
4. ÉCOLE MILITA...

This affluent quarter, with its wide vistas and straight avenues, has a military air about it. The major roads which cross it today were once large avenues cutting through

☑ **One day**

woods and fields, whose function was purely decorative. The Avenue de Breteuil, which was opened in 1680, leads nowhere. The Avenue de Ségur was built in 1770; leading toward Grenelle; the Avenue de Villars was built in the direction of Montparnasse, which did not exist at the time. All these roads date from the same era as the Invalides and the École Militaire, grand institutions created by Louis XIV and Louis XV for military use and the glory of the monarchy. After the First and Second empires, the republics used the Invalides for displays of patriotism and dedicated the Champ-de-Mars, today one of Paris's largest parks, to the great exhibitions of the industrial era. The Eiffel Tower stands as a record of these grand events. At the crossroads of today's Rue

6. CHURCH OF
ST-PIERRE-DU-GROS-CAILLOU
7. ST-FRANÇOIS-XAVIER
8. CHAMP-
DE-MARS
EL TOWER ✪

**THE INVALIDES
AT NIGHTFALL**
The long boulevard,
named after the
famous Hôtel des
Invalides, is lit up by
beacons.

Clerc and Rue St-Dominique was a village
built on land which was previously used
for truck farming. This village, Gros-
Caillou, expanded rapidly when the Hôtel
des Invalides was built and was swamped
by urban expansion at the end of the 19th
century. The laundresses of this village
were famous at the time: a "rugged band
of women armed with paddles", as
Michelet described them.

LES INVALIDES

(1 EF7)

Louis XIV built the Hôtel des Invalides, the largest
architectural project of his reign after Versailles, for his
wounded soldiers who previously had no option but to live by
stealing if they refused to join the abbeys, which were obliged
to take them in.

CONSTRUCTION. Libéral Bruant, who had just completed
the Hôpital de la Salpêtrière, built the eastern half of
the building on the Grenelle plain between 1671
and 1674. The first group of veterans moved in
immediately. Before the western section was
completed, Louis replaced Bruant with
Jules Hardouin-Mansart, who built
the double church of the Invalides.
The Soldiers' Church, for the
pensioners' use, was opened
in 1677, while the Domed
Church, reserved for
the king and his
entourage, was opened in
1706. At this stage they were
not separated by a glass wall,
as they are now.

THE SOLDIERS' CHURCH. The
church is entered through a gallery
on the second story of the main court.
Its austere barrel vault is 230 feet long,
without a transept and very bright. The
custom of hanging captured enemy
flags from the ceiling goes back to the Empire.

**PARMENTIER'S
LABORATORY**
A number of
scientists also lived at
the Invalides. It was

from here that
Antoine Augustin
Parmentier
introduced the potato
to the French by
writing his famous
report on the dietary
merits of this tuber.
He came up against
stubborn opposition
from the "gray nuns"
assigned to look after
invalid veterans, who
saw Parmentier as a
threat to their control
of medical matters.
They put up a tough
fight and thought they
had won when
Parmentier lost his
laboratory in 1773.
Nonetheless, he did
not give up and
converted the
flowerbeds of the
Invalides gardens into
vegetable patches.

The opening of the
Invalides Church by
Louis XIV, painted by
Pierre Denis Martin
the Younger.

NAPOLEON'S VISIT TO THE INVALIDES
Just like the kings who preceded him, Napoleon was eager to present himself as an attentive and paternal benefactor to the veterans.

TONS OF 24-CARAT GOLD
More than 27,830 pounds of gold (555,000 gold leaves) were used on the dome, where up to ten master goldsmiths worked in 1989. From this viewpoint, the long roof of the Soldiers' Church can be seen flanked by two courtyards, then the main court, which has further buildings and side courts on either side. The infirmaries are on the right-hand side, out of view. Straight ahead is the Esplanade des Invalides, extending the main lines of the building into the distance.

The flags hung there all date from after March 17, 1814: on this date the allies entered Paris, and Marshal Sérurier, the Governor of the Invalides, ordered the destruction of all trophies. Marshals of the French army are buried in the crypts, which are not open to the public. On July 14, 1789, the crowd which later stormed the Bastille came here first; with the veterans' assistance they took some twenty-three thousand rifles and twenty-four cannons from the cellars.

THE DÔME. The young Jules Hardouin found the design for this building among the papers of his great-uncle François Mansart; the plan was originally conceived for a mausoleum of the Bourbons at St-Denis but had never been carried out. The complex, centralized design of the building allowed for optimal light, which gave prominence to Charles de la Fosse's paintings in the dome. Mansart's nephew was able to perfect the building's internal arrangement, following the classical model of a Greek cross set in a square, with a central dome and circular chapels at each of the corners. All parts of the church can be seen from the central rotonda, which can itself be admired from each of the chapels. After December 15, 1840, when Napoleon's ashes were brought back to Paris, the dome became the mausoleum of the Bonapartes. It took more than twenty-one years to adapt Mansart's church to its imperial function. The crypt, which was completed in 1861, is twenty feet deep, with an opening of forty-nine feet in diameter: it holds the Emperor's tomb, made in Finnish red porphyry, following a design by Louis-Joachim Visconti.

AROUND THE MAIN COURT. Projections and pediments do little to relieve the classical severity of this court, which is bordered by cloisters on the first floor, like those typically found in convents or hospitals. There are two stories of arcades above this. Richly decorated refectories were located on either side of the court. Administrative offices were housed in the 640-foot-long central building facing the Esplanade.

A RESOLUTELY MODERN INSTITUTION. The pensioners lived in the ancillary buildings. Ordinary soldiers slept five or six to a room, and officers' rooms had one or two beds. This set new standards for the time, as did the facilities for invalid pensioners, who had individual rooms in the infirmary. Ten years of military service was the requirement for admittance to the Invalides, and prayers and mass were compulsory. Misdemeanors were punished with a seat at the "water drinkers' table" in the center of the refectory; however, anyone "found sleeping with a man or woman" was displayed on the "wooden horse", a large rack suspended by ropes. The building was designed to accommodate between fifteen hundred to two thousand veterans but had three thousand in 1710. It functioned as a small town.

WORKSHOPS. The pensioners could devote themselves to work. There were flourishing workshops for tapestry and ceramics, calligraphy and illumination: the Versailles *Antiphonary* and Louis XIV's *Book of Hours* were produced at the Invalides. Courses in anatomy and chemistry were also held here and the institution's surgeons were highly regarded. The Abbé Jean-Antoine Nollet's experiments with electricity inflamed the public's imagination in the mid-18th century, and this cure was used on paralyzed soldiers at the Invalides.

DECLINE. After the return of Napoleon's ashes, the mausoleum began to take precedence over the soldiers' home, which was the scene of a brief uprising in 1848. By this stage the number of pensioners had declined significantly: there were now only eighty or so. Today cannons no longer fire at the Invalides to announce great events, but it still has a very modern surgical hospital, and its buildings house the museums of the Army, of Relief Maps and Plans, and of the Liberation ▲ 145.

THE FAÇADE
The central pavilion with the entrance to the Invalides is rounded in shape. The pavilion is decorated with a carved pediment depicting the Sun King.

THE DÔME PAINTINGS
These were produced between 1702 and 1706 by several artists who worked for the glory of God and the monarchy: Charles de La Fosse painted the calotte (above) and Jouvenet the inner cupola. Coypel was brought in to paint the roof of the shrine, and Bon Boullogne decorated the corner chapels.

A COMPLEX ARRANGEMENT
Mansart's dome has two internal cupolas. The first ends at the second row of windows on the drum of the dome; the second forms a calotte, or cap, over the first. This double structure maximizes the lighting of the ceiling paintings. The device is perfect: from ground level the viewer is unaware of the complex construction. This ingenious arrangement was later used by Soufflot for the Panthéon ▲ 257.

293

RACETRACK FROM 1833 TO 1860
The Jockey Club, created under the July Monarchy, converted the Champ-de-Mars into a racetrack facing the Military Academy, as shown in this painting (below). The prevailing fashion for all things English ensured that the venture was a success. However, after 1854 the Society for the Promotion and Improvement of Horse racing moved to Longchamp, which had a better track.

LE CHAMP-DE-MARS (1 BC7 and 8)

In 1751, Louis XV decreed the establishment of a military academy, to be built on the Grenelle plain: his aim was to secure the allegiance of France's impoverished nobility by guaranteeing its younger members a military education. The vast area stretching to the Seine was given the name Champ-de-Mars and dedicated to military exercises. Great national celebrations were held on the Champ-de-Mars during the Revolution: the Festival of the Federation on July 14, 1790, during which Louis XVI pledged allegiance to the constitution (a year later, in the same place, La Fayette ordered soldiers to shoot into the crowd, which was calling for the king's deposition), and the Festival of the Supreme Being on June 8, 1794, presided over by Robespierre. Napoleon came to the Champ-de-Mars on December 3, 1804, just after he had been made Emperor, to present imperial standards to the officers who had gathered to pledge their loyalty.

THE UNIVERSAL EXHIBITIONS. The tradition of great exhibitions on the Champ-de-Mars began under the Second Empire ● 30. After exhibitions in 1867 and 1878, the Exhibition of 1889, on the centenary of the Revolution, was the most brilliant of all. Twenty-six million visitors came to see the Eiffel Tower, which had been built as the main attraction on the Champ-de-Mars. Another attraction was the GALERIE DES MACHINES, built by the architect Dutert and the engineer Contamin, which stood until 1909: its framework, in a single unit measuring 1,400 by 360 feet, heralded an architectural style which was to develop on an even grander scale with the advent of concrete. ELECTRICITY made a triumphant entrance at the Exhibition of 1900: the Champ-de-Mars was illuminated by a Palace of Electricity designed by the architect Hénart. The Great Wheel built on the corner of the Avenue Suffren and the Avenue de La Motte-Picquet towered over the area until 1937.

REDEVELOPMENT OF THE CHAMP-DE-MARS. In order to dispose of buildings left over from exhibitions and to raise funds, the City of Paris sold off plots of land around the perimeter of the Champ-de-Mars, which is now built up. Joseph Bouvard, Director of Promenades and Plantings, converted the central area into a garden of around 60 acres, which has become one of the most popular parks in the capital.

A patch of green: the Champ-de-Mars viewed from above.

THE ÉCOLE MILITAIRE (1 D8). The design of the building was entrusted to Jacques-Ange Gabriel, who also designed the Place Louis-XV (now Place de la Concorde). Construction work continued up to the eve of the Revolution. The long neoclassical façade overlooking the Champ-de-Mars is reproduced on the other side, which is not open to the public. The quadrangular dome can be seen from both sides. The wings, dating from the Second Empire, bear the inscriptions CAVALERIE and ARTILLERIE. The academy took in military cadets between 1777 and 1787 – among them Bonaparte. Today Gabriel's building houses the Institute of Advanced Studies for National Defense, as well as the Military Academy for Advanced Studies.

ART NOUVEAU FAÇADES
Jules Lavirotte designed this stunning façade at 29, avenue Rapp, in 1901 (1 C6). Curved lines form the basis of the ornamentation.

UNESCO (1 D9) 7, place de Fontenoy. The Y-shaped main building houses the general secretariat of Unesco. The building, which opened in 1958, was the work of Breuer (US), Nervi (Italy) and Zehrfuss (France). Works of art by Matta, Appel, Picasso and others decorate this major international institution.

295

▲ THE EIFFEL TOWER

The Eiffel Tower: this 1,000 feet of metal has come to symbolize Paris throughout the world. The tower was chosen among 107 projects as the centerpiece of the Universal Exhibition of 1889. Gustave Eiffel and his team of 50 engineers and 132 laborers took less than two years to achieve this technical feat, joining together 18,000 iron sections with 2.5 million rivets. The tower was originally designed to stand for twenty years but was saved for scientific purposes. Highly controversial and sneered at by artists from the very beginning, this paragon of metal architecture has attracted over 120 million visitors.

FAST WORK

The foundations were started on January 28, 1887, and took five months to complete. The four pillars were joined together by March 1888. The tower grew at a rate of 30 feet per month from the second story (190 feet high) to the third (370 feet high). After this, it grew more rapidly, rising to nearly 100 feet per month as it neared the summit. The sections arrived in preassembled 16-foot-long pieces.

Gustave Eiffel
(1832–1923)
Eiffel was a designer of
metal frameworks and an
unconventional engineer. His
creations included the viaducts
of Garabit (central France) and
Porto (Portugal), Pest Station
(Hungary) and the framework of the
Statue of Liberty.

New lighting
Sodium lamps were installed in 1985,
casting a yellow-orange light from inside
the tower.

"Bergère ô tour Eiffel..." ✪
Apollinaire might
have written that
the Eiffel Tower
watches over the
bridges of Paris
like a shepherd
over his sheep, but
it is the whole of the
city that seems to
nestle beneath it.
The stunning
view means that
it is almost
permanently
besieged by tourists.
On a fine day, it is
best to climb up on
foot to the second
or third level (go at
your own pace),
then take the lift up
to the fourth: it is
cheaper and less
crowded; the view
unfolds as you go,
and you get a much
better idea of the
tower's subtlety
and complexity.

SCIENTIFIC USES
The Eiffel Tower was intended only as a temporary construction. Eiffel incorporated laboratories for meteorology, aerodynamics and instrument calibration, in order to demonstrate the tower's scientific utility. The tower later became a telegraph station (1898), a radio station (1921) and a television station (1959).

A SUCCESS WITH THE PUBLIC

The Eiffel Tower was opened on March 31, 1889. Gustave Eiffel climbed the 1,710 steps to place the French flag at the top. For six months the tower had twelve thousand visitors a day. After this, the number of visitors trailed off, until 1963. During those sixty years the tower had captured the hearts of new generations of poets and painters ● 92.

THE ICARUS OF PARIS

February 4, 1912, a tailor from Longjumeau named Reichelt threw himself from the first level of the tower strapped into a large waterproof canvas: he flew . . . then crashed to the ground, 190 feet below.

🕐 **One day**

"In my spare time I would wander through the surrounding streets, which were named after painters: Scheffer, La Tour, David."

Alfonso Reyes

The 16th arrondissement came into being in 1860 ● *21*, when three very rural villages were amalgamated. This soon became one of the capital's most elegant quarters. It is now an architectural goldmine, offering a unique overview of Art Nouveau and Art Deco styles, alongside charming little hamlets, a remnant of the area's rural past.

PASSY
(8 CJ 5 to 10)

At first a simple hamlet, Passy was raised to the status of *seigneurie* (a lord's domain) in the 15th century. The presence of the court at the royal Château de la Muette and the development of thermal springs in the 18th century attracted wealthy Parisians to these vine-covered slopes. Under the Revolution the village, with only half a dozen streets, became an independent commune or parish. In 1825 Passy was divided into lots, creating the Élysée-Charles X quarter around Place Victor-Hugo: this was the first stage of urbanization.

Balzac's house overlooks the Hôtel de Lamballe, now the Turkish Embassy, where Maupassant died. Below, the Château de la Muette, which no longer exists.

RANELAGH GARDENS (8 F9 and 10). This green triangle frequented by children and joggers is all that remains of La Muette estate: it is bordered by quiet, opulent streets. It was from one of these streets, Allée Pilâtre-de-Rozier, that the first hot-air balloon flight took place in 1783. The Ancien Régime danced at the famous Ranelagh ball which was held in the gardens up to the Second Empire. Modern apartment blocks have largely replaced the Belle Époque houses around the gardens: only three of these remain, one of them the MUSÉE MARMOTTAN ▲ *155*.

BOULEVARD BEAUSÉJOUR (8 F10). The boulevard crosses what used to be a rural area, where Mme Récamier, Chateaubriand and Rossini stayed. Villa Beauséjour, at no. 7, has a surprise for passersby: three chocolate-colored *isbas* (log huts), remnants of the Universal Exhibition of 1867.

RUE DE PASSY (8 GI10). Formerly the main street of the village, this is still the area's liveliest road. It follows the same winding course as before, but fashionable shops have replaced the old stalls. The building where Louis XV kept his collection of scientific instruments is now occupied by Frank & Fils store: a sign of the times. The small Place de Passy, where the old town hall used to be, has kept something of its former rustic charm.

CIMETIERE DE PASSY (8 I8). (2, rue du-Commandant-Schloesing). Debussy, Manet and the poetess Renée Vivien are buried in this small, shady cemetery, the highlight of the quarter. Other tombs worthy of note include that of stage designer Ruhlmann and the Moorish tomb of Marie Baskirtseff, a painter and poetess who died in her prime, acquiring posthumous fame through her diary.

CHAILLOT   (8 J8)

THE INSPIRED HILL. Up to the Revolution Chaillot was the preserve of two religious orders. The monastery of the Minims, more often known as the Bonshommes, was directly next to that of the Visitandines which was destroyed in 1794 when the Grenelle powder magazine exploded. The hill was leveled during building works undertaken by Napoleon I and Napoleon III and Davioud built a Moorish palace on it for the Universal Exhibition in 1878. The palace was rebuilt in its present form in 1937 when the organizers of the

RANELAGH MOVIE-THEATER
The theater dates from the 18th century. Its neo-Renaissance auditorium saw the premiere of Wagner's *Rheingold* in 1900.

THE PERRET BROTHERS
Auguste (1874–1954), Gustave (1876–1952) and Claude (1880–1960) achieved new heights in concrete architecture, throughout the 16th arrondissement: (below) a detail of *25 bis*, rue Franklin (1903).

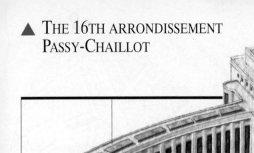

Above, the Palais
de Chaillot

THE TROCADÉRO
Davioud's temporary
palace replaced the
elegant Couvent de la
Visitation (Convent
of the Visitation),
founded in 1651 by

Henriette de France,
itself on the site of
Catherine de'
Medici's country
house. Chaillot has
attracted all kinds of
architectural fantasies
Napoleon wanted to
build a palace for the
King of Rome here
and the 1848
Revolutionaries
dreamed of building a
vast palace of the
people of France.

International
Exhibition of Arts and
Technology located the
exhibition's entrance on Place
du Trocadéro. The palace of Davioud
was built on the site of the palace of Chaillot,
and the palace of Tokyo on the site of the former
Savonnerie, carpet manufacturers to the royal family.

PALAIS DE CHAILLOT (8 J8) Place du Trocadéro.
A competition was held for the new Trocadéro in 1932.
Jacques Carlu was victorious, together with his partners
Louis-Hippolyte Boileau and Léon Azéma, beating Auguste
Perret ▲ *301* and Le Corbusier ▲ *307*. The project set out to
achieve the impossible: Davioud's palace was to be rebuilt,
but retaining its basic structure in order to minimize public
expenditure. The architects destroyed the minarets and
rotonda of the old palace and separated its two wings.
Ignoring academic precepts they chose not to add a
campanile to balance the structure. The completed building
opens majestically onto the Champ-de-Mars. The project's
many critics were finally won over by the effectiveness of
its horizontal structure.

A STOREHOUSE OF 1930'S ART. The aim of the Exhibition was
to stimulate a renaissance in the decorative arts. The interior
of the palace was therefore decorated by seventy-one painters
and sculptors, representing all aspects of contemporary
French art. The architects had the task of making a
harmonious whole from this
diverse range of works, which has
been criticized for its eclecticism.

THE EXTERNAL DECORATION
is thoroughly classical in its
sobriety. Metopes mark the lower
entrance to the theater, while the
blind façades on the street sides
of the Passy wing (right-hand
side) and Paris wing (left-hand
side) feature bas-reliefs on
themes relating to the museums inside. Sculptures
are arranged with equal care around the square,
the terrace, the gardens and the ornamental lake.
The central pavilions, bearing quotations from
Paul Valéry on two sides, are each surmounted
by a monumental group in bronze: by
Delamare on the left and by Sarrabezolles on
the right. The graceful lines of the bronzes in
the square (right) contrast with the monumental
groups on the terrace: *Apollo* by Bouchard and
Hercules by Pommier.

THE THEATER. Its wide galleries, halls and
staircases still have their original decoration

created by artists of the period: Vuillard, Bonnard and Roussel. The Palais de Chaillot houses the MUSÉE DE LA MARINE (Naval Museum) ▲ 155, the MUSÉE DE L'HOMME (Museum of Mankind) ▲ 144, the CINÉMATHÈQUE and the THÉATRE NATIONAL DE CHAILLOT, which retains its original lobby.

PALAIS DE TOKYO

(8 1B4) 11–13, av. du Pont-Wilson.

It was decided to create a museum of modern art for the International Exhibition of Arts and Technology of 1937.

A competition was held and four architects – Dondel, Aubert, Viard and Dastugue – won the commission to build this elegant building, designed entirely to achieve optimal interior lighting. It is called the "Palais de Tokyo" because its riverside street, which dates back to 1572, was named Avenue de Tokio in 1918; in 1945 it was changed to Avenue de New York. A colonnade of white stone forms a portico around a central patio, joining the two wings; one houses the Museum of Modern Art of the City of Paris, the other the Site de Création Contemporaine, Palais de Tokyo, opened in 2002. This huge multi-disciplinary "laboratory" for contemporary creation holds exhibitions, events and meetings with the artists; a wonderful initiative or a fashionable mess, according to your point of view. New gardens were also planted in 2002. In both wings, most rooms are lit from above. The only decoration is in the courtyard, arranged around an ornamental lake dominated by *France*, a bronze by Rodin's associate and chief assistant Bourdelle, who also created *Strength* and *Victory*, on either side of the peristyle.

FOR THE **MUSÉE GUIMET** SEE ▲ 142.

The Joys of Life by Léon Drivier, a group for the Trocadéro Gardens.

THE TNP (National Theater of Paris)

The predecessor of the National Theater of Chaillot was founded in 1920 by Firmin Gémier, a supporter of popular theater. It was first located in Davioud's palace then relocated to the great hall of the new Trocadéro designed by the Niermans brothers. Jean Vilar made this into the leading stage of the French theater with a troupe of young stars including Gérard Philipe and Jeanne Moreau. Under his direction, between 1951 and 1963, the theater-going public became accustomed to seeing the classics and rediscovered Kleist, Brecht and O'Casey.

Auteuil was an ecclesiastical domain from the 11th century to the Revolution. The village, famed for its vines, survived the ups and downs of history unscathed under the monks' supervision. It was separated from the hamlet of Boulogne in the 14th century and from the village of Passy three centuries later. Auteuil became a refuge for the literary and aristocratic elite seeking sanctuary from the turbulence of Paris. Thermal springs contributed to its popularity: famous visitors included Molière, Racine and Boileau, followed later by Chateaubriand, Bonaparte and Marcel Proust. Auteuil, like neighboring Passy, was annexed to Paris in 1860.

RUE LA FONTAINE (7 EF3). Proust was born on the site of no. 96, but this affluent street is chiefly famous for its architectural attractions, dominated by the work of Hector Guimard ● 78.

CASTEL BÉRANGER (no. 14). This Art Nouveau masterpiece was originally a block of low-rent apartments: the years have given it a sheen of age without detracting from its striking originality. When construction started in 1895, Auteuil was merely an outlying suburb full of factories and warehouses. A careful economy was observed in all aspects of its design, from the choice of materials to the mass production of stained-glass windows, balconies and mosaics. This did not prevent Guimard from giving full rein to his fertile imagination, with the consent of his patron Mme Fournier. Castel Béranger is three buildings grouped around a courtyard. The asymmetrical façades feature gables, barbizons and corbeled

THE CAFÉ-BAR AT 17, RUE LA FONTAINE Unlike its neighbors, this café-bar with its crimson façade has survived in its original state and is currently being classified as an historical monument. The interior is strictly authentic, with its original decorations and mirrors speckled with age.

alconies decorated with clinging foliage nd seahorses. The materials used are ery diverse, including brick, cast iron, eramics, millstone and freestone. The esult, achieved with minimal expense, is ibrant and colorful, with yellow, red, eige and blue-green used to emphasize ie building's design. Stone, an npressive and expensive material, is eserved for the shell of the building and ie main façade. The luxuriant rnamentation makes great use of curved lines which are ypical of Art Nouveau. Interior decorations display the same iventiveness: Guimard achieved optimal lighting and spatial onditions while creating a cohesive structural and rchitectural whole. Everything bears his mark, from the itchen ranges to the brass door handles whose shape he etermined by clasping a piece of clay in his hand. The uilding, nicknamed Castel Dérangé (Crazy Castle), won a rize in the first competition for façades in the city of Paris, nd launched Guimard's brilliant but controversial career.

NEW AUSTERITY. Guimard's other creations on Rue La ontaine show how his work evolved after this first nasterpiece. Some fifteen years after Castel Béranger, usterity has taken over from imaginative exuberance. In the roup of buildings comprising nos. 17, 19 and 21, RUE LA ONTAINE, 8 and 10, RUE AGAR (7 G2) and no. 43, RUE GROS 7 G2) Guimard acted as property developer as well as rchitect. Eleven apartment buildings were planned, but only ix were completed. The architect took great care over details, esigning the shop fronts on the Rue Gros and the Rue La Fontaine as well as the street signs and numbers on the Rue Agar.

HÔTEL MEZZARA (no. 60, visit by permission of the Rector of the University of Paris). This is one of the few works by Guimard to retain its original interior decorations. The interior is arranged around a vast central hall with a gallery on the second floor, lit by a glass roof.

CHARITABLE ORPHANAGE OF AUTEUIL (7 F3) (no. 40). This was founded in 1860 to take in orphans, who were then trained for manual work. A collection of neo-Gothic buildings surrounds a popular garden: the movie theater here was the only one in the quarter for a long time.

HECTOR GUIMARD (1867–1942) Guimard studied and later taught at the École des Beaux-Arts: his role models were Horta, leader of Belgian Art Nouveau and Viollet-le-Duc. From his earliest works he exhibited an originality which was often misunderstood. Guimard's work, dismissed by his critics as "noodle" style, found expression in his apartment blocks, mostly built in the suburbs and in the 16th arrondissement, as well as in his furniture designs and kiosks for the Paris Métro. His last creations, influenced by the Art Deco movement, made no impact on the architectural world. Guimard died in the United States, forgotten by everyone.

THE 1882 DECREE
In the 19th century, the relaxation of building regulations freed Parisian architecture from the shackles imposed by Haussmann ● 72. Architects were allowed to incorporate projections and bow windows in their buildings.

THE BOILEAU ESTATE
After 1830 the parks which made up most of Auteuil were divided into lots, allowing the development of private estates. The Boileau estate was built on the site where the 17th-century author lived and convalesced. In 1838 the printer Lemercier acquired the southern part of the estate where he built squares, alleys and country houses. Strict regulations were enforced to preserve the peacefulness of the area. Lemercier later built Villa Montmorency on the site of Boufflers' former home at 12, rue Poussin.

STUDIO BUILDING (no. 65). As an architect, Henri Sauvage (1873–1932) does not fit into any categories. Initially a supporter of Art Nouveau, he later concentrated on white, tiered apartment blocks ● 78, ▲ 283. This series of split-level studios is clearly different from his earlier work: the style is monumental, using cool-colored tiles in geometric patterns to emphasize the design.

PLACE D'AUTEUIL (7 F4). This square stands on the site of the first cemetery in Auteuil: a small obelisk opposite the church is the only remnant. It marks the tomb of Chancellor d'Aguesseau (1668–1751), a French legal reformer. The church of NOTRE-DAME-D'AUTEUIL, begun in 1319, was rebuilt by Vaudremer in 1877 in a Romano-Byzantine style.

RUE D'AUTEUIL (7 DE4). Here you will find the HÔTEL PUSHER, built in the 17th century (no. 16) and the HÔTEL DE VERRIERES (nos. 43–47), scene of the love affair between the Maréchal de Saxe and the actress Marie de Verrières, George Sand's ancestors. This former thoroughfare served as a refuge for philosophers and writers escaping the turmoil of the capital from the 17th century onward.

LITERATURE IN RUE D'AUTEUIL. Racine wrote *Les Plaideurs* (*The Litigants*) in a house on the site of today's Lycée Jean-Baptiste-Say (no. 11 *bis*) and Molière wrote *Amphitryon* at no 2. Both Racine and Molière frequented the Auberge du Mouton-Blanc, which has since become a restaurant (no. 40) other visitors to the inn included Boileau, La Fontaine, the actress Mme Champmeslé and Mme de Sévigné. After Molière's death in 1763 the parish priest of Auteuil accompanied his widow Armande Béjart to an audience with Louis XIV. The king allowed them to bury the writer on consecrated ground even though actors were generally excommunicated at the time.

THE SALON OF MME HELVETIUS. The house at 59, rue d'Auteuil was built around 1720 and then rebuilt at the end of the 19th century. In 1772 the widow of philosopher Helvetius bought it from the painter Quentin de La Tour. Her guests here included Diderot, Condorcet, d'Alembert, Chénier, Talleyrand, Chateaubriand and two future presidents of the United States Jefferson and Adams. She received offers of marriage from two gallant octogenarians Tugot and Benjamin

Franklin. "Our Lady of Auteuil", as she was known, outlived her salon and died peacefully in 1800.

CHÂTEAU DU COQ (nos. 63–73). Just a wall separated 59, rue d'Auteuil from this "petite maison" which Louis XV used for his secret liaisons. The king, who was passionately interested in botany, added a vast nursery to the house, which survives as the basis for the Auteuil Flower Garden. The land was divided up in 1862, making way for the Rue Michel-Ange, Rue Erlanger and Rue Molitor.

RUE DU BUIS ★ (7 E4). This street, lined with white houses decorated with gargoyles, has kept all its original charm. At no. 6 a plaque commemorates Olympe de Gouges, a writer and feminist who was guillotined in 1793: legend has it that she was a natural daughter of Louis XV.

FONDATION LE CORBUSIER (7 E1) 8–10, square du Docteur-Blanche ▲ *302*, ● *78*. Le Corbusier prepared an overall plan for this cul-de-sac which stands on poor building land but had to be content with building two terraced houses in 1924, which now house the Fondation Le Corbusier. One was intended for his brother Albert Jeanneret (no. 8), the other for his friend La Roche (no. 10). The houses have the piles, roof terraces, window ledges, and free-style ground plans and façades which are typical of his style.

RUE MALLET-STEVENS (7 E1). The cream of Paris society, a minister and two prefects gathered for the opening of this masterpiece by Robert Mallet-Stevens ● *78* in 1927. The owners of the different plots had accepted an overall design for the site. Five individual houses are arranged along the avenue – all have sleek white façades incorporating terraces and recesses. Every house is different but overall harmony is achieved through the use of shapes, building materials, the dado which surrounds the buildings, the flower beds and street lamps. The architect's office (no. 12, right) was added later. Sculptors Joël and Jan Martel live and work in a home studio at no. 10.

LE CORBUSIER (1888–1965) This French painter, town planner and polemicist, originally from Switzerland, became one of the leading architects of the modern era. Villa Laroche (above) was used as a setting for its owner's art collections.

16ᴹᴱ Aᵀ. RUE DU CAPITAINE OLCHANSKI

A ROYAL VIEW

The four-mile-long axis which runs from the Place de la Concorde to the Arche of

Half a day

THE THREE ARCHES

Napoleon decided to build the Arc du Carrousel and the Arc de Triomphe in February 1806. The demolition of the Tuileries Palace in 1882 opened up the view from one to the other. The opening of the Grande Arche of La Défense seems to point toward an extension of the Great Avenue.

AMUSEMENTS OF THE PAST.

The Coliseum, demolished in 1780, began the tradition of open-air entertainment. Many other establishments flourished, attracting large crowds. They all disappeared by the end of the 19th century.

La Défense was started more than three centuries ago, under the supervision of Le Nôtre. Louis XIV commissioned him to redesign the gardens of the Tuileries in 1664. In doing so Le Nôtre gave prominence to the central avenue, which he extended beyond the park, up to today's Rond-Point des Champs-Élysées, without making any changes to the area in between (which was to become the Place de la Concorde). There was no need for this: from his palace the king could not

1. ARC DE TRIOMPHE
2. PARIS CHAMBER OF COMMERCE AND INDUSTRY
3. CLARIDGE, LIDO, ARCADES DU LIDO
4. HÔTEL DE LA PAÏVA
5. ROND-POINT DES CHAMPS-ÉLYSÉES
6. THÉÂTRE MARIGNY
7. PALAIS DE L'ÉLYSÉE
8. ESPACE CARDIN
9. PETIT PALAIS
10. GRAND PALAIS
11. PALAIS DE LA DÉCOUVERTE
12. THÉÂTRE DES CHAMPS-ÉLYSÉES
13. ANGLICAN CHURCH

see this area, and the only view that mattered was the view created for the king's eyes.
THE GLORIOUS VISTA. The avenue duplicates the Rue du Faubourg-St-Honoré. The old Normandy road, it was built initially for purely esthetic reasons rather than practical ones, although its extension to Neuilly in the 18th century was undertaken in response to more tangible needs. Especially since the development of La Défense in the 1980's, the great avenue is basically monumental in function, punctuating the landscape and enhancing the capital's prestigious image. The road's main landmarks are the Place de la Concorde, the Arc de Triomphe and the Grande Arche; the Porte Maillot is rather a poor relation, while the Pyramide du Louvre to the east is the latest addition, marking the origins of this grand design. The stretches of road in between serve merely to mark the distance from one monument to the next. From the Arc de Triomphe to the Grande Arche, it is the view which gives the great avenue its meaning. It may be extended farther, beyond La Défense, as there are plans to incorporate the road which runs through Nanterre. Only the long stretch between the Arc de Triomphe and the Place de la Concorde has any real character. This avenue has become a symbol of patriotism and French power.

SHOWCASE OF MODERNISM. The gardens of the Champs-Élysées have a long history. The history of the avenue and its surrounding area goes back only to the beginning of the last century, when the capital expanded toward the west and a new quarter sprang up, studded with opulent private residences. However, the stretch between Concorde and the Arc de Triomphe seems to have been used for strolling and recreation from early times. Although few people live there, many come to visit its numerous places of entertainment: from the Bal Mabille to the Lido, the Café des Ambassadeurs to Fouquet's, the Panorama to the movie theaters. Traditionally, the gardens and the avenue have been a showcase for the latest technologies: for industry, the car and the movies. At the other end of the avenue, La Défense transposes this modernist tradition into the architectural sphere. Here, the Grande Arche looks back over Paris from the height of its stone platform: this subtle shift of perspective is appropriate, as the city center now has fewer inhabitants than the suburbs.

NATIONAL TRIUMPHS
Immense crowds gathered on the Champs-Élysées, the pathway of national pride, to greet Napoleon I, to honor the internment procession of Victor Hugo in 1885, and to celebrate the liberation of Paris in 1944 or, most recently, France's 1998 World Cup triumph.

309

La fontaine nord, La Navigation fluviale

THE OBELISK

Louis-Philippe wanted to put up a monument which would not arouse violent passions of the revolutionary or royalist variety. The Luxor Obelisk, a perfectly neutral monument, was erected in 1836 before a crowd of 200,000 spectators.

PLACE DE LA CONCORDE

The square was intended as the setting for a statue of Louis XV, which stood there for only thirty years. It broke with the tradition of enclosed royal squares ● *62* in order to preserve the view from the Tuileries to the Champs-Élysées. The royal architect Jacques-Ange Gabriel adopted Germain Boffrand's solution and bordered only one side of the square with monumental façades. He opened up the space to the spectacle of "nature", a concept much admired in the 18th century – in this case the woods which stood on the site of today's gardens.

A SQUARE FOR THE CROWDS. The eight statues on stone pedestals represent the eight great towns of France. They mark the access to the dry moat, filled in 1854 and now planted as flowerbeds. Public celebrations were held on the square under the Ancien Régime, but it was later the setting for less happy events. The guillotine was set up here for the execution of Louis XVI; Danton, Robespierre and many others were to follow the king. The naval headquarters moved into the building behind Gabriel's façades, which were inspired by the Louvre colonnade. This building, the HÔTEL DE LA MARINE, still retains furnishings from the 18th and 19th centuries. West of the Rue Royale is the luxurious Hôtel de Crillon. The square today is largely the product of alterations made from the 1830's onward, under the direction of the architect Hittorff, who built two fountains on either side of the obelisk, adding a number of columns decorated with ship's prows, the symbol of the capital.

THE MARLY HORSES

These sculptures by Coustou have stood at the entrance to the gardens since 1794.

HÔTEL DE CRILLON

THE CHAMPS-ÉLYSÉES GARDENS

(1 FG3) The avenue of the Champs-Élysées was created to give the king an impressive view from the Tuileries. Originally it was bordered by undergrowth and insalubrious establishments where petty crooks and prostitutes met. The gardens first became popular during the Revolution, when the spectacle of "patriotic shortenings" (beheadings) attracted crowds thirsty for blood and wine. When the Empire fell, Russian and Prussian troops camped out in the gardens for two years, destroying all the vegetation. The most popular promenade in Europe and its establishments fell into decline.

RENAISSANCE OF THE GARDENS. The gardens were renovated in the 1830's and 1840's by Hittorff while work was under way on the Place de la Concorde. He added bronze candelabras to illuminate the gardens, seven fountains to cool the air, and a number of buildings, of which the pavilions Ledoyen and Laurent are the only ones to survive today. Theaters, circuses, panoramas and cafés attracted crowds avid for entertainment, which until then had been limited to the large boulevards. The Summer Circus arena, which no longer exists, had excellent acoustics which meant that concerts could be held there: Berlioz was among the conductors. Offenbach directed the Théâtre des Bouffes-Parisiens, which was later replaced by the Théâtre Marigny. There was also a fashion for panoramas – painted canvases arranged in a circle, which recreated a landscape in the round for viewers standing in the center. Hittorff's panorama opened with *The Fire of Moscow*; a second panorama, built by Davioud, followed in 1860. The public could admire seas and continents at the Géorama, a sort of early-day "Géode" ▲ *429*.

MUSIC IN THE PARK. In 1859, Alphand ▲ *208* redesigned the gardens in the English style: groups of trees and winding pathways replaced the formal squares. There had always been music in the Champs-Élysées: dances had always been popular, and at the end of the 19th and the beginning of the 20th century the café-concert became fashionable. Yvette Guilbert, Mistinguett and Maurice Chevalier performed at the Ambassadeurs at the height of its popularity. The Théâtre Marigny was built in 1880, followed by the Pavillon de l'Élysée (now Élysée-Lenôtre) in 1898. The Pavillon des Ambassadeurs (now the Espace Pierre Cardin) was the most recent addition to the garden's buildings, dating from 1931. The gardens currently have four restaurants, two theaters and one pavilion.

PAVILLON LEDOYEN
This charming restaurant ▲ *497*, rebuilt by Hittorff in 1848, has been restored to its original colors. Its visitors have included many celebrated painters and writers: Flaubert, Maupassant, Zola, Gide and Cocteau. In 1993, Robert Altman shot one of the scenes here for his film *Ready-to-Wear.*

RENAUD-BARRAULT, A LEGENDARY THEATER
Jean-Louis Barrault and Madeleine Renaud, legends of French theater, directed the Marigny, Odéon and Orsay theaters before founding the Théâtre du Rond-Point (1 E3) in the early 1980's, in Davioud's panorama which had been converted into a skating rink at the end of the 19th century.

GRAND PALAIS (1 E3)

GRAND PALAIS
Since opening, this colossus of a building – 790 feet long and 148 feet high – has been criticized for its academic façades, whose stone

The Universal Exhibitions were initially dedicated to industry and technology but gradually opened their doors to the creative arts. The 1900 Exhibition replaced the Palace of Industry, built in 1855 for the first exhibition, with the Petit Palais and the Grand Palais, a monument dedicated to the glory of French art. Art exhibitions held at the GRAND PALAIS (Avenue Winston Churchill) included the Salon d'Automne, featuring Gauguin in 1906 and Cézanne the following year; the Salon des Indépendants, the most revolutionary exhibition of all; and part of the International Exhibition of Decorative Arts in 1925, which saw the appearance of Art Deco style. Recently it has housed

colonnades crowned with statues hide the iron construction behind them. Inside, metal spirals and foliage are an integral part of the structure, breaking with the tradition of adding separate cast-iron ornaments. This integration of ornament and structure is typical of Art Nouveau.

shows like FIAC (International Fair of Contemporary Art) and major art exhibitions: Renoir, the Etruscans and Toulouse-Lautrec attracted several hundred thousand visitors. It is currently closed for renovation. In 1937 the PALAIS DE LA DÉCOUVERTE (1 E3) opened in the wing facing the Avenue Franklin D. Roosevelt. It was created to popularize science and invites visitors to take part in experiments covering the fields of astronomy, biology, medicine, chemistry, mathematics, physics and earth sciences. The PETIT PALAIS (1 F4) ▲ *169* has housed the municipal art collections since 1902. It has a dome reminiscent of the Invalides: its high gilded gateway and rich ornamentation give it an indisputable charm.

FIAC PARIS

GRAND PALAIS

20

9-17 OCTOBRE 93

SALON d'AUTOMNE

THE FRANÇOIS-I QUARTER (1 D3)

This was the first area of Paris to be divided into lots: it was created in 1823 on a star-shaped plan imitating classical parks. The project did not match developers' expectations, however; by 1830, Victor Hugo was living in the only house on Rue Jean-Goujon. The area became fully built up during the Second Empire. The Hôtel Clermont-Tonnerre and the Hôtel Vilgruy, built around 1865, stand opposite each other in Place François-I on either side of Davioud's fountain.

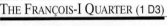

THE FIRE OF THE BAZAR DE LA CHARITÉ
The church of Notre-Dame-de-la-Consolation (23, rue Jean-Goujon) was built to commemorate the victims of the fire at the Bazar de la Charité, a charity sale attended by the cream of Paris society. The sister of Empress Elizabeth of Austria died in the fire, which claimed 125 victims, of whom 120 were women. A number of men had beaten their way to safety using their walking sticks, dispelling some illusions regarding gentlemanly behavior.

AVENUE MONTAIGNE

(1 D3). The great fashion designers, jewelers, perfumers and leather artisans make this the most expensive street in the quarter. Buildings worth a look here include the Hôtel Plaza Athénée (nos. 23–27). However, the pride of the avenue is still the THÉÂTRE DES CHAMPS-ÉLYSÉES ★ (nos. 13–15), built just before World War One. Bourdelle was responsible for the bas-reliefs on the outside; the painters Maurice Denis, Vuillard and Roussel also contributed to the decoration. The theater was highly innovative in its programming: Nijinsky's choreography and Stravinsky's music for *The Rite of Spring* created a sensation. From Richard Strauss to Boulez, the theater has stuck to its policy of presenting high culture.

A NABIS DOME
Maurice Denis, of the Nabis group of artists, produced four paintings representing the *History of Music* for the dome of the auditorium of the Théâtre des Champs-Élysées (left).

Jean-Paul Belmondo and Jean Seberg on the Champs-Élysées in Jean-Luc Godard's *Breathless*.

AVENUE DES CHAMPS-ÉLYSÉES (1 B to G 1 to 4)

Was the Avenue des Champs-Élysées, nicknamed "les Champs" by Parisians, ever as magnificent as its reputation? Maybe in the Belle Époque, when it boasted apartment blocks with monumental façades and luxury hotels. The legend still lives on today, despite the noisy commercialism which has taken it over. In 1994 the Paris city council took steps to clean up the avenue, diverting cars to side roads and creating new street furniture. Although the Champs may not be able to match its former glory, it has regained a good deal of its charm as a place to stroll.

BRIEF HISTORY OF THE CHAMPS. The avenue's history is scarcely a century old. It only reached just beyond the Rond-Point in the 17th century and was extended to the Place de l'Étoile and then to Neuilly at the end of the 18th century. In 1800 only six buildings stood along the avenue, which gradually became more built up during the following decades. In the mid-19th century, under the Second Empire, the division between rich Paris and poor Paris became clearer: the avenue became part of the new wealthy district to the west of the capital. Only a few houses have survived from this period, among them HÔTEL DE LA PAÏVA (no. 25). The real boom dates from the beginning of this century. The avenue was on the first Métro line, which opened in 1900, and several large hotels were built here, including the ÉLYSÉE PALACE in 1897 (no. 103, now a bank headquarters) and the CLARIDGE (no. 74, now residential). Luxury shops also began to appear at this time: the perfumer Guerlain (no. 68) arrived in 1913.

AVENUE OF FASHION. Palatial car showrooms were opened on the avenue during the 1920's; today's relatively modest successors are the PUB RENAULT (nos. 51–53), which shows some cars from the collection, and HIPPO CITROËN (no. 40). Two splendid office buildings survive from the 1930's (nos. 52–60 and no. 101). During the same decade the avenue boasted a number of first-run movie theaters. The movie industry is still celebrated here every year when the César awards are presented at FOUQUET'S (no. 99). The Arcades des Champs-Élysées (no. 78) – better known as the ARCADES DU LIDO, as they used to house the famous cabaret, now located at no. 116 *bis* – still have their splendid pink marble columns and original Lalique lamps.

HÔTEL DE LA PAÏVA
Following various amorous conquests, Thérèse Lachman, one of the many courtesans of the Second Empire, became the marquise de la Païva. In 1852 she met the hugely rich Count Guido Henkel von Donnersmark. His unlimited financial resources enabled her to build the most opulent town house in Paris. She employed famous decorators and sculptors, including Dalou, Carrier-Belleuse and Paul Baudry (who designed the ceiling of the Opéra's auditorium). The house still has its splendid onyx

CHAMPS-ÉLYSÉES: A ROYAL AVENUE ✪
Of the many vistas in Paris, that of "les Champs" is the grandest. This is the very heart of the modern, cosmopolitain city. The sunny north side is filled with window-shoppers and lined with famous international brand names. The south side has pavement cafes and its own set of prestigious establishments. The best view is from the top of the Arc de Triomphe, a center from which radiate eleven other avenues.

315

▲ THE ARC DE TRIOMPHE

THE GIANT ARCH
Only this massive arch, with its single arcade, could provide a suitably majestic conclusion to the view down the avenue.

When Napoleon decided to build the Arc de Triomphe in 1806, he wanted not only to celebrate the victories of the Grande Armée but also to "feed French sculpture for ten years". When the arch was completed in 1836 it had achieved this aim: "this pile of stone for a pile of glory", as Victor Hugo described it, provides a backdrop for the works of great 19th-century artists. As for its function as a triumphal arch, this has continued to the present day: conquerors and liberators of this century have processed here, and in peacetime this is the setting for the July 14 military parade.

TRIUMPHAL ELEPHANT
After 1722, the leveling and redevelopment of the Étoile hill gave rise to a number of grandiose and eccentric projects. In 1758 an architect proposed building an elephant fountain with rooms inside.

NATIONAL GLORY
After Napoleon in 1840, Victor Hugo was accorded posthumous honors under the arch designed by Chalgrin. The plaster chariot which had crowned the monument for three years was destroyed the following year and has never been replaced. Since 1921 the arch has housed the tomb of the Unknown Soldier.

TRIUMPH
Cortot, who created the *Triumph of Napoleon*, was one of the sculptors, connected with the Romantic movement, who sought to revitalize the classical tradition.

RESISTANCE
Adolphe Thiers was Minister of the Interior under Louis-Philippe and an art lover; it was to him that Étex owed the commission for the two high reliefs facing Neuilly.

"La Marseillaise"
The absence of columns left large spaces free for sculpture on the arch: some twenty artists contributed to it. Rude's *Marseillaise*, on the side facing central Paris, shows the Romantic influence in sculpture. Unlike a number of sculptors who received public commissions, Rude adopted a very personal tone here, which proved far more successful than the other reliefs.

"Peace"
Where modernist sculptors depicted dramatic subjects the stone is worked in a rougher, more abrupt fashion, as can be seen in the two works by Étex.

Misuses of the Arc
This pompous edifice has inspired a number of irreverent gestures, like this harvest organized by farmers in 1990. Other pranksters have also become legendary, like the mysterious Baron Noir, who flew a plane through the arch several times in the 1980's.

Three hours

COEUR DÉFENSE

CNIT
The CNIT
● *82*
(opposite,
below), which
opened in 1958,
was a technical feat
for its time. Its
arched roof, made
of a double shell
of thin concrete,
stretches over
650 feet. The
building initially
housed the great
thematic exhibitions
of the 1960's and
1970's, including
the Ideal Home
Exhibition and
the Exhibition of
Childhood. It was
reorganized in 1989
and now incorporates
a hotel, restaurants,
shops, exhibition
spaces and
conference halls.
Its roof and façades
are classified
as historical
monuments. The
engineer Jean Prouvé
was responsible for
the CNIT's immense
glass windows and the
façade of the Hoechst
Marion Roussel
Tower – evidence of
the major role played
by engineers in the
construction of La
Défense, which has a
series of technical
innovations, from the
CNIT to the Arche.

LA DÉFENSE

The history of La Défense began in the 1950's. Paris was
faced with increasing traffic congestion and growth in the
service sector. The old city seemed incapable of adapting to
society's new requirements: a complete transformation of the
urban infrastructure seemed necessary. This was difficult to
put into practice in Paris itself, and so La Défense was used
as an experimental site straddling the districts of Courbevoie
and Puteaux: in 1959 its only buildings were small houses
and, farther west, the shantytowns of Nanterre, the largest in
France. Sheep could still be seen on the wasteland and cows
in backyards. Since 1883, a statue of the *Defense of Paris*, in
memory of the 1870 war, had stood on a site dating back to
before the Revolution, in alignment with the Champs-Élysées
axis. This statue gave its name to the project, which picked
up on an old idea: Napoleon I had dreamed of an imperial
avenue and the Third Republic of a triumphal avenue. In
1931, the City of Paris organized a competition for the
development of the axis from the Arc de Triomphe to La
Défense with two objectives: to solve traffic problems and to
give the capital a ceremonial avenue worthy of its status. This
competition defined the monumental ambition which gave
shape to today's Défense.

PROTOTYPE OF THE MODERN TOWN. The first project of La
Défense at the end of the 1950's was still quite conventional.
In the tradition of great avenues built in the 19th century,
ÉPAD, the state organization developing the project, planned

to build a complete quarter around the new road, with housing, gardens, offices and shops. The designers of the first plan (1960), Camelot, Mailly and Zehrfuss, followed the theories of the modernist movement and decided it was more appropriate to create buildings specially adapted to their function, allowing for the use of industrial modes of construction. As a result, offices and residential accommodations had separate areas and towers. A small section of this plan was carried out in the Bellini area, near the Pont de Neuilly. The architectural vocabulary of La Défense was evolving, and this international style was characterized by geometric abstraction, clear shapes and glass halls. The Hoechst Marion Roussel Tower, built by Mailly, creates a striking glass-curtain effect: a non-load-bearing wall is built around a load-bearing concrete nucleus.

THE GREAT PLATFORM. The second stage of plans (1964), moved away from the idea of a French-style Manhattan with

FROM SCULPTURE ...
The gigantic scale of the buildings in La Défense is counteracted by a large number of open-air sculptures. From top to bottom: Calder's *Stabile*, Takis's water mirror and Miró's fantastic figures.

... TO RELIGION
A new addition to the existing Protestant Evangelical and Roman Catholic churches at La Défense is to be the church of Notre-Dame-de-Pentecôte. Now under construction, the building's front elevation will face onto the square.

319

DUE WEST
From Pont de Neuilly the level rises in a series of landings, the last and most ornate stage of which is the staircase of the Grande Arche, which manages to be at once imposing and welcoming. The huge scale of the project underlines the power of the central state administration, which imposed its will on reluctant district authorities. On the other side of the Arche, development projects are gradually taking shape.

O. VON SPRECKELSEN
This Danish architect had built only three churches and a house when his project was accepted. He was very exacting and abandoned the project when part

traffic circulating between skyscrapers. A pedestrian platform, surrounded by a circular boulevard, was built to cover the complex traffic system underneath. Residential accommodation was arranged along this platform, built around square courts which have been nicknamed "palais royaux". Office towers, which were limited to 330 feet in height, were kept separate from residential areas. The Europe, EDF, Aurore and Crédit Lyonnais towers were built according to these guidelines, as were the residential buildings of Place des Corolles. At the end of the 1960's the demand for office space grew, and the idea of a diversified quarter gave way to the need for a commercial center. At the same time, the principle of building groups of identical buildings was called into question. ÉPAD granted permission to build the twin Manhattan Towers and increased the limits for height and width. This made way for the green GAN Tower and the black granite Framatome Tower, the latter the highest tower of La Défense, measuring 584 feet. This second stage of development was characterized by an explosion of shapes and colors, and different design principles.

THE THIRD GENERATION. The scandal of 1972, when Parisians first became conscious of the GAN Tower looming behind the Arc de Triomphe, combined with the oil crisis and the fear of a "towering inferno", brought the project to a sharp halt.

> "An open cube. A window on the world.
> A temporary stopping point on the avenue.
> With one eye on the future."
>
> Otto von Spreckelsen

La Défense seemed to symbolize the failure of modern architecture, with its oversized, neon-lit offices whose air-conditioning often failed to work and was always expensive to run. La Défense took off again at the beginning of the 1980's, when the enormous Quatre-Temps shopping center was built, making La Défense a regional focus for commercial activity. A third generation of towers was built with more complex internal spaces, halls reaching over several stories and natural lighting for every office. Under the requirement to ensure that every office has natural l ight – which cannot be met in a tower which is 150 feet thick – a new type of design emerged, exemplifed by the Athena and Elf towers: these buildings are slimmer, hollowed out and split apart.

THE 21ST ARRONDISSEMENT. In 1971, ÉPAD organized a competition for plans to extend La Défense toward the west. Should the view be closed? Should a square be built in order to get back to manageable urban dimensions? The outcome two decades later, after years of debate, is the Grande Arche ● *82* by Otto von Spreckelsen. Today this monumental construction houses the Ministry of Equipment and private offices in its side walls. The roof can be reached by elevators, offering spectacular views. The Grande Arche attracts 100,000 visitors each month, finally giving this satellite town the tourist focus it needed and helping to make La Défense, with its 130,000 workers, the "21st arrondissement" of Paris. New towers have been built, such as the Coeur Défense complex (2001), comprising twin towers 590 feet tall linked by an atrium containing a luxury conference center. These new spaces, totalling 215,280 square yards, were designed by Jean-Paul Viguier.

THE GRANDE ARCHE
This 330-foot hollow cube represents a true technological feat, as well as a subtle response to the question of whether the avenue should be closed or left open on the threshold of the suburb. It marks a border while at the same time allowing the eye to roam.

THE TOWERS
The architects of the first towers expressed their creativity only on the surface of the building, as in the Aurore Tower (top). When size restrictions were relaxed, La Défense moved into the avant-garde of architectural audacity, as represented by the PFA Tower (middle) and the Elf Tower (bottom).

☑ **One to three days**

THE LOUVRE, THE KING OF MUSEUMS ✪

The Louvre has been under permanent construction for eight hundred years, each successive ruler and architect adding to its size and splendor. The result is daunting and several days are needed to take in its architecture and the masterpieces that it contains. Because of restoration work, the pieces you want to see may have been moved, so check with the museum before you visit. The best time to visit is out of school times, very early or in the evening on late-opening days. Those with limited time will find the "Guide for the visitor in a hurry" useful. Note that the *Mona Lisa* (room 13, Italian painting, until 2004) and the *Wedding at Cana* (Denon Wing) are always besieged.

A ROYAL RESIDENCE
Charles V moved into the Louvre in 1358, by which time the château no longer played a defensive role. The architect Raymond du Temple converted the Louvre into an elegant Gothic palace, setting windows into the walls. It became a royal residence fit for the king, surrounded by gardens.

The Louvre was first a fortress and then a royal residence; in the 17th century the Tuileries Palace was built on its western side. This center of royal power, built outside the city to avoid problems of congestion, was surrounded by ministers' residences grouped around Richelieu's palace. These new quarters, which also included two royal squares, gradually became a focus of power in several spheres: financial institutions moved into the area around the Rue Vivienne; culture was represented by the Bibliothèque Royale, later Nationale, where Molière created his most important work in a theater built by Richelieu in the east wing; and finally there was the Palais-Royal, pleasure palace of the great. The area was redeveloped under the First

16. JARDINS DU PALAIS-ROYAL
17. BANQUE DE FRANCE
18. PLACE DES VICTOIRES
19. MUSÉE DES ARTS DÉCORATIFS
20. COUR CARRÉE (SULLY)
21. COLONNADE
22. TOWN HALL OF THE 1ST ARRONDISSEMENT
23. CHURCH OF ST-GERMAIN L'AUXERROIS

Empire.
Even though the Louvre
is no longer the focal point of the power of
the State, it is nevertheless a prestigious showcase for France,
as demonstrated by its glass pyramid and its ambitious
museum scheme.

THE LOUVRE

A DEFENSIVE ROLE. The Louvre came into being under
Philippe-Auguste: before leaving for the Crusades in 1190, he
built a city wall to protect the Right Bank during his absence.
A fortress with an imposing keep at its center was the first
part of this defensive plan, located at the northwest of the
present-day Cour Carrée. The Great Tower, a symbol of
feudal power, was completed in 1202 to house the Royal
Treasury, the archives and the arsenal as well as to hold high-
ranking prisoners. This Louvre was later dismantled; only the
foundations remain today (these can be seen in the museum's
archeological crypt).

I.M. PEI'S PYRAMID
The glass building's
silhouette crowns the
Grand Louvre, which
was renovated and
enlarged as part of the
project undertaken
between 1981 and 1993.

THE FORTRESS TO THE GRAND LOUVRE

Philippe-Auguste's Louvre, completed in 1202, was built strictly as a fortress. In 1358 Charles V moved into the Louvre and spent ten years converting it into a royal residence. After destroying the keep, François I commissioned Pierre Lescot to make the old château into a Renaissance palace. This was completed by Henri II (1546–59). In 1594, Henri IV continued Catherine de'Medici's plan to connect the Louvre and the Tuileries.

1610: Henri IV's Grand Plan.

1870: Napoleon III's Louvre in its completed state.

CARROUSEL ENTRANCE AND STAIRCASE

1

Henri IV's Grand Plan included making the Cour Carrée four times larger. The 17th century saw the addition of the Pavillon de l'Horloge by Le Mercier, the Galerie d'Apollon by Le Vau and Le Brun, and the Colonnade by Perrault. Le Vau also completed the enlargement of Le Mercier's Cour Carrée. The Grande Galerie museum was opened on August 10, 1793. From 1804 to 1848, Percier and Fontaine resumed the old Grand Plan in keeping with Lescot's style: by contrast, Visconti and Lefuel made the Louvre into a showpiece of Napoleon III architecture. A century after the Tuileries Palace burned, Pei's Grand Louvre became part of the Grand Plan.

A ROYAL RESIDENCE
Charles V's architect, Raymond du Temple, made the castle into an elegant Gothic building with bay windows and surrounded by gardens.

GRANDE GALERIE (1)
The gallery, started in 1595 by Louis Métezeau and Jacques Androuet Du Cerceau, was put up along the Seine to connect the Louvre with the Tuileries Palace, b... in 1563.

Cour Carrée (5)

Following the Grand Plan laid out by his father, Henri IV, Louis XIII commissioned the architect Jacques Le Mercier to make the Cour Carrée four times larger, to build the Pavillon de l'Horloge (1624–40) and to extend the Lescot Wing to the north. The alternation of vertical pavilions and horizontal wings, the formal austerity of the buildings (tempered by elegant ornamentation), the French-style columns with fleurs-de-lys, the curved and triangular pediments, and the carved monograms of kings all conspired to create a new architectural style which was called classicism. Nearly two centuries later Napoleon III's architects Hector Lefuel and Louis Visconti built the Pavillon Denon to match the elevation of the Pavillon de l'Horloge.

Salle St-Louis (6)

All that remains of the medieval residence is this low room, which was discovered by chance in 1882. It was opened to the public and was for a long time the only part of the medieval Louvre which could be seen. However, since the excavations of 1984–5, the remains of Philippe-Auguste's castle (the moats and the perfectly circular keep) have been open to visitors.

Salle des Cariatides (7)

Second floor

THE RAFT OF THE MEDUSA
(1819) This painting by Théodore Géricault shows the shipwreck of the frigate *Medusa*, from which only 15 men escaped alive. The Romantics restored nature and emotion to the place which neoclassicism had denied them.

LA GIOCONDA
(1503–6) This painting by Leonardo da Vinci, *Portrait of Lisa Gherardini* (known as *La Gioconda* or the *Mona Lisa*), is the most famous in the Louvre. It was the centerpiece of François I's collection. The delicate modeling of the figure, the serene, misty lighting, the enigmatic smile and the gracious gestures are features which can be seen in most of the artist's paintings.

WEDDING FEAST AT CANA
(1562–3) This painting by Paolo Veronese was commissioned for the refectory of the San Giorgio Maggiore monastery in Venice. The huge canvas (23 by 33 feet) was restored on site between 1989 and 1992, as it was too large to be transported. Restoration uncovered the original colors of the work under layers of repainting and dirt. Venetian painting, with its emphasis on color (in the works of Bellini, Giorgione, Titian, Veronese and Tintoretto) traditionally contrasted with the Florentine emphasis on draftsmanship. Venetian classicism was just as influential as that of Florence.

The Louvre is the largest museum in the world, with seven departments and collections which date back to the 7th millennium BC. A few of the major exhibits are presented here as an encouragement to seek out and discover the others.

THE SLAVES
(1513–15)
Both figures were carved by Michelangelo as part of the first plan for the monumental tomb of Pope Julius II in Rome. Above, *Dying Slave*, the counterpart of *Rebellious Slave*. The figures were not completed because of faults which appeared in the marble; they were to have been part of a series of six or seven statues.

Before leaving Paris for Versailles, the young Louis XIV decided to go ahead with work on the Louvre. His aim was to complete the Cour Carrée and the Tuileries, and to build the Colonnade, a façade facing the town which has become a symbol of French classical architecture.

COLONNADE (8)
The competition for the Louvre façade pitted Bernini and Pietro da Cortona against a trio of French architects (Claude Perrault, Louis Le Vau and Charles Le Brun). The French group was victorious.

PYRAMIDE (11)
Exactly 793 glass diamonds and triangles, assembled with minute accuracy.

THE PERCIER AND FONTAINE STAIRCASE (9)
Napoleon I's two architects built a second story on three sides of the Cour Carrée and added the hallways and staircases the museum needed.

COUR MARLY (10)
Three new covered courts were created during the redevelopment of the Richelieu Wing: Cour Marly and Cour Puget, devoted to French sculpture of the 17th century, and Cour Khorsabad, which reconstructs the Assyrian palace of Sargon II. Cour Marly is covered with a huge glass roof reaching a height of 90 feet, giving it the benefit of natural overhead lighting.

GRAND LOUVRE
The renovation of the Louvre was entrusted to I.M. Pei, an American architect of Chinese origin. It observed two basic principles: to respect the old buildings showing them to advantage while making a resolutely contemporary contribution, free of pastiche, in the Richelieu Wing and the underground areas, the Hall Napoléon and the Carrousel

INVERTED PYRAMIDE (12)
This is held together by a similar system of cables (here shown during assembly).

APHRODITE, OR THE VENUS DE MILO
(2nd century BC)
This statue was discovered on Milo, or Melos, one of the Cycladic islands, in 1820. It is regarded as a masterpiece of classical Greek art. The Marquis de Rivière claimed ownership of the work along with all the other pieces found with it. He brought it to France and gave it to Louis XVIII who in turn gave it to the museum in May 1821. Many theories have been proposed concerning the position of Venus' lost arms: the right arm must have been in front of the body, with the hand toward the left hip, and the left arm was probably raised.

THE MEDIEVAL LOUVRE
The remains of Philippe-Auguste's castle were brought to light during the excavation of 1984–5 and are now open to the public. Visitors can walk along the old moats and around the Grosse Tour, the circular keep which symbolized feudal power and housed the royal treasury, archives, arsenal and high-ranking prisoners. The monarchs themselves spent little time there.

Entresol

SULLY

First floor

SULLY

THE VICTORY OF SAMOTHRACE
(c. 190 BC)
This winged figure was discovered in 1863 during excavations on the island of the same name, in the Aegean Sea. It had been placed at the top of a promontory, perhaps to commemorate a naval victory by Rhodes. This perfect example of classical Greek art was found by Charles François Champoiseau, broken in pieces. The figure's hand was discovered in 1950 and is also on display.

THE BULLS OF KHORSABAD
The five bulls with wings and human heads were intended to act as beneficent guards of the Assyrian palace of Sargon II at Khorsabad. They are now exhibited in the Cour Khorsabad, where reliefs from the palace are displayed at their original height so as to reproduce the monumental effect of Assyrian architecture.

THE MARLY HORSES
This group of four sculptures were commissioned for the royal park at Marly. *Fame* and *Mercury* (1706), by Antoine Coysevox, were later replaced by Guillaume Coustou's *Horses Restrained by Grooms* (1745). The first pair was moved to the entrance of the Tuileries in 1719, and the second to the Place de la Concorde during the Revolution.

OLEON III APARTMENTS (2)
e rooms have been open to the public
1993: they are the former state
s of Napoleon III's Ministry of State
ater housed the Ministry of Finance
1989. The paintings and stucco work,
e gold and silk of the furniture, the
marbles and bronzes of the
fireplaces all demonstrate
Napoleon III style
at its peak.

99, RUE DE RIVOLI
ENTRANCE

PASSAGE
RICHELIEU
ENTRANCE

PYRAMIDE
ENTRANCE

PETITE GALERIE (3)
This was begun under
Charles IX, and another story was added by
Louis Métezeau under Henri IV. The upper
tory housed the Gallery of Kings, decorated
with portraits of France's kings and queens.
The style of the arcades matches Pierre
Lescot's architecture, but the style of
decoration is new: pilasters with rustic or
vermiculated bosses and ornamentation
abound with fleurs-de-lys and royal initials.

GALERIE
D'APOLLON (4)

PORTRAIT OF THE ARTIST AT HIS EASEL (1660) Rembrandt developed a style that powerfully combined the magnificence of baroque painting with a sober, introspective quality. He was a master of light, of dark glazes and of muted golds. The Louvre has three of his self-portraits.

THE LACEMAKER (c. 1670) An interest in everyday life and meticulous attention to detail are typical of Jan Vermeer. The Louvre has two of his most famous works. He worked within the tradition of Dutch painting, creating exquisite harmonies with cool tones, especially blues and yellows. His technical skill matched the subtlety with which he conveyed human emotions.

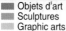

PORTRAIT OF JEAN LE BON (c. 1350) This anonymous work is the first individual profile portrait known in Europe.

THE MEDICI GALLERY The group of 24 paintings produced by Rubens between 1622 and 1625 for the Medici Gallery of the Palais du Luxembourg is a series of allegories recounting the life of Marie de' Medici. This masterpiece combines realism and the fantastic, creating an overall effect of dynamism and movement.
Left: *Marie de' Medici Landing at the Port of Marseille*

THE CHEAT WITH THE ACE OF DIAMONDS Georges de La Tour, an artist from Lorraine who was long undervalued, has been compared to Caravaggio. Nocturnal scenes are lit with candlelight, in contrast to the cool light of the daytime scenes.

THE SKATE (1728) Jean-Baptiste Siméon Chardin celebrated the object in his work, elevating it almost to the status of an independent being. Cauldrons, pipes, glasses, brass fountains, saucepans and pots are painted with sculptural precision, a love of form and a predilection for soft halftones.

A RENAISSANCE PALACE. Charles V transformed the château into a royal residence, but his successors neglected the building. In 1515, François I took up residence at the Louvre in order to ensure the Parisians' support. He replaced the Great Tower with a paved court and commissioned the architect Pierre Lescot to embellish the old palace with the help of the sculptor Jean Goujon. Under Henri II the southwest section of today's Cour Carrée was built, up to the central pavilion (now known as the Pavillon de l'Horloge), as well as the Pavillon du Roi, overlooking the Seine. Inside the palace the Salle des Cariatides was built, as well as the staircase now known as the Henri II Staircase.

THE GRAND PLAN. In 1594, Henri IV revived Catherine de' Medici's plan to join the Louvre and the Tuileries. The king bought up all the surrounding land so that he could make the Cour Carrée four times larger; he also built the Grande Galerie in 1595, designed by Louis Métezeau and Jacques II Androuet Du Cerceau. The Petite Galerie, with its famous Gallery of Kings on the second story, was started in 1566 in order to connect the two façades. In 1624, during the reign of Louis XIII, Le Mercier built the Pavillon de l'Horloge (or Pavillon de Sully) and extended the Lescot Wing to the north. The Gallery of Kings was destroyed by fire in 1661. When it was rebuilt, the architect Louis Le Vau made it twice the size and created the Galerie d'Apollon on the second story, which was decorated by Charles Le Brun, among others. Louis XIV wanted the palace to have a monumental entrance on the Paris side and chose Claude Perrault's design with its famous colonnade, a "true manifesto of the classical style". Built between 1667 and 1670, it measured over 570 feet in length and faced the Place St-Germain-l'Auxerrois.

IMPERIAL FESTIVITIES
Van Elven's painting depicts a soirée held at the Tuileries to celebrate the Universal Exhibition of 1867: Empress Eugénie, dressed by Worth ● *117* accompanies the Czar, followed by Napoleon III and the King of Prussia. The emperor and his entourage were very fond of entertainment: for seventeen years the palace witnessed a series of lavish festivities.

ARC DE TRIOMPHE DU CARROUSEL (2 A5)
Napoleon had this arch built between the Louvre and the Tuileries in 1806. On top of it he placed the bronze chariot made by the Greek sculptor Lysippos in 300 BC, which he had taken from the portico of St Mark's in Venice during the Italian campaign (the Venetians themselves had taken it from Constantinople in 1204). The famous horses were given back in 1815 and replaced by a copy.

TUILERIES PALACE

After the fire started by the Communards, the ruins of the palace were left standing until 1882. This former royal residence, with a vast garden opening onto what was then countryside, had been built by Catherine de' Medici starting in 1564, after a design by Philippe Delorme. She chose the site of the old *tuileries* (tile works) outside Charles V's city wall. Henri IV, Mazarin and Colbert continued work on the palace following the original designs but planned new galleries to connect the central pavilion with the Louvre, and new wings. The aim was to create a more intimate residence than the Louvre. The interior was repeatedly redesigned: Mazarin even had a theater built in the palace, which staged the first opera performances in France. Later the palace was neglected in favor of Versailles and in the 17th and 18th centuries it had numerous tenants. Louis XVI's forced return to Paris in 1789 and the later arrival of Revolutionary committees in the palace made it a center of political power; this also ensured that its furniture survived. The Tuileries Palace was redesigned under Napoleon I, who created the Place du Carrousel and added the gallery running along the Rue de Rivoli. The Tuileries was the official royal residence from 1814 to 1870.

A CULTURAL CENTER. Two Second Empire buildings stand opposite each other at the entrance to the Tuileries Gardens ▲ *200* on the Place de la Concorde. Since its conversion, completed in 1991, the Jeu de Paume (1 H4) has been a gallery of contemporary art. The Orangerie ▲ *168* houses the Walter-Guillaume collection and Monet's *Waterlilies*.

RUE DE RIVOLI   (1 H4 to 2 F7)

This road was built by consular decree between 1802 and 1835, representing a new vision of town planning. Rue de Rivoli took over from the old Rue St-Honoré, giving Paris a second east-west axis.

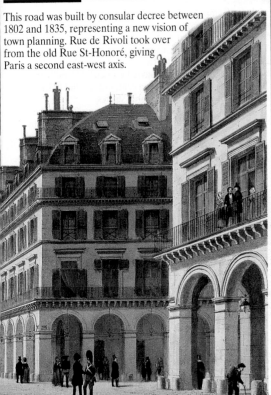

THE TUILERIES ON FIRE
The palace was set on fire in March 1871, and its remains were destroyed for political reasons in 1882. Remnants can be found in Paris' parks and at St-Raphaël (Var). *Le Figaro* even bought some of the marble: the pieces were cut down into paperweights and sold to subscribers.

GALIGNANI BOOKSHOP
The bust of founder Giovanni Galignani is on display here: an ancestor of his was editing books in Padua as early as 1520. The bookshop was initially located in Rue Vivienne but moved to Rue de Rivoli in 1854. Giovanni married the daughter of an English printer and founded *Galignani's Messenger* in 1814; this publication functioned as an international newspaper for twenty-four years.

RUE DE RIVOLI AROUND 1840
Chateaubriand described how slowly work was progressing in 1813: "So far you can only see the arcades put up by the government and a few houses being built here and there, with their jagged outline of expectant stones."

333

▲ THE LOUVRE AND THE TUILERIES

ROBESPIERRE AND THE MAISON DES DUPLAY
Robespierre moved to Rue St-Honoré above a carpenter's shop in 1791.

FAÇADES AND ARCADES. The Rue de Rivoli was built from the Rue St-Florentin up to the Place des Pyramides on ground which had formerly belonged to a monastery. Freestone façades were built along it following plans by the architects Charles Percier and Pierre-François Fontaine, the organizers of festivities under the First Empire. The façades consisted of a first story with arcades and three further stories, the last under a convex zinc roof. As part of the project, a new quarter was created around Rue Mont-Thabor, Rue Cambon and Rue de Castiglione. The road was extended up to Rue St-Antoine in 1848, without matching façades.

LUXURY SHOPS AND GRAND HOTELS. Today the arcades house elegant shops and a few luxury hotels, like the Meurice, at no. 228 (1 l4). This hotel, founded in 1907, has preserved a number of opulent drawing rooms in the 18th-century style designed by Henri-Paul Nénot, the architect of the new Sorbonne. Angélina, the tea room at no. 226, was founded in 1903 by the pâtissier Rumpelmayer: it is a favorite haunt of hot chocolate afficionados. At no. 224 is Galignani, the first English bookshop established in Paris, in 1800.

One of the drawing rooms at the Meurice.

THE FLAMBOYANT PORCH OF ST-GERMAIN
A neo-Gothic belfry (1861) by Théodore Ballu (who also built the Église de la Trinité) joins the church to the town hall of the 1st arrondissement (1859). The town hall was built by Jacques-Ignace Hittorff, who also designed the Gare du Nord.

THE LOUVRE DES ANTIQUAIRES (2 B5). This huge arcaded building between Rue de Rivoli and Rue St-Honoré housed the Grands Magasins du Louvre between 1878 and 1960. Today this is the only shopping center of its kind in Europe, with 250 antique dealers on three stories.

ST-GERMAIN-L'AUXERROIS (2 B6). The first church dedicated to the bishop of Auxerre Saint Germain was built on this site at the end of the 7th century.

The church was rebuilt in the first half of the 12th century and then altered repeatedly. It became the royal parish when the Valois moved to the Louvre, and from the 17th century onward this was the traditional burial place for royal artists, including Le Vau, Gabriel, Soufflot, Boucher, Van Loo and Chardin. The superb porch in the Flamboyant Gothic style (1435–9) bears the mark of Burgundian influence. The choir was altered in the 18th century, and the church lost its famous white marble rood screen, carved by Jean Goujon in 1541 after plans by Pierre Lescot; fragments can be seen in the Louvre. Nearly all the original furniture has been lost, although the church still has some beautiful pieces, including the royal pew made in 1682 after a design by Le Brun and the Flemish Retable, a vast altarpiece in carved oak from the early 16th century.

RUE ST-HONORÉ   (1 H3 to 2 C5)

Rue St-Honoré crosses three of the old gates of Paris as it runs between Rue du Louvre and Rue Royale. The first of these gates, demolished in 1535, was around the site of the Oratory, at no. 115. The second gate was called Porte des Aveugles (Blind Men's Gate) because it was close to the Quinze-Vingts hospice ▲ *405* which moved to Rue de Charenton under Louis XVI; the gate was demolished around 1636. The third gate was built in 1631, when the Rue Royale was widened, and was destroyed in 1730. From the end of the 16th century onward, religious communities and businesses moved into the new quarter (including À la Civette, the tobacconist's shop at no. 157, founded in 1716). Today they have mostly been replaced by luxury boutiques.

CHURCH OF ST-ROCH (1 J4). This church, designed as a series of chapels, was built on a hillock between 1653 and 1754. Corneille, Le Nôtre and Diderot are buried here. The architect of the Sorbonne, Jacques Lemercier, designed the choir and the nave; the vault was added under the Regency, donated by a new parishioner, the financier John Law. The façade was built around 1738 after a design by Robert de Cotte but has since lost its decorative carvings. Father Marduel, the parish priest, had the

GRANDS MAGASINS DU LOUVRE
These department stores were created by Alfred Chauchard, a dealer and art lover who left his collections to the Louvre in 1906. The stores were famous for having electric lighting in their window displays before World War One. In addition to its magnificent antique stores, the Louvre des Antiquaires has an exhibition room which has shows on such subjects as heraldry or the decorative arts.

CHAPELS OF ST-ROCH
Among the most remarkable chapels of the church are the chapel dedicated to the Virgin, designed by Jules Hardouin-Mansart in 1705, and the Chapelle du Calvaire, by Étienne-Louis Boullée, built in 1754. The building contains religious works of art which were formerly held in neighboring monasteries.

COMMUNARDS AGAINST THE COLUMN
The revolutionaries saw the Vendôme column as a "symbol of brute force and false glory" and demolished it on May 16, 1871.

MAGNIFICENT JEWELRY
Paris's grandest jewelers ▲ 128 have been located on and around Place Vendôme since the Second Empire.

church decorated with religious scenes: he appointed the sculptor Étienne-Maurice Falconet and the painter Jean-Baptiste Pierre, who painted *The Triumph of the Virgin* on the dome.

PLACE DU MARCHÉ-ST-HONORÉ (1 J3). The Rue du Marché-St-Honoré leads to this square. The Jacobin monastery, which became famous as a meeting place for revolutionaries (Jacobins), used to stand here. The market was established in 1810 and in 1954 was replaced by a multi-story car park now torn down. A glass-fronted office building designed by architect Ricardo Bofill has recently been completed.

CHURCH OF THE ASSUMPTION (1 H3). The enormous dome at no. 266 *bis* belongs to the chapel of the Dames de l'Assomption convent. It was built in 1670 following designs sent from Rome by Errard and acquired the nickname *sot dôme* (silly dome). The church became a Polish parish in 1850. At no. 398 is the MAISON DES DUPLAY, where Robespierre lived during the Revolution.

PLACE VENDÔME   (1 I3) ● 62 ▲ 128

Place Vendôme, formerly Place Louis-le-Grand, was designed by Jules Hardouin-Mansart and is regarded as the ultimate in classical city planning. Planned as a home for the academies and royal library, it was built at the end of the 17th century at the instigation of the minister Louvois. At the center of the square, the column erected by Napoleon stands out against the austere, magnificent geometry of the whole.

THE FIRST PLAN FAILS. Mansart had originally planned a three-sided square, open to the south, on the site of a house belonging to the Duc de Vendôme. Arcaded façades with a retaining wall but no roof had been built around half of the square, and an equestrian statue of Louis XIV as a Roman emperor, by François Girardon, had just been placed at the center. Then, on April 7, 1699, the king announced a change of plan: he wanted the square to be octagonal in shape.

A CLOSED AREA. Mansart made the new square into an enclosed area of 480 by 450 feet built on four sides with cut-off corners and narrow openings to Rue St-Honoré to the south and the Capuchin monastery to the north. Rue de Castiglione and Rue de la Paix were built under the Empire, increasing traffic on the square. Among the first to acquire property here were Mansart himself and the banker Law, who built magnificent private homes behind the 80-foot-high façades. The MINISTRY OF JUSTICE is located at nos. 11–13; one of these houses was built for the financier Lhuillier, while the other, which is sometimes open to the public, was owned by Paul Poisson de Bourvallais, the model for Lesage's Turcaret, in 1706. The famous RITZ HOTEL, at no. 15, is next door to the Hôtel Crozat, which held the art collection of the same name, and the Hôtel d'Évreux, at nos. 17–19 (headquarters of the Crédit Foncier bank, which owns several buildings on the square). The small exhibition hall at no. 20, which cannot be seen from the square, is an example of a folly from the early 20th century built in 18th-century style; it is now the headquarters of the Republic National Bank. The great names of the jewelry world ▲ 128 have turned the square into a glittering showcase and have spread into Rue de la Paix. The square itself has been resurfaced since 1992: paving stones of grey granite form a checkerboard design, while steel bands mark out the pedestrian area.

PALAIS-ROYAL   (2 AB4) ▲ 202

Richelieu's guards no longer haunt
the corridors and outbuildings seeking

IN HONOR OF AUSTERLITZ
The Vendôme column was covered with a total of 425 bronze plaques, made from guns taken from the Russian and Austrian armies. It was erected between 1806 and 1810 to celebrate the victory of Napoleonic troops in one of the greatest battles in history.

The painter Gustave Courbet (1819–77) was a man of great conviction and a friend of Proudhon. In the excitement of May 1871, he incited the Communards to destroy the column and went to prison as a result.

A STYLISH QUARTER
During the 1800's, the Place Vendôme and Rue de la Paix were quietly prosperous and bourgeois areas until the arrival of luxury stores like the couture houses of Worth and Doucet made it extremely chic ▲ 116.

revenge on the king's musketeers. Luxury shops, prostitution and gambling have long since disappeared, but the Palais-Royal still attracts many strollers, drawn by the peaceful atmosphere of the arcades and the gardens. The buildings now house the Council of State, the Constitutional Council and the Ministry of Culture.

THE PALAIS CARDINAL. Richelieu built his palace, designed by Jacques Lemercier, on land which he had acquired in 1624. All that remains of the original building is the balcony supported by lions' heads at no. 6, rue de Valoi,s and the Gallery of Prows, which formed the eastern wing of what is today the main court: its maritime trophies commemorate Richelieu's time as superintendant of shipping. When Richelieu died in 1642, he bequeathed the building to the monarchy. Anne of Austria moved here with the young Louis XIV but had to leave this poorly protected residence during the disturbances of the Fronde.

RESIDENCE OF THE ORLÉANS FAMILY. In 1692 the Sun King gave the Palais-Royal to his brother Philippe, and it became the property of the Orléans family, who kept it until 1848. The king's brother, and then his son the Regent built extensions and employed the greatest artists of the time, including Jules Hardouin-Mansart. The gardens ▲ *202* became fashionable, and the Regent held elegant dinners here. After the terrible fire of 1763, which destroyed the east wing of the palace and part of the main building, the palace was rebuilt and entirely redesigned. The architect Pierre Moreau-Desproux built the Cour de l'Horloge. The buildings overlooking the Rue St-Honoré were built in their present form, as was the north façade. In 1765, Contant d'Ivry built the great staircase; it has a handrail of wrought iron made by Corbin after a design by Jean-Jacques Caffieri and can be seen through the glazed entrance door of the Council of State (on the right-hand side when leaving the entrance court).

SHOPS AND PROSTITUTION. In 1780 the Duc de Chartres, later Philippe Égalité, leased out the area around the gardens for commercial purposes in order to reduce his mountain of debts. Victor Louis built sixty houses with uniform façades; there were shops and 180 arcades on the street level. After this, Rue de Valois, Rue de Beaujolais and Rue de Montpensier were built, named after the three sons of the Duc de Chartres. The curious flocked to this "temple of pleasure", which, according to Louis-Sébastien Mercier, had "banished the very semblance of modesty". As the police were not allowed to set foot on Orléans property, the place became a center of political agitation in 1789.

GARDEN OF THE REVOLUTION. It was at the Palais-Royal that Camille Desmoulins gave his speech of July 12, 1789, after Necker's dismissal had been announced. Clubs – for reading, gambling and debating – had sprung up under the arcades since February. La Fayette and Talleyrand crossed paths at the Club des Valois, the Jacobins held their meetings

at the Corazza café, and the *sans-culottes* met at the Caveau des Aveugles. The place was soon nicknamed "Palais-Égalité" (Equality Palace): it became public property after its owner was beheaded on November 6, 1793.

PROFITS FOR THE EMPIRE. Gambling was permitted at the Palais-Royal and became a source of income for the state, as the police allowed gambling businesses to operate on payment of a tax. The Orléans family returned in 1814 and built the gallery which bears its name, a double portico separating the main court from the garden, originally glazed and with shops at street level. Louis-Philippe closed the gambling houses and cafés in 1836, and the place fell into rapid decline.

TRADITIONS UPHELD. A small cannon is fired in the garden at midday every day, and the Grand Véfour, a restaurant established in 1784, still has decorations dating from the Restoration in its Beaujolais Gallery. The Constitutional Council, the Council of State and the Ministry of Culture illustrate the splendors of the First Empire, July monarchy and Third Republic. The Grand Salon in the Ministry (dating from the Empire) has been impressively restored.

THÉÂTRE FRANÇAIS
This was built by the Duc de Chartres between 1786 and 1790 after plans by Victor Louis. It is now the home of the Comédie-Française. The use of iron in the balconies and dome caused a fuss. The exterior was given its present form by Prosper Chabrol in 1860. The theater was totally destroyed by fire in 1900 but was rebuilt exactly as it had been.

SALLE DES IMPRIMÉS
This room can accommodate up to 360 readers. It is built on a basilica-style plan with a central walkway; the ceiling has nine metallic domes supported by thin columns, decorated with colored ceramic tiles.

AROUND THE PLACE DES VICTOIRES (2 B4) ● 63

Place des Victoires, the second royal square in Paris, was built by the Duc de Feuillade, who wanted to display a statue of Louis XIV which he had commissioned from the sculptor Martin Desjardins after the Peace of Nimègue in 1678. Jules Hardouin-Mansart designed an almost circular area, in the Italian style, creating the illusion of an enclosed space. The arrangement of the whole was destroyed when the Rue Étienne-Marcel was built in 1883, and stories were added to the buildings. A new equestrian statue of the king, by François-Joseph Bosio, was erected in 1822.

BASILICA OF NOTRE-DAME-DES-VICTOIRES. This church is located on the pretty Place des Petits Pères: it is all that remains of the Augustine monastery whose foundation stone was laid by Louis XIII in 1629. Seven large paintings by Van Loo can be seen in the choir, as well as ex-votos and Lully's tomb.

A ROYAL SQUARE
"Feuillade, my God, I think you're fooling us/ To put the sun between four lanterns". This is how Parisians mocked the duke's square, made up of façades built according to the four classical architectural orders, with lanterns on top of four columns, which lit the square both day and night.

THE VIVIENNE AND COLBERT ARCADES (2 B3) 4 and 6, rue des Petits-Champs. These arcades join with each other and Rue Vivienne, and date from 1823 and 1826. Many arcades were built at this time so that the central part of the plot could be divided into sections while at the same time offering passers-by a place to stroll away from the dangers of traffic (sidewalks had not yet been introduced). The arcades were restored in 1985, revealing the richness of their ornamentation which features the symbols of trade.

THE BANQUE DE FRANCE
AND ITS SURROUNDINGS (2 B4)

The Banque de France was founded in 1800. Eight years later, it moved into one of the city's most beautiful aristocratic

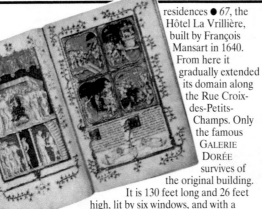

residences ● *67*, the Hôtel La Vrillière, built by François Mansart in 1640. From here it gradually extended its domain along the Rue Croix-des-Petits-Champs. Only the famous GALERIE DORÉE survives of the original building. It is 130 feet long and 26 feet high, lit by six windows, and with a ceiling painted by François Perrier depicting the four elements. For the Comte de Toulouse, Louis XIV's second legitimate son, and for Mme de Montespan, who acquired the house in 1713, François-Antoine Vassé produced carvings in gilded wood showing marine and hunting scenes: these gave the gallery its golden appearance. The striking GALERIE VÉRO-DODAT at no. 2, rue du Bouloi is similar in style to the Galerie Vivienne (below). It was built in 1826 by the butchers Véro and Dodat. Aubert, who edited the periodicals *La Caricature* and *Charivari*, exhibited drawings by Gavarni and Daumier here. Shops in the arcade include Capia, which sells antique dolls.

THE BIBLIOTHÈQUE NATIONALE   (2 B3)

Rue des Petits-Champs, Rue Vivienne, Rue Colbert and Rue Richelieu form a square which borders the area occupied by the Bibliothèque Nationale. Most of the library's collections have now been relocated to the glass buildings of the Bibliothèque Mitterrand at Tolbiac ▲ *232*.

ROYAL, THEN NATIONAL. Colbert broke the royal tradition of transporting libraries with each change of royal residence when he installed the Royal Library in two houses on the Rue Vivienne in 1666. Gradually the Palais Mazarin was surrounded. Under the Revolution the library became national property, and its collections expanded as books and works of art were confiscated from religious bodies and émigrés. The Bibliothèque Nationale is organized in departments – Theatrical Arts, Maps and Plans, Prints and Photographs, Music, Manuscripts, Coins and Medals ▲ *172*, Printed Books, Periodicals, and Sound and Image (the last three departments are to be transferred to Tolbiac). It has been affiliated with the Ministry of Culture since 1981. The architect Henri Labrouste modernized the building in 1854, creating the printed-book reading room and the adjoining central shop.

REGISTRATION OF COPYRIGHT
The law established by François I in 1537 stated that a copy of each printed book should be deposited at the library of the Château de Blois. This meant that an ever-increasing number of books flooded into the Bibliothèque Nationale: 390 works in 1780, over 38,000 in 1980. Gilding irons for bindings and ink-pads for stamping became indispensable.

TREASURES OF THE BANQUE DE FRANCE
The Galerie Dorée displays copies of major works from the Vrillière collection, including a Poussin. The originals are kept at the Louvre.

🕐 **One day**

**REMAINS OF THE
TUILERIES PALACE**
(9 E9)
These (top) were relocated to the courtyard of an apartment block (9, rue de Murillo) after the palace was demolished in 1882.

CHARTRES ROTONDA
The Duc de Chartres partly financed this observation post, obtaining permission to install a living room under the dome, from which he had views over all the north of Paris.

LOO GALLERY
This strange pagoda (right) on the corner of the Rue Rembrandt and Rue de Courcelles was built by the architect F. Bloch in 1926 for C.T. Loo, whose gallery helped popularize Oriental art in France.

NAUMACHIA
This Corinthian colonnade, which borders the lake in Parc Monceau, is supposed to have come from the tomb planned for Henri II at St-Denis.

The area of Paris between Monceau and Drouot underwent a

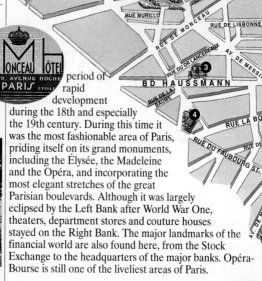

period of rapid development during the 18th and especially the 19th century. During this time it was the most fashionable area of Paris, priding itself on its grand monuments, including the Élysée, the Madeleine and the Opéra, and incorporating the most elegant stretches of the great Parisian boulevards. Although it was largely eclipsed by the Left Bank after World War One, theaters, department stores and couture houses stayed on the Right Bank. The major landmarks of the financial world are also found here, from the Stock Exchange to the headquarters of the major banks. Opéra-Bourse is still one of the liveliest areas of Paris.

PARC MONCEAU (9 DE8) ▲ 206

THE CHARTRES FOLLY. The Duc de Chartres, later Philippe Égalité, built his folly in the village of Monceau, where Joan of Arc camped in 1429. It was created by the designer and playwright L. Carrogis, known as Carmontelle, with the help of Thomas Blaikie, the landscape gardener of Bagatelle ▲ 207. This "garden of illusions" was completed in 1778 and featured an

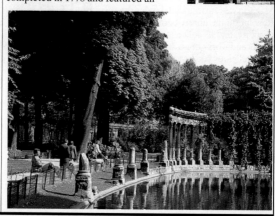

Egyptian pyramid, a pagoda, and a Tartar tent. It was here that the world's first parachutist, J. Garnerin, threw himself from a balloon and landed safely on October 22, 1797. In 1860, when the village of Monceau became part of Paris, the garden at Chartres was cut down to half its size; a year later, it was converted into an English-style garden by Alphand ▲ 208. The park is still delightful, with its long avenues, pyramid (the only one of Carmontelle's creations to survive), Naumachia, colonnade, arcade from the Hôtel de Ville (which was burnt down by the Communards in 1871) and its many monuments dedicated to writers and artists.

Avenue Van-Dyck.

THE CHARTRES ROTUNDA. This building to the north of

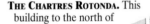

the park is surrounded by a peristyle of sixteen columns and has the appearance of a neoclassical temple. It is a remnant of the Farmers General Wall built by Ledoux in 1784 ● 68.

MAISON OPÉRA-GARNIER (Rue du Docteur Lancereaux) The interiors of the houses in Monceau,

ARCHITECTURE OF THE BELLE ÉPOQUE

ENTREPRENEURS OF THE 19TH CENTURY. In 1837 the Pereire brothers were permitted to build a railway, passing under the hill of Monceau. This began a major phase of urban development, which would later inspire Zola's novel *La Curée* (*The Quarry*). The splendid residences built in Monceau after the end of the Second Empire constitute a unique architectural ensemble.
A RESIDENTIAL QUARTER. Two short avenues lead into the park, ending with gilded gates designed by Ducros. They are still lined with opulent buildings: on the Avenue Velasquez (9 EF8) are the HÔTEL CHAUCHART (no. 5) and the MUSÉE CERNUSCHI (no. 7), the former home of the banker of that name ▲ 139. The surrounding area has buildings in the official style inspired by Haussmann, as well as the RUSSIAN ORTHODOX CHURCH (9 C9) at 12, rue Daru and a number of Gothic and Renaissance pastiches. The MUSÉE JACQUEMART-ANDRÉ (9 E10) at 158, bd. Haussmann resembles an Italian Renaissance palace, while the Musée Camondo (9 F9) at 63, rue de Monceau, recreates an 18th-century private residence.

like the one shown here, illustrate the displays of opulence favored by the upper classes in the Belle Époque.

343

FAUBOURG ST-HONORÉ

THE ROAD TO ROULE. The Rue du Faubourg-St-Honoré, stretching from the Place des Ternes up to the church of St-Philippe-du-Roule, still follows the winding course which goes back to the Middle Ages, when this was the road leading to the village of Roule.

THE CHURCH OF ST-PHILIPPE-DU-ROULE (1 E1). This basilica-style church is fronted by a peristyle with four columns supporting a triangular pediment. It was built by J.F. Chalgrin between 1774 and 1784, and set a fashion in Paris for churches in the neoclassical style. The *Descent from the Cross* in the half-domed vault of the choir was painted by Chassériau in 1855; it was the artist's last work.

HÔTELS OF THE FAUBOURG. During the 18th century the aristocracy moved into the areas around the Champs-Élysées and the new Place Louis XV (later Place de la Concorde). Here, as in the Faubourg St-Germain ▲ *262*, they built magnificent residences, some of which still survive on the odd-numbered side of the road, on either side of the Élysée Palace (1 G23). At no. 33, the CERCLE DE

L'UNION INTERALLIÉE occupies the former Hôtel Levieux, built sometime after 1713; a swimming pool, opening onto the garden, has been added to this elegant setting. Further on, at no. 39, is the HÔTEL CHAROST, built around 1720; it was richly decorated by Napoleon's sister Pauline Bonaparte, who built a gallery for the famous Borghese collection. This has been the home of the British Embassy since 1825, and its interior decorations have been carefully preserved. The former Hôtel Pontalba at no. 41 was built in 1836 and redesigned by Baron Edmond de Rothschild at the end of the 19th century; it has since become the residence of the United States ambassador.

SHOWCASE FOR LUXURY GOODS AND FASHION. The Faubourg-St-Honoré, like the area around Avenue Montaigne, has become a center of Parisian haute couture. Jeanne Lanvin moved into no. 22 (1 H3) in 1890; it was here that she made the collections inspired by designs created for her daughter.

Paul Valéry purchased the first "green coat" (the official dress for members of the French Academy) in the men's boutique on the other side of the street. Many other fashion houses have moved in, including Pierre Cardin (1 G2, no. 59), Christian Lacroix (1 G2; no. 73) and Karl Lagerfeld (1 H3; no. 19). Important jewelers and stores selling luxury goods have also settled here. The house opposite the Élysée Palace (1 F2), which was built in 1768 for the Prince de Beauvau, is now occupied by the Ministry of the Interior (1 FG2).

ÉLYSÉE PALACE (1 F2) ● 66

HÔTEL D'ÉVREUX. This was one of the first private houses on the Faubourg, built in 1718 by the architect Armand-Claude Mollet for Hervé-Louis de La Tour d'Auverge, Comte d'Évreux. Louis XV's mistress, Mme de Pompadour, bought the house, located between the court and the gardens, in 1753. In 1764 it became the king's property, and it was sold seven years later to the immensely wealthy banker Beaujon, who gave it to Louis XVI in return for a lifetime allowance (only to die four months later).

ÉLYSÉE-BOURBON. This house was given to the Duchesse de Bourbon-Condé and renamed Élysée-Bourbon. Under the Revolution it became an amusement park before being divided up into stores and apartments. The young Alfred de Musset was one of its inhabitants and later wrote: "This was my childhood home, my place of study, my school."

ÉLYSÉE-NAPOLÉON. In 1805, Napoleon gave the house to his sister Caroline Murat, who had it decorated in opulent style. The emperor himself lived here for a time and then gave the house to Josephine as a parting gift before returning to sign his abdication here at the end of the Hundred Days. Later the Élysée fell to Louis-Philippe, and then to Louis-Napoléon Bonaparte; it was here that the latter planned his coup d'état of December 2, 1851.

THE "CHÂTEAU". The Élysée Palace has been the official residence of presidents of the Republic since 1871. Republican guards parade here for official visits and keep watch over the Council of Ministers, which takes place each Wednesday morning. The main building is still the original Hôtel d'Évreux, although wings were added to the palace under the Second Empire where neighboring houses had once stood. On the Champs-Élysées side the palace opens onto the Avenue Gabriel through the Grille du Coq (above), which was added in 1900. The magnificent interior is decorated with countless Gobelins tapestries and with 18th-century French furniture and paintings in the Murat, Doré, Argent and Pompadour rooms.

▲ FROM THE FAUBOURG ST-HONORÉ TO THE OPÉRA

CHURCH OF ST-AUGUSTIN
The church has a cast-iron framework covered with stone, and the vault of the nave is supported by visible arches of chased metal. The use of iron allowed the monumental dome to be raised to a height of 160 feet.

BOULEVARD MALESHERBES

When this road was built between 1800 and 1866, it put an end to the Little Poland area, which is supposed to have inspired Eugène Sue's *Mysteries of Paris*.

ST-AUGUSTIN (9 G9). This church was built by Baltard beginning in 1861, in an eclectic style which combines Roman, Gothic, Renaissance and neo-Byzantine elements on an ingenious groundplan defined by the triangular plot. It was in this church that Charles de Foucauld was converted in 1886.

CHAPELLE EXPIATOIRE (9 H10). This chapel, with its Greco-Roman appearance, was built by Fontaine in 1815; it is framed by two galleries housing what Chateaubriand called a "string of tombs". The bodies of Louis XVI and Marie-Antoinette lay here until they were transferred to St-Denis ▲ *432*, with the bodies of three thousand other victims of the Revolution. In 1815 Louis XVIII decided to build a commemorative monument which is located in the peaceful Square Louis XVI; in it is a crypt where a tomb-shaped altar is framed by two marble sculptures, *Louis XVI Supported by an Angel* (by Bosco), and *Marie-Antoinette Praying at the Feet of Religion* (by Cortot).

ÉGLISE DE LA MADELEINE (1 H2)

MARCEL PROUST
Proust lived with his parents at 9, place de la Madeleine, whose first floor has housed the Lucas Carton restaurant ▲ *216* since 1880.

CHANGES OF PLAN. Contant d'Ivry was commissioned to build the church in 1764, in order to provide "a pleasant conclusion to the Rue Royale" facing the Bourbon Palace. In 1806 Napoleon altered the purpose of the building, charging Pierre Vignon to construct a "temple to the glory of the French armies". The building, surrounded on all sides by a colonnade, was to form "a monument such as there used to be at Athens, and such as does not exist in Paris". The church, once again dedicated to religious worship, was finally finished in 1842 under the July Monarchy.

A TOUR-DE-FORCE OF CLASSICAL STYLE. The church has the imposing appearance of a classical temple: it is 350 feet long, 140 feet wide, surrounded by 52 Corinthian columns each measuring 64 feet. There is no external bell or cross to show that this is a church, although the two monumental bronze doors (weighing over 3 tons) feature bas-reliefs of the Ten Commandments by Henri de Triqueti, while the niches hold 32 statues of saints. Inside, the building's religious purpose is clear, expressed in the official style typical of 1830–40. The interior is arranged around a vast nave (260 feet long), with three bays surmounted by flattened domes. Two beautiful sculptures stand out: *The Rapture of Mary Magdalene*, a marble group by Marochetti, and *The Baptism of Christ*, by François Rude. On the surface of the half-dome in the chancel, which covers 23 square feet, is a stunning fresco by Jules Ziegler, *The History and Glorification of Christianity*.

PLACE DE LA MADELEINE. Since 1834 there has been a flower market on this square, which is also the place to come for fine groceries. Two names stand out particularly: Hédiard (no. 21), which has been at this address for over 130 years, and Fauchon (nos. 24–30). The Fauchon buildings were designed by Théodore Charpentier in 1842.

MAXIM'S (1 H3)
This restaurant opened at 3, rue Royale, in 1893 and has preserved its Art-Nouveau decoration, along with the traditional corridor arrangement, allowing diners to see and be seen.

RUE ROYALE (1 H3)
The florist Lachaume (above) has been at no. 10 since 1845, in one of the grandest stores on the street. Lalique (glassware, a precursor of the modern style) is at no. 11, Christofle (silver) is at no. 12 ▲ *130*, and Ladurée pâtisserie is at no. 16.

"This is where life is," exclaimed Balzac in his "physiology of the boulevards of Paris", in which he recounted their history since 1670, when Louis XIV decided to convert Charles V's city wall into a public promenade. From the mid-18th century through the 19th century, the Grand Boulevards were the height of fashion. Stylish Parisians flocked to these avenues crammed with famous cafés, theaters and places of entertainment, while strollers simply enjoyed the theatrical ambiance of the place.

REX MOVIE THEATER
Lamps in the ceiling simulating a starry sky, a classical Hispanic town illuminated with lighting displays, fountains at Christmas ... This movie theater was designed in 1932, after American

models, and has been declared a historical monument. It continues the tradition of spectacular places of entertainment along the Grand Boulevards, which include the Bains Chinois (Chinese baths), Café Frascati, Olympia music hall and Musée Grévin.

MONTAGNES RUSSES
In wintertime, the Russians built wooden scaffolds on the River Neva, with steep slopes for sleds to hurtle down. These "Russian Mountains" were introduced to France in the 19th century, thrilling the public and becoming one of the most popular attractions at amusement parks.

MUSIC HALL
All the great variety artists established themselves at the Olympia under the direction of Bruno Coquatrix. Later the Olympia came up against competition from the Zenith and the Palais de Bercy.

"I LOVE TO STROLL . . ."
"I love to stroll along the Grand Boulevards, there is so much, so much to see," sang Yves Montand, in praise of the great avenues, which reached the height of their popularity during the Belle Époque, under the Third Republic.

MAURICE CHEVALIER
Maurice Chevalier, with his famous boater, popularized the "boulevard spirit" and cheeky Parisian humor as far afield as the United States. He tackled all the genres: café-concert, variety shows with Mistinguett, and operettas, as well as movies and music hall.

▲ From the Faubourg St-Honoré to the Opéra

Showpiece of the Second Empire
The Opéra was a temple of the bourgeoisie, at the heart of the city's commercial center; it had to act as a showcase for the splendors of the Second Empire.

Worldly splendor
The Opéra's interior, with its many different colored marbles, creates a magnificent display of worldly splendor. The great ceremonial staircase decorated with female figures carrying torches (made by Carrier-Belleuse), divides into two divergent flights of stairs that lead to the gallery of the Grand Foyer. This hall, designed by Garnier as a "drawing room for Paris society", opens onto an outside loggia, with the Salon de la Lune and Salon du Soleil at either end.

THE OPÉRA

(1 J2)

GARNIER'S PALACE. Napoleon III had a narrow escape from an assassination attempt led by Orsini as he left the Salle Le Peletier in 1858. This prompted him to build a new opera house in a safe location, provided with better escape routes. Charles Garnier was commissioned to fulfill the project, which proved to be fraught with pitfalls. At the outset the empress criticized his lack of style, to which he replied "But this is Napoleon III style, Madam." Then he had to lay the foundations over an underground water source (this later provided the setting for Gaston Leroux's *Phantom of the Opera*). Building work was delayed due to lack of funds, but the Opéra was finally opened in 1875 – under the Third Republic.

A "WORLDLY CATHEDRAL OF CIVILIZATION". This verdict by Théophile Gautier is a perfect description of Charles Garnier's project: Garnier

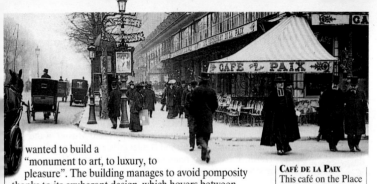

wanted to build a "monument to art, to luxury, to pleasure". The building manages to avoid pomposity thanks to its exuberant design, which hovers between Baroque and neo-Renaissance styles. On the outside, the monumental façade has seven arcades beneath the seven bays of the loggia, which are separated by pairs of columns. The whole building from top to bottom is crammed with sculptures: busts of composers, classical masks and large allegorical groups, including a replica of Carpeaux's *La Danse*. There are more sculptures on the flattened dome over the auditorium, including *Apollo Raising His Lyre* by Millet, which is surrounded by winged horses.

RED AND GOLD. The red-and-gold auditorium itself is relatively small, accommodating 2,130 spectators in front of its Italian-style stage. André Malraux had the ceiling renovated in 1964; Lenepveu's decorations were painted over by Chagall, who depicted famous operas and ballets.

EMINENTLY FUNCTIONAL. The building is an impressive size, 560 feet long and 330 feet wide; it covers an area of nearly 120,000 square feet and has a grand total of 6,319 stairs in its many basements and mazes of corridors. The size of the auditorium was restricted by the fact that escape routes were a priority. The stage machinery was unique for its period, with scenery stacked up to a height of over 200 feet. For opera performances, the building has now been superseded by the Opéra-Bastille; it was renamed Palais de la Danse in 1985.

PLACE DE L'OPÉRA. This is a major crossroads, with traffic heading for the Grand Boulevards and the department stores of the Boulevard Haussmann. The Grand Hôtel, built for the Universal Exhibition of 1867, echoes Garnier's Opéra building with its 700 rooms and 70 drawing rooms, its courtyard crowned with a glass roof, and its glittering golden dining room.

CAFÉ DE LA PAIX
This café on the Place de l'Opéra, on the first floor of the Grand Hôtel, counted Maupassant and Zola among its regular customers.

DEPARTMENT STORES OF THE BOULEVARD HAUSSMANN (1 l1)
The main Printemps building (no. 64) dates from 1865 and was rebuilt in its present form by Paul Sédille in 1881. The second Printemps building was rebuilt in 1921 after a fire: on its seventh story is a tea room under the great glass dome designed by Binet in 1911. The nearby Galeries Lafayette (no. 40) has also kept its façade from 1910 and its stained-glass dome, supported by ten metal pillars ● 77.

BOULEVARD DES ITALIENS (2 AB2)

BOULEVARD OF ELEGANCE. "Everyone comes here, the whole world is here, within a hundred steps", said Musset of the most famous of the Grand Boulevards, renowned for its Café Hardi, Tortoni ice cream parlor, Chinese baths, Hanover pavilion (reassembled in the Parc de Sceaux in 1935) and Passage des Princes shopping arcade, with its glass roof and metal arches, opened in 1860 and recently renovated. The mood of the boulevard changed at the end of the 19th century, when the large banks moved into the quarter to be close to the Stock Exchange. The BNP (Banque Nationale de Paris) still occupies the Art Deco building (no. 16) built in 1933 on the site of the former Café Riche, where the Goncourt brothers, Zola, Daudet and Turgenev held their "dinners for unpopular authors". The bank has an annex in the Maison Dorée (no. 29), which was built in 1838 and takes its name from its gilded balconies. The headquarters of the Crédit Lyonnais (nos. 17–23), dating from 1878, is another perfect illustration of the "irresistible golden trap, blazing in the sun", depicted by Zola in his novel *L'Argent* in 1891.

CRÉDIT LYONNAIS
Behind its Louis XIV-style façade is the largest privately built construction in Paris.

BOULEVARD MONTMARTRE (2 BC2)

TEEMING CROWDS OF PARIS. Along the lively Boulevard Montmartre streamed "the teeming crowds of Paris", in the words of Jules Vallès. Buildings which survive from its golden days include the Café Madrid (no. 6) and the THÉÂTRE DES VARIÉTÉS (no. 7), built in 1806 in an elegant classical style. The theater, originally the home of vaudeville, later staged Offenbach's operettas and the witty boulevard plays of Tristan Bernard and Sacha Guitry. On the other side of the street is the MUSÉE GRÉVIN ▲ *141* (no. 10), which opened in 1882. Its exhibits include wax models of French historical figures, the giant kaleidoscope from the palace of illusions, and the fin-de-siècle style Théâtre Joli, which is decorated with Bourdelle's bas-relief *The Clouds*.

SHOPPING ARCADES. These were very fashionable at the beginning of the 19th century, until the advent of electricity and sidewalks

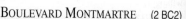

COMÉDIE-ITALIENNE
The Salle Favart, or Opéra-Comique, was built in 1781 for the Italian actors after whom the nearby boulevard is named. It was rebuilt in 1898. The most popular comic operas were performed here, as were Offenbach's operettas.

"TEMPLE OF MONEY"
The main façade of the Bourse (Stock Exchange) is built in a neoclassical style which gave rise to Hugo's ironic description. It is decorated with statues of *Commerce* and *Industry* by Dumont and Duret.

under the Second Empire.

Around twenty of them can still be seen in Paris, and two perfect examples give onto Boulevard Montmartre. The Passage des Panoramas (no. 11) opened in 1799; it was named after the landscapes painted by the American artist Fulton, which gave 19th-century visitors the illusion of being in London or Athens. The arcade still houses the engraver Stern, founded in 1840, and the Arbre à Cannelle tea rooms, with their Napoleon III décor. The PASSAGE JOUFFROY opens on the other side of the street (no. 12); this arcade has secondhandbook stalls and toy stores.

THE BOURSE   (2 B2)

This edifice by the architect Brongniart was begun in 1808 and completed in 1826; its two wings were added between 1902 and 1907. The original rectangular building is bordered by a peristyle of Corinthian columns, and the central hall has an 80-foot-high glass dome surrounded by arcaded galleries. The old stockbrokers' enclosure has been superseded by computer screens installed in 1987, but the trading floor is as noisy as ever.

"HUMAN AQUARIA"
This is how Aragon described the Parisian arcades. Although they no longer serve as a refuge from bad weather (their prime function before the advent of sidewalks), many of them still have an exotic air of the Oriental bazaar.

⏱ **One day**

The Île de la Cité is the historical heart of Paris: from the time of the Late Empire (3rd to 5th centuries AD), this strip of land was the focus of royal, judiciary and religious power. The Gallo-Roman palace which stood on the western part of the island was later taken over by the Merovingians and then rebuilt by Philippe le Bel in the 14th century. Today's Palais de Justice stands on the same site. The Parlement and other institutions were based here, including the Chambre des Comptes (Chamber of Revenue), the Chambre du Trésor (Treasury) and so on. The eastern part of the island was devoted to religion from the Gallo-Roman era onward. A cathedral already stood on the site of today's Notre-Dame in 362. Gradually an entire ecclesiastical center grew up around this building: a baptistry, bishop's palace, the Hôtel-Dieu (general hospital),

PONT-NEUF
This was the first bridge across the Seine without houses on it. The humpback bridge with semicircular arches was designed by the architects Pierre Désilles and Androuet du Cerceau and opened in 1607. The statue of Henri IV which dates from 1818, replaced a statue by Franqueville which was erected in 1635 and destroyed in 1792.

and 46 houses occupied by canons. As these institutions were built it became necessary to raise the level of the island, which has grown in size from 20 to 43 acres over ten centuries. The island was completely transformed under Haussmann, who razed the medieval city to create an administrative center. This center is now the base of two institutions devoted to maintaining public order – the judiciary and the police.

In the 19th century, the island's population was regarded as the most destitute in Paris: it fell from 15,000 inhabitants in 1858 to 5,000 in 1868.

A HIVE OF ACTIVITY
Up until the 19th century, the Pont-Neuf (above, during construction) buzzed with activity. Below, opposite: the bridge in the 17th century.

PLACE DAUPHINE AND THE PONT-NEUF ★ (2 C7)

In 1584, Henri III decided to sell off the end of the Île de la Cité in order to raise funds to build the Pont-Neuf: an area of sand and water made up of three small islands which had to be filled in and joined together, significantly increasing the island's surface area. In 1601, Henri IV decided to build a three-sided square here (the base of the triangle, on the Rue de Harlay, was demolished in

1874). The land was sold in 12 lots, on which 32 identical houses were built in red brick with stone facing. The houses had an arcade on the first floor, and three stories above this; the façades on the Seine side were identical. Only the two symmetrical buildings at the end of the square are still in their original form. The square itself is charming – the poet Malherbe, in the 17th century, described it as "the most beautiful and the most practical in Paris".

NOTRE-DAME DE PARIS ★ (2 D8)

A CLASSICAL CATHEDRAL. It is now thought that the Île de la Cité had a

NOTRE-DAME, AT THE ORIGINS OF PARIS ✪
This masterpiece of architecture set between the arms of the Seine justly deserves the moniker "ship of stone". Building began when Paris was chosen as the capital of France. In the crypt is the Musée de l'Histoire de Paris. Do not miss the view from the top of the towers and the official center of Paris, marked in the square in front of the west end.

cathedral as far back as the 4th century, at a time when Christianity was spreading, thanks to the policies of Emperor Constantine. A group of episcopal buildings was established, consisting of the bishop's house, the baptistry (destroyed in 1748) and an exceptionally long basilica (230 to 260 feet long). The beginnings of what was to become the Hôtel-Dieu (general hospital) probably go back to this period. This episcopal

RADICAL CHANGES
In the 19th century
the Île de la Cité
underwent major
alterations, mainly as
a result of
Haussmann's
schemes: an
enormous

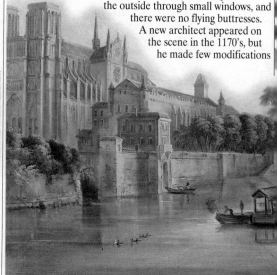

square was cleared in
front of Notre-Dame;
the Tribunal de
Commerce was built,
as was the barracks
which later became
the police
headquarters; and a
new general hospital
was built to the north
of the island. The
archbishop's palace
was demolished in
1831 and partially
replaced by the
sacristy, which was
restored by Viollet-le-
Duc.

POINT OF DEPARTURE
A bronze star outside
Notre-Dame marks
the center not only of
Paris but of the whole
country: this is the
point from which
road distances from
Paris to the towns of
France have been
measured since the
Ancien Régime.

center grew during the course of the 8th and 9th centuries
with the addition of a canonical chapter; it became, in effect,
a sort of urban monastery, with independent houses and
gardens. Gradually the chapter expanded: a choir was built
between the shrine and the nave and later, to the west, two
halls were added on either side of a tower-
porchway. In 1148, Archdeacon Étienne de
Garlande, a leading figure within the chapter,
built a portal with carved
columns dedicated to the Virgin.
When the old basilica was
demolished around 1160, only
Étienne de Garlande's
portal survived, becoming
part of the later western
façade (Ste-Anne Portal).
At this time Louis VII's
kingdom was flourishing;
the old basilica seemed
very out-of-date, and
Bishop Maurice de Sully
decided it should be
rebuilt.

THE MAJOR PHASES OF CONSTRUCTION. Sully's ambitious
project was conceived on a huge scale: covering a surface area
of nearly 60,000 square feet, it entailed significant alterations
to the surrounding urban fabric. Everything was demolished
except the canons' enclosure and the baptistry, and the
western façade was moved toward the east to make way for a
square in front of the cathedral. The anonymous architect
evidently had considerable funds at his disposal, which meant
that building could begin immediately, starting with the
chevet. The interior was planned on four levels, with a line of
rose windows above the galleries. The bays were opened to
the outside through small windows, and
there were no flying buttresses.
A new architect appeared on
the scene in the 1170's, but
he made few modifications

to the design, except for technical innovations which allowed the bays to be joined to the nave by three openings rather than two. A third architect tackled the western body of the building and the square in front of the church; at this stage the nave was not yet complete. Around 1210–20, a fourth architect joined the façade to the nave: he altered the original plan significantly, abandoning the use of columns in favor of a more complex arrangement, similar to devices used for the cathedral at Chartres. During the 1220's and 1230's, the cathedral underwent further modification, mostly to allow more light into the building, in the spirit of High Gothic style. As a result, the windows of the nave became larger and the rose windows disappeared; the roof over the bays was lowered and replaced by terraces; and large flying buttresses were added, serving also as drainage pipes for rainwater. A spire was built over the crossing of the transept at this time. Around 1250 the architect Jean de Chelles was commissioned to build new façades at the far ends of the transept and to complete the northern end. Pierre de Montreuil continued work on the southern end. From this time up to 1325, side chapels were built between the buttresses, enclosed by a continuous wall, in the nave, the choir and the chevet. The cathedral was badly damaged during the Revolution and was restored after 1845 by Jean-Baptiste Lassus and Eugène Viollet-le-Duc. The latter continued the work alone from 1857 to 1864, when it was completed.

RUE CHANOINESSE
This street is named after the canons who lived in the cloisters of Notre-Dame. Its buildings have quiet internal courtyards.

TYMPANUM OF THE LAST JUDGMENT
The central portal of Notre-Dame depicts the Last Judgment, drawing not only on the Apocalypse but also on the Gospel of Saint Matthew. Its iconography is very simple and easily understood by those who cannot read: Good and Bad are clearly contrasted, without any superfluous ornamentation. The central section shows the weighing of souls, presided over by Saint Michael: good souls are directed to the left, toward Abraham, while the bad, on the right, are thrown headfirst into Hell.

▲ NOTRE-DAME

Notre-Dame de Paris, at the geographic and historical heart of the capital, illustrates the splendors and variations of Gothic architecture between the mid-12th and the early 14th centuries. The simplicity and harmony of this impressive building derive from a skillful combination of horizontals and verticals. After a century of gradual deterioration, the Romantic 19th century brought the building back to life, restoring most of its magnificent sculptures.

LOUIS XIII'S VOW
(1708–26)
Louis XIV decided to carry out his father's vow and ordered the architect Robert de Cotte to renovate the choir of Notre-Dame. The high altar was created by Antoine Vassé, the *Virgin of Compassion* sculpture by Nicolas Coustou. The kneeling statues of Louis XIV and Louis XIII (right) were carved, respectively, by Antoine Coysevoix and Guillaume Coustou. The six angels of gilded bronze by the pilasters carry the instruments of the Passion.

FLYING BUTTRESSES
The chevet was first modified around 1220–30, when the flying buttresses were built. These incorporated a channel which was intended to solve the problem of rainwater runoff, created when the roofs were replaced by terraces.

SIDE CHAPELS
Between 1250 and 1325, chapels were built between the buttresses, encased by a continuo wall, in the nave, the choir and the chevet (by Pierre de Chelles and Jean Ravy).

GRAND AUSTERITY
The building consists of a nave with five double bays flanked by double aisles, a very short transept, and a round apse with seven sections. The square vaults – six over the central nave and four over the side aisles – would normally have resulted in alternating strong and weak pillars, but the architect used a single type of pillar throughout to produce an effect of structural unity. At the crossing of the transept is an elevation with four levels: this is roughly how the earlier cathedral looked, as re-created by Viollet-le-Duc.

11

DECORATIVE PANELS

These form a background mosaic with a variety of motifs, some taken from the heraldic vocabulary. Each lancet – like that of the Passion (left) – is framed by a narrow border, which also shows a heraldic influence.

6

STAINED-GLASS WINDOWS: A TRIPLE FUNCTION

These beautiful windows fulfill historical and decorative functions and they also have an architectural role in creating an enclosed space.

COLORS

Variations from one window to another are apparent mainly in the background mosaics, where the same decorative motifs are repeated. These motifs form a colored screen. In the historical panels, by contrast, the colors are distributed in an irregular fashion on a blue background. The dominant colors are blue and red, although other tones are prominent in places, yellow in particular.

5
4
3
2
1

HISTORICAL PANELS

The series covers the eight large windows with four lancets on the nave – four to the north and four to the south – and the seven windows with two lancets on the apse,

ending with the great rose window in the western façade, which was completed in the final decade of the 5th century. The sequence as a whole presents the entire history of the Hebrew people from the Creation to their arrival in Israel. It ends with Louis IX receiving the relics of the Passion. This historical sequence is accompanied by a prophetic cycle on the life of Christ framed by the lives of Saint John the Baptist and Saint John the Evangelist. These saints fit into the sequence through their roles as prophets: the Baptist announces the Lamb of God and the Evangelist the vision of the Apocalypse.

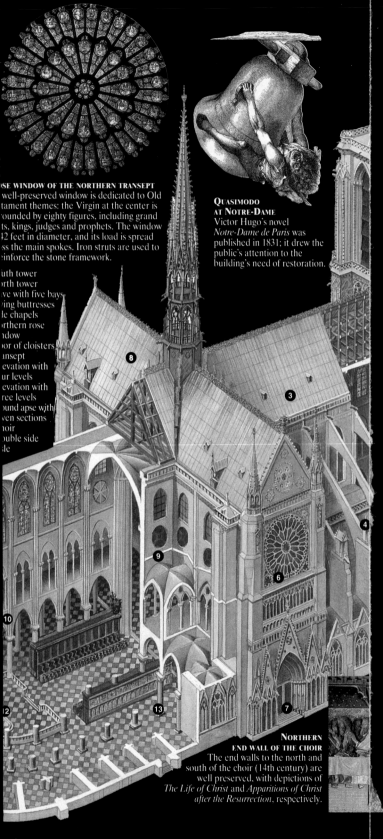

OSE WINDOW OF THE NORTHERN TRANSEPT
well-preserved window is dedicated to Old
tament themes: the Virgin at the center is
ounded by eighty figures, including grand
ts, kings, judges and prophets. The window
42 feet in diameter, and its load is spread
ss the main spokes. Iron struts are used to
einforce the stone framework.

uth tower
orth tower
ve with five bays
ving buttresses
le chapels
orthern rose
ndow
oor of cloisters
unsept
evation with
ur levels
evation with
ree levels
ound apse with
ven sections
noir
ouble side
le

**QUASIMODO
AT NOTRE-DAME**
Victor Hugo's novel
Notre-Dame de Paris was
published in 1831; it drew the
public's attention to the
building's need of restoration.

**NORTHERN
END WALL OF THE CHOIR**
The end walls to the north and
south of the choir (14th century) are
well preserved, with depictions of
The Life of Christ and *Apparitions of Christ
after the Resurrection*, respectively.

Saint Louis built the Ste-Chapelle between 1241 and 1248, to provide a worthy setting for the relics of the Passion. This archetype of monumental Gothic art is therefore not only a palatine chapel (with a lower chapel for the public and a higher chapel for the king) but first and foremost a reliquary chapel. The exterior of the building has an original design, with very strong buttresses, but no flying buttresses, allowing the architect to build enormous windows. The verticality of the design is accentuated by the long spire.

A ROYAL MANIFESTO
The Ste-Chapelle was traditionally attributed to Pierre de Montreuil, but it has also been ascribed to Thomas de Cormont and to Robert de Luzarches. It was set into the structure of the Palais de la Cité and had a political as well as a religious function. Here the king refers to his double

function, as temporal and spiritual leader of the people, whose mission is to lead them to eternal life.

A 19TH-CENTURY MONUMENT
The Ste-Chapelle was badly damaged during the Revolution and restored in the 19th century by Félix Duban, Jean-Baptiste Lassus, Émile Boeswilldald and Viollet-le-Duc. They replaced the roof, the external staircase, the spire (for the fourth time in 1853), the interior decorations and some of the stained-glass windows.

A UNIQUE NAVE
The Ste-Chapelle building consists of a single unit with four bays, ending in a chevet with seven sections.

LOWER CHAPEL
The Lower Chapel has something of the air of a crypt. Its two rows of columns strengthen the building structurally, as well as forming two side aisles which join together in the apse.

UPPER CHAPEL
The Upper Chapel is striking for its simplicity and unity. The traditional Gothic three-level elevation has given way to an elevation on two levels, or even on a single level, as the dominant window section seems to encroach upon the base section.

VERTICALITY
Powerful protruding buttresses, very close together at the apse end, allowed the architect to do without flying buttresses.

KINGS OF JUDAH
The Gallery of Kings, a horizontal version of the tree of Jesse, displayed twenty-eight statues of Christ's ancestors up until 1793. They were restored in the 19th century. Twenty-one heads, pulled down and mutilated during the Revolution, were found in the basement of a Parisian bank in 1977.

STE-ANNE PORTAL
▲ 356. An additional lintel and a lower row of voussoirs were needed when the old portal was reassembled on the Gothic façade. The portal derives its effect from its formal structure and stylistic unity.

PORTAL OF THE VIRGIN
This was created at the height of Gothic sculpture in the 13th century, when the monumental tradition was tempered by a trend toward greater humanity. It is striking for its balanced composition, in which archivolts highlight the interplay of diagonals and horizontals.

PORTAL OF THE LAST JUDGMENT ▲ 357
The humanization of iconograpy led to the introduction of new subjects at the beginning of the 13th century. The Gallery of Kings, Saint Anne and the Last Judgment are all new motifs.

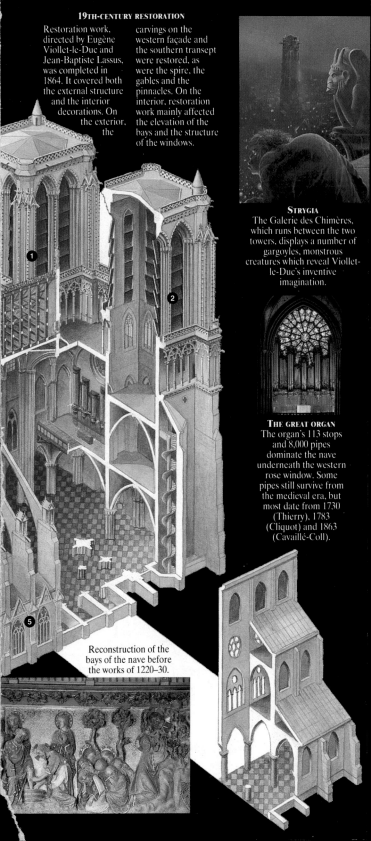

19TH-CENTURY RESTORATION

Restoration work, directed by Eugène Viollet-le-Duc and Jean-Baptiste Lassus, was completed in 1864. It covered both the external structure and the interior decorations. On the exterior, the carvings on the western façade and the southern transept were restored, as were the spire, the gables and the pinnacles. On the interior, restoration work mainly affected the elevation of the bays and the structure of the windows.

STRYGIA

The Galerie des Chimères, which runs between the two towers, displays a number of gargoyles, monstrous creatures which reveal Viollet-le-Duc's inventive imagination.

THE GREAT ORGAN

The organ's 113 stops and 8,000 pipes dominate the nave underneath the western rose window. Some pipes still survive from the medieval era, but most date from 1730 (Thierry), 1783 (Cliquot) and 1863 (Cavaillé-Coll).

Reconstruction of the bays of the nave before the works of 1220–30.

INGENIOUS TECHNICAL DEVICES
The architect used extra metal
supports to connect the bays as well
as iron struts running across the
transoms and right through the
supports. Care was taken to hide
these thick iron bars by making
them coincide with the framework
of the stained-glass windows where
possible.

SCHOLARLY ICONOGRAPHY
The iconography of the Ste-Chapelle
presents a theological reflection on
Christ's Passion, drawing on the
Ideas of the Mendicants and
Franciscans, Saint Louis' favorite
orders.

1. Upper Chapel
2. Lower Chapel

Genesis
Exodus
Numbers
Deuteronomy,
Joshua
Judges
Isaiah (left),
the Tree of Jesse
(right)

8

9

10

9. Saint John the Baptist
(left), the Book of Daniel
(right)
10. Ezekiel
11. Jeremiah (left),
Tobias (right)
12. Judith and Job
13. Esther
14. The Book
of Kings
15. The Translation
of the Relics
16. The Apocalypse

11

12

13

14

15

16

Saint John the Evangelist
(left), the Childhood of
Christ (right)
The
Passion

PALAIS DE JUSTICE (2 C7)

This diverse group of buildings, which houses the law courts, covers nearly all the western section of the island. This was probably the site of a citadel in the Gallo-Roman period, which was later used by the first Merovingian kings. The fortress was at its height under the Capetians. Philippe-Auguste was born here in 1165 and later restored the palace. His grandson Louis IX (1214–70), later Saint Louis, stayed here often. In 1242 he decided to build the Ste-Chapelle ▲ *362*, joining it to the palace by a gallery to house the relics of Christ's Passion, which he had just acquired. Finally, Philippe le Bel extended the buildings between 1296 and 1313 to accommodate his financial, administrative and judicial services. However, civil unrest during the 14th century forced the monarchs to move to the Hôtel St-Paul, leaving the palace on the island to the Parliament of Paris, a supreme judicial court which also functioned as a prison. After repeated fires and destruction during the Revolution, most of the palace had to be rebuilt. The Ste-Chapelle, the towers and the lower sections of the north façade are the only parts of the medieval palace standing today. During the last century, magnificent interior decorations were added in the Salle des Pas Perdus, the Vestibule de Harlay and the Cour de Cassation: although these are quite impressive, visitors who are pushed for time might restrict themselves to visiting the Conciergerie.

THE CONCIERGERIE PRISON. The building is named after the Concierge, the king's steward, who had many powers and highly lucrative privileges. It incorporated both the Concierge's residence and a prison which was used by the Concierge, and later by the Parliament. The Parliament was replaced by the Criminal Tribunal after the fall of the monarchy and by the Revolutionary Tribunal in 1793. During those two years over 2,700 people who had been condemned to death spent their last hours here. Among the victims was Queen

in the 12th century. The Rue de la Cité was known as the Rue de la Juiverie (Street of the Jewish Quarter) until 1834.

Marie-Antoinette, who was guillotined on October 16, 1793. Famous prisoners held here during the 19th century include the royalist Cadoudal, Maréchal Ney, Prince Napoleon and the anarchists Orsini and Ravachol. In 1914 part of the prison was converted into a historical monument open to the public. The latest alterations were made for the bicentenary of the Revolution in 1989: there are reconstructions of the room where the clerk kept the registers and of the *toilette des condamnés*, where prisoners went before being led to the Cour de Mai. Upstairs the dungeons can be viewed, including the cell kept for high-ranking prisoners. Marie-Antoinette's cell has been arranged as it was under the Restoration: a chapel of atonement is located in the part where the queen lived, and paintings recount the story of her captivity.

THE MEDIEVAL PALACE (entrance on the Quai de l'Horloge). The first room, the Salle des Gardes (guards' room), was built under the reign of Philippe le Bel (beginning of the 14th century): three huge pillars divide it into two naves with four bays and rib vaulting, while two staircases lead to the César and Argent towers, which date from the same period. After this is the magnificent Salle des Gens d'Armes (officers' room),

reserved for officers on duty, which was built around 1300. This large Gothic construction has often been compared to the rooms in the Palais des Papes at Avignon. The rectangular space is divided into four naves by three rows of sturdy pillars. The room was heated by four large fireplaces. Later modifications are easily spotted: the raised passageway known as the Rue de Paris, which was formerly divided into tiny dungeons without light or air; the extra pillars added to the middle row to reinforce the upper room, rebuilt by Salomon de Brosse in 1622; and the spiral staircase in openwork stone renovated in the 19th century. Finally, there are the basement kitchens at river level, built around 1353.

CHAPELLE DES GIRONDINS
The chapel in the Conciergerie bears this name in memory of the twenty-one Girondin deputies who were condemned to death by the Revolutionary Tribunal. They spent their last night here before being executed on October 30, 1793. *The Call for the Last Victims of the Terror*, by Charles Louis Müller (1815–92), depicts this tragic episode in the history of the Conciergerie (above); Boilly and Delaroche also painted this subject.

A PLANNED ISLAND
The present layout of the Île St-Louis was the work of engineer Christophe Marie. He was commissioned by Louis XIII to join the island to the banks of

the Seine by two stone bridges, to border it with stone quaysides, and to build its roads and houses. This urban-development plan was carried out between 1614 and 1660. The Pont Marie was completed in 1630, Pont de la Tournelle fifteen years later.

ÎLE ST-LOUIS ★   (2 EF8 and 2 F9)

People come to the Île St-Louis in large numbers to stroll through its streets and enjoy the island's astonishingly tranquil atmosphere. Two centuries ago, Louis-Sébastien Mercier observed that the island "seems to have escaped the great corruption of the city, which has not yet reached here". Little has changed in the island's appearance since this time. Its quaysides are lined with beautiful houses offering unique views of the Seine and the city.

A RECENT CREATION. Buildings began to appear on the Île St-Louis in the 17th century: it was given its present name in 1726. Before this, the island, which was known as the Île Notre-Dame, was nothing but a pasture subject to regular flooding. Washerwomen came here to dry their linen; since medieval times, this has been the place where duels were held: the sword, supposedly inspired by God, was used to settle legal disputes.

AN ATTRACTIVE PROJECT. Christophe Marie, an engineer and official Parisian bridge builder, began the development of the island in April 1614. He directed the project in collaboration with Lugles Poulletier, a military superintendent and François Le Regrattier, treasurer of the Cent-Suisses (a military company). The project's finances were very volatile. The Pont Marie was completed in 1630, Pont de la Tournelle fifteen years later.

Marie bears the name of its creator who died in poverty in 1653, and carries an inscription proclaiming that he "deserves the sympathy of all visitors to Old Paris and the gratitude of the island's inhabitants". Two streets bear the names of his associates. The quays, around 32 feet high, form a parallelogram measuring 2,000 by 560 feet; they were completed in 1650. The new quarter was a huge success, and its airy houses and well-arranged streets represented an entirely different kind of urban design. The main part of the houses were built to overlook the quays rather than the courtyards (as formerly), making the most of the fresh air and river views. Another innovation was the use of freestone on its own rather than as a facing for brickwork.

A MAIN THOROUGHFARE
Rue St-Louis-en-l'Île is peaceful during the week and more lively during the weekend. The shops are its main attraction, including the bookshop Ulysse at no. 26, specializing in travel books, and the DAAVP bookshop, at

RUE ST-LOUIS-EN-L'ÎLE

This central street was built between 1614 and 1646. Visitors approaching the island by the Pont St-Louis (rebuilt in 1970 and reserved for pedestrians) will find the inn Aux Anysetiers du Roy at no. 61, on the corner of Rue Le Regrattier. The inn still has grilles and a statuette from the Petit Bacchus, a 17th-century tavern.

HÔTEL DE CHENIZOT. The house at no. 51 is named after the tax collector who acquired it in 1719, one hundred years after it had been built. This owner was also responsible for the rococo-style decoration of the façades overlooking the courtyard and the street. A staircase and handrail have been preserved at the far end of the courtyard on the right-hand side. The structure of a *jeu de paume* (tennis court) built in 1634 survives at no. 54; it can be seen from inside the house which currently stands on this site.

no. 25, which stocks a wide range of books on Paris. The ice-cream maker

Berthillon is at no. 31.

CHURCH INTERIOR
The church was built following Le Vau's design. It is a perfect example of French 17th-century Baroque style, showing a new religious sensitivity. The interior is very bright, an impression heightened by the use of white stone and shining gold highlights.

CHURCH OF ST-LOUIS-EN-L'ÎLE. The church, dedicated to Saint Louis, was started in 1664 and completed in 1726. The steeple clock (1741) hangs at a right angle to the road. The church has a number of notable works of art, including *The Pilgrims of Emmaüs* by Coypel (1746), an *Annunciation* after Fra Angelico, a *Saint François de Sales* by Noël Hallé (18th century) and *Saint John and Saint Peter Healing a Lame Man* by Carle Van Loo (1742).

CABINET DES MUSES
Eustache Le Sueur (1616–55) was one of the famous artists who contributed to the decoration of the Hôtel Lambert. The artist produced a group of five paintings depicting the muses (above), after which one of the rooms is named.

HÔTEL LAMBERT. This palace was owned by the family of Prince Adam Czartoryski between 1842 and 1976, and was the artistic center of the Polish bohemian community. It was built by Le Vau at no. 2, rue St-Louis for Jean-Baptiste Lambert de Thorigny, a financier and advisor to the king. The magnificent interior decorations were produced for Nicolas Lambert, Jean-Baptiste's brother and president of the Chambre des Comptes (Chamber of Accounts): among the artists who contributed were François Perrier, Charles Le Brun, Giovanni Romanelli, Bertholet Flémalle and Pierre Patel. The decorations were purchased by the king in 1776 and dismantled. Some of the painted panels are now in the Louvre, but the majority of the paintings and sculptures are in their original places. Plates produced by the engraver Bernard Picart show us what the Galerie d'Hercule, the Salon de l'Amour and the Cabinet des Muses were like. The house is not open to the public.

QUAI D'ANJOU

This quay invites nostalgia. The description by Funck-Brentano conjures up an image of what it was like three-quarters of a century ago: "This stretch of the Seine is not used by shipping: singing can be heard in the washing places and the bridge of moored barges makes a platform for the life of the bargemen". Louis Le Vau had his house built at no. 5, next to the Hôtel Lambert, to which it is joined by a long balcony. The small Hôtel Marigny has beautiful wrought-iron railings.

HÔTEL DE LAUZUN. This house with its magnificent interior decorations was completed by Le Vau in 1657 for Charles Gruyn, son of a prosperous innkeeper. It was bought in 1682 by the Comte de Lauzun, a favorite of Louis XIV and lover of La Grande Mademoiselle (the king's cousin). After this, the house had various owners: in 1779 it was acquired by the Marquis de Pimodan, who gave it his own name. In 1842 the Hôtel de Pimodan was bought by Jérôme Pichon, a bibliophile and art lover, who restored its former name. The house was a meeting place for the "Haschischins club", whose members included Baudelaire, Balzac and Théophile Gautier. Gautier wrote a story about these drug-experimentation

HÔTEL DE LAUZUN
The façade of the Hôtel de Lauzun displays a magnificent wrought-iron balcony. The gutters decorated with dolphins date from 1910.

meetings. The house was beautifully restored by Louis Pichon in 1910 and was purchased by the City of Paris in 1928. Unfortunately, this building is no longer open to the public.

QUAI DE BOURBON (2 E8)

Le Franc-Pinot, at no. 1, with its grille decorated with vines and grapes, is a former bargemen's tavern. The Hôtel Le Charron, at no. 15, was built by Sébastien Bruant between 1637 and 1640 for Jean Charron, a military inspector in Picardy. In the corner of the courtyard is a projecting room supported by a squinch, an appendage which was common in the early 17th century. The Maison du Centaure, at no. 45, was built after 1658 by François Le Vau, brother of Louis; it is named after the two bas-reliefs depicting Hercules' victory over Nessus.

QUAI D'ORLÉANS AND QUAI DE BÉTHUNE (2 EF9)

The SOCIÉTÉ HISTORIQUE ET LITTÉRAIRE (society of history and literature) stands at 6, quai d'Orléans; it was founded by refugees in 1838. On the same site is a museum dedicated to the poet Adam Mickiewicz (1798–1855). In the 18th century the Quai de Béthune was known as the Quai des Balcons: Le Vau had decreed that all its façades should have balconies. The Hôtel de Richelieu, at no. 18, was built, probably by Le Vau, on a plot which once belonged to Madame de Sévigné's grandfather. The tour of the island ends between the two arches of the Pont Sully (1874–7), at the first houses on the Boulevard Henri-IV. At no. 1 is a store called La Maison de la Mouche (House of the Fly), which sells fishing equipment.

HÔTEL HESSELIN
This house by Louis Le Vau (below) was one of the finest on the Quai de Béthune. It was demolished in 1935, and only the carriage entrance, carved by Étienne Le Hongre still stands, at no. 24.

▲ Beaubourg – Les Halles

One day

A SQUALID AREA
"The whole area is miserable, but it exudes a delightful stench of old roguery" wrote Huysmans in 1902. Beaubourg takes its name from a village which became part of Paris when Philippe-Auguste built his city wall. During the last century it became thoroughly squalid, and it was razed in 1939, becoming a wasteland before being incorporated into the development project around Les Halles (the former market).

RUE DU SENTIER

RUE DE CLÉRY

RUE D'ABOUKIR

RUE RÉAUMUR

RUE MONTMARTRE

RUE MONTORGUEIL

RUE DUSSOUBS

RUE DE SÉBASTOPOL

RUE ÉTIENNE MARCEL

RUE DE TURBIGO

RUE PIERRE LESCOT

RUE SAINT-DENIS

BD DE SÉBASTOPOL

RUE QUINCAMPOIX

RUE SAINT-MARTIN

RUE BERGER

RUE SAINT-HONORÉ

RUE DE RIVOLI

RUE DES HALLES

RUE DE LA MONNAIE

RUE DU RENARD

QUAI DE LA MÉGISSERIE

PLACE DU CHÂTELET

AV. VICTORIA

PONT AU CHANGE

QUAI DE

ESVRES

1. BOURSE DU COMMERCE
2. SAMARITAINE DEPARTMENT STORE
3. CHURCH OF ST-EUSTACHE
4. FORUM DES HALLES
5. TOUR SAINT-JACQUES
6. HÔTEL DE VILLE
7. CHURCH OF SAINT-NICOLAS-DES-CHAMPS
8. CONSERVATOIRE DES ARTS ET MÉTIERS
9. GEORGES-POMPIDOU CENTER ❂
10. FONTAINE DES INNOCENTS
11. TOUR DE JEAN-SANS-PEUR
12. CHURCH OF ST-MERRI
13. CHURCH OF NOTRE-DAME-DE-BONNE-NOUVELLE

From the Gallo-Roman era, the *cardo*, or main south–north road of Lutetia, crossed this section of the Right Bank, running along the course of today's Rue St-Martin. However, it was not until the 11th century that the area became built up. Louis VI constructed his Châtelet fortress here, and the area became a center of commercial activity and the focus of municipal administration. The area is not resting on its laurels, however: following major redevelopment projects it now boasts the largest pedestrian mall in Europe. With the Forum des Halles and the Pompidou Center, it is (sometimes exaggeratedly) considered the heart of contemporary Paris.

RUE ND DE NAZARETH

RUE DU VERT-BOIS

RUE VAUCANSON

RUE MONTGOLFIER

8

7

BIGO

HÔTEL DE VILLE (2 E7)

PLACE DE GRÈVE. This square stood on the site of today's Place de l'Hôtel de Ville, as it was renamed in 1830. The headquarters of the Parisian municipal administration moved to this square in 1357 and has remained here ever since. In the 12th century Saint Louis entrusted the administration of Paris to the *hanse,* or guild of water merchants, who controlled shipping on the Seine. After this Paris had elected representatives, based close to Châtelet: four aldermen with the merchants' provost at their head. In 1357 the provost, Étienne Marcel, transferred the headquarters of the town council to the Maison aux Piliers, on the site of today's town hall. Crowds used to gather on the Place de Grève, standing around the huge braziers of St-Jean (whose saint's day, June 24, is celebrated with huge bonfires) to see the king. But this was also the setting for the somber spectacle of executions, from the 12th century up to 1830: criminals of the middle and lower classes were hanged, noblemen were decapitated, and heretics and sorcerers were burned alive, while criminals guilty of *lèse-majesté* were tortured. In 1610, Raviallac was quartered by four horses after being scalded and mutilated. During the last century, laborers without work used to gather on the square, which gave rise to the expression "*être en grève*" (to be on strike).

AN OPEN, WELCOMING PLACE
The Pompidou Center is one of the largest cultural centers in the world, attracting crowds of visitors to the quarter since its opening in 1977. Street artists and acrobats entertain a good-natured audience on its piazza. Today it is a focal point of the city's life, especially in the summer.

PORT DE GRÈVE
In medieval times, the Place de Grève formed a gently sloping bank descending toward the Seine where ships could land. Produce for the nearby market was unloaded at the port.

LUXURIOUS DÉCOR
The gilt decorations and paneling of the Hôtel de Ville show the splendors of the Republic: chandeliers by Baccarat in the Salle des Fêtes and works by Puvis de Chavannes decorate the southern Salon d'Arrivée.

HÔTEL DE VILLE (2 E7). This was built on the site of the Maison aux Piliers from 1553 to the early 17th century, after plans by the Italian architect Domenico Bernabei, then burnt down under the Commune, on May 24, 1871 ● 28. Ballu and Deperthes rebuilt it in its original style between 1874 and 1882. Its four façades are decorated with an abundance of niches, containing 108 statues of celebrated persons born in Paris. On the entablature are 30 statues representing the provincial towns of France, while an allegorical female figure represents the city of Paris on top of the clock pediment. It was here, in 1789, that Louis XIV was given the tricolor flag by Jean Sylvais Brouilly, mayor of Paris. It was also here that Robespierre was arrested and taken to the guillotine on July 28, 1794, thus ending the Reign of Terror.

CHÂTELET (2 D6)

PLACE DU CHÂTELET. The square was overshadowed by the silhouette of the Grand Châtelet up until 1808. Louis VI built this fortress near the Pont-Neuf in 1130 to defend the bridge to the Île de la Cité. Initially it was the headquarters of the merchants' provost; later, it became a prison specializing in refined methods of torture. The famous funnel-shaped Chamber of Hypocras forced prisoners to remain constantly standing. Today the square is one of the busiest crossroads in Paris. It is flanked by twin theaters built by Davioud in 1862 ● 74. On the western side is the Théâtre du Châtelet. It was here that the Colonne concerts came into being in 1874; now it presents dance companies like those of Pina Bausch and the New York City Ballet. On the eastern side is the Théâtre de la Ville, where Sarah Bernhardt triumphed in Edmond Rostand's *Eaglet* in 1900.
QUAI DE LA MÉGISSERIE (2 C6). This is one of the two liveliest places in the area, with its secondhand-book

ART DECO FAÇADE
Bay windows and recesses are the
main features of La Samaritaine's
stone facing. This is the only large-
scale Art Deco façade in Paris.

sellers by the Seine opposite colorful sidewalks crowded with
merchants selling plants and pets. However, in medieval times
this area was the home of the slaughterhouses, whose
pestilential stench made it one of the most unpleasant parts of
the capital. Beyond the quay are quiet roads like the Rue des
Orfèvres, which have kept their medieval course and their
peaceful atmosphere.

LA SAMARITAINE (2 C6) 19, rue de la Monnaie. Ernest
Cognacq and his wife, Louise Jay, transformed the original
1869 shop into a vast hive filling four buildings.
Between 1905 and 1910 the architect Frantz
Jourdain put up the revolutionary building at
2, rue de la Monnaie. The terrace at the top of
this Art Deco monument (on the 11th story)
offers a magnificent view over Paris. Jourdain
collaborated with Henri Sauvage ▲ *306* to build
the store at no. 3, facing the Seine.

TOUR ST-JACQUES (2 D6). This curious High
Gothic steeple (right) is all that remains of the
church of St-Jacques-de-la-Boucherie, built in
the 16th century and demolished in 1797. At
ground level, under a vault, is a statue of Pascal
commemorating his reproduction here of the
barometric experiments he first conducted at
Puy-de-Dôme. On the northwestern corner is
a statue of Saint Jacques the Elder
over a platform with a small
meteorological station. On the
other corners are carved
symbols representing the four
evangelists (lion, eagle, bull
and man): these were
restored in the 19th
century, as were the
gargoyle and the
eighteen statues of
saints on the sides
of the tower.

**FONTAINE AUX
PALMIERS**
This was built in 1806
to celebrate
Napoleon's victories
and stands on the site
of the Parloir aux
Bourgeois.

LES HALLES

(2 CD5)

THE BELLY OF PARIS. Les Halles de Paris were founded in the 12th century by Louis VI "le Gros" ("the Fat") on the site of the Champeaux, ancient marshes which were partially cultivated. In 1534, François I put up new buildings surrounded by a covered gallery, whose pillars survived until 1854. A colorful population developed, made up of market porters and fishwives, who enjoyed the privilege of being received by the king at the new year.

BALTARD'S HALLES. In 1851, Napoleon III decided to bring the different markets together in one place, near the church of St-Eustache. He had been impressed by the new metal architecture used for the Gare de l'Est and told the architect Baltard : "Make me umbrellas . . . made of iron, nothing but iron". Ten pavilions with iron frameworks resulted, constructed between 1854 and 1912. Zola celebrated them in his 1873 novel *Le Ventre de Paris* (*The Belly of Paris*). By 1962 this market at the very heart of Paris had become outdated and overcrowded: the problem was solved by transferring it to Rungis, 9 miles south of the capital, in 1969. All but two of Baltard's pavilions were destroyed: one of these was reassembled at Nogent-sur-Marne, the other at Yokohama, in Japan.

MARKET PORTERS
The guild of market porters (*Forts des Halles*) was founded by Saint Louis in 1250. The porters also functioned as security guards. There were still three thousand of them in 1965.

REDEVELOPMENT. For years there was a gaping hole where the market had stood. A wide range of projects was proposed, including an immense hanging garden and a gigantic hexahedron construction devised by the architect Ricardo Bofill. It was not until 1979 that the Halles project finally took shape, transforming the whole area up to the Rue Beaubourg. Everything changed around the new colossus: apartment buildings were renovated, and the area's activities and population were transformed, producing a commercial and cultural boom. The quarter is served by the huge Châtelet-les-Halles station, the hub of the RER network, which draws people from all over the suburbs toward Europe's largest pedestrian mall.

> "I found myself before the vast pantry which would provide the food for the day's orgy. In the pale light I spied piles of red meat, . . . mountains of vegetables piercing the shadows with splashes of green and white"
>
> Émile Zola

FORUM. Every day, crowds hurry toward the doors of the Forum from Rue Rambuteau, Rue Pierre-Lescot and Rue Berger. This vast subterranean complex has shopping arcades on four levels: it is the capital's largest shopping center, catering to a broad market, but especially to the stylish young shoppers who congregate around the square decorated by Julio Silva's *Pygmalion*. Farther to the west the section arranged around the

Place Carrée has a more cultural purpose: its swimming pool is surrounded by a tropical greenhouse, a center for music and dance, a photography exhibition space and a book and video library (*médiathèque*) with internet facilities. From the outside, the Lescot building seems to group its pavilions of reflecting glass together in the shape of mushrooms, housing conservatoires, studios and exhibition spaces. On top of the building is a terrace with a view over the whole quarter.

FONTAINE DES INNOCENTS
Not far from the Halles is the only Renaissance fountain in Paris. Dating from 1549, it is decorated with delicate nymphs by Jean Goujon.

GARDEN. The garden is quieter, reaching southward through a series of metal arcades. At the center is a pleasant mall planted with young trees, running from the Forum to the glass pyramids which cover the tropical conservatory close to the Commodity Market. Opposite the southern portal of the church of St-Eustache is the statue by Henri de Miller, a stunning contemporary work. This colossal head, which weighs 70 tons, is made of Massaugis stone (from Burgundy) and seems to lend its ear both to the city's noise and to the quiet of the sanctuary.

BOURSE DU COMMERCE (2 C5). This ring-shaped former grain exchange, built in the 18th century, stands to the west of Les Halles (below). It was given a metallic dome in 1811, which was covered with copper sheets and later with glass. On the eastern

side the building is flanked by a strange column, formerly part of the Hôtel de Soissons, built by Catherine de' Medici. The tower is supposed to have been an observatory for Ruggieri, the queen's astrologer. The Hôtel de Nesles also stood on this site: Blanche de Castille, Saint Louis' mother, died there in 1252.

PEACE AND QUIET
The terrace on top of the Lescot building and the arbors in the garden: two places of peace and quiet amid the bustle of Les Halles.

THE QUARTER OF LES HALLES

SQUARE DES INNOCENTS (2 D5). Many Parisians were buried in the Cimetière des Innocents, which stood here from the late Middle Ages. Before the 17th century the place was not always treated with respect: shops were set up inside the cemetery which inspired François Villon's *Testament*. In 1549, the only Renaissance fountain in Paris was set against the cemetery wall, with

CHURCH OF ST-EUSTACHE
The building's interior is 290 feet long and 110 feet high: the dimensions are similar to those of Notre-Dame, and the ground plan is identical.

delicate carved nymphs by Jean Goujon. In 1786 the cemetery was closed, and a sinister nocturnal procession threaded the streets of Paris, transporting the remains of two million corpses buried in these graves to the catacombs of St-Jacques ▲ *274*. The Fontaine des Innocents was skillfully separated from the wall, given a fourth side

by Pajou in 1788, and then set in the middle of the square. This is one of the most popular meeting places around the Forum des Halles.

RUE DE LA FERRONNERIE (2 D6). At night this road is popular with young people attracted by its bars and lively restaurants. Opposite no. 11 is a plaque set into the road, bearing three fleurs-de-lys. It was here that Henri IV's carriage was held up on May 14, 1610 (the road was much narrower at the time). Ravillac had followed the carriage from the Louvre: he stood on a stone block and dealt the king three fatal blows with a knife.

RUE ST-HONORÉ (2 A4 to 2 C5). From the 12th century onward, this very old road took the place of the Chaussée du Roule, a major route through the capital since the Roman era. Many 17th- and 18th-century buildings still stand along the street. The pharmacy at no. 115 goes back to 1715, while a

A REFUGE FOR JEAN SANS PEUR
Jean sans Peur, the Duke of Burgundy, ordered the assassination of the Duc d'Orléans in 1407. He had a tower built a year later to protect himself from possible reprisals. Despite this precaution he was assassinated in 1419 on the Pont de Montereau.

plaque at no. 96 indicates that Molière was born on this site in 1622. The Fontaine du Trahoir, at no. 111, was rebuilt by Soufflot in 1776, replacing the fountain built by Jean Goujon in 1519 at the crossroads with Rue de l'Arbre-Sec, whose name refers to the gallows which used to stand here.

CHURCH OF ST-EUSTACHE (2 C4). The church came to the fore again when the old market was demolished: its Gothic buttresses and its elegant shape can now be fully appreciated. It was built between 1532 and 1637 on the site of a 12th-century chapel; unfortunately, its Gothic structure was disfigured by a classical façade added in the 18th century. It was restored by Baltard after a fire in 1840. The interior decorations are mainly Renaissance, even classical, in contrast with the Gothic style of the building. Among the church's valuable works of art are a *Martyrdom of Saint Eustache* by Simon Vouet and a statue of the Virgin by Jean-Baptiste Pigalle. St-Eustache's organ concerts have a high reputation, as does its choir; the church is one of the most attractive in the capital.

TOWER OF JEAN SANS PEUR (2 D4). The tower stands at 20, rue Étienne-Marcel; it does not look its age. The tower is square with sides measuring 90 feet; it has a spiral staircase with 140 steps leading to a turret with machicolations. It was recently restored and represents one of the few surviving examples of feudal military architecture in Paris ● *61*.

RUE ST-DENIS (2 DE6 to 2 E3). For many years this street benefited from the special status of the St-Denis basilica ▲ *432*. The kings of France processed along this holy route to their second coronation, before the people. Triumphal arches were built for the occasion, and fountains flowed with free wine and milk. One of the fountains, rebuilt in 1732, still stands on the corner of no. 142. The Rue St-Denis, which is now a pedestrian mall from the Rue Étienne-Marcel to the Rue des Lombards, has changed greatly since the development of the Forum close by: many of the establishments in this former red-light district on the north side of the street have now become food stores. A number of the historical buildings in this area still have brightly lit neon signs.

BEAUBOURG

CHURCH OF ST-MERRI. As was the case with St-Eustache, this church is tightly enclosed by buildings, in keeping with the medieval tradition. The church goes back to the 9th century; it was rebuilt in the 12th century, and again from 1520 to 1620, preserving the building's High Gothic style. The contrast between the flying buttresses on the Place Stravinski and the interior of the church is striking. In the 18th century the Gothic decorations in the crossing of the transept were extensively modified and adapted to the Baroque taste of the day. Michel-Ange Slodtz decorated the choir with stucco and marble, while his brother Paul-Ambroise decorated the chapel (its top lighting was

BAPTISMS AND FUNERALS
The Church of St-Eustache (below) was the setting for ceremonies involving many famous people: Richelieu and Molière were baptized here, and the church held the funerals of La Fontaine and Colbert (a benefactor of the building). Colbert's tomb, designed by Le Brun, stands in a chapel near the chevet.

TINGUELY FOUNTAIN
Jean Tinguely, a maker of mobiles, collaborated with the designer Niki de Saint-Phalle to produce the figures on the Place Igor-Stravinski, paying tribute to the composer of *Firebird*. Strange objects and grotesque figures twirl on the fountain, spraying water and delighting onlookers.

added by Boffrand in 1744). The church also lost some of its 16th-century stained-glass windows, which were replaced by plain glass. Despite the damage suffered under the Revolution, it still has many paintings, including *Mary the Egyptian* by Chassériau and *Saint Merri Releasing the Prisoners* by Vouet. To the left of the façade is a small tower with a campanile, which contains the oldest bell in Paris, the "Merri", cast in 1331.

QUARTIER DE L'HORLOGE (2 E5). On the Rue Rambuteau, to one side of the Georges-Pompidou Center, a statue of Prometheus by Ossip Zadkine marks the entrance to this quarter. The renovation of the area was organized by its residents. It is named after the curious electronic clock by Jacques Monestier on Rue Bernard-de-Clairvaux: a man armed with a sword and shield is fighting a dragon, a bird and a crab, confronting each of these separately every hour and all of them together at midday and at six o'clock in the evening.

GEORGES-POMPIDOU CENTER

"I should passionately like Paris to have a cultural center which would be at once a museum and a center of creation." These words spoken by President Pompidou in 1969 paved the way for the great international competition to build the center which would bear his name. The design by the Italian architect Renzo Piano and the British architect Richard Rogers was chosen from among 681 entries. Their creation continues to arouse passionate reactions, but the Pompidou Center has become a part of the Parisian landscape: eight million visitors every year demonstrate its popular success.

AN ARCHITECTURAL FEAT. The architects created an avant-garde building, a gigantic block measuring 550 by 200 feet, 140 feet high, with a steel framework and glass walls, and painted in bright colors. Piano and Rogers focused the interior space by banishing all functional elements – escalators, ventilation shafts, heating ducts – to the exterior. This allowed them to create a space of 80,000 square feet on each of the six stories. The

cross-section opposite shows one of the center's thirteen sections. The color of the girders and shafts corresponds to their function: blue for air conditioning, green for liquids, red for communications and yellow for electricity. A huge escalator, set in a glass tube held in place by arches, diagonally crosses the face of the building on the piazza side.
A CULTURAL CENTER (2 E5 and 6). The center's originality lies in its multidisciplinary character: it houses many events in all spheres of contemporary creativity. From the piazza a monumental porch leads into the large information hall on the first floor. The signing is large and bold, yet is striking for its simplicity. The hall is also a meeting place: besides the information center, there is a café, a shop selling design items, a bookshop and a children's area. The hall gives access to the various levels. Level 1 has three theaters and a movie theater. On Levels 2 and 3 is the Bibliothèque Publique d'Information (BPI), which is notable for its large stock of books and for giving direct access to its readers. Documentary films, CDs, videodisks and language-learning audiotapes for three hundred foreign languages and dialects illustrate the center's aim of making learning accessible and promoting all aspects of culture in which the center specializes. Levels 4 and 5 are taken up by the Musée National d'Art Moderne (MNAM). Level 6 is devoted to major temporary exhibitions. It also has a bookshop and a restaurant with a balcony overlooking Paris and the piazza below.

THE MNAM ▲ 134. The large exhibition spaces, with views over the capital, are filled with 1400 works of art. The comparative approach is original; the juxtaposition of painting, architecture, photography, design, and video allows each phase in the development of 20th-century art, as well as present-day movements, to be appreciated from many angles. It is the largest museum of modern art in the world.

en bleu: l'air conditionné
en rouge: circulations
en vert: les fluides
en jaune: l'électricité
en rouge: circulations

EGYPTOMANIA
The façade at 2, Place du Caire, is covered with Egyptian motifs – hieroglyphics, sphinxes and lotus flowers. The building itself opens onto the Passage du Caire, which was inspired by the Great Bazaar of the Egyptian capital.

THE REX
The Hollywood-style façade of the Rex cinema stands out on the Boulevard Poissonnière. This movie theater, which opened in 1932, was created by the architects Bluysen and Eberson. It is strikingly innovative on the outside with its white wedding-cake-style tiers, so incongruous in the Parisian landscape. The interior was modeled on American-style movie theaters.

RÉAUMUR (2 CE3)

RUE RÉAUMUR. The great textiles companies and institutions of the press were based on this street at the beginning of the century; they put up spectacular buildings combining stone façades with metal structures. Huge glass bays supplied the light necessary to both types of business. Three buildings standing close to each other (nos. 101, 124 and 126) show how iron and glass gradually replaced stone as a construction material.

CONSERVATOIRE DES ARTS ET MÉTIERS 136 (2 EF3). This institution, too often missed by visitors, is located in the grounds of the St-Martin-des-Champs abbey, the "third daughter of Cluny", which was founded in 1060. The buildings were dismantled in the 19th century but the church (opposite) is still standing. Its nave, built around 1130, had the first rib vaulting in Paris and the first flying buttresses in France. The superb monks' refectory, now a library, was supposedly built by Pierre de Montreuil, the architect of the Ste-Chapelle, who also contributed to Notre-Dame ▲ 358.

CHURCH OF ST-NICOLAS-DES-CHAMPS (2 E4). This parish church was founded in 1184 and rebuilt at the end of the 12th century and again in the 15th century. It is a very good example of Renaissance church architecture: the southern side portal with carved doors was built after a design by Philibert Delorme. The church did not escape the inevitable 18th-century modifications: the stained-glass windows were replaced by painted windows. The interior is richly decorated, with paintings by Simon Vouet (1629) on either side of the choir.

SENTIER (2 CD3)

CHURCH OF NOTRE-DAME-DE-BONNE-NOUVELLE (2 D2). This church was rebuilt by Godde between 1823 and 1830, retaining only its steeple, built between 1628 and 1652, whose first stone was laid by Queen Anne of Austria. The queen, who was barren for twenty-three years before finally giving birth to Louis XIV, was a generous benefactress of the church. The interior still displays magnificent paintings by Philippe de Champaigne and Le Brun, as well as *Anne d'Autriche and Henriette de France* by Mignard. A silk chasuble from the 18th century, displayed in a former sacristy, is supposed to be the one worn by Abbé Edgeworth de Firmont when he said the last mass for Louis XVI at the scaffold.

QUARTIER DU CAIRE (2 D3). Right at the heart of the Sentier, the street names – Rue d'Aboukir, Rue du Nil, Rue Damiette – commemorate Bonaparte's expedition to Egypt. This was no great political success, but it did leave a lasting impression on French art. Up to 1667 this area was the domain of beggars, who took refuge in the *cours des miracles*: their name is supposed to derive from the "miracles" which happened every evening, when crippled beggars suddenly recovered the use of their limbs and their senses. The most famous of these courts stood on today's Rue du Nil. The beggars (who were led by an elected king) were evicted in 1667 by La Reynie, the Lieutenant-General of Police.

THE BOULEVARDS

BOULEVARD POISSONNIÈRE (2 CE2). This road has many shops and is still very lively, especially at night. The Hôtel de Montholon, at no. 23, was built in 1775: it stands out from the row of Haussmann-style buildings, a memento of the golden age of the boulevards ▲ *348*. The Café Brabant at no. 32 is where the Naturalists, led by Zola, met for their *diner du boeuf nature* (dinner of plain beef).

BOULEVARD ST-MARTIN (2 FG3). This boulevard ends on the Place de la République and was built through public garbage pits near the city wall. Two theaters stand next to each other on the even-numbered side. The façade of the Théâtre de la Porte-St-Martin, at no. 16, is decorated with carved masks of classical actors; its auditorium was rebuilt in 1873 after the fire of the Commune. Sarah Bernhardt played in *Tosca* and Alexandre Dumas' *Dame aux Camélias* here, and the first performance of Edmond Rostand's *Cyrano de Bergerac* was also given here in 1897. The Théâtre de la Renaissance, at no. 20, was directed by Sarah Bernhardt from 1893 to 1899. Further on, the Porte-St-Martin stands 56 feet high. On it, Louis XIV is shown leading his armies, depicted as a naked Hercules wearing a wig. The traditional fig leaf is replaced by a lion's paw.

PORTE ST-DENIS
The arch, which is 75 feet high, was built by Blondel in 1672 and carved by Michel Anguier. Its ornamentation and inscriptions celebrate Louis XIV's greatness and his victories in Holland.

CENTER OF THE RAG TRADE
The whole of the Sentier (whose name is supposed to have derived from *chantier*, or building site) is a hive of activity: bales of fabric, materials of all sorts, trolleys, hand trucks and traffic jams reflect the vibrant activity of this area. This is the kingdom of the clothing industry, with manufacturing and wholesale businesses.

▲ THE MARAIS

☑ Two days

In 1961, the engineer Michel Raude discovered remarkable painted beams and joists in the Hôtel de Vigny, which was about to be destroyed.

So he organized puppet performances there – this was the start of the Marais Festival – and created two associations which helped carry through a plan to protect and promote the Marais.

384

A HISTORIC AREA

The Marais quarter occupies a triangle formed by the Hôtel de Ville, the Place de la Bastille and the Place de la République. This is the historical heart of Paris. It was to have been razed like the Île de la Cité, but the fall of the Empire allowed it to escape Haussmann's development plans. In the 19th century it became an industrial district: businesses and small-scale manufacturers moved into the buildings, adding annexes in courtyards and gravely damaging interior decorations. Nonetheless, their presence saved the buildings of the Marais from being altered to suit the tastes of the day. After André Malraux's law for the protection of the national heritage was passed in 1962, the city's first area of conservation underwent a striking renaissance. The main drawback of this splendid restoration work is that the traditional crafts are gradually disappearing from the area.

FROM THE TEMPLE
TO THE GOLDEN AGE

From the 12th century onward, the Knights Templars and other religious groups cleared the marshy land to the north of Philippe-Auguste's city wall. This provided the foundations for the later development of the area. Further to the south, the area close to the Seine was invigorated when Charles V built the Hôtel St-Pol in 1385, before the royal residence was moved to the Hôtel des Tournelles, to the north of the Rue St-Antoine. After Henri IV created the Place Royale, which later became the Place des Vosges ● 62 ▲ 396, in 1605, the whole quarter became the center of a brilliant social scene in which the arts and literature flourished. Mme de Sévigné lived here her whole life, changing homes ten times: she is a central figure in this golden age of the Marais in the 17th century. When Louis XIV came to the throne, the Marais both reached its peak and began to decline as the aristocracy steadily moved off to the Faubourgs St-Germain ▲ 262 and St-Honoré ▲ 344.

HÔTEL DE SENS
This building has a thoroughly medieval appearance with its irregular design, its Gothic porch and its corbeled turrets at the corners. Along with the Hôtel de Cluny and the Jacques-Coeur house, this is one of the few remaining examples of civil architecture from the Middle Ages in Paris ● 58. The portal, the turrets and the square keep with its gatehouse are original; the rest has been reconstructed, sometimes very badly (for example, the façade facing the garden).

THE MARAIS, VESTIGE OF PARIS OF THE ANCIEN RÉGIME ✪
The only way to fully appreciate the Marais, the only surviving quarter of old Paris, is to explore the warren of narrow streets lined with town houses. With the Place des Vosges – the first square to be created in Paris – or the Place Ste-Catherine, the rue des Francs-Bourgeois and rue des Rosiers, the heart of the Jewish Quarter since the Middle Ages, the Marais has always had a busy atmosphere. It is a very pleasant place to shop, stroll and relax: the shops here are open on Sundays. In the past ten years, it has become on of the city's main gay areas, where most of the gay restaurants, bars and shops are found.

385

TEMPLE ENCLOSURE
Its 4,000 inhabitants
enjoyed legal and
fiscal privileges, and
its craftsmen were
exempted from the
regulations of the
guilds.

OLD TEMPLARS ENCLOSURE

The SQUARE DU TEMPLE (2 G4), in the north of the Marais,
stands on the site of one of the nine thousand outposts of the
Knights Templars. The building was established here in the
12th century and housed the grand master of the order from
the 13th century onward. The enclosure was effectively a self-
contained fortified town surrounded by 26-foot-
high crenelated walls. After the Templars were
suppressed, by order of Philippe IV and Pope
Clement V in the Council of Vienne (1311–12), the
enclosure was owned by the Knights Hospitalers,
better known as the Knights of Malta, until the
Revolution.

SQUARE DU TEMPLE

This garden is located on the site of the former
Grand Prior's Palace, which was destroyed in 1853.
The garden was designed in the English style by
Jean-Charles Alphand ▲ 208 in 1857.

CHURCH OF STE-ÉLISABETH (195, rue du Temple).
This church has a beautiful, timeworn classical façade: its first
stone was placed by Marie de' Medici in 1628, and its huge
neoclassical choir was built by Godde in 1822. One hundred
17th-century wooden panels with carvings of biblical scenes
were added in 1845 from the Abbaye de St-Vaast in Arras.

CARREAU DU TEMPLE (2 G4). This stands behind the town
hall, occupying six metal halls built in 1863. Secondhand
clothes are still sold here every morning.

TEMPLE PRISONERS
The site of the Temple
keep, built under
Saint Louis around
1265, is marked in the
road to the north of
today's Square du
Temple, opposite the
town hall of the 3rd
arrondissement. This
imposing square
tower had sides
measuring 50 feet and
large corner turrets
with pepperpot
watchtowers. The
royal family was held
here after August 13,
1792. On January 21,
1793, Louis XVI left
the tower to be led to
the scaffold, while the
young Louis XVII is
thought to have died
here under
circumstances which
are still shrouded in
mystery.

RUE DU TEMPLE

This winding road with its old façades is still charming. By day, the area is a hive of activity: jewelry businesses to the north, then leather goods and finally, to the south, wholesale businesses and import-export houses run by Chinese immigrants from the Zhejang region ▲ *VIII*.

HÔTEL D'AVAUX DE ST-AIGNAN, MUSÉE D'ART ET D'HISTOIRE DU JUDAISME (2 F5) nos. 71–5. This handsome house was built 1640–50 by one of the delegates to the treaty of Westphalia (1648). The Museum of the Art and History of Judaism, inside, relates the changes in Jewish communities from the Middle Ages to the 21st century through cultural and historical displays.

HÔTEL DE BERLIZE no. 41. The rather dilapidated appearance of the façades and the windows with curved pediments add to this building's charm. It houses the Café-Théâtre de la Gare in its large paved courtyard.

HÔTEL D'HALLWYLL (2 E5) 28, rue Michel-le-Comte. This is one of the rare 18th-century buildings in the Marais and the only work by Claude-Nicolas Ledoux still standing in Paris. The heavy Doric columns and the design of the street façade and main building are typical of Ledoux's austere style, modeled on classical architecture. Germaine Necker, later Mme de Staël, was born in this house in 1766.

RUE DES ARCHIVES

This lively street, which was widened in the 19th century, has many shops, bars and restaurants.

CLOÎTRE DES BILLETTES (2 E6) nos. 22–6. In the 12th century, so the story goes, a communion host which was stabbed and thrown into boiling oil began to bleed. A place of pilgrimage grew up around this legend, and the reformed Carmelites, or *Billettes*, rebuilt the church between 1756 and 1778; today it is a Protestant church. The cloister of 1427–8 still has three of its original galeries with triangular arcades and carved keystones.

HÔTEL GUÉNÉGAUD DES BROSSES (2 F5) no. 60. This grand, sober house was built by François Mansart between 1651 and 1655. It narrowly escaped destruction: one of its 20th-century owners made a hole in the roof to speed up a demolition permit. After 1967 it was restored by a foundation established by the industrialist and patron of the arts François Sommer; he set up the Musée de la Chasse et de la Nature here ▲ *139*.

MAISON COEUR
This building at 40, rue du Temple, one of the oldest houses in Paris, now contains a primary school. It was built by the granddaughter of Jacques Coeur, Charles VII's great Minister of Finance. The neat varnished red and black bricks of the façade and the windows with their stone transoms are typical of late-15th-century architecture.

FRANÇOIS MANSART
The severe style of the Hôtel Guénégaud des Brosses, without even a pediment, illustrates Mansart's minimalist approach. It is the architect's only complete house to survive in Paris. François Mansart was known for his preference for the roofs that now bear his name ● *67*: he played a key role in the evolution of French classical architecture.

MEDIEVAL REMAINS
A fortified Gothic gateway, flanked by two corbeled towers with pepperpot watchtowers, marks the site of the Hôtel de Clisson. The gateway was

preserved because of its impressive appearance and is the only surviving example of civil architecture from the end of the 14th century in Paris.

DELAMAIR'S DEVICE
He radically altered the ground plan of the Hôtel de Soubise by building this majestic main court. It is 200 feet long and 130 feet wide and surrounded by a huge peristyle made of 56 coupled columns, modeled on the peristyle of the Hôtel des Grands Prieurs du Temple.

THE NATIONAL ARCHIVES

ARCHIVE QUADRANGLE. Napoleon I moved the national archives into the Soubise Palace in 1808. Soon they had taken over the Hôtel de Rohan and four adjacent houses (54–8 *bis*, rue des Francs-Bourgeois). The collection grew steadily and now takes up some 300 miles of shelf space. In response to this expansion the architect Filzer added a reception area and research center, CARAN, on the Rue des Quatre-Fils. The dark glazed façade with steel pillars blends well with the old architecture.

FORMER HÔTEL DE CLISSON 58, rue des Archives. This house was built around 1371–5 by Olivier de Clisson, who was Constable under Charles V and an ally of Du Guesclin. In 1556 it passed into the ownership of the Ducs de Guise, who gave it magnificent interior decorations, employing famous Renaissance artists like Niccolò dell'Abbate and Primaticcio. It was in this center of League activity, under Henri de Guise (lover of the future Queen Margot), that final preparations were made for the St Bartholomew's Day Massacre of 1572 ● *24*. In the 1660's, Duc Henri II de Lorraine received Corneille here.

HÔTEL DE SOUBISE (2 F6) 60, rue des Francs-Bourgeois. In 1700, the Hôtel de Clisson was acquired by François de Rohan, Prince de Soubise. He was able to rebuild the palace thanks to financial assistance obtained from Louis XIV through his wife. Pierre-Alexis Delamair was the architect appointed for the project. The austere main building features the same columns as those of the peristyle around the main court: its projections are decorated with copies of Robert de Lorrain's allegorical sculptures of *The Four Seasons* and sculptures symbolizing *The Spirits of the Arts* on the cornice. The interior is just as remarkable, although a complete contrast to this beautiful classical design. It was created by Germain Boffrand in between 1735 and 1739, and is one of the most lavish décors in the rococo Louis XV style to be seen in Paris. The palace is one of Paris' most attractive architectural landmarks. It was the home of the Maréchal de Soubise, an intimate friend of Louis XV and the only one of the king's courtiers to follow the royal coffin all the way to St-Denis.

HÔTEL DE ROHAN (2 G6)

This building at 87, rue Vieille-du-Temple, is inseparable from the Palais Soubise, whose gardens it shares. The same

architect, Delamair, built it, for one of the Prince de Soubise's four sons, Armand de Rohan-Strasbourg. The house has a monumental classical façade with colonnades and pilasters: it has formed part of the National Archives complex since 1927. Its outbuildings in the Rue des Quatre-Fils house the records of Paris notaries. The interiors were ruined when the Imprimerie Nationale (National Press) was located here in the 19th century; nonetheless, they are still among the most beautiful in Paris, featuring two remarkable rooms, the Cabinet des Singes by Christophe Huet from 1745 and the beautiful Cabinet des Fables d'Ésope ▲ *393*.

HÔTEL SALÉ (2G6)

This imposing house, at 5, rue de Thorigny, was built between 1656 and 1659 for Pierre Aubert de Fontenay. It now houses the Musée Picasso ▲ *170*, which was opened in 1985 and has helped revitalize this part of the Marais.

Aubert, a former footman, made his fortune collecting the *gabelle* (salt tax). His house kept the nickname *salé* (salty) even after Aubert had been ruined, a victim of Fouquet's demise in 1661 ▲ *446*. After this, the building had many occupants before its restoration: these included the embassy of Venice and the business of the bronzesmith Vian, father of the novelist Boris Vian ▲ *234*. At the far end of the semicircular courtyard, is a pediment decorated with dogs' heads (the owner's coat of arms): sphinx volutes join it to the two wings. The left wing is a trompe l'oeil construction, while the right wing houses kitchens and stables running along the Rue des Coutures-St-Gervais. The façade facing the garden is even more monumental, on a scale unique in the Marais.

HÔTEL LIBÉRAL-BRUAND (2 G6). The architect of the same name, who created the Invalides, built this elegant house at 1, rue de la Perle, between 1685 and 1687, prefiguring Louis XVI style. The main façade is decorated with busts of Roman emperors set in niches: on either side of the oculus on the pediment are horns of plenty spilling branches of flowers and fruits. After the building was renovated, the Bricard company established its Musée de la Serrure (Museum of Locksmithing) here.

HORSES OF THE SUN

This famous bas-relief was carved by Robert le Lorrain in 1735: it is set on the façade of the former stables in the Hôtel de Rohan. Lorrain also produced sculptures for Versailles and Marly.

ARMAND DE ROHAN-STRASBOURG

He was the first in a series of four cardinal-bishops of Strasbourg who lived in the Hôtel de Rohan. The fourth of these, Louis-René de Rohan-Guéméné, became famous through the affair of the queen's necklace at the end of the 18th century.

AN OSTENTATIOUS RESIDENCE

J.P. Babelon called the Hôtel Salé a "typical nouveau riche house" because of its ostentatious grandeur. The main building, which is very wide, houses this magnificent carved staircase (below).

Picasso

▲ THE MARAIS – CARNAVALET

This bronze statue of Louis XIV, made by Coysevox in 1689, was the only royal statue to escape destruction under the Revolution: it stands in the main

court of the Hôtel Carnavalet.

A RENAISSANCE BUILDING
Jacques de Ligneris, the first president of the Parlement de Paris, built his house in 1545; the

Renaissance portal with bosses and the Italian-style main building with transomed windows still stand today within the Hôtel Carnavalet. The building is lavishly decorated with bas-reliefs of *The Four Seasons*, attributed to Jean Goujon ▲ *378*. Goujon also produced the allegorical bas-relief *Abundance* for the portal on the Rue de Sévigné.

HÔTEL CARNAVALET

(2 G6). This building, at 23, rue de Sévigné ▲ *138*, derives its unusual name from a corruption of the surname of Françoise de Kerneveroy, lady in waiting to Queen Margot. Despite many alterations, the building still holds immense architectural interest. François Mansart redesigned the whole building in 1660–1, skillfully combining the Renaissance residence with classical additions. He built the two wings decorated with bas-reliefs by Gérard von Obstal, crowning the whole with double-sloped roofs. In the 19th century the architect Parmentier subjected the building to some unfortunate modifications, which completely disfigured the garden façade.

MUSÉE DE L'HISTOIRE DE FRANCE (2 F6). The museum's rooms display reconstructions of historical interiors. These give visitors a fascinating overall view of what the interiors of houses in the Marais looked like in the past: wood paneling, trompe l'oeil paintings, painted beams and joists. Buildings from other locations have also been reconstructed around the museum, stone by stone, including the 16th-century Arch of Nazareth in the Rue des Francs-Bourgeois, which originally came from the Palais de Justice on the Île de la Cité, and the Pavillon des Drapiers in the Rue Payenne, which was built by Jacques Bruand in 1660.

HÔTEL LE PELLETIER DE ST-FARGEAU (2 G6). This house, at 29, rue de Sévigné, was acquired by the Musée Carnavalet in 1889 to serve as an annex dedicated to the history of Paris since the Revolution. Built between 1686 and 1689, it was owned, very unusually, by the same family until 1811. One of the members of this family, Louis-Michel Le Pelletier de St-Fargeau, voted for Louis XVI's execution and was assassinated in 1793 by Pâris, a bodyguard of the king; the Convention gave him a state funeral. The house is built in a very simple style. On the pediment of the main building is the figure of an old man carrying an hourglass, a striking allegory of Time.

AROUND CARNAVALET

The streets around the Hôtel Carnavalet make for a pleasant walk. They have kept their residential character and are lined with attractive houses.

RUE DU PARC-ROYAL. The colorful façade of the HÔTEL DE CANILLAC (4, rue de Sévigné), made of brick and stone, should not cast doubt on its authenticity. In fact, the white façades of restored houses in the Marais sometimes belie their original colorful appearance: bright, even garish colors were often used in Louis XIII's time.

The restoration of the HÔTEL DURET DE CHEVRY (no. 8) seems less careful: the stonework has been daubed with white paint. This was the home of Philippe-Emmanuel de Coulanges, a cousin of Mme de Sévigné, who composed songs and burlesque poems. The HÔTEL DE VIGNY (2 G6), at no. 10, houses the Ministry of Culture's architectural department and its library, and has an Italian-style ceiling dating from 1669.

HÔTEL DE MARLE (2 G6). This elegant building, at 11, rue Payenne, stands opposite the Square Georges-Cain and is a perfect example of successful restoration. It houses the Swedish Cultural Center and the Tessin Foundation, which mounts exhibitions of contemporary art on the second floor. The building dates mainly from 1572.

Restoration work revealed unusual ship's-hull roofs under later two-sloped roofs: these were invented by the architect Philibert Delorme, who built the Château d'Anet (Eure-et-Loir *département*).

HÔTEL DONON 8, rue Elzévir. This house was built in the late 16th century for Médéric de Donon, general inspector of the king's buildings; today it houses the Cognacq-Jay Museum ▲ *141*. The main building has an elegant, impressively simple pyramid-style façade. Behind the pediment is the Great Roof, which slopes to a height of nearly 26 feet.

"CARNAVALETTE"
Mme de Sévigné, the Hôtel Carnavalet's most famous resident, lived here from 1677 until her death in 1696. She called it her *carnavalette*, praising its "lovely air, lovely court, lovely garden and lovely neighborhood".

RENOVATIONS
The Louis XIII-style houses on the Rue du Parc-Royal were mainly built between 1619 and 1621, and have been extensively restored. The façade of the Hôtel de Châtillon (13, rue Payenne) is an exception, with its covering of Virginia creeper.

ORANGERY
The Hôtel Le Pelletier de St-Fargeau still has its orangery, one of the few to survive in Paris (the Hôtel de Sully has another).

391

The interior decorations of houses in the Marais are among the richest in Paris, illustrating the development of architectural styles between the 16th and 18th centuries: painted beams and joists under Henri IV, paneling and Italianate trompe l'oeil views from Louis XIII's reign, panels interspersed with paintings under Louis XIV, stucco work and gilding in the rococo style under Louis XV. These miraculously preserved interiors conjure up an image of splendors which have been lost forever.

CUPIDS AND SPHINXES
These archivolts on the painted ceiling of the Grand Salon in the Hôtel Mansart de Sagonne are attributed to Jean-Baptiste Corneille. They illustrate the mythological style which was typical under the reign of Louis XIV.

PAINTED BEAMS
"French-style" beams and joists decorated with painted medallions and monograms, and with floral or geometrical motifs, are common in the Marais. They were typical decorative features in private residences up to the age of Louis XIII.

MONKEY TRICKS
Christophe Huet created these imaginative pictures of monkeys between 1749 and 1752, for the famous Cabinet des Singes of Hôtel de Rohan.

ROCOCO STYLE
The Salon Ovale of the Hôtel de Soubise was decorated under the direction of Boffrand around 1737–40. Its stucco work and its white and gold paneling with allegorical high-reliefs in plaster make it a fine example of rococo style.

CHINOISERIE
This type of picture was common in the 18th century; here it appears with rural motifs on the painted panels in the Cabinet des Singes of the Hôtel de Rohan.

CABINET DES FABLES
These carved wooden medallions came from the Hôtel de Soubise: they have been relocated to the Hôtel de Rohan. The subjects are taken from Aesop's *Fables*.

HÔTEL AMELOT
This magnificent Italian-style dome from the late 17th century is decorated with highly restored Baroque paintings by Louis Boullongne showing *The Marriage of Hercules and Hebe*.

HÔTEL D'ALBRET

The balcony on the street side is supported by consoles in the form of lions' heads. At the end of the garden is a tower, originally part of Philippe-Auguste's city wall, which was converted into a chapel in the 17th century. The Paris city council chose this house as the base for its cultural service and redesigned the

interior in a striking modern style.

HÔTEL AMELOT DE BISSEUIL

This building is known for the Medusa heads sticking their tongues out at passersby on the doors of its carriage entrance. It has a fascinating history. La Bruyère mocked its first owner, who hesitated to move into his house, "so splendid, so rich and so ornate". In 1776, Beaumarchais set up a company here called Rodriguez, Hortolez & Co., for supplying arms to the American rebels; he also wrote *The Marriage of Figaro* here.

RUE DES FRANCS-BOURGEOIS

This is a favorite place for a Sunday stroll, stretching from Beaubourg to the Place des Vosges, following the outer path of Philippe-Auguste's city wall ● 54, some parts of which can still be seen. This street lined with private homes at the heart of the Marais derives its name from an almshouse for citizens exempt from taxes. It is also typical of the new Marais, in that luxury boutiques are gradually replacing the traditional shops: the baker at no. 23, with its Belle Époque signs, has now become a fashion boutique.

HÔTEL DE SANDREVILLE (2 G7) no. 26. The superb Renaissance façade on the garden side dates from 1586. On the street side, the building was later given a Louis XVI-style façade with monumental fluted pilasters.

HÔTEL D'ALBRET (2 G6) nos. 29 *bis*–31. It is here that the meeting between Mme de Maintenon and the Marquise de Montespan took place, the latter entrusting the former with the care of the Duc de Maine, illegitimate son of Louis XIV. The ambitious Mme de Maintenon, widow of the poet Scarron, made the most of this chance to displace her rival in the king's affections. The 16th-century building underwent a number of later alterations, notably by François Mansart around 1640.

HÔTEL D'ALMÉRAS (2 G6) no. 30. The main building was constructed in 1611 in red brick and stone, and is a typical example of Henri IV style. The Mannerist-style portico is ornamented with rams' heads on either side of a tympanum decorated with chimeras.

RUE VIEILLE-DU-TEMPLE

Some old shop fronts can still be seen on the street, like the horsemeat butcher's at no. 15, from the early 20th century, with its red earthenware tiles. However, art galleries and shops selling clothes or trinkets are rapidly taking over.

HÔTEL AMELOT DE BISSEUIL (2 F6) no. 47. This house, built around 1660, is also known as the Hôtel des Ambassadeurs de Hollande. On the other side of the splendid portal is a bas-relief carved by Regnaudin showing the Roman wolf suckling Romulus and Remus. The first court is lavishly decorated with cherubs, gargoyles and sundials bearing golden mottos.

HÔTEL HÉROUET (2 F6) no. 54. This Gothic-style building, with a corbeled turret and fine stone carvings around the transomed windows, adds to the charm of its location. The Hôtel Hérouet dates back to 1510–20, but the building which stands today is a 19th-century reconstruction in the troubadour style.

FROM THE BLANCS-MANTEAUX TO THE RUE PAVÉE

THE BLANCS-MANTEAUX QUARTER. Its name derives from the order of Serfs of the Virgin Mary, who dressed in white coats, which was established here by Saint Louis around 1250. The church which stands today at 12, rue des Blancs-Manteaux, has a magnificent Bavarian rococo pulpit, which dates from 1749. The façade added by Baltard in 1863 came from the church of St-Éloi-des-Barnabites, built on the Île de la Cité in 1703.

RUE DES ROSIERS. The street has a unique atmosphere, with its kosher shops, Eastern specialties and shops selling Jewish religious objects. The restaurant Chez Jo Goldenberg (nos. 7–10) is typical of the street. However, some modernization is evident: the St-Paul Turkish baths at no. 4, for example, have been converted into a café.

HÔTEL LAMOIGNON (2 G7) 24, rue Pavée. At the end of the 17th century, President Guillaume de Lamoignon received the leading intellectuals of his day here, including Racine, Mme de Sévigné, Boileau and Louis Bourdaloue. The building now houses the Bibliothèque Historique de la Ville de Paris and is open to the public. Its monumental Corinthian pilasters on two stories are supposed to have been the first of this type built in Paris. The decorative motifs reflect Diane de France's passion for the hunt.

395

MONTGOMERY'S LANCE

"Montgomery's lance created the Place des Vosges," wrote Victor Hugo, one of the square's famous inhabitants. Henri II was accidentally wounded in the eye by the lance of Montgomery, his captain of guards, during a tournament in July 1559: he died after ten days of agony. His widow, Catherine de' Medici, persuaded her son to demolish the Hôtel des Tournelles, where both Louis XI and Louis XII died. A horse market moved into the space left vacant, before Henri IV decided to establish a silk factory on the northern side, with accommodation for the workers on the other three sides of the square. The factory soon foundered, and the square, close to the church of St-Louis-des-Jésuites, was gradually taken over by the aristocracy of the Marais. Corneille paid tribute to it by calling one of his plays *Place Royale*. After this, the Place des Vosges went into decline, but it has now recaptured all its former prestige: once again it counts famous people among its inhabitants, while galleries, luxury shops and restaurants have taken up residence under its arcades.

The lavish carrousel of 1612 marked the opening of the Place Royale.

THE PAVILLON DU ROI
This is higher than the buildings around the rest of the square.

A ROYAL SQUARE   (2 H7)

The striking thing about the square is its stylistic unity: this goes back to Henri IV's decree of 1604, which laid down strict building regulations. In contrast to the harmonious façade on the square, on the other side (the court side) its buildings have always been a complete mixture. The brilliant social life of the Marais took place behind this stage setting: nearly all the pavilions on the square have a fascinating history. The

HÔTEL DE COULANGES (no.1 *bis*) was the birthplace of the Marquise de Sévigné. For a time in the 19th century, the Hôtel de Rotrou (no. 4) housed the kitchens of the Compagnie des Wagons-Lits railway company. The HÔTEL DE CHAULNES (no. 9), one of the most magnificent pavilions, was the headquarters of the Academy of Architecture. It was also the model for the Metaxas Palace in the 17th-century sentimental novel *Le Grand Cyrus* and housed the royal stands in the 1612 Carrousel ● 86: on the court side is a wing with pediment built by Jules Hardouin-Mansart in 1676–7. The

HÔTEL DE BASSOMPIÈRE (no. 23) has one of the most striking staircases in the Marais: its handrail has carved balustrades decorated with bowls of fruit, women's faces and grimacing men's faces. In the HÔTEL DE ROHAN-GUÉMÉNÉ (no. 6) is a museum dedicated to Victor Hugo: the writer lived on the third story between 1832 and 1848 and wrote *Ruy Blas* here. The HÔTEL LA RIVIÈRE (no. 14) had some decorations by Le Brun, now in the Musée Carnavalet. For a time it was a town hall (the thoroughly incongruous campanile was added in 1860). Since the Second Empire it has been the residence of the Chief Rabbi of France, connecting at the back with the Ashkenazi Synagogue (22 *bis*, rue des Tournelles), the structure of which was designed by Gustave Eiffel. The HÔTEL CAULET D'HAUTEVILLE (no. 28) was a famous gaming house under Louis XIII. On the court side it was rebuilt in neoclassical style at the end of the 18th century. Since 1982 it has been a hotel, fitting discreetly into this prestigious setting.

PLACE DE L'ARSENAL

The square is decorated with a statue of Beaumarchais; until 1789 it stood in a private residence, which has since disappeared. The statue stands close to the boulevard named after the author.

HÔTEL DE SULLY

The palace is entered by a portal flanked with pavilions connected by a balustrade. The main buildings and the wings are decorated in Renaissance style. On the garden side, the left wing (1661) houses the apartments of the Duchesse de Sully – an example of 17th-century interior decoration, including an Italian-style room with a dome on which Antoine Paillet painted *The Abduction of Endymion*.

At the end of the garden is one of the few surviving orangeries in Paris, which gives access to the Place des Vosges.

RUE ST-ANTOINE

This old, wide royal road was a favorite place for jousts and ceremonial entries into the city, such as that of Louis XIV and Marie-Thérèse in 1660.

TEMPLE DE L'ORDRE DES FILLES DE LA VISITATION (2 H8) no. 17. This is part of a convent where Saint Francis de Paul was chaplain for eighteen years. Dating from 1632–4, this is was one of François Mansart's first works. Under the building, with its centralized ground plan and cupola, is a crypt which holds the remains of Nicolas Fouquet ▲ *446* and the Marquis de Sévigné.

HÔTEL DE MAYENNE (2 H8) no. 21. One of the oldest buildings of the Marais; the Brothers of the Christian Schools have been housed here since 1870. Built in 1606–9 for the dukes of Mayenne, members of the Guise family, after plans by Jacques Androuet du Cerceau, it was modified and embellished by Germain Boffrand a century later. The recently-restored west wing contrasts starkly with the shabby grayness of the rest of the building: this symbolizes the architectural history of the Marais as a whole, marked by an alternating pattern of decline and renewal.

HÔTEL DE SULLY   (2G7)

62, rue St-Antoine. The National Office for Historical Monuments moved here in 1965, choosing one of the most impressive and beautiful buildings in the Marais as its home. It has been meticulously restored. It was built between 1625 and 1630 for Mesmes Gallet, general inspector of finances, and was bought by Maximilien de Béthune, Duc de Sully, in 1634: the former minister of Henri IV was seventy-four years old at the time. The dukes of Sully made this palace into one of the centers of social and intellectual life in the Marais.

ST-PAUL QUARTER

THE VILLAGE OF ST-PAUL. This village consists of a maze of courtyards full of antiques stores. As you leave the village, the Rue des Jardins-St-Paul, where Rabelais died on April 9, 1553, offers a good view of two towers from Philippe-Auguste's city wall built in 1190 ● *54*.

CONVENT OF THE GREAT JESUITS (14, rue Charlemagne). This Jesuit establishment was built during the reigns of Louis XIII and Louis XIV; since 1802 it has housed the Lycée Charlemagne. To the east is the main staircase, set in a tower from Philippe-Auguste's city wall. The staircase leads up to a dome with a trompe-l'oeil painting of *The Apotheosis of Saint Louis* by the Italian artist Gherardini.

CHURCH OF ST-PAUL-ST-LOUIS (2 G7)

CHURCH OF ST-PAUL-ST-LOUIS
The building is very bright, since it is lit from the dome lantern and the high windows of its barrel vault.

This church was built 1627–41 and its first mass was given by Cardinal Richelieu. The tomb of the great Maréchal de Condé, inside the church, was destroyed during the Revolution. The Jesuits promoted the Counter Reformation with militant fervor: their church was therefore duty bound to move and impress the faithful. The façade, on three levels, is impressive, as is the large dome crowned with a lantern, which rises to a height of 180 feet. The ground plan of the church conforms to the Jesuit formula established by the Society of Jesus in Rome: a simple axis without ambulatory or side aisles. This center of Christian and aristocratic life was designed to highlight the magnificence of its decorations and furniture. Many of the works which contributed to this splendor have disappeared: the marble high altar was once decorated with four paintings, of which only *The Presentation at the Temple* by Simon Vouet survives (it is now displayed in the Louvre). Nonetheless, some works of art remain, giving an impression of former glories: they include *The Virgin of Sorrows* carved by Germain Pilon in 1586 and *Christ in the Garden of Olives* by Delacroix.

ST-GERVAIS QUARTER

Between the churches of St-Paul-St-Louis and St-Gervais is a network of quiet, narrow, winding streets which still follow their medieval course. This ancient *Quartier de la Mortellerie* – the area of all the building trades – narrowly escaped total destruction. It had record rates of tuberculosis in the 19th and early 20th century and because of this was classified "unhealthy little island no. 16" and designated for demolition. The plan to raze the district was indeed set in motion, leaving a few unhappy marks, like the dismal block of the Cité des Arts (10–48, rue de l'Hôtel-de-Ville), which houses some 230 artists' studios.

HÔTEL D'AUMONT. This house, at 7, rue de Jouy, was built in 1649 by the financier Antoine Scarron. His son-in-law Antoine d'Aumont, nicknamed Tarquin le Superbe, added lavish interior decorations, some by the artist Le Brun. His descendants perpetuated the solid family traditions of magnificent art collections, dissipated life style and death by apoplexy. The building now houses the administrative tribunal of Paris. Little remains of the interior decorations apart from a *History of Romulus and Remus* by Le Brun. The garden façade was adapted to suit the needs of the tribunal.

HÔTEL DE SENS (2 F8)

This fortress-palace at 1, rue du Figuier, was built between 1475 and 1519 for Tristan de Salazar, the 9th archbishop of Sens. The building has a rich history: it was the site of the Council of Sens, which condemned Luther's Theses in 1528, and of Monsignor de Pellevé's death in 1594, at the very moment Henri IV was entering Paris. The building was used for the most diverse purposes in the 19th century, among them a coach and carriage service and a jam factory. It was rebuilt in 1940 by the architect Halley in a rather dry neo-Gothic style. Nonetheless, the building has retained its irregular medieval design on the court side, as well as the portal with its Gothic arch and the dungeon with a bartizan and machicolations. Today it houses the Forney library, dedicated to the decorative arts.

RUE FRANÇOIS-MIRON

This was formerly part of the Rue St-Antoine. It still has shops all along its winding course (Izraël, at no. 30, offers a huge array of groceries).
HÔTEL DE BEAUVAIS (no. 68). This house was built sometime after 1654 for Catherine Bellier, nicknamed "One-Eyed Cathau", whose physical defects did not prevent her from deflowering the young Louis XIV. On the street side

the building has been disfigured, but beyond the concave door of the portal is an original Baroque construction, ingeniously devised by the architect Le Pautre. An open vestibule with Doric columns runs along the convex forebuilding on the court, following the court's irregular outline. The decorative motifs include several rams' heads, emblem of Catherine Bellier. Mozart stayed here in 1763, when he was seven years old, on his first European tour.

MAISONS D'OURSCAMP (nos. 44–6). At the end of the 16th century these houses were built to replace the former townhouse of the Abbey of Ourscamp (Oise), whose vast medieval cellar, built around 1250, still survives. The buildings were taken over and restored by the Association of Historical Paris. On the second floor they look out over a curious little court with wooden panels and corbeled privies.

CHURCH OF ST-GERVAIS-ST-PROTAIS

This church was built on the Place St-Gervais, on the site of a 6th-century chapel. Construction lasted over two centuries, which led to a curious mixture of styles. From 1494 to 1540, in the middle of the Renaissance, Martin Chambiges built a nave in the purest High Gothic style. The façade offers a total contrast: it was built by another great architect, Salomon de Brosse, from 1616 to 1621 (he also built the Palais de Luxembourg). Voltaire called the façade a masterpiece: it is a typical classical construction and the first example in Paris of a combination of Doric, Ionic and Corinthian orders. The building has splendid interior decorations, including a stunning crown of openwork stone, 8 feet in diameter, on the keystone of the Chapel of the Virgin. The superb tomb for chancellor Michel le Tellier was made after a design by Jules Hardouin-Mansart. In 1528 a statue of the Virgin was installed near the choir: it had been vandalized on the corner of the Rue de Sicile. Beyond the façade are the great organs of 1628, played by members of the Couperin dynasty between 1653 and 1789. The great François Couperin composed two masses here in 1685.

Half a day

THE VIADUC DES ARTS

Beneath the old viaduct that runs the length of the Avenue Daumesnil are the workshops and sales outlets of numerous artist-craftsmen. Above them, the old rail tracks have gone, replaced by a 3-mile planted walkway.

THE ELEPHANT OF THE BASTILLE

Napoleon I planned to build a fountain in the shape of an elephant on the Place de la Bastille. A mock-up of the animal, 80 feet high and 52 feet long, was set up to the east of the present-day column. It stood there from 1813 to 1847. Gavroche sheltered underneath it in Victor Hugo's novel *Les Misérables*.

The Bastille, the starting point for worker demonstrations in the capital, holds a special place in the collective French psyche. It leads to two other squares with equally evocative names – Place de la République and Place de la Nation. The storming of the Bastille on July 14, 1789, has become a myth in its own right, but it resulted in large part from actions taken by the inhabitants of the Faubourg St-Antoine. This street still has a high level of creative activity, with numerous artists' studios and architects' offices. New types of residents are beginning to move into this area, which has started to become fashionable, but it retains its popular, colorful atmosphere along with its traditional passageways and backyards.

PLACE DE LA BASTILLE

(2 I8)

FORTRESS AND PRISON. The Bastille was built by Hugues Aubriot, provost of the merchants of Paris between 1370 and 1382, to defend the capital against invaders from the east and to protect the Hôtel St-Pol, residence of Charles V. Paving stones in the road opposite 49, avenue Henri-IV mark the outline of one tower of this fortress, which stood to the west of today's square. The fortress was 80 feet high and had eight round towers; it was surrounded by an 80-foot ditch. Despite this impressive appearance, it played only a minor military role, except during the Fronde in 1649, when La Grande Mademoiselle, niece of Louis XIII, turned the cannons on the royal troops led by Turenne in order to protect the Prince de Condé. From Richelieu's time the Bastille was a state prison and a symbol of the arbitrary use of royal power. Many famous prisoners were held here, sent to prison simply by a *lettre de cachet* (a letter bearing the royal seal which, under the Ancien Régime, gave order of public ceremony, imprisonment or even exile). They include Fouquet, Cagliostro, the famous Man in the Iron Mask and Voltaire, who completed his play *Oedipe* during a year of captivity in 1717. Although the dungeons were unpleasant, the regime was especially lenient toward high-ranking prisoners, and the number of inmates rarely exceeded fifty or so after Louis XIV became king. This did not prevent the Marquis de Sade from haranguing passersby from his window with his cries that "the prisoners of the Bastille are being assassinated, you must come to their rescue". He was transferred to the Charenton insane asylum, on July 4, 1789.

GREAT MOMENTS OF THE REVOLUTION. On July 14, 1789, the Bastille entered into the mythology of the Revolution. After Minister Necker had been dismissed by Louis XVI, 900 rioters, mostly from the Faubourg St-Antoine, gathered in front of the fortress with the aim of obtaining weapons. In the afternoon they were reinforced by 100 French guards; the governor, De Launay, capitulated but was massacred along with his garrison of 32 Swiss Guards and 82 veterans. The prisoners of the Bastille were given an ovation and carried off in triumph – all seven of them, including two swindlers, one nobleman guilty of incest, and a lunatic. This victory by the "conquerors of the Bastille", achieved at a cost of 100 dead and 73 injured, acquired a mythical status out of all proportion to the significance of the military events. One man wasted no time in making the most of the situation: the "Patriote" Palloy took charge of demolishing the Bastille, making 83 models of the fortress which he sent to all 83 French *départements* to "perpetuate the horror of despotism there". This astute businessman also made jewelry, chains and keys from the remains of the fortress: some examples can be seen at the Musée Carnavalet. Some of the stones were also used to build the Pont de la Concorde.

COLONNE DE JUILLET
A law of 1830 decreed the erection of a monument to commemorate the victims of the Three Glorious Days of the Revolution – July 27, 28 and 29, 1830 ● 20. This was the origin of the July Column, inspired by the Trajan Column in Rome and completed by Duc in 1840. Its bronze shaft is 150 feet high and is surmounted by the Spirit of Liberty, which is shown "in flight, rending its chains asunder and scattering light". It is modeled on a sculpture by Drumont. Beneath the column are two tombs holding the remains of victims of the revolutions in 1830 and 1848.

AV. DU BEL-AIR

▲ BASTILLE
FAUBOURG ST-ANTOINE

OPÉRA-BASTILLE. The building is striking for its austerity and its monumental style of architecture composed of geometric shapes: the sober glass wall of the main façade is fronted by a dark gray marble portico. The architect Carlos Ott kept to the typical shape of building lots in the surrounding area: his building is worth seeing in the evening, when the whole glass façade is lit up. The Grand Auditorium, in gray granite and oak, has 2,700 seats. Its double stage, along with the hall's nine aisles, allow different productions to be alternated without dismantling the scenery.

THE ARSENAL (2 G9)

The cannon foundry of the Royal Arsenal was established in the 16th century and closed under Louis XIII. The furnaces continued to operate, however, producing large statues for the Palace of Versailles, for example. This was once a huge collection of buildings stretching as far as the Bastille; now only the wing built by Germain Boffrand between 1718 and 1745 is still standing. This wing, built in a very austere style, formerly belonged to the residence of the Great Master of the Artillery (1–3, rue de Sully).

THE LIBRARY. Paulmy d'Argenson, a diplomat and minister of war, assembled his magnificent collection of medieval illuminated manuscripts and prints here in 1757. This formed the basis of today's library, which acquired the archives of the Bastille during the Revolution, as well as books confiscated from convents and monasteries. The Arsenal library has a calm atmosphere, warm-colored paneling and shelves full of leather-bound books; its collection includes 14,000 manuscripts – among them the *Psautier de Saint Louis* and the *Heures du Maître-aux-Fleurs* – as well as 120,000 prints. The library also specializes in works dedicated to the arts and theater.

A POPULAR OPERA HOUSE
The Opéra-Bastille was built in the east of the capital, in a deliberate move away from the elitist character of the more affluent areas. Its date of opening was just as significant: July 14, 1989, the bicentenary of the French Revolution. It has yet to be seen if the opera house can achieve its social aims; meanwhile, the building itself has aroused lively controversy.

Faubourg St-Antoine

TRADITIONAL CRAFTS. The royal Cistercian abbey of St-Antoine-des-Champs was founded in 1198 by Foulques, parish priest of Neuilly-sur-Marne and a preacher in the Fourth Crusade. It became one of the richest convents in Paris. The "Lady of the Faubourg", its abbess, was often a member of one of the most eminent families in the kingdom. The abbey, on the site of the present Hôpital St-Antoine, enjoyed an unusual privilege: in the 15th century, Louis XI exempted the craftsmen working here from membership in the guilds. After this, the faubourg grew and prospered. The woodworkers, freed from the restrictive regulations of the guilds, were able to depart from prescribed models and the use of oak in order to work with marquetry and rare woods.

REVOLTS IN THE FAUBOURG. The high level of industrial activity made this working-class area one of the most restless in Paris. The workers here were open to new ideas and were easily aroused; this fostered an atmosphere of social agitation and rebellion. On April 28, 1789, a riot took place among the four thousand workers under Réveillon, who introduced wallpaper in France: this was a prelude to the Revolution. The population of the faubourg played a key role not only in the storming of the Bastille but also in the social unrest of the 19th century: barricades were raised in the streets in 1830 and 1848 and under the Commune in 1871 ● *26*.

RUE DU FAUBOURG ST-ANTOINE. Although mechanization has transformed working conditions, there are still many workshops here and a large number of furniture shops, especially around the Bastille. Hidden curiosities include the paved courtyard of the Étoile-d'Or (2 J8) at no. 75, with its artists' studios and a sundial from 1751. The courtyard of the Bel-Air (2 J8) at no. 56 is one of the most beautiful in Paris: its walls are covered in Virginia creeper, sometimes even with grapes and tomatoes on the southern side. At no. 50, Passage de la Boule-Blanche (2 J8) opens onto the Rue de Charenton, opposite the Hôpital des Quinze-Vingts (2 I9). This institution was founded by Saint Louis in 1260 to

INTERIORS OF THE ARSENAL (2 G9) Mme de La Meilleraye's room is very well preserved: it was decorated in 1637 with a ceiling attributed to Simon Vouet (*Apollo and the Muses*) and wall panels with a delicate floral pattern. In the Oratory are paintings in the grotesque style from the 17th century, depicting famous women of history. The Salon de Musique is a very good example of Louis XV style, with grisaille paintings over the doors.

FAUBOURG ST-ANTOINE
This quarter was the most industrial area of Paris under the Ancien Régime: it was renowned throughout Europe for its furniture, earthenware and textiles. Today the street of the same name is well known for its furniture shops and the craft workshops in its many courtyards and passageways, such as the Passage du Chantier at no. 66.

405

house three hundred blind people ("fifteen times twenty").

RUE DE CHARONNE (3 A8 to 3 D7). A café on the corner of Avenue Ledru-Rollin still has its turn-of-the-century decorations: its window still advertises a cup of coffee at ten centimes in gold lettering. The view of the Hôtel de Mortagne (no. 53) is spoiled by the ugly modern building next to it: the older house was built in 1660 for Delisle Mansart, with gargoyles on its façade and an octagonal rotonda. Jacques Vaucanson assembled his collection of machines and automata here in 1746; this was the start of the Conservatory of Arts and Crafts ▲ *136*.

RUE DE LAPPE (2 I8). This street is quiet and undistinguished by day, but in the evenings it still has something of its early 20th-century atmosphere, when it was a favorite place for dancing. Settlers from the Auvergne and from Italy made it into a center for *bals musette*, popular dance halls with accordion music, frequented by *apaches*, the local hooligans ▲ *410*. The Balajo (no. 9) is still the leading establishment; it was decorated by Mahé (who also decorated the Rex Cinéma) and opened in 1936. A traditional Auvergne shop at no. 6 still has its old display shelves for salted meats and fish, while bars and restaurants like the Bar à Nénette (no. 26) have a delightful prewar atmosphere.

FROM BASTILLE TO NATION

GARE DE LYON (5 J1). This station was built between 1847 and 1852, and rebuilt for the Universal Exhibition of 1900 in the academic style fashionable at the time. It is dominated by its belfry: the clock's hands are 10 feet long. The arrival of the TGV (high-speed train service) gave a modern dimension to this old station.

ALIGRE MARKET (3 A9). This market, selling food and bric-a-brac, is held every day ▲ *IV*.

BUILDING PROJECTS OF THE GRAND EST PARISIEN ● *80*. This enormous urban development project is based around a few major architectural creations: the Opéra-Bastille, the pleasure port in the Arsenal basin, and the impressive 1,200-foot-long viaduct-like new Ministry of Finance building, which was completed in 1988. The Bercy warehouse district was formerly the site of the largest wine market in France, covering an area of 86 acres; this has been replaced by a huge modern park, preserving the two rows of listed wine storehouses, which now house boutiques, wine bars and restaurants, and the hundred-year-old trees. The architecturally innovative former American Cultural Center (4 B3), designed with overlapping sloping sections by Frank O. Gehry, is to become the future

Maison du Cinéma. If the project gets the financial backing it needs, it will be the most ambitious cultural center dedicated to movies (and one of the most interesting architecturally). Other ambitious development projects for offices and residential and leisure complexes are also underway, and the area will be served by the new driverless metro. With the Bibliothèque de France and the MK2 movie complex on the Left Bank, this is fast becoming an attractive area.

CHURCH OF STE-MARGUERITE (3 B8). Behind its discreet façade is the Chapel of Souls in Purgatory, built in 1760 and decorated with curious trompe-l'oeil frescos by Brunetti. It was in its cemetery (now disused), on June 10, 1795, that the burial of a young boy who had died at the Temple took place. It was thought that this might have been Louis XVII, but two examinations by forensic surgeons in 1846 and 1894 showed that the body was that of a boy aged 15 to 18: the Dauphin was 10 years old when he disappeared.

PLACE DE LA NATION (3 E9 10). On August 26, 1660, a royal throne was set up here for the ceremonial entry of Louis XIV and Marie-Thérèse into Paris. Thereafter, the square kept the name Place du Trône. During the Revolution the square was the site of a guillotine, which claimed over 1,300 victims, including the poet André Chénier. It was given its present name in 1880, on the occasion of celebrations for July 14 (decreed a public holiday). At the center of the square is *The Triumph of the Republic*, a bronze statue by Jules Dalou originally intended for the Place de la République.

GARE DE LYON
The Train Bleu restaurant on the second floor is lavishly decorated with gilded paneling and paintings by the official artists of the Third Republic. The magnificent decoration indicates the important position of the railways in the 19th century.

BERCY
This stadium (4 A3), with its turf-covered steel roof, can hold 17,000 spectators, in a multifunctional area adaptable for sports and other events.

⏱ **Half a day**

THE WATERS OF BELLEVILLE

Springs were common here, and some of Belleville's street names still hark back to a time when water ran down its slopes. The footbridge of the Rue de la Mare was rebuilt in 1900 (shown around 1940, below): it crosses the railway of the former Petite Ceinture.

RUE DE LA MARE

Alleys running down the slopes, stalls and workshops, old bistros, villas, gardens hidden away behind carriage entrances – Belleville and its former hamlet, Ménilmontant, still bear the mark of their rural and working-class past. The village came into being in medieval times on the vine-covered slopes owned by the great Parisian abbeys (St-Merri, St-Martin et al.). In the 18th century and up to the Restoration, this was the kingdom of *guinguettes*, or open-air cafés. Parisians used to come here on Sundays to drink a vinegarish wine called *guinguet*. After 1840 Belleville grew rapidly, becoming one of the largest towns in France. Workers came here in large numbers, forced out of the center of Paris by the grand urban projects under way there. In 1860 the town was annexed to Paris and cut in two: its main thoroughfare marks the boundary between the 19th and 20th arrondissements. The former wine-growing village became a place of poverty and revolt, its population banding together in the revolt of the Commune: Belleville's barricades were the last to fall under attack by the Versaillais. In the 20th century Belleville became home to many immigrant groups. Today its population is one of the most diverse and cosmopolitan in Paris, as can be seen in the extraordinary market held every Wednesday and Friday morning on the boulevards between Métro stations Belleville and Ménilmontant.

RUE DE BELLEVILLE AND ITS SURROUNDINGS

CITÉ DU PALAIS-ROYAL (11 D10) 151, rue de Belleville. Hidden away from the bustle of the street is one of Belleville's many secret "garden cities". These houses and small apartment blocks with little gardens, grouped around private roads, are typical of the area. From 1840 until the first decades of the 20th century, Belleville developed as a working-class area, its land divided into very small plots. Disdained by the grand urban-development projects, the town grew up haphazardly, following the schemes and projects of its small tenants (near right: the Villa de l'Ermitage).

REGARD DE LA LANTERNE (11 D9) Place des Fêtes. From the 12th century onward, abbeys which owned land on the Belleville plateau drained off its water with underground aqueducts to supply their monasteries in Paris. Little buildings were put up along the course of the aqueducts to give access to them for inspection. The Lanterne manhole (1613) stands out amid glass-and-steel towers: it marked the head of the Belleville aqueduct.

ON THE ROAD TO MÉNILMONTANT ★. The network of alleys and passages between the Rue de Belleville and the Rue de Ménilmontant – mostly following old paths between the vines – still has a prewar atmosphere. The Rue Piat led to two windmills in the 19th century: today it ends at the PARC DE BELLEVILLE ▲ *210*, where a vine has been symbolically replanted. The RUE DES ENVIERGES (3 C1) rings out each evening to the accordion music of its cafés-chantants. From the Passage Plantin you can see the maisonettes of the Villa Castel, where François Truffaut filmed scenes for *Jules et Jim* (1962). The RUE DES CASCADES (3 D2), with its dollhouses, bistro, glass-blower and manholes (nos. 42 and 17), is the site of one of the few restoration projects (nos. 15–23) which has respected the traditional social and urban fabric of the area.

DESCENTE DE LA COURTILLE
Under the Restoration a riotous carnival was held at Belleville every year, attracting all of Paris society to the area.

BELLEVILLE TO BE SCRAPPED?
The Parc de Belleville offers a splendid view over Paris (above), but the staircase of the Passage Julien-Lacroix was destroyed to make way for this development. Belleville is a developers' target, but it is holding out: many artists have now moved into its old factories.

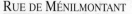

The real Casque d'Or (opposite), with *apaches* on either side. Simone Signoret immortalized the character in the 1952 film by Jacques Becker.

"APACHES"
Around 1900 the *apaches* reigned in the streets of Belleville. These gangs of young people fought bitterly over their territory, took great care with their appearance and treated their women as equals. Casque d'Or (Golden Cap) was one of the most famous *apache* women.

REBELLIOUS BELLEVILLE
"I'm from Belleville, this word terrifies you! It is the devil's quarter! It's Dante's hell!" These words were declaimed from the Belleville theater the day after the Commune. This

RUE DE MÉNILMONTANT

(3 BF7 to 3E2)
This was a favorite walk for Parisians in the 18th century, rising in a steep slope up to the plateau. In 1778 seven Parisians died here, engulfed by a collapsing quarry. The name Ménilmontant comes from *Mesnil Mautemps* (home of bad weather), the name of a house on these hills. Around the 16th century this was corrupted to *Mesnil Montant* (rising home).

LA BELLEVILLOISE ★ (3 D3) 23–5, rue Boyer. This building from 1927 is decorated with Marxist symbols, reflecting the strong communist tradition which grew up in Belleville after the Commune. La Bellevilloise, founded in 1877, continued to be very active up to the last war. Its shops, library and social club were open only to members.

MAISON DES SAINT-SIMONIENS (3 E2) 145, rue de Ménilmontant. The house is hidden by a block: it can be seen from the neighboring square. This was the mecca of Saint-Simonianism. In 1832, Prosper Enfantin, one of the apostles of this utopian thinker, put into practice his ideas regarding intimate relationships, based on the primacy of passion. This grand priest of the new religion was searching for a woman-messiah. On Sunday, the Saint-Simonians opened their house to the population of Belleville, sang canticles and wore their uniform (white trousers, red waistcoat and violet tunic, the colors of love, work and faith). Enfantin was prosecuted for offending public morals and forced to disband the society.

DOMAINE DE ST-FARGEAU

The Château de St-Fargeau and its grounds were broken up after the Revolution: they covered a vast area between the Rue Pelleport and the Boulevard Mortier (3 FH2). The last

center of political opposition terrified the middle classes of Paris. The population of Belleville was decimated by the Commune, falling from 50,000 to 20,000 in five months.
Above: the inner court of a workers' housing development in the Rue Ernest Lefèvre at the end of the 19th century.

occupant, the member of parliament Michel Le Pelletier, was assassinated in 1793 for voting in favor of the king's death.

CIMETIÈRE DE BELLEVILLE (11 F10) 40, rue du Télégraphe. The trees of this cemetery (1804) are all that remain of the park of St-Fargeau where Rousseau came to collect plants. In 1792, Claude Chappe chose this place – the highest point of eastern Paris – to test his telegraph machine. However, the *sans-culottes* of Belleville wrecked his signaling device. The cemetery houses the tomb of one of the pioneers of cinema, Léon Gaumont, who came from Belleville.

NOTRE-DAME-DES-OTAGES (11 F10) 81, rue Haxo. This church (1938) commemorates a bloody episode of the Commune ● *28*. On May 26, 1871, the mob massacred fifty-two Federate hostages here, mostly monks and national guards. The remains of the wall where they were executed can be seen on Rue Borrégo, behind courtyard railings.

VILLAS OF THE AMERICAN QUARTER
A developer created

CHAUMONT AND AMÉRIQUE QUARTERS

QUARRIES. Just over a century ago, this was a dangerous area, hollowed out by gypsum quarries. The underground tunnels served as nocturnal meeting places for criminals, and the police raided them regularly (above). Today, the parks of the Buttes-Chaumont and Butte du Chapeau-Rouge and the many villas around them make this one of the most picturesque areas of Paris.

AMÉRIQUE QUARTER ★ (MAP 11). The name of this area supposedly comes from the fact that gypsum from here was sent to Louisiana. The quarries ceased operation in 1872, but the roads built after they were filled in remained empty until the beginning of this century, as no one dared to build on such unstable ground.

PARC DES BUTTES-CHAUMONT.
See *Nature* ▲ *208*.

HÔTEL DES IMPÔTS (11 B9) 35, rue du Plateau. Léon Gaumont, who started his working life in a photographic studio in Belleville, built up an empire here until he went bankrupt in 1930. The studios and offices of the Elgé City (from his initials "LG") covered the entire area between the Rue Botzaris and the Rue

Fessart. Now only this building (1925) survives, with its splendid Art Deco entrance decorated with marguerites, in honor of his mother's name.

54, AVENUE SIMON-BOLIVAR ★ (11 B10). The staircase which passes through this building leads to five small streets created in 1927 on the circular site of a former stadium. At the far western end is an extraordinary view of Paris and its great monuments.

these small alleyways between the Rue Mouzaïa, Rue Général-Brunet and Rue Miguel-Hidalgo in 1901. However, the city council would not allow houses to be built over one story high because of the unstable subsoil, which had been weakened by the quarries. Gradually, villas intended for working-class families were built on either side of these streets.

20ᵉ Ar.

RUE DU REPOS

With its shady avenues, winding streets, forests and esplanades, its fashionable areas, its poor districts, its history, folklore, mysteries, police and outlaws – the Père-Lachaise Cemetery, opened by Prefect Frochot in 1804, is a city of the dead within a city of the living. It is located on the old hill of Champ-l'Évêque, where a rich merchant built his house in 1430. In the 17th century the Jesuits converted it into a hospice for members of their order: it became a meeting place for high society under the influence of the Père La Chaise, Louis XIV's confessor.

THE PÈRE-LACHAISE, CEMETERY: LIFE AND DEATH ✪
Covering 108 acres, this cemetery on the east side of Paris is the city's largest green space. With its valleys and steep gradiients, including the famous Allée aux Chèvres, it is quite a taxing experience. The 23-acre area known as "le secteur romantique" is worth a visit. It is the oldest part of the cemetery and, with its moss-covered trees, fallen gravestones and eroded inscriptions, is classified as a beauty spot and site of historic interest. It is particularly pleasant in summer, or in the fall, when the leaves are turning red.

A HISTORY BOOK
Like this one in the Egyptian style that was so fashionable after Napoleon's Egyptian campaign (1798–1802), each tomb reflects the

fashions and preoccupations of its period. Contemporary styles are, however, conspicuously absent from the design of modern tombs.

COLOMBARIUM
A long gallery surrounds the Moorish-style crematorium at the center of the cemetery. Both were built at the end of the last century by the architect Formige. Small niches in the gallery hold the ashes of the dead.

OSSUARY
This high relief, made in 1895, decorates the entrance to the ossuary in the Père-Lachaise cemetery. The sculptor Bartholomé portrayed the anguish of the living as two of their number cross over the threshold of death. The ossuary is a repository for bones from derelict graves.

Tomb of Jim Morrison (6th division)

TOMB OF ABÉLARD AND HÉLOÏSE (7th division)

Victor Noir (92)

ROCK AND SPIRITUALISM
Jim Morrison, whose bust was taken by fans, has stolen the limelight from Abélard and Héloïse, entombed under a neo-Gothic canopy since 1817. Morrison has a cult following equaled only by that of the spiritualist Allan Kardec (24th division). The statue of the journalist Yvan Salmon, alias Victor Noir

Frédéric Chopin (11th)

(92nd division), is believed to have fertility-enhancing powers. The tomb of Frédéric Chopin (11th division) has a sculpture of a muse by Clésinger or Vivant Denon, the diplomat-artist whose monument is by Cartellier (above, 10th division).

Honoré de Balzac (48th)

Allan Kardec (44nd)

413

One day

Paris viewed from
Montmartre by
Louis-Jacques
Mandé-Daguerre.

Little has
changed in
Montmartre since Nerval sang
its praises in the 19th century.
Though this butte has always had
a defiantly independent character, it was nonetheless
annexed to Paris in 1860 and has not escaped the relentless
sprawl of the city. This hill devoted to art and to pleasure is also
a place of paradoxes. At once mystical and libertarian, touristy
and insular, it has remained one of the last villages of Paris,
along with the Butte-aux-Cailles in the 13th arrondissement.
FROM SAINT DENIS TO PICASSO. Montmartre has been a place
of worship since the time of the Gauls. In the Middle Ages it
was an important pilgrimage stop dedicated to Saint Denis,
the saint who converted Paris to Christianity. Legend has it
that after his decapitation Saint Denis walked to Catullanum,
now St-Denis, where he was buried ▲ *432*. In 1133,
Montmartre passed into the hands of the Benedictine monks,
whose territory, stretching as far as today's 9th
arrondissement, was famous for its vines and its windmills.
This was also a strategic site: it was occupied by Henri de
Navarre in 1590, by the Cossacks in 1814, and by the
English in 1815. It was made into a separate

JEHAN RICTUS
This "cursed poet" had a belated revenge on the injustices of fate when a square was named after him.

MONTMARTRE CEMETERY
This necropolis covers 27 acres. It was opened in 1825 on the site of former gypsum quarries, which had earned the area its name of Barrière-Blanche (white barrier). The quarries had served as a communal grave, especially during the Revolution. Berlioz liked this "field of tranquility" so much that he chose it as his final resting place, as did Degas, Vigny, Stendhal, Fragonard and Marguerite

municipality under the Revolution and was the birthplace of the Commune in 1870 ● *28*. Montmartre was colonized by artists from the 19th century onward. Its bars and its painters, from Corot to Picasso, have made it legendary.

PLACE DES ABBESSES (10 B7). The name of this square refers to the former Benedictine convent which stretched from the summit to halfway down the hill. Here, in the shade of the plane trees, you can see one of the two surviving windows made by Guimard for the Métro. This one, reassembled in 1976, came from the Hôtel-de-Ville station. The CHURCH OF ST-JEAN-L'ÉVANGÉLISTE, the first religious building made of reinforced concrete, was built between 1894 and 1904 by Anatole de Baudot, a follower of Viollet-le-Duc. His design was chosen because it was the least expensive: it was partly financed by the parish priest. The project had to overcome numerous bureaucratic obstacles before it could be carried out: officials of the time had little faith in this new type of construction. The church has been nicknamed St-Jean-des-Briques after its external facing. Its somber Art-Nouveau interior decorations offer a stark contrast to the façade, whose crossed arches were inspired by Muslim architecture.

THE COMMUNARDS AT THE TOWN HALL. The former town hall stood on the Square Jehan-Rictus. Verlaine was married here

Gautier, Alexandre Dumas' model for *La Dame aux Camélias*. Above, Théophile Gautier's funeral.

415

Temps des Cerises

BATEAU-LAVOIR
The building (right) was a "manor of surprises . . . shaky, dark, all staircases, corners, nooks and crannies", wrote Roland Dorgelès in his *Bouquets of Bohemia*.

LOUISE MICHEL
(1833–1905)
This teacher at the Batignolles was a militant, writer and poet. The natural daughter of a country squire and a housekeeper, she later became an ambulance driver and figurehead of the Federates in Montmartre. She was deported to New Caledonia, but Paris gave her a triumphal welcome when she returned in 1880 after the Communards' general amnesty.

and Georges Clémenceau, a doctor of Montmartre, held the position of mayor when the Commune ● *28* was proclaimed in Paris on March 26, 1871. On the same day he was accused of complying with the authorities and

forced to give way to Jean-Baptiste Clément (1836–1903), who wrote "Le Temps des Cerises" ("Cherry Time"), the love song charged with revolutionary nostalgia which accompanied Zola's last journey, to the North Cemetery. Clément was exiled after the revolt had been put down. He continued his militant activities in London, and again in France after his return in 1880. One of Montmartre's squares is named after him, and a cherry tree was planted there in his memory.

BATEAU-LAVOIR (10 B6) Place Émile-Goudeau. Artists started coming to live in Montmartre in the 19th century, attracted by its light and its cheap rents. The first to come was Georges Michel (1763–1843). He was soon followed by Géricault, Corot, Renoir, and Degas, and in the early 20th century, the Fauves, Cubists and Futurists. The Bateau-Lavoir was their headquarters. The name given to this ramshackle building referred to its peculiar layout, reminiscent of a ship's gangways, and, ironically, to its single tap. It was also called the trapper's cabin, and Max Jacob nicknamed it the central laboratory. Artists and writers who lived here included Van Dongen, Juan Gris, Vlaminck and Braque, as well as Renoir, Cézanne, Max Jacob and Apollinaire. Picasso, its most famous inhabitant, painted his Cubist manifesto *Les Demoiselles d'Avignon* here in 1907. The Bateau-Lavoir was destroyed by fire soon after it was accorded landmark status in 1970; it was replaced by a block of artists' studios.

PLACE DU TERTRE (10 B6). This tourist mecca is now the preserve of restaurants and artists offering modestly priced, mediocre paintings. The ubiquitous easels and café terraces have almost destroyed the charm of this rustic square, where the abbey's shackles and gallows once stood. The first local council of Montmartre set up its town hall here in 1790, at no. 3. There is another town hall at no. 19, which organizes local festivities.

CHURCH OF ST-PIERRE DE MONTMARTRE (10 B6). This venerable edifice, one of the oldest in the capital, is supposed to have been built on the site of a temple to Mercury. But history has treated it roughly: it was dedicated by Eugène III in 1147; it became a "Temple of Reason" under the Revolution; the Commune made it into a clothing factory; and in 1793 the engineer Chappe put a telegraph pole on top of it. The church was saved in 1897 by a group of artists who persuaded the public authorities to restore it.

THE TWO ABBEYS OF MONTMARTRE. The church was the chapel of the Benedictine convent, founded in 1133 by Adélaïde de Savoie, wife of Louis VI. The nuns derived substantial revenues from the SANCTUM MARTYRIUM (10 B7), built in the 12th century on the site where Saint Denis met his death, according to legend; it was replaced by a memorial chapel in 1887 (9, rue Yvonne-Le-Tac). On August 15, 1534, Ignatius de Loyola founded his Company of Jesus in this famous shrine, visited by the faithful from all over Europe. From the 15th

LA MÈRE CATHERINE
This famous restaurant on the Place du Tertre opened in 1793. It is here that the word *bistro* (Russian for "quick") entered the French language, introduced by the Cossack occupying forces in 1814. It was, understandably, mistranslated as a synonym for "café" ● *42*.

BALLOONS ON THE PLACE ST-PIERRE
At the suggestion of the photographer Nadar, balloons were sent up from here to survey the enemy lines during the siege of Paris in 1870. Gambetta, in charge of organizing the resistance outside Paris, flew off for Orléans from here on October 7.

The sign of *Au Clairon des Chasseurs*. (right). *The Building of the Sacré-Cœur* by Borrel (below).

century the convent gradually declined, ruined by the Hundred Years War and the decline in pilgrimages. Its finances were at an all-time low when, in 1661, building works in the Martyrium led to the discovery of a crypt marking the site of Saint Denis' martyrdom. This timely discovery brought back the pilgrims. As money poured in, the Martyrium was incorporated in a new priory, called the Lower Abbey. The Upper Abbey was abandoned and demolished; only the church of St-Pierre remained. The Lower Abbey was demolished under the Revolution.

HISTORY. Behind the 18th-century façade and the modern doors carved by Gismoni lies a fascinating historical site. The vault of the choir, with its thick moldings, is the oldest in Paris, predating the one in St-Martin-des-Champs. It dates from the mid-12th century, as do the choir, the two apsidioles, the transept and the bay next to the nave. Originally the apse had a half-domed roof; it was rebuilt in the 12th century. The first three bays of the nave date from the same period, although their vaults date from the 15th century. Four marble columns at the entrance and in the choir are from an earlier building. The church also has some interesting tombstones. The tomb of Adélaïde de Savoie is in the northern apse.

SACRÉ-COEUR (10 C6). This church is an integral part of the Montmartre landscape, with its Byzantine-Romanesque façade, its dazzling white domes and bell towers, and the constant procession of pilgrims climbing its steps. Its striking presence almost erases the memory of its turbulent beginnings, which were dogged by a political and religious conflict reflecting the state of the nation after two national crises, the defeat of 1870 and the Commune.

A PROJECT FOR THE NATION. 1870 was a black year for Catholic France: the loss of Alsace-Lorraine, the Commune rebellion and the annexation of the pontifical states seemed like a punishment for a century without religion. Although many pilgrimages were made to save the Pope and the nation, it was two laymen, Alexandre Legentil and Hubert Rohault de Fleury, who vowed to build a church dedicated to the cult of the Sacred Heart. The archbishop of Paris, Monsignor Guibert, was unenthusiastic at first but soon became the project's champion. The basilica was to overlook the capital from the top of the Montmartre hill, sanctified by the martyrdom of Saint Denis and defiled by Communard reprisals. In 1873 the General Assembly declared that the project was to be financed by private funds.

TOUR OF THE CHURCH. The building was modeled on the church of St-Front in Périgueux. The vault of the choir is decorated with a mosaic by Luc-Olivier Merson, who also produced the mosaics for the side chapels. Alongside the

MONTMARTRE, SACRÉ-CŒUR ✪
The steep streets and dizzying flights of steps on the hill of Montmartre are well known. But it is not only the topography but also the way of life that gives this typically Parisian village – one of the last to survive in the capital – its unique character. It is best exemplified by the grape harvest festival, a blend of ceremony and burlesque, in which many of the inhabitants take part on the first weekend in October. There are also the street banquets which take place in summer, when local friends and neighbors gather around tables set out in the street. From the Place des Abbesses, a walk through the quiet streets will bring you out at the Sacré-Cœur. Magnificent sunrises and sunsets can be seen from the cathedral square.

THE QUARRIES
The Montmartre quarries were rich in montmartrite, a type of gypsum used since Roman times. Cuvier, the father of paleontology, found them invaluable for his field studies. Hermits and outlaws – among them Ignatius Loyola, Marat and the rebels of June 23, 1843 – hid in their tunnels.

The Quarries of Montmartre by Bouhot (right).

CONSTRUCTION OF THE SACRÉ-COEUR
The project was punctuated by skirmishes with opponents and fraught with problems. The foundations had to be dug deeper than

anticipated because of the quarries under the hill, thus increasing the cost and delaying the building work. Construction began in 1877, and the church was completed forty years later. Three architects separately managed the project: Paul Abadie, who restored the church of St-Front in Périgueux, Hervé Rauline and Lucien Magne.

PILLARS IN THE HILL
Eighty-three pillars were driven into the hill to support the walls and columns of the Sacré-Coeur. They stand on stone shafts, some 16 feet thick. It has been claimed that it is the basilica which holds up the hill, and not the other way round.

FRANCISQUE POULBOT (1879–1946) This draftsman created the image of the typical Montmartre urchin. In 1921 he opened a clinic for local children with the help of the manager of the Pomponette restaurant. His urchins, known as *poulbots*, have outlived their creator.

MAQUIS This scrubland covered with copses, wild grasses and picturesque huts was located between Rue Girardon and Rue Caulaincourt. It disappeared in 1911 when Avenue Junot was built. The avenue's residents have included Tristan Tzara (no. 15) and Poulbot (no. 13).

Virgin, the pope and the saints of France, the mosaic depicts the Parisian cardinals and bishops and the project's initiators (a chapel in the CRYPT also pays tribute to the founders). The DOME offers a dizzying view, while the CAMPANILE has one of the world's largest bells, the Savoyarde (1895).

WORSHIP AT THE SACRÉ-COEUR. The basilica is not a parish church but a place of pilgrimage, drawing Catholics from all over the world. A continuous service is held here, manned at night by delegates from the different Parisian parishes.

RUE ST-RUSTIQUE (10 B6). This narrow street is nine centuries old and has kept its old paving and its central gutter. The restaurant À la Bonne Franquette, on the corner of Rue des Saules, once called Aux Billards de Bois, was the meeting-place of Sisley, Cézanne, Toulouse-Lautrec, Pissarro, Renoir, Monet and Zola. The little garden where Van Gogh painted *The Open-Air Café* can still be seen.

CHÂTEAU DES BROUILLARDS (10 B5). The mysterious Allée des Brouillards runs through an old estate which used to reach as far as Rue Caulaincourt. The château, a beautiful pre-Revolution house, was made famous by Roland Dorgelès' novel. Gérard de Nerval is supposed to have lived there in 1846. Renoir lived in an ordinary house on the other side of the street.

MUSÉE DE MONTMARTRE (10 B6). This museum, at 12, rue Cortot, opened in 1860 in the former residence of Roze de Rosimond, an actor in Molière's troupe who died on stage (like Molière himself). This house, the oldest in Montmartre, had a more bohemian flavor at the beginning of the century. Its outbuildings housed the painter Raoul Dufy, the writers Léon Bloy and Pierre Reverdy, the theatrical manager André Antoine, and a talented but eccentric trio: Suzanne Valadon, her husband André Utter and his son Maurice Utrillo. Renoir rented an apartment here, and this is where he painted *The Swing*.

LE "PLACARD" DE SATIE (10 B6) ▲ *477.*
THE VINEYARD OF MONTMARTRE. In 1929 there
was a rumor that an apartment building was to
be built on the site of Aristide Bruant's garden,
on the corner of Rue des Saules and the Rue St-
Vincent. The resistance, led by Poulbot and the
painter Willette, decided to confront the authorities with a
fait accompli, so they created a square here to prevent the
demolition. The operation was a success. Later, a grapevine
was planted here to make good use of the ground which had
been saved. Ever since then, the harvest festival has been a
major local event. The Montmartre wine,
or *picolo*, is auctioned for charity.
LE LAPIN AGILE (10 B6) 4, rue des Saules.
This small pink building on the corner of
Rue St-Vincent was once famous for its
risqué poetry. Inside there are timeworn
walls covered with engravings and
paintings, old-fashioned curtains, a
disused fireplace and a large Christ figure
by Wasley above the wooden tables. The
establishment was formerly called the
Cabaret des Assassins but it changed its
name when the caricaturist André Gill
produced a new sign showing a
mischievous rabbit leaping from a cooking
pot. Le Lapin à Gill became Le Lapin
Agile (The Agile Rabbit). Aristide Bruant
bought the business in 1902, entrusting its
management to Frédéric Gérard, known
as Frédé. Regulars included Utrillo,
Picasso, Braque, Derain, Vlaminck and
Modigliani, as well as Apollinaire, Max Jacob, Carco, and
Charles Dullin. The place became legendary. It has a
reputation for discovering new talent: its Cabaret du Quai des
Brumes is one of the few stages in Paris open to newcomers.

LA MAISON ROSE
This small house at 2,
rue de l'Abreuvoir,
was immortalized by
Utrillo (1883–1955).
He was an alcoholic
from childhood; he
never left his easel
and worked mainly
from postcards. The
artist was generally
regarded as the
village idiot and

avoided painting
from life in order to
escape gibes.

BAL au Moulin Rou

Montmartre ended the 19th century to the tune of a quadrille. There was much dancing on Boulevard de Clichy and Boulevard de Rochechouart. A cosmopolitan crowd of pleasure-seekers, members of the demimonde and ordinary Parisians frequented the "unchastity belt" of Montmartre, where the Boule-Noire and the Élysée-Montmartre had packed houses. While the Moulin-Rouge invented the cancan and Toulouse-Lautrec sketched its performers, satirical cabaret was born at Le Chat-Noir.

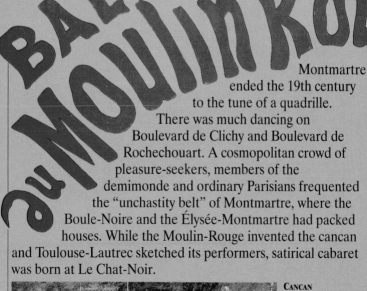

CANCAN

It is just a stone's throw from the Moulin-Rouge to the Place Pigalle, where the market for artists' models was held. Some *grisettes* (a term meaning a young coquettish factory worker, taken from the verb *griser*, "to make tipsy") who had left the studios achieved their brief moment of glory on the stage, including Jane Avril, known as *La Mélinite*; Cricri, who died doing splits; and La Goulue, who ended her life as a tramp. Below: Nini Patte-en-l'Air (Nini Foot-in-the-Air).

LE MOULIN DE LA GALETTE

This was one of thirty mills in Montmartre which were used to grind not only grain but also gypsum and stone. It was owned by the Debray family of millers, who lived in the Rue Lepic. They decided to open a dance hall here, selling flat cakes called *galettes* as a refreshment for customers between polkas. The Moulin de la Galette was born. Its good-natured atmosphere delighted Renoir and Dufy, both of whom lived at 12, rue Cortot, and came here to paint. It soon faced competition from another mill: Le Moulin-Rouge.

LE CHAT-NOIR

In 1881, Rodolphe Salis leased a disused post office on the Boulevard de Rochechouart and opened a cabaret under the patronage of the *chansonnier* Émile Goudeau. A *chansonnier* is a singer-songwriter who writes satirical songs about current affairs. Le Chat-Noir was a great success. A huge painting by Willette, *Farce Domine*, complemented its somber Louis-XIII-style décor.

Salis made fun of the institutions of the day and scolded his audiences. He also opened a shadow theater and founded a satirical journal. Bruant later took over Le Chat-Noir, renaming it Le Mirliton. Intellectuals and monarchs were among those attracted by his cheeky humor.

Above: *La Goulue and Valentin le Désossé at the Moulin-Rouge* by Toulouse-Lautrec.

ARISTIDE BRUANT (1851–1925)

"Corduroy trousers, a vest with lapels and a hunting jacket with brass buttons. A red scarf. A huge, extravagant hat, and under it the gentle, handsome face of a determined royalist." This is how the critic Courteline described *chansonnier* Aristide Bruant. Bruant, anarchist and entertainer of Le Chat-Noir, became famous after writing the popular song "Nini Peau d'Chien".

🕐 **Half a day**

TIME FOR ALL
Two sculptures by
Arman were put up in
the Cour du Havre and
the Cour de
Rome in 1985:
L'Heure pour tous
(Time for All) and
Consigne à vue
(Baggage Check),
assemblages of clocks
and suitcases,
respectively.

**PONT DE LA PLACE
DE L'EUROPE**
The bridge allowed
onlookers to watch
the new railway at the
heart of an area
where many writers
and artists lived,
including Huysmans,
Jules Romains,
Manet, Caillebotte
and Apollinaire.

A fter the end of the
18th century the capital expanded into the areas north of
the city walls destroyed under Louis XIV ● *54*. Private
houses, places of entertainment and development projects
like the "New Athens" around the Place St-Georges sprang
up between St-Lazare and the Faubourg Poissonnière. Writers
and artists of the Romantic age adopted this as their favorite
area. The 19th century saw the construction of churches and
railway stations (temples of the industrial age), as well as the
St-Martin Canal, with its provincial charm.

ST-LAZARE

FACTORY OF DREAMS. The Gare St-Lazare (9 I9) was built in
1851, with the iron structures which were to inspire Baltard
when he designed Les Halles. The station was rebuilt by
J. Litsch in 1885. Marcel Proust described this glass
construction as a "great glass workshop", while Jacques de
Lacretelle called it a "factory of dreams".
CHAUSSÉE D'ANTIN. Although less famous than the Faubourg
St-Honoré, the Chaussée d'Antin has just as many fashion
boutiques. The house at nos. 18–22, rue de la Chaussée
d'Antin (1 J2), is where the twenty-one heads of the kings of

Judah were discovered in 1977. They had been taken from the façade of Notre-Dame ▲ *358* in 1789 and are now on display in the Musée de Cluny.

LYCÉE CONDORCET (9 |10) 63, rue Caumartin. This school, formerly the Lycée Napoléon, is housed in a former Capuchin monastery. Famous pupils include Marcel Proust and Alexandre Dumas. It has a neoclassical façade and a cloister with Doric columns built by Brongniard in 1780.

PLACE ST-GEORGES

STE-TRINITÉ – NOTRE-DAME-DE-LORETTE

AROUND THE CHURCH (9 J9) 3, rue de la Trinité. A belfry flanked by two pinnacles gives this church its distinctive outline. It was built in 1861 in the Florentine style of the 16th and 17th centuries. The decorations include many paintings: the fresco *The Trinity and Angels* by F. Barrias stands out among these. Olivier Messiaen was the organist here for forty years. The Casino de Paris (16, rue de Clichy) is where Josephine Baker became famous; it was built in the Art Nouveau style in 1922.

NEW ATHENS. This huge residential development to the north of St-Lazare became famous for its neoclassical apartment buildings on the Rue de la Tour-des-Dames: its name reflected the Romantic fashion for Greece. At 27, place St-Georges (10 A9), Adolphe Thiers rebuilt his father-in-law's house in a grand, plain style (it had been demolished by the Communards).

A SORT OF WEDDING CAKE
This is how Léon-Paul Fargue described the church of the Ste-Trinité, designed by Ballu (below).

Opposite, the Marquise de Païva's house (no. 28) is
decorated with a multitude of sculptures in a striking
Gothic-Renaissance style. Near this is the Musée de la Vie
Romantique, in Rue Chaptal: this country-style residence
once housed the studio of A. Scheffer, who painted Stendhal.
In Rue La Rochefoucauld the symbolist painter Gustave
Moreau ▲ *142* turned his house into a museum dedicated
to his work. The nearby Square d'Orléans (10 A9) has seen
many famous residents, including Gounod, Bizet, George
Sand (no. 5) and Chopin (no. 9).

CHURCH OF NOTRE-DAME-DE-LORETTE (10 B9). According
to Viollet-le-Duc, this was the "parish of the demi-monde".
It gave its name to the *lorettes*, local courtesans of the 1830's,
who were immortalized in sculptures by Gavarni and in the
novels of Flaubert and Zola. The church was built by
H. Lebas in 1823; the austere outer structure of this building
(modeled on early Christian basilicas) contrasts with its
pompous interior decorations in the Louis-Philippe style.

FAUBOURGS MONTMARTRE AND POISSONNIÈRE

FAUBOURG MONTMARTRE. This working-class area used
to be the home of the Parisian fur trade. It still has a
19th-century atmosphere, with its shopping arcades and its
traditional shops, like the grocery store À la Mère de Famille
(35, rue du Faubourg-Montmartre), founded in 1761 and
still displaying its original gold lettering (2 C1). In the Rue
Richer is the music hall Folies-Bergères (2 C1), which

presents one of
the capital's major
variety shows. It
was established
in 1869 and at first
was called the
Theater of Elastic
Mattresses: it was
redecorated by Pico
in the Art Nouveau
style in 1929 ("in an exquisitely offensive style", according to
J.K. Huysmans).

FAUBOURG POISSONNIÈRE. Magnificent houses were
built around this street, formerly the route serving the
northern ports. The brasserie Flo (2 E1) 7, cour des
Petites-Écuries, was opened in 1886; its present décor
dates from 1910.

ST-MARTIN CANAL

The canal was built between 1822 and 1825 as an extension of the Ourcq canal, built by Napoleon I to supply Paris with drinking water. The waterway is 3 miles long, with a series of locks, swing bridges and humpback bridges; there is still some shipping activity. The banks have been redeveloped into charming walkways with an almost Venetian atmosphere. In the past they were occupied by tanneries,

paper mills and china factories. These industrial activities, which needed a lot of water, left their mark on this industrial, working-class area, as depicted on the façade of the Hôtel du Nord (2 G1) 102, quai de Jemmapes.

HÔPITAL ST-LOUIS (2 H1) 2, place du Docteur-Alfred-Fournier. This hospital, built of brick and stone, was erected in 1607; it was located outside the city walls in order to isolate plague victims. The building has survived virtually intact.

PLACE DE LA RÉPUBLIQUE AND BOULEVARD DU TEMPLE

Haussmann built the huge Place de la République (2 G3) in 1854, at the junction of the new boulevards. Moricet's *Monument de la République* was installed here in 1883. The project involved the demolition of the liveliest section of the Boulevard du Temple, which was alternatively known as the Boulevard of Crime because of the melodramas performed in its theaters, among them, the Théâtre de l'Ambigu-Comique and the Théâtre des Funambules, where the mime-artist Deburau performed during the Restoration.

DEBURAU
The mime-artist Deburau was immortalized in Marcel Carné's film *Les Enfants du Paradis* (1945). He was hugely successful with the *paradis* (the cheap seats in the gallery) and established the definitive version of the Pierrot costume.

ATMOSPHERE
In *Hôtel du Nord* (1938), Carné re-created the mood of prewar Paris. Arletty's famous words to Louis Jouvet on a footbridge over the canal – "Atmosphere, atmosphere, I've had my fill of atmosphere" – were, in fact, filmed in the studio.

One day

PORTE DE LA VILLETTE

La Villette may have lost its colorful working-class atmosphere, with its many bistros and its old slaughterhouses, but it has become one of the most dynamic cultural and educational centers of Paris. The City of Science and Industry stands out as an emblem of the renaissance of eastern Paris.

LA VILLETTE: INTO THE FUTURE ✪
There is nothing quite like La Villette anywhere in the world. It contains the city's largest landscaped park, the Cité des Sciences et de l'Industrie – a huge workshop devoted to popular science and technology – and the Cité de la Musique. A wide range of games and educational activities are available to children all year round. The park is the only one in Paris open day and night. In summer open-air movies and Sunday dancing attract many Parisians.

AN UNDERGROUND CANAL
The St-Martin canal runs for 3 miles from the marina at the Bassin de l'Arsenal (south of Place de la Bastille) to the Bassin de La Villette, passing underground for beneath the Boulevard Richard Lenoir and the Place de la Bastille.

FROM THE SLAUGHTERHOUSES TO THE CITY

CONSTRUCTION OF THE OURCQ CANAL. Napoleon I opened the canal between the Ourcq and the Seine on December 2, 1808; it was built to supply Paris with drinking water and to create a new shipping route. The Bassin de la Villette and the St-Martin canal were incorporated in the project. Today this "little Parisian Venice", bordered on the east by the St-Denis canal, is again used for shipping, and its quaysides have been redeveloped as walkways. At the southern end is the most attractive of the four tollhouses from the Farmers General wall, LA ROTONDE, built in 1784 by Claude Nicolas Ledoux ● *26, 55,* ▲ *387*. The canal allowed the town of La Villette, located outside the toll boundaries, to develop into a large industrial center. Evidence of this can be seen in the two warehouses of the Magasins Généraux, for sugar and grain, at 41, quai de la Loire, and in the hydraulic crane on the Rue de Crimée, built in 1885. This metal construction has four gigantic pulleys.

THE SLAUGHTERHOUSES OF LA VILLETTE. Huge slaughterhouses were built here in 1867, and a cattle market which could accommodate 1,300 head a day was constructed to the south of the canal. Two buildings survive: the ROTONDE DES VÉTÉRINAIRES, at the northern entrance to the City (this now houses the MAISON DE LA VILLETTE, a performance space), and the GRANDE HALLE, to the south of the Ourcq. Enormous new slaughterhouses were built in the 1960's, but these proved obsolete as soon as they were opened: progress in refrigeration technology meant that animals could now be slaughtered on the farm. Huge losses led to their being shut down in 1974. The quarter was rescued by a well-judged redevelopment project, centered on the City of Science and Industry.

CITY OF SCIENCE AND INDUSTRY (11 C3)

MAIN BUILDING. This giant edifice opened its doors on the day Halley's comet shot through the skies: March 13, 1986. Since then it has had some 35 million visitors each year. Moats filled with water surround the building, light enters through two 56-foot domes, and three large greenhouses full of plants open onto the park. The huge entrance hall leads off to the various centers of activity: the Children's City, the Crafts arcade, the Louis Lumière movie theater (in 3-D), the Mediathèque library (with a collection of 300,000 titles) and a giant aquarium in the basement.

PERMANENT AND TEMPORARY EXHIBITIONS. These educational exhibitions explore different subject areas in displays which cover several rooms interconnected by stairways and footbridges. Enjoyable experiments are used to tackle subjects like the oceans or energy, and to examine all the scientific disciplines. The planetarium displays the stars and planets.

GÉODE. This has come to stand as an emblem of the City as a whole. It is a sphere 120 feet in diameter, covered with 6,433 triangles of polished stainless steel, which reflect its surroundings. Its movie theater has the largest hemispherical screen in the world.

GRANDE HALLE
This masterpiece of metal architecture is 800 feet long and 260 feet wide: it is the only surviving hall of the four built by Jules Mérindol in 1876.

ARCHITECTURAL HARMONY
Adrien Fainsilber designed the project, skillfully combining the vast structures of the slaughterhouses with modern technologies using glass and steel.

THE CINAXE AND THE ARGONAUTE. The Cinaxe is a projection booth with sixty seats, mounted on bearings that can tip it 30 degrees in any direction: the spectator experiences the same kind of simulation which is used in training air pilots. The *Argonaute* submarine traveled around the world several times before taking up residence in the museum, where visitors can explore its gangways and passageways.

PARC DE LA VILLETTE   (11 CD3 and 11 D4)

GARDENS ▲ *210*. This is the largest landscaped park in Paris, stretching over 86 acres to the south of the city. It offers a variety of facilities, including a giant-screen open-air movie theater in the summer. The Zenith, to the east, has become a popular venue for musical events and can accommodate 6,400 spectators.

GRANDE HALLE. This impressive metal building from the former cattle market stands to the south of the park. It has been converted into a multipurpose cultural facility. Inside, partitions, stands and platforms can be arranged to adapt the space for the concerts, exhibitions and festivals held here. Two buildings stand on either side of it: the old Leather Market to the east, which now houses the Théâtre Paris-Villette, and the Janvier building to the west, which functions as a reception center. The *Lions of Nubia* fountain (1811) stood on the Place de la République, where it served as a watering place for animals; it was moved here in 1867 and now stands on the huge esplanade at the entrance to the park.

CITÉ DE LA MUSIQUE (11 D5). This complex is the highlight of the southern section of the park. It was designed by Christian de Portzamparc in the form of a village and houses the Higher National Conservatory of Music and Dance. It also houses two concert halls, as well as a wide range of musical equipment and a library. Exhibits in the newly opened MUSÉE DE LA MUSIQUE ▲ *159* range from Italian lutes to instruments by Amati and Stradivarius, up to the latest devices such as Frank Zappa's E-Mu modular synthesizer.

Excursions outside Paris

▲ St-Denis basilica

St-Denis, the cemetery of the kings, has suffered greatly. It was vandalized under the Revolution, then clumsily restored. It has been stripped of its most beautiful works which are now in the Louvre and the Bibliothèque Nationale. Nonetheless, this Gothic masterpiece remains a major historical landmark.

The eastern façade. The Regalia, the instruments of the coronation, were kept in this church – an indication of its importance.

The basilica of the kings

The original church was built in the 5th century over the tombs of Saint Denis ▲ 417 and his followers Rusticus and Eleutherius. An abbey grew up around the shrine, funded by large donations from the Merovingian kings, like Dagobert, who was buried here in 639. Under the Carolingians, who took over from the Merovingians with the support of the abbot of St-Denis, the church became the main location for royal ceremonies. In 1122, Louis VI made this the official burial place for French monarchs, at the request of Abbé Suger. Saint Louis reserved it for monarchs alone, a rule which was broken several times, and had the remains of his predecessors transferred to tombs in the crossing of the transept. They were arranged in dynastic order, proclaiming the continuity of the French monarchy. Over the centuries the abbey's power gradually waned, and Louis XIV placed it under the jurisdiction of the archbishop of Paris.

A museum of monumental sculpture

The church was seriously damaged under the Revolution. Afterward, Louis XVIII reinstated it as the royal necropolis, returning to the crypt the remains which had been thrown into a common grave; he also had the remains of Louis XVI and Marie-Antoinette transferred here. At the same time, the tombs which had survived the Revolution were brought back to the basilica, along with other tombs from various churches around Paris: this made St-Denis a unique museum of monumental sculpture. Restoration of the building started under Napoleon I and Louis XVIII, and it was continued by Viollet-le-Duc under Napoleon III.

A Gothic masterpiece

The Carolingians rebuilt the old Merovingian

basilica. Suger, in his turn, also decided to improve St-Denis and rebuilt the Carolingian basilica. The western façade was dedicated in 1140 and the chevet in 1144, but the building remained incomplete after the abbé's death in 1151. Suger's church represents a landmark in the development of

The tomb of Louis XII and Anne de Bretagne was designed by Guido Mazzoni and produced by the Florentine artist Jean Juste in 1507. It is made in the form of a catafalque and for the first time shows its royal subjects both as recumbent figures and in prayer.

Gothic architecture. Intersecting ribs were used here on a large scale for the first time. In this way, the architect could do without walls between the

Christ carrying the cross: detail from the portal.

pillars. Vaulting could be extended throughout the ambulatories, and the radiating chapels and huge windows could be incorporated in the chevet. This is how Suger realized his concept: for him, light had a thoroughly metaphysical significance. Another innovative feature is the rose window on the west façade. In 1231, Abbé Eudes Clément began work on the new nave. The first stage was directed by an anonymous

architect; he was succeeded by Pierre de Montreuil. The choir was rebuilt, although the double ambulatory, crypt and radiating chapels were kept, as was the western façade. The ground plan of the nave was altered. Flying buttresses on the exterior meant that the walls could be built to a greater height and on a larger scale, and the bays were divided into three levels (large arcades, triforium and high windows). This marked the transition toward High Gothic style.

TOMB OF THE KINGS
Before the 13th century, monarchs were buried near the altar under paving stones. Saint Louis transferred their remains to tombs decorated with recumbent stone figures. Later, the Valois were buried in impressive Renaissance-style tombs decorated with realistic recumbent and praying figures. The Bourbons were buried in the crypt, in wooden coffins placed on iron trestles.

The 9th-century crypt of Hilduin. The central barrel-vaulted nave can be seen in the crypt today.

▲ VERSAILLES

Versailles, an architectural fantasy conjured up by Louis XIV, was both a showcase for and an instrument of his power. The Sun King made this into a theater for the monarchy and a model for royal palaces.

BIRTH OF A PALACE

The palace of Versailles was constructed around a hunting lodge which had been rebuilt for Louis XIII by Philibert Le Roy. In 1661, Louis XIV had the estate modernized by the architect Le Vau and landscape designer Le Nôtre, and it became the setting for royal festivities. Soon the king decided to extend this modest château, and large-scale construction began. In 1668, Le Vau added a majestic stone façade to the three external faces of the U-shaped building around the Cour de Marne, creating the *château neuf*, the main building of the new palace. A vast terrace was added to the west, and the flat roofs were hidden behind ornamental balustrades. In 1678, Louis XIV decided to make Versailles his official residence, for reasons of politics and prestige. Construction was undertaken on a colossal scale in order to accommodate the royal family, the court and the government. On the garden side, the terrace was covered over and made into the Hall of Mirrors.

Everything in the palace revolved around the king, the sun in the universe of Versailles. Below: Louis XIV in coronation robes, by Hyacinthe Rigaud.

Jules-Hardouin Mansart built two long symmetrical structures, the Midi wing (1682) and the North wing (1689), set back from the main building. The town side of the palace was built around three branching avenues; the original façades of the Cour de Marbre were preserved. Mansart retained the Louis XIII-style buildings: the four pavilions built by Le Vau were joined in pairs to form the ministers' wings, which housed offices and apartments allocated to civil servants.

In front of the palace is a huge proscenium, the

Place d'Armes, bordered on the east by the Grande Écurie and the Petite Écurie (the Great and Small Stables). Even these functional buildings have a palatial appearance.

Above: the king's bedroom. Left: Colbert, by Claude Lefebvre. Colbert directed the project, aiming to create an unrivaled palace for Louis XIV while containing costs.

THE APARTMENTS

These were arranged in a strict hierarchy. The princes and leading courtiers lived in the north wing and the south wing on the garden side, while minor courtiers lived on the town side. The royal apartments were located on the second story of the main building – the king in the Grand Appartement to the north, the queen to the south. They were reached by two marble staircases, which has not survived, and that of the Queen.

ROYAL APARTMENTS OF THE GRAND SIÈCLE
The GRAND APPARTEMENT was decorated in the Italian style by a group of skilled painters working under Charles Le Brun. The paintings on the ceiling depicted gods and heroes of antiquity; the walls were decorated with statues and gold brocades. Images of planets revolving around the sun and mythological figures were used as allegories of royal power.

Festivities and ceremonies were central to palace life. Below: "Masked Ball Held at Versailles for the Marriage of the Dauphin" by Charles-Nicolas Cochin.

When the king finally moved to Versailles in 1682, he took up residence in the APPARTEMENT DU ROI, leaving the

The portraitist Nattier was a favorite with the daughters of Louis XV. Below: his likeness of Madame Adélaïde, the king's sixth child.

Grand Appartement for ceremonial uses. The king's apartment was located, symbolically, at the heart of the palace. Its mirrors, its pale ceilings and its carved white-and-gold paneling radiated light and warmth. The king's life was more comfortable here, but it was still subject to the implacable machinery of official rituals.

GABRIEL'S CONTRIBUTION
Under Louis XV, this warmer style achieved perfection. Two masters of this style, Jacques and Jacques-Ange Gabriel, decorated the CHAMBRE DE LA REINE (1730), the CABINET DU CONSEIL (1755) and the private apartments, where Jacques-Ange created magnificent paneling which was either carved and gilded or painted with a glaze which gave it the appearance of china. The gilded paneling of the APPARTEMENT INTÉRIEUR on the second floor is matched by the colored, glazed paneling of the PETITS APPARTEMENTS on the third floor,

Right: chapel by Vuillard. Each day Louis XIV attended services here, taking his place in the upper central gallery. The courtiers were seated on the first floor.

where Louis XV could live more privately. Gabriel produced a final masterpiece in 1774 – Louis XVI's LIBRARY, a refuge for the king, who was an avid reader with a keen interest in geography.

HALL OF MIRRORS
This 240-foot-long gallery has seventeen windows and seventeen arcades covered with mirrors. Le Brun devised the French-order capitals combining the inevitable sun motif with the royal lily and the French cock. The ceiling depicts the great deeds of Louis XIV, who is shown as a hero dressed in classical style.

CHAPEL
The last years of Louis XIV's reign were marked by the pious influence of his morganatic wife, Mme de Maintenon. During this time, Louis XIV built the chapel which rises above the palace roofs. It was started by Mansart and completed by Robert de Cotte in 1710. It has one of the few painted church ceilings to survive in France, produced by Jouvenet, Coypel and La Fosse, pupils of Le Brun. The magnificent interior combines gilding and white carved stone.

OPERA
Versailles did not have a proper theater until the marriage of the Dauphin to Marie-

The wooden décor of the Opéra de Gabriel, painted to look like marble, gives the Opéra its excellent acoustics.

Antoinette in 1770. Oval in shape, the auditorium can accommodate over seven hundred spectators, in tiered seating that goes from the orchestra pit to the back colonnade. Built by Gabriel, it has ingenious machinery that allows the stage and auditorium to be converted for balls and banquets. On May 16, the day of the wedding, the floor was raised up in order to set up the royal table.

TRIANON
Louis XIV was an avid builder. Once Versailles was completed, he ordered Mansart to build the GRAND TRIANON, a long, Italianate palace

consisting of two wings connected by a peristyle, with borders and perspectives created by Le Nôtre. The greenhouses and gardens were redeveloped in Louis XV's reign under the direction

of the botanist Jussieu. At this time Gabriel reached the height of his powers, building the PETIT TRIANON for Mme de Pompadour: it was a modern residence in a sober, neoclassical style. The king's mistress died in 1768, before it was finished. Marie-Antoinette had the gardens redesigned in the fashionable English style adding ornamental constructions including the TEMPLE OF LOVE, the BELVEDERE, the THEATER and the MODEL VILLAGE.

Above: Grand Trianon. The columns and pilasters of its façades create a harmonious, multicolored whole. Below: the English garden of Marie-Antoinette's village, redesigned by Richard Mique in the style of Hubert Robert. This miniature village has a dairy, a farm and a windmill.

437

THE GARDENS OF VERSAILLES

Two factors determined the design of the Versailles gardens: the palace's position at the top of a hill with irregular slopes, and the layout of the ground, divided by a central axis and crisscrossed with avenues from Louis XIII's reign. Le Nôtre, the royal landscape architect, opened up vast perspectives with ornamental lakes, which reflect the changing skies.

AN OPEN-AIR SCULPTURE MUSEUM

Three hundred urns and statues of lead, marble and bronze populate the groves designed by Mansart and Le Nôtre. Among them are copies of classical works and works by pupils of the new French Academy in Rome. The twenty-four marble statues of the Great Commission (1674) were commissioned by Colbert, superintendent of the Royal Buildings, following designs by Le Brun.

The lakes are central to the tour devised by the Sun King in the pamphlet he wrote for visitors, *How to View the Gardens of Versailles.* The Grand Canal, 5,400 feet in length, connected Versailles and the Trianon: this major aquatic feature was a setting for lavish festivities. Below: the Marais cascade (section and elevation).

"The borders and gardens are an open-air drawing room . . .
This is not a place for solitude and relaxation but a place
to stroll around, meeting people."

Hippolyte Taine

RESTORATION OF THE GARDENS

The gardens are currently undergoing reforestation. Some of the groves will also be restored, including the Bosquet de l'Encelade. The previous reforestation took place under Louis XVI; it was immortalized by the painter Hubert Robert.

NATURE TAMED

Creating the gardens of Versailles was a considerable undertaking: the site was a difficult one, with unfavorable contours. After the marsh had been drained, there was the problem of supplying water for the lakes and for watering the gardens. This was solved using Marly's machine, which pumped water from the Seine and conveyed it to its destination by means of aqueducts. The garden was divided into three distinct areas. Near the palace were gardens stretching to the horizon. After this came the groves and spinneys. Beyond this was the forest. The Labyrinth (above) no longer exists. Opposite: the Bosquet de l'Étoile.

Although it looks wild, the forest of Fontainebleau has been carefully maintained for seven centuries. The kings of France used this as their hunting ground and built one of their loveliest palaces here, using sandstone from local quarries. The landscapes of Fontainebleau inspired the painters of Barbizon, who were the first to take their easels outdoors, creating a famous school of painting.

1. PARIS
2. PORTE D'ITALIE
3. PORTE D'IVRY
4. PORTE DE BERCY
5. MELUN
6. FONTAINEBLEAU

The palace of Fontainebleau was originally a manor house where Louis VII (1120–80) stayed while hunting.

THE CHÂTEAU OF FONTAINEBLEAU

The château was a favorite with the kings of France and was repeatedly altered over the centuries. It is striking for its composite appearance: eight hundred years of architectural history can be read here. When François I returned from exile after the defeat of Pavia (1525), he brought leading Italian artists with him, including Il Rosso and Primaticcio. They created magnificent frescos and stucco work for the CHAMBRE DE LA DUCHESSE D'ÉTAMPES', the FRANÇOIS I GALLERY and the BALLROOM (the last was completed under Henri II). Henri IV and Louis XIII created the LOUIS XIII ROOM, where royal ceremonies were held up to 1773. Louis XV started the THRONE ROOM, the only one in France to retain its original furniture; Louis XVI created the GAMES ROOM and the QUEEN'S BOUDOIR. The palace was refurnished under Napoleon I. It still has a good deal of furniture from the Ancien Régime and the First Empire, as well as later pieces.

The Gallery of Diana, where Napoleon III housed the library. The globe dates from Napoleon I.

The palace of Fontainebleau (originally Fontaine-Belle-Eau or Fontaine Bliaut) may have been named after a nearby spring or after Bliaut – the name either of its owner or of the dog from the royal pack which first discovered the palace during a hunt.

The emperor Napoleon did not make any major alterations to Fontainebleau. However, he is commemorated here in the MUSÉE NAPOLÉON, dedicated to the years 1804–15. The MUSÉE CHINOIS, where Empress Eugénie displayed her Oriental collections, dates from the reign of Napoleon III. Its displays have been carefully reconstructed.

"Shepherdess Guarding Her Sheep" by Jean-François Millet.

FONTAINEBLEAU MASSIF

This is one of the most beautiful forests in France. It covers an area of 61,750 acres, incorporating three separate forests: Commanderie, Trois Pignons and Fontainebleau. The Fontainebleau forest itself is the second-largest in France, covering 41,990 acres. The first roads were built through the forest in medieval times. Henri IV built the ROUTE RONDE which leads to the heart of the forest by a series of crossroads: this network was extended by Louis XV. In the 19th century Dénecourt, a former soldier under Napoleon, created 93 miles of pathways through the forest, the basis of today's network (which covers 190 miles). The paths connect various sites of interest: ruins, lakes, caves and notable trees. In 1849 the railway brought tourists to the forest – and their garbage: four garbage trucks now cover the area on a fulltime basis. Fontainebleau also has other attractions for tourists and sports lovers: the GORGES D'APREMONT, the

ERMITAGE DE FRANCHARD and the CARREFOUR DE L'ÉPINE. Other, more sheltered attractions are the MARE AUX FÉES, GROTTE BÉATRIX and VALLÉE JAUBERTON.

BARBIZON

Between 1830 and 1875, this hamlet on the edge of the forest was the home of a group of landscape painters. They were attracted by the huge skies and by the modest prices of the AUBERGE GANNE, now a municipal museum. The inn's interior

Oak, beech and pine trees populate this forest, along with some spruce trees, larch trees and even sequoias.

decorations have recently been restored; they were produced on rainy days by its occupants (including Corot, Millet and Théodore Rousseau).

441

1. PARIS   2. PORTE DE LA CHAPELLE   3. LE BOURGET AIRPORT, MUSÉE DE L'AIR ET DE L'ESPACE   4. CHANTILLY

The former estate of the Great Condé is now dedicated to art and horses: the Museum of the Horse is housed in its Great Stables, while Chantilly palace itself has one of the richest art collections in France.

CHEMIN DE FER DU NORD

CHÂTEAU DE CHANTILLY

VISITE DU CHÂTEAU ET DU MUSÉE

PICTURE GALLERIES OF MUSÉE CONDÉ

Their originality lies in the arrangement of the pictures, determined by Aumale himself in the 19th-century style. The works are displayed cheek-by-jowl, and different schools and periods are mixed together with no regard for chronological order. Italian paintings predominate, with 98 works by Fra Angelico, Piero di Cosimo, Salvator Rosa, Sassetta and Raphael (including his *Three Graces* and the *Orleans Madonna*).

DUC D'AUMALE (1822–97)
This soldier, historian and enlightened collector was exiled twice, despite his republican leanings.

CHÂTEAU DE CHANTILLY

The palace comprises two separate buildings, set in grounds designed by Le Nôtre and crisscrossed by a network of lakes and streams. The PETIT CHÂTEAU was built by Jean Bullant in the 16th century for Anne de Montmorency. The neighboring

GRAND CHÂTEAU was built in the 19th century on the foundations of the original fortress: it was designed to house the art collection of the Duc d'Aumale. The overhead lighting of its best rooms – the Gallery, the Tribune and the Santuario – reflects this purpose.

Northern schools are represented by several Flemish primitives and three portraits by Van Dyck, while Clouet, Nattier, Ingres, Philippe de Champaigne, Poussin, Watteau and Delacroix illustrate the history of French painting. The entrance gallery and the CHAPEL contain treasures from the Château of Écouen ▲ 444.

LIBRARY
The collection is unique. The extremely precious illuminated manuscripts – including the *Psalter of Queen Ingeburge of Denmark* and *Les Très Riches Heures du Duc de Berry* – are not on display, but facsimiles are shown, as are bindings from the 11th to 14th centuries, early printed books and a huge collection of historical documents.

APARTMENTS
These are in the 16th-century building and boast a Riesener commode made for Louis XVI and a cabinet from Gustave III of Sweden.

The Great Stables, 600 feet long, are made of ten naves forming a vast octagon. They were built by a horselover who thought he would be reincarnated as a horse himself.

Left: "The Three Graces" by Raphael. Below: "Simonetta Vespucci" by Piero de Cosimo. The Florentine beauty is portrayed ten years after her death, as symbolized by the snake which is coiled around her neck. Top: "Landscape with Two Nymphs" by Poussin.

MUSÉE VIVANT DU CHEVAL: THE GREAT STABLES
In 1719 the seventh prince of Condé commissioned the architect Jean Aubert to build the Great Stables, a masterpiece of 18th-century architecture. Since 1982 the stables have housed a museum dedicated to the horse. All aspects of the equine world are explored in around thirty rooms. The star attractions are the forty real horses in the stalls and the educational equestrian displays.

▲ ÉCOUEN

1. PARIS
2. PORTE DE LA CHAPELLE
3. PARC DE LA COURNEUVE
4. ÉCOUEN

The beautiful castle of Écouen combines a French style of architecture with Italian ornamental motifs. The greatest artists of the Renaissance contributed to this exceptional building, which is today the Musée National de la Renaissance.

JEWEL OF RENAISSANCE ARCHITECTURE

CHÂTEAU DU CONNÉTABLE

Anne de Montmorency rebuilt the family manor of Écouen after being appointed constable by

Below: "The Trojan Horse", painted wood panel on a marriage chest (Florence, 15th century).

François I in 1538. He was known for his progressive tastes as a collector: when he fell from favor, he used the enforced leisure to embellish his château, one of the most beautiful in the kingdom.

The château forms a regular quadrangle around an internal court. The architect replaced the traditional towers with rectangular corner pavilions, and the two residential wings, to the right and the left of the entrance, were joined by galleries. The entrance gallery (1807) has replaced the original wing, which was destroyed shortly before the Revolution.

ARCHITECTURAL ORNAMENTATION The development of architectural styles can be seen

in the ever-more elaborate design of the windows, by which the different sections of the château can be dated. The west wing was the first to be completed (1542), followed by the south wing, the north wing and the east gallery. The first phase of construction was characterized by a very plain style. Examples of this are the scallops and related motifs on the turrets of the staircase in the south wing. The cartouches with indented edges in the north wing show a much more sophisticated style. The columns of the portico in the south wing are the first example of colossal-order columns in French architecture. This portico by Jean Bullant was doubtless designed to house the two *Slaves* by Michelangelo, now held in the Louvre.

This celestial globe in gilded bronze (1502) is a symbol of the union of science and art, and is extremely accurate.

INTERIOR DECORATIONS

The interiors seem relatively bare: most of the decorations were, in fact, transferred to Chantilly ▲ 442. This former estate of the Montmorencys houses the panels and stained-glass windows of the chapel and the forty-two grisaille windows of the Gallery of Psyche. The *Pietà* by Il Rosso, a masterpiece from the Connétable's collection, is now in the Louvre. The painted fireplaces were an original feature; they probably date from the reign of Henri II. Their Old Testament imagery depicts the life and virtues of the Connétable. The frame of the marble fireplace in the Grande Salle is attributed to Bullant.

MUSÉE NATIONAL DE LA RENAISSANCE

Much of the collection comes from the Musée de Cluny. The tapestry of the *History of David and Bathsheba*, a cup with the coat of arms of Anne de Bretagne, the large enamels by Pierre Courteys, the ship supposedly by Charles V and medallions by Luca Della Robbia are some of the major exhibits. On the second floor the surviving decorations and exhibits convey an impression of how the château once looked. Elsewhere, exhibits are arranged thematically. The third floor is devoted to the arts of the kiln, with a magnificent collection of enamels, glass and ceramics.

Detail of "The Tribute to Caesar". This scene from the Gospels is depicted on the central medallion of a painted fireplace.

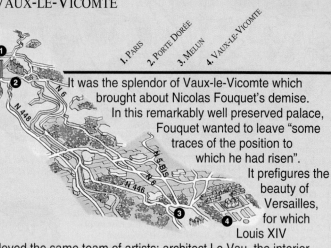

1. Paris 2. Porte Dorée 3. Melun 4. Vaux-le-Vicomte

It was the splendor of Vaux-le-Vicomte which brought about Nicolas Fouquet's demise. In this remarkably well preserved palace, Fouquet wanted to leave "some traces of the position to which he had risen". It prefigures the beauty of Versailles, for which Louis XIV employed the same team of artists: architect Le Vau, the interior decorator Le Brun and the landscape designer Le Nôtre.

Quo non ascendet?

Nicolas Fouquet (1615–80) rose rapidly to power, finally achieving the post of superintendent of finances. He grew richer as he grew more powerful: the loans he arranged for the king were secured by his own fortune and brought him substantial profits. He was a lover of literature and the fine arts, and made his palace at Vaux the most beautiful in France. Its pediments displayed the highly appropriate motto: *Quo non ascendet?* (To what heights will he not ascend?).

The last festivities at Vaux

On August 17, 1661, Fouquet held a magnificent celebration in honor of the king. The lavish festivities sealed his fate. Louis XIV, already won over by Fouquet's rival Colbert, was

Nicolas Fouquet, who represents the rise of senior civil servants under Louis XIV.

irritated by this opulent display and set investigations under way. After a dubious trial, Fouquet was imprisoned in the fortress of Pignerol in Piedmont. His palace was confiscated; it was returned to his family in 1673. Vaux-le-Vicomte was refurnished repeatedly by later owners.

A thoroughly royal splendor

The early stages of classicism can be seen here. The north façade is surmounted by a pediment set back from the corner pavilions. On the garden side, the Oval Room is crowned by a dome which stands out at the center of the façade.

It took only five years to transform a marshy area halfway between the royal palaces of Vincennes and Fontainebleau into a dream palace. Fouquet did not hestitate to demolish three villages which stood in his way.

Fouquet's arrest interrupted the painting of the dome in the Oval Room. It has not been altered since.

INTERIOR DECORATIONS

The statues, furniture and paneling designed by Le Brun are a perfect match for Le Vau's building. The ceremonial rooms and the private apartments have been carefully reconstructed; their effect is almost magical, conjuring up a life of freedom and opulence. The paintings in Fouquet's bedroom have survived intact, but Le Brun's most beautiful ceiling is in the Salon des Muses. Also in this room is the tapestry of the *History of Diana*, one of many which decorate the palace walls. (A special factory was established in the vicinity to supply the palace.) This splendor contrasts with the magnificent austerity of the Oval Room, located between the garden, the ceremonial rooms and the vestibule (which rises to roof level).

THE FIRST GARDEN IN THE FRENCH STYLE

Le Nôtre and Fouquet dreamed of huge perspectives and a balance between the building and its setting. They saw the garden as a theater: a stage setting to display the central object, the palace. Le Nôtre created optical illusions and effects to enhance this impression. The garden, with borders and ornamental lakes, opens onto the horizon. Its slope hides the Canal de la Poêle, which appears

unexpectedly at the vistor's feet. From afar, the palace seems to be held up by its terraces. The low buildings on either side add to this effect.

▲ DISNEYLAND® PARIS

1. PARIS 2. PORTE DE BERCY 3. PORTE DE VINCENNES 4. LAGNY 5. DISNEYLAND® PARIS

Carnival parades and spectacular entertainments, fairground attractions, restaurants and stores provide colorful variety in the five "lands" that make up the theme park. Seven themed hotels in fairytale settings offer a choice of accommodations to delight young and old alike. Walt Disney Studios, the most recent attraction, offers an interactive exploration of animated film, cinema and television.

MAIN STREET, U.S.A. The street is lined with wooden houses in soft colors, re-creating the a small American town at the beginning of the century. Parades of Disney characters pass by, and a steam locomotive waits

and a Cheyenne encampment (LEGENDS OF THE WILD WEST). Two thrilling attractions are BIG THUNDER MOUNTAIN, an expedition with dynamite explosions, and a journey through PHANTOM MANOR, a haunted house.

ROBINSON'S TREEHOUSE or take an adventure ride through the ruins of the Lost City (INDIANA JONES AND THE TEMPLE OF DOOM).
FANTASYLAND Beyond SLEEPING BEAUTY'S CASTLE, which rises above the park, is a

DISCOVERYLAND This futuristic city full of special effects will fascinate science-fiction fans. Start with an interstellar journey designed by George Lucas (creator of *Star Wars*). Then there is the VISIONARIUM, which projects films in 360 degrees. After a tour in CAPTAIN NEMO'S SUBMARINE, fans of Jules Verne will be catapulted to the stars by the COLUMBIAD cannon, inspired by the novel *From the Earth to the Moon*. This takes off from the SPACE MOUNTAIN, which is 118 feet high.
WALT DISNEY STUDIOS Animated film, cinema and television: you could spend a day on the other side of the screen.

for passengers at MAIN STREET STATION to take them on a tour of the park.
FRONTIERLAND The legendary Wild West, with saloons, cowboys, paddle steamers

ADVENTURELAND An exotic kingdom of pirates. You can join a buccaneer expedition (PIRATES OF THE CARIBBEAN), visit the SWISS FAMILY

fairytale village full of turrets and half-timbered houses. Attractions here include favorite fairytale heros, from Snow White to Pinocchio.

©Disney

World cultures in Paris

Since the 19th century Paris has been a refuge for large numbers of Eastern Europeans, especially Poles and Russians fleeing revolutions and repressions. These groups of immigrants have left their mark on the city, creating "little Russias" or "little Polands" which now act as magnets attracting new arrivals. However Paris has also taken in thousands of emigrants from the poorest areas of Italy, Spain and Portugal: these groups are the largest foreign communities in the capital.

THE "WHITE CITY"

Paris had a distinctly Russian air about it in the 1920's, when aristocrats and bourgeoisie settled in the city, fleeing the Revolution. Cossacks and White Army officers became factory workers, taxi drivers, or dancers and musicians in the cabarets which were very popular with Parisians at the time.

THE "LITTLE RUSSIAS"

Besides St-Alexandre-Nevsky, Paris has a number of Russian churches in the 15th and 19th arrondissements, where magnificent chanted masses are held. The most attractive of these are St-Séraphin-de-Sarov and St-Serge, the latter decorated with frescos by Dmitri Stelletsky and 16th-century iconostasis doors.

ST-ALEXANDRE-NEVSKY

This masterpiece of cultural transplantation, located at 12, rue Daru (9C9), was built between 1859 and 1861 by Kouzmine and Strohm, architects of the Imperial court. It follows the traditional orthodox design – "onion" domes and a ground plan in the shape of a Greek cross – but the exterior is distinctly Muscovite. The Christ figure on the façade is copied from a mosaic in Ravenna.

CUBISM, SURREALISM AND SPAIN

At the start of the century, Paris attracted artists and intellectuals from all over the world. These included Picasso (above, painted by Marevna along with Ehrenburg, Chagall and Léger), Miró, Juan Gris and Dali. There is now a special museum dedicated to Dali, christened "the emperor of Montmartre" by his artist friends, on the "Butte". (Above, *L'Éléphant spatial*, a sculpture from 1890.) The Spanish Civil War and then Francoism produced a steady exodus to France which lasted up to the 1960's. Since Franco's death in 1975 Spain has become fashionable in Paris, with a proliferation of tapas bars and flamenco schools.

ITALY

Peasants from the Piedmontese Alps and the Apennines streamed into France from 1870 onward. Immigration from Italy reached its height between 1920 and 1930, when Paris became the center of Italian anti-fascism (above, Italian workers are welcomed at Puteaux). Italians, or "ritals" as they were pejoratively known, formed the largest foreign community in France at this time and became a target for racial hostility. Today Italian restaurants, trattorias and couturiers have pride of place in Paris.

PORTUGUESE

The Portuguese community in Paris gathers at the Bastille (left) to celebrate their national day and commemorate the 16th-century poet Camoens, author of a national epic, the *Lusiade*.

REFUGE ...

From 1831 Paris became the place of refuge for Polish exiles. One of the main Polish centers is on Île St-Louis, with the Bibliothèque Polonaise and a museum dedicated to the revolutionary poet Adam Mickiewicz (1798-1855). The museum also has an impressive room devoted to Chopin.

OXFORD IN PARIS

The Cité Internationale Universitaire was built between 1923 and 1968; several European architects contributed to this striking campus. The Italian House (1958) was built in Italian villa style (asymmetrical ground plan, loggia, arcades, classical pediment), and the Deutsch-de-la-Meurthe Foundation (1925), was inspired by English college buildings (below).

...FOR POLISH EXILES

The church of the Assumption was presented to the Polish community in 1844. The Polish School was founded in the Batignolles quarter in 1842 (below).

THE "PLATZEL" (2F7)

Antisemitic pogroms in Russia, the Ukraine and Poland brought thousands of immigrants to Paris between 1880 and 1930. Many settled in the Marais, around Rue des Rosiers and Place St-Paul (the "Platzel"). Guimard was commissioned to build the synagogue in Rue Pavée in 1913.

World cultures in Paris
North Africa and the Middle East

The influence of the Mediterranean world is tangible in Paris. You can enjoy a *couscous* or have a feast of Lebanese *mezze*, walk in the gardens of the Grande Mosquée, spend an evening in a *raï* discotheque or an eastern cabaret, hear a concert of Arabo-Andalusian music at the Institute of the Arab World (IMA) or the Algerian Cultural Center,

Goutte-d'Or, Belleville and cultural centers.

unwind in a hammam or visit the souks of Belleville and Goutted'Or ... virtually all the communities of North Africa and the Middle East are represented in the city. North Africans are the largest single community, of which the dominant group is the Algerians.

ARABIC STYLE
The southern façade of the Institut du Monde Arabe is covered with motifs reminiscent of macharabiehs. Originally these were part of a sophisticated lighting system.

A CULTURAL CENTER
The IMA is not content simply to attract Parisians to its highly reputed exhibitions and museum ▲ *144* (above, a 19th-century Egyptian ewer); it has also become a place where the Arab community in Paris and French citizens of Arabic origin can express and explore their own culture. The institute organizes debates, theatrical performances and concerts; its library is unique in Europe, with a collection of fifty thousand books and one thousand periodicals. The restaurant and the council room on the top floor have one of the most beautiful views in Paris.

"GOUTTE-D'OR"
Long ago a highly reputed wine known as *goutte d'or* (drop of gold) was produced on these slopes. The Goutte-d'Or quarter has been the main district for settlers from North Africa since the 1950's. Its streets teem with shops selling oriental fabrics, cafés, and oil wholesalers which supply shops and businesses throughout France.

ISLAMIC CENTER
The Grande Mosquée in Paris was built between 1922 and 1926 on the model of the Fez mosques. It is one of the most disorienting places in the city, with its garden paved with mosaics – a symbolic representation of paradise – its immaculate white central courtyard, its Moorish café, bazaar and restaurant ▲ *261*.

ARABIAN MUSIC
The many and diverse types of music from North Africa and the Middle East can be heard in a number of Parisian venues. However, it is *rai* music above all – music from Oran celebrating love and the joys of life – which has taken Paris by storm during the last decade. *Raï* can be heard in the cafés of Barbès and Belleville and in the nightclubs of Paris (the Bagdad, the Bejaïa Club) and the suburbs (La Marquise in Montreuil).

HAMMAM
The Turks introduced the hammam (which means "hot bath" in Turkish) throughout North Africa and the Middle East. There are many hammams in Paris and its suburbs, including the magnificent example in the Grande Mosquée and the luxurious Hammam Pacha at St-Denis (right).

THE CORNER STORE
Many Parisian groceries are run by Moroccans from Sous and Tunisians from Djerba; they stay open late into the night, seven days a week. Grocers from Djerba and Sous dominate the food business in their own countries; they were just as important in Algeria up to Independence, when many left to set up shop in France.

SOUKS
The markets of Barbès, Belleville and Aligre are meeting places for the North African community in Paris. They have the appearance of Mediterranean souks, with stalls selling eastern fabrics, editions of the Koran, cassettes of Arab music, meats, spices, dried fruits and couscous. There are Tunisian groceries and cake shops in the small streets of Belleville (below).

PASSAGE DU CAIRE (CAIRO PASSAGE) (2C3)
The façade of the building at 2, place du Caire, was built between 1798 and 1799; it incorporates Egyptian-style motifs (heads of the goddess Hathor, frieze of pharaohs, imitation hieroglyphics) alongside neo-Gothic and neo-Byzantine elements. A speculator designed this bizarre composition to attract customers into the first Parisian passageway directly inspired by oriental bazaars.

WORLD CULTURES IN PARIS
AFRICA AND THE WEST INDIES

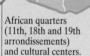

African quarters (11th, 18th and 19th arrondissements) and cultural centers.

From the 1920's onward the rhythms of drums and of the *biguine* (a West Indian dance) took Paris by storm and an Afro-Caribbean elite became established in a general climate of racial awareness. Paris' *colonie noire* (black community) has grown considerably since the 1960's with the arrival of large numbers of immigrants from French-speaking Africa and French citizens from the overseas territories, mainly Martinique and Guadeloupe.

WEST INDIAN FESTIVALS

The West Indians in Paris love to get together to dance *zouk* and *soukous* (particularly the *collé-serré* and the *touffé nyen-nyen* styles, in which dancers are press together closely). The "Zénith" (www.le-zenith.com) is one of their grand annual venues, where the West Indian Kassav band perform. The Paris Overseas Carnival, which takes place in the 12th arrondissement at the end of June, is also a must.

AFRICAN TROUBADOURS

In some small African restaurants in Paris you can hear a *griot* from Mali or Senegal singing and playing the *kora* (harp-lute). *Griots* are the story-tellers and musicians of West Africa: they act as the repositories of local oral tradition, travelling from village to village to retell historical epics and legends.

BLACK PARIS IN THE "ANNÉES FOLLES"

Between the wars a "negro craze" hit Paris: Parisians flocked to the "Bal nègre", captivated by the exotic attractions of jazz, Josephine Baker and the West-Indian *biguine* dance. Ethnologists discovered the riches of African art and civilization which became a source of inspiration for artists of the avant-garde (Picasso, Cendrars and Breton). Paris became the center of an Afro-Caribbean elite which mounted a campaign against the image of the "jolly negro".

AFRO-CARIBBEAN MUSIC

In the 1980's tomtoms and other Afro-Caribbean drums joined forces with synthesizers and electric guitars: Paris became the world capital of Afro-Caribbean music (right, Mory Kanté). Venues for listening or dancing to the rhythms of this music include jazz clubs (New Morning, Trabendo) and discotheques (Keur Samba, L'Alizé, BB Antilles, and Cinquième Dimension).

MARABOUTS

"Professor Z., genuine African marabout": a typical boast on business cards handed out by Métro exits. In Muslim Africa, a marabout is a spiritual guide endowed with supernatural powers.

AFRICA IN MUSEUMS

African art can be seen in Paris at the Musée des Arts d'Afrique et d'Océanie ▲ 158, at the Musée de l'Homme ▲ 144, in many galleries of St-Germain-des-Prés, and in the Musée Dapper (8J6).

BATIK AND "BOUBOUS" (10D6)

Fabric stores in the Château-Rouge quarter offer a profusion of shimmering materials and brightly colored batiks which are used to make the *boubous* or long tunics still worn by Africans in Paris. Batik, which originated in Indonesia, was introduced to Africa by Dutch merchants. This quarter also has a number of African tailors (Rue Myrha).

FRENCH ARTISTS FROM OVERSEAS

Nearly two hundred painters and sculptors from French overseas territories currently live in Paris. Works by around fifty of them are shown each year at an exhibition held in Espace Reuilly. Above, a painting by Shuck, an artist from Guadeloupe.

Founded in 1986, the Musée Dapper organizes exhibitions that aim to provide new insights into an art that is still relatively unknown; story-telling sessions are held each Wednesday. The museum is named after a 16th-century Dutch humanist who wrote one of the first books on Africa. Above, a statuette from Gabon.

CHÂTEAU-ROUGE

The stalls and markets of the Château-Rouge quarter, the hub of Afro-Caribbean life in Paris, are crammed with specialities: tropical fish (*capitaine*, *thiof*, *marachon*), tropical crabs, giant snails, cassavas and yams, African drinks (beer with ginger) and West Indian drinks (champagne-cola, lemonade with aniseed).

WORLD CULTURES IN PARIS
THE FAR EAST

Asian quarters (2nd and 13th arrondissements), and cultural centers.

In the early 1900's Paris already had a few Chinese restaurants, craftsmen and trinket sellers. However since the 1970's refugees from Southeast Asia have established their own distinct quarters within the city, bringing with them the exotic aromas of their markets, their huge canteen-style restaurants and their colorful festivities – like the Chinese New Year with its paper dragon.

THE "WENZHOU" QUARTER

Hidden away in the 2nd arrondissement is an unobtrusive "Chinatown". Originally from Zhejiangh, the "Wenzhou Chinese" have been emigrating to France since the 1920's. They form a close-knit group, speaking a dialect incomprehensible even to other Chinese

communities in Paris. They have taken over the workshops and wholesale businesses of the "Arts et Métiers" quarter (2EF4) devoted to the leather trade.

THE "CHOISY TRIANGLE" (5GH8)

This is the name sometimes given to the most famous Chinese quarter in Paris, located in the 13th arrondissement between Avenue d'Ivry, Avenue de Choisy and Boulevard Masséna. The quarter came into being after 1975 when large numbers of refugees arrived from former French territories in Indochina: Vietnamese, Laotians and Cambodians. This quarter, previously occupied by the Panhard factory buildings, had undergone extensive renovation. The refugees poured into the tower blocks snubbed by Parisians when they were first put up for rent in the early 1970's.

THE FIRST CHINESE QUARTER IN PARIS

This came into being after World War One, close to the Gare de Lyon. China had entered the war in 1917 on the side of the Allies, and had sent 140,000 volunteers to take part in the war effort. The volunteers worked in ports, on building sites and in arms factories; several thousand chose to stay in France at the end of the war, becoming workers in car factories, craftsmen or peddlers. A small group moved into the Chalon estate (now destroyed) and set up businesses there; they were followed by immigrants from North Africa in the 1950's.

VIII

THE TEMPLES OF THE OLYMPIADES

The huge Olympiades building at the heart of the "Choisy triangle" houses two Buddhist temples: the meditation center of the Teochew Association (below) and the altar of the Cult of Buddha, whose sign shines out in the half-light of a parking lot. Prayers are held several times each day, accompanied by traditional music. Worshippers also come to consult their guardian divinities using divining rods.

CHINESE OR INDOCHINESE?

Much of the Asian population in the 13th arrondissement is Chinese in origin: in the 19th century they had emigrated to Vietnam, Laos and Cambodia where they were partly assimilated into the local culture. Many came originally from Teochew, a region of southern China with an emigrant tradition going back to the 17th century when foreign explorers landed here.

THE "PARIS BUDDHA"

The International Buddhist Institute of Paris (4E9), open to Buddhists of all persuasions, is located in the Bois de Vincennes, in a group of African buildings dating from the colonial exhibition of 1931. The largest of these, the former Cameroon pavilion, houses a huge Buddha covered in gold (above). The thirty-foot high figure is known as the Paris Buddha. A Tibetan temple was added to the institute in 1984. A sculpture by Japanese artist Tarao Yazaki depicting zen pilgrims – "Pilgrims of Clouds and Water" – marks the entrance to the site.

DANCE OF THE DRAGON

The Dance of the Dragon is the most spectacular event in the Chinese New Year festivities. The dragon passes through the streets of the Chinese quarter chasing away evil spirits and receiving "good-luck money": new banknotes in red envelopes. Parades and Buddhist processions are held throughout the week.

UNDER THE SIGN OF THE COCK

Rambutans, bamboo shoots, lotus roots, dried fish – produce from all over Southeast Asia is unloaded every day at Tang Frères in Avenue d'Ivry. The company's emblem is a cock: the astrological sign of the Tang brothers' grandfather, who emigrated from Teochew to Laos at the beginning of the 20th century.

CHINA SQUARE

In China it is generally believed that a building placed where two rivers meet will bring prosperity to its inhabitants. This augurs well for Chinagora (literally, "China Square"), which was built where the Seine joins the Marne in 1992. This striking group of buildings is owned by a large Chinese state-controlled company; it was designed in the Manchu style and intended as a showcase for China, past and present.

Chinagora incorporates an exhibition hall built in a style reminiscent of Peking's Forbidden City, the delightful "Garden of Nine Dragons" which is entirely hidden from view on the outside, and a tea house where visitors can attend Chinese tea ceremonies.

BELLEVILLE TURNS CHINESE

The Belleville quarter has become home to many immigrant communities since the 19th century: Jews from Eastern Europe, Armenians, Spanish, Greeks, and North Africans followed one after the other. Today it is the Asian community's turn – refugees from Indochina and Wenzhou Chinese have moved into northeast Belleville. Asian markets have opened and the area is now famous for its Chinese restaurants, including Nioullaville and the sumptuous President (Royal Belleville).

ORCHESTRA WITHOUT VOICES

In Japanese, karaoke means "orchestra without voices". The word is used to describe the facility offered by certain restaurants or bars whereby customers can take the stage to sing popular songs accompanied by a backing tape. Karaoke is very popular in Japan, throughout Southeast Asia and in China. The craze has also hit Paris. Japanese karaoke clubs are often difficult to get into; Chinese karaoke clubs, by contrast, are open to everyone, and all kinds of songs are performed. The Chinagora karaoke (below).

MAGIC WANDS

The first Asian restaurants appeared in the Latin Quarter at the beginning of the 20th century. More followed in the 1950's, when the War of Indochina brought in a first wave of Vietnamese immigrants; another wave followed this in the 1970's. The restaurant business, a traditional immigrant activity, gave the refugees a springboard for social integration and success. Today some 15 percent of Parisian restaurants are Asian.

MAISON DES CULTURES DU MONDE
(1110)
The Maison des Cultures du Monde, based in the theater of the Alliance Française, was established in 1982. It was one of the first theaters to welcome artists from all over the world, giving priority to the least-known traditional cultures. This venue is used for all types of performance all year round, including Chinese opera, Japanese theater, African, Islamic and Indian music and dance.

JAPAN IN THE OPÉRA QUARTER

The Opéra quarter has the largest number of Japanese shops, restaurants and bars; it is known as the Japanese quarter of Paris. However Japanese influence is also felt in the rooms dedicated to Japanese Buddhism in Musée Guimet ▲ *142* and in the Japan House of the Cité Internationale Universitaire (5 B9) and the Japanese Cultural Center (7 J1). The painter Fujita

produced two magnificent works for this building, combining Western and Japanese techniques (painting on gold-leaf). One of them depicts the first meeting of Japanese and Westerners in the port of Nagasaki in the 16th century.

THE HOUSE OF CHING TSAI LOO

This gallery of Asian art at 48, rue de Courcelles (9D9) is open to the public; it was built by Fernand Bloch between 1926 and 1928 following instructions from his patron Ching Tsai Loo, a Chinese antique dealer. The pagoda is striking: placed on the corner of the building, its colored façade contrasts with its surroundings. Apart from the roof and the canopies covered with varnished tiles on each story, the building is very simple in design. Inside, the exhibition hall on the second story is decorated with lacquer panels, some dating from the 16th century (Ch'ing period).

TAI CHI CHUAN

A disciple of Lao-tseu said: "To live well you must stretch your body like an animal." Tai Chi Chuan, an ancient Chinese martial art, is based on this principle. Slow, precise movements are performed in a fixed sequence, allied with deep breathing to achieve relaxation and self healing. In the 1960's the practise became a common sight in the cities of China. The fashion has also arrived in Paris, where Tai Chi Chuan is practised in the squares of the Chinese quarters, in the Bois de Boulogne, in the Jardin du Luxembourg and the Buttes-Chaumont.

FILM SETS

In 1927 Fujita laid the first stone of the Japan House in the Cité Internationale Universitaire.

Southeast Asia House, on the same campus, is often used as a film set.

WORLD CULTURES IN PARIS
INDIA, PAKISTAN AND SRI LANKA

The 10th and 18th arrondissements and cultural centers.

Up to the early 1970's India was still a mysterious continent whose music, dance and cinema were known only to a few initiates in Paris. However in the last twenty or so years increasing numbers of Indians have arrived in Paris and its surrounding region, especially since Great Britain closed its doors to foreign immigrants. These new arrivals often come into the country secretly and work at whatever odd jobs they can get.

INDIAN QUARTERS
Bazaars, groceries and cassette stores have sprung up at the top end of Rue du Faubourg-St-Denis. This is where the Indians of Paris come for their supplies; it is close to the Sentier where many of them work.

WHO ARE THE INDIANS OF PARIS?
Pakistanis from the Punjab have been coming to Paris since the 1970's. Recently they have been joined by Indians from Gujerat and the Punjab – the latter including many Sikhs fleeing ethnic conflicts. The Indian community in Paris also includes Tamils from Sri Lanka and thousands of people from the Pondicherry Territory who chose French nationality after the French trading post there was closed down.

PASSAGE BRADY (2E1)
The sounds, smells and colors of India have taken over all the stalls in this passage (left) connecting Rue du Faubourg-St-Denis with Boulevard de Strasbourg. Hindu statuettes, saris, jewelry, mountains of rice, jars of chutney, crockery and magazines are heaped chaotically on the stalls. In summer all the restaurants have their tables out of doors and the sound of Indian chants echoes under the arches.

INDIAN DANCE
Courses and performances of folk and classical Indian dance are offered at the Mandapa and Soleil d'Or centers. Below, the Bindi pose.

RESTAURANTS
Many Indians and Pakistanis from the Punjab opened restaurants in Paris. They serve mainly Mongolian-influenced northern Indian food: tandooris and curries. There are a few restaurants, notably in Passage Brady, serving southern Indian cuisine, which boasts thousands of vegetarian dishes. The sumptuous decor of Lalqila in the 15th arrondissement (above): a stucco reproduction of the Taj Mahal.

Practical information

◆ GETTING THERE

CONSULATES

→ IN THE UK
– 21 Cromwell Road
London SW7 2EN
Tel. 020 7838 2000
– 11 Randolf
Crescent
Edinburgh EH3 7TT
Tel. 0131 225 7954

→ IN THE US
– 934 Fifth Ave.
New York, NY 10021
Tel. 212 606 3600
– 737 North
Michigan Ave.
Suite 2020
Chicago, IL 60611
Tel. 312 787 5359
– 10990 Wilshire Bvd
Suite 300
Los Angeles
CA 90024
Tel. 310 235 3200

FORMALITIES

→ DOCUMENTS
EU nationals need
only their identity
card or passport.
US citizens do not
require a visa, but
need a passport
valid for 3 months
beyond the
intended stay and
proof of onward or
return travel.
■ **Authorization to
leave the country**
Required for
unaccompanied
minors entering
France and traveling
around the country.

→ DRIVING
Must comply
with European
law: a valid
driving license, car
registration papers
and proof of
international car
insurance required.

TRAVEL

→ BY AIR
Daily flights at
very low prices
are now widely
available from
London, New York
and most other
major cities direct to
Paris Roissy-Charles-
de-Gaulle and
Orly airports.
Flight information
(Roissy and Orly):
www.adp.fr

London–Paris
Prices from £65
excl. airport taxes
Duration 55 mins
New York–Paris
Prices from $270
Duration 7 hours
Chicago–Paris
Prices from $285
Duration 9½ hours
Los Angeles–Paris
Prices from $300
Duration 11 hours

→ IN THE UK
■ **Air France**
Tel. 0845 082 0162
www.airfrance.co.uk
■ **British Airways**
Tel. 0845 773 3377
*www.british
airways.com*
■ **Easyjet**
Tel. 0870 600 000
www.easyjet.com

→ IN THE US
■ **Air France**
Tel. 1-800 237 2747
www.airfrance.com
■ **American Airlines**
Tel. 1 800 433 7300
www.aa.com
■ **Delta Airlines**
Tel. 1 800 241 4141
www.delta.com

→ BY TRAIN: EUROSTAR
Frequent trains from
London Waterloo to
Paris Gare de Nord.
To book in the UK:
Tel. 08705 186 186
www.eurostar.com
From the US/Canada:
US Tel. 1 800 257 2887
CA Tel. 1 800 361 RAIL
www.raileurope.com

**→ BY CAR AND TRAIN
(LE SHUTTLE)**
From Folkestone
to Calais via the
Channel Tunnel in
35 mins.
To book in the UK:
0870 535 3535
www.eurotunnel.co.uk

→ BY CAR AND FERRY
Ferry services
operate to the
European mainland.
■ **Brittany Ferries**
Tel. 0870 566 5333
*www.brittany-
ferries.co.uk*
■ **Hoverspeed**
Tel. 0870 240 8070
www.hoverspeed.co.uk

→ CAR
See the map at the
end of the book.
Main highways:
A1 and A16 (north),
A4 (east), A5 and A6
(southeast), A10 and
A11 (southwest) and
A13 (west).
*Warning: Parking
in Paris is difficult
at all times.*

HEALTH

**→ MEMBERS OF THE
EUROPEAN UNION**
Form E111, issued
by the Health
Authorities of EU
countries, entitles
their members to
emergency medical
treatment.

→ OTHER COUNTRIES
Non-EU members
are advised to take
take out personal
medical insurance
before departure.

→ VACCINATIONS
No specific
vaccination required.

MONEY

→ CURRENCY
The monetary
unit is the European
euro (€), divided
into 100 cents.

→ CREDIT CARDS
Automatic teller
machines and most
stores accept the
main international
credit cards.

→ EXCHANGE RATES
£1 = €1.44
US$1 = €0.90
€10 = £6.91/US$11
(at time of research)

TELEPHONE

→ FROM ABROAD
Dial the
international dialing
code, then 33, then
the number in
France, omitting
the initial 0 (so a
total of 9 digits).

TIME DIFFERENCE

GMT + 1.
When it is noon
in Paris, it is 11am
in London and
6am in New York.

TOURIST OFFICES

→ IN THE US
– 444 Madison Ave.
16th Floor
New York, NY 10022
Tel. 212 838 7800
– 676 North
Michigan Ave,
Chicago, IL 60611
Tel. 312 751 7800
– 9454 Wilshire Bvd
Suite 715
Beverley Hills
CA 90212
Tel. 310 271 6665

WEBSITES

*www.paris-
touristoffice.com*
www.paris.fr
*www.francetourism.
com*
■ **Cybercafés in Paris**
www.cybercaptive.com
■ **French Youth
Hostel Federation**
www.fuaj.org

WHEN TO GO

→ CLIMATE
■ **Spring**
Good weather starts
in May, but possible
thunderstorms end
of May and June.
■ **Summer**
Pleasant. Can be
quite hot during the
day, with thunder
storms at night.
■ **Fall**
In general, good
weather until Oct.
■ **Winter**
Can be quite cold.
Snow possible in
Jan. and Feb.
Showery.

→ PARISIAN LIFE
■ **Spring**
Easter school hols.
Many public hols in
May. End of cultural
season in June.
■ **Summer**
Summer sales in July,
but many stores
closed in Aug. Few
Parisians stay in
Paris from mid-July
until mid-Aug.
Traffic is lighter.
■ **Fall**
New school year
from early Sep.
New cultural season.
■ **Winter**
Christmas and
Feb. school hols.
Jan. sales.

STAYING IN PARIS FROM A TO Z ◆

Access for the disabled – Air travel – Beaches – Boats – Budget

The letters and figures (e.g. 10 I7) give grid references for the maps at the end of the guide.

ACCESS FOR THE DISABLED
Around 20 bus, metro and RER lines are accessible for wheelchair users. The website of the RATP (runs public transports in Paris) has all the information you need (in French only)
www.citefutee. com/informer/ accessibilite.php
Email: *mission. accessibilite@ratp.fr*

AIR TRAVEL
Two airports in Paris: Roissy-Charles-de-Gaulle (CDG) and Orly (ORY).
Flight information:
Tel. 08 36 68 10 48
www.adp.fr

→ **AIRPORT-TO-AIRPORT**
■ **Air France Coach Line 3:** Every 30 mins, 6am–10.30pm. Duration: 50 mins. Cost: €15.
■ **RER B and Orlyval** Every 4–10 mins, 6am–10.30pm (7am–11pm Sun). Duration: 1¼ hr. Cost: €16.
Note: *there is one change at Antony station.*
■ **Taxi** Duration: 1 hr. Cost: around €46.
■ **CDG1–CDG2** Free transfer every 10 mins.

→ **FROM ROISSY (CDG) TO THE CITY CENTER**
15½ miles north of Paris.
■ **Air France Coach Line 2:** To Porte Maillot (rue Gouvion-St-Cyr) and Place de l'Étoile (1, ave. Carnot). Every 15 mins, 6am–11pm. Duration: 40 mins. Cost: €13.
■ **Air France Coach Line 4:** To Gare Montparnasse (opposite the Méridien Hotel) via Gare de Lyon (Blvrd Diderot). No need to fly Air

France. Every 30 mins, 7am–9pm. Duration: 1 hr. Cost: €15.
■ **Roissybus** to Opéra (Rue Scribe). Every 15 mins, 6am–11pm. Duration: 45 mins/ 1 hr. Cost: €8.
■ **RER B to Chatelêt Les Halles** Every 4–15 mins, 5am–midnight (7am–9pm Sat. and Sun). Duration: 30 mins. Cost: €8.
Note: *direct access to CDG2 only. Free shuttle between CDG1 and RER.*
■ **Taxi** Duration: 30 mins/ 1 hr. Cost: around €38+.

→ **FROM ORLY TO THE CITY CENTER**
9½ miles south of Paris.
■ **ORLYBUS** to Denfert-Rochereau metro station. Every 15 mins, 6am–11.30pm. Duration: 30 mins. Cost: €5.50.
■ **Air France Coach Line 1** to the Invalides (Air France Terminal) via Montparnasse (opposite the Méridien Hotel). No need to fly Air France. Every 15 mins, 5.45am–11pm. Duration: 30 mins/ 1 hr. Cost: €7.50.
■ **RER C** to Saint-Michel station. Every 15 mins, 5.45am–10.30pm (every 30 mins after 9pm). Duration: 40 mins. Cost: €5.
■ **Jetbus** to Villejuif-Louis-Aragon metro station (line 7) Every 15 mins, 6.30am–10.30pm. Duration: 15 mins. Cost: €5
■ **RER B and Orlyval** Orly to Antony station with Orlyval metro then RER B to les Halles. Every 4–8 mins

6am–10.30pm (7am–11pm Sun.). Duration: 30 mins. Cost: €8.75.
Note: *You have to change at Antony.*

→ **ORLY SUD-OUEST**
Free transfer from Orlyval (2 mins). Every 4–7 mins.

BEACHES
→ **PARIS-PLAGE**
During the summer, 2 miles of embankment from Quai Henri IV to the Quai des Tuileries are reserved for pedestrians, roller-skaters and cyclists: a space right in the middle of Paris, with sand and palm trees, for walks, cultural and sports activities, or simply for resting on a deckchair.

BOATS
→ **BATOBUS**
Tel. 01 44 11 33 99
www.batobus.com/eg
■ **Times**
Apr.–Nov. daily 10am–7pm (until 9pm June–Sep.). Every 25 mins.
■ **8 stopovers**
Eiffel Tower, Orsay museum, Saint-Germain-des-Prés, Notre-Dame, Jardin des Plantes, Hôtel-de-Ville, Louvre, Champs-Élysées.
■ **Fares**
€3.50–€10 according to the journey.
1-day ticket: €10
2-day ticket: €12.50; children half price.
Season ticket: €42.

→ **CRUISES**
Times may vary with the season. No reservations are necessary for basic tours, but they are essential for canal cruises, special visits and dinner-cruises (smart dress for dinner).
■ **Bateaux-Mouches** Port de la Conférence 75008 (1 D4)
Tel. 01 42 25 96 10

■ **Bateaux Parisiens** Port de la Bourdonnais 75007 (1 A6)
Tel. 01 44 11 33 44
■ **Paris Canal**
Tel. 01 42 40 96 97
Route: Musée d'Orsay–La Villette (morning) and La Villette–Orsay (afternoon).
■ **Vedettes du Pont-Neuf** Square du Vert-Galant 75001 (2 B7)
Tel. 01 46 33 98 38

→ **LEISURE BOATING**
■ **Port Autonome de Paris**
2, quai de Grenelle 75015 (7 J1)
Tel. 01 40 58 29 99
■ **Section des Canaux de Paris** 6, quai de Seine 75019 (10 I6)
Tel. 01 44 89 14 14
Info on waterways.

BUDGET
Like most European capitals, Paris is an expensive city to visit.

→ **TRANSPORT**
Public transport: Standard weekly travel card: €13.75.
Taxi: €10–€13 for central journeys.

→ **MEALS**
Breakfast: Around €5 in sandwich bars, cafés and tearooms.
Lunch: Set menus from €15. Salads and sandwiches can be bought at sandwich bars, bakers or delis.
Brunch: From around €15 in cafés and trendy eateries.
Dinner: From around €23 min. per person. Gourmet menus start at €46.
Note: *Wine is rarely included in the set menu price. Tap water is free.*

→ **ACCOMMODATION**
Per night for a double room:
2 stars: €76– €90.
3 stars: €130– €140.
4 stars: €155– €185.

451

→ LEISURE
Budget may vary according to the individual traveler, but expect to spend from €15 to €30 per day and per person. Coffee, at the bar: around €1; on the terrace: €1.60–€2.50. Glass of wine: €2.50– €5. Sandwich: €4–€5.50. Museum: €4– €7. Movie: around €8. Cabaret and dinner: from €110.

CARS
→ CAR RENTAL
Ada
www.ada.fr
Tel. 08 25 16 91 69 (from France)
Agencies at the Gare du Nord, Gare de Lyon and throughout the city.
Avis
www.avis.fr
Orly airport, Ouest and Sud terminals
Tel. 01 49 75 44 91
Roissy airport 1 & 2
Tel. 01 48 62 34 34
Plus agencies at all railway stations.
Hertz
www.hertz.fr
Orly airport, Ouest terminal
Tel. 08 25 88 92 65
Roissy airport
Tel. 08 25 88 97 55
Many other agencies throughout the city.

→ DRIVING IN PARIS
Traffic can be very congested in central Paris, and the French tend to be very assertive drivers. Speed is limited to 35 miles an hour in the center and to 50 miles per hour on the Périphérique (circular road). Seat belts must be worn both in the front and the back. The use of mobile phones while driving is not permitted.
Warning: There is a growing number of bicycles and roller skates on the roads.

→ PARKING
Parking prohibited at all times in red zones (main roads). Unless otherwise indicated, metered parking in all streets.
■ **Parking meters**
Mon.–Fri. (or Sat. according to the zones) 9am–7pm. Parking limited to 2 hours; charges vary with the area (€1– €3 per hour). Payment in coins or by special cards (€15 or €30) available from tobacconists.
■ **Parking lots**
Numerous. Similar charges.
■ **Free parking**
Sat. and in Aug. in certain areas; on Sun. and public hols.
■ **Towing**
Quite common. To get your car back, contact the nearest police station or the Préfecture de Paris. Tel. 01 40 37 79 20
■ **Police checks**
Very frequent. Fines from €12 to €150.

→ TRAFFIC NEWS
■ **Information**
– Bison futé
www.bison-fute.equipement.gouv.fr
Tel. 01 48 05 56 55
– RATP
www.ratp.fr
Tel. 08 92 68 77 14
■ **Radio**
95.2 FM Traffic news
Every 15 mins 6.30–10am and 5–8.30pm.
Autoroute info (107.7 FM)
Highway traffic news every 15 mins.
FIP (105.1 FM)
Traffic news every 15 mins.

CHILDREN
Aquaboulevard
4, rue Louis-Armand 75015. Balard metro station (**7** G9)
Tel. 01 40 60 10 00
Sports complex with swimming pools.
Jardin d'Acclimatation
Bois de Boulogne 75116 (**8** F1)

Tel. 01 40 67 99 16
The best theme park for children in Paris.
Musée Grévin
10, bd Montmartre 75009 (**2** B2)
Tel. 01 47 70 85 05
Wax model museum.
Musée de la Magie
11, rue St-Paul 75004 (**2** G8)
Tel. 01 42 72 13 26
Magic fun and games, see *p. 141*.
Palais de la Découverte
Av. Franklin-D.-Roosevelt 75008 (**1** E4)
Tel. 01 56 43 20 20
Science museum
See *p. 312*.
Parc de la Villette
30, av. C.-Cariou 75019 (**11** D4)
Tel. 01 40 05 70 00
Containing the Cité des Sciences and la Géode, IMAX cinema, see *p. 429*.
Zoo de Vincennes
53, av. Saint-Maurice 75012 (**4** E8)
Tel. 01 44 75 20 10
Paris' biggest zoo.

CYCLING
→ RENTAL AND TOURS
See *Pariscope* or *Officiel* magazines for more information on tours.
■ **Roue Libre**
1, passage Mondétour 75001 (**2** D5)
Tel. 08 10 44 15 34
Open daily 9am–7pm.
Hiring, storage, advice and guided tours. Plus 40 thematic rides in Paris and around.
■ **Paris-Vélo**
2, rue du Fer-à-Moulin 75005 (**5** E3)
Tel. 01 42 81 24 72
■ **Paris à Vélo C'est Sympa!**
37, bd Bourdon 75004 (**2** H8)
Tel. 01 48 87 60 01
www.parisvelosympa.com
Hour-long, day or night rides. Also city bikes and tandem rentals.
Note: For all rentals a deposit of €300 will be asked.

DUTY FREE
13% reduction for non EU members for goods with a minimum value of €185 purchased in the same store.

ELECTRICITY
220 volts, and plugs with two round pins.

EMERGENCY NUMBERS
Ambulance 15
Fire 18
Police 17 (from mobile phone122)
SOS Médecins
01 47 07 77 77

ETIQUETTE
→ SMOKING
Is not allowed in public places (metro, train stations etc.). There are designated areas in restaurants and cafés. The rules are flexible, but generally respected.

→ TIPPING
■ **Cafés, restaurants**
Service (15%) is always included, but the *pourboire*, or tip (5–10%), is entirely at the client's discretion so do not be deterred by the frosty way in which the *garçons* eye you when they see you haven't left anything.
■ **Shows, movies, concerts, private theaters**
Tipping expected. Keep at least €2 in coins for the usher or the cloakroom attendant.
■ **National theaters**
Tipping not allowed.
■ **Taxi**
Tipping expected (10-15% of the overall amount).

FESTIVALS AND EVENTS
■ **End Feb.–March:**
Banlieues Bleues (jazz festival at Seine-St-Denis); Agricultural Fair; IMAX film festival at La Villette.

The letters and figures (e.g. 10 I7) give grid references for the maps at the end of the guide.

■ **Mid-March**
International Contemporary Art Fair; Salon du Livre (book fair).
■ **Early April**
Paris Marathon.
■ **End April–May**
Paris Fair.
■ **End May–June**
French Open Championship (tennis) at Rolland-Garros.
■ **June**
Music festival (21st); Cinema festival (last weekend); Gay Pride.
■ **July**
Bastille Day (Firemen's Ball and fireworks display, 13th; military parade, 14th); the Tour de France ends at the Champs-Elysées end of July.
■ **July–Aug.**
Free open-air film festival (La Villette); Paris quartiers, summer festival (dance, concerts).
■ **Sep.**
Heritage Open Days (properties usually closed to the public open for the day).
■ **Mid-Sep–end Dec.**
Fall festival: dance, theater, music (*www.festival-automne.com*)
■ **Oct.**
Nuits Blanches: well-known and little-known locations in Paris are transformed by artists of all kinds. Free to the public (*www.paris-france.org*); grape picking in Montmartre (1st weekend)

HEALTH

Parisians suffering from flu' or bronchitis tend to call a mobile medical team rather than a doctor.
■ **Gare médicale de Paris**
Sends the local duty doctor within an hour of receiving a call.
Tel. 01 42 72 88 88

→ **PHARMACIES**
■ **Open 24 hours**
Derhy
84, av. des Champs-Élysées 75008 (**1** D2)
Tel. 01 45 62 02 41
Pharmacie Européenne
6, place de Clichy 75009 (**9** I7)
Tel. 01 48 74 65 18
Pharmacie Daumesnil
6, place Félix-Éboué 75012 (**4** E2)
Tel. 01 43 43 19 03
■ **Open until 2am**
Pharmacie Internationale
17, bd Rochechouart 75009 (**10** D7)
Tel. 01 48 78 03 01
Pharmacie Forum Santé de la Porte de Vincennes
86, bd Soult 75012 (**3** H10)
Tel. 01 43 43 13 68

LEISURE
■ **Bastille**
Lively area. Trendy.
■ **Beaubourg/ Les Halles**
The most diverse area in Paris.
■ **Champs-Élysées**
Late-opening movie theaters, restaurants, cafés. Mixed crowd, mostly tourists.
■ **Grands Boulevards** (Opéra/Madeleine/ St Lazare)
Late-opening movie theaters and cafés. Mixed crowd, mostly tourists.
■ **Marais**
Predominantly gay, trendy area.
■ **Ménilmontant**
Latest fashionable area.
■ **Montparnasse**
Late-openeing movie theaters, cafés, restaurants. Mixed crowd, mostly tourists.
■ **Pigalle**
Cafés and discos, back in fashion.
■ **Les Quais (the Embankment)**
Floating restaurants from Javel to the Eiffel Tower. "Bateaux-concerts" and "péniches-théâtre" (river boats

holding plays and concerts) on the canals and near the Bibliothèque François-Mitterrand.
■ **Saint-Michel**
Movie theaters, late-opening restaurants and cafés. Mixed crowd of both locals and tourists.

LOST PROPERTY
■ **Bureau des Objets Trouvés**
36, rue des Morillons 75015 (**6** C5)
Tel. 01 55 76 20 20
Open Mon.-Fri. 8.30am–5pm

MARKETS
Many markets open 2 or 3 mornings a week in each arrondissement; there are also some permanent food stalls and specialized markets.

→ **ANTIQUE BOOKS**
■ **Porte de Brancion**
Parc G.-Brassens 75015 (**6** C5)
Sat.–Sun. 9am–6pm.

→ **STAMPS**
■ **Rond-Point des Champs-Élysées**
Corner of avenues Matignon and Gabriel 75008 (**1** E2)
Thur., Sat., Sun. and public hols. 9am–7pm.

→ **BIRDS, SMALL ANIMALS**
■ **Île de la Cité**
Place Louis-Lépine 75004 (**2** D7)
Sun. 8am–7pm.
■ **Quai de la Mégisserie**
75004 (**2** C6)
Mon.–Sat. 10am–7pm.
Not for animal-loving souls.

→ **FLEA MARKETS**
■ **Montreuil**
Porte de Montreuil 75020.
Open Sat.–Mon. 7am–7.30pm
■ **Saint-Ouen**
Between Porte de

Saint-Ouen and Porte de Clignancourt.
Open Fri. 6am–2pm, Sat.–Mon. 7am–5.30pm.
■ **Vanves**
Avenue Georges-Lafenestre 75014
Open Sat.–Sun. 2–7.30pm

→ **FLOWERS**
■ **Île de la Cité**
Place Louis-Lépine 75004 (**2** D7)
Mon.–Sat. 8am–7.30pm.
■ **Madeleine**
To the right of the church, 75008 (**1** H2)
Tue.–Sun. 8am–7.30pm.
■ **Ternes**
Place des Ternes 750017 (**9** B9)
Tue.–Sun. 8am–7pm.

→ **ORGANIC PRODUCE**
■ **Batignolles**
Bd des Batignolles 75017 (**9** H7)
Sat. 9am–2pm.
■ **Raspail**
From Rue de Rennes to Sèvres-Babylone 75006 (**1** I9)
Sun. 9am–2pm.
■ **Place Constantin Brancusi**
on the square 75014 (**6** G3)
Sat. 9am–2pm.

→ **GENERAL FOOD MARKETS**
There are food markets in all arrondissements except the 1st and 9th. Some of the best-known general markets are:
■ **Rue Montorgueil**
75002 (**2** D4) Daily.
■ **Rue Mouffetard**
75005 (**5** D2)
Tue., Thur. and Sat.
■ **Rue d'Aligre**
75012 (**3** A9)
Tue.–Sun.
■ **Rue de Lévis**
75017 (**9** F7)
Tue.–Sat. and Sun. am.
■ **Rue Poncelet**
75017 (**9** B9)
Mon.–Sat.
■ **Rue Lepic**
75018 (**10** A6)
Tue.–Sun.

→ TEXTILES
■ **Halles Saint-Pierre**
2, rue Charles-
Nodier 75018 (**10** C7)
Mon. 1.15–6.30pm,
Tue.–Sat.
9.15am–6.30pm.

MEDIA
→ **NEWSPAPERS
AND MAGAZINES**
■ **Cultural programs**
The *Officiel des
spectacles* and
Pariscope magazines
(out every Wed.)
cover all the cultural
events and other
activities taking
place in Paris and its
environs.
■ **Specialized
newspapers**
Le Parisien
(the only regional
newspaper), *Nova*
magazine (monthly
review for night-
owls), *TimeOut Paris*
(a British view of the
French capital), *Lylo*
(fringe shows and
concerts – out every
three weeks), *Paris
capitale* (monthly
publication for
smart and trendy
places), *Le 18e
du Mois* (the
18th-district's own
newspaper), *À nous
Paris* (free weekly
magazine produced
by the RATP), *Paris,
le Journal* (free
monthly review
from the Mairie de
Paris) and *Île* (free
quarterly magazine
distributed by the
Comité Régional du
Tourisme).
■ **Supplements**
Figaroscope of
the daily *Le Figaro*
and *Aden* of the
daily *Le Monde*
(both out on Wed.);
Libération, *Les
Inrockuptibles*, *La
Croix*, *Télérama*,
out every Wed.;
and the weeklies'
supplements.

→ **INTERNATIONAL
NEWSPAPERS**
Available at most
newsagents.
■ **24 hours a day**
– 33, av. des Champs-

Élysées 75008 (**1** D2)
– 52, av. des Champs-
Élysées 75008 (**1** C2)
– 2, bd Montmartre
75009 (**2** C2)
– 16, bd de la
Madeleine 75008
(**1** H2)

→ **RADIO**
■ **95.2**
City Radio gives
general information
on sports, music,
traffic, as well as
news bulletins.
■ **FG (98.2)**
House, techno and
garage programs.
■ **Nova (101.5)**
World techno
programming.

→ **TELEVISION**
During the week
France 3 broadcasts
a regional news
bulletin, 7–7.30pm.

MONEY
Take euros with you
in case you arrive
late and cannot
change money, or to
avoid exchange
charges.

→ **BANKERS CARDS**
■ **Cashpoints**
Most cashpoints
accept Eurocard,
MasterCard and
Visa.
■ **Loss or theft**
Contact the nearest
police station to get
proof of theft for
later dealings with
your insurance
company.
– American Express
Tel. 01 47 77 72 00
– Diner's Club
Tel. 01 49 06 17 50
– Eurocard-
MasterCard
Tel. 01 45 67 84 84
– Visa
Tel. 08 36 69 08 80

→ **EXCHANGE**
Proof of identity
is required when
changing cash,
traveler's checks or
Eurocheques.
■ **Banks**
Open Mon.–Fri.
9am–5pm.
Some open on
Sat. 9am–noon.

■ **Bureaux de
Change**
Open Mon.–Sat.
9am–6pm, and
found in all tourist
areas, such as Rue
de Rivoli, Les Halles,
Champs-Élysées and
department stores.
– **Chèque Point**
150, avenue des
Champs-Élysées
75008 (**1** B1)
Tel. 01 42 56 48 63
Open 7 days a week,
24 hours a day.
– **Thomas Cook**
Over 20 addresses,
including one at
52, avenue des
Champs-Élysées
75008 (**1** D2)
Tel. 01 42 89 80 33
Open daily 8.30am–
10.30pm.

OPENING TIMES
■ **Banks**
Banks are open
Mon.–Fri. 9am–
5pm. An increasing
number of branches
open on Sat. 9am–
noon (and even
until 5pm).
■ **Cafés–Restaurants**
Cafés and brasseries
open early and offer
continuous service
until very late all
week. Restaurants
are usually open
noon–2pm, 7–10pm.
Some are shut Sat.
lunchtime and Sun.
■ **Meals**
Parisians usually
have lunch
between 12.30
and 2.30pm, and
dinner between
8 and 10pm.
■ **Museums**
Usually open 10am–
6pm. The main
museums are shut
on Mon. or Tue.
Late-night opening
once a week.
■ **Rush hour**
7–9am and 5–7pm.
*Warning: Friday:
weekend exodus.
Saturday is a
shopping day.*
■ **Stores**
Open Mon.–Sat.
10am–7pm. Some
department stores
stay open later one
evening a week.

Grocery stores:
Supermarkets are
open Mon.–Sat.
9am–8pm, 9pm
or 10pm. Smaller
stores are open on
Sun. morning but
shut on Mon.
**Neighbourhood
stores:** Open every
day until late.
August: Many are
closed in Aug.
Sunday: Department
stores tend to open
on the Sundays
leading up to
Chrismas and during
the sales. Boutiques
situated in tourist
areas are open on
Sun. all year round
(Place des Vosges
and Rue des Francs-
Bourgeois, etc.).

POST
→ **POST OFFICES**
Open Mon.–Fri.
8am–7pm and
Sat. 8am–noon.
■ **Central post office**
52, rue du Louvre
75001 (**2** C4)
Tel. 01 40 28 23 27
Open 24 hours daily.
■ **Stamps**
On sale at post
offices (counter or
automatic machines)
or at tobacconists.
Pre-stamped
envelopes also
available.

PUBLIC
CONVENIENCES
■ **Cafés, restaurants**
Toilets are usually
reserved for clients.
■ **Coin-operated
public toilets**
About 400 units all
over Paris, open
from 6am to 10pm
(€0.30). Cleaning is
automatic. After
15 mins, the light
switches itself off
and the door opens
automatically.
■ **Madeleine**
Authentic Art
Nouveau toilets
underground, right
by the church at the
corner of the Place
and the Boulevard
de la Madeleine.
Have a coin ready to
tip the attendant.

The letters and figures (e.g. 10 I7) give grid references for the maps at the end of the guide.

PUBLIC HOLIDAYS
Jan. 1 (New Year's Day); Easter Sun and Mon; May 1 (Labour Day); May 8 (Victory of 1945); Ascension Thur; Pentecost Mon; July 14 (Bastille National Day); Aug 15 (Assumption); Nov. 1 (All Saints); Nov. 11 (Armistice of 1918); Dec. 25 (Christmas).

PUBLIC TRANSPORT
Cheap, efficient network.
The metro and RER complement each other, connecting at Châtelet-Les-Halles, Auber, Saint-Michel and Charles-de-Gaulle–Étoile stations. In many cases, tickets are valid for any type of transport (metro, RER, bus, etc.) within the same zone.

■ **RATP**
54, quai de la Rapée 75012 (5 I1)
Tel. 08 92 68 77 14
www.ratp.fr
The RAPT manages public transport in Paris and its suburb (bus, metro, tram and two of the five RER lines). Its website is excellent.
■ **SNCF**
Tel. 08 36 35 35 35
www.idf.sncf.fr
The SNCF national rail company runs suburban trains and three RER lines.

→ **INSPECTIONS**
Tickets can be checked at any time by inspectors on buses, RER trains and in the metro.

→ **CHILDREN**
Free for children under 4 years, half-price from 4 to 10 years.

→ **SALES POINTS**
In the metro, RER and railway stations (ticket office or automatic machines) or tobacconists that display the green ticket sign. Only single tickets can be purchased on the buses.
Warning: Do not buy a ticket second-hand.

→ **ZONES**
■ **Paris**
The metro covers the basic zone (1–2), which more or less corresponds to central Paris.
■ **Suburbs**
RER and suburban trains serve zones 1–3 to 1–8. The fares increase according to the distance traveled.

→ **TICKETS AND PASSES**
■ **Ticket T**
Since January 2003 you only need a single ticket, the purple "T", for use on the bus, metro, and RER within Paris. However, you cannot use it on the Orlyval, or Roissy/Orly coaches (*see p. 451*). Single "T" ticket €1.30; book of 10: €9.60
■ **Weekly pass**
The "Carte Orange hebdomadaire" is valid Mon.–Sun. Cost: €13.75 for zones 1–2, €18.35 for zones 1–3, etc.
■ **Monthly pass**
The "Carte Orange mensuelle" is valid from the first to the last day of the month. Cost: €46.05 for zones 1–2, €60.85 for zones 1–3, etc.
Note: Fares go up every summer.
■ **Day pass (Mobilis)**
Valid for 1 day, zones 1–2 to 1–8. Cost: €5–€17.95. This pass can be combined with the Musées et Monuments card, which gives access to 70 sites in Paris and around (*see next page*).

■ **Visitor's pass**
"Paris Visite": Cards for 1, 2, 3 or 5 days for zones 1–3, 1–5 or 1–8. Cost: €8.35–€53.35. Also gives reduced admission fees for monuments in Paris and surrounding areas.

→ **BUSES** (Map *p. 532*)
Some 58 bus lines operated by the RATP, including the Petite Ceinture (inner belt) which circles the city.
■ **Times**
All buses run from 5.30am–8.30pm Mon.– Sat. Some lines operate until 12.30am on Sun. and public hols.
■ **How to find them**
Each line is given a different color, and the main stops are indicated on the sides of the bus. Details of times and routes, as well as a map of the area, can be found at bus stops.
■ **How to get around**
Show your bus pass to the driver or validate a single ticket for each journey by running it though the machine.
Warning: During rush hour (Fri. evening and Sat. afternoon) buses become crowded and slow.

→ **LOCABUS**
Old or new buses may be hired from €125.
Tel. 01 49 28 48 97
www.ratp.fr

→ **NOCTAMBUS**
There are 18 lines of night buses. Departure from Av. Victoria, between the Hôtel de Ville and Place du Châtelet.
Tel. 08 36 68 77 14
■ **Times**
Every night between 1am and 5.30am.
■ **Fares**
€2.40 for each journey, with or without transfers, or using your pass (within the zone or zones for which it is valid).

→ **METRO** (Map *p. 530*)
Only a few lines go as far as the immediate suburbs. 14 lines, numbered 1 to 14.
■ **Times**
The metro runs daily 5.30am–12.30am.
■ **Getting around**
Run your ticket or your pass through the validating machine, and make sure you keep it until you come out at your final destination. One ticket is used for each journey, with an unlimited number of changes.

→ **RER** (Map *p. 530*)
The Réseau Express Régional goes through the whole of Paris, with 5 lines (A, B, C, D, E) divided into branches that connect it to the suburbs.
■ **Times**
The RER operates daily 5.30am–12.30am.
A timetable is displayed on every platform. Check the times carefully if you're planning to go out at night.
■ **Getting around in Paris**
Same conditions as for the metro.
■ **Outside Paris**
The cost of a ticket or pass varies according to the distance you wish to travel. Tickets must be bought at the point of origin.
■ **Services**
You can find public telephones and photo booths in most stations. Larger stations will also have an information point, newsagents, cafés, bakeries, flower stores, etc.

◆ STAYING IN PARIS FROM A TO Z

Reductions – Roller-skating – Security – Shopping – Sightseeing tours

→ **LONG-DISTANCE COACHES**
International coach terminal: Porte de Bagnolet (**3** H4) – the last stop of metro line no. 3 (Gallieni).
Eurolines
28, av. Ch.-de-Gaulle
93170 Bagnolet
Tel. 08 36 69 52 52
Open daily
6.30am–11.30pm
www.eurolines.fr

REDUCTIONS

→ **"LA MAIRIE DE PARIS VOUS INVITE..."**
(PARIS TOWN HALL INVITES YOU...)
■ ... **to the theater**
For a period of 3 days, 1 free seat for each paid ticket.
■ ... **to a concert**
For a period of 10 days, 1 seat free for each seat purchased.
Note: Dates may vary from one year to the next.

→ **MOVIES**
■ **Special offers**
Both large movie houses and smaller theaters offer special cards or subscription rates.
■ **Times**
Some showings may be cheaper, depending on the program or on the theater, (before 6pm on weekdays, first showing, etc.).
■ **Movie festival**
During the last weekend in June, all showings are priced at €1.50, with the exception of the first show which is charged at the normal price.
■ **"Paris Fait son Cinéma" (Paris makes movies)**
During the summer, seats are at €3 for all movie-goers under the age of 25.

→ **MUSEUMS**
■ **Carte Musées-Monuments**
This card gives free access to about 70 museums (permanent exhibitions only)

and monuments in Paris and its region. Passes are valid for 1, 3 or 5 consecutive days (€15– €45). They are available from museums and monuments that are members of the scheme, from main metro stations, tourist offices and the Espace de Tourisme d'Île-de-France (see *Useful addresses p. 457*).

→ **SHOWS**
■ **Kiosques Théâtre**
Half-priced seats available for that evening's show. Open Tue.–Sat. 12.30pm–8pm, Sun. 12.30–4pm.
Madeleine
To the left of the church, on the side of the Hédiard deli/store (**1** H2)
Montparnasse
On the square, between the station and the tower (**6** G2)
Warning: Bankers' cards are not accepted.
■ **Spectateur Service**
Yearly subscriptions (€25) and various reduced rates.
252, rue du Faubourg-St-Honoré
75008 (**9** C9)
Tel. 01 53 53 58 58
■ **General information**
Reduced rates and conditions may vary according to the theater. For example, national theaters, such as Chaillot and Comédie Française, sell seats for €8 every Thur. In every case, the number of reduced tickets is limited.

→ **TOURIST SITES**
■ **Carte Paris Visite**
For every ticket bought, another is given free. Paris and surrounding area. Cards are valid for 1, 2, 3 or 5 consecutive days in zones 1–3, 1–5 or 1–8 (from €8.35 to €45.70).

You may buy them in museums and main metro stations. *Advantages: This card includes both transport and the admission fees.*

ROLLER-SKATING

→ **HIRE**
Bike'n Roller
36, rue Fabert, Esplanade des Invalides
75007 (**1** E5)
Tel. 01 45 50 38 27
Nomades
37, bd Boudon
75004 (**2** H10)
Tel. 01 44 54 07 44
Suggested routes for experienced and beginners on Fri. and Sun.
Pari Roller
Tel. 01 43 36 89 81
www.pari-roller.com
Organizes the Paris Friday Night Fever, a free 15-mile outing every rain-free Friday. The starting point is between the Montparnasse tower and the railway station, and skaters gather for a 10pm start. Beware, this is absolutely not for beginners.

SECURITY

Paris is not a dangerous city, but it may be sensible to be careful at the start of the metro and RER lines in the evening and at the weekend. Beware of pickpockets in touristic Châtelet, Les Halles, St Michel and so on.

→ **POLICE**
■ **Telephone**
Police: 17
■ **Police stations**
There is a main police station in each arrondissement, open 7 days a week, 24 hours a day.
■ **Small police units**
Smaller police units are located in various neighborhoods, open Mon.–Fri. 9am– 8pm.

SHOPPING

See also above *Markets*, and *Shopping p. 479*.

→ **SHOPPING AREAS**
■ **Opéra/Madeleine/ Saint-Lazare/**
Department stores, major labels and brand names.
■ **Rues St-Honoré/ du Fbg-St-Honoré**
Designers.
■ **Champs-Élysées/ Avenue Montaigne**
Top labels, designers.
■ **Les Halles/Sentier**
Second-hand clothes, major names.
■ **Saint-Michel**
Second-hand clothes.
■ **Sèvres-Babylone/ St-Germain-des-Prés**
Designers, interior decoration.

→ **ANTIQUE AND SECOND-HAND STORES**
■ **Louvre des Antiquaires**
In the former Grands Magasins du Louvre, opposite the Place du Palais-Royal. 75001 (**2** B5)
■ **Carré Rive Gauche**
Between Quai Voltaire, rues du Bac, des Saints-Pères and de l'Université
75007 (**1** IJ6)
■ **Village Suisse**
Near the École militaire, 75015 (**1** C8)
■ **Village Saint-Paul**
Between Quai des Célestins and Rue Charlemagne
75004 (**2** F8)

→ **SALES**
Sales last for 6 weeks twice a year (Mid-Jan. and July).

SIGHTSEEING TOURS

→ **TOURIST BUSES**
■ **Balabus**
Runs like an ordinary bus, but stops at all the main points of interest between the Gare de Lyon and the Grande Arche de La Défense. There is no running commentary.

456

The letters and figures (e.g. 10 I7) give grid references for the maps at the end of the guide.

– TIMES
Sun. and public hols. from the 1st Sun. in Apr. to the last Sun. in Sep.
– FARES
Validate 1 ticket (3 for the Grande Arche) or show your pass.

■ **Montmartrobus**
This is the only bus service to operate on the Butte Montmartre hill. It runs between Pigalle and the 18th-district townhall.
– TIMES
Daily from 8am to 8pm, every 15 mins.
– FARES
Same as for buses.

■ **Open Tour**
Green panoramic double-decker buses. Run daily. (Tel. 01 42 66 56 56 info, Mon.–Fri.)
www.paris-opentour.com
– MAIN ROUTE
From the Madeleine back to the Madeleine, via the Opéra, Louvre, Latin Quarter, Orsay, Champs-Élysées, Trocadéro and Invalides. Complete tour: 2 hours, with commentary in French and English.
– OTHER ROUTES
Bastille–Bercy (1 hr); Madeleine–Montmartre (1 hour).
– COST
Passes: 1 day (€24), 2 consecutive days (€26), children from 4 to 11: €12. Unlimited stops.

STRIKES
Some notice is usually given. The current trend is "micro-strikes", which can affect one metro line or one museum for a few days.

TAXIS
There are around 15,000 cabs in Paris. A taxi is free only when the "taxi" light is on. It is not available

when only the smaller lights on the side are on.
Warning: Avoid using unlicensed taxis.

→ **RATES**
Basic charge of €2 to which one must add the following:
■ **Variable rates**
There are different tariffs (classified as A, B and C), in force according to the zone and the time of travel.
Three area zones
Paris, Boulevard périphérique and suburbs.
Two time zones
7am–7pm and 7pm–7am, Sun. and public hols.
Tip: A list of tariffs is given on the left-hand passenger window of the cab. The rate applied by the driver appears on the meter, next to the fare.
■ **Fixed rates**
4th passenger (€2.29), large pieces of luggage (€0.90 per unit), pets (€0.60 per animal), pick-up from a railway station (€0.76), waiting time (€23.63 per hour).

→ **CAB COMPANIES**
■ **Alpha Taxi**
Tel. 01 45 85 85 85
■ **Taxis Bleus**
Tel. 08 25 16 10 10
■ **Taxis G7**
Tel. 01 47 39 47 39
Warning: Few cabs are available on Friday and Saturday nights. It is also very difficult to find a cab driver willing to take you back to the suburbs late at night.

TELEPHONE
→ **CALLING ABROAD FROM FRANCE**
Dial 00 + the country code and the number you wish to call: 44 for UK, 1 for US and Canada.

→ **CALLING WITHIN FRANCE**
Dial all ten digits, including the initial 0, even if you are calling within the same zone or city.

→ **SPECIAL NUMBERS**
Start with 08, but only numbers starting with 0800 are free.

→ **PUBLIC TELEPHONES**
Plentiful, but they only take cards; these can be bought at tobacconists and metro stations. Coin-operated telephones may be found in cafés.

USEFUL ADDRESSES
→ **CONSULATES**
■ **UK**
16, rue d'Anjou
75008 Paris
Tel. 01 44 51 31 02
■ **US**
2, rue St-Florentin
75382 Paris Cedex 08
Tel. 01 43 12 22 22
www.amb-usa.fr

→ **TOURIST OFFICES**
■ **Office de Tourisme de Paris**
127, avenue des Champs-Élysées
75008 (1 B1)
Tel. 08 36 68 31 12
www.paris-touristoffice.com
Open Mon.–Sat. 9am–8pm,
Sun 11am–7pm.
Branches at the Gare de Lyon and the Eiffel Tower.
■ **Espace du Tourisme d'Île-de-France**
Carrousel du Louvre
99, rue de Rivoli
75001 (2 A5)
Tel. 01 44 50 19 98
www.paris-ile-de-france.com
Open 10am–7pm. Other office at Disneyland® Paris.

→ **INTERNET CAFÉS**
■ **WebBar**
32, rue de Picardie
75003 (2 G4)
Tel. 01 42 72 66 55
www.webbar.fr

Open Mon.–Fri. 8.30am–2am, Sat. and Sun. 11am–2am. Also bar, snacks, events, exhibitions.
■ **Le Rendez-Vous Toyota**
79, av. des Champs-Élysées
75008 (2nd floor of the store) (1 C2)
www.rv-toyota.com
Open Tue.–Sun. 10.30am–9pm (midnight Fri., Sat.)
Also bar, restaurant, cybercafé and exhibitions.
■ **Clickside**
14, rue Domat
75005 (2 D9)
Tel. 01 56 81 03 00
www.clickside.com
Open Mon.–Sat. 10am–midnight, Sun. 1–11pm. Self-service drinks, student discounts. For more addresses consult:
www.cybercaptive.com

VISITS
The *Officiel* and *Pariscope* magazines (out every Wed.) give the week's programs. If you have not registered in advance, just go to the place at the time indicated. Partial list:
■ **Paris-Story**
11bis, rue Scribe
75009 (1 J2)
Tel. 01 42 66 62 16
www.paris-story.com
Hourly, 9am–7pm. A 40-minute film on 2,000 years of Paris history. Commentary in 13 languages.
■ **Caisse Nationale des Monuments Historiques et des Sites**
Hôtel de Sully
62, rue St-Antoine
75004 (2 H8)
Tel. 01 44 61 20 00
Organizes visits to monuments and sites normally closed to the public.
■ **Paris et son Histoire**
82, rue Taitbout
75009 (10 A9)
Tel. 01 45 26 26 77

◆ HOTELS

The letters and figures (e.g. ◆ 1 G3) give grid references for the maps at the end of the guide.

SAINT-GERMAIN-DES-PRÉS

Artus Hotel
◆ 2 A8
34, rue de Buci
75006
Tel. 01 43 29 07 20
Fax 01 43 29 67 44
www.artushotel.com
A six-story house by rue de Seine and its food stalls and market, previously known as the Buci Latin. The Artus has some surprising features: curious objects dotted around the reception rooms, wonderful bedroom doors, some with door handles like pétanque bowls, animal-print décor, warm hues in the rooms, colored graffiti running up the staircase, and rooms with a very individual and original décor devised by one of seven artists. The whole place is slightly avant-garde, often surprising but with a restful feel to it, and in a wonderful location.
27 rooms: €190

Duc de St Simon
◆ 1 H7
14, rue St-Simon
75007
Tel. 01 44 39 20 20
Fax 01 45 48 68 25
Quiet, quaint and elegant, the Saint-Simon is housed in a former 18th-century townhouse, off the Boulevard St Germain. It has period furniture, objets d'art here and there, beautiful Pierre Frey fabrics in the bedrooms and gilded panels. The rooms are not too large but bright and comfortable – some have balconies overlooking the back garden or the courtyard. Bar in the vaulted cellar. All in all, the place is

a real treat.
34 suites and rooms: from €190

Esmeralda
◆ 2 D8
34, rue Saint-Julien-le-Pauvre
75005
Tel. 01 43 54 19 20
The attraction of this quaint one-star hotel is its location, in a 17th-century building (a listed monument) opposite Notre-Dame. There are beamed ceilings, old stonework, faded wallpaper, wonky floors and a decoration straight out of flea markets. The rooms are basic – it is only a one-star hotel after all – but if you have one with a view over the

LE RELAIS-CHRISTINE

cathedral, it won't matter. The place has its fans so book early.
19 rooms: from €85

Hôtel de l'Abbaye
◆ 1 J9
18, rue Cassette
75006
Tel. 01 45 44 38 11
www.hotel-abbaye.com
A small, warm, inviting luxury hotel, housed in a 17th-century convent. It is an oasis of calm, two minutes' walk from the Luxembourg gardens. It hides a pretty flower-filled courtyard where you can have breakfast in summer, or a drink in the evening. In winter an open fire blazes in the hearth of the downstairs

bar. Room 301 has a terrace overlooking the rooftops of Paris.
46 rooms and suites: €185–399

Hôtel des Marronniers
◆ 2 A7
21, rue Jacob
75006
Tel. 01 43 25 30 60
The Marronniers if full of charm and character and situated in one of the prettiest streets in the area, with antique shops and galleries. There is a conservatory where breakfast is served, and a small garden. The rooms are on the smallish side but are perfectly adequate; they give onto the garden or the courtyard (and are therefore quiet) and if you ask for one on the fourth story you'll get views of the rooftops and of the clocktower of the church of Saint-Germain. As with all hotels in this area, book well in advance.
37 rooms: €160–210

Relais Christine
◆ 2 B8
3 rue Christine 75006
Tel. 01 40 51 60 80
www.relais-christine.com
A 16th-century villa built on the remains of an Augustinian abbey founded by Saint Louis in 1231. The hotel has retained the original well, fireplace and medieval cellars; it

also has an inner garden. Like the Hôtel de l'Abbaye (above), it is an oasis of quiet and elegance in the middle of St-Germain-des-Prés. A romantic treat. From €350

Relais Saint-Germain
◆ 2 B8
9, carrefour de l'Odéon
75006
Tel. 01 43 29 12 05
Fax 01 46 33 45 30
A number of artists have fallen under the spell of this 17th-century, Anglo-Provençal style residence. The rooms are beautifully decorated, some to a surprising degree of luxury, with both high-tech facilities and valuable works of art.
5 suites: €400
17 rooms: €210–370

LATIN QUARTER

Hôtel des Grandes-Écoles
◆ 5 D1
75, rue du Cardinal-Lemoine
75005
Tel. 01 43 26 79 23
A rare thing: a villa resembling a country manor with a private garden, in the middle of Paris and just a few yards from the Contrescarpe (city walls). Complete peace and quiet, and a large terrace where breakfast is served when the weather allows. The décor of this late 19th-century bourgeois house is immaculate: floral wallpaper, antique furniture.
51 rooms: €90–120

Hôtel des Grands Hommes
◆ 2 C10
Place du Panthéon
75005
Tel. 01 46 34 19 60

This elegant 18th-century hotel has spacious rooms with exposed beams and wrought-iron bedsteads. Views of the Panthéon dome from the 6th-floor balconies.
32 rooms: from €183

Hôtel des Jardins du Luxembourg
◆ 5 B2
5, Impasse Royer-Collar
75005
Tel. 01 40 46 08 88
The people who run this splendid hotel have exquisite taste: kilims, wood paneling, balconies, flowers and tiling give the rooms an unforgettable charm. The rooms aren't huge but are very comfortable. Room 1, on the ground floor, is very spacious and has its own entrance. Sauna, elevator, patio and air-conditioning. Very quiet.
25 rooms: from €135

Les Rives de Notre-Dame
◆ 2 C8
15, quai Saint-Michel
75005
Tel. 01 43 54 81 16
Fax 01 43 26 27 09
Steinbeck once lived in this 16th-century residence located on the banks of the Seine. Inside, it has a warm and cosy décor inspired by Provence. There are unrivaled views of Notre-Dame cathedral.
1 suite: €266-381
9 rooms: €183-289

Vert Galant
◆ 5 D5
41-43, rue Croulebarbe
75013
Tel. 01 44 08 83 50
Fax 01 44 08 83 69
How good it feels to be in this ancient inn in the Gobelins

quarter where the Laborde family's welcome is charming, and the bedrooms open out onto a garden bordered by restful vines. Some rooms are equipped with small kitchens.
15 rooms: €87–90

L'Atelier Montparnasse
◆ 6 I1
49, rue vavin
75006
Tel. 01 46 33 60 00
Fax 01 40 51 04 21
A five-minute walk from St Germain des Prés or the Luxembourg gardens and just behind the legendary cafés and brasseries of Montparnasse – such as La Coupole and Le Dôme – the Atelier is perfectly located. The floor of the entrance hall is covered with a multi-colored floral carpet and its walls are hung with the works of contemporary artists. The rooms have no air conditioning and are small, but they are full of light and comfortable. They are named after artists who made the area famous: Picasso, Gauguin, Fujita... The bathrooms have reproductions of their artists' works in mosaics.
17 rooms: from €140

Sainte-Beuve
◆ 6 I1
9, rue Sainte-Beuve
75006
Tel. 01 45 48 20 07
Fax 01 45 48 67 52
In a wonderful position between the Jardin du Luxembourg and Montparnasse, this hotel offers light and spacious rooms furnished with

antiques. Each room has its own name: Sainte-Beuve is the nicest.
22 rooms: €126–265

Le Tourville
◆ 1 E8
16, av. de Tourville
75007
Tel. 01 47 05 62 62
Fax 01 47 05 43 90
This beautiful house has a cozy charm. Four of the bedrooms open onto well-laid-out terraces and bathrooms are fitted with Jacuzzis – all at a stone's throw from the Invalides.
3 suites: €310
27 rooms: €145–240

Raphael
◆ 1 A2
17, av. Kléber
75016
Tel. 01 53 64 32 00
Fax 01 53 64 32 01
From the warm paneling of the English Bar, to the paintings hung in the lounges, the chandeliers, silk taffetas and Louis-XV chest of drawers in the rooms – everything has been designed with meticulous concern for sophistication. For instance: the 540-foot-square suite with garden terrace planted with lavander and bamboo.
39 suites: €1,124–5,100
51 rooms: €315–905

Saint-James Paris
◆ 8 I6
43, av. Bugeaud
75016
Tel. 01 44 05 81 81
Fax 01 44 05 81 82
The only "château-hôtel" in central Paris, this splendid 19th-century neo-classical residence offers a flower-filled garden, pretty fountain, magnificent listed stone staircase and a cosy, very British bar-cum-library. On the top floor, the rooms, which have private terraces, are set out around a glass roof. Fitness center and sauna. Restaurant.
29 suites: €570–730
19 rooms: €340–470

Crillon
◆ 1 G4
10, place de la Concorde 75008
Tel. 01 44 71 15 00
Fax 01 44 71 15 02
This palace prides itself on being among the most beautifully decorated of its kind, with its painted paneling, parquet floors from Hungary, Baccarat crystal chandeliers and Flemish tapestries. It also boasts a huge suite (not less than 1,320 foot square) situated on the 5th floor, with panoramic views over the Seine. Guerlain beauty center on the

L'ATELIER MONTPARNASSE

premises.
57 suites: €1,100–13,850
90 rooms: €575–855

Costes
◆ **2** A4
239, rue Saint-Honoré 75001
Tel. 01 42 44 50 00
Fax 01 42 44 50 01
Someone wrote of this hotel "Super fashionable designer hotel in eclectic French Empire brothel style". See for yourself. It is an unusual hotel arranged around a lovely Italian-style patio and much loved by the trendy set. The bedrooms and common rooms are decorated in a mixture of oriental, Empire or baroque styles. There are private terraces and a fitness center with vaulted-roofed snf swimming-pool. A well-known DJ manages the music in the evening in the restaurant and bar (there are now four volumes of "Hotel Costes" music CDs). The whole place feels cozy though, and would be the right destination for honeymooning trendsetters.
4 suites: €500–1,400
78 rooms: €350–400

Meurice
◆ **1** I4
228, rue de Rivoli 75001
Tel. 01 44 58 10 10
Fax 01 44 58 10 15
This palace, surrounded by its winter garden, topped with a magnificent Art Nouveau glass roof, seems to have rediscovered its past. Many of its original features have been restored, mostly in the Louis XVI or Empire style. Views over the Tuileries,

the Louvre and the Champs-Élysées.
36 suites: €1,250–10,000
124 rooms: €600–1,150

Westminster
◆ **1** J3
13, rue de la Paix 75002
Tel. 01 42 61 57 46
Fax 01 42 60 30 66
Entirely refurbished by Pierre Rochon, the suites of this former cloistered convent between L'Opéra and the place Vendôme feature bronze clocks and Louis XV marquetry furniture. Fitness center.
21 suites: €950–2,500
80 rooms: €420–900

Banville
◆ **9** B6
166, boulevard Berthier 75017
Tel. 01 42 67 70 16
Fax 01 44 40 42 77
The Lambert family have run the Banville for three generations. All the rooms are beautifully decorated and have an individual charm. Particularly recommended is the Théodore de Banville room, although the Amélie room and the Marie suite certainly have their followers. A lovely atmosphere pervades the whole house.
1 suite: €250
37 rooms: €132–187

Hôtel Chopin
◆ **2** B1
46, passage Jouffroy (entrance at 10 bd Montmartre) 75009
Tel. 01 47 70 58 10
This is a small hotel hidden away at the end of the pretty Passage Jouffroy, a lovely old-fashioned covered walkway with small

boutiques, and close to the Grands Boulevards. The rooms, recently redone, are comfortable, light, attractive and very quiet as they do not give onto the street but onto the passageway. Those ending with number 7 are the best, as well as 409, 310 and 412.
From €110

Hôtel Langlois
◆ **9** I10
63, rue Saint-Lazare 75009
Tel. 01 48 74 78 24
The former Hôtel des Croisés was built as a bank in 1870 and red carpets lead to the superb retro-style reception and the old elevator with a wrought-iron gate. The rooms are very spacious, fitted out with handsome period-style furniture, some with marble fireplaces and wood paneling. Those on the first and second stories are larger but from the 5th or 6th stories you have lovely views over the rooftops and the Sacré Cœur (rooms 62 and 63). The hotel changed its name in 2002 after being used as a set for the French movie Langlois. The address is not a well-kept secret any more – book well ahead.
27 room: from €110

Scribe
◆ **1** I2
1, rue Scribe 75009
Tel. 01 44 71 24 24
Fax 01 42 65 39 97
Experience elegance and the height of luxury in this Haussmann-designed hotel. The rooms are decorated in Louis-Philippe or Second Empire style, the best among them being elegant suites

featuring mahogany décor.
11 suites: €900-1,152
206 rooms: €335-518

Hotel de Noailles
◆ **2** A2
9, rue de la Michodière 75002
Tel. 01 47 42 92 90
Fax 01 49 24 92 71
Situated just 100 yards from the Place de l'Opéra, this hotel is surprisingly quiet and has great charm. Most of the rooms – all newly refurbished and designed in a sober modern style reminiscent of Philippe Starck's – overlook the central courtyard, and 10 of them have private terraces. There is a library and a Petit Salon decorated with contemporary furniture, exotic woods and warm tones. In fine weather you can sit outside in the Japanese Garden and terrace.
61 rooms, 5 suites: €165–250

Au Relais du Louvre
◆ **2** C6
19, rue des Prêtres Saint-Germain-l'Auxerrois 75001
Tél. 01 40 41 96 42
Fax 01 10 41 96 44
The former Café Momus, once frequented by Voltaire, Victor Hugo and Puccini, today contains rooms in Louis-Philippe style with views over St-Germain-L'Auxerrois and the Louvre.
3 suites: €205–380
18 rooms: €99–180

Bretonnerie
◆ **2** F6
22, rue Sainte-Croix-de-la Bretonnerie 75004

The letters and figures (e.g. ◆ 1 G3) give grid references for the maps at the end of the guide.

Tel. 01 48 87 77 63
Fax 01 42 77 26 78
This old hotel, characteristic of the 17th century, with lovely lounge and bedrooms, fits in perfectly with the spirit of the Marais. Room number 1 is the nicest of the lot.
7 suites: €180–230
22 rooms: €110–145

Hotel du Bourg-Tibourg
◆ 2 F7
19, rue du Bourg-Tibourg 75004
Tel. 01 42 78 47 39
Fax 01 40 29 07 00
Hailed as one of the most charming hotels in Paris, the Bourg Tibourg (formely Rivoli-Notre Dame) was completely renovated in 2002 and refurbished by Jacques Garcia. The rooms are comfortable, cozy and romantic in style (especially those in the attic), and decorated in the warm, Moorish tones of an oriental palace. Interior garden. A fine hotel in a fascinating area of Paris.
31 rooms: €200–350

Hotel Caron de Beaumarchais
◆ 2 G6
12, rue Vieille-du-Temple 75004
Tel. 01 42 72 34 12
Fax 01 42 72 34 63
www.caronde
beaumarchais.com
Beaumarchais, the author of The Marriage of Figaro, lived at no.47 rue Vieille-du-Temple, and some of his letters are displayed on the hotel's wall. The hotel is in the style of an 18th-century bourgeois town house; the rooms are large and comfortable, decorated with pretty wall fabrics and curtains, hand-

painted tiles in the bathroom, gilded mirrors and beams on the ceilings. All rooms are sound-proofed and have air conditioning.
19 rooms: from €122

Hôtel Jeanne d'Arc
3, rue de Jarente 75004
Tel. 01 48 87 62 11
Fax 01 48 87 37 31
◆ 2 G7 (NOT MARKED)
This attractive stone-built 17th-century hotel is on the corner of a quiet, pretty street off the Place des Vosges in the Marais. It has been decorated with the works of artists who are regulars to the hotel so there are frescoes in the dining room and a bizarre and a huge, outrageous, mirror which has pride of place in the small reception. The rooms vary in size but most are fairly spacious, light, and comfortable. The area can be quite noisy so ask to be on the higher stories. The staff are friendly and pleasant, the hotel is inexpensive, and the area is one of the best in Paris: you have to book months ahead.
From €120

Pavillon de la Reine
◆ 2 H7
28, place des Vosges 75003
Tél. 01 40 29 19 19
Fax 01 40 29 19 20
www.pavillon-de-la-reine.com
With its heavy scarlet and gold fabrics, walls densely interlaced with beams, Louis XIII furniture, and wrought-iron four-poster beds, this former residence of Catherine de Medici has an irresistible charm. The hotel's

position and flower-filled courtyards assure it a precious tranquillity.
25 suites: €590–720
30 rooms: €335–375

Hôtel du Vieux Saule
◆ 2 G4 (NOT MARKED)
6, rue de Picardie 75003
Tel. 01 42 72 01 14
In a quiet street of the Marais and a 10-minute walk away from the Pompidou center, this beautiful hotel is easily identifiable from its flower-covered façade. It dates back to 1830 and was built where the seat of the Order of the Templars used to be. The rooms are comfortable, modern with air conditioning and free sauna. Breakfast is served in the vaulted cellars. Small garden and exhibition of antiques in the prudly displayed "high-tech" lobby.
31 rooms: € 91–121

BASTILLE

Beaumarchais
◆ 2 H5
3, rue Oberkampf 75011
Tel. 01 53 36 86 86
Fax 01 43 38 32 86
A former architect has skilfully refurbished this hotel, a neighbor of the Cirque d'Hiver. It is endowed with a flower-filled patio, and colorful contemporary bedrooms.
2 suites: €120–130
29 rooms: €59–100

Nouvel Hôtel
◆ 3 E10
24, av. du Bel-Air 75012
Tel. 01 43 43 01 81
Fax 01 43 44 64 13
This former annexe of a girls' boarding school is a wonderful place. The delightful

little bedrooms are decorated in Laura Ashley fabrics, and there's a lovely garden which some of the rooms overlook. The owners are very obliging.
28 rooms: €60–93

MONTMARTRE

Ermitage Hôtel
◆ 10 C5
24, rue Lamarck 75018
Tél. 01 42 64 79 22
Fax 01 42 64 10 33
There is only a small number of rooms in this old, typically Napoleon III-style hotel which has been run by the Canipel family for decades. The rooms with beamed ceilings, decorated with English fabrics and boasting a terraced garden and vines behind, are the most in demand. No televisions.
12 rooms: €74–124

TROCADÉRO/ PORTE MAILLOT

Le Pergolèse
◆ 8 I4
3, rue Pergolèse 75016
Tel. 01 53 64 04 04
Fax 01 53 64 04 40
www.hotelpergolese.com
A resolutely contemporary style by Rena Dumas, and carpets and fabrics specially created by Hilton McConnico; Bang & Olufsen television in all rooms. The interior combines mahogany doors with chrome highlights, pale ash furniture in the pastel-colored rooms and cheerful accessories in gold yellow, apricot, royal blue, green or deep red. The rooms are sound-proofed and air-conditioned.
40 rooms: €195–350

◆ RESTAURANTS

The prices listed for both menus and à la carte do not include wine.
Unless otherwise indicated, all restaurants accept credit cards.
Unless otherwise stated, lunch is served noon–2.30pm, dinner 7.30–10.30pm.

Restaurants are listed alphabetically within the following categories:

GASTRONOMIC STARS

Among the very best France has to offer.

Alain Ducasse Restaurant Plaza Athénée
◆ **1** D4
25, av. Montaigne
75008
Tel. 01 53 67 65 00
Open for lunch Thur.–Fri., diner Mon–Fri.
If you want to be bowled over, the Plaza Athénée is the palace to come to. The seemingly unstoppable super-chef with a politician's drive – Alain Ducasse – opened this three-star restaurant in September 2000, in one of France's most prestigious hotels. His aim is to bring absolute excellence and elegance to the table. And of course being Mr Ducasse, he's done it. Memorable langoustines with caviar, Brittany turbot cooked in chestnut leaves and served with autumnal mushrooms, a wonderfully aromatic and lightly spiced lamb tian, are some of the delights on the menu. Perfect service.
€200–250

L'Ambroisie
◆ **2** H4
9, place des Vosges
75004
Tel. 01 42 78 51 45
Open Tue.–Sat.
Discretion is the key word in this restaurant, where famous people dine away from the crowds. Bernard Pascaud, unlike most of the three-star chefs in France, hates being talked about. You'll see no photos of him shaking hands with various heads of state for example. However, he once gave an hour-long television interview that was so moving one had to fight back the tears. Pascaud is a perfectionist. Each individual vegetable is perfectly peeled and shaped, the food placed with precision on the plates, the 12 tables themselves laid as if for royalty. There are no clever uses of trendy ingredients but pure classicism shines through with absolute brilliance. The terrine de foie gras de canard aux épices with a quince chutney has become an all-time favorite, as has the perfectly roasted poulette de Bresse au beurre de romarin citronné, purée de persil (Bresse chicken with rosemary and lemon butter sauce and parsley purée). You leave having spent a highly civilized moment – a feeling that one rarely gets nowadays.
€170–260

L'Arpège
◆ **1** G7
84, rue de Varenne
75007
Tel. 01 45 51 47 33
Open Mon.–Fri.
Alain Passard got his third Michelin star a few years ago. This young and extremely inventive chef was the first to treat vegetables as if they were caviar – and charge as if they were as well! He manages to conjure up astonishing flavors and textures from a carrot, a couple of leeks and a black radish. Although recently he has let an outstanding lobster, and occasionally even a young pigeon from the Landes region, back on the menu. Mainly their presence is to underline the fragrance and finesse of his ultra-fresh vegetables. Favorites include a light carrot soup cooked with verbena, and a

The letters and figures (e.g. ◆ 1 G3) give grid references for the maps at the end of the guide.

fabulous dish simply entitled Collection de légumes: *tender vegetables cooked in liquorice. The classic house dessert is la tomate farcie aux douze saveurs, with an interesting play between touches of acidity and the ripeness of the stuffed tomato. With such complex, unique dishes, it's best to follow the advice of the inspired wine waiters.*
€260–400

Carré des Feuillants
◆ 1 I4
14, rue de Castiglione
75001
Tel. 01 42 86 82 82
Open Mon.–Fri.
Alain Dutournier has a number of passions apart from his kitchens: one is his native Gascony where he spends most week-ends in fall "à la chasse". Nobody knows better than he how to choose and cook game – it's part of his upbringing. His other great passion is wine – his wine list doesn't read like a snob's guide to wine, but like a book full of wonderful temptations. There are even a few unusual bottles served by the glass, to help his clientele become a little more adventurous. But back to the kitchen: dishes emerge that are each more tempting than the last: venison pâté en croûte with foie gras, wood-pigeon cooked on embers, roast guinea-fowl with a fricassée of asparagus and purple artichokes, peaches served up roasted with pepper, and also iced with rose water. These

meals are delicious moments of happiness!
€100–200

Lucas Carton
◆ 1 H2
9, place de la Madeleine
75008
Tel 01 42 65 22 90
Open Tue.–Fri. lunch and dinner; Mon., Sat. dinner only
In his exquisite original Art Nouveau restaurant, Alain Senderens has refined to an art the difficult task of marrying specific dishes to a wine. With every one of his dishes comes a recommended wine, sourced from some of the best wine producers in the world. These wines can be ordered by the glass. No other top restaurant carries out such intensive matching, making sure that the food and wine work harmoniously together. Senderens continues to be amazingly active and creative in his kitchen. Some of his dishes are inspired from royal recipes in past centuries, others stay closer to regional cooking and the seasons such as polenta with white truffles, or the duck roasted in honey and spices. Senderens is also a great cigar lover, giving yet more clever matching between wines and cigars.
€180–285

The tastiest food from different regions of France.

L'Ambassade d'Auvergne
◆ 2 E5 (NOT MARKED)
22, rue du Grenier-St-Lazare

75003
Tel 01 42 72 31 22
Open daily
Untouched by minimalist designers, this rustic house groans under the weight of hams hanging from the beams. Françoise Petrucci, who worked with her father for 30 years, has now taken over the restaurant and continues to promote specialties from the Auvergne: exceptional jambon de pays, saucisson, Puy lentils served as a warm salad, cabbage and Roquefort soup (sounds awful but is amazing), Salers beef, chestnut boudin. The dish which must be tasted is the aligot – creamy mashed potatoes mixed with melted Tomme cheese served by the cook with panache. Then there are of course the splendid spread of local cheeses. The only thing one could miss out on are the desserts, but then again…
€30–45

Au Bascou
◆ 2 E4
38, rue Réaumur
75003
Tel. 01 42 72 69 25
Open Mon.–Fri.
Jean-Guy Lousteau is a genuinely generous person. The helpings at his Basque restaurant are also wonderfully generous, to such an extent that it is advisable to dine here at the beginning of your stay in Paris when your appetite is still keen! Almost everything on his menu (including the wines) comes from small producers in the Basque country: the anchovies

prepared in a mille-feuille, the juicy tender veal, the wild duck. Most dishes are spiced up with the local piment d'Espelette. The Basque cheese is served with the traditional black cherry jam.
€30–40

Maison de l'Aubrac
◆ 1 D3
37, rue Marbeuf
75008
Tel. 01 43 59 05 14
Open daily
This address is essential if (a) you like red meat and (b) your flight arrives in Paris at some awful time at night. Open all the time, this restaurant specializes in food from the Auvergne: charcuterie du pays, pot-au-feu, a sizeable côte de bœuf for two, aligot (see above L'Ambassade d'Auvergne). An interesting choice of wines from the Languedoc-Roussillon.
€25–46

Le Quincy
◆ 2 J9
28, av. Ledru-Rollin
75012
Tel. 01 46 28 46 76
Open Tue.–Fri.
Let it be clearly stated: this restaurant is not for the faint-hearted. The patron can't stand customers with small appetites and he never takes credit cards! In this kitsch bistro beyond the Bastille, the faithful flock, ready to put up with the patron's moods, tie their napkins around their necks and tuck into the generous cassoulet au confit d'oie, the fricassée de volaille, the traditional stuffed cabbage. When it's

time to ask for the bill, "Bobosse" the owner usually serves "on the house" a generous glass of eau de vie de prune, equivalent, according to him, to the percentage the credit card companies would charge.
€65–80. Credit cards not accepted.

Le Régalade
♦ **6** H7
49, av. Jean Moulin 75014
Tel. 01 45 45 68 58
Open Mon.–Fri. lunch and dinner, Sat. dinner only
For over ten years La Régalade has remained the *favorite eating place for Parisian gourmets. It all started when Yves Camdeborde left the kitchens of a starred restaurant because he was fed up with simply doling out spoons of caviar on every dish. He opened up a small restaurant dedicated to authentic cooking, on a most untrendy edge of the 14th arrondissement. Ever since, the restaurant is full all the time (book at least three weeks in advance – longer than is needed for the three-star restaurants). His secret certainly has nothing to do with the location, or the décor, or the seating! It lies in the exceptional quality of Camdeborde's cooking. The influence comes of course from his native province, the Béarn, in southwest France. The menu changes constantly. Favorites include coquilles St-Jacques (scallops) roasted in their shells with black olives and* seaweed, parmentier de boudin noir *(black pudding),* cassoulet made with the rare haricots Tarbais *(delicious white beans). The wine list is interesting and incredibly reasonably priced. There is one big drawback – the desserts too good to refuse.*
€30–45

Au Trou Gascon
♦ **4** D3
40, rue Taine 75012
Tel. 01 43 44 34 26
Open Mon.–Fri.
This is where you'll get the best cassoulet *in town. Here you are in the southwest of France, the heart of "gourmand-land", the land of foie gras, roast game, ceps and armagnac. The restaurant has shed its more "ethnic" look and gone in for a grey and white décor, but the chef's exceptional talent and flourish are untouched.*
€35–65

TREND
Without a doubt the places to be seen in.

Bon 2
♦ **2** A2
2, rue du Quatre Septembre 75002
Tel. 01 44 55 51 55
Open daily to midnight
This is the second Parisian restaurant opened by three partners including the French designer Philippe Starck and the talented chef Jean-Marie Amat. You can sit on one of the seven steel stools and have a quick meal at the white-tiled bar, or enter the comfortable dining room with an almost English club atmosphere to it. There is food for the open-minded such as tuna with peanut and coffee sauce, but also food as good as home cooking used to be – such as roast chicken with thick-sliced french fries. Bon 2 is open for breakfast, lunch, tea, cocktails and dinner. The first-class patisserie comes from Ladurée.

Hotel Costes
♦ **1** I3
239, rue St-Honoré 75001
Tel. 01 42 44 50 00
Open daily to 1am
If you want to be seen, this is where to go. French food critics tend to advise to drop by for a drink and thus avoid the dangers of being "tainted" by world cuisine. But in fact the food is surprisingly good. There's something for everyone on the menu. "Just a glass of freshly pressed carrot juice" for the slimmest of the slim (plenty of them around); a copious dish of fresh steam-cooked vegetables for the non-meat eaters; and for the plain old-fashioned (not many of them around), roasted duck foie gras, followed by a wickedly soft chocolate cake. In the summer, dine outside in the Tuscan courtyard atmosphere. There's even a touch of a Moroccan souk ambience.
€35–75

Spoon, Food and Wine
♦ **1** D3
14, rue de Marignan 75008
Tel. 01 40 76 34 44
Open Mon.–Fri.
Another one of Alain Ducasse's brilliant ideas that attracts people who don't like to be tied down with the weight of tradition (see also Plaza Athénée p. 462 and Au Lyonnais p. 467). The base products are of top quality. It's up to you to decide on what goes with what. Your sole can be served with lemon, a Béarnaise sauce or be eaten with chopsticks and wok-cooked vegetables. Put simply, you become the composer of this fusion food: just do what you want! You can even end your meal with a bubble-gum flavor ice-cream.
€60–80

FABULOUS VIEWS AND LISTED INTERIORS
Restaurants with exceptional views or surroundings and… good food.

Café Marly
♦ **1** J5
Palais du Louvre Richelieu wing 93, rue de Rivoli 75001
Tel. 01 49 26 06 60
Open daily to 2am
Try to grab an outside table along the colonnade in the Louvre, overlooking the Louvre courtyard and Pei's glass pyramid. There's a wonderful forceful Parisian yet also Italian, feel to the place. The Costes brothers (who now own 25 eating places in Paris) run this café with flair and efficiency. The food is perfectly decent, and the clientele a good mixture of business people unwinding, chic Parisians and tourists.
€20–40

Le Chalet des Iles
◆ **8** E5
Lac du Bois de
Boulogne
75016
Tel. 01 42 88 04 69
Last boat crossing to
the island 10.30pm
Closed Sun. evenings
*You have to take a
little boat (1 minute
ride) to reach an
uninhabited island
in the middle of the
Bois de Boulogne.
In the summer the
restaurant spreads
out onto various
terraces, but in the
winter meals are
served in the original
chalet where a
blazing fire burns.
Whatever the
season, the
exceptional setting
makes for a lovely
break from cars and
monuments. The
restaurant has
recently been
bought out, and the
new chef is a
definite
improvement
on the last.*
€50–60

Clown Bar
◆ **2** H5 (NOT MARKED)
114, rue Amelot
75011
Tel. 01 43 55 87 35
Open Mon.–Sat.
lunch and dinner to
1am, Sun. lunch only
*The décor of this
enchanting original
Art Nouveau bistrot,
next to the circus, is
entirely dedicated
to life at the circus.
The clever selection
of off-the-beaten-
track wines, no
doubt helps kick
up a lively ambience
till late at night. The
presence of circus
artists helps too!
The small kitchen
turns out tasty
traditional dishes
such as bœuf aux
carottes, or the
poelée de foie de
canard au Rivesaltes
(duck liver pan-fried
with Muscat wine)
See also Bars p475.*
€20–30

Georges
◆ **2** E6
Place Georges
Pompidou
75004
Tel 01 44 78 12 33
Closed Tue.
Last orders midnight
*This is another of the
Costes' dining places
(see also Hotel
Costes p. 464 and
Café Marly p. 464).
And what a
spectacular place it
is. Right on the top
of the Pompidou
Center, it embraces
Paris. The food is
light, such as
carpaccio with
roquette, steamed
vegetables, the sort
of food trendy girls
seem to grow tall
and thin on. It is
constantly full so
book well in
advance. It's best
to double-check
on the day of the
reservation: if the
museum staff
happen to be on
strike, the restaurant
is sometimes forced
to close.*
€35–60

Le Grand Véfour
◆ **1** I4
17, rue de Beaujolais
75001
Tel. 01 42 96 56 27
Open Mon.–Thur.
lunch and dinner,
Fri. lunch only
*Pleasure and
sophistication
mingle in this, surely
the most beautiful
restaurant in Paris,
dating back to 1784.
Wonderfully rich gilt
Directoire interior,
plush red velvet
banquettes and staff
who quickly put you
at ease. The chef,
Guy Martin, has
earned his three
stars with classic
favorites such as
ravioles de foie gras
with cream of truffle
sauce and the*

LE GRAND VÉFOUR

LE TRAIN BLEU

*famous Pigeon
Prince Rainier III. The
selection of cheeses
is particularly good
and there are always
imaginative desserts,
such as the one
made with
artichokes.*
Lunch set menu
€72 excl. wine.
Dinner €200–250

Le Jules Vernes
◆ **1** A6
2nd Floor,
Tour Eiffel
Champs de Mars
75007
Tel. 01 45 55 61 44
Open daily
*The ride up to
dizzying heights in
a private lift, the
modern décor and
of course the most
stupendous 360°
view of Paris are
already quite a lot to
take in. Then comes
the astonishing
menu where choices
are difficult to make,
they all sounds so
enticing. Alain Reix
continues, with
tremendous flair, to
create delicious
dishes such as the
extremely subtle
tartare of
langoustines, the
skewer of coquilles
St-Jacques, the classic
foie gras en terrine
or the guinea fowl
from Challans with
its crispy potatoes
and foie gras cake.
The cheese trolley
has a wide selection
of pungent French
cheeses; the desserts
end on a lighter
note, such as the
rose ice-cream. Book
well in advance.*
Lunch set menu €50
excl wine; à la carte
€110–150

Au Petit Riche
◆ **2** B1
25, rue Le Peletier
75009
Tel. 01 47 70 68 68
Open Mon.–Sat.
lunch and evening to
12.30am
*This restaurant used
to be the rendez-*

◆ RESTAURANTS

The letters and figures (e.g. ◆ 1 G3) give grid references for the maps at the end of the guide.

vous for thirsty coachmen when it opened in 1880. The décor has remained untouched, with walk-through dining rooms, rather like a railway coach, and lots of brass and mirrors and chandeliers. The Petit Riche has always remained faithful to Loire wines and food: rillons (pork belly cooked in lard), filet de sandre (zander fillet) cooked in Vouvray, gelinette de Touraine (a recently rediscovered variety of particularly delicious chicken), all classic dishes that go well with a Chinon or a Saumur-Champigny. The restaurant also has a very good selection of oysters, including the famous Gillardau oysters.
€30–40

Le Train Bleu
◆ 2 I10
Gare de Lyon
75012
Tel. 01 43 43 09 06
Open daily to 11pm
The fabulous interior of this restaurant above the Gare de Lyon, with its 1880 rococo frescoes portraying the journey in those days from Paris to the Mediterranean, is a pure delight. The well spaced-out tables are an invitation to take your time over your meal. The chef, André Signoret, has worked in the top kitchens in Paris. He creates with flair great French classics, such as foie gras de canard confit served with brioche and a fig marmalade, the côte de veau (a favorite here), the hare when in season, and the well-doused in rum baba.
€40–55

Le Ziryab
◆ 2 F9 (NOT MARKED)
Institut du Monde Arabe
1, rue des Fossés-St-Bernard
75005
Tel. 01 53 10 10 20
Open Tue.–Sat. lunch and dinner, Sun. lunch only
Perched on the top floor of the ultra-modern Institut du Monde Arabe, designed by Jean Nouvel, this Moroccan restaurant with colorful cooking offers fabulous views: Notre-Dame, l'Ile St- Louis and a stretch of the Seine. Fresh herbs and spices are used generously in the kitchen to create tasty Mediterranean/ oriental dishes such as tagines. As soon as it's warm enough the terrace is opened up.
€40–55

BISTROTS
Having previously turned their back on bistrot cooking, Parisians are now rediscovering the simple pleasures of homely cooking.

L'Assiette
◆ 6 H4
181, rue du Château
75014
Tel. 01 43 22 64 86
Closed Mon.–Tue.
For over twenty years, the well-known chef Lulu has transformed fabulously fresh ingredients into gastronomic delights. Prime ministers, fashion designers and the Left Bank intelligentsia have treated, over the years, this small but enchanting converted charcuterie as their Sunday evening canteen. The emphasis tends to

be on fish, but duck also figures on the menu, with the flavorful magret de canard an all-time favorite.
Lunch set menu €35 excl. wine;
à la carte €75–90

L'Avant–Goût
◆ 5 E6
26, rue Bobillot
75013
Tel. 01 53 80 24 00
Open Tue.–Fri.
The chef/owner worked in a number of three-starred restaurants before opening up on his own a few years ago. His imaginative cooking, with an unusual and subtle use of spices, and the excellent value, mean that this modern, brightly lit restaurant is always full. The menu is re-invented every three weeks, only the classic pot-au-feu de cochon aux épices stays on the blackboard throughout the year. Well chosen selection of small wineries.
€30–40

Bistrot Paul Bert
◆ 3 B8
18, rue Paul-Bert
75011
Tel. 01 43 72 24 01
Open Tue.–Sat..
This is the sort of bistrot one imagines Paris to be full of. But the truth is – "genuine ambience" such as found here, is hard to come by. Everything about this place is just right: the 1940's tiled floor, the long wooden bar where you can taste a selection of wines sourced from up-and-coming producers, the clientele who clearly very much enjoy food and drinking, and the patron. The menu changes

daily and includes bistrot classics such as a croustillant de pied de cochon (pig's trotter). The Paul Bert is slightly off the beaten track, but definitely worth the effort.
€25–35

Au Bon Accueil
◆ 1 B6
14, rue de Monttessuy
75007
Tel. 01 47 05 46 11
Open Mon.– Fri.
In the summer book early if you want a table on the pavement, with a particularly lovely view of the Eiffel Tower. The bistrot is chic, with a mixture of French and international clientele. The ultra-classic menu (no "clever" use of exotic spices or vegetables turned into desserts here) changes with the seasons. The all-time favorite – the côte de veau de lait, luscious melt-in-the mouth veal – is hard to beat.
€45–60

Le Café d'Angel
◆ 9 B9 (NOT MARKED)
16, rue Brey
75017
Tel. 01 47 54 03 33
Open Mon.–Fri.
Two minutes from the Place de L'Etoile, this small bistrot with its red banquettes and tiled walls, draws in a lively – gourmet – lunchtime crowd. The menu is short but original (squid with fresh herbs and gésiers de canard) and the dishes are attractively presented. Two delicious wines on the list are the exceptional white Macon Guillemet and the velvety red Cairanne Richaud.
€35–50

Café des Délices

◆ **1** J10
87, rue d'Assas
75006
Tel. 01 43 54 70 00
Open Mon.–Fri.
Gilles Choukroum, who has worked in various top restaurants, attracted French media attention when he opened this small restaurant just off the Luxembourg gardens. A light Moroccan flavor to the décor and the food, although it would seem that his inspiration is moving increasingly toward "world" cuisine.
€35–40

Aux Charpentiers

◆ **2** A8 (NOT MARKED)
10, rue Mabillon
75006
Tel. 01 43 26 30 05
Closed Sun. and public holidays
This is one of the old favorites in the quartier, and one of the last restaurants to have remained unchanged over the past hundred years. Classic bourgeois cooking such as célerie rémoulade, pâté de tête, roast chicken (now organic), and a traditional plat du jour such as pot-au-feu, that changes every day. The staff and owner have been there forever, adding to the nostalgic yet curiously delightful charm.
€30–40

Le Dirigeable

◆ **6** C3
37, rue d'Alleray
75015
Tel. 01 45 32 01 54
Open Tue.–Sat.
This little gem, a turn-of-the-century bistrot with wooden floors and mirrors on the walls, is full every day. Etienne, the patron, pours out glasses of chilled

beaujolais from Métras for his regular customers as they tuck into generous helpings of deliciously traditional, comforting bistrot dishes. What could be better?
€25–38

Fish

◆ **2** A8
69, rue de Seine
75006
Tel. 01 43 54 34 69
Open Tue.–Sun.
Owned by a wine-loving New Zealander, this cozy restaurant often gets listed in French guides as a fish restaurant. Indeed there is always a fair amount of fish on the menu, but the inspiration for the restaurant's name actually comes from the expression "drinks like a fish"! Great-value dishes with a light Mediterranean influence and a lovely selection of wines, a dozen available by the glass. The place is always full, with an international, fairly laid-back clientele. You can also eat at the bar.
Lunch set menu €20; à la carte €35

Flora

◆ **1** C3
36, av. Georges V
75008
Tel. 01 40 70 10 49
Open Mon.–Fri. lunch and dinner; Sat. dinner only
The young Flora first opened a much-acclaimed restaurant on the Left Bank where her inspiration came mainly from Provence. She has just moved to a grander neighborhood, and has decided to allow herself more freedom with her

creative cuisine: croustillant de crabe with aniseed, lobster risotto, roast turbot with artichokes and gnocci, fine tarte aux figues with almond milk ice cream. You hardly ever catch a glimpse of Flora – she's always in her kitchen.
€35–70

Georgette

◆ **10** A9 (NOT MARKED)
29, rue St Georges
75009
Tel. 01 42 80 39 13
Open Mon.–Fri. lunch, and Thur., Fri. dinner
This recently opened 1940's-style bistrot is run by the contagiously generous and enthusiastic Marie-Odile. Her dishes are original – she often uses unusual salads and vegetables – and cleverly prepared, combining originality with her good common sense of home cooking. Get there before it becomes the trendy lunchtime venue.
€30–35

Aux Lyonnais

◆ **2** B2 (NOT MARKED)
32, rue St Marc
75002
Tel. 01 42 96 65 04
Open Tue.–Fri. lunch and dinner; Sat. dinner only
This is Alain Ducasse's very latest restaurant (see also Plaza Athénée p. 462 and Spoon, Food and Wine p. 464). It's very frustrating because with Ducasse, food critics can't find anything to criticize. With this bistrot he has moved away from the land of the classic three stars and the trendy minimalists to get closer to the "terroir". A very professional busy bistrot atmosphere,

serving local specialties such as charcuterie, frogs' legs, roast poultry and a wide range of wines from the Lyons/Rhône region. Dining rooms on two levels.
€28–40

Le Soleil

◆ OFF MAP, NORTH OF **10** C1
109, av. Michelet
93400 St Ouen
(métro Porte de Clignancourt)
Tel. 01 40 10 08 08
www.lesoleil.com.fr
Open daily for lunch, dinner Thur.–Sat.
Opened in 1999, on the edge of the St-Ouen flea market, this place has become the meeting point for weekend strollers looking for a bargain but also, for other restaurateurs eating out – always a sign that good food is served. Stall owners lunch here early, tucking in on the perfectly seasoned foie gras mi-cuit au torchon, the classic carré d'agneau, and the extravagant baba au rhum. (Don't forget this is the flea market, keep mobile phones and valuables out of sight.)
€40–50

La Table d'Hélène

◆ **1** I9
4, rue d'Assas
75006
Tel. 01 42 22 00 11
Open Tue.–Sat.
Hélène Darroze's grandfather, father and then herself ran a famous Michelin-starred restaurant in southwest France. Three years ago the young Hélène moved to Paris to open up on her own. There is a smart, expensive restaurant on the first floor. On the ground floor is a more relaxed atmosphere with an

◆ RESTAURANTS

extremely inventive tapas menu, as well as a more classic menu du jour. For a comfortable meal, book a table with a banquette and enjoy to the full the soft orange and purple velvet cushions while watching others sit upright on bar stools!
€40–65

Le Villaret
◆ 2 J4 (NOT MARKED)
13, rue Ternaux
75011
Tel. 01 43 57 89 76
Open noon–2pm, 7.30pm–1am (Mon. and Tue. to midnight). Closed Sat. lunch, all day Sun.
The owner opened this small bistrot in this untrendy neighborhood on purpose – it was his way of targeting the clientele he wanted. He figured that Parisians who really cared about food wouldn't mind crossing Paris. His marketing sense paid off. The chef, Olivier Gaslain, goes to the Rungis wholesale market at 3am to select the best seasonal produce. It is only when he is back in his kitchen with his ingredients laid out that he creates his recipes. The menu changes an amazing twice a day. The restaurant is full til late, the food is outstandingly good, the wines well chosen and reasonably priced.
Set menu €24; à la carte €50

BRASSERIES
These are wonderfully noisy places, full of atmosphere, where waiters rush around carrying tray loads of oysters and choucroute.

Bofinger
◆ 2 H8
5, rue de la Bastille
74004
Tel. 01 42 72 87 82
Open daily to 1am
The wonderful décor of this brasserie built in 1864 delights even the most blasé of Parisians. The chandeliers, glass dome, extravagant flower arrangements and the highly efficient waiters dressed in black and white, all contribute to the warm and incredibly busy brasserie atmosphere. Oysters, choucroute, steak tartare and pig's trotters are favorites here.
€30–50

Brasserie Balzar
◆ 2 E10
49, rue des Ecoles
75005
Tel. 01 43 54 13 67
Open daily to midnight
A great storm blew up a couple of years ago when the owners of La Coupole (see Cafés p473) bought this intimate, authentic 1920's brasserie. The Left Bank intellectuals – who treat this place as their canteen – drew up a petition. But nothing was to be done, the big "bad" group bought the small restaurant. The outcome? Before you never dared complain when you crunched your way through sand in the poorly washed leeks vinaigrette, your steak was overcooked, your chips cold. With the new owners the quality of the food has been hiked up, the waiters are the same, and the Left Bank intellectuals have returned.
€30–45

Brasserie de l'Ile St-Louis
◆ 2 E8 (NOT MARKED)
55, Quai de Bourbon
75004
Tel. 01 43 54 02 59
Open Thur.–Tue. to midnight
This friendly, family-run brasserie, with its rough wooden floors, dates back to the 19th century. It's always crowded, with a mixture of Parisians and foreigners ordering the house specialties: choucroute, coq au Riesling, onion tart, and tarte tatin with cream. As you step out of the brasserie, all you have to do is cross the bridge over the Seine, and you're at Notre-Dame.
€35–45

Chez Jenny
◆ 2 H4
39, bd du Temple
75003
Tel. 01 44 54 39 00
Open daily to 1am
This traditional Alsace brasserie, with its authentic early 20th-century wooden carvings, serves first and foremost de la choucroute. As you enter the brasserie, an imposing spit roasts suckling pigs. Wines and beers from Alsace flow freely.
€30–50

Closerie des Lilas
◆ 6 J2
171, Bd du Montparnasse
75006
Tel. 01 40 51 34 50
Open daily

This famous brasserie, with its wonderful piano bar where Hemingway used to hang out, has been bought out by the quality-conscious owner of the Café de Flore (see below Salads and Light Meals, and Cafés p472). The chef, thankfully, is new, the food much improved but prices are still steep. In the summer book outside.
€45–80

Flo
◆ 2 E2
7, cours des Petites Ecuries
75010
Tel. 01 42 46 15 80 or 01 47 70 13 59
Open daily to 1.30am
This is the first brasserie bought by Mr Bucher, who now owns eight of the most beautiful brasseries in Paris, including Julien, the Vaudeville, Bofinger and La Coupole (see Cafés p. 472). The owner has a soft spot for this place with its 1880's décor, its mirrors, wood paneling and banquettes. Oysters are eaten in great quantities, the plats du jour are classic such as dorade (sea bream) with fennel, suprême de volaille with softened leeks, and of course the formidable choucroute paysanne.
€28–50

Julien
◆ **2** E2
16, rue du Faubourg
St-Denis
75010
Tel. 01 47 70 12 06
Open daily to
1.30am
*Post-theater crowds
come to this
outstanding Art
Nouveau gem for
late-night dinners.
The classic menu
lists dishes such as
foie gras et crème
de porto, steak
béarnaise and
chocolate
profiteroles. The
service is friendly
and professional,
the atmosphere
great.*
€30–53

Lipp
◆ **1** J8
151, bd St Germain
75006
Tel. 01 45 48 53 91
Open daily to 1am
*This remains one of
the classic smart
brasseries of the Left
Bank. Lovely listed
Belle Epoque
interior. It used to
be that credit cards
were not accepted,
that tourists were
immediately
dispatched with
disdain to the
upstairs dining
room. Things have
changed a little,
foreigners are
sometimes allowed
to eat in the main
dining room where
left-wing politicians,
lawyers and the
press like to be seen.
Keep to the simple
things on the menu:
herring, faux-filet
and for dessert the
mille-feuille.*
€40–60

Terminus du Nord
◆ **10** D8
23, rue Dunkerque
75010
Tel. 01 42 85 05 15
Open daily to
12.30am
*If the Eurostar is
delayed, it's almost a
blessing. Pop across*

*the road and settle
down to a meal in
this welcoming
1930's brasserie
where the waiters
couldn't be more
friendly, helping
you settle down
and enjoy your
unexpected time
off. This restaurant,
part of the Bucher
group (see above),
offers classics such
as plateau de fruits
de mer, confit de
canard and île
flottante for dessert.
Try the fruity, well-
made wine from
Touraine, the
Domaine de la
Charmoise.*
€25–41

Le Vaudeville
◆ **2** B3
29, rue Vivienne
75002
Tel. 01 40 20 04 62
Open daily to 1am
*This brasserie has
got it just right: the
bustling atmosphere,
the waiters rushing
with trays of oysters
held high, the
original 1930's décor
and the potatoes
mashed with truffle
juice.*
€30–55

Wepler
◆ **9** I7
14, place Clichy
75018
Tel. 01 45 22 53 24
Open daily to 1am
*This privately-owned
brasserie was
opened 115 years
ago, but was entirely
redecorated in 1930.
Bustling atmosphere
with late-night
diners enjoying a
good selection of
oysters, blanquette
of veal and
andouillette.*
€30–35

FISH
*... of the freshest
sort!*

Le Cagouille
◆ **6** G3
10, place Brancusi
75014

Tel. 01 43 22 09 01
Open daily lunch
and dinner
*This fish restaurant
has never served
meat since it opened
20 years ago. Three
partners share the
running of the
restaurant, so it
therefore manages
to stay open every
day of the year. The
oysters are bred by
David Hervé, the
oyster farmer in
the Charentes.
The fish, cooked to
perfection, is served
with the most
delicate of sauces,
just enough to
reveal, or simply
underline, the fresh
sea flavors. The
restaurant claims
to have the largest
collection of cognacs
in France. Book a
table on the large
outdoor terrace as
soon as it is warm
enough.*
Set menu €38;
à la carte €55

Le Duc
◆ **6** J2
243, bd Raspail
75014
Tel. 01 43 20 96 30
Open Tue.–Fri. lunch
and dinner, Sat lunch
only
*This upmarket fish
restaurant, with its
deluxe cabin décor,
has been going
for 35 years. The
regular clientele
come here for its
truly exceptional
quality of fish and
they appear to be
prepared to pay
handsomely for it.
Jeanine Minchelli
puts a huge
emphasis on the
freshness of her
products, but she
also explains to us
how they travel from
the small fishing
ports. The oysters,
for example, must
never travel on ice,
only on seaweed.
Try the langoustines
with ginger, the
steam-cooked*

*turbot, the red
mullet flipped over
in olive oil.*
Lunch set menu €45
exc. wine;
à la carte €76–110

L'Ecailler du Bistrot
◆ **3** B8 (NOT MARKED)
22, rue Paul-Bert
75011
Tel. 01 43 72 76 77
Open Tue.–Sat. lunch
and dinner
*Gwenaëlle Cadoret
comes from Brittany,
where her father is
one of the last
remaining oyster
breeders to
specialize in the
"huître plate" – the
flat, native oyster.
Most brasseries serve
two types of oysters
in various sizes;
Gwenaëlle however
offers 10 different
types – Spéciale du
Belon, Pied the
Cheval, Papillon,
Spéciale Utah Beach
– each with its
distinctive flavor. It's
not surprising that
the city's real oyster
lovers converge
here. Seating is
often tight, but the
bistrot has just taken
over the next-door
premises which
should ease the
oyster rush hour! For
those who don't like
oysters, the bistrot
also serves fish,
direct, of course,
from Brittany.*
€30–35

Marius et Jeanette
◆ **1** C2
4, av. Georges V
75008
Tel. 01 47 23 41 88
Open daily
*The French media,
people in advertising
and actors all
congregate here to
escape from le stress
parisien and get a
soupçon of a
sensation that
they've had lunch in
Marseilles. As soon
as it's warm, the
outside tables are
booked up, white*

◆ RESTAURANTS

The letters and figures (e.g. ◆ 1 G3) give grid references for the maps at the end of the guide.

wine flows with the order for soupe de poisson, *crab, and tartare* of coquilles St-Jacques. *By the time the strawberry mille-feuille is ordered, afternoon business meetings may just as well be cancelled.*
€48–95

La Méditerranée
◆ **2** B8
2, place de l'Odéon
75006
Tel. 01 43 26 02 30
Open daily
This restaurant near the Luxembourg Gardens, with its original wall frescoes by Cocteau, its terrace looking onto a charming square and the Odeon theater, has had its ups and downs. It would seem that the new team have decided to pull it together and have put the emphasis back on fresh fish again. Try the red tuna tartare with olive oil, or the daurade royale with fragrant spices.
€30–42

SALADS AND LIGHT MEALS

A necessary breathing space before the next gastronomic experience.

L'Alcazar Mezzanine
◆ **2** B7
62, rue Mazarine
75006
Tel. 01 53 10 19 99
Open daily
noon–3pm and
7pm–2am
This renowned Parisian music hall was bought by Englishman Sir Terrance Conran a few years ago. There's a brasserie on the ground floor but it's more fun to be on the mezzanine level with a bar, dim lights and

comfortable seating around coffee tables. *The reasonably priced set menu at the bar includes a choice of a traditional dish (such as confit de canard) or a generous salad and a glass of wine. From 10.30pm Wednesdays through Saturdays there's a DJ – food is then no longer served.*
€25–40

A Priori Thé
◆ **2** B3
35–37, Galerie
Vivienne
75002
Tel. 01 42 97 48 75
Open Mon.–Fri
9am–6pm,
Sat. 9am–6.30pm,
Sun. noon–6.30pm
Walk through the Palais Royal to reach one of the most beautiful passageways in Paris. This salon de thé, which also serves a couple of well chosen wines, is fully booked every lunchtime with fashion-conscious Parisians delighted with Peggy Hancock's generous helpings of inventive salads. As soon as it's warm enough, book a table outside. Brunch served at the weekend.
€25–30

Café de Flore
◆ **1** I7
172, bd St Germain
75006
Tel. 01 45 48 55 26
Open daily to
1.30am
The whole point of the Flore is to watch Paris life go by. If you want the Flore with more Parisians than tourists, your only hope is to get there for an early breakfast. The food, served all day and night, is simple and delicious, such as

croque monsieur and salade niçoise.
€30–40

Emporio Armani Caffè
◆ **1** J8
149, bd St Germain,
75006
Tel. 01 45 48 62 15
Open Mon.–Sat.
noon–6pm and
8–10.30pm
This is one of the very few places in France where you can try the ultra–rare jambon de pays Culatello di Zibello. All the produce (tomatoes included) are delivered direct from Italy where you obsessively carefully selected producers, so that even the basic pasta with tomato and basil sauce hits perfection. The clientele – definitely fashion victim – seems quite happy to eat on the somewhat squashed-up mezzanine level, overhanging the entrance of the Armani shop. Food served all afternoon.
€30–45

Westminster Hotel Bar
◆ **1** J3
13, rue de la Paix
75002
Tel. 01 42 61 57 46
When shopping near the Opéra it's worth knowing that there's a quiet haven for lunch at the bar of the Westminster Hotel. In this comfortable English club atmosphere, the lunch menu includes a starter or a main course, a glass of wine and a dessert. Discrete service.
Lunch set menu €27

WINE BARS

Don't forget we are in France – good wines are not enough, the food has to be delicious as well.

Le Baratin
◆ **3** B1 (NOT MARKED)
3, rue Jouye-Rouve
75020
Tel. 01 43 49 39 70
Open Tue.–Fri. and
Sat. evening
In this almost guaranteed tourist-free zone is a small, authentic, no-frills wine bar, with an incredible range of unusual wines. The tasty home cooking is just right. This is one of the capital's few interesting wine bars, where people tend to linger late into the night.
€20–25 plus wine

Café de la Nouvelle Mairie
◆ OFF MAP, SOUTH OF **2** C10
19–21, rue des
Fossés St-Jacques
75005
Tel. 01 44 07 04 41
Open Mon.–Fri.
9am–10pm; dinner
Tue. and Thur. only
Just behind the Panthéon is a charming little square – a fast food-free enclave of the Latin Quarter. At the slightest ray of sun, book a table for lunch outside, as a micro-climate seems to bless this wine bar. Really interesting lesser-known wines, top-quality saucissons secs, simple yet delicious plats du jour (tagine of lamb with lemon) and home-made tarts for dessert. The staff are genuinely jolly and enthusiastic – which is unusual in Paris.
€20–30. Credit cards not accepted

Caves Petrissans
◆ **9** B7
30bis, av. Niel
75017
Tel. 01 42 27 52 03
Open Mon.–Fri.
French food critics love this 1900 bistro: not only is there a fantastic selection of wines (800

references), but equally important serious, classic, old-fashioned cooking goes on here. The wine can be ordered either from the small wine list, or you can browse round the annexe wine shop and pick up your choice from the shelf. A €16 corkage fee is charged. €30–50

Juveniles
◆ **2** A4
47, rue de Richelieu
75001
Tel. 01 42 97 46 49
Open Mon.–Sat.
Despite many decades spent in France, Englishman Tim Johnston remains staunchly un-Frenchified. His small wine bar/shop serves a wide range of Tuscan, Spanish and Australian wines and a very reduced selection of French wines. However

those that do get on his list are truly exceptional, like the Château de Roquefort, a bio-dynamic Côtes de Provence. The evening clientele tends to be young, in this chummy, almost pub-esque ambience. Tapas, andouillette with mashed potatoes and Donald's chocolate cake are house favorites. €25–35

Le Rubis
◆ **1** J3 (NOT MARKED)
10, rue du Marché
St Honoré
75001
Tel. 01 42 61 03 34
Open Mon.–Fri.
Chilled Beaujolais for the very thirsty has been served for decades in this minute old-fashioned wine bar. The owner, Albert, is completely un-phased by the

trendiest of Paris fashion shops that have now taken over what used to be a very foodie neighborhood. He continues to serve rillettes. *Everything about this place is straightforward – plat du jour, dessert maison and a short, uncomplicated wine list – therein lies its charm.* €20–30

Aux Tonneaux des Halles
◆ **2** D4
28, rue Montorgueil
75001
Tel 01 42 33 36 19
Open Mon.–Sat.
7.30am–11.30pm
You can drop in here at any time of day or evening for a plate of charcuterie and a refreshing glass of Beaujolais. The plats du jour, served at mealtimes only, are not for the faint-hearted:

kidneys, wild boar – dishes that cry out for voluptuous, lusty wines. Luckily Patrick Fabre has plenty of them: try the robust wines from the Languedoc-Roussilon. €20–30

Willy's Wine Bar
◆ **2** B3
13, rue des Petits
Champs
75001
Tel. 01 42 61 05 09
Open Mon.–Sat.
How many people over the past 20 years have discovered what real wine is about by sipping wines, by the glass, at the long wooden bar in this upmarket wine bar? The interesting menu sticks closely to the seasons (even for the cheeses), and the quality wine list contains rare gems. €45–50

◆ CAFÉS, TEAROOMS

The letters and figures (e.g. ◆ 1 G3) give grid references for the maps at the end of the guide.

CAFÉS

Bar Hemingway
◆ **1** I3
Hôtel Ritz
15, place Vendôme
75001
Tel. 01 43 16 30 30
Open Tue.–Sat.
6.30pm–2am
When Hemingway dreamt of life after death, he imagined himself at the Ritz, and was one of the first to help liberate it in 1944. The bar bearing his name has been extended. Another bar opens out onto a patio on summer evenings.

Café Beaubourg
◆ **2** E6
100, rue Saint-Martin
75004
Tel. 01 48 87 63 96
Open Sun.–Wed.
8am–1am,
Thu.–Sat. 8am–2am
A few steps from the Saint Phalle fountain and the Modern Art Museum. Sharp, elegant marble décor (passageway on mezzanine level), designed by Christian de Portzamparc. Pleasant terrace.

Colette Water Bar
◆ **1** J4
213, rue St-Honoré
75001
Tel. 01 55 35 33 90
Open Mon.–Sat.
10.30am–7.30pm.
Incredibly still in fashion six years after opening, this is the place to come to relax between heavy shopping sessions. In the basement of a fashion and design boutique, it offers 90 types of water served with the care and respect usually reserved for the best wine vintages. Plus fruit juices, snacks and patisseries.

Dokhan's
◆ **8** J7
Hôtel Trocadéro
Dokhan's
117, rue Lauriston
75016

Tel. 01 53 65 66 99
Open daily 6.30am–2am
Champagne bar with an open fire and candlelight in the evening. The best of its kind in Paris, serving more than 50 different types of champagne.

Le Fumoir
◆ **2** B5
6, rue de l'Amiral-de-Coligny 75001
Tel. 01 42 92 00 24
Open daily 11am–2am; Sun. brunch noon–3pm
Opulent yet simple décor, with large bay windows partly overlooking the Louvre colonnade. Trendy clientele.

Hôtel Lutétia
◆ **1** I9
45, bd Raspail 75006
Tel. 01 49 54 46 46
Open daily
9.30am–11pm
Every weekend, this luxury Left Bank hotel offers the opportunity to listen to a small jazz band in the Art Deco setting designed by Sonia Rykiel. Phone for details of times.

Jacquemart-André
◆ **9** E10
158, bd Haussmann
75008
Tel. 01 45 62 04 44
Open daily for lunch
11.45am–3pm
Afternoon tea
3–5.30pm; Sun.
brunch 11am–3pm
After a visit to the opulent Jacquemart-André museum, sit at the attractive terrace of its swanky café. The patisseries are excellent and it is a favorite among chic Parisian ladies.

Café Marly
◆ **1** J5
Palais du Louvre
Richelieu wing
93 rue de Rivoli
75001
Tel. 01 49 26 06 60
Open daily 8am–2am

Popular for its Louvre courtyard setting and its view of the glass pyramid. Secluded terrace under the arcades and some rooms lead into the French sculpture section of the Louvre. See also Restaurants p462.

Véry
◆ **1** I4
Jardin des Tuileries
75001
Tel. 01 47 03 94 84
Open daily
noon–9pm (last orders 7pm), summer noon–midnight
A favorite among the Louvre's visitors, park strollers and people working in the neighborhood. Pleasant spot under linden trees.

Virgin Café
◆ **1** D2
Virgin Megastore
52, av. des Champs-Élysées 75008
Tel. 01 49 53 50 00
Open Mon.–Sat.
10am–midnight,
Sun. noon–midnight
Located at the top of an impressive staircase worthy of this former bank. Fussy but friendly welcome.

The World Bar
◆ **9** I10
Le Printemps store
Rue de Provence
75009
Tel. 01 42 82 50 00
Open Mon.–Sat.
9.30am–7pm (until
9.30pm Thur.)
Decorated by British designer Paul Smith and located on the fifth story of the Printemps department store, this café-restaurant is a pleasant place to rest after a spot of shopping. For animation and techno enthusiasts, Level 1 offers quick muffins at the long table of Bar 01.

GREAT CLASSICS

Café de Flore
◆ **1** I7
172, bd St-Germain
75006
Tel. 01 45 48 55 26
Open daily
7.30am–1.30am
Regular clientele from the nearby publishing houses, as well as tourists who come to drink what is probably the most expensive expresso in one of the most legendary cafés in Paris. See also Restaurants p462.

CAFÉS, TEAROOMS ◆

Le Café de la Paix

◆ **1** J2

12, bd des Capucines 75009

Tel. 01 40 07 30 20

Open daily 10am–1.30am.

Designed by the same Charles Garnier who designed the Opéra Garnier opposite, the décor is pure 19th century. The covered terrace – the longest in Paris – looks onto the frantic traffic of the Place de l'Opéra.

La Closerie des Lilas

◆ **5** A2

171 Bd du Montparnasse 75014

Tel. 01 40 51 34 50

Open daily noon–1.30am

A dance hall in the 19th century where Zola and Cézanne came to fool around, the Closerie became the mecca of literary café society during the golden age of Montparnasse at the beginning of the 20th century. Lenin, Trotsky, the Surrealists, Hemingway all came here. The terrace, in summer, is a delight.

La Coupole

◆ **6** I1

102, bd du Montparnasse 75014

Tel. 01 43 20 14 20

Open daily 8.30am–1am.

When the Coupole brasserie was opened in 1927, the 1200 bottles of Mum champagne were not enough to quench the thirst of the 2500 guests! The name wittily refers to the neighboring bars La Rotonde and Le Dôme (at 105 and 108 Bd du Montparnasse), but there was of course no cupola in sight. The basement was dedicated to dancing and the ground floor to a brasserie. The fabulous décor is Art

Deco and you can still imagine the wild nights some spent in Montparnasse in the 1920s. There is still a nightclub in the basement, playing cha cha cha, paso doble but sometimes also house or garage.

Les Deux Magots

◆ **1** J7

6, pl. St-Germain-des-Prés 75006

Tel. 01 45 48 55 25

Open daily 7.30am–1am

The terraces are well located overlooking the beautiful church or the crossroads. The trays of cakes, presented at regular intervals, are very tempting, but watch out for the bill.

Le Fouquet's

◆ **1** C2

99, av. des Champs-Élysées 75008

Tel. 01 47 23 70 60

Open daily 8am–2am

Restaurant: open noon–3pm and 7.15pm–midnight. One of the most attractive terraces on the Champs-Élysées with a bourgeois and distinguished clientele.

CAFÉ MARLY

TEAROOMS

Angélina

◆ **1** I4

226, rue de Rivoli 75001

Tel. 01 42 60 82 00

Open daily 9.30am–6.45pm

Opened in 1903 under the arcades of the rue de Rivoli, Angelina is a Parisian institution. Classics, like the montblanc (meringue and chestnut cream), are served in a pleasant "Versailles" décor.

A Priori Thé

◆ **2** B3

35–37, galerie Vivienne 75002

Tel. 01 42 97 48 75

Open Mon.–Fri. 9am–6pm, Sat. 9am –6.30pm, Sun. noon–6.30pm

Quiet location in the Galerie Vivienne. Excellent teas, cakes and snacks. See also Restaurants p462.

La Fourmi Ailée

◆ **2** D8

8, rue du Fouarre 75005

Tel. 01 43 29 40 99

Open daily noon–midnight

Former bookshop specializing in

feminist literature, converted into a small snack bar. Books on the walls.

Ladurée

◆ **1** D2

75, av. des Champs-Élysées 75008

Tel. 01 40 75 08 75

Open daily 7.30am–12.30am

Restaurant open daily 7.30–11.30pm (teas at the bar). The uneven-numbered side of the Champs-Élysées is back in fashion. This second Ladurée tearoom was decorated by Jacques Garcia. Ladurée's trademark, the famous macaroons, come in 30 flavors that include rose petal and Guérande caramel, all served against a backdrop of stucco, gilt and marble. Genteel service. The original Ladurée, opened in 1865 as a bakery, is in Place de la Madeleine at 16, rue Royale (8th).

Le Loir dans la Théière

◆ **2** G7

3, rue des Rosiers 75006

Tel. 01 42 72 90 61

Mon.–Fri. 11.30am–7pm; Sat.–Sun. 10am–7pm

Light, warm tearoom in the Marais district, with comfortable old leather armchairs and a bohemian air. Patisseries, salads and savory tarts.

Mosquée de Paris

◆ **5** E2

39, rue Geoffroy-Saint-Hilaire 75005

Tel. 01 43 31 38 20

Open daily 9am–11.30pm

The central courtyard and Moorish lounges will take you into a different world. Oriental sweets and mint tea de rigueur.

◆ BARS

Under each heading addresses are listed according to districts.
The letters and figures (e.g. ◆ 1 G3) give grid references for the maps
at the end of the guide.

BARS

HALLES

Le Café Noir
◆ 2 C4
65, rue Montmartre
75002
Tel. 01 40 39 07 36
Open Mon.–Fri.
7.30am–2am,
Sat. 2.30pm–2am
*Quiet neighborhood
café during the day,
but quite lively in
the evening. Some
tables outside on
the terrace.*

Café Oz
◆ 2 D6
18, rue Saint-Denis
75001
Tel. 01 40 39 00 18
Open daily 3pm–2am
*Australian bar with
a 72-foot-long
counter. Rowdy,
mostly Anglo-Saxon
clientele.*

Le Comptoir
◆ 2 C5
14, rue Vauvilliers
75001
Tel. 01 40 26 26 66
*Dance floor until
4am Fri.–Sat. Bar
and restaurant daily
noon–2am
(3am Fri.–Sat.)
Large tapas bar
designed by
Jonathan Amar
(who also created
Les Bains) opposite
St-Eustache. It
becomes a mini
nightclub every
weekend and has
enjoyed undisputed
popularity for the
past seven years.
One of the best
places in the area.*

Le Sous-Bock
◆ 2 C5
49, rue Saint-Honoré
75001
Tel. 01 40 26 46 61
Open daily
11am–5am
*A must for those
who want to taste
some of the 400
types of beer on
offer here, including
Fischer from Alsace
and Lutèce from the
capital. Also owns
the store next door.*

The Frog and Rosbif
◆ 2 D4
116, rue Saint-Denis
75002
Tel. 01 42 36 34 73
Open daily
noon–1.30am
*A micro-brasserie
that brews its own
beer on site. As its
name indicates, this
place is an attempt
at uniting France
and Britain. Pub
atmosphere.
Brunch on Sun.*

MARAIS/RÉPUBLIQUE

La Belle Hortense
◆ 2 F6
31, rue Vieille-du-
Temple 75004
Tel. 01 48 04 71 60
Open daily 1pm–2am
*Bookstore-cum-
winebar in the heart
of the Marais.*

Le Clown Bar
◆ 2 H5
114, rue Amelot
75011
Tel. 01 43 55 87 35
Open noon–3pm
and 7pm–1am
Closed Sun. lunch.
*Excellent place with
a superb Art Deco
setting and a circus-
inspired décor (The
Cirque d'Hiver is
nearby). Cooked
meat platters, snacks
and daily specials are
served with côtes-
du-rhône wines.
Quite lively. See also
Restaurants p462.*

Satellit Café
◆ 2 I4
44, rue de la Folie-
Méricourt 75011
Tel. 01 47 00 48 87
Open Tue.–Thur.
8pm–3am (until
dawn Fri. and Sat.)
*Discotheque with
impeccable sound
and just about every
style of music from
rock, soul, jazz, to
French songs and
world music. A must
for true music lovers.*

Le Web Bar
◆ 2 G4
32, rue de Picardie
75003
Tel. 01 42 72 66 55

www.webbar.fr
Open Mon.–Fri.
8.30am–2am,
Sat.–Sun.
10.30am–2am
*Web bar: Old
silversmith workshop
converted into an
internet café in the
midle of Le Marais.
Set on two stories –
mezzanine for net
surfing and ground
floor for drinks.
Exhibitions, events.
Good meeting place.*

BASTILLE

Le Café de l'Industrie
◆ 2 I7
16, rue Saint-Sabin
75011
Tel. 01 47 00 13 53
Open Sun.–Fri.
10am–2am
*Bright place in which
to hang out and
soak in the lively
atmosphere of the
neighborhood.*

La Fabrique
◆ 2 I8
53, rue du Faubourg-
Saint-Antoine 75011
Tel. 01 43 07 67 07
Open Mon.–Fri.
12.30am–5am,
Sat. 6pm–5am
*This micro-brasserie
offers reasonably
priced house beers
and cooked meals
made with produce
from its own
delicatessen store.*

Le Sanz Sans
◆ 2 I8
49, rue du Faubourg-
Saint-Antoine 75011
Tel. 01 44 75 78 78.
Open Tue.–Sat.
9am–5am,
Mon. 9am–2am,
Sun. 6pm– 2am.
*Fashionable music-
bar-restaurant. Its
bric-à-brac décor
harbors a few
surprises.*

MONTPARNASSE

Les Mousquetaires
◆ 6 H3
77, av. du Maine
75014
Tel. 01 43 22 50 46
Open daily
7am–3 or 4am
Eleven billiard tables.

L'Utopia
◆ 6 G4
79, rue de l'Ouest
75014
Tel. 01 43 22 79 66
Open Mon.–Sat.
10pm–2am (6am at
the weekend)
*A different band
every evening,
playing blues, R&B
and rock 'n' roll.*

ST-GERMAIN-
DES-PRÉS

Le Bar du Marché
◆ 2 A8
75, rue de Seine
75006
Tel. 01 43 26 55 15
Open daily 8am–2am
*Strategic spot near
the Rue de Buci
market. Friendly
clientele, but often
crowded.*

Horse's Tavern
◆ 2 B8
16, carrefour de
l'Odéon 75006
Tel. 01 43 54 96 91
Open Sun.–Thur.
8am–2am, Fri.–Sat.
until 4pm
*Incredible place with
a huge choice of
beer (12 types on
draft and over 200
bottled brands).
Expert advice.*

La Palette
◆ 2 A7
43, rue de Seine
75006
Tel. 01 43 26 68 15
Open Mon.–Sat.
8am–2am
*One of the oldest
bistrots in the area,
close to the École
des Beaux-Arts.
Large, peaceful
terrace and a
backroom with a
truly Parisian
atmosphere. A
favorite.*

ÉTOILE

Le Floridita
◆ 1 A1
19, rue de Presbourg
75016
Tel. 01 45 00 84 84
Open Tue.–Sat.
noon–5am,
Mon. noon–6pm
*"Cigar bar". Well-
behaved clientele.*

PIGALLE

Le Dépanneur
◆ **9** J7
27, rue Fontaine
75009
Tel. 01 40 16 40 20
Open daily
11am–7am

La Fourmi
◆ **10** B7
74, rue des Martyrs
75018
Tel. 01 42 64 70 35
Open Mon.–Thur.
8.30am–2am, Fri.–
Sat. 8.30am–4am,
Sun. 10am–noon
*Perfect for drinks
before a concert at
Divan du Monde or
at La Cigale. One of
the most popular
places in Pigalle.
Very crowded in the
evening and at the
weekend.*

Aux Noctambules
◆ **10** A7
24, bd de Clichy
75018
Tel. 01 46 06 16 38
Open daily
10am–4am.
*From tourists in
search of the
picturesque to young
Parisians yearning
for authenticity,
everyone enjoys the
kitsch atmosphere
of this caf'conc'
(music-bar).*

Le Sancerre
◆ **10** A6
35, rue des Abbesses
75018
Tel. 01 42 58 08 20
Open daily 7am–2am
*Trendy meeting
place for lovers
of the Abbesses
neighborhood, not
far from Pigalle.*

BUTTE-AUX-CAILLES

La Folie en Tête
◆ **5** D6
33, rue de la Butte-
aux-Cailles 75013
Tel. 01 45 80 65 99
Open Mon.–Sat.
5pm–2am
*Small music-bar that
holds concerts of
rock, jazz and
traditional French
songs on Thur. and
Fri. 9pm–midnight.*

ST-BLAISE

La Flèche d'Or
◆ **3** F6
102 bis, rue de
Bagnolet 75020
Tel. 01 43 72 04 23
www.flechedor.com
Open Mon.–Fri.
6pm–2am, Sat.–Sun.
10am–2am
*Café located in
a former railway
station. Rock
concerts, French
song evenings or
Salsa on Sun.*

CANALS

Le Café de la Musique
◆ **11** D5
213, av. Jean-Jaurès
75019
Tel. 01 48 03 15 91
Open daily 8am–2am.
*Designer café with a
superb terrace. Jazz
every Fri. evening.*

L'Opus
◆ **10** H9
167, quai de Valmy
75010
Tel. 01 40 34 70 00
Open Tue.–Wed.
8pm–2am,
Thur.–Sat. 9pm–4am
*A British officers'
mess during World
War I, this café has
been converted into
a music loft-bar
looking over Canal
Saint-Martin. Soul
music on Wed., funk
on Thur., opus-jam
on Sun. and club at
the weekend.*

GAMBETTA

MK2 Project Café
◆ **3** E4
4, rue Belgrand
75020
Tel. 01 43 49 01 99
Open Tue.–Sat.
noon–2am, Sun.–
Mon. noon–midnight
*Music-bar showing
performing artists'
videos. Close to the
MK2 movie theater.*

MÉNILMONTANT

Blue Billard
◆ **2** J3
111, rue Saint-Maur
75011
Tel. 01 43 55 87 21
Open daily
11am–2am
18 billiard tables

*over 3,280 square
feet, two rooms and
a mezzanine. Free
game for two if you
have lunch there.*

Le Charbon
◆ **3** A3
109, rue Oberkampf
75011
Tel. 01 43 57 55 13
Open daily 9am–
2am (4am Fri.–Sat.)
*One of the first
fashionable places
to open on Rue
Oberkampf.
Authentic décor of
natural patina, old
mirrors and seats.
Trendy clientele.
Music venue.*

Cithéa
◆ **3** A3
114, rue Oberkampf
75011
Tel. 01 40 21 70 95
Open daily
10pm–6am
*Dance bar dedicated
to live jazz, funk,
rock and groove.
Regular DJs.*

La Maroquinerie
◆ **3** D3
23, rue Boyer 75020
Tel. 01 40 33 30 60
Open Mon.–Sat.
11am–1am
*Literary café close
to the Bellevilloise.
Various events.*

NIGHTCLUBS

BASTILLE

Le Réservoir
◆ **3** A9
16, rue de la Forge-
Royale, 75011
Tel. 01 43 56 39 60
*Bar-restaurant that
plays excellent world
music. Themed
evenings during the
week and live music
at the weekend.
Rock, salsa or world
music. Café-theater
on Mon.*

CHAMPS-ÉLYSÉES

Queen
◆ **1** C2
102, av des Champs-
Élysées 75008
Tel. 08 92 70 73 30
Open every evening
Ten years after its

**GAY AND LESBIAN
PARIS**
Recent years have
seen the birth of an
impressive number
of establishments,
mainly located in
the four central
arrondissements
and in particular in
the Marais (4th
arrondissement). It
is here that most of
the restaurants,
bars and stores are
found. In other
districts, gays and
lesbians are no less
of a presence but
may be more
discreet. Bars
generally open at
the beginning or
middle of the
afternoon and
close at two in
the morning (as
required by law),
apart from those
with a special
license that stay
open until the early
hours. Nightclubs
open at 11pm or
midnight and close
in the morning.
Information:
www.paris-gay.com

BARS

Amnésia Café
42, rue Vieille-du-
Temple 75004

Banana Café
13, rue de la
Ferronnerie 75001

Open Café
17, rue des Archives
75004

Le Cox
15, rue des
Archives 75004

Le Scorp
25, bd Poissonnière
75002

CLUBS

Le Queen
102, av. des
Champs-Élysées
75008

Red Light
34, rue du Départ
75015

◆ NIGHTCLUBS

*Under each heading addresses are listed according to districts.
The letters and figures (e.g. ◆ 1 G3) give grid references for the maps
at the end of the guide.*

opening, Queen has lost some of its gay followers and the clientele is now mixed most nights, except on Sun and Mon evening when loyal drag queens come back for the special evenings. The golden rule here is to be stylish, sexy and ready to party, and never, ever arrive before 2am!

GRANDS-BOULEVARDS

El Globo
◆ 2 E2
8, bd de Strasbourg 75010
Tel. 01 42 41 55 70
Open 11.30pm–6am
Don't arrive before 1 or 2am and be prepared to queue. Ideal for groups keen to enjoy the atmosphere rather than the eclectic music.

Le New Morning
◆ 2 E1
7, rue des Petites-Écuries 75010
Tel. 01 45 23 51 41
In a class of its own, this is Parisian nightclub has an international reputation. Top jazz musicians, as well as blues, rock, folk, etc., artists meet and perform here.

Rex Club
◆ 2 D2
5, bd Poissonnière 75002
Tel. 01 42 36 10 96
Open Tue.–Sat. from 11.30pm
Top international techno club: D-Club on Wed evenings, Watch-out on Sun, and many more! A must for techno-house and garage enthusiasts.

HALLES

Les Bains
◆ 2 E4
7, rue du Bourg-l'Abbé 75003
Tel. 01 48 87 01 80
Open Mon.–Sat.
Restaurant:

8.30pm–1am
Club: 11.30pm–6am.
For a long time the preserve of a happy few, Les Bains has regained its original atmosphere thanks to the Guetta pair.

LA PALETTE'S TERRACE

QUEEN NIGHTCLUB

They left last year and some feared the worst for the future of the club. It is, however, still going strong, peopled with models and wannabes. The Café Con Leche evenings on Sun, or Rush on Fri and Sat, still attract a very trendy, but more mixed crowd. Restaurant inside. Private parties: call for information.

Lombards sur Jazz
◆ 2 D6
– **Le Baiser Salé**
58, rue des Lombards 75001
Tel. 01 42 33 37 71
– **Duc des Lombards**
42, rue des Lombards 75001
Tel. 01 42 33 22 88
– **Sunset**
60, rue des Lombards 75001
Tel. 01 40 26 46 60
The Lombards-sur-jazz association, grouping the three

clubs listed above, organizes joint music events that are open to young musicians, with preferential tickets and monthly venues called "Une entrée, trois clubs" (one ticket, three clubs). Additional programs include acoustic jazz-rock at the Sunset; Latino-funk, jamming sessions and Afro-jazz at the Baiser Salé, and traditional jazz at the Duc des Lombards.*

Le Petit Opportun
◆ 2 C6
15, rue des Lavandières-Sainte-Opportune 75001
Tel. 01 42 36 01 36
A landmark in top-quality jazz. Bar on the ground floor and small vaulted cellar.

EAST PARIS

Les Instants Chavirés
7, rue Richard-Lenoir 93100 Montreuil
M° Robespierre
Tel. 01 42 87 25 91
Here improvisation reigns supreme. A must for jazz experimentation enthusiasts.

LATIN QUARTER

Le Petit Journal
◆ 2 B10
71, bd Saint-Michel 75005
Tel. 01 43 26 28 59
Specializing in New-Orleans-style jazz, this club welcomes such regular artists as Benny Bailey and Marcel Zanini.

MARAIS

Les 7 Lézards
◆ 2 G7
10, rue des Rosiers 75004
Tel. 01 48 87 08 97
Café-restaurant with a terrace. Friendly setting. Anything from current jazz, from free to Afro.

PIGALLE

Le Divan du Monde
◆ 10 B7
75, rue Martyrs 75018
Tel. 01 44 92 77 66
Wide range of world music (rai, hip-hop, etc.) and regular performances.

Élysée Montmartre
◆ 10 C7
72, bd de Rochechouart 75018
Tel. 01 42 23 46 50
Open from 11.30pm.
Formerly the temple of wrestling, the Élysée now puts on very different performances, such as the Scream evenings offering endless variations on the seven deadly sins, and a traditional ball (twice a month) of French musette and popular music.

Folie's Pigalle
◆ 10 A7
11, pl. Pigalle 75009
Tel. 01 48 78 25 26
Open Tue.–Sun.
from midnight
After-hours at the weekend, Black-Blanc-Beur tea dance on Sundays at 5pm. A mostly gay crowd and techno music are regular features at this former peep-show venue.

MOVIE THEATERS ◆

QUAI DE LA GARE

Batofar

◆ **5** J4

Quai François-
Mauriac 75013
Tel. 01 56 29 10 00
www.batofar.lagare.fr
Open Tue.–Sat.
9pm–5am.
*This former Irish
lightship rescued
from demolition has
become one of the
main places for
experimental techno
music and all its
current variations. It
also regularly invites
artists from other
capital cities and
gives them exposure
for a few months.*

ST-GERMAIN-DES-PRÉS

La Villa

◆ **2** A7

29, rue Jacob 75006
Tel. 01 43 26 60 00
*Opened in 1991, La
Villa has already
earned itself quite
a reputation for its
creative and inspired
jazz programs.
Shirley Horn,
Kenny Baron and
Ahmad Jama have
all performed here.
The minimalist décor
of the ground floor
bar is the work of
Marie-Christine
Dorner.*

MOVIE THEATERS

The original or
French versions of all
types of movies are
shown at large
complexes (UGC,
Gaumont, etc.) and
at neighborhood
theaters (5th and
6th arrondissements,
MK2 group).
A small selection
is listed here.

BALARD

Grand Pavois

◆ **7** I7

364, rue Lecourbe
75015
Tel. 01 45 54 46 85
*This theater, which
resembles a ship,
complete with fake
portholes and four
rooms bearing
maritime names*

*(Port, Starboard...),
specializes in fantasy
or cult movies.
Good selection of
children's movies.*

BERCY

UGC Ciné Cité Bercy

◆ **4** C5

114, quai de Bercy
75012
*This extremely
modern multiplex
has the latest high-
definition sound
system. Perfect
location in a
pedestrian zone
close to the Parc de
Bercy and to the old
restored stonework
and sunny terraces
of the Cour Saint-
Émilion.*

CANALS

La Géode

◆ **11** C3

Parc de la Villette
26, av. Corentin-
Cariou 75019
Tel. 01 40 05 12 12
*The image projected
on the 3,280-square-
foot hemispheric
screen exceeds
the human visual
field. With around
1 million of visitors
every year, La Géode
is one of the most
popular attractions
in Paris.*

MK2 Quai de Seine

◆ **10** I6

14, quai de Seine
75019
*Set up on a metal
structure left over
from the 1872 World
Fair, this MK2
overlooks the Villette
embankment. It also
boasts a restaurant-
cum-bar-cum-
tearoom with a
popular terrace.*

ÉCOLE MILITAIRE

**Gaumont
Kinopanorama**

◆ **1** C9

60, av. La Motte-
Picquet 75015
Tel. 01 43 06 50 50
*Only one cinema,
but with an
impressive 650
square-foot curved
screen.*

ÉTOILE

Mac-Mahon

◆ **9** B10

5, av. Mac-Mahon
75017
Tel. 01 43 80 24 81
*A temple to all great
American movie
classics and their
stars (Audrey
Hepburn, Billy
Wilder, etc.)*

GRANDS BOULEVARDS

**Cinémathèque
Française**

◆ **2** D2

42, bd de Bonne-
Nouvelle 75010
Tel. 01 56 26 01 01
*Built after the
Musée du Cinéma
was destroyed by a
fire, this theater
follows the same
philosophy as the
Cinemathèque
in Chaillot, which
has now reopened.*

**Max Linder
Panorama**

◆ **2** C2

24, bd Poissonnière
75009
Tel. 08 36 68 50 52
*The slightly curved,
panoramic 59-by-
32-feet screen
guarantees superb
viewing. The marble
décor in the
entrance hall as well
as the black-colored
theater, mezzanine
and balcony all
combine to create
the perfect setting
for independent
movies.*

Rex

◆ **2** D9

1, bd Poissonnière
75002
Tel. 01 42 36 83 93
*This prestigious
theater, created in
1932, is classified as
historical monument.
Its main attraction
is the atmospheric
room which contains
2,800 seats. A huge
starry sky and a
pasteboard "pueblo
español" decorate
the ceiling and the
walls. The screen
measures
59 by 27 feet.*

HALLES

Forum des Images

◆ **2** C5

Forum des Halles
Porte Saint-Eustache
2, Grande Galerie
75001
Tel. 01 44 76 62 00
*Genre movies are
presented in three
different theaters or
on the screen of the
interactive video
stations.*

LATIN QUARTER

Accattone

◆ **2** C10

20, rue Cujas
75005
Tel. 01 46 33 86 86
*The Accattone puts
on the great classics
that were widely
talked about or
controversial when
they first came out.*

Action Écoles

◆ **2** D9

23, rue des Écoles
75005
Tel. 01 43 29 79 89
*The two theaters
of Action Écoles
present the best
North-American
comedies from the
1940s and 1950s.
Original décor.*

Escurial Panorama

◆ **5** D3

11, bd de Port-Royal
75013
Tel. 01 47 07 28 04
*New movies as
well as reruns are
shown here. This
place has retained
its old neighborhood
theater fittings and
shows the best
contemporary
movies on a
panoramic
backcloth.*

MONTPARNASSE

Entrepôt

◆ **6** F4

7–9, rue Francis-
de-Pressensé
75014
*An original feature
of the Entrepôt is
the opportunity to
discuss certain
movies with their
directors after their
showing.*

477

Under each heading addresses are listed according to districts. The letters and figures (e.g. ◆ 1 G3) give grid references for the maps at the end of the guide.

PLACE D'ITALIE

Gaumont
Grand Écran Italie
◆ **5** E5
30, pl. d'Italie
75013
Tel. 01 45 80 77 00
The largest screen in Paris (860sq ft). Laser beam show with digital display before the presentation of the movies.

QUAI DE LA GARE

MK2 Bibliothèque
◆ **5** I3
128–162 av. de France 75013
Tel. 08 92 68 14 07
The MK2 Bibliothèque is the newborn of the MK2 group – a movie complex erected on a triangle of free ground between the Bibliothèque and the railtracks of the Gare d'Austerlitz. Dreamed up by film producer Marin Karmitz, it is 1,100ft long and 98ft wide at its largest! Inside are 14 movie screens, two music stores and four restaurants. The latest stylish addition to a fast developing district and the ideal destination if you have not seen the Bibliothèque yet.

TROCADÉRO

Cinémathèque Française
Palais de Chaillot
◆ **8** J8
7, av. Albert-de-Mun 75116
Tel. 01 56 26 01 01
Here you can discover or rediscover the great movie classics.

SHOWS

BASTILLE

Opéra-Bastille
◆ **2** I8
120, rue de Lyon 75012
Information:
Tel. 01 44 73 13 99
The most famous operas by Mozart,

Puccini, Wagner, etc., are staged here. The Amphithéâtre, on the other hand, specializes in chamber music and the Autumn Festival.

Théâtre de la Bastille
◆ **2** J7
76, rue de la Roquette 75011
Reservations:
Tel. 01 43 57 42 14
Contemporary dance performances.

CANALS

Cité de la Musique
◆ **11** C3
221, av. Jean-Jaurès 75019
Tel. 01 44 84 45 00
Wide range of music from medieval to modern, jazz, songs and world music. The Cité de la Musique also puts on dress rehearsals that are open to the public, summer courses, Javanese percussion workshops, conferences and a Musée de la Musique.

CHAMPS-ÉLYSÉES

Salle Gaveau
◆ **1** E1
15, rue La Boétie 75008
Res. 01 49 53 05 07
The programs here have always been dedicated mostly to piano and chamber music, but also include some orchestral music.

Salle Pleyel
◆ **9** C9
252, rue du Faubourg-Saint-Honoré 75008
Tel. 08 25 00 02 52
Many works had their first performance in this prestigious concert hall, and many great conductors, soloists, and symphonic orchestras have performed here.

Théâtre des Champs-Élysées
◆ **1** C4
15, av. Montaigne 75008
Reservations:
Tel. 01 49 52 50 50
The program at this theater includes opera, recitals, chamber music as well as dance performances.

GRANDS BOULEVARDS

L'Opéra-Comique
◆ **2** B2
5, rue Favart 75002
Reservations:
Tel. 01 42 44 45 46
This opera house dedicates itself to the presentation of the French repertory of the period, but also to Baroque and 20th-century music.

Opéra-Garnier
◆ **1** J2
Place de l'Opéra 75009
Reservations:
Tel. 01 44 73 13 99
The program gives priority to ballet, with performances by the Ballet de l'Opéra de Paris. A non-resident ballet company is invited for a few days every season.

HALLES

Théâtre du Châtelet
◆ **2** D6
1, place du Châtelet 75001
Information:
Tel. 01 40 28 28 28
The Châtelet's program includes opera and 20th-century music. It also invites international choreographers every year to present their work.

Théâtre de la Ville
◆ **2** D6
2, place du Châtelet 75001
Tel. 01 48 87 54 42
Concerts of classical and modern music, consisting mostly of song recitals,

single instrument performances and chamber music.

MAISON DE LA RADIO

Radio France
◆ **7** H2
116, av. du Président-Kennedy 75116
Tel. 01 42 30 15 16
The Orchestre national de Radio France performs mostly French music, from Berlioz to Varèse.

MARAIS

Centre National de la Danse
◆ **2** F7
9, rue Geoffroy-L'Asnier 75004
Tel. 01 42 74 44 22
The national dance center puts on performances by young French and foreign companies.

PIGALLE

Théâtre des Abbesses
◆ **10** B7
31, rue des Abbesses 75018
Tel. 01 48 87 54 42
Complements its Châtelet counterpart by giving concerts of classical and modern music. The program includes song recitals, single instrument performances and chamber music.

PLACE DES FÊTES

Le Studio du Regard des Cygnes
◆ **11** E10
210, rue de Belleville 75020
Tel. 01 43 58 55 93
Eclectic and exciting program by young French and foreign companies.

PORTE DE ST-OUEN

L'Étoile du Nord
◆ **9** J3
16, rue Georgette-Agutte 75018
Reservations:
Tel. 01 42 26 47 47
Dance performances.

The letters and figures (e.g. ◆ 1 G3) give grid references for the maps at the end of the guide.

BREAD

Boulangerie Poilâne
◆ **1** I9
8, rue du Cherche-Midi 75006
Tel. 01 45 48 42 59
Open Mon.–Sat. 7.15am–8.15pm
This is the original boutique opened in 1932 by Pierre Poilâne. Lionel, his son, took over the business in the 1970's. One of his favorite projects was the cage that he and Salvador Dali made together out of bread dough. "The bird could eat its way out of the cage." Between 7,000 and 8,000 country loaves come out of Poilâne's ovens every day to be enjoyed by Parisians as well as by people living in the provinces – Poilâne's bread is dispatched by special postal service to different places in France and FedExed to 20 countries around the world. Parisians come a long way to queue for the hot croissants, apple pies and butter pastries.

Flûte Gana
◆ **3** E3
226, rue des Pyrénées 75020
Tel. 01 43 58 42 62
Open Tue.–Sat. 7.30am–8pm
The Ganachaud sisters' specialty is the Gana "flûte", a thin type of baguette whose dough undergoes six hours of fermentation before being kneaded and shaped by hand according to an old recipe which brought fame and fortune to the Parisian baguette at the turn of the century. They also make organic bread, bread with walnuts, hazelnuts and raisins, and wheatgerm-enriched country loaves.

Max Poilâne
◆ **6** C5
87, rue Brancion 75015
Tel. 01 48 28 45 90
Open Mon.–Sat. 7.30am–8pm,
Sun. 9am–7pm
Not as well known as his brother Lionel (see above), Max Poilâne bakes the same classics just as competently: fabulous country loaves, rye bread with currants or walnuts from the Périgord region, personalized bread (two days' notice required) and yes, even plain white bread.

Le Moulin de la Vierge
◆ **1** D10
166, av. de Suffren 75015
Tel. 01 47 83 45 55
Open Mon.–Sat. 7am–8pm
Beautiful décor. Basile Kamir, a former reporter, uses only a woodfire oven for his organic bread, country loaves and Provençal "fougasse". Other specialties and two more outlets in the 14th and 17th arrondissements.

Au Pain Bien Cuit
◆ **9** J10
111, bd Haussmann 75008
Tel. 01 42 65 06 25
Open Mon.–Sat. 8am–7.30pm
Over 350 different types of bread are baked here in all shapes and forms by the supplier to the Élysées Palace: choose, for instance, between turtles, hearts (with or without messages) and the ever-popular Eiffel Tower.

Au Panetier
◆ **2** B3
10, pl. des Petits-Pères 75002
Tel. 01 42 60 90 23
Open Mon.–Fri. 8am–7.15pm
This fine 1896 bakery sells leavened bread baked in a woodfire oven. House specialties: the "Saint-fiacre" and the "Pavé des Petits-Pères", made with flour from a traditional millstone.

Poujauran
◆ **1** D5
20, rue Jean-Nicot 75007
Tel. 01 47 05 80 88
Open Tue.–Sat. 8am–8.30pm
Rue Jean-Nicot wakes up every day to the delights of JL Poujauran's bakery. He has introduced Paris to the "cannelés" from Bordeaux (a cake whose taste is similar to pancakes), specialties from his own region (Landes) and from the Basque country. Leavened bread and other interesting bread made with corn flour, figs or poppy seeds. The simple baguette is especially delicious at 5pm when it's fresh out from the oven.

PÂTISSERIES

Dalloyau
◆ **1** EF1
101, rue du Faubourg-Saint-Honoré 75008
Tel. 01 42 99 90 00
Open daily 8am–9pm
An institution. There are six Dalloyau stores-cum-tearooms in Paris, offering top-quality cakes (works of art really) and impeccable service. Founded in 1802, this great establishment is the inventor of the famous "Opéra" cake (layer upon layer of chocolate), which to this day remains unchallenged and unrivalled. Other classics include "Louvre", shaped like a pyramid, a chocolate mousse covered with a dark chocolate exterior. For new creations try the "chocolate autumn leaf" and the "Tonkinois" which can be eaten on the spot, or the small "Market crate", with nougatine. Heaven on Earth.

Gérard Mulot
◆ **2** A8
76, rue de Seine 75006
Tel. 01 43 26 85 77
Open Thu.–Tue. 6.45am–8pm
A huge, light store with an incredible range of tempting pâtisseries. "Cœur-frivole" (frivolous heart) and "Jour-et-nuit" (day and night) are two of the lovely names given by Gérard Mulot to his delicious, delightfully presented creations. Tarts and Danish pastries are equally delectable. Difficult to resist.

Jean Millet
◆ **1** D6
103, rue Saint-Dominique 75007
Tel. 01 45 51 49 80
Open Mon.–Sat. 9am–7pm,
Sun. 8am–1pm
Jean Millet, recipient of the "Meilleur ouvrier de France" award (best craftsman), and his wife have been running this store for over 30 years. The selection of individual cakes is rather small but of undisputed quality. Unusual creations use "tuiles" (thin

biscuits in the shape of roof tiles) and a decoration of delicious mousse. Don't miss the superb charlotte, which you can eat on the spot if you can't wait.

Pierre Hermé

◆ **1** J9
72 rue Bonaparte
75006
Tel. 01 43 54 47 77
The "Picasso of pastry" is renowned throughout the world. He was apprenticed to Gaston Lenôtre at 14, took over Fauchon's pastry quarters at only 24, went on to open Ladurée's store on the Champs-Elysées and has written several book on desserts. In 2002 this patissier extraordinaire finally opened his first shop, in St-Germain-des-Prés, near the Place St Sulpice. You may think that the black glass façade with no apparent sign is that of a discreetly luxurious jeweler. In a way it is, but people rarely queue on the sidewalk to buy a diamond ring! Inside, cakes, biscuits, and Hermé's macaroons – try the olive oil one.

CHOCOLATE

The following are a few addresses of master chocolatiers, who count among the best in France, if not the world.

Christian Constant

◆ **1** I9
37, rue d'Assas
75006
Tel. 01 53 63 15 15
Open Mon.–Sat. 8.30am–9pm, Sun. 8am–7pm
Christian Constant, who was awarded the "Ordre du Mérite" in 1998, creates chocolates using the essence of subtle flowers such as jasmine from Yemen or ylang-ylang from the Comoro Islands. The more classic lines include chocolates with dried fruit, honey and pine kernels, or the amazing "Conquistador" (100% cocoa, with hazelnut, honey and cinnamon from Sri Lanka). If you prefer sorbets and ice creams, the unusual green-tea sorbet is exceptional. Catering available.

Debauve et Gallais

◆ **1** J7
30, rue des Saints-Pères
75007
Tel. 01 45 48 54 67
www.debauve-et-gallais.com
Open Mon.–Sat. 9.30am–7pm
While choosing your chocolates, admire the elegant décor dating from 1800, and interesting images recalling the medicinal origins of chocolate. Two other stores in Paris.

L'Étoile d'Or

◆ **10** A7
30, rue Fontaine
75009
Tel. 01 48 74 59 55
Open Tue.–Sat. 10.30am–8pm, Sun.–Mon. 2.30–8pm
Run by Denise Acabo, this Art Deco boutique sells some of the best chocolates France has to offer.

Jean-Paul Hévin

◆ **1** E7
23 bis, av. de La Motte-Picquet
75007
Tel. 01 45 51 77 48
www.jphevin.com
Open Tue.–Sat. 10am–7.30pm
If you're a chocolate addict, go for the house specialty: the 5-lb bar (the equivalent of 10 standard-size bars). The height of sophistication is a combination of coffee and dried fruit on a chocolate base (fig-ginger, dried apricot or walnut). Other delicious items include cocoa sorbet and tea ganache.

La Maison du Chocolat

◆ **9** C9
225, rue du Faubourg-Saint-Honoré
75008
Tel. 01 42 27 39 44
www.lamaisonduchocolat.com
Open Mon.–Sat. 10am–7.30pm (until 7pm in summer)
This is undoubtedly one of finest chocolate makers in France. In Robert Linxe's store – as dark as his chocolates – you will find chocolates with truffle filling, quayaquils, quitos and bacchus with rum and raisins (even the fennel chocolates are convincing!), a long-life chocolate cake that keeps for 4–5 days, the "Pleyel", which can be sent anywhere in France, and the famous hot chocolate. Many outlets throughout Paris.

Richart

◆ **1** H6
258, bd Saint-Germain
75007
Tel. 01 45 55 66 00
www.richart.com
Open Mon.–Sat. 10am–7pm
Established in 1925, Michel Richart sells, among other well-designed produce, chocolates spiced with saffron, cloves or three peppers, and ultrathin wafers to savor with coffee, packaged in lovely white boxes with small drawers.

ICE CREAM

Glaciers Berthillon

◆ **2** F8
31, rue Saint-Louis-en-l'Île
75004
Tel. 01 43 54 31 61
Open Wed.–Sun. 10am–8pm. Closed mid July–end Aug
These renowned ice cream makers on Île Saint-Louis are so successful they can

DEBAUVE ET GALLAIS

À LA MÈRE DE FAMILLE

The letters and figures (e.g. ◆ 1 G3) give grid references for the maps at the end of the guide.

afford to shut for a significant part of summer. The most popular items are "marrons glacés" in winter, wild strawberry ices in summer and vanilla with forest fruit coulis, plus raspberry, mirabelle, nougat, plum, honey and fig sorbets – easily the best in Paris.

Pascal le Glacier
◆ 8 G10
17, rue Bois-le-Vent 75016
Tel. 01 45 27 61 84
Open Tue.–Sat. 10.30am–7pm
Located in the posh heart of the 16th arrondissement, these fine ice cream makers are the kings of take-out sales (choose between cones and small pots) as the former sitting area is now an annex of the store's laboratory. Pavé de Passy (available from December to March, dark chocolate with marron glacé filling), nine varieties of chocolate (the latest filling being candied apricot), blood orange, melon or pink guava. Also served at the terrace of the Flore (see p. 462, p. 472).

Raimo
◆ 4 E2
59–61, bd de Reuilly 75012
Tel. 01 43 43 70 17
Open Tue.–Sun. 9am–midnight
Although this store is not centrally located, its vanilla ice cream is well worth the journey, following a walk in Parc de Bercy for example. You also have a hoice of some 30 other flavors of ice cream, plus ginger, cinnamon, honeydew melon sorbets.

CONFECTIONERS
À la Mère de Famille
◆ 2 C1
35, rue du Faubourg-Montmartre 75009
Tel. 01 47 70 83 69
Open Tue.–Fri. 9am–7pm, Mon. and Sat. 10am–7pm
The oldest confectioner's in Paris. A delightful façade (stamped glass dating back from 1761), and neatly displayed French specialties ("madeleines" from Commercy, "bergamotes" from Nancy). Everything is made on the premises.

Les Bonbons
◆ 6 I1
6, rue Bréa 75006
Tel. 01 43 26 21 15
Open Tue.–Sat. 10.30am–1.30pm and 2–7.45pm, Mon. 3–7.45pm
Marie-Claude Lesueur's store is narrow, but the shelves carry all the traditional French sweets: barley sugar from Tours, "bêtises" from Cambrai, "fondants" from Lyon, the king of sweets – the "négus" from Nevers – and authentic "violets" from Toulouse. Buy a selection from all the different jars.

Fouquet
◆ 1 D3
22, rue François-Ier 75008
Tel. 01 47 23 30 36
Open Mon.–Sat. 10am–7.30pm
Ultra-Parisian store, first opened in 1852. Violet, poppy, "salvator", "palet" Bourbon, Graca, ginger-flavored chocs – everything is made on the premises. Decorations for cakes (rose petals, mimosa, coriander berries) and, for

Easter, the prettiest sugar molds (vanilla egg, raspberry, lemon, orange) you've ever seen.

La Maison des Bonbons
◆ 6 I5
14, rue Mouton-Duvernet 75014
Tel. 01 45 41 25 55
Open Tue.–Sat. 10.30am–8pm, Mon. 3–8pm
This sweet-store is run by Anne-Laurence Dalloz, who has something of a sweet tooth herself. Her moussy chocolate heads, marshmallow mice, gelatine Eiffel Towers, Coco Boer capsules (liquorice powder) and plain old-fashioned sweets are as tempting to adults as they are to children.

CHEESES
Alléosse
◆ 9 B8
13, rue Poncelet 75017
Tel. 01 46 22 50 45
Open Tue.–Sat. 9.30am–1pm and 4–7pm, Sun. 9am–1pm
Goumard, Senderens, Faugeron... No restaurant chef

can resist Roger Alléosse's amazing array of cheeses: goat's cheese from Savoie and Corsica, manchego from Spain, lavort from Puy-de-Dôme, ewe's milk cheese from the Basque Country, Braisoir from Alsace and the ubiquitous camemberts (Vardon and Jort).

Barthélemy
◆ 1 I7
51, rue de Grenelle 75007
Tel. 01 45 48 56 75
Open Tue.–Sat. 8am–1pm and 4–7.15pm
Closed Sat. during school holidays
For the past 25 years the owner of this small store, Savoyard Roland Barthélemy, has been supplying the capital with cheeses matured to perfection in the store's cellars: bries from Meaux, Melun and Malesherbes (kept ten weeks under ashes), and camemberts from the Pays d'Auge, Cotentin and Orne (three regions which guarantee him continued supplies).

BARTHÉLEMY

CHEESES FROM FRANCE

Boursault-Vernier
◆ **6** I6
71, av. du Général-Leclerc
75014
Tel. 01 43 27 93 30
Open Tue.–Fri.
8.30am–12.30pm
and 4.15–9.15pm,
Sat. 8.30am–1pm
and 3.30– 7.15pm,
Sun. 8.30am–1pm
At Boursault-Vernier, fresh milk is taken as seriously as cheese. For years Jacques Vernier has been traveling throughout the length and breadth of France during his holidays in search of fine blue cheeses from the Auvergne, high-mountain pasture beauforts and – in season – some 20 different goat's cheeses (one of them made by the monks of a monastery in the Hérault département). Another favourite to watch out for is Vernier's Termignon blue, whose marbling does not come from a fungus, unlike other blue cheeses. The store has new maturing cellars in the basement.

REGIONAL PRODUCE

L'Ambassade du Sud-Ouest
◆ **1** C6
46, av. de La Bourdonnais 75007
Tel. 01 45 55 59 59
Open daily
10am–11pm
There is a small restaurant through the store. In both, you can try foie gras, goose and duck conserves from Périgord and fine Bordeaux wines. Don't miss the fruit preserved in armagnac and walnut cream from Souillac.

Produits de Campagne
◆ **6** I4
21, rue Daguerre
75014
Tel. 01 43 20 02 72
Open Tue.–Sat.
8.45am–1.45pm and
3.45–7.45pm,
Sun. 8.45am–1pm
A boutique fitting for the Rue Daguerre and its residents, selling a wide range of "country products". On offer are specialties from different parts of France: wines from Savoie, cheese from Laguiole, etc.

À la Ville de Rodez
◆ **2** F7
22, rue Vieille-du Temple 75004
Tel. 01 48 87 79 36
Open Tue.–Sat.
8am–1pm and
3–7.30pm.
Closed August.
This charming store sells all the best produce from Aveyron: hams, sausages, cheeses and the famous "fricandeaux d'Espalion".

TEA AND COFFEE, HERBAL TEAS

Betjeman and Barton
◆ **1** H2
23, bd Malesherbes
75008
Tel. 01 42 65 86 17
Open Mon.–Sat.
10am–7pm
Behind the window display of old, white metal teapots, over 240 different types of tea are offered. The specialty of the house is Pushkin, a very popular mix. Not to be missed either are Eden Rose – the latest creation by Didier Jumeau-Lafond – Japanese Genmaicha made from black rice, Vietnamese Royal Lotus and the latest green teas from Japan and China.

Les Herbes du Luxembourg
◆ **2** B10
3, rue de Médicis
75006
Tel. 01 43 26 91 53
Open Tue.–Fri.
10.30am–7pm, Mon. and Sat. 11am–7pm
The lovely fragrance of 250 different types of medicinal plants mingle, surprisingly, with the aroma of fresh bread and eggs.

Herboristerie du Palais-Royal
◆ **2** B3
11, rue des Petits-Champs 75001
Tel. 01 42 97 54 68

Open Mon.–Fri.
9.30am–7pm,
Sat. 10.30am–
6.30pm
This is undoubtedly the finest herbalist's in Paris. The ladders propped against its wooden shelves are used to reach some of the store's 500 medicinal plants and herbs (all of them unpackaged).

Lapeyronie
◆ **2** E5
3, rue Brantôme,
Quartier de l'Horloge
75003
Tel. 01 40 27 97 57
Open Mon.–Fri.
8.30am–7.30pm,
Sat. 10am–7.30pm
Tempting pale-wood store with a small, surprisingly quiet terrace. Bruno Saguez not only sells excellent coffee (including Harrar mocha from Ethiopia and Blue Mountain from Jamaica) and some 60 varieties of tea, but also invites you to sample them.

Mariage Frères
◆ **2** F6
30, rue du Bourg-Tibourg
75004
Tel. 01 42 72 28 11
Open daily
10.30am–7.30pm;
tearoom open
noon–7pm
Mariage Frères, the main tea importers in France, sell over 500 varieties (including the extremely rare five-dynasty yellow tea from Mount Jun-Hunnan). The main store is located in the heart of the Marais and has a small exhibition of old-fashioned cash registers, scales and sifters on the upper floor, and reproductions of old teapots. There are many other outlets in Paris.

FAUCHON

HÉDIARD

The letters and figures (e.g. ◆ 1 G3) give grid references for the maps at the end of the guide.

Le Palais des Thés
◆ 1 H10
35, rue de l'Abbé-Grégoire
75006
Tel. 01 45 48 85 81
Open Tue.–Fri.
11am–7pm,
Mon. noon–7pm,
Sat. 10.30am–7pm
François-Xavier Delmas has been importing some 300 varieties of tea (around 30 tons every year) from various parts of the world since 1987, including a mysterious tea from the garden of a Tibetan monastery. The store also sells tea-related objects such as teapots, filters and confectionery (chocolate bonbons, etc.).

WINES

Caves des Gobelins
◆ 5 E4
56, av. des Gobelins
75013
Tel. 01 43 31 66 79
Open Tue.–Sat.
9am–1pm and
3–8pm
It is Éric Merlet who now bottles all the vintages, but Bernard Merlet is not far away. Both divide their time between the vineyards and their store. Top-quality selection of wines and expert advice in these authentic Left Bank cellars.

Cave Taillevent
◆ 9 C10
199, rue du Faubourg-Saint-Honoré 75008
Tel. 01 45 61 14 09
Open Tue.–Sat.
9am–7.30pm,
Mon. 2–7.30pm
Cellar and restaurant owner at the very top of his profession. Outstanding old vintages as well as more modest wines (from less than €10) chosen with great

expertise. Wine sampling on Saturdays. Advice given. Cellar tours are available.

Estève
◆ 2 H8
10, rue de la Cerisaie
75004
Tel. 01 42 72 33 05
Open Tue.–Sat.
10am–1.30pm and
3–7.30pm
Jean-Christophe Estève, president of the Fédération Nationale des Cavistes Indépendants (national federation of independant cellarmen), represents his trade and fellow members with honor. Personal choice of wines with a strong emphasis on southwestern France.

Legrand Filles et Fils
◆ 2 B3
1, rue de la Banque
75001
Tel. 01 42 60 07 12
Open Tue.–Fri.
10am–7.30pm,
Sat. 10am–7pm
One of the prettiest early 20th-century stores in Paris. Run by the third generation of Legrands, it offers a huge and most reliable selection of wines. It also sells objects related to the wine business (carafes, glasses, etc.). Warehouse and sales outlet in the 13th arrondissement.

LUXURY GROCERIES

Fauchon
◆ 1 H2
26–30, pl. de la Madeleine
75008
Tel. 01 47 42 60 11
Open Mon.–Sat.
9.30am–7pm.
One of the finest Parisian delicatessens selling thousands of items from the rare

CAVES DES GOBELINS

BETTMAN AND BARTON

(redcurrant jam from Bar-le-Duc deseeded with goose feathers) to the unusual (honey made from bees living on the roof of the Opera). It is almost a museum of chic food. Huge selection of more usual items as well. Many catering and eating outlets. Stunning window display at Christmas. Very expensive, of course.

La Grande Épicerie de Paris
Bon Marché
◆ 1 H9
38, rue de Sèvres
75007
Tel. 01 44 39 81 00
Open 8.30am–9pm
Mon.–Fri, Sat. till
8pm
Everything from basic consumables to the more unusual items expected of a luxury grocery store (homemade lemonade, ravioli with chocolate). Fine Italian selection among the many products arranged according to country of origin. In just a few years, Philippe Thomas has succeeded in creating on the Left

Bank a store that is both functional and of high gastronomic standards.

Hédiard
◆ 1 H2
21, pl. de la Madeleine
75008
Tel. 01 43 12 88 88
Open Mon.–Sat.
8.30am–9pm
Delicatessen store par excellence, Hédiard offers, with a touch of exoticism, fruit and vegetables from around the world, rare condiments, some 60 different types of spices, almost as many jams (banana, green tomato, ginger, etc.), and wonderful candied fruits. Excellent selection of wines and spirits. Many outlets in Paris.

Izraël
◆ 2 F7
30, rue François-Miron
75004
Tel. 01 42 72 66 23
Open Tue.–Fri.
9.30am–1pm and 2.30–7pm,
Sat. 9am–7pm
Closed Aug.
Picture-postcard

of a typical French delicatessen store. It is run by a bearded enthusiast who sells products from all over the world: from garlands of hot red peppers to African baskets.

Lafayette Gourmet
◆ 1 J1
Galeries Lafayette
40, bd Haussmann
75009
Tel. 01 48 74 46 06
Open Mon.–Sat.
9.30am–8.30pm
(until 9pm on Thur.)
An original feature here is the mini-restaurant counter in each of the eight food sections (such as the sushi bar, right by the entrance). You can enjoy a fresh-fruit cocktail while you're shopping in the fruit-and-veg section, sample a few cheeses in the cheese department, and finish with the special of the day in the tea-and-coffee section. Service available between 11am and 6pm. Be prepared to wait to be served.

Lenôtre
◆ 8 J5
48, av. Victor-Hugo
75016
Tel. 01 45 02 21 21
Open daily 9am–9pm
With its many outlets in Paris and all over France, Lenôtre is a real gourmet empire.

DEPARTEMENT STORES

BHV
◆ 2 E7
52-56, rue de Rivoli
75001
Tel. 01 42 74 90 00
Open Mon.–Sat.
9.30am–7pm (until
10pm on Thur)
The BHV is known for its fabulous do-it-yourself and interior decoration departments.

Bon Marché
◆ 1 H9
22, rue de Sèvres
75007
Tel. 01 44 39 80 00
www.lebonmarche.fr
Open Mon.–Fri.
9.30am–7pm (until
9pm on Thur., 8pm
on Sat.)
The first of Paris' department store, Bon Marché has also become in the past decade the chicest of them all, the French equivalent of Harvey Nichols or Bergdorf Goodman, selling top names in fashion, accessories, cosmetics etc. It has

LA SAMARITAINE

recently opened La Grande Epicerie, a huge deli store selling all the best delicacies the world has to offer, rivalizing with the luxury stores Fauchon or Hédiard (see p. 483).

Galeries Lafayette
◆ 1 J1
40, bd Haussmann,
75009
Tel. 01 42 82 34 56
www.galerieslafayette.
com
Open Mon.–Sat.
9.30am–7.30pm
(until 9pm on Thur.)
The listed 19th-

century building and its famous cupola alone are worth a visit. As for the contents of this luxury "bazaar", you will find the usual top fashion designers, street brands, accessories, shoes, perfume and avast array of services. Plus next door, the Lafayette Gourmet, a fantastic deli (see above).

Madelios
◆ 1 H2
23, bd de la
Madeleine, 75001
Tel. 01 53 45 00 00
Open Mon.–Sat.
10am–7pm
Department store exclusively for men: prêt-à-porter and designer accessories. VIP services: shoe-shiner, cobbler and beauty salon. Café.

Printemps
◆ 1 I1
64, bd Haussmann
75009
Tel. 01 42 82 57 87
www.printemps.com
Open Mon.–Sat.
9.30am–7pm (until
10pm on Thur.).
Three buildings that make up the Printemps are linked

to one another by bridges: Printemps Femme (fashion for women, all top brands and services such as personal shopper), Printemps Homme (the same for men), and Decoration (perfume, tableware, fabrics, bedlinen).

Samaritaine
◆ 2 C6
Rue de Rivoli
75001
Tel. 01 40 41 20 20
Open Mon.–Sat.
9.30am–7pm (until
9pm on Thur., 8pm
on Sat.)
Splendid Art Deco building overlooking the river Seine, with beautiful elaborate polychrome cast-iron staircase. Panoramic restaurant on the top floor. Top names in decoration and clothing.

FASHION ACCESSORIES

BUTTONS

Entrée des Fournisseurs
◆ 2 G7
8, rue des Francs-Bourgeois
75003
Tel. 01 48 87 58 98
Open Tue.–Fri.
10.30am–7pm,
Sat. 11am–7pm,
Mon. 2.30–7pm
This haberdasher's has everything: beads arranged according to country or color; buttons; and embroidery sets.

HATS

Elvis Pompilio
◆ 1 I8
62, rue des Saints-Pères 75006
Tel. 01 45 44 82 02
Open Wed.–Sat.
11am–7pm
Displayed in the window, perched on different stands at different heights, are unique models or limited editions of hats. In the workshop, which

The letters and figures (e.g. ◆ 1 G3) give grid references for the maps at the end of the guide.

resembles a garden, hats are made for some of the greatest fashion designers.

Marie Mercié
◆ 2 D4
56, rue Tiquetonne
75001
Tel. 01 40 26 60 68
Open Mon.–Sat.
11am–7pm
Hats made to measure take ten days. You wish it were compulsory to wear a hat.

HATS & SHOES
Philippe Model
◆ 1 J3
33, pl. du Marché-Saint-Honoré
75001
Tel. 01 42 96 89 02
Open Mon.–Sat.
10am– 7pm
Closed in Aug.
Hat designer Philippe Model – his finest designs are frequently seen at the Grand Prix de Diane (the French Ascot) – has now added shoes and accessories to his collections.

LUXURY LEATHER GOODS
Hermès
◆ 1 H3
24, rue du Faubourg-Saint-Honoré
75008
Tel. 01 40 17 47 17
Open Mon.–Sat.
10.30am–6.30pm
The atmosphere of the tiny Hermès museum, in the founders' former office above the store (visits by appointment) gives a glimpse of a past which contrasts sharply with the modern store.

Louis Vuitton
◆ 1 C2
101, av. des Champs-Élysées
75008
Tel. 01 53 57 24 00
Open Mon.–Sat.
10am–8pm
The latest of Louis

Vuitton boutiques to be opened in Paris, this has the full range of Louis Vuitton products: travel goods and fine leatherwork, of course, but also shoes and the prêt-à-porter line created by the American Max Jacobs.

MISCELLANEOUS
Cerize
◆ 1 I3
380, rue Saint-Honoré
75001
Tel. 01 42 60 84 84
Open Mon.–Sat.
10am–7.30pm
Very impressive boutique with impressive costume jewelry, embroidered bags, even T-shirts. The word "accessory" takes on a whole new meaning here. The best designs are regularly displayed on two levels, and every month a young unknown artist or a well-established craftsman is put in the spotlight.

Colette
◆ 1 J4
213, rue Saint-Honoré
75001
Tel. 01 55 35 33 90
Open Mon.–Sat.
10.30am–7.30pm
On display are three levels of selected products by designers from around the world who follow the "Colette" concept of lifestyle, exclusive designs and minimalism. Names change but the spirit remains: everything related to art, design, accessories, cosmetics, electronics, etc. is given special prominence here. There is also an art gallery and water bar (see p. 472)

PURSES
Renaud Pellegrino
◆ 1 H3
14, rue du Faubourg-Saint-Honoré
75008
Tel. 01 42 65 35 52
Open Mon.–Sat.
9am–7pm.
The epitomy of Parisian chic, these designs boast surprising materials and unusual colors. Here you will find casual and evening purses such as the classic "Novella" or "Shirley" models with handles with pearls made from Bohemia glass.

SHOES
Christian Louboutin
◆ 2 B5
19, rue J.-J.-Rousseau
75001
Tel. 01 42 36 05 31
Open Mon.–Sat.
10.30am–7pm
Formerly assistant to Roger Vivier and nicknamed "The Man with the Red Shoe Soles", Christian Louboutin is fond of designing unusual shoes recognized the world over.

Delage
◆ 2 B4
15, rue de Valois
75001
Tel. 01 42 84 15 24
Open Wed.–Fri.
10.30am–6.30pm,
Mon. and Sat.
10.30am–1pm
and 2–6.30pm
Simple, weightless shapes, maximum comfort and unusual colors.

Pierre Corthay
◆ 1 I2
1, rue Volney 75002
Tel. 01 42 61 08 89
Open Mon.–Sat.
9.30am–7pm
Pierre Corthay makes shoes and boots for men and women, for town and riding. He only works to order, carefully molding a cast for each foot,

using selected, noble leathers. Watch him at work though the store window. On Saturday, knock on the door to be let in.

Raymond Massaro
◆ 1 I3
2, rue de la Paix
75002
Tel. 01 42 61 00 29
Open Mon.–Fri.
9.30am–12.30pm
and 2–6pm
The Massaro bussiness started a century ago. Today Raymond Massaro, an artist and craftsman, perpetuates his ancestral and renowned trade, producing entirely hand-made shoes, supplying Chanel, Dior, Lagerfeld and a few other lucky mortals with his unique creations.

Sidonie Larizzi
◆ 1 D3
8, rue de Marignan
75008
Tel. 01 43 59 38 87
Open Mon.–Sat.
10.30am–7pm
Sidonie Larizzi's own unique style (instep, materials used, etc.) has conquered many a great designer.

JEWELRY
Place Vendôme
Alltogether the most expensive square in Paris. On either side of the Ritz Hotel you will find the most luxurious jewelers in the country: **Boucheron** (no. 26), on the square since 1893; **Chaumet** (no. 12) who designed Napoleon I's coronation jewels; **Mauboussin** (no. 20) who mixes colors like no one else; **Van Cleef & Arpels** (no. 22) who perfected the technique of jewel setting without apparent claws; and last but not least,

Cartier, whose trademark, the bestiary, first appeared in 1914 in the shape of a panther.

Mellerio
◆ **1** I3
9, rue de la Paix
75002
Tel. 01 42 61 57 53
Open Mon.–Sat.
10am–1pm and
2–6.30pm
The oldest jewelers in this famous street.

On Aura Tout Vu
◆ **2** A4
Palais-Royal
30, galerie de Montpensier
75001
Tel. 01 42 60 70 55
Open Tue.–Sat.
10am–7pm; Mon.
by appointment
Designer jewelry and haute couture buttons. This boutique-cum-gallery-cum-meeting place was born out of the association of three designers. As a regular event, different artists are commissioned to create jewelry and present their work.

Sic Amor
◆ **2** F7
20, rue du Pont-Louis-Philippe
75004
Tel. 01 42 76 02 37
Open Tue.–Sat.
10.30am–2pm,
3–7.30pm; Sun.–
Mon. 2–7.30pm.
A store full of tempting items where the designers take turns on "guard duty". Stefano Poletti's "Botanicus" collection, in colored Murano glass, is absolutely beautiful.

Annick Goutal
◆ **1** H6
16, rue de Bellechasse 75007
Tel. 01 45 51 36 13
Open Mon.–Sat.
10am–1.30pm and
2.30–7pm

Small, sand-colored boutique whose décor consists mostly of perfume bottles. The collection includes Goutal's first creation, "Sables" and 13 more recent scents and eaux de toilette.

Guerlain
◆ **1** D2
68, av. des
Champs-Élysées
75008
Tel. 01 45 62 52 57
Open Mon.–Sat.
10.30am–8pm,
Sun. 3–7pm
One of the first perfume makers in Paris, who now sells over 300 different scents. The building dates from 1913 and remains one of the most beautiful on the avenue.

Les Salons du Palais-Royal Shiseido
◆ **2** B4
142, galerie de Valois
75001
Tel. 01 49 27 09 09
www.salons-shiseido.com
Open Mon.–Sat.
10am–7pm
This store, decorated in lush Directoire style and in shades of purple, is the only place that sells the 17 "Eaux exclusives" by Serge Lutens (Bois de Violette, Iris, Ambre Sultan). Mail order also available.

Miller & Bertaux
◆ **2** F7
7, rue Ferdinand-Duval 75004
Tel. 01 42 78 28 39
Open Tue.–Sat.
11am–1.30pm and
2–7pm, Mon. 2–7pm
A store with 1,001 ideas from all over the world: clothes, objects and small, simply designed

items of furniture, as well as stationery, collage-maps, toys and amulets and burning oils (Cedarwood, El Nil)...

Couleurs du quai Voltaire
◆ **1** J6
3, quai Voltaire
75007
Tel. 01 42 60 72 15
Open Mon. 2–
6.30pm, Tue.–Sat.
9.30am–12.30pm
and 2–6.30pm
Walking into this century-old store is akin to opening an old, well-loved box of paints. Its three floors are crammed full of everything an artist could possibly need, from portable easels to lapis-lazuli in powder form.

Baccarat
◆ **10** E10
30 bis, rue de Paradis
75010
Tel. 01 47 70 64 30
Open Mon.–Sat.
10am–6.30pm
Following a visit to the cristal museum, you will probably be tempted to buy everything in the boutique which sells unique pieces, among which are contemporary designs.

Lalique
◆ **1** H3
11, rue Royale
75008
Tel. 01 53 05 12 12
Open Mon.–Fri.
10am–6.30pm (Sat.
until 7pm)
Originally a jeweler, René Lalique did not become involved in the creation of perfume bottles until 1911. Time has not stood still in this store which now also sells table glassware, decorative objects for the office and jewelry bearing the famous name.

Galerie Sentou
◆ **1** H7
26, bd Raspail
75007
Tel. 01 45 49 00 05
Open Mon. 2–7pm,
Tue.–Sat. 11am–7pm
As well as producing and selling the work of industrial designer Roger Tallon, the Galerie Sentou is also the sole importer and distributor in Europe for the 120 paper lamps by the sculptor Nogushi. There is a second outlet at nos.18 and 24, rue du Pont-Louis-Philippe, 75004.

Galerie Bamyan
◆ **2** F8
24 and 51, rue Saint-Louis-en-l'Île
75004
Tel. 01 46 33 69 66
Open Tue.–Sat.
11.30am–8pm,
Sun. 2.30pm–8pm
She is blonde, he is Afghan. Together they make regular trips to central Asia to bring back furniture, carpets and textiles, as well as jewelry from Pakistan, southern Russia, India, Nepal and Iran.

La Tuile à Loup
◆ **5** E2
35, rue Daubenton
75005
Tel. 01 47 07 28 90
Open Tue.–Sat.
10.30am– 7pm
It is difficult to know where to look in this boutique with its French provincial crafts and works by contemporary artists. The place is full of wicker objects hanging from the ceiling, glazed terracotta pots piled up on huge tables, "santons" from Provence, textiles. A wide range of quality items.

*The letters and figures (e.g. ◆ 1 G3) give grid
references for the maps at the end of the guide.*

FRAMING
Eugénie Seigneur
◆ 2 G5
16, rue Charlot
75003
Tel. 01 48 04 81 96
Open Mon.–Fri.
10am–1pm and
2–7pm, Sat. 10am–
1pm and 3–7pm
*Framed by a
painting, the front
of this store is an
example of the
originality of its
owner who, with
the help of her
assistants, creates
personalized frames.
Her range of mirrors
"reinvented" from
old frames is truly
remarkable (from
€137).*

FURNITURE AND ACCESSORIES
Liwan
◆ 2 A9
8, rue Saint-Sulpice
75006
Tel. 01 43 26 07 40
Open Mon. 2–7pm,
Tue.–Sat. 10.30am–
7pm
*Three stories of
superbly arranged
space. From top to
bottom: the
Hammam (a floor
dedicated to
bathrobes, friction
gloves, soaps...),
the Djelabba (for
clothes), and the
Liwan (set as the
interior courtyard of
a Lebanese house
and selling crockery,
tablelinen, etc.).*

Maison de Famille
◆ 2 A9
29, rue Saint-Sulpice
75006
Tel. 01 40 46 97 47
Open Mon.–Sat.
10.30am–7pm
*Everything here is
displayed in a warm,
personal manner.
The owner of this
boutique has
devoted most of its
space to recreating
the interior of a real
home, with hidden
staircases, moldings
and floorboards.
The various rooms
are filled with*
*furniture, objects
and clothes (on the
first floor).*

Victoria Perry Higgins
◆ 2 A8
24, rue de Buci
75006
Tel. 01 43 54 27 27
Open Tue.–Sat.
11am–7.30pm,
Mon. 2pm–7.30pm,
Sun. 11am–1pm and
3pm–7.30pm.
*The bright, heavy
decoration of the
store front, which
is changed every
season, is the first
thing to greet you
as you approach the
store. Once inside,
you will discover
treasures, such as
a wide array of
furniture, lamps,
mirrors and pictures.
All are top-quality
reproductions of
18th- or 19th-
century objects from
Italy. The various
styles (Louis XV,
Empire, Restoration,
etc.) are all displayed
together in a
cheerful, fictional
opulence.*

PÂTE DE VERRE
Daum
◆ 1 I3
4, rue de la Paix
75002
Tel. 01 42 61 25 25
Open Mon.–Sat.
10am–7pm
*Pâte de verre
specialists.*

POTTERY
Gien
◆ 1 H1
18, rue de l'Arcade
75008
Tel. 01 42 66 52 32
Open Tue.–Fri.
10.30am–7pm,
Sat. 11am–6.30pm.
*Gien pottery is
widely admired,
and pieces of both
antique and
contemporary
designs are displayed
here on tables or
hung on a wall.
The wall display
is particularly
stunning.*

RARE BOOKS
La Maison Rustique
◆ 2 A7
26, rue Jacob, 75006
Tel. 01 42 34 96 60
Open Mon.–Sat.
10am–7pm
*A charming,
decorative
bookstore. Hundreds
of richly illustrated
art books and
specialist works from
all over the world:
interior decoration,
gardening, botany
(wonderful books
on roses, from
detailed Anglo-
Saxon works to
photographic
reproductions of
interior designer
Jacques Garcia's
arrangements).
The bookstore
opposite specializes
in nautical works.*

SILVERSMITHING
Christofle
◆ 1 H3
9, rue Royale
75008
Tel. 01 55 27 99 00
Open Mon.–Sat.
10am–7pm
*Interesting little
museum above the
store in the Rue
Royale (visits by
appointment)
displaying some
extremely beautiful
pieces.*

STATIONERY
Calligrane
◆ 2 F7
4 and 6, rue du
Pont-Louis-Philippe
75004
Tel. 01 40 27 00 74
Open Tue.–Sat.
noon–7pm
*The rue du Pont-
Louis-Philippe is the
street par excellence
for those who love
writing and fine
paper. Calligrane –
undoubtedly the
most innovative
designer in this field
– offers a range of
Calligrane stationery,
a selection of
Fabriano paper
(17 colors) and
designer office*
*accessories. The store
also sells a large
selection of papers
from countries all
over the world.*

TEXTILES
Galerie de Textiles
◆ 2 A8
5, rue Lobineau
75006
Tel. 01 43 25 01 64
Open Tue.–Sat.
11am–7pm
*Stacked on shelves,
draped over sofas
or hanging from
wooden rails, textiles
from Asia, Africa and
America pay homage
to a particular artist,
technique or color.*

Le Jardin Moghol
◆ 2 F6
53, rue Vieille-du-
Temple 75004
Tel. 01 48 87 41 32
Open Tue.–Fri.
11am–7pm,
Sat. 11am–7.30pm
*Fabrics designed by
two artists living in
India: Brigitte Singh
creates a beautiful
range of colored
textiles (shirts,
tablecloths, etc.)
whose colors relate
to the 18th-century
Mogul court; Neeru
Kumar designs
geometric weaves
(jackets, car rugs,
etc.) in brown, beige
and black.*

Maison de Vacances
◆ 2 A4
63–64, galerie
Montpensier 75001
Tel. 01 47 03 99 74
Open Mon.–Sat.
10.30am–1pm and
2–7pm
*It is deeply satisfying
to see fabrics lying
side by side here,
where the
expression "the art
of the table" means
just what it says.
House linen can be
ordered in matching
colors. Where else
would you find
household linen
catering to your
needs, on this
sort of scale?*

◆ PLACES TO VISIT

The ▲ symbol refers to the Itineraries section, while the ◆ refers to the map section.
We have only listed here places that are open to the public.

PARIS

(FORMER) ABBEY OF PORT-ROYAL DE PARIS Maternité Baudelocque 123–125, bd de Port-Royal 75014	*Site open daily.*	▲ 259 ◆ 5 B3
ABBEY OF ST-MARTIN-DES-CHAMPS Rue Réaumur 75002	*See Musée des Arts et Métiers.*	▲ 382 ◆ 2 F3
ALIGRE MARKET Rue d'Aligre 75012	*Open Tue.–Sun. 7am–1.30pm.*	▲ 406 ◆ 3 A9
ARC DE TRIOMPHE Place Charles-de-Gaulle 75008 Tel. 01 44 09 89 94	*Triumphal Arch open daily 10am–11pm (April–Sep.);* *10am–10.30pm (Oct.–Mar.).*	▲ 316 ◆ 1 B1
ARCHE (GRANDE) Le Parvis de La Défense 92044 Puteaux Tel. 01 49 07 27 27	*Open daily.* *Summer: 10am–8pm; winter: 10am–7pm.* *Closed public hols.*	▲ 321
THE ARSENAL 21, bd Morland 75004 Tel. 01 42 76 33 97	*Open Tue.–Sat. 10.30am–6.30pm, Sun. 11am–7pm.*	▲ 404 ◆ 2 G9
ASSEMBLÉE NATIONALE 126, rue de l'Université 75007 Visitors' entrance: 33 bis, quai d'Orsay Tel. 01 40 63 99 99 (recorded information) or 01 40 63 60 00 *www.assemblee-nationale.fr*	*Individual visits Sat. 10am, 2pm and 3pm.* *Closed when the Assemblée is in session,* *Sun., public hols and June 5.* *Free admission. Proof of identity required.* *Reservations for group visits (Tel. 01 40 63 64 08).*	▲ 265 ◆ 1 G5
BANQUE NATIONALE DE PARIS 16, bd des Italiens 75009	*Not open to the public.*	▲ 352 ◆ 2 B2
BASILICA OF NOTRE-DAME-DES-VICTOIRES Place des Petits-Pères 75002 Tel. 01 42 60 90 47	*Basilica open Mon.–Fri. 7.30am–7.45pm,* *Sat. 7.30am–7.30pm, Sun. and public hols* *8.30am–12.30pm and 2.30–7.30pm.*	▲ 340 ◆ 2 B3
BASILICA OF STE-CLOTILDE 12, rue Martignac 75007 Tel. 01 44 18 62 63	*Basilica open daily 9am–6.30pm.*	▲ 267 ◆ 1 G6
LE BELLEVILLOISE 23–25, rue Boyer 75020	*Office building.*	▲ 410 ◆ 3 D3
BIBLIOTHÈQUE NATIONALE – FRANÇOIS-MITTERRAND SITE 11, quai François-Mauriac 75013 Entrance on esplanade level Tour des Nombres Tel. 01 53 79 53 79 *www.bnf.fr*	*Library: open to visitors over the age of 16* *Tue.–Sat. 10am–8pm, Sun. noon–7pm.* *Exhibition room: Tue.–Sat. 9am–8pm,* *Sun. noon–7pm.* *Closed public hols.*	▲ 232 ◆ 5 J5
BIBLIOTHÈQUE NATIONALE – RICHELIEU SITE 58, rue de Richelieu 75002 Tel. 01 53 79 59 59 CABINET DES MÉDAILLES ET DES ANTIQUES Tel. 01 47 03 83 30	*Library: open Mon.–Sat. 9am–5pm.* *(Opening times vary according to departments.)* *Medal room: open Mon.–Fri. 9am–6pm,* *Sat. 9am–5pm.*	▲ 341 ◆ 2 B3 ▲ 172
BIBLIOTHÈQUE STE-GENEVIÈVE 10, place du Panthéon 75005 Tel. 01 44 41 97 97	*Open Mon.–Sat. 10am–6pm.* *The reading room closes at 10pm.* *Closed public hols and Aug.*	▲ 255 ◆ 2 C10

BOIS DE BOULOGNE 75016 JARDIN D'ACCLIMATATION Tel. 01 40 67 99 16 PARC DE BAGATELLE Tel. 01 45 01 20 50 SERRES D'AUTEUIL 1, av. Gordon-Bennet 3, av. d'Auteuil 75016 Tel. 01 40 71 74 00	*The storms that took place in Dec. 1999 caused a great deal of damage to the woods.* *Garden: open daily 10am–7pm (June–Sep.); 10am–6pm (Oct.–May).* *Park: open daily 9am–5pm (fall and winter); 9am–8pm (summer); 9am–7pm (Sep.).* *Auteuil greenhouses: open daily 10am–5pm, (Oct.–March); 9am–6pm (April–Sep.).*	▲ 212 ◆ 8 ▲ 213 ◆ 8 F1 ▲ 207 ◆ 8 D3 ▲ 205 ◆ 8 D7
BOIS DE VINCENNES 53, av. Saint-Maurice 75012 Tel. 01 44 75 20 10 FLORAL GARDENS CASTLE ESPLANADE 9, cours Lumière Route de la Pyramide 75012 Tel. 01 55 94 20 20 VINCENNES ZOO	*The storms that took place in Dec. 1999 caused a great deal of damage to the woods.* *Floral garden and castle esplanade: open daily sunrise–5pm (winter); sunrise–6pm (spring); sunrise–8pm (summer); sunrise–7pm (fall).* *Zoo: open daily 9am–6pm (until 6.30pm on Sun. and public hols).*	▲ 214 ◆ 4 ▲ 205 ◆ 4 G7 ▲ 214 ◆ 4 E8
BOURSE (STOCK EXCHANGE) Palais Brongniart Place de la Bourse 75002 Tel. 01 49 27 55 55 *www.bourse-de-paris.fr*	*Group visits by appointment only.*	▲ 353 ◆ 2 B2
BRASSERIE FLO 7, cour des Petites-Écuries 75010 Tel. 01 47 70 13 59	*Service noon–3pm and 7pm–1.30am.*	▲ 426 ◆ 2 E1
CARREAU DU TEMPLE (MARKET) 2, rue Pérrée 75003	*Open Tue.–Sun. 8.30am–12.30pm.*	▲ 386 ◆ 2 G4
CATACOMBS 1, place Denfert-Rochereau 75014	*Open Tue. 11am–4pm, Wed.–Sun. 9am–4pm. Closed Mon. and public hols.*	▲ 274 ◆ 6 J4
CHAPELLE EXPIATOIRE 29, rue Pasquier 75008 Tel. 01 44 32 18 01	*Open Thur.–Sat. 1–5pm.*	▲ 346 ◆ 9 H10
CHAPELLE DE LA MÉDAILLE MIRACULEUSE 140, rue du Bac 75007 Tel. 01 49 54 78 88	*Open Mon.–Sat. 7.45am–1pm and 2.30–7pm.*	▲ 270 ◆ 1 H9
CHAPELLE DES PRÊTRES-DE-LA-CONGRÉGATION-DE-LA-MISSION 95, rue de Sèvres 75007 Tel. 01 45 49 84 84	*Open daily 7am–noon and 1.30–6.30pm.*	▲ 271 ◆ 1 H9
CHINAGORA 1, place du Confluent-France-Chine 94000 Alfortville Tel. 01 45 18 33 06	*Open noon–2.30pm and 7–11pm.*	▲ X
CHURCH OF LA MADELEINE Place de la Madeleine 75008	*Open Mon.–Sat. 7am–7pm, Sun. and public hols 7am–1.30pm and 3.30–7pm.*	▲ 347 ◆ 1 H2
CHURCH OF NOTRE-DAME-DE-L'ASSOMPTION 263 bis, rue Saint-Honoré 75016 Tel. 01 42 61 37 47	*Open Mon.–Fri. 8.30am–noon and 2–7pm, Sat.–Sun. 8am–1pm and 5–8pm.*	▲ 336 ◆ 1 H3
CHURCH OF NOTRE-DAME-D'AUTEUIL 1, rue Corot 75016 Tel. 01 42 30 50 01	*Open Mon.–Fri. 8.15am–noon and 2–7pm, Sat.–Sun. 9am–noon and 3–7.30pm.*	▲ 306 ◆ 7 E4

◆ PLACES TO VISIT

The ▲ symbol refers to the Itineraries section,
while the ◆ refers to the maps

CHURCH OF NOTRE-DAME-DE BONNE-NOUVELLE 19 bis, rue Beauregard 75002 Tel. 01 42 33 65 74	*Open Mon.–Fri. 9am–noon and 4–7pm, Sat.–Sun. 8.30am–noon (summer); Mon.–Fri 8am–7pm, Sat.–Sun. 8.30am–noon (winter).*	▲ 382 ◆ 2 D2
CHURCH OF NOTRE-DAME-DE-LA-CONSOLATION 23, rue Jean-Goujon 75008 Tel. 01 42 25 61 84	*Open daily 8am–7pm.*	▲ 313 ◆ 1 D4
CHURCH OF NOTRE-DAME-DE-LORETTE 18, rue de Châteaudun 75009 Tel. 01 48 78 92 72	*Open Mon.–Sat. 8am–7pm.*	▲ 426 ◆ 10 B9
CHURCH OF NOTRE-DAME-DES-OTAGES 51, rue Borrégo 75020 Tel. 01 43 64 60 70	*Open Mon.–Sat. 8am–7pm, Sun. 8am–noon.*	▲ 410 ◆ 11 F10
CHURCH OF NOTRE-DAME-DU-TRAVAIL-DE-PLAISANCE 59, rue Vercingétorix 75014 Tel. 01 44 10 72 92	*Open Tue.–Fri. 9.30am–12.15pm and 2.30–6.30pm, Sat. 3–7pm, Sun. 10am–noon.*	▲ 287 ◆ 6 G4
CHURCH OF ST-AUGUSTIN Place Saint-Augustin 75008 Tel. 01 45 22 23 12	*Open Tue.–Fri. 10am–12.45pm and 3.30–6pm, Sat. 10am–noon and 4–7.30pm, Sun. 10am–noon and 5.30–7.30pm. Open later in winter.*	▲ 346 ◆ 9 G9
CHURCH OF ST-ÉTIENNE-DU-MONT Place Sainte-Geneviève 75005 Tel. 01 43 54 11 79	*Open Mon.–Fri. and Sun. 8am–8pm, Sat. 8am–noon and 2–8pm (Sep.–June); daily 10am–noon and 4–7pm (July–Aug.).*	▲ 254 ◆ 2 D10
CHURCH OF ST-EUSTACHE 2, rue du Jour 75001 Tel. 01 42 33 77 87	*Open Mon.–Sat. 9am–7pm, Sun. 8.15am–12.30pm and 2.30–7pm.*	▲ 378 ◆ 2 C4
CHURCH OF ST-GERMAIN-L'AUXERROIS 2, place du Louvre 75001 Tél 01 42 60 13 96	*Open daily 8am–8pm. No visits during services.*	▲ 334 ◆ 2 B6
CHURCH OF ST-GERMAIN-DES-PRÉS 3, place Saint-Germain-des-Prés 75006 Tel. 01 46 33 15 05 CHAPELLE SAINT-SYMPHORIEN	*Church: open Mon.–Fri. 8am–7.30pm, Sat.–Sun. 8.30am–7.30pm.* *Chapel: open Tue. and Thur. 1.30am–5.30pm.*	▲ 236 ◆ 1 I8
CHURCH OF ST-GERVAIS-SAINT-PROTAIS 13, rue des Barres 75004 Tel. 01 48 87 32 02	*Open daily 6am–9pm.*	▲ 401 ◆ 2 E7
CHURCH OF ST-JACQUES-DU-HAUT-PAS 252, rue Saint-Jacques 75005 Tel. 01 43 25 91 70	*Open Tue.–Sun. 11.45am–12.45pm and 3–7pm (July–Aug.), Tue.–Sun. 8am–12.30pm and 3–7.30pm (Sep.–June).*	▲ 247 ◆ 5 B1
CHURCH OF ST-JEAN-L'ÉVANGÉLISTE 19, rue des Abbesses 75018 Tel. 01 46 06 43 96	*Open Tue.–Sun. 10am–noon and 4–7.30pm (summer), 9am–noon and 3–7pm (winter).*	▲ 415 ◆ 10 B7
CHURCH OF ST-JULIEN-LE-PAUVRE 79, rue Galande 75005 Tel. 01 43 54 52 16	*Open Mon.–Sat. 9.30am–1pm and 3–6.30pm, Sun. 9.30am–1pm and 3–6.30pm.*	▲ 249 ◆ 2 D8
CHURCH OF ST-LOUIS-EN-L'ÎLE 19 bis, rue Saint-Louis-en-l'île 75004 Tel. 01 46 34 11 60	*Open Tue.–Sun. 9am–noon and 3–7pm.*	▲ 369 ◆ 2 F9
CHURCH OF ST-LOUIS-DES INVALIDES Ministry of Defense Hôtel National des Invalides 129, rue Grenelle 75007 Tel. 01 44 42 37 65 *www.invalides.org* ÉGLISE DES SOLDATS Esplanade des Invalides 75007	*Open daily 10am–6pm (summer), 10am–5pm (winter).*	▲ 291 ◆ 1 F7

CHURCH OF ST-MARTIN-DES-CHAMPS 36, rue Albert-Thomas 75010 Tel. 01 42 08 36 60	*Open daily 8.30am–noon and 4–7pm.*	▲ 382 ◆ **2** G2
CHURCH OF ST-MÉDARD 141, rue Mouffetard 75005 Tel. 01 44 08 87 00	*Open Tue.–Sun. 8am–12.30pm and 2.30–7.30pm.*	▲ 260 ◆ **5** D2
CHURCH OF ST-MERRI 76, rue de la Verrerie 75004 Tel. 01 42 71 93 93	*Open daily noon–1pm and 3–7pm.*	▲ 379 ◆ **2** D6
CHURCH OF ST-NICOLAS-DES-CHAMPS 254, rue Saint-Martin 75004 Tel. 01 42 72 92 54 *www.asaintnicolas.net*	*Open 9.30am–1pm and 3.30–7pm (summer).* *Ask for information on winter opening times.* *Closed 1st Fri. of every month.*	▲ 382 ◆ **2** E4
CHURCH OF ST-NICOLAS-DU-CHARDONNET 23, rue des Bernardins 75005 Tel. 01 44 27 07 90	*Traditionalist church.* *Open Mon.–Fri. 7.45am–7pm, Sat. 10.30am–1pm and* *3–7.30pm, Sun. 8.30am–1pm and 5–6.30pm.*	▲ 247 ◆ **2** D9
CHURCH OF ST-PAUL-ST-LOUIS 19, rue Saint-Antoine 75004 Tel. 01 42 72 30 32	*Open daily 9am–8pm (July–Aug.), 8am–8pm* *(Sep.–June).*	▲ 399 ◆ **2** G7
CHURCH OF ST-PHILIPPE-DU-ROULE 9, rue de Courcelles 75008 Tel. 01 53 53 00 40	*Open Mon.–Fri. 7.45am–1.15pm and 5–7pm,* *Sat. 3–7.45pm, Sun. 10.30am–1.15pm and* *5.30–7.30pm (July–Aug.); 8.45am–7pm (Sep.–June).*	▲ 344 ◆ **1** E1
CHURCH OF ST-PIERRE-DE-MONTMARTRE 2, rue du Mont-Cenis 75018 Tel. 01 46 06 57 63	*Open daily 8.45am–7.30pm.* *Closed afternoon on public holidays.*	▲ 417 ◆ **10** B6
CHURCH OF ST-ROCH 296, rue Saint-Honoré 75001 Tel. 01 42 44 13 20	*Open daily 8am–7.30pm.*	▲ 335 ◆ **1** J4
CHURCH OF ST-SERGE (RUSSIAN ORTHODOX CHURCH) 93, rue de Crimée 75019 Tel. 01 42 01 96 10	*Open during services Mon.-Fri. 8–9am, 6–6.45pm,* *Sat. 6–8pm, Sun. 10am–noon.* *Group visits by appointment.*	▲ II ◆ **11** D4
CHURCH OF ST-SÉVERIN 1, rue des Prêtres-Saint-Séverin 75005 Tel. 01 42 34 93 50	*Open Mon.–Sat. 11am–7.30pm, Sun. 9am–8.30pm.*	▲ 248 ◆ **2** C8
CHURCH OF ST-SULPICE 2, rue Palatine 75006 Tel. 01 46 33 21 78	*Open daily 7.30am–7.30pm.*	▲ 238 ◆ **2** A9
CHURCH OF ST-THOMAS-AQUINAS 1, rue de Montalembert 75007 Tel. 01 42 22 59 74	*Open Mon.–Sat. 8.30am–7pm, Sun. 9am–noon and* *4–7pm.*	▲ 264 ◆ **1** I7
CHURCH OF ST-VINCENT-DE PAUL 5, rue de Belzunce 75010 Tel. 01 48 78 47 47	*Open 8am–noon and 5–7pm.*	● 70 ◆ **10** E9
CHURCH OF STE-ÉLISABETH 195, rue du Temple 75003 Tel. 01 49 96 49 10	*Open Mon.–Sat. 8am–7pm, Sun. 8am–noon.* *Opening times can vary slightly; ask for information.*	▲ 386 ◆ **2** G4
CHURCH OF STE-MARGUERITE Chapel of Souls in Purgatory 36, rue Saint-Bernard 75011 Tel. 01 43 71 34 24	*Open Mon.–Sat. 8.30am–noon and 4–7.30pm,* *Sun. 8.30am–noon (July–Aug.); Mon.–Sat. 8.30am–* *noon and 2–7.30pm, Sun. 8.30am–noon (Sep.–June).*	▲ 407 ◆ **3** B8
CHURCH OF THE TRINITÉ 3, rue de la Trinité 75009 Tel./Fax 01 42 85 09 88	*Open Mon.–Sat. 7.15am–7pm,* *Sun. 8.30am–1pm and 5–8pm.*	▲ 425 ◆ **9** J9
CIMETIÈRE BELLEVILLE (DE) 40, rue du Télégraphe 75020 Tel. 01 46 36 66 23	*Open 8am–5.30pm (Nov.–March),* *8am–6pm (March–Nov.), Sundays from 9am.*	▲ 410 ◆ **11** C10
CIMETIÈRE PASSY (DE) 2, rue du Commandant-Schloesing 75016 Tel. 01 47 27 51 42	*Open Mon–Fri 8am–5.30pm (Nov.–March),* *8am–6pm (March–Nov.), Sat. from 8.30am and* *Sun. from 9am.*	▲ 301 ◆ **8** I8

◆ PLACES TO VISIT

The ▲ symbol refers to the Itineraries section,
while the ◆ refers to the maps

CITÉ DES ARTS 18, rue de l'Hôtel-de-Ville 75004 Tel. 01 42 78 71 72	*Exhibition room open Mon.–Fri. 2–7pm.* *Occasionally closed in summer.*	▲ *400* ◆ **2** F8
CITÉ INTERNATIONALE **UNIVERSITAIRE** 19, bd Jourdan 75014 Tel. 01 43 13 65 00	*Open 24 hours a day.*	◆ **5** B10
CITÉ DES SCIENCES **ET DE L'INDUSTRIE** **(CITY OF SCIENCE AND INDUSTRY)** Parc de la Villette 30, av. Corentin-Cariou 75019 Tel. 01 40 05 80 00 (recorded information) Information and reservations: 01 40 05 12 12 *www.cite-sciences.fr*	*Open Tue.–Sun.* EXHIBITIONS: *Explora: Tue.–Sat. 10am–6pm, Sun. 10am–7pm.* *Cité des enfants: Tue.–Sun.* *Poussières d'étoiles: 9pm and different times during* *school hols.* *Salle des Sciences et Actualités: noon–8pm.* *Aquarium: Tue.–Sat. 10am–6pm, Sun. 10am–7pm.* *Submarine: Tue.–Fri. 10.30am–5.30pm,* *Sat.–Sun. 11am–6pm.* SHOWS: *Planetarium: additional charge.* *Cinéma Louis-Lumière: access with Carte d'entrée* *aux expositions;* *Géode: Tue.–Sat. 10.30am–9.30pm,* *Sun. until 7.30pm.* *Two films are shown every evening from 6.30pm.* CONSULTATION: free access *Médiathèque: Tue. noon–8pm,* *Wed.–Sun. noon–7pm.* *Cité des métiers: Tue.–Fri.10am–6pm,* *Sat. noon–6pm.*	▲ *429* ◆ **11** C3
CLOÎTRE DES BILLETTES 22, rue des Archives 75003 Tel. 01 42 72 37 08	*Open during exhibitions.*	▲ *387* ◆ **2** E6
CLOS MONTMARTRE Corner of rues des Saules and Saint-Vincent 75018	*No access to the vineyards.* *Fête des Vendanges (grape harvest celebrations)* *1st weekend in Oct.*	▲ *421* ◆ **10** B5
CNIT 2, place Défense 92053 Paris-La Défense Tel. 01 46 92 11 11	*Open Mon.–Sat. 7am–11pm, stores 10am–7pm.*	▲ *318*
COLBERT ARCADE 32, rue Penthièvre 75008 Tel. 01 40 76 00 08	*Open during the day.*	▲ *340* ◆ **2** B3
COLLÈGE DE FRANCE 11, place Marcelin-Berthelot 75005 Tel. 01 44 27 12 11	*Access only as part of conferences.*	▲ *253* ◆ **2** C9
CONCIERGERIE 1, quai de l'Horloge 2, bd du Palais 75001 Tel. 01 53 73 78 50	*Open daily 9.30am–6pm. Closed public hols.* *Guided tours at 11am and 3pm; children's tour Wed.* *at 2.30pm.*	▲ *366* ◆ **2** C7
COUVENT DES GRANDS-JÉSUITES Lycée Charlemagne 14, rue Charlemagne 75004 Tel. 01 53 01 98 30	*Not open to the public.* *Contact the headmaster for permission to visit the* *college.*	▲ *399* ◆ **2** G7
ÉCOLE DES BEAUX-ARTS COUVENT DES PETITS-AUGUSTINS MUSÉE DES MOULAGES DE LA RENAISSANCE 14, rue Bonaparte 75006 Tel. 01 47 03 50 00	*Visits by appointment Mon. at 2pm.* *Temporary exhibitions: 1–7pm except Mon.*	▲ *242* ◆ **2** A7
ÉCOLE DE MÉDECINE ET CHIRURGIE 12, rue de l'École-de-Médecine 75006	*Opening times may vary.*	▲ *241* ◆ **2** B8
ÉCOLE MILITAIRE 1, place Joffre 75007 Tel. 01 44 42 30 11	*To arrange a visit contact the Caisse Nationale* *des Monuments Historiques et des Sites* *(Tel. 01 44 61 20 00)*	▲ *295* ◆ **1** D8

EIFFEL TOWER Champ-de-Mars 75007 Tel. 01 44 11 23 23 *www.tour-eiffel.fr*	*Open daily 9.30am–11pm (Sep.–June),* *9am–midnight (July–Aug.).*	▲ 296 ◆ 1 A6
ÉLYSÉE PALACE French President's residence 55, rue du Faubourg- Saint-Honoré 75008 Tel. 01 42 92 81 00	*Open on National Heritage days.*	▲ 345 ◆ 1 F2
FONDATION CARTIER **FOR CONTEMPORARY ART** 261, bd Raspail 75014 Tel. 01 42 18 56 50 *www.fondation-cartier.fr*	*Open Tue.–Sun. noon–8pm, Thur. noon–10pm.*	▲ 287 ◆ 6 J4
FONDATION LE CORBUSIER 10, square du Docteur-Blanche 75016 Tel. 01 42 88 41 53	*Villa Laroche: open Mon. 1.30–6pm,* *Tue.–Thur. 10.30am–12.30pm and 1.30–6pm.* *Libary: open by appointment.*	▲ 307 ◆ 7 E1
GALERIE VÉRO-DODAT 2, rue Bouloi 75001	*Open during the day.*	▲ 341 ◆ 2 B5
GEORGES-POMPIDOU CENTER 19, rue Beaubourg 75004 Tel. 01 44 78 12 33 *www.centrepompidou.fr*	*Museum and exhibitions:* *Open Wed.–Mon. 11am–9pm.* *Atelier Brancusi: open Wed.–Sun. 2–6pm.* *Public reference library: open Wed.–Fri. noon–10pm,* *Sat.–Sun. 11am–10pm. Closed May 1.*	▲ 380 ◆ 2 E5
GRAND PALAIS 3, av. du Général-Eisenhower 75008 Tel. 01 44 13 17 17	*Open Thur.–Mon. 10am–8pm, Wed. 10am–10pm.* *Reservations essential until 1pm.* *Closed May 1 and Dec. 25.* *Admission fees vary according to exhibitions.*	▲ 312 ◆ 1 E4
HAMMAM PACHA 147, rue Gabriel-Péri 93200 Saint-Denis Tel. 01 48 29 11 11	*Open Mon.–Wed. and Fri. noon–midnight,* *Thur. 10am–midnight, Sat.–Sun. and public hols* *10am–8pm.* *Women only.*	▲ V
HEURE JOYEUSE LIBRARY 6, rue des Prêtres- Saint-Séverin 75005 Tel. 01 43 25 83 24	*Open Tue., Thur.–Fri. 2–6.15pm,* *Wed. and Sat. 10.30am–6.15pm.*	▲ 248 ◆ 2 C8
HÔTEL ALBRET (D') Cultural service of Paris city council 29 bis–31, rue des Francs- Bourgeois 75003 Tel. 01 42 76 67 00	*Open Mon.–Fri. 9.30am–5.45pm.* *Documentation available on historic sites in Paris.*	▲ 394 ◆ 2 G6
HÔTEL AUMONT (D') Administrative tribunal of Paris 7, rue de Jouy 75004	*Requests for permission to visit must be made in* *writing to the president of the Tribunal.*	▲ 400 ◆ 2 G7
HÔTEL DE BEAUVAIS (DE) Paris administrative court of appeal 68, rue François-Miron 75004	*Renovation works currently being carried out.*	▲ 400 ◆ 2 F7
HÔTEL BERLIZE (DE) Café-Théâtre de la Gare 41, rue du Temple 75003	*Façade and courtyard.*	▲ 387 ◆ 2 E6
HÔTEL BOISGELIN (DE) Italian Embassy 51, rue de Varenne 75007 Tel. 01 49 54 03 00.	*Open on National Heritage days.*	▲ 268 ◆ 1 H8
HÔTEL DURET DE CHEVRY German Historical Institute 8, rue du Parc-Royal 75003 Tel. 01 42 71 02 11	*Open Mon.–Thur. 9am–5.30pm, Fri. 9am–4pm.*	▲ 391 ◆ 2 G6
HÔTEL GALLIFET (DE) Italian Cultural Institute 50, rue de Varenne 75007 Tel. 01 44 39 49 39 *www.iicparis.org*	*Library: open Mon.–Fri. 9.30am–1pm and 3–6pm.* *Teachers' services: open Mon.–Fri. 3–6pm.* *Cultural events.* *Closed April 25, July 14 and Nov. 1.*	▲ 269 ◆ 1 G7

The ▲ symbol refers to the Itineraries section,
while the ◆ refers to the maps

HÔTEL LAMOIGNON Bibliothèque Historique de la Ville de Paris 24, rue Pavée 75004 Tel. 01 44 59 29 40	*Open Mon.–Sat. 9.30am–6pm.* *Closed public hols.*	▲ 395 ◆ 2 G7
HÔTEL LAUZUN (DE) 17, quai d'Anjou 75004 *www.monuments-france.fr*	*For permission to visit, apply to the Caisse* *nationale des monuments historiques et des sites* *(Tel. 01 44 61 20 00).*	▲ 370 ◆ 2 F8
HÔTEL MARLE (DE) Swedish Cultural Center Fondation Tessin 11, rue Payenne 75003 Tel. 01 44 78 80 20	*Reception: open Tue.–Fri. 10am–1pm and 2–6pm.* *Exhibitions: open Tue.–Fri. 2–6pm, Sat. 2–7pm.* *Library: Tue. 2–5pm, Thur. 10am–1pm and by* *appointment.*	▲ 391 ◆ 2 G6
HÔTEL MATIGNON Residence of the Prime Minister 64, rue de Varenne 75007	*Normally closed to the public, but open on National* *Heritage days.*	▲ 269 ◆ 1 G7
HÔTEL RITZ 15, place Vendôme 75001 Tel. 01 43 16 30 30 *www.ritzparis.com*	*Visits by appointment with the commercial and* *reservations departments.*	▲ 337 ◆ 1 I3
HÔTEL ROHAN (DE) 87, rue Vieille-du-Temple 75003 Tel. 01 40 27 60 09	*Open during exhibitions.* *Program available from the Hôtel de Soubise.*	▲ 389 ◆ 2 G6
HÔTEL SENS (DE) Bibliothèque Fornay 1, rue du Figuier 75004 Tel. 01 42 78 14 60	*Library: open Tue.–Fri. 1.30–8.15pm,* *Sat. 10am–8.15pm.* *Temporary exhibitions.*	▲ 400 ◆ 2 F8
HÔTEL SOUBISE (DE) 60, rue des Francs-Bourgeois 75003	*Houses the Museum of French History.*	▲ 388 ◆ 2 F6
HÔTEL SULLY (DE) National Office for Historical Monuments 62, rue Saint-Antoine 75004 Tel. 01 44 61 20 00	*Open Tue.–Sat. 9am–7pm.* *Closed Jan. 1, May 1, Nov. 1 and 11, Dec. 25.* *Tours. Thu. 5pm.* *Heritage library: open Tue.–Fri. 10am–7pm.* *Access to the courtyard and the garden from Place* *des Vosges.*	▲ 398 ◆ 2 G7
HÔTEL VIGNY (DE) Ministère de la Culture Centre National de Conservation du Patrimoine 10, rue du Parc-Royal 75003 Tel. 01 40 15 73 00	*Ministry of Culture's documentation center:* *phone for opening times.* *Hôtel not open to the public.*	▲ 391 ◆ 2 G6
HÔTEL VILLARS (DE) Mayor's office of the 7th arrdt. 116, rue de Grenelle 75007	*Write to the Secrétaire Général to request* *permission to visit.*	▲ 267 ◆ 1 G7
HÔTEL VILLE (DE) Office of the Mayor of Paris Pl. de l'Hôtel de Ville 75004 Tel. 01 42 76 40 40 *www.paris-france.org*	*Visits depend on official events.* *Groups: by appointment (1 or 2 months' notice:* *Tel. 01 42 76 54 04).*	▲ 374 ◆ 2 E7
INSTITUT DE FRANCE 23, quai de Conti 75006 Tel. 01 44 41 44 41	*Open Sat., Sun and public holidays.* *Guided tours at 10.30am and 3pm.*	▲ 242 ◆ 2 B7
INSTITUT DU MONDE ARABE 1, rue des Fossés-Saint-Bernard 75005 Tel. 01 40 51 38 38 *www.imarabe.fr*	*Open Tue.–Sun. 10am–6pm.*	▲ 144 ◆ 2 F9
INTERNATIONAL BUDDHIST **INSTITUTE OF PARIS** 40 bis, route Ceinture-du-Lac Daumesnil 75012 Tel. 01 43 41 54 48	*Group visits by appointment Mon.–Fri. 2–6pm.*	▲ IX ◆ 4 H5
JARDIN DE BABYLONE **(BABYLON GARDEN)** 33, rue de Babylone 75007	*Open daily 9am–5.30pm (winter),* *9am–10pm (summer).* *Atelier Vert: nature discovery for children.*	▲ 270 ◆ 1 G9

JARDIN LUXEMBOURG (DU) Bd Saint-Michel 75006	*Open daily. Opens between 7.15 and 8.15am.* *Closes between 2.45 and 9.30pm, depending on* *the time of year.*	▲ 202 ◆ 2 A10
JARDIN PALAIS-ROYAL (DU) 6, rue Montpensier 75001 Tel. 01 47 03 92 16	*Open daily 7.30am–8.30pm (Oct.–March);* *7am–10.15pm (April–May); 7am–11pm (June–Aug.);* *7am–9.30pm (Sep.).*	▲ 202 ◆ 2 B4
JARDIN PLANTES (DES) 57, rue Cuvier 75005 Tel. 01 40 79 30 00	*Open daily 7.30am–5.30pm (winter);* *7.30am–8pm (summer).*	▲ 204 ◆ 5 F1
JEU DE PAUME **(GALERIES NATIONALES DU)** 1, place de la Concorde 75008 Tel. 01 47 03 12 50	*Open Tue. noon–9.30pm, Wed.–Fri. noon–7pm,* *Sat.–Sun. 10am–7pm.* *Closed public hols.*	▲ 333 ◆ 1 H4
LAPIN AGILE (LE) 22, rue des Saules 75018 Tel. 01 46 06 85 87	*Artistic cabaret: open daily 9pm–2am.*	▲ 421 ◆ 10 B6
LE PLATEAU Corner of rue des Alouettes and rue Carducci 75019	*Open Wed.–Fri. 2–7pm, Sat.–Sun. 11am–7pm.* *Contemporary art space: exhibitions, debates,* *events. Free entry.*	◆ 11 C9
LOO GALLERY 48, rue de Courcelles 75008 Tel. 01 45 62 53 15	*Open during the day. Telephone for opening times.*	▲ 342 ◆ 9 D9
LUTETIAN ARENA 49, rue Monge 75005 Tel. 01 45 35 02 56	*Open daily 9am–9.30pm (summer),* *8am–5.30pm (winter).*	▲ 260 ◆ 5 E1
LYCÉE CONDORCET 8, rue du Havre 75009 Tel. 01 48 74 25 95	*Visits allowed. Go to the porter's lodge and ask for* *the headmaster.* *Open on National Heritage days.*	▲ 425 ◆ 9 I10
LYCÉE HENRI-IV 23, rue Clovis 75005 Tel. 01 44 41 21 21	*Write to the headmaster to request permission to* *visit the college.*	▲ 247 ◆ 2 D10
LYCÉE LOUIS-LE-GRAND 123, rue Saint-Jacques 75005 Tel. 01 44 32 82 00	*Write to the headmaster to request permission to* *visit the college. Open to the public once a year on* *special "open-door" days.*	▲ 247 ◆ 2 C1
MAISON DE BALZAC 47, rue Raynouard 75016 Tel. 01 55 74 41 80	*Open Tue.–Sun. 10am–5.40pm.* *Closed public hols.* *L'Alliance française theater.*	▲ 300 ◆ 7 H1
MAISON DES CULTURES DU MONDE 101, bd Raspail 75006 Tel. 01 45 44 72 30	*Visits by appointment.*	▲ X ◆ 1 I10
MAISON OPÉRA-GARNIER 5, rue du Docteur-Lancereaux 75008 Tel. 01 45 61 91 82	*Visits by appointment.*	▲ 343 ◆ 9 E9
MAISONS D'OURSCAMP Association of Historical Paris 44–46, rue François-Miron 75004 Tel. 01 48 87 74 31	*Documentation center.* *Open daily 2–6pm.*	▲ 401 ◆ 2 F7
MAISON ROSE 2, rue de l'Abreuvoir 75018 Tel. 01 42 57 60 75	*Restaurant open daily 10am–11pm.*	▲ 421 ◆ 10 B6
MAISON DE VICTOR-HUGO Hôtel de Rohan-Guéméné 6, pl. des Vosges 75004 Tel. 01 42 72 10 16	*Open Tue.–Sun. 10am–5.40pm.* *Closed Mon. and public hols.* *Library by appointment.*	▲ 397 ◆ 2 H7
MARCHÉ AUX FLEURS **(FLOWER MARKET)** Place Louis-Lépine, Île de la Cité 75004	*Open Mon.–Sat. 8am–7.30pm.*	▲ 366 ◆ 2 C7

◆ PLACES TO VISIT

The ▲ symbol refers to the Itineraries section,
while the ◆ refers to the maps

MAZARINE LIBRARY 23, quai Conti 75006 Tel. 01 44 41 44 06	*Open Mon.–Fri. 10am–6pm.* *Closed Aug. 1–15.*	▲ 243 ◆ 2 A7
MONTMARTRE CEMETERY 20, rue Rachel 75018 Tel. 01 43 87 64 24	*Open Mon.–Sat. 8am–5.30pm (Nov.–March),* *8am–6pm (March–Nov.), Sun. from 9am.*	▲ 415 ◆ 9 I5
MONTPARNASSE CEMETERY 3, bd Edgar-Quinet 75014 Tel. 01 44 10 86 50	*Open Mon.–Sat. 8am–5.30pm (Nov.–March),* *8am–6pm (March–Nov.), Sun. from 9am.*	▲ 287 ◆ 6 I3
MOSQUE OF PARIS 1, place du Puits-de-l'Ermite 75005 Tel. 01 45 35 97 33 *www.mosquee-de-paris.com*	*Open Sat.–Thur. 9am–noon and 2–6pm* *(until 7pm in summer).* *Restaurant, hammam, café.*	▲ 261 ◆ 5 E1
MUSÉE ADAM-MICKIEWICZ 6, quai d'Orléans 75004 Tel. 01 55 42 83 83	*Open Thur. 2–5pm.* *Group visits by appointment Wed.–Fri.* *Closed at Christmas, Easter and during the summer.*	▲ 371 ◆ 2 E8
MUSÉE ART MODERNE (D') Georges-Pompidou Center Place Beaubourg 75004 Tel. 01 44 78 12 33 *www.centrepompidou.fr*	*Open Wed.–Mon. 11am–9pm.* *Closed May 1.*	▲ 156 ◆ 2 E5
MUSÉE ART MODERNE DE LA VILLE DE PARIS (D') Palais de Tokyo 11, av. du Président-Wilson 75016 Tel. 01 53 67 40 00 *www.paris-france.org*	*Open Tue.–Fri. 10am–5.40pm, Sat.–Sun. 10am–7pm.* *Closed public hols.*	▲ 134 ◆ 1 B4
MUSÉE ARTS D'AFRIQUE ET D'OCÉANIE (DES) 293, av. Daumesnil 75012 Tel. 01 43 46 51 61	*Open Mon.,Wed. and Fri. 10am–noon and* *1.30–5.30pm, Sat.–Sun. 12.30–6pm.* *Closed May 1.*	▲ 158 ◆ 4 H4
MUSÉE ARTS DÉCORATIFS (DES) Palais du Louvre 107, rue de Rivoli 75001 Tel. 01 44 55 57 50 *www.ucad.fr*	*Open Tue., Thu.–Fri. 11am–6pm, Wed. 11am–9pm,* *Sat.–Sun. 10am–6pm.* *Closed public hols.*	▲ 135 ◆ 1 A5
MUSÉE ARTS ET MÉTIERS (DES) Église Saint-Martin-des-Champs 60, rue Réaumur 75003 Tel. 01 53 01 82 00 *www.arts-et-metiers.net*	*Open Tue.–Sun. 10am–6pm (Wed. until 9.30pm).* *Closed public hols.*	▲ 136 ▲ 382 ◆ 2 E3
MUSÉE DES ARTS ET TRADITIONS POPULAIRES (DES) 6, av. du Mahatma-Gandhi Jardin d'Acclimatation 75106 Tel. 01 44 17 60 00	*Open Wed.–Mon. 9.30am–5.15pm.* *Closed Jan. 1, May 1, Dec. 25.*	▲ 136 ◆ 8 E1
MUSÉE ASSISTANCE PUBLIQUE (DE L') 47, quai de la Tournelle 75005 Tel. 01 46 33 01 43	*Open Tue.–Sun. 10am–6pm.* *Closed public hols, Aug.*	▲ 136 ◆ 2 E9
MUSÉE BOURDELLE 18, rue Antoine-Bourdelle 75015 Tel. 01 49 54 73 73	*Open Tue.–Sun. 10am–5.40pm.* *Closed public hols.*	▲ 137 ◆ 6 G1
MUSÉE CARNAVALET 23, rue de Sévigné 75003 Tel. 01 44 59 58 58	*Open Tue.–Sun. 10am–5.40pm.* *Closed public hols.*	▲ 138 ◆ 2 G6
MUSÉE CERNUSCHI 7, av. Vélasquez 75008 Tel. 01 45 63 50 75	*Closed for renovation until 2004.*	▲ 139 ◆ 9 E8
MUSÉE CHASSE ET DE LA NATURE (DE LA) Hôtel Guénégaud-des-Brosses 60, rue des Archives 75003 Tel. 01 53 01 92 40	*Open Tue.–Sun. 11am–6pm.* *Closed Jan. 1, July 14 and Dec. 25.*	▲ 139 ◆ 2 F5

MUSÉE CLUNY (DE) **MUSÉE NATIONAL DU MOYEN-ÂGE** 6, place Paul-Painlevé 75005 Tel. 01 53 73 78 16	*Open Wed.–Mon. 9.15am–5.45pm.*	▲ *140* ◆ **2** C8
MUSÉE COGNACQ-JAY Hôtel Donon 8, rue Elzévir 75003 Tel. 01 40 27 07 21	*Open Tue.–Sun. 10am–5.40pm.*	▲ *140* ◆ **2** G6
MUSÉE CURIOSITÉ ET DE LA MAGIE **(DE LA)** 11, rue Saint-Paul 75004 Tel. 01 42 72 13 26	*Open Wed., Sat.–Sun. 2–7pm, and daily during* *school hols 2–7pm.*	▲ *141* ◆ **2** G8
MUSÉE DAPPER 50, av. Victor-Hugo 75016 Tel. 01 45 00 01 50	*Open daily 11am–7pm only during exhibitions.* *Bookstore.*	▲ *VII* ◆ **8** J6
MUSÉE GRÉVIN 10, bd Montmartre 75009 Tel. 01 47 70 85 05 www.musee-grevin.com	*Open daily 10am–7pm.*	▲ *141* ◆ **2** B2
MUSÉE GUIMET 6, place d'Iéna 75116 Tel. 01 56 52 53 00	*Open Wed.–Mon. 10am–5.45pm.*	▲ *142* ◆ **1** A4
MUSÉE GUSTAVE-MOREAU 14, rue de La Rochefoucauld 75009 Tel. 01 48 74 38 50	*Open Mon. and Wed. 11am–5.15pm,* *Thur.–Sun. 10am–12.45pm and 2–5.15pm.* *Group visits by appointment. Closed public hols.*	▲ *142* ◆ **10** A9
MUSÉE HISTOIRE DE FRANCE (DE L') Hôtel de Soubise 60, rue des Francs-Bourgeois 75003 Tel. 01 40 27 60 96	*Open Mon., Wed.–Fri. 10am–12.30pm and* *2–5.30pm, Sat.–Sun. 2–5.30pm.* *Closed public hols.*	▲ *390* ◆ **2** F6
MUSÉE HISTOIRE **DE LA MÉDECINE (D')** Université René-Descartes 12, rue de l'École-de-Médecine 75006 Tel. 01 40 46 16 93	*Open Mon.–Wed., Fri.–Sat. 2–5.30pm.* *Closed public hols.*	▲ *241* ◆ **2** B9
MUSÉE HOMME (DE L') Palais de Chaillot 17, place du Trocadéro 75016 Tel. 01 44 05 72 72 www.mnhm.fr	*Open Wed.–Mon. 9.45am–5.15pm.* *Closed public hols.*	▲ *144* ◆ **8** J8
MUSÉES INVALIDES (DES) MUSÉE DE L'ARMÉE MUSÉE DES PLANS ET RELIEFS Hôtel national des Invalides 129, rue de Grenelle 75007 Tel. 01 44 42 37 72 MUSÉE DE L'ORDRE DE LA LIBÉRATION 51 bis, bd de La Tour-Maubourg 75007 Tel. 01 47 05 04 10	*Open daily 10am–6pm (April–Sep.),* *10am–5pm (Oct.–March).* *Closed Jan. 1, May 1, June 17 (Musée de l'Ordre* *de la Libération), Nov. 1, Dec. 25 and 1st Mon. of* *the month.*	▲ *145* ◆ **1** F7
MUSÉE JACQUEMART-ANDRÉ 158, bd Haussmann 75008 Tel. 01 42 89 04 91 www.musee-jacquemart- andre.com	*Open daily 10am–6pm.*	▲ *343* ◆ **9** E10
MUSÉE DE LA LÉGION D'HONNEUR Hôtel de Salm 2, rue de Bellechasse 75007 Tel. 01 40 62 84 25	*Open Tue.–Sun. 11am–5pm.* *Closed for renovation until mid 2003.* *Palace visits by appointment: Tel. 01 40 62 84 28*	▲ *265* ◆ **1** H5
MUSÉE LOUVRE (DU) Cour Napoléon 75001 Tel. 01 40 20 53 17 www.louvre.fr	*Open Mon. and Wed. 9am–9.45pm,* *Thur.–Sun. 9am–6pm.* *Closed public hols.* *Free admission 1st Sun. of the month.*	▲ *146–* *154* ◆ **2** A5
MUSÉE MARINE (DE LA) Palais de Chaillot 17, place du Trocadéro 75016 Tel. 01 53 65 69 69	*Open Wed.–Mon. 10am–5.45pm.* *Closed May 1.*	▲ *155* ◆ **8** J8

◆ PLACES TO VISIT

The ▲ symbol refers to the Itineraries section,
while the ◆ refers to the maps

MUSÉE MARMOTTAN–CLAUDE MONET 2, rue Louis-Boilly 75016 Tel. 01 42 24 07 02	*Open Tue.–Sun. 10am–6pm.* *Closed some public hols.*	▲ 155 ◆ **8** E9
MUSÉE MODE ET DU TEXTILE (DE LA) Palais du Louvre 107, rue de Rivoli 75001 Tel. 01 44 55 57 50	*Open Tue., Thur.–Fri. 11am–6pm,* *Wed. 11am–9pm, Sat.–Sun. 10am–6pm.*	▲ 135 ◆ **2** A5
MUSÉE MONNAIE (DE LA) Hôtel de la Monnaie 11, quai Conti 75006 Tel. 01 40 46 55 35 *www.monnaiedeparis.fr*	*Open Tue.–Fri. 11am–5.30pm,* *Sat.–Sun. noon–5.30pm.* *Personal guided tour Sun. at 3pm.* *Closed Jan. 1, July 14, May 1 and Dec. 25.*	▲ 156 ◆ **2** B7
MUSÉE MONTMARTRE (DE) 12, rue Cortot 75018 Tel. 01 46 06 61 11	*Open Tue.–Sun. 11am–6pm.*	▲ 420 ◆ **10** B6
MUSÉE MUSIQUE (DE LA) Cité de la Musique 221, av. Jean-Jaurès 75019 Tel. 01 44 84 45 45 *www.cite-musique.fr*	*Open Tue.–Sat. noon–6pm, Sun. 10am–6pm.*	▲ 430 ◆ **11** D5
MUSÉE NISSIM-DE-CAMONDO 63, rue de Monceau 75008 Tel. 01 53 89 06 40	*Open Wed.–Sun. 10am–5pm.* *Closed Jan. 1, May 1, Aug. 15 and Dec. 25.*	▲ 343 ◆ **9** F8
MUSÉE ORANGERIE (DE L') Place de la Concorde 75001	*Closed for renovation until 2004.*	▲ 168 ◆ **1** H4
MUSÉE ORSAY (D') 1, rue Bellechasse 75007 Tel. 01 40 49 48 48 *www.musee-orsay.fr*	*Open Tue.–Wed., Fri.–Sat. 10am–6pm,* *Thur. 10am–9.45pm, Sun. 9am–6pm.* *Closed Jan. 1, May 1 and Dec. 25.*	▲ 160 ◆ **1** I6
MUSÉE PETIT PALAIS Av. Winston-Churchill 75008 Tel. 01 42 65 12 73	*Closed for renovation until Jan. 2005.*	▲ 169 ◆ **1** F4
MUSÉE PICASSO Hôtel Salé 5, rue de Thorigny 75003 Tel. 01 42 71 25 21	*Open Tue.–Sun. 9.30am–6pm (April–Sep.),* *9.30am–5.30pm (Oct.–March).* *Closed Jan. 1 and Dec. 25.*	▲ 170 ◆ **2** G6
MUSÉE RODIN Hôtel Biron 77, rue de Varenne 75007 Tel. 01 44 18 61 10	*Open Tue.–Sun. 9.30am–5.45pm (April–Sep.),* *9.30am–4.45pm (Oct.–March).*	▲ 171 ◆ **1** F6
MUSÉE VIE ROMANTIQUE (DE LA) 16, rue Chaptal 75009 Tel. 01 48 74 95 38	*Open Tue.–Sun. 10am–6pm.* *Closed public hols.*	▲ 426 ◆ **9** J8
MUSÉE ZADKINE 100 bis, rue d'Assas 75006 Tel. 01 43 26 91 90	*Open Tue.–Sun. 10am–5.30pm.* *Closed public hols.*	▲ 172 ◆ **5** A1
MUSÉUM HISTOIRE NATURELLE (D') Jardin des Plantes 57, rue Cuvier 75005 Tel. 01 40 79 30 00 *www.mnhn.fr*	*Open Mon., Wed., Fri.–Sun. 10am–6pm,* *Thur. 10am–10pm.* *Closed May 1.*	▲ 143 ◆ **2** F10
NOTRE-DAME DE PARIS 6, place du Parvis de Notre-Dame 75004 CATHEDRAL Tel. 01 42 34 56 10 TOWERS Tel. 01 44 32 16 70 CRYPT Tel. 01 43 29 83 51 MUSEUM 10, rue du Cloître-Notre-Dame *www.catholique-paris.com*	*CATHEDRAL: open daily 8am–6pm.* *TOWERS: open daily 9.30am–7.30pm (April–June and* *Sep.), Fri.–Sun. until 9pm (July–Aug.);* *10am–5.30pm (Oct.–March).* *Closed Jan. 1, May 1 and Dec 25.* *CRYPT: open Tue.–Sun. 10am–6pm.* *Closed Jan. 1, May 1 and Dec 25* *MUSEUM: open Wed., Sat.–Sun. 2.30–6pm.* *Closed Pentecost, Dec. 25.*	▲ 355 ◆ **2** D8

OBSERVATOIRE DE PARIS 61, av. de l'Observatoire 75014 Tel. 01 40 51 22 21	Visits by appointment Mon.–Fri.	▲ 259 ◆ 5 A3
ŒUVRE DES ORPHELINS D'AUTEUIL 40, rue La Fontaine 75016 Tel. 01 44 14 75 75	School visits by appointment. Charitable orphanage	▲ 305 ◆ 7 F3
OPÉRA-BASTILLE Place de la Bastille 75012 Tel. 01 40 01 17 89 (recorded information)	Group bookings may be arranged in writing only (120, rue de Lyon 75012). Sometimes shut in summer.	▲ 404 ◆ 2 I8
OPÉRA-GARNIER Palais Garnier place de l'Opéra 75009 Tel. 01 40 01 17 89 www.opera-de-paris.fr	Open 10am–6pm (summer), 10am–5pm (winter). Closed during matinées and on special occasions. Museum–Library open daily 10am–5pm (tel.: 01 47 42 07 02)	▲ 350 ◆ 1 J2
PAGODE 57 bis, rue de Babylone 75007 Tel. 01 45 55 48 48	Movie theater open for performances.	▲ 271 ◆ 1 G8
PALAIS DÉCOUVERTE (DE LA) Av. Franklin-D.-Roosevelt 75008 Tel. 01 56 43 20 21 www.palais-decouverte.fr	Open Tue.–Sat. 9.30am–6pm, Sun. 10am–7pm. Closed some public hols.	▲ 312 ◆ 1 E4
PALAIS JUSTICE (DE) 4, bd du Palais 75001 Tel. 01 44 32 50 50	School visits only, by appointment. Apply to the Caisse Nationale des Monuments Historiques et des Sites (Tel. 01 44 61 20 00).	▲ 366 ◆ 2 C7
PALAIS DE TOKYO 13, av. du Président Wilson 75116 Tel. 01 47 23 54 01 www.palaisdetokyo.com	Open Tue.–Sun. noon–midnight. Contemporary art exhibitions. See alsp Musée d'Art Moderne de la Ville de Paris.	▲ 303 ◆ 1 B4
PANTHÉON Place du Panthéon 75005 Tel. 01 44 32 18 00	Open daily 9.30am–6.30pm (April–Sep.); 10am–6.15pm (Oct.–March). Closed Jan. 1, May 1, Nov. 11 and Dec. 25.	▲ 256 ◆ 2 C10
PARC ANDRÉ-CITROËN Quai André-Citroën 75015 Tel. 01 45 58 35 40	Open daily Mon.–Fri. 8am–5.30pm, Sat.–Sun. 9am– 5.30pm (winter); Mon.–Fri. 8am–9pm, Sat.–Sun 9am– 9pm (summer).	▲ 211 ◆ 7 G6
PARC BELLEVILLE (DE) Rue des Couronnes 75020 Tel. 08 20 00 75 75	Open daily Mon.–Fri. 8am–5.30pm, Sat.–Sun. 9am– 5.30pm (winter); Mon.–Fri. 8am–9pm, Sat.–Sun 9am– 9pm (summer).	▲ 210 ◆ 3 B2
PARC BERCY (DE) 210, quai de Bercy 75012	Open daily Mon.–Fri. 7.30am–5.30pm, Sat.–Sun. 9am– 5.30pm (winter); Mon.–Fri. 7.30am–9pm, Sat.–Sun 9am–9pm (summer).	▲ 210 ◆ 4 B4
PARC BUTTES-CHAUMONT (DES) Rues Botzaris and Manin 75019 Tel. 01 42 38 02 63	Open daily 7.30am–9pm (winter), 7.30am–11pm (summer).	▲ 208 ◆ 11 B8
PARC MONCEAU Bd de Courcelles 75008 Tel. 01 44 15 93 40	Open daily 7am–8pm (winter); 7am–10pm (summer).	▲ 206 ◆ 9 E8
PARC MONTSOURIS Bd Jourdan 75014 Tel. 01 45 88 28 60	Open daily Mon.–Fri. 7.30am–5.30pm, Sat.–Sun. 9am–5.30pm (winter); Mon.–Fri. 7.30am–9pm, Sat.–Sun 9am–9pm (summer).	▲ 209 ◆ 5 B8
PARC VILLETTE (DE LA) 30, av. Corentin-Cariou 75019 Tel. 01 40 03 75 75	Access 24 hours a day. Many events.	▲ 210 ◆ 11 D4
PÈRE-LACHAISE CEMETERY 16, rue du Repos 75020 Tel. 01 55 25 82 10	Open Mon.–Fri. 8am–5.30pm (Nov.–March), 8am–6pm (March–Nov.), Sat. from 8.30am and Sun. from 9am.	▲ 412 ◆ 3 D5
PLACARD DE SATIE 6, rue Cortot 75018 Tel. 01 42 78 15 18	View from outside only. Closed to the public.	▲ 421 ◆ 10 B6

◆ PLACES TO VISIT

The ▲ symbol refers to the Itineraries section,
while the ◆ refers to the maps

POMPIDOU CENTER	*See Musée d'Art Moderne*	
REX MOVIE THEATER 1, bd Poissonnière 75002 Tel. 08 92 68 05 96	*Guided tours Wed.–Sun. 10am–7pm, daily during school hols.*	▲ 348 ◆ 2 D2
RUSSIAN ORTHODOX CHURCH 12, rue Daru 75008 Tel. 01 42 27 37 34	*Open Tue.–Fri. 3–5pm, Sun. 10am–12.30pm and 3–6pm.*	▲ 343 ◆ 9 C9
SACRÉ-CŒUR DE MONTMARTRE 35, rue Chevalier-de-la-Barre 75018 Tel. 01 53 41 89 00	*Basilica open daily 6am–10.30pm; Dome and crypt: open daily 10am–5.45pm.*	▲ 418 ◆ 10 C6
STE-CHAPELLE 4, bd du Palais 75001 Tel. 01 53 73 78 50	*Open daily 9.30am–6.30pm (April–Sep.); 10am–5pm (Oct.–March).*	▲ 362 ◆ 2 C7
SÉMINAIRE DES MISSIONS ÉTRANGÈRES 128, rue du Bac 75007 Tel. 01 44 39 10 40	*Salle des Martyrs: visits 9–11.30am, 2–6pm. Tour of the garden: request permission from the Father Superior.*	▲ 270 ◆ 1 H8
LE SÉNAT Palais du Luxembourg 15, rue de Vaugirard 75006 Tel. 01 42 34 20 00 *www.senat.fr*	*Open Mon.–Sat. Visits on Mon., Fri. and Sat.*	▲ 239 ◆ 2 A9
SEWERS OF PARIS (LES ÉGOUTS DE PARIS) Place de la Résistance (left bank of the Alma bridge, corner of Quai d'Orsay) 75007	*Visits Sat.–Wed. 11am–4pm.*	▲ 278 ◆ 1 C5
SORBONNE 47, rue des Écoles 75005 Tel. 01 40 46 20 15 CHAPELLE SAINTE-URSULE-DE-LA-SORBONNE	*Sorbonne: access Mon.–Fri. during the academic year (Sep.–June), but with some exceptions.* *Chapel: only open during exhibitions.*	▲ 251 ◆ 2 C9
SQUARE D'ORLÉANS 80, rue Taitbout 75009	*Access 24 hours a day.*	▲ 426 ◆ 10 A9
SQUARE DU TEMPLE Rue du Temple 75003	*Open daily Mon.–Fri. 7.30am–5.30pm, Sat.–Sun. 9am–5.30pm (winter); Mon.–Fri. 7.30am–9pm, Sat.–Sun. 9am–9pm (summer).*	▲ 386 ◆ 2 G4
SYNAGOGUE 10, rue Pavée 75004 Tel. 01 48 87 21 54	*Visits on request.*	▲ 395 ◆ 2 G7
SYNAGOGUE 21 bis, rue des Tournelles 75004	*Free access daily.*	▲ 397 ◆ 2 H7
TOUR DE JEAN-SANS-PEUR 20, rue Étienne-Marcel 75002 Tel. 01 40 26 20 28	*Open Wed., Sat.–Sun. during school year 1.30–6pm, Tue.–Sun. during school hols 1.30–6pm. Guided tour at 3pm.*	▲ 379 ◆ 2 D4
TOUR MONTPARNASSE 33, av. du Maine 75015 Tel. 01 45 38 91 51 (reservations) *www.tourmontparnasse56.com*	*Open daily. 9.30am–10.30pm (winter); 9.30am–11.30pm (summer).*	▲ 286 ◆ 6 H1
TUILERIES GARDENS Place de la Concorde 75001 Tel. 01 40 20 90 43	*Open daily 7.30am–9pm (April–Sep.); 7.30am–7.30pm (Oct.–March); Mon.–Fri. 7.30am–11.45pm, Sat.–Sun. 7.30am–12.45am (July–Aug.).*	▲ 200 ◆ 1 I4
UNESCO 7, place Fontenoy 75007 Tel. 01 45 68 16 42 *www.unesco.org*	*Open Mon.–Fri. 9am–6pm.*	▲ 295 ◆ 1 D9
VAL-DE-GRÂCE 1, place Alphonse-Laverand 75005	*Chapel: open Mon.–Sat. 2–6pm, Sun. 9am–noon and 2–6pm.*	▲ 258 ◆ 5 B2
VIVIENNE ARCADE Rue Vivienne 75002 Tel. 01 42 96 37 32	*Open during the day.* *Several entrances: 4, rue des Petits-Champs.*	▲ 340 ◆ 2 B3

EXCURSIONS		
BARBIZON MUSÉE MUNICIPAL DE L'ÉCOLE DE BARBIZON Auberge Ganne 92, Grande-Rue 77630 Tel. 01 60 66 22 27	*By car: highway A6, exit Fontainebleau, then N37 and D64.* *By train: Gare de Lyon to Fontainebleau-Avon.* *MUSEUM: open Wed.–Mon.* *10am–12.30pm and 2–5pm (Mid Oct.–April);* *10am–12.30pm and 2–6pm (May–mid Oct.).*	▲ 441
LE BOURGET MUSÉE DE L'AIR AND DE L'ESPACE Aéroport de Paris-Le Bourget Tel. 01 49 92 70 62 *www.mac.org*	*Five miles to the north of Paris.* *MUSEUM: open Tue.–Sun. 10am–6pm (May–Oct.),* *10am–5pm (Nov.–April).* *Closed Jan. 1, Dec. 25.*	442
CHANTILLY CHÂTEAU-MUSÉE CONDÉ Tel. 03 44 62 62 62 MUSÉE VIVANT DU CHEVAL Tel. 03 44 57 13 13 *www.chateaudechantilly.com*	*By car: highway A1, exit Chantilly.* *By train: Gare du Nord to Chantilly station.* *By RER D: Gare du Nord, Gare de Lyon, Les Halles.* *CASTLE-MUSEUM:* *open Mon., Wed.–Fri. 10am–6pm, Sat.–Sun. and* *public hols 10.30am–5pm (March–Oct.);* *Mon., Wed.–Fri. 10.30am–12.45pm and 2–5pm,* *Sat.–Sun. and public hols 10.30am–5pm (Nov.–Feb.).* *MUSEUM OF THE HORSE: open daily 10.30am–5.30pm* *(April–Oct.); Mon.–Fri. 2–7pm, Sat.–Sun.* *10.30am–5.30pm (Nov.–March).* *Riding shows at 11.30am, 3.30pm and 5.15pm.*	▲ 442
DISNEYLAND® PARIS Tel. 01 60 30 60 30	*By car: highway A4, exit 14. 20 miles from Paris.* *By train: TGV to Marne-la-Vallée-Chessy station.* *Shuttle buses from Orly and CDG-Roissy airports.* *Times and admission fees vary according to season.*	▲ 448
ÉCOUEN MUSÉE NATIONAL DE LA RENAISSANCE Rue Jean-Bullant 95440 Tel. 01 34 38 38 51	*By car: highway A1, exit Pierrefitte, towards* *Beauvais then D28 and N1 towards Chantilly.* *By train: Gare du Nord to Écouen-Ézanville station,* *then bus line no. 269 to Place de la Mairie.* *Museum: open Wed.–Mon. 9.30am–12.45pm and* *2–5.15pm.*	▲ 444
FONTAINEBLEAU CHÂTEAU DE FONTAINEBLEAU Tel. 01 60 71 50 70 Reservations: Tel. 01 60 71 50 77 MUSÉE NAPOLÉON Tel. 01 60 71 50 60	*By car: highway A6, exit Fontainebleau, then N37.* *By train: Gare de Lyon to Fontainebleau-Avon.* *CASTLE: open Wed.–Mon. 9.30am–5pm (Oct.–May);* *9.30am–6pm (June–Sep.).* *MUSÉE NAPOLÉON: guided tour Mon.,Thur. and Sat.* *by appointment.*	▲ 440 ◆ 13
ST-DENIS BASILICA 1, rue de la Légion-d'Honneur 93200 Saint-Denis Tel. 01 48 09 83 54 STADE DE FRANCE Zac Cornillon-Nord Rue Francis-de Pressensé Tel. 08 92 70 09 00	*BASILICA: open (Oct.–March) Mon.–Sat. 10am–5pm,* *Sun. noon–5pm ; (April–Sep.) Mon.–Sat. 10am–7pm,* *Sun. noon–7pm .* *Closed Jan. 1, May 1, Dec. 25.* *STADIUM: visits daily when events are not taking* *place. It is best to telephone ahead.*	▲ 432
VAUX-LE-VICOMTE CHÂTEAU, JARDIN ET MUSÉE DES ÉQUIPAGES Tel. 01 64 14 41 90 *www.vaux-le-vicomte.com* JEUX D'EAUX VISITES AUX CHANDELLES	*By car: highway A6, exit Melun-Sénart.* *CASTLE, GARDEN AND MUSEUM: open mid March–mid* *Nov. Mon.–Fri. 10am–1pm and 2–6pm,* *Sat.–Sun. 10am–6pm.* *FOUNTAINS: 2nd and final Sat. of the month 3–6pm.* *VISITS BY CANDLELIGHT: Sat. 8pm–midnight* *(May–Oct.).*	▲ 446
VERSAILLES CASTLE Tel. 01 30 83 78 00 *www.chateauversailles.fr* GRAND TRIANON PETIT TRIANON AILES DE TRIANON-SOUS-BOIS JARDINS	*By car: highway A13, exit Versailles-Château.* *By train: Gare Saint-Lazare to Versailles-Rive-Droite,* *Gare Montparnasse to Versailles-Chantiers.* *By RER C to Versailles-Rive-Gauche.* *By bus: line no. 171 to Pont-de-Sèvres.* *CASTLE: open Tue.–Sun. 9am–5.30pm (Oct.–April),* *9am–6.30pm (May–Sep.).* *GRAND TRIANON AND PETIT TRIANON: open daily noon–* *5.30pm (Nov.–March), noon–6.30pm (April–Oct.).* *REAL TENNIS COURT: open Sat.–Sun. 12.30–6.30pm* *(April–Oct.).* *GARDENS: access daily from 7am in summer and 8am* *in winter until dusk. The Dec. 1999 storms caused* *great damage to the woods.*	▲ 434 ◆ 12

◆ BIBLIOGRAPHY

ESSENTIAL READING

◆ BRASSAI:
The Secret Paris of the Thirties: Brassai, Trans. Miller (R.), Thames & Hudson, London, 1978
◆ DE BALZAC (H.):
Cousin Bette, Trans. James Waring, Everyman's Library, London/AA Knopf, New York 1991
◆ DE BALZAC (H.):
Old Goriot, Trans. Ellen Marriage, Everyman's Library/AA Knopf 1991
◆ HEMINGWAY (E.):
A Moveable Feast, Bantam, New York, 1965
◆ HUGO (V.):
The Hunchback of Notre-Dame, Trans. Shoberl (F.), Richard Bentley, London, 1838
◆ ORWELL (G.):
Down and Out in Paris and London, Penguin Books, London, 1940
◆ STEIN (G.):
The Autobiography of Alice B. Toklas, Harcourt, Brace, New York, 1933

GENERAL INTEREST

◆ BENNETT (A.):
Paris Nights, Hodder & Stoughton, London, 1905
◆ BRILLAT-SAVARIN:
Physiologie du Goût, Flammarion, Paris, 1982
◆ CRONIN (V.):
Paris, city of light 1919-1939, HarperCollins, London, 1994
◆ LE DANTEC (J.P.) AND LE DANTEC (D.): *Paris in Bloom*, London, Thames & Hudson, 1991
◆ EHRLICH (B.):
Paris on the Seine Weidenfeld & Nicolson, London 1962
◆ HEROLD (C.):
Mistress to an age, Bobbs-Merrill, New York, 1958
◆ LONERGAN (W.F.):
Forty Years of Paris, T. Fisher Unwin, London, 1907
◆ MONTAGNÉ (P.):
New Larousse Gastronomique, Trans. Froud (N.), Gray (P.), Murdoch (M.),and Taylor (B.M.), Hamlyn, London and New York, 1960
◆ OSTER (D.) AND GOULEMOT (J.):
La vie Parisienne: Anthologie des Moeurs du XIXe siècle, SAND-CONTI, PARIS, 1989
◆ RICHARDSON (J.):
The Bohemians: La vie de Bohème in Paris 1830-1914, Macmillan, 1969
◆ ROBERTSON (W. J.):
Life was worth living, Harper & Bros., New York, 1931
◆ ROTHENSTEIN (W.):
Men and Memories, Faber and Faber, London, 1931-39
◆ RUSSEL (J.):
Paris, Thames & Hudson, London, 1960
◆ SKINNER (C.O.):
Elegant Wits and Grand Horizontals: Paris – La Belle Epoque, Michael Joseph, London, 1963
◆ TROLLOPE (F.):
Paris and the Parisians in 1835, Bentley, London, 1836
◆ WISER (W.):
The Crazy Years: Paris in the Twenties, Thames & Hudson, London, 1983

TRAVELERS' TALES

◆ BINGHAM (HON.D.):
Recollections of Paris, Chapman & Hall, London, 1896
◆ CORYATE (T.):
Coryat's Crudities, Vol.1, James MacLehose and Sons, Glasgow, 1905
◆ HAZLITT (W.):
Notes of a journey through France and Italy, Hunt and Clarke, London, 1826
◆ SAINT-SIMON:
Historical Memoirs of the Duc de Saint-Simon, Vol. III: 1715–23, Edited and translated by Lucy Norton, Hamish Hamilton, London 1972
◆ SAUVAN (M.):
Picturesque Tour of the Seine from Paris to the Sea, R. Ackermann, London, 1821
◆ SCOTT (J.):
Picturesque views of the City of Paris and its Environs, Longman, Hunt, Rees, Orme & Brown, London, 1820
◆ SMOLLETT (T.):
Travels through France and Italy, Oxford University Press, London, 1979
◆ YOUNG (A.):
Travels in France during the years 1787, 1788 and 1789, Cambridge University Press, Cambridge, 1950

HISTORY

◆ BICKNELL (A.L.):
Life in the Tuileries under the Second Empire, The Century Co., New York, 1895
◆ CARLYLE (T.):
The French Revolution, J.M. Dent Ltd. /E.P. Dutton, New York, 1955
◆ KERSHAW (A.):
A History of the Guillotine, Calder, London, 1957
◆ LUTHY (H.):
France against herself, Meridian Books, New York, 1959
◆ MAUROIS (A.):
A History of France, trans. Binsse (H.L.), Jonathan Cape, London, 1949
◆ NOVICK (P.):
The resistance versus Vichy, Chatto & Windus, London, 1968
◆ DE ROTHSCHILD (G.):
The Whims of Fortune, Granada, London, 1985
◆ SAINT-SIMON: *Saint-Simon at Versailles*, Sel. and trans. by Lucy Norton, Penguin, Harmondsworth, 1985
◆ STEEGMULLER (F.):
The Grande Mademoiselle, Farrar Strauss, New York, 1955
◆ WHITEHURST (F.M.):
Court and Social Life in France under Napoleon III, Tinsley, London, 1873
◆ ZELDIN (T.):
France 1845–1945, OUP, 5 volumes

ARCHITECTURE

◆ ARNOLD (W.):
The Historic Hotels of Paris, Thames & Hudson, London, 1990
◆ ATGET (E.):
Atget's Paris, Thames & Hudson, London, 1993
◆ BALLON (H.):
The Paris of Henri IV: architecture and urbanism, MIT Press, Cambridge (Mass.), 1991
◆ BEAL (M.):
British Embassy, Paris: the house and its works of art, Government Art Collection, London, 1992
◆ BERGER (R.W.):
A Royal Passion: Louis XIV as Patron of Architecture, Cambridge University Press, Cambridge, 1994
◆ BOSSI (F.):
Paris1900: Architecture and Design, Trans. Palmes (J.C.), Rizzoli, New york, 1989
◆ BOXER (M.): *The Paris Ritz*, Thames & Hudson, London, 1991
◆ BRAHAM (A.):
The architecture of the French Enlightment, Thames & Hudson, London, 1989
◆ BRASSAI:
The Arts of my Life, Trans. Miller (R.), Thames & Hudson, London, 1982
◆ BRASSAI AND MOREAU (P.): *Paris after Dark: Brassai*, Thames & Hudson, London, 1987
◆ CHAMPOLLION (H.):
Paris, Thames & Hudson, London, 1988
◆ CHEVALIER (L.):
The assassination of Paris, Trans. Jodan (D.P.), University of Chicago Press, Chicago, 1994
◆ KERTESZ (A.):
André Kertesz of Paris and London, Thames & Hudson, London, 1985
◆ LOYER (F.):
Paris, Nineteenth century Architecture and Urbanism, Trans. Clark (C.L.), Abbeville, New York, c1984
◆ MIDDLETON (R.) ED.:
The Beaux Art and Nineteenth century French Architecture, Thames & Hudson, London, 1984
◆ OLSEN (D.J.):
The City as a Work of Art: London, Paris, Vienna, Yale University Press, New Haven, 1986
◆ PADAILLÉ-GALABRUN (A.): *The Birth of Intimacy: Privacy and Domestic Life in early Modern Paris*, Trans. Phelps (J.), Polity Press, Cambridge, c1991
◆ ROWE (C.):
Royal Châteaux of Paris, Putnam, London, 1956
◆ RUSSELL (J.):
Paris, Thames & Hudson, London, 1983
◆ SILVER (K.E.):
Esprit de Corps-The Art of the Parisian Avant-Garde and the First World War, Thames & Hudson, London, 1989
◆ SUTCLIFFE (A.):
Paris, an Architectural History, Yale University Press, New Haven, 1993
◆ TAYLOR (B.B.):
Le Corbusier, The City of Refuge, Paris 1929-33, University of Chicago Press, Chicago, 1987
◆ THOMPSON (D.):
Renaissance Paris: Architecture and Growth, Zwemmer, London, 1984

INTELLECTUAL AND ARTISTIC LIFE

◆ BALDICK (R.):
The First Bohemian. The Life of Henry Mauger, Hamish Hamilton, London, 1961
◆ BARRAULT (J.L.):
Memories for Tomorrow, Thames & Hudson, London, 1974

◆ BEACH (S.):
*Shakespeare &
Company,* Harcourt
Brace, New York, 1959
◆ CAUTE (D.):
*Communism and the
French Intellectuals,*
André Deutsch,
London, 1994
◆ CÉZANNE (P.): *Letters
of Paul Cézanne,* Ed.
Rewald (J.), Trans. Kay
(M.), Bruno Cassirer,
Oxford, 1976
◆ CLERGUE (H.):
*The Salon: A Study of
French Society and
Personalities in the
Eighteenth Century,* G.P.
Putnam & Sons, New
York, 1907
◆ DE GONCOURT (E.)
AND DE GONCOURT (J.):
*Pages from the
Goncourt Journal,* Ed.
and Trans. Baldick (R.),
Oxford University Press,
Oxford, 1978
◆ HUDDLESTON (S.):
*Paris, Salons, Cafés,
Studios: Being Social,
Artistic and Literary
Memories,*
J.B. Lippincott,
Philadelphia, 1928
◆ SHATTUCK (R.):
*The Banquet Years. The
Arts in France 1885-
1918,* Faber & Faber,
London, 1959
◆ WALL (I.):
*French Communism in
the Era of Stalinism,*
Greenwood Press,
Westport, Conn., 1983
◆ WHITE (E.):
Jean Genet, Chatto &
Windus, London, 1993
◆ WILSON (E.):
*A Literary Chronicle of
the Forties,* W.H. Allen,
London, 1951
◆ ZELDIN (T.):
The French, Collins
Harwill, 1989

PAINTING
AND SCULPTURE

◆ Besnard-BERNADAC
(M.L.):*The Musée
Picasso, Paris,* Vol.1,
Thames & Hudson,
London, 1990
◆ BOUVET (F.): *Bonnard:
The Complete Graphic
Works,* Thames &
Hudson, London, 1981
◆ BRUNHAMMER (Y.):
*L'art de vivre:
Decorative Arts and
Design in France 1789-
1989,* Thames &
Hudson, London, 1989
◆ CHAMPIGNEULLE (B.):
Rodin, Thames &
Hudson, London, 1987
◆ CLARK (T.J.):
*The Painting of Modern
Life: Paris in the art of
Manet and his Followers.*
Thames & Hudson,
London, 1990

◆ COURTION (P.):
Manet, Thames &
Hudson, London, 1963
◆ DAIX (P.) AND ROSSELET
(J.): *Picasso: The Cubist
Years 1907-1916. A
Catalogue Raisonné of
the paintings and
Related Works,* Thames
& Hudson, London,
1979
◆ DENVIR (B.):
Toulouse-Lautrec,
Thames & Hudson,
London, 1991
◆ ELDERFIELD (J.):
*Henri Matisse: A
Retrospective,* Thames
& Hudson, London,
1992
◆ FRIEDMANN (J.):
*Inside Paris:
Discovering the Period
Interiors of Paris,*
Phaidon, Oxford, 1989
◆ GUSE (E.G.):
*Rodin: Drawings and
Watercolours,* Thames &
Hudson, London, 1985
◆ LACLOTTE (M.), LUCIE-
SMITH (E.) ET AL:
*Impressionist and Post-
Impressionist at the
Musée d' Orsay,*
Thames & Hudson,
London, 1986
◆ MELLY (G.):
*Paris and the
Surrealists,* Thames &
Hudson, London, 1991
◆ PACH (W.):
Renoir, Thames &
Hudson, London, 1975
◆ PINET (H.):
*Rodin-The Hands of a
Genius,* Thames &
Hudson, London, 1992
◆ RICH (D.C.):
Degas, Thames &
Hudson, London, 1954
◆ RICHET (M.):
*The Musée Picasso,
Paris,* Vol.II, Thames &
Hudson, London, 1982
◆ WHITFIELD (S.):
Fauvism, Thames &
Hudson, London, 1991

FASHION

◆ BRABEC (D.) AND
SALVY (E.):
*Paris Chic – The
Parisian's own Insider
Shopping Guide,*
Thames & Hudson,
London, 1993
◆ COLEMAN (E.A.):
*The Opulent Era –
Fashions of Worth,
Doucet and Pingat,*
Thames & Hudson,
London, 1989
◆ DIOR (C.):
Dior by Dior, Weidenfeld
& Nicolson, London,
1974
◆ GIROUD (F.):
*Dior: Christian Dior
1905-1957,* Thames &
Hudson, London, 1987
◆ WORTH (J.P.):
A Century of Fashion,

Trans. Scott (R.M.),
Little Brown, Boston,
1928

LITERATURE

◆ DE BALZAC (H.):
Cousin Pons, Trans.
Marriage (E.), J.M. Dent
& Sons, London/E.P.
Dutton, New York, 1960
◆ DE BEAUVOIR (S.):
*Memoirs of a dutiful
daughter,* Trans. Kirkup
(J.), André Deutsch and
Weidenfeld and
Nicolson, London, 1959
◆ CAPOTE (T.):
Answered Prayers,
Random House, New
York, 1987
◆ DICKENS (C.):
A Tale of Two Cities,
Everyman's Library/
AA Knopf 1993
◆ DUMAS (A.):
Le Demi-Monde, Paris,
Levy, 1855
◆ DU MAURIER (G.):
Trilby, Osgood, Mc
Ilvaine, London, 1892
◆ FITZGERALD (F. S.):
*The Crack-Up,*Penguin
Books, London, 1965
◆ FLAUBERT (G.):
Sentimental Education,
Trans. Baldick (R.),
Penguin Books,
London, 1964
◆ GELLHORN (M.):
A Honeyed Peace,
André Deutsch,
London, 1954
◆ HALL (R.):
The well of Loneliness,
Paris, Pegasus, 1928
◆ HUGO (V.):
Les Misérables, Hodder
& Stoughton, London,
1925
◆ IRVING (W.):
*Journals and
Notebooks, 1803-1806,*
Vol. 1, Ed. Wright (N.),
University of Wisconsin
Press, Madison, 1969
◆ JAMES (H.):
*A Small Boy and
Others,* Charles
Scribner's Sons, New
York, 1913
◆ JAMES (H.):
The Tragic Muse,
Houghton Miffin & Co.
New York and Boston,
1890
◆ KEROUAC (J.):
Satori in Paris, Grove,
New york, 1967
◆ KOESTLER (A.) AND
(C.): *Stranger on the
Square,* Hutchinson,
London, 1983
◆ LEWIS (D.B.W.):
François Villon,
Doubleday Anchor, New
York, 1958
◆ LEWIS (P.W.):
Tarr, Chatto and
Windus, London, 1928
◆ LITTLEWOOD (I.):
*Paris, a Literary
Companion,* Murray,

London, 1987
◆ MCCARTHY (M.):
Birds of America,
Penguin Books,
London, 1973
◆ MAUPASSANT (G. DE):
Bel-ami, Victor-Havard,
Paris, 1886
◆ MILLER (H.):
Black Spring, Obelisk
Press, Paris, 1936
◆ MITFORD (N.):
The Blessing, Hamish
Hamilton, London, 1951
◆ PROUST (M.):
*A la recherche du
temps perdu,* Trans.
Scott-Moncrieff,
Kilmartin (T.) and Mayor
(A.), Chatto & Windus,
London, 1981
◆ QUENEAU (R.):
Zazie dans le Métro,
Trans. del Piombo (A.)
and Kahane (E.),
Olympia Press, Paris,
1959
◆ RHYS (J.):
*After Leaving Mr.
Mackenzie,* Penguin
Books, London, 1975
◆ RHYS (J.):
Quartet, André
Deutsch, London, 1969
◆ ROLLAND (R.):
Jean-Christophe, Trans.
Cannan (G.), William
Heinemann, London,
1910-1913, Paris, 1905
◆ STEIN (G.):
Paris France, Batsford,
London, 1940
◆ STEIN (G.):
Wars I Have Seen,
Random House, New
York, 1945
◆ STERN (L.):
A Sentimental Journey,
J.M. Dent & Sons,
London, 1960
◆ THACKERAY (W.M.):
The Paris Sketch-Book,
Tauchnitz, Leipzig, 1873
◆ TWAIN (M.):
The Innocent Abroad,
Routledge, London,
1872
◆ VIDAL (G.):
The Judgment of Paris,
Panther Books, London,
1976
◆ WHARTON (E.):
*The Custom of the
Country,* Constable,
London, 1965
◆ ZOLA (E.):
Thérèse Raquin, Trans.
Tancock (L.), Folio
Society, London, 1969
◆ ZOLA (E.):
The Masterpiece, Trans.
Walton (J.), Paul Elek,
London/New York, 1950
◆ ZOLA (E.):
Le ventre de Paris,
Trans. Hughes (D.) and
Mason (M. J.), Paul
Elek, London, 1958
◆ ZOLA (E.):
Les Trois Villes, Paris,
Trans. Vizetelly (E.A.),
Chatto & Windus, 1898

◆ LIST OF ILLUSTRATIONS

LIST OF ILLUSTRATIONS ◆

◆ LIST OF ILLUSTRATIONS

◆ LIST OF ILLUSTRATIONS

LIST OF ILLUSTRATIONS ◆

◆ LIST OF ILLUSTRATIONS

Abbreviations :
ADAGP : Société
des Auteurs dans les Arts
graphiques et plastiques.
AN : Archives nationales.
ATP : Musée des Arts et
Traditions populaires.
BN : Bibliothèque nationale.
CNMHS : Centre national
des Monuments historiques.
Com. Vieux Paris :
Commission du Vieux Paris.
DAC : Direction des
Affaires culturelles
(Ville de Paris).
EPAD : Établissement public
d'aménagement de la
Défense.
MAAO : Musée des Arts
africains et océaniens.
MNAM : Musée national d'art
moderne
PMVP : Photothèque des
musées de la Ville de
Paris/Philippe Joffre, Philippe
Ladet, Patrick Pierrain, Rémi
Briant, Lyliane Degraces,
Daniel Lifermann by Spadem,
199.
RMN : Réunion des
Musées nationaux.

In some cases we have
been unable to contact the
heirs to certain documents,
or their publishers; an
account remains open for
them at our offices.

**Grateful
acknowledgment is
made to the following
for permission to reprint
previously published
material:**

◆ HARCOURT BRACE &
COMPANY: Excerpt from
Shakespeare and Company
by Sylvia Beach, copyright ©
1959 by Sylvia Beach,
copyright renewed 1987 by
Frederic Beach Dennis;
excerpt from *Birds of
America* by Mary McCarthy,
copyright © 1971 by Mary
McCarthy. Reprinted by
permission of Harcourt Brace
& Company.

◆ HARVARD UNIVERSITY
PRESS: Excerpt from two
letters, April 2, 1845, and
June 1, 1853, from *The
Letters of Gustave Flaubert
1830–57,* edited and
translated by Francis
Steegmuller, copyright
© 1979, 1980 by Francis
Steegmuller. Reprinted by
permission of Harvard
University Press, Cambridge,
Mass.

◆ RANDOM HOUSE, INC.:
Excerpt from *The
Autobiography of Alice B.
Toklas,* by Gertrude Stein,
copyright © 1933 by Alice B.
Toklas, copyright renewed
1961 by Alice B. Toklas.
Reprinted by permission of
Random House, Inc.

◆ CHARLES SCRIBNER'S SONS:
Excerpt from "Miss Stein
Instructs" from *A Moveable
Feast,* by Ernest Hemingway,
copyright © 1964 by Mary
Hemingway, copyright
renewed 1992 by John H.
Hemingway, Patrick
Hemingway, and Gregory
Hemingway. Reprinted by
permission of Charles
Scribner's Sons, a division of
Simon & Schuster Inc.

◆ CHRISTOPHER SINCLAIR-
STEVENSON: Excerpts from
*Historical Memoirs of the Duc
de Saint-Simon: A Shortened
Version, Volume III: 1715–23,*
edited and translated by
Lucy Norton (Hamish
Hamilton Ltd., London),
copyright © 1972 by Lucy
Norton. Reprinted by
permission of Christopher
Sinclair-Stevenson, literary
executor for the Estate of
Lucy Norton.

◆ INDEX

◆ INDEX

◆ INDEX

Map section

Key

▀▀	Freeway
═	Main road
▭▭	Railroad
··	*Département* limit
⊞	Cemetery
✈	Airport
Ⓜ	Métro station
RER	RER station
✚	Hospital
🛢	Gas station
P	Parking
✉	Mail box
☏	Police

◆ MÉTRO PLAN

◆ TOURIST BUS MAP

Lignes de bus touristiques
Tourist bus services
Linee di autobus turistici

RATP

82
Neuilly
Hôpital Américain

Roissybus

73 Balabus
La Défense
Grande Arche

82

73

Palais des congrès

Porte
Maillot

Arc de Triomphe

La Madelein

Balabus

L'OpenTour

Champs-Elysées
Etoile

Rd Pt des
Champs-Elysées

Porte de la Muette
63

Victor
Hugo

82

42

Grand
Palais

73

Alma-Marceau

63

Trocadéro

63

82

42

Palais de Chaillot

42

Musée d'Orsay 7

69

Tour Eiffel
69

Champ
de Mars

69

Invalides

St-

Maison de la Radio

82

Duroc

42

42

Tour
Montparnasse

André Citroën **42**

Denfert-Ro
ORLY

RATP-CML-IV Agence Cartographique
LBT 98-02-005-C, JG
Reproduction interdite

(BUS) **Dimanches et fêtes**
de 7 h à 20 h 30 environ
Sundays and Bank Holidays
from 7:00 a.m. to approximately 8.30 p.m.
Domeniche e giorni festivi
dalle ore 7.00 alle ore 20.30 circa

20 **21** **27**
63 **82** Montmartrobus
ORLYBUS ROISSYBUS

Balabus De 12h00 à 21h00 d'avril à septembre
12 noon to 9 p.m. from April to September
Dalle ore 12.00 alle ore 21.00 da aprile a settembre

.... L'OpenTour
de 9h00 à 19h00, 7 jours sur 7.
from 9 a.m. to 7 p.m., daily all year round.
dalle ore 9.00 alle ore 19.00, 7 giorni su 7.

(BUS) **Soirées**
de 20 h 30 à 0 h 30 environ
Evenings
8.30 p.m. to approximately 0.30 a.m.
Serate
dalle ore 20.30 alle ore 0.30 circa

21 **27** **63**
PC ORLYBUS ROISSYBUS

ROISSYBUS **Aéroport Charles de Gaulle** ✈
Ligne directe – Direct line – Linea diretta

Porte de La Villette 75

Montmartrobus
Mairie du XVIIIe

Sacré-Cœur

Pigalle

Funiculaire
de Montmartre

L'OpenTour

Montmartrobus

42 47
Gare du Nord

Gare St-Lazare
20 21 27

42

42

Richelieu
Drouot

47

47

20

Opéra
ROISSYBUS ✈
Ligne directe

Strasbourg
St-Denis

20

20

75

*Place de
la République*

Gambetta
69

21 27

rde
Musée
Louvre

La Pyramide

47

Centre Pompidou

Oberkampf

Châtelet

69

Pont Neuf
75

75

Hôtel de Ville

69

Place des Vosges

*Place de
la Nation*

*St-Germain
des-Prés*

ac
ain

63

St-Michel

47

Notre-Dame

Balabus

Bastille

Cluny

Maubert
Mutualité

uxembourg 82

27

63

47

20 63
Balabus
Gare de Lyon

Panthéon

Gare
d'Austerlitz

L'OpenTour
Bercy

Observatoire

21

Gobelins

u ✈
Orlybus ✈

27

Place
d'Italie

Patay-Tolbiac

47

**Glacière
Tolbiac**

Tolbiac

Universitaire

27

21

Porte
d'Italie

27 **Porte de Vitry
Claude Regaud**

21
Porte de Gentilly

Orly Ouest/Sud ✈ ORLYBUS

▼ 47 **Fort du Kremlin Bicêtre**

◆LOUVRE, MARAIS, ÎLE DE LA CITÉ, LATIN QUARTER

2

◆ BERCY, DAUMESNIL, BOIS DE VINCENNES

4

A B C D E

R. DE RAMBOUILLET

SAINT-ELOI
DIACONESSES
CIMETIÈRE DE PICPU

R. DE CHARENTON

AVENUE DAUMESNIL

MONTGALLET

RUE

RUE DE CHARENTON

JARDIN DE REUILLY

RUE RENARD

RUE DE REUILLY

ALLÉE VIVALDI

RUE DE LA GARE DE REUILLY

1

BERCY

MAIRIE DU 12ÈME

AVENUE DAUMESNIL

R. LAMBLARDIE

BD

RUE DE BERCY

DE

BERCY

RUE CHARLOTAIS

DUGOMMIER

SQUARE J. MORIN

BOULEVARD

Place Félix Éboué

DE RE

DAUMESNIL

2

PALAIS OMNISPORT DE PARIS-BERCY

P

RUE TAINE

DE

RUE DE LA BRÈCHE AUX LOUPS

ST-ESPRIT

SQUARE CORITERIOT

RUE DE LA LANCETTE

RUE DE LA

3

QUAI DE BERCY

RUE DE BERCY

PARC DE BERCY

Place Lachambeaudie

NOTRE-DAME DE LA NATIVITÉ DE BERCY

CORIOLIS

RUE DE

CHARENTON

WATTIGNIES

RUE DES MEUNIERS

RUE DE GRAVEL

QUAI DE LA GARE

R. JOSEPH KESSEL

COUR SAINT-ÉMILION

RUE G.

RUE DU BARON LE ROY

RUE FRANÇOIS TRUFFAUT

LAMÉ

CIMETIÈRE DE BERC

4

BIBLIOTHÈQUE NATIONALE DE FRANCE F. MITTERRAND

PONT DE TOLBIAC

RUE DES PIROGUES BERCY

Place des Vins de France

AV. DES TERROIRS DE FRANCE

AV. DE

R. DE TOLBIAC

QUAI PANHARD ET LEVASSOR

SEINE

QUAI DE BERCY

5

BIBLIOTHÈQUE F. MITTERRAND

BOULEVARD PONIATOWSKI

R. DU CHEVALERET

RUE

WATT

RUE J.A. DE BAÏF

PONT NATIONAL

QUAI D'IVRY

6

BOULE

BOULEVARD MASSÉNA

RER

MASSÉNA

PARIS

SAINT MANDÉ

7

AV. DE LA PORTE DE VITRY

BOULEVARD

PÉRIPHÉRIQUE

BOULEVARD

AVENUE DAUMESNIL

PORTE DORÉE

PORTE DE CHARENTON

LAC DAUMESNIL

PARC ZOOLOGIQUE

8

AVENUE

PIERRE

SÉNARD

IVRY-SUR-SEINE

PELOUSES DE REUILLY

TEMPLE BOUDDHIQUE

9

CHARENTON LE PONT

AVENUE DE GRAVELLE

0 ——— 150 m
0 ——— 490 feet

LA SEINE

A4

10

A B   C D E

5

SQ. DES ARÈNES DE LUTÈCE

LUXEMBOURG RER

JARDIN R. CAVALIER DE LA SALLE

ST-JACQUES-DU-HAUT-PAS

P. ET M. CURIE RUE

N-D-DU-LIBAN

RUE ST-MÉDARD

LACÉPÈDE

PLACE MONGE

RUE D'ASSAS

R. J. BARA

RUE DE L'OBSERVATOIRE

BARBUSSE

RUE GAY LUSSAC

RUE D'ULM

RUE ÉRASME

RUE ST-JACQUES

RUE TOURNEFORT

SQUARE ORTOLAN

MAISON FRATERNELLE

DAUBENTON

TARNIER

JARDIN MARCO POLO

SAINT-MARCEL

Place E. Denis

PORT ROYAL RER

RUE HENRI

RUE PIERRE

NICOLE

RUE RATAUD

CHAPELLE DU VAL-DE-GRÂCE

VAL-DE-GRÂCE

RUE CLAUDE

RUE VALLUBERT

SÉMINAIRE ISRAÉLITE DE FRANCE

CENSIER DAUBENTON P

SAINT-MÉDARD

CENSIER

RUE DE LA CLEF

SANTEUIL

BD MONTPARNASSE

R. BOISSONADE

BOULEVARD

RUE ST-JACQUES

DE

BERTHOLLET

RUE DES LYONNAIS

RUE DE BROCA

PORT-ROYAL

RUE DU FER À MOULIN

SQUARE SCIPION

RUE VÉSALE

BOULE

SAINT-VINCENT-DE-PAUL

BAUDELOCQUE

AVENUE

COCHIN

PÉAN

SANTÉ

DE LA GLACIÈRE

GOBELINS

RUE DE LA REINE BLANCHE

RUE LE BRU

OBSERVATOIRE DE PARIS

RUE ST-HIPPOLYTE

RUE BERBER DUHETS

PORT-ROYAL

ARAGO

DES

BOULEVARD DU FBG

ARAGO

BOULEVARD

BROCA

GOBELINS

BD

RUE

RUE JEAN DOLENT

RUE J.-M. NORDMANN

JARDIN ARAGO

RUE DES CORDELIÈRES

RUE DES RECOLLETTES

CROULEBARBE

SAINT JACQUES RER

ST-JACQUES

SQUARE RENÉ LE GALL

ST-DOMINIQUE

RUE É. DUBOIS

DAREAU

FERRUS

ST-JACQUES BOULEVARD

CORVISARD

STE-IRÉNÉE

RUE A. HOVELACQUE

GLACIÈRE

AV. DE LA TOMBE ISSOIRE

RUE DAREAU

RUE CABANIS

SANTÉ

DE LA

AUGUSTE

SAINTE ROSALIE

BLANQUI

RENÉ

RUE DU ST-GOTHARD

RUE BROUSSAIS

SAINTE-ANNE

DE

VERGNIAUD

CORVISART

RUE DES CINQ DIAMANTS

BOBILLOT

BILLOT

RUE

D'ALÉSIA

SAINT-ALBERT-LE-GRAND

RUE

DAVIEL

RUE DE LA BUTTE AUX CAILLES

RUE DU MOULIN DES

COTY

RUE SAINT-YVES

SAINTE-JEANNE-D'ARC

AV. REILLE

RUE

DE

WURTZ

RUE

RUE BUOT

MICHAL

STE-ANNE-DE-LA-PROVIDENCE

RUE G. MOREAU

RUE

DE LA

RUE

BOBILLOT

DE

SQUARE DES PEUPLIERS

C. FOURIER

AVENUE

REILLE

RUE DE L'AMIRAL

TOLBIAC

VERGNIAUD

BRILLAT SAVARIN

BOUSSINGAULT

RUE BARRAULT

RUE DE LA FONTAINE À MULARD

COLONIE

HÔPITAL DES PEUPLIERS

PARC MONTSOURIS

GAZAN

MOUCHEZ

DE RUNGIS

R. KUSS

BRILLAT-SAVARIN

CITÉ UNIVERSITAIRE RER

RUE DES LONGUES RAIES

RUE CACHÉUX

BOULEVARD

JOURDAN

BOULEVARD

CAFFIÉRI

RUE F. DE MONTANDRE

AV. DE L'HISTOIRE

RUE A. MOROT

RUE STE-HÉLÈNE

GOUTIÈRE

RUE M. JACO

PARC KELLERMANN

AV. D. WEILL

CIMETIÈRE DE GENTILLY

CITÉ INTERNATIONALE UNIVERSITAIRE

AV. DE LA PORTE DE GENTILLY

P

STADE SÉBASTIEN CHARLÉTY

BOULEVARD

GENTILLY

PORTE DE GENTILLY

0   150 m
0   490 feet

A   B   C   D   E

10

◆ RUE DE VAUGIRARD, ALÉSIA, MONTPARNASSE

7

A B C D E

LAC SUPÉRIEUR

NOTRE-DAME-DE-L'ASSOMPTION-DE-PASSY

PÉRIPHÉRIQUE

BOULEVARD

R. L.

1

BOIS DE BOULOGNE

HIPPODROME D'AUTEUIL

Fortifications

AVENUE DU MARÉCHAL FRANCHET

SO. M. BATAILLE

AVENUE DU MARÉCHAL

SUCHET

RUE DU DOCTEUR BLANCHE

R. HENRI HEINE

RAFFET

JASMI

2

DES

ALLÉE DU MARÉCHAL

AV. DU MARÉCHAL

SQUARE A. CAPUS

SQUARE TOLSTOÏ

BOULEVARD

BOULEVARD DE MONTMORENCY

RUE

VILLA DE MONTMORENCY

RUE DE

AVENUE

RUE LE

3

PORTE D'AUTEUIL

PORTE D'AUTEUIL

AVENUE DE LA PORTE D'AUTEUIL

PORTE D'AUTEUIL

RUE POUSSIN

MICHEL-ANGE AUTEUIL

RUE

D'AUTEUIL

4

BOULEVARD

D'AUTEUIL

SARRAIL

MURAT

PÉRIPHÉRIQUE

AV. DU GÉN

RUE CHANEZ

RUE SAINT-FRANÇOIS

ERLANGER

RUE MICHEL ANGE

RUE

MARIE RÉPARATRICE

RUE BOILEAU

CHARDON LAGACHE

MOLITOR

RUE DU CHÂTEAU

SCHURAN

STADE JEAN BOUIN

BD.

CIMV.

MICHEL-ANGE MOLITOR

AUTEUIL

HAMEAU BOILEAU

RUE BOILEAU

CHARDON

LAGACHE

SAINT PÉRIN

ROBERT

RUE DU

RUE DE

RUE D. CELESTRAIN

APPARITION DE LA SAINTE VIERGE

EXELMANS

EXELMANS

JOUVENE

POINT DU JOUR

5

PARC DES PRINCES

BOULEVARD

AV. DU GÉN

RUE C. VARIZE

RUE MICHEL

ANGE

RUE C LORRAIN

SAINTE-GENEVIÈVE

CIMETIÈRE D'AUTEUIL

TOUS LES SAINTS DE LA TERRE RUSSE

RUE

MUSSET

AVENUE

RUE VAN LO

PONT D. GARIGLIAN

AVENUE

BOULEVARD

PARENT DE ROSAN

HENRI DUNANT

AVENUE DE VERSAILLES

6

ROUTE DE LA REINE

AV. DE LA PORTE DE ST-CLOUD

SAINTE-JEANNE-DE-CHANTAL

PORTE DE SAINT CLOUD

RUE LE MAROIS

CLAUDE TERRASSE

MURAT

SAINT-EXUPÉRY

7

BOULOGNE-BILLANCOURT

BOULEVARD

RUE DU GÉN. MALLETERRE

RUE

A. FERRY

QUAI

QUAI D'ISSY

BOULEVARD PÉRI

8

AVENUE EDOUARD VAILLANT

BOULEVARD

RUE PIERRE GRENIER

RUE DE LA

DU

SEINE

QUAI DU PRÉSIDENT ROOSEVELT

BOULEVARD

GALLIENI

9

BOULEVARD JEAN JAURÈS

AVENUE

RÉPUBLIQUE

POINT

DU

PONT D'ISSY

ISSY-LES-MOULINEAUX

RUE ROUGET DE LISLE

QUAI

0 150 m
0 490 feet

10

A B C D E

◆BOIS DE BOULOGNE, TROCADÉRO, PORTE MAILLOT

8

NEUILLY
SUR SEINE

JARDIN
D'ACCLIMATATION

PUTEAUX

BOULEVARD R. WALLACE

CHAMP
D'ENTRAINEMENT

PARC DE
BAGATELLE

ALLÉE DE LONGCHAMP

ROUTE DE SÈVRES A NEUILLY

SURESNES

PRÉ
CATELAN

BOIS

LAC
INFÉRIEUR

DE

BOULOGNE

ROUTE DE L'HIPPODROME

SEINE

ROUTE DE SÈVRES A NEUILLY

ALLÉE DE LA REINE MARGUERITE

ROUTE DE L'HIPPODROME

HIPPODROME
DE LONGCHAMP

LAC
SUPÉRIEUR

HIPPODROME

D'AUTEUIL

BOULEVARD ANATOLE FRANCE

PORTE
D'AUTEUIL

Carrefour
des Anciens
Combattants

AVENUE DE LA PORTE D'AUTEUIL

BOULEVARD D'AUTEUIL

BOULOGNE-BILLANCOURT

PORTE
DE LA MUETTE

AVENUE DE SAINT-CLOU

BOIS

DE

BOULOGNE

BOULEVARD PÉRIPHÉRIQUE

AV. DU MARÉCHAL MAUNOURY

BOULEVARD SUCHET

PORTE
DE PASSY

AVENUE
RAPHA

0   150 m
0   490 feet

AVENUE
BD DE

9

A B C D E

CLICHY

1

2

PORTE DE CLICHY

AV. DE LA PORTE DE CLICHY

LEVALLOIS-PERRET

3

PORTE D'ASNIÈRES

PÉRIPHÉRIQUE

BD DE DOUAUMONT

BD DU FORT DE VAUX

BOULEVARD BERTHIER

4

BOULEVARD DE REIMS

AV. DE LA PORTE D'ASNIÈRES

SQUARE A. ULMANN

Avenue BRUNETIÈRE

SQUARE P. PARAY

RUE DE SAUSSURE

BOULEVARD J. LAMBERT

RUE PHILIBERT DELORME

BOULEVARD BERTHIER

5

BOULEVARD DE COURCELLES

SQUARE STE ODILE

RUE E. ET A. MASSARD

A. ROLL

RUE VERNIQUET

PÉREIRE NORD

PÉREIRE SUD

BD

BD

RUE DE LA FÉLICITÉ

TOCQUEVILLE

D'ABBANS

SAINTE-ODILE

PORTE DE CHAMPERRET

SQUARE J. BELLOT

PÉREIRE-LEVALLOIS RER

BOULEVARD

RUE A. DE NEUVILLE

R. DE

AV. DE VILLIERS

PÉREIRE-LEVALLOIS

RER

RUE

AMPÈRE

AVENUE DE WAGRAM

MALESHERBES

JOUFFROY

6

RUE DESCOMBES

RUE LAUGIER

R. GALVANI

RUE VERNIER

BOULEVARD PÉREIRE

BOULEVARD PÉREIRE

PÉREIRE

AVENUE NIEL

RUE DE PRONY

AVENUE DE VILLIERS

ST-FRANÇOIS-DE-SALES

WAGRAM

D'ABBANS

RUE VIÈTE

RUE DE

7

RUE FARADAY

RENNEQUIN

R. PIERRE DEMOURS

RUE TH. DE BANVILLE

RUE DE GOUNOD

AVENUE DE WAGRAM

CARDINET

RUE DE PRONY

RUE DE FORTUNY

MÉDÉRIC

AV.

MALESHERBES

DE

8

AVENUE DES TERNES

RUE PIERRE DEMOURS

RUE NIEL

RUE FOURCROY

RENAUDES

RUE LAUGIER

RUE PONCELET

RUE DE COURCELLES

RUE MARGUERITE

SVENSKA KYRKAN

RUE T. RIBOT

RUE PROST

RUE DE CHAZELLES

BOULEVARD DE COURCELLES

COMTESSE DE SÉGUR

ALLÉE

PARC DE MONCEAU

MONCEAU

BD DE

ST-FERDINAND STE-THÉRÈSE-DE-L'ENFANT-JÉSUS

AVENUE DES TERNES

TERNES

Place des Ternes

BOULEVARD

RUE DARU

CATHÉDRALE SAINT-ALEXANDRE NEVSKY

COURCELLES

RUE DE COURCELLES

RUE DE MONCEAU

DE

AV.

9

R. DES ACACIAS

AV. CARNOT

AV. MAC MAHON

RUE DE L'ÉTOILE

RUE TROYON

RUE

RUE HOCHE

SALLE PLEYEL

AVENUE DE FRIEDLAND

NOTRE-DAME-DE-L'ANNONCIATION

RUE DU FAUBOURG SAINT-HONORÉ

BALZAC

RUE DE BERRI

BOULEVARD

RUE

DE COURCELLES

ARGENTINE

RER

RER

SAINT-JOSEPH

AVENUE BEAUJON

DE

CHARLES-DE-GAULLE-ÉTOILE

0 ——— 50 m
0 ——— 490 ft

ARC DE TRIOMPHE

10

DE TILSITT

AV.

DE

FRIEDLAND

CORPUS CHRISTI

R. DE BERRI

A B C D E

10

A   B   C   D   E

PORTE DE CLIGNANCOURT

RUE JEAN HENRI FABRE   RUE DU PROFESSEUR GOSSET

BOULEVARD   PÉRIPHÉRIQUE

1

STADE BERTRAND DAUVIN

STADE DES POISSONNIERS

RUE   RUE M. SEMBAT   RUE R. FLAMMARION   RUE C. FOURNIÈRE   RUE BINET   RUE F. LABORI   AV. DE LA PORTE DE CLIGNANCOURT   AV. DE LA PORTE DES POISSONNIERS

RUE F. DE CROISSET   R. JEAN COCTEAU

PORTE DE CLIGNANCOURT

BOULEVARD NEY

2

BOULEVARD NEY   RUE BELLIARD

RUE BELLIARD   RUE BELLIARD

RUE G. ROUANET   RUE   STE-HÉLÈNE   SQUARE STE-HÉLÈNE   BOULEVARD   CENIS   RUE DES POISSONNIERS

CHAMPIONNET   MONT   RUE CHAMPIONNET

SAINTE-GENEVIÈVE-DES-GRANDES-CARRIÈRES   RUE   RUE DU RUISSEAU   RUE DU POTEAU   DUHESME   SIMPLON   NOTRE-DAME DU BON CONSEIL

3

RUE   MONTCALM   ORDENER   RUE DU SIMPLON   ORNANO   RUE   RUE DES

RUE DAMBEMONT   RUE VAUVENARGUES   SQUARE LÉON SERPOLLET   JULES JOFFRIN   NOTRE-DAME-DE-CLIGNANCOURT   SQ. DE CLIGNANCOURT   R. HERMEL   R. J. DIJON   BAUDELIQUE   SAINT-SAVA   SAINT-PAUL

RUE MARCADET   RUE   DUC   MAIRIE DU 18ÈME   MARCADET POISSONNIERS   R. MARCADET

4

LAMARCK CAULAINCOURT   RUE DUHESME   RUE MARCADET   RUE   MARCADET   R. E. SUE   R. SIMART   SAINT PAUL   RUE ERNESTINE

RUE FRANCŒUR   MAISON VERTE   BARBÈS   R. LABAT

RUE CAULAINCOURT   CIMETIÈRE ST VINCENT   LAMARCK   RUE   CLIGNANCOURT   R. LABAT   RUE MARCADET

5

AV. JUNOT   SQUARE S. BUISSON   VIGNES DE MONTMARTRE   RAMEY   CUSTINE   RUE DOUDEAUVILLE   R. DE LAGHOUAT

RUE LEPIC   PARC DE LA TURLURE   CHÂTEAU ROUGE   DES   MYRH   R. CAV   SAINT-BERNARD-DE-LA-CHAPELL

Place du Tertre   BASILIQUE DU SACRÉ CŒUR   DE   RUE   RUE RICHOMME   SQUARE LÉON

SAINT-PIERRE-DE-MONTMARTRE

6

RUE DURANTIN   RUE DES ABBESSES   SQUARE NADAR   FUNICULAIRE   SQUARE WILLETTE   BOULEVARD   RUE DE LA GOUTTE D'OR   RUE DE CHARTRES

RUE LEPIC   SQ. J. RICTUS   RUE DES TROIS FRÈRES   CHAPELLE SAINTE-ANNE   BARBÈS ROCHECHOUART   BOULEVARD

ABBESSES   D'ORSEL

BLANCHE   SAINT-JEAN-DE-MONTMARTRE   RUE   ANVERS   LARIBOISIÈRE

PIGALLE   MARTYRS   ROCHECHOUART   R. GUY PATIN

7

R. HOUDON   BOULEVARD   ROCHECHOUART   RUE DU DELTA   BOULEVARD   GARE DU NORD

Place Pigalle   SQUARE D'ANVERS   Place d'Anvers   RUE A. PARÉ   DE MAUBEUGE

R. FONTAINE   RUE V. MASSÉ   AVENUE TRUDAINE   RODIER   RUE DE DUNKERQUE   GARE DU NORD

8

RUE N-D   DES   RUE DE LA T. D'AUVERGNE   RUE TURGO   RUE   CONDORCET   RUE PÉTRELLE   DE MAGENTA

RUE LA BRUYÈRE   R. DE NAVARIN   R. CLAUZEL   RUE   R. SEHARD   ST-VINCENT-DE-PAUL

RUE DE LA ROCHEFOUCAULD   SQ. A. BISCARRE   SAINT GEORGES   DE MAUBEUGE   RUE FÉNELON   RUE DE CHABROL

9

RUE D'AUMALE   FAUBOURG   ST-CONSTANTIN STE-HÉLÈNE   RUE MILTON   RUE CHORON   SQUARE DE MONTHOLON   LA FAYETTE   RENCONTRE

RUE ST-LAZARE   N. D. DE LORETTE   N-D DE LORETTE   CADET   POISSONNIÈRE   SAINT LAZARE   SQUARE SATRAGN

RUE   DE CHÂTEAUDUN   RUE   DE   D'HAUTEVILLE   DE   PARADIS

10

RUE DE LA VICTOIRE   LE PELETIER   RUE CADET   RUE SAULNIER   RUE DE TRÉVISE   RUE   RICHER

RUE   LA FAYETTE   RÉDEMPTION   RUE DROUOT   RUE FG MONTMARTRE   RUE DU FBG POISSONNIÈRE   RUE DES PTES ÉCURIES   SAINTE-CÉCILE

0 —— 150 m
0 —— 490 feet

11

AUBERVILLIERS

BOULEVARD PÉRIPHÉRIQUE

BOULEVARD MACDONALD

QUAI DE L'ALLIER
DULLOT

QUAI DE LA CHARENTE

AV. DE LA PORTE DE LA VILLETTE

AV. J. JAURÈS

AV. ÉDOUARD VAILLANT

RUE DU CHEMIN DE FER

PORTE DE LA VILLETTE

BOULEVARD MACDONALD

BOULEVARD SÉRURIER

PÉRIPHÉRIQUE

PANTIN

RUE CURIAL

RUE DE CAMBRAI

AV. DE FLANDRE

CORENTIN CARIOU

CANAL SAINT-DENIS

CITÉ DES SCIENCES ET DE L'INDUSTRIE

LA GÉODE

ZÉNITH

CANAL DE L'OURCQ

RUE DE CAMBRAI

RUE DE NANTES

RUE DE L'ARGONNE

AV. DE LA GIRONDE

PARC DE LA VILLETTE

AV. DE L'OURCQ

CRIMÉE

QUAI DE L'OISE

CANAL DE L'OURCQ

QUAI DE LA MARNE

QUAI DE METZ

RUE DES ARDENNES

PORTE DE PANTIN

LA GRANDE HALLE

CITÉ DE LA MUSIQUE (MUSÉE)

PORTE DE PANTIN

SAINT-JACQUES-SAINT-CHRISTOPHE

RUE DE THIONVILLE

RUE DE L'OURCQ

CITÉ DE LA MUSIQUE

SAINTE-CLAIRE

QUAI DE LA SEINE

BASSIN DE LA VILLETTE

QUAI DE LA LOIRE

RUE DE CRIMÉE

RUE LÉON GIRAUDON

OURCQ

AVENUE JEAN JAURÈS

LAUMIÈRE

AVENUE JEAN JAURÈS

RUE DE MEAUX

RUE

PETPPPIT

PETIT

CIMETIÈRE DE LA VILLETTE

AV. DE LA PORTE CHAUMON

BOULEVARD SÉRURIER

RUE DE CRIMÉE

N.D. DES BUTTES-CHAUMONT

ST-SERGE

R. ARMAND CARREL

RUE MANIN

MANIN

STE-COLETTE

RUE D'HAUTPOUL

RUE

RUE DE LA SOLIDARITÉ

R. G. BRUNET

DAVID R. DE LA PRÉVOYANCE

Place de Rhin et Danube

DANUBE

RUE D'ANGERS

PARC DE LA BUTTE R

SQUARE DU VEX

RUE PAILLERON

SAINT-PIERRE

PARC DES BUTTES CHAUMONT

RUE M. HIDALGO

R. DU GÉN. BRUNET

SAINT-FRANÇOIS-D'ASSISE

RUE DE

MOUZAIA

RUE SECRETAN

RUE MANIN

RUE

BOTZARIS

BOTZARIS

RUE DE BELLEVUE

RUE JANSSI

RUE DU PLATEAU

ROTHSCHILD

BUTTES CHAUMONT

RUE DE LA VILLETTE

RUE DES ANNELETS

RUE DE CRIMÉE

RUE COMPANS

PLACE DES FÊTES

RUE DU PRÉ SAINT-GERV

RUE

RUE

R. CARDUCCI RUE

DES SOLITAIRES

Place des Fêtes

RUE SIMON BOLIVAR

FESSART

0   150 m

0   490 feet

AV. SIMON BOLIVAR

RUE CLAVEL

R. MÉLINGUE

SAINT-J-B-DE-BELLEVILLE

JOURDAIN

R. DE BELLEVILLE

R. DU GÉN. LASALLE

PYRÉNÉES

RUE DE BELLEVILLE

RUE DES PYRÉNÉES

RUE LEVERT

RUE F. LEMAÎTRE

RUE PIXÉRÉCOURT

RUE PELLEPORT

◆ VERSAILLES (12) AND FONTAINEBLEAU (13)

12

VERSAILLES RIVE DROITE

VERSAILLES

BASSIN DE NEPTUNE

BOULEVARD DE LA REINE

BD DU ROI

RUE DE LA PAROISSE

BOULEVARD DE LA REINE

RUE DES RÉSERVOIRS

CHÂTEAU

Place d'Armes

GRANDES ÉCURIES

HÔTEL DE VILLE

AVENUE DE SAINT - CLOUD

ORANGERIE

PETITES ÉCURIES

AV. DE SCEAUX

AVENUE DE PARIS

R. DES ÉTATS GÉNÉRAUX

AVENUE DE PARIS

RUE DE L'ORANGERIE

RUE DU MARÉCHAL JOFFRE

POTAGER DU ROI

VERSAILLES RIVE GAUCHE

RUE D'ANJOU

Carrés St-Louis

RUE ROYALE ST-LOUIS

VERSAILLES CHANTIER

0 0 0 m
1/00 000 - 1 cm = 0 m

13

FONTAINEBLEAU

BOULEVARD DU MARÉCHAL JOFFRE

RUE LAGORSSE

RUE GRANDE

RUE A. BRIAND

Carrefour de la Libération

RUE SAINT-MERRY

RUE SAINT-HONORÉ

Place de l'Étape aux Vins

BD A. MAGINOT

RUE DE FRANCE

RUE GRANDE

RUE ROYALE

RUE DU PARC

BOULEVARD DE CONSTANTINE

RUE SAINT-MERRY

Place Napoléon Bonaparte

Place de Boischyver

RUE ROYALE

R. SAINT-HONORÉ

RUE SAINT-HONORÉ

RUE DE L'ARBRE SEC

CHÂTEAU

LE TIBRE

AVENUE DES CASCADES

BOULEVARD MAGENTA

ÉTANG DES CARPES

LE ROMULUS

Carrefour de l'Obélisque

BOULEVARD DU MARÉCHAL JUIN

Carrefour de Maintenon

RN 6

ARRONDISSEMENTS OF PARIS

AREA
40 sq miles
(33 sq miles minus
the Bois de
Boulogne and Bois
de Vincennes);
0.022% of French
territory.
POPULATION
2.125 million

(4 % of French
population); density
52,400 people per sq
mile; 10.952 million
in the urban area.
**ADMINISTRATIVE
DISTRICTS**
20 *arrondissements*
arranged in spiral
fashion starting

from the center. A
mayor and twenty
local mayors elected
every six years.
THE CITY COUNCIL
Annual budget
5.8 billion euros;
44,625 employees; 38
bridges; 3341 streets
and 348 avenues;

9515 public benches;
415 squares; 80,500
street signs;
22 million visitors
per year; 73,000
hotel rooms; 11,500
restaurants.
ECONOMY
Since1979 the
world leader for